MODERN BRITAIN

FLORIDA STATE
UNIVERSITY LIBRARIES

JUN 18 2001

TALLAHASSEE, FLORIDA

MODERN BRITAIN

A Social History 1750–1997

Second Edition

EDWARD ROYLE

Reader in History,
University of York, England

A member of the Hodder Headline Group
LONDON • NEW YORK • SYDNEY • AUCKLAND

HN
385
.R665
1997

First published in Great Britain in 1987
Second edition published in 1997 by
Arnold, a member of the Hodder Headline Group
338 Euston Road, London NW1 3BH
175 Fifth Avenue, New York, NY 10010
http:\\www.arnoldpublishers.com

Distributed exclusively in the USA by
St Martin's Press, Inc.
175 Fifth Avenue, New York, NY 10010

© 1987, 1997 Edward Royle

All rights reserved. No part of this publication may be reproduced or transmitted in any form or by any means, electronically or mechanically, including photocopying, recording or any information storage or retrieval system, without either prior permission in writing from the publisher or a licence permitting restricted copying. In the United Kingdom such licences are issued by the Copyright Licensing Agency: 90 Tottenham Court Road, London W1P 9HE.

British Library Cataloguing in Publication Data
A catalogue entry for this book is available from the British Library

Library of Congress Cataloging-in-Publication Data
A catalog entry for this book is available from the Library of Congress

ISBN 0 340 57944 7 (pb)

Production Editor: Liz Gooster
Production Controller: Sarah Kett
Cover design: Terry Griffiths

Composition by Scribe Design, Gillingham, Kent, UK
Printed and bound in Great Britain by J W Arrowsmith Ltd, Bristol

Contents

List of maps and tables

List of maps

List of tables

Map 1 Britain: counties before 1974 and major towns in 1831

Source: Ordnance Survey Atlas of Great Britain and *Census of Population* (1831).
Note: Towns over 25,000 population are as shown in the 1831 Census.

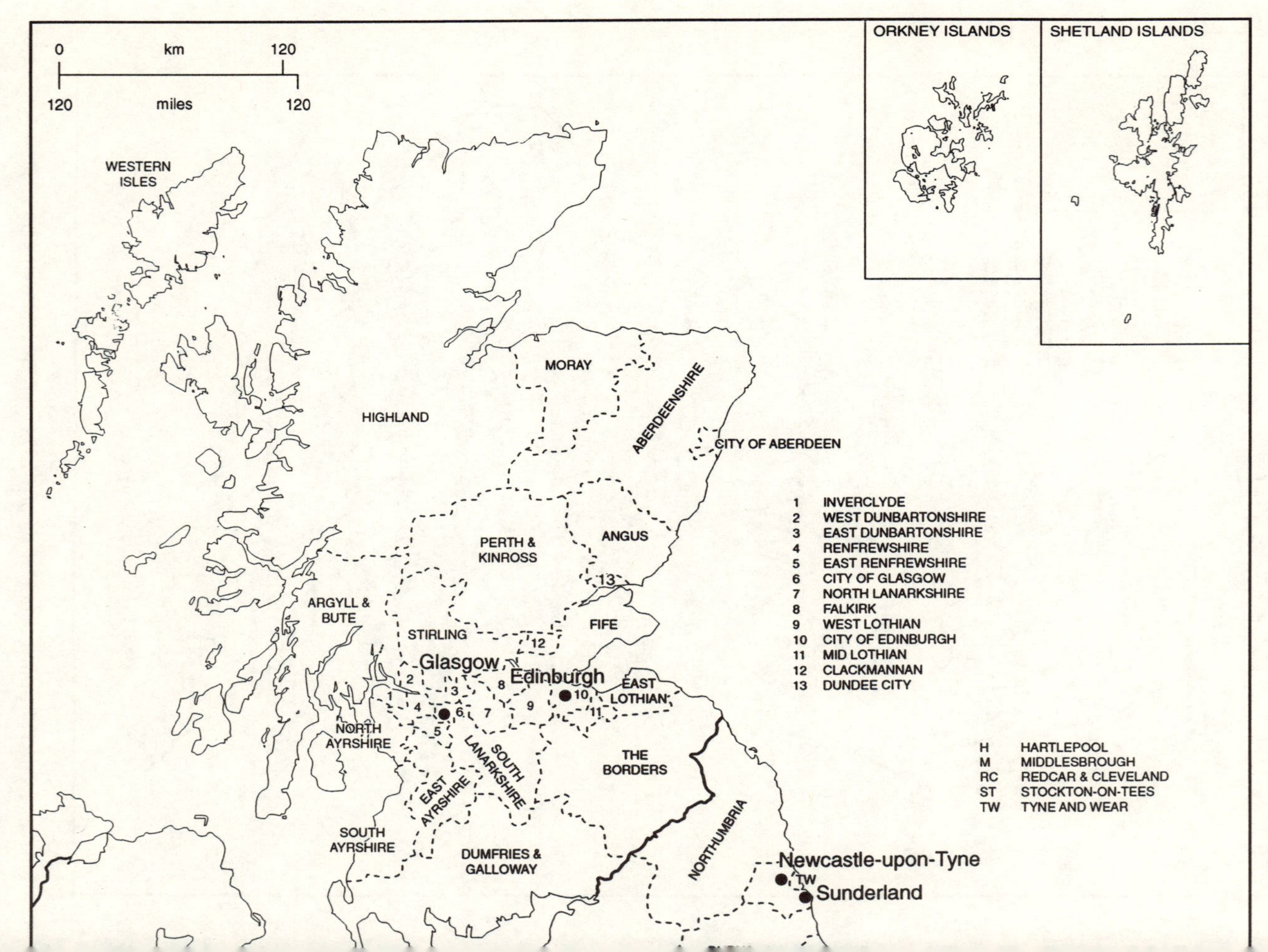

0
km
120
120
miles
120
ORKNEY ISLANDS
SHETLAND ISLANDS
WESTERN ISLES
HIGHLAND
MORAY
ABERDEENSHIRE
CITY OF ABERDEEN
PERTH & KINROSS
ANGUS
ARGYLL & BUTE
STIRLING
FIFE
Glasgow
Edinburgh
EAST LOTHIAN
NORTH AYRSHIRE
SOUTH LANARKSHIRE
EAST AYRSHIRE
THE BORDERS
SOUTH AYRSHIRE
DUMFRIES & GALLOWAY
NORTHUMBRIA
Newcastle-upon-Tyne
TW
Sunderland
1 INVERCLYDE
2 WEST DUNBARTONSHIRE
3 EAST DUNBARTONSHIRE
4 RENFREWSHIRE
5 EAST RENFREWSHIRE
6 CITY OF GLASGOW
7 NORTH LANARKSHIRE
8 FALKIRK
9 WEST LOTHIAN
10 CITY OF EDINBURGH
11 MID LOTHIAN
12 CLACKMANNAN
13 DUNDEE CITY
H HARTLEPOOL
M MIDDLESBROUGH
RC REDCAR & CLEVELAND
ST STOCKTON-ON-TEES
TW TYNE AND WEAR

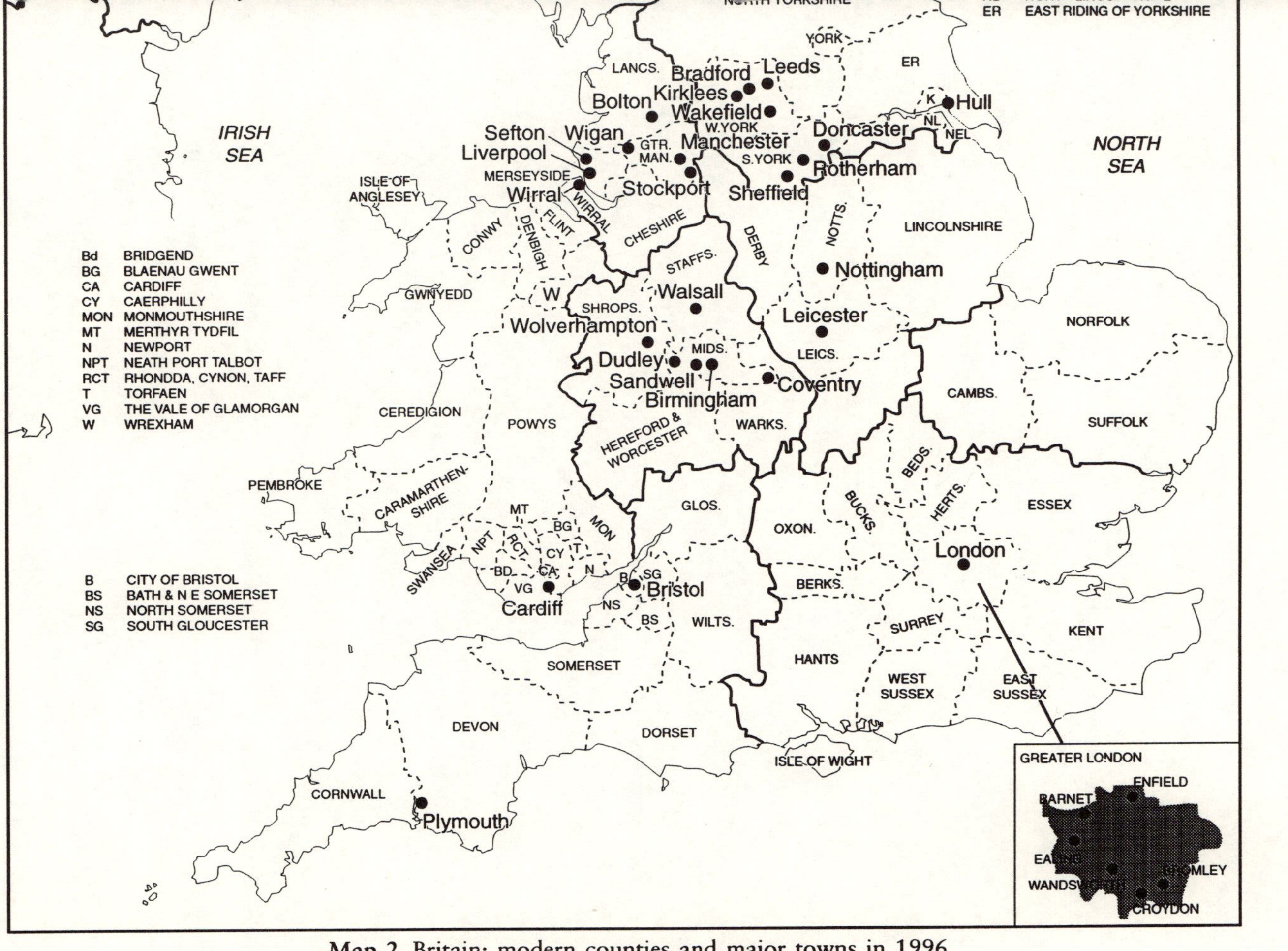

Map 2 Britain: modern counties and major towns in 1996

Source: Social Trends (1977) and *Census of Population* (1991).

Note: Names are as given in the 1991 Census for towns, London boroughs and metropolitan districts with populations over 250,000.

Preface

Social history touches upon human relationships in every part of life, and as such is beyond detailed treatment in any single textbook. Three principles of selection have therefore been applied to the subject matter of this volume. First, I have been aware of those topics – such as the standard of living, class, radicalism, the labour movement, the poor law and the welfare state – which are conventionally regarded as 'social history' in courses offered in schools, colleges and universities, and by those responsible for examining students in these institutions. Second, I have tried to give emphasis to some of those topics which have been attracting the attention of scholars working in the broad field of social history – urban history, demography, the family, women's history, crime, leisure, popular religion and literacy studies. Third, I have attempted to follow some of those themes which are currently of interest to all students of modern Britain in the hope that a historical perspective may lead to a clearer understanding of some of the major concerns about late twentieth-century British society – the environment, immigration, changing moral values, consumerism, poverty, unemployment and the decline of Britain.

Critics of the first edition of *Modern Britain* regretted that my Britain did not include Ireland. This omission is deliberate, not only on account of length but also of definition. The boundaries of the United Kingdom changed significantly twice during the period covered by this book. The island of Great Britain is a relative constant, so this is the Britain of the present study – the history of society in England, Wales and Scotland. Even so, the three countries have not been treated evenly throughout. Many published social statistics bracket England and Wales, and make the task of isolating the separate history of Wales a difficult one. And though Scotland has recently benefited from excellent work on its own history, coverage remains patchy for some topics dealt with extensively in English history. I hope I have nevertheless done enough to show English students that Wales is different and that Scotland does have its own past to be appreciated within the overall context of British history.

The approach is thematic, and largely chronological within each theme, although centres of discussion vary in accordance with the principles outlined above. Most themes begin around the middle of the eighteenth century, generously defined in either direction of 1750, and end with the present day. The conclusions reached about the latter are necessarily even more personal and temporary than historical judgements usually are. They are not intended to be party-polemical, though that danger is inescapable. I do not wish to imply that 'History' suggests any particular course of action for the reorganisation of modern social life, for history is inanimate and teaches only those lessons which people choose to attribute to it. What the historian can claim is that a knowledge of the past helps clear away some of the misinformed prejudices on which those who wish to enlist the past in their own cause have frequently built. Those who would honestly seek the wisdom to shape the future are invited first to understand the past for its own sake and in its own context.

This second edition differs from the first in a number of ways. Most importantly, I have tried to bring the themes up to date, which has meant sometimes a salutary recasting of my views about present trends, and sometimes a confirmation of them. I have also tried to incorporate the most significant new material that has been published over the past decade, although I have not felt compelled by this to undertake a complete rewriting of the text. Since I first wrote, women's history has become more settled in the mainstream of historical understanding than in its earlier, pioneering days; even greater suspicion has fallen on the language of class, especially as used in the nineteenth century; cultural history has become the vehicle for examining all aspects of human life and activity; and sociological ideas about secularisation have been resolutely repelled by historians, who now take religious experience more seriously than was once fashionable. These and other matters of emphasis will be found in the relevant sections of the book. I have also improved the detail in the references, and extended the bibliography by adding just a few of the many works which have poured from the presses over the past decade.

In the preparation of this work I have been helped by many scholars whose books and articles have taught me a great deal about unfamiliar things. The decision not to use notes except for direct quotations and references to historians by name means I have no means of acknowledging personally all who have made this book possible. The bibliography gives some of their names, but by no means all. I should, however, like to thank my immediate colleagues in the Department of History at York for their encouragement, and those many generations of school and university students who have challenged me with their insights, and have told me through their examination scripts what it is which they have found hard to understand. I hope this book helps them as they have helped me.

Edward Royle
York, 1997

1

The changing environment

The countryside

People, not the environment, make history; yet the conditions under which history is made are circumscribed by the physical environment – mountains, marshes, fertile or infertile soils, access to river transport and coastal waters, climate. Within these limits man has exercised his ingenuity throughout the ages to control, exploit and intentionally or otherwise change his environment for better or worse. When the poet William Cowper wrote 'God made the country, and man made the town', he was indulging in a romantic fiction.[1] In fact much of the environment as we know it is the product of human habitation and a part of our social history. During the past 200 years man has exerted control over his environment in ways undreamt of by his ancestors, and emancipated himself from many of the age-old constraints which kept his life, in Hobbes's celebrated words, 'solitary, poor, nasty, brutish, and short'.[2]

The age of enclosure and improvement, 1750–1830

Figures for land use in the early eighteenth century are scarce and unreliable. According to Gregory King in 1696, over a quarter of the 37.3 million acres (15.1 hectares) in England and Wales was under arable cultivation, with another quarter under pasture and meadow and a further quarter waste and barren land. At the same time, approaching three-quarters of the land area of Scotland was thought to be uncultivable. In 1801 arable acreage in England and Wales remained about the same, but the total acreage under pasture and meadow had increased by some 20 per cent, and there had been a similar decline in the acreage described as commons and wastes. Figures are not available for Scotland, but it seems likely that the same trend occurred, though a larger proportion of Scotland's 19 million acres (7.7 hectares) remained waste, and a smaller proportion was under arable. Much of this waste lay in the upland areas of northern and western Britain, but some land remained to be reclaimed even on the outskirts of London.

The most striking change to the rural environment in many parts of the countryside came with the enclosure of open fields, commons and wastes. The extent of enclosure must not be exaggerated. In England, where much land was already enclosed at the start of the eighteenth century, the main areas affected lay in a central belt running north-eastwards from Berkshire and Oxfordshire through the south and east Midlands into Norfolk, Lincolnshire and the East Riding of Yorkshire. Here enclosure could mean both changing field patterns and changing land use. Open strip-fields, radiating from nucleated settlements, were replaced by hedged and ditched fields under single ownership, giving the countryside a chequered appearance.

Crop yields increased by some 40 per cent during the course of the eighteenth century. About two-thirds of this increase can be attributed to the more intensive use of land, but historians are now less ready than were contemporary propagandists of improvement to accept that enclosure was a necessary part of this progress, or that the human costs were always outweighed by the alleged benefits. Many of the advantages associated with enclosure could have been secured without it by local co-operation, but during the later eighteenth century parliamentary enclosure became the norm, involving not only legal fees but also the costs of hedging, providing roads, and allowing land in lieu of a commuted tithe, all of which could bring the total costs of enclosure to as much as £12 an acre (£5 a hectare). Where arable strips were enclosed, those small proprietors who were unable to bear such costs could find themselves reduced to labouring for those who had prospered from the improvements. A more frequent problem, though, was the plight of those who lived off the so-called 'wastes' – common land, to which they had no title – who, when the commons were enclosed, found themselves without means of support other than those offered by day labour, the poor law, or emigration to the towns.

In Scotland the situation was slightly different, but the outcome was the same. Improvers initially tried to take account of the welfare of the small landholders, who were invariably tenants, not owners as in England. New planned villages were created to act as markets and centres of alternative employment, but this was possible only so long as rural industry was able to compete with the growing specialist production of the towns. On many estates in the Highlands the improvers were reluctant to disrupt settled communities and enclosure took place mainly on commons and in the outfields, but some crofters were driven to seek a new livelihood gathering kelp along the shoreline as an expansion in sheep-farming pushed them off their holdings inland.

Enclosure did not become widespread until the second half of the eighteenth century, when grain prices rose with population growth. New peaks were reached in the 1770s, and again during the French and Napoleonic Wars, when high prices justified investment in enclosing and improving commons and marginal or 'waste' land. But the drive for enclosure and general agricultural improvement has been attributed not only to the market, but also to fashion, and the demands of an increasingly expensive aristocratic lifestyle calling for a maximisation of rent-rolls. These two factors came together in that most striking feature of the eighteenth-century landscape, the enclosed park, of which several hundred were designed during the course of the century – nearly 200 by Lancelot ('Capability') Brown (1715–83) alone. By the beginning of the nineteenth century the results of this work were evident in thousands of acres of rolling 'natural' parkland, liberally planted with trees. Seldom can the indulgence of a few have contributed so greatly to the enrichment of the environment of the many in later generations.

The significance of this agricultural improvement lies not simply in its effect on the environment as perceived in field patterns, drained fens, reclaimed wastes and country parks, but in its economic and social importance for the lives of all the people of Britain. For, without a strong agricultural sector, the economy could not have supported the rapidly growing population, an increasing proportion of which was engaged in non-agricultural pursuits and lived in an urban environment.

The Victorian countryside, 1830–1914

Those changes in the appearance of the countryside which are usually associated with the age of enclosure were largely (though not entirely) completed by 1830, but it would be a mistake to think of the rest of the nineteenth century as a period of stability. Changes continued to take place, the cumulative effects of which were quite as dramatic as those of the earlier period. And though the characteristic land pattern of the nineteenth century was of roughly equal-sized, rectangular fields (easier to plough and convenient for crop rotation), regional variations were still paramount. Change occurred unevenly, and in different ways according to soil type, distance from markets and local custom. The major natural determinants of land use were altitude and the nature of the soil, whether light chalk or sand, or heavy clay. The great achievement of the agricultural improvers of the later eighteenth century had been to bring the light soils into arable cultivation, especially in the south-eastern part of England. Once suitably cared for with manures, liming, marling and crop rotations, they were by far superior to the heavy clays for growing wheat. The clays, by contrast, were less efficient and always liable to become uneconomic in times of depression such as followed the ending of the wars in 1815. It was to help farmers on these lands that Sir Robert Peel in 1846 associated government aid for land drainage with the removal of agricultural protection. The invention of the mole plough to cut underground drainage channels, and the use of cheap clay pipes in place of the old ridge-and-furrow system of surface drainage created the possibility of a more efficient High Farming even on heavy clay soils, but the latter remained second best to the lighter soils which retained their warmth into the autumn, released their nutrients more readily, offered dry grazing for sheep and were more easily and cheaply worked.

The late 1870s proved a turning-point in the history of land usage in the wheat-growing areas of England – areas which provided the financial backbone of two of the main institutions of political England, the Church and the aristocracy. Cold wet summers were reported every year between 1877 and 1882, at a time when alternative supplies of wheat were available from North America. This competition reduced prices everywhere, but it was the clay lands which suffered most. In western and northern parts, where arable farming had usually taken second place to pasture, much land passed out of tillage completely as farmers concentrated on supplying beef cattle for the expanding urban market. Cattle-breeding prospered in North-Eastern Scotland, and in Cumberland. As the acreage under wheat fell in the last third of the century, the number of cattle rose from 104,184 in 1867 to 149,313 in 1899.

The response of some farmers on the more depressed clay lands of the south-east was to economise on labour by allowing arable land to go to grass, even rough grass, and to maintain their hedges and ditches less regularly. Some land went out of production entirely in parts of Essex, and tenancies were taken over by Scotsmen from Ayrshire who turned to milk production for the London market. Between 1866 and 1880 the volume of milk being imported into the capital by rail rose from 7 million gallons to 20 million. Other urban centres throughout the country had a similar effect on their agricultural environments. Leicestershire sent milk to the West Riding and even Newcastle; Ayrshire supplied Glasgow; Cheshire provided for Manchester and Liverpool. Urban demand, rail transport and the need of farmers to diversify production also encouraged the development of market gardening. Carrots were grown in the fens round Chatteris, and peas in Essex; Cornwall specialised in broccoli and early potatoes. Lincolnshire around Spalding turned to flowers as a commercial crop. Over 300 acres were under glass in the Lea Valley in the 1890s, supplying tomatoes, grapes and flowers to London. Fruit farming spread from the West Country to Kent, where hop farmers were suffering from over-production, and to Cambridgeshire, where Chivers opened his jam factory at Histon in 1873. Everywhere local specialisation in response to accessible markets was transforming the face of agriculture, and the definition of 'accessible' was constantly changing as the railway network reached into the furthest corners of the kingdom.

Increasingly the demands of industry and city-dwellers made their impact on the face of the countryside, as land was given over for quarries, mines, spoil heaps and reservoirs, as well as railway lines, embankments and stations. The landscaped park of the eighteenth century continued in fashion, as men who had made money in industry sought rural retreats appropriate to their wealth and social standing, and away from the dirt and smoke which had generated their fortunes. The new rich also made their impact on the countryside as they followed their Queen into the Scottish Highlands, where sheep-farming was giving way before the higher rentals which could be had from deer forests, grouse-shooting, and river-fishing. At the beginning of the 1870s the sporting valuations of parishes in the Highland Region represented 13.4 per cent of their total valuations; by 1911–12 the proportion had risen to 27.7 per cent, and was as high as 38 per cent in the west. Shooting also came to play a prominent part in the economy of parts of England. The partridge was said to be 'the salvation of Norfolk farming', as houses and land were let out to shooting tenants.[3]

The twentieth-century countryside

The First World War temporarily restored some of that protection which improvements in transportation had removed in the 1870s. The acreage devoted to cereal production was increased, especially following the poor harvest of 1916, when the government intervened with guaranteed cereal prices to encourage output: in 1918 more acres were under wheat than at any time since 1884, while the area under permanent pasture was at its lowest since 1890. But with the return to normal conditions and the repeal of the Corn Production Act in 1921, agricultural depression returned as imports flooded the country. The value of farm produce was halved between 1920 and 1922 and, although meat prices held up better than most, no sector of the farming community was immune. Marginal land again reverted to rough pasture, and uneconomic holdings were abandoned. Output fell by 3.1 per cent per annum in the inter-war years. The victims of depression were, as often as not, small farmers, many of whom had only recently purchased tenancies from their landlords in the boom years of 1918–21. With the collapse in farm incomes, their *de facto* new landlords became the banks.

Economic prospects were as bleak in the countryside as in the old industrial areas. Protection in 1932 brought some relief, but it was the Second World War which marked the real turning-point in the fortunes of agriculture. After the war the policy of loans, subsidies and controls which had increased the acreage devoted to cereals and root crops by over 60 per cent between 1939 and 1945 was continued, to ensure that, unlike the 1820s and 1920s, the 1950s would not see a collapse in post-war farm prices. Guaranteed prosperity ensured investment in new machinery and fertilisers. Though the number of horses in agriculture had been falling in the 1930s, a dramatic increase in the use of tractors on the farms of Britain came during the war. Thereafter, agriculture increasingly came to be thought of as another industry, using sophisticated and expensive machinery and pushing productivity up to record levels. Wheat production by the mid-1960s actually exceeded that of the best war years, although the acreage was 27 per cent less. Much of this higher output was due to the exploitation of large farms in the south and east of England, increasingly owned by City interests with the necessary capital to invest in the efficient maximisation of productivity in land and labour. The result by the 1980s was a greatly expanded output at artificially high prices without regard to the level of demand.

The same measure of success was enjoyed by other groups of farmers, especially in dairying, and government grants brought some aid even to those experiencing most difficulties – the upland farmers, especially of Wales and northern Scotland. British farms had 12 per cent more cattle, 46 per cent more sheep, 173 per cent more pigs and 43 per cent more poultry in 1965 than in 1950, and the numbers of all animals (except horses) were higher at this date than they had been even at the beginning of the century, despite the fact that the country was less rural, and the countryside less agricultural, than ever before.

Such economic success was achieved only at the cost of considerable change in the appearance of the countryside. In the 1950s, about 50,000 acres (over 20,000 hectares) of wetland were being reclaimed each year; by 1980 the figure had risen to 300,000 (120,000 hectares). About a third of the 60,000 acres (25,000 hectares) of Exmoor was ploughed up between 1945 and 1980; a quarter of the chalk downland of Dorset was put to the plough in the 1950s and 1960s; and by 1980 half the pre-war acreage of the Wiltshire downs had similarly been lost. To economise on labour and save valuable land, hedgerows were everywhere being grubbed out and trees destroyed, either to be replaced by wire fences or to make way for 'prairie'-style farming, with huge fields more suited to the use of large machinery. On top of this came one of the greatest ecological disasters of the century, when two-thirds of the 23 million elm trees south of a line from Birmingham to the Wash were destroyed by Dutch Elm Disease in the 1970s. But if such developments were of great concern to conservationists, the latter were equally unhappy with the policy of afforestation which radically altered the appearance of many highland parts of Britain.

The Forestry Commission was set up in 1919 to buy land and grow timber for strategic use in war or to help the peacetime economy. The Second World War underlined the importance of the Commission's task, and after 1945 a target was set of 5 million acres (over 2 million hectares) of usable forest within 50 years. The Commission became one of the largest landowners in the country (and by far the largest in Scotland), owning about half of the 4.2 million acres (1.7 million hectares) of forest in Britain. Until the early 1980s the Commission was acquiring new land at the rate of over 30,000 acres (12,000 hectares) a year, a policy then reversed as government thinking on the economy shifted in favour of the private ownership of production. By the end of the 1980s, over a quarter of a million acres (100,000 hectares) of forest had been disposed of, with a similar target fixed for the 1990s. Public and private enterprise together, though, ensured the planting of 618,000 acres (nearly 250,000 hectares) of new forest in the 1980s and early 1990s, contributing to a doubling of the forest area of Britain since 1919 to around 5.4 million acres (2.2 million hectares) of productive forest, of which 37 per cent was still owned by the Forestry Commission.

Other major landowners with increasing stakes in the British countryside included the army, which had held large sections of Salisbury plain since before the First World War, and controlled other extensive training grounds even in those areas designated under the Countryside Act of 1949 as National Parks; and the Royal Air Force, which acquired thousands of acres for airfields in the east of England during the Second World War, some of which were gradually relinquished in peacetime and reverted to agricultural, light industrial or commercial use.

Water authorities also became important landowners. By 1904 over 80,000 acres (32,000 hectares) in England and 6,000 acres (2,400 hectares) in Wales were owned by local authorities as gathering grounds for reservoirs; and as the appetite of modern industrial society for water continued to grow in the twentieth century, so the areas flooded increased in size. Huge man-made lakes filled valleys in the Pennines and Wales, and even an English lowland area, the ancient county of Rutland, was extensively flooded to make a reservoir in 1970. Perhaps the best example of this new kind of landscaping on a vast scale is to be found in Kielder in the North Tyne Valley. Here, in one of the largest man-made forest plantations in Europe – a quarter of a million acres (100,000 hectares) – a lake was created in the 1970s with a surface area of 2,684 acres (1,087 hectares – larger than Ullswater in the Lake District), coupled with a 6.2-megawatt hydroelectric generating capacity. As with forests, so with water, government policy in the 1980s led to the transfer of this land to the private sector, making the newly created and sometimes foreign-owned water companies among the largest private landlords in the country.

Everywhere during the past 250 years there has been increasing evidence of man's impact on his environment, even in the depths of the countryside. To the quarries and pit-head spoil heaps of earlier years – many of which were now merging with the 'natural' countryside scene – were added drilling rigs for oil and gas in areas like Dorset, remote from the cradles of the first industrial revolution. By the mid-twentieth century hardly a view could avoid the ubiquitous electricity power cables and pylons, vital if unattractive arteries bringing the possibilities of modern living to even the remotest corners of the land. Stricter planning controls then led to a policy of burying these cables in environmentally 'sensitive' areas, though the development of wind farms – clusters of giant wind-propelled generators – on prominent ridges and exposed coasts posed a new dilemma for defenders of the environment, anxious both to avoid intrusive signs of technology and to promote electricity production from renewable and non-polluting energy sources.

Although the word 'environmentalist' was first used about 1916, from the late nineteenth century this intensification of economic exploitation has been challenged by those who have seen the countryside as an amenity to be enjoyed by all the people, a majority of whom could only ever be visitors from urban areas. Such an awareness of the value of the countryside has in part been prompted by the realisation that it has become a rapidly wasting asset. During much of the twentieth century around 50,000 acres (20,000 hectares) of agricultural land have been lost on average each year to the needs of industry, housing and roads. By the 1990s, 10 per cent of the area of England and 7 per cent of Britain was designated urban, over 30,000 acres (12,000 hectares) alone being covered with motorway. This process was not new, and had been a necessary feature of the changing British economy since the mid-eighteenth century; but the extent of the change became more marked in the later twentieth century as improvements in private transport and the desire to escape large cities finally broke down the fading distinctions between town and country. The paradox at the end of the twentieth century is that catering for such refugees from the city has itself become a form of exploitation and a threat to the very things that people wish to see and enjoy.

The countryside as a place for leisure, not merely for the aristocracy in their country parks, but for all, has led to the view that farmers were not merely producers from the land but also conservers of it. This change in attitude, which was gaining ground in closing decades of the twentieth century, was aided by grants made by the European Union to control the use made of agricultural land. By 1994, 39 environmentally sensitive sites had been identified, covering over 7.6 million acres (3.1 million hectares), with farmers receiving nearly £19 million to use less intensive methods of cultivation and grazing and to preserve grasslands. In addition, over 1.5 million acres (0.63 million hectares) of land were 'set aside', with farmers being paid not to cultivate it. Nevertheless, total government subsidies to promote intensive farming still exceeded grants to encourage the reverse.

Transportation

Historians of the railway age might sometimes seem to imply that economic growth and social change in the nineteenth century were in large part a consequence of the application of steam locomotion to the transportation of goods and people. This might be true of most countries which industrialised between 1830 and 1914, but the roots of British growth are to be found in the earlier and, by railway standards, relatively modest investment in roads and canals. Even after the coming of the railways, the older means of transport did not lose all importance. Coastal shipping experienced its own technological revolution with the application of steam power; and though the roads lost most of their long-distance traffic to the railways, the latter were never as important as the roads over short distances, especially in towns. Moreover, the social consequences of developments in transportation should not be exaggerated. The wealthier classes benefited disproportionately; travel other than by foot was a luxury for the poor right through the nineteenth century. For many of the less well-off, liberation from the limitations of a pedestrian existence came only at the end of the century, with the electric tram and the bicycle.

Turnpikes and canals, 1750–1830

As Adam Smith accurately observed in his *Wealth of Nations*:

> Good roads, canals and navigable rivers, by diminishing the expense of carriage, put the remote parts of the country nearly on a level with those in the neighbourhood of a town: they are, upon that account, the greatest of all improvements.[4]

Toll-gates and turnpikes had become acceptable as means of improving the roads of Britain at the very end of the seventeenth century. Defoe praised them in the 1720s, but only in the second half of the century did they become widespread. Even so, Arthur Young still found much fault with the roads during his travels in the 1770s. Turnpike trusts were local and often inefficient, unable to maintain adequately those most heavily used roads which invariably degenerated in bad weather into muddy, rutted tracks. Towards the end of the century the situation was somewhat improved with the emergence of what can be called serious civil engineering, pioneered by John Metcalfe, John McAdam and Thomas Telford, whose network of roads consolidated links between England and Scotland and across North Wales and Galloway to the Irish ports.

With around 22,000 miles of turnpiked roads in England by 1836 (about 20 per cent of the total mileage), travelling times were significantly reduced. A journey from London to Shrewsbury, which had taken four days in April 1753, took only a day and a half in the summer of 1772, and only 12 hours and 40 minutes in June 1835. Traffic correspondingly increased. Seven coaches left Chester daily in 1801; this had risen to 26 by 1831. Fly vans brought perishable agricultural produce into London, and stage-wagons bearing light non-perishable goods to and from the major centres of manufacture and consumption enabled six draught horses to do the work of 30 pack-horses. Above all, the carriage of the Royal Mail caught the imagination after John Palmer of Bristol had persuaded the government to replace post 'boys' on horseback with regular mail-coaches, cutting delivery times between Bristol and London from over 30 hours to only 16 in 1784.

For every 16 miles of turnpike road in 1830, one mile of river navigation had been improved and nearly two miles of canal completed. For the carriage of heavy goods and those with a low weight/value ratio, water transport was slow but essential. It is hard to find a growing industrial centre at the beginning of the nineteenth century which was not served by, or which had not grown up by, adequate communications by water. River navigations predominated in the east and south, canals in the north and west. By 1790 the four major river systems of England – the Humber, Mersey, Severn and Thames – had been linked by canals, though the first direct trans-Pennine canal from the Humber to the Mersey was not completed until 1801. In Scotland similar developments occurred, with early canals from the 1760s focusing on the Clyde, and linking the Forth and Clyde by 1791. By the early nineteenth century a network of inland waterways had been created along which farmers could send their crops to distant markets and bring in lime to improve the soil. Stone could now be carried long distances, enabling road-makers to take advantage of the innovations of McAdam and Telford, and providing the builders of factories, warehouses and domestic dwellings in expanding manufacturing areas with cheaper and more easily accessible constructional materials. Passenger traffic also thrived in certain areas: the number of passengers carried annually on the Forth-Clyde canal rose from 44,000 in 1812 to nearly 200,000 in 1836, while the introduction of fast passenger boats between Paisley and Glasgow on the uncompleted Ardrossan canal resulted in 363,000 using the service in 1836. But coal was the most important item of bulk transported on the canals of Britain, supplying both domestic and industrial customers; and it was the need to move coal to the canal-side (or, in the North East and South Wales, to the coast) which led to the development of the railway.

The railway age, 1830–1914

It is difficult to think of any aspect of life which was not touched and changed by the coming of the railways and steam locomotion. For the first time, heavy goods could be carried long distances over land at high speed, and people were able to cross the country in a matter of hours instead of days. Economically, the railways united the whole country as never before, but they also strengthened regionalism by encouraging specialisation in production through economy in distribution. They brought the furthest corners of the land into close contact with the centre, but they also helped to define what was the centre and what were the margins. And as always, though the poor certainly benefited by the railways, the rich were in a position to gain most from them whilst at the same time having the means to escape some of their less desirable side-effects.

The railway age is traditionally dated from the opening of the Liverpool to Manchester line in 1830, the first line in the world built specifically with passengers as well as goods in mind, and relying solely on steam locomotive power. Initially the railway provided no more of a national network than had the canals or turnpike roads. Indeed, the new railways were thought of as a kind of turnpike, to which traffic would have public access, and, as with the canals, there was no agreement on the width of the track. Nevertheless, by 1838 around 500 miles of track had been completed, nearly half of which ran between London, Liverpool, Manchester and Birmingham. The next decade then saw the foundations of a national network – what John Ruskin in 1849 called 'the iron veins that traverse the frame of our country'.[5] By 1850 over 6,000 miles of track had been opened in Great Britain. Despite a good deal of wasteful competition, what emerged was in fact surprisingly efficient. A Railway Clearing House facilitated the conveyance of passengers between various company lines from 1842, and goods from 1848, whilst amalgamations such as that which produced George Hudson's Midland Railway in 1844 and the London and North Western in 1846 brought a measure of rationalisation to the scene. Most major towns in England were connected to the railway by 1850, with trunk lines radiating from London, and dense local networks across the industrial West Riding and south-east Lancashire. Robert Stephenson had also built his North Wales coastal line to Holyhead, and three lines connected Scotland and England; but much of Wales, the South-West and Scotland outside the Central Valley still awaited the railway. Glasgow and Edinburgh were connected in 1842, but the West Highland line was not opened until 1889, and some lines in the Highlands were never built. The total rail network by 1912 was over three times that of 1850, but many of these late arrivals were to be the least economic and would be among the first to be closed – including the last trunk line in England, the Great Central, which reached Marylebone from Sheffield in 1899.

Such was the impact of the railway that its early consequences are frequently exaggerated. The full social benefits came only with the completion of the basic network after 1850, and affected the bulk of the population rather later than the wealthier classes. The economic consequences were also slow to emerge. The Post Office used the railways for the letter post from the start, and the Penny Post of 1840 would not have been possible without them. But although the revenue of the turnpikes reached its peak in 1837, the mileage continued to grow, and was higher in 1848 than at any other time in the century. What was lost were the profitable long-distance routes, and the people hardest hit were the innkeepers and others engaged in servicing the coaching trade. Local haulage was, by contrast, stimulated by the railways. There were slightly more horses being used for commercial purposes in 1851 than in 1811, and the number quadrupled in the second half of the century. The canals similarly did not reach their maximum mileage until 1858, and some continued to pose sufficient of a threat to the railways' carriage of goods to keep railway rates well below those permitted by Parliament. Not until 1850 did railway receipts from the transportation of goods exceed those arising from the carriage of passengers. The canals fought with the railway between Liverpool and Manchester for 20 years, and in 1848 carried twice the tonnage of the railway. But in general only those canals prospered which were, in effect, extensions of the coastal shipping trade – like the Aire and Calder Navigation connecting the West Riding to the Humber and, above all, the new Manchester Ship Canal, constructed in 1894.

Coastal shipping certainly benefited from the stimulus to the economy which the railways helped create, as shipping and railways were closely integrated. Not until 1867 did more coal reach London by rail than by sea. The economy of the valleys of industrialising South Wales expanded dramatically as short lines like that from Merthyr to Cardiff, opened in 1841 – the first railway line in Wales – poured out coal and iron products through the expanding docks of the Monmouth and Glamorgan coast to the rest of Britain and the world. In much of Scotland passenger transport also necessarily relied upon the new steam-powered sea-going ferries, as important an innovation as the railways. Steam navigation also lay behind the continuing commercial prosperity and growth of Glasgow and Liverpool. Not only did a network of local railways confirm their positions as entrepôts for the world's trade, but the establishment of international passenger lines (such as Cunard in 1840) made them gateways to the west for hundreds of thousands of emigrants seeking work and riches in the New World.

The most immediate impact of the transport revolution was on the landscape. The hostility with which the building of the first railways was greeted was not unlike that which was aroused by proposals to build motorways in the later twentieth century. As John Ruskin wrote of the Derby to Manchester railway line:

> There was a rocky valley between Buxton and Bakewell, once upon a time divine as the Vale of Tempe; . . . You enterprised a railroad through it – you blasted its rocks away. . . . The valley is gone and the Gods with it. And now every fool in Buxton can be at Bakewell in half-an-hour and every fool in Bakewell at Buxton; which you think a lucrative progress of exchange – you fools everywhere.[6]

Most people, however, saw the railways as progress, and realised that not to be on the railway was to be left off the map of civilisation and prosperity. They took a pride in the great earthworks, cuttings, viaducts, tunnels and bridges which remain monuments to the skill and vision of engineers like Robert Stephenson and Isambard Brunel. Great vaulted train sheds at station termini rose above the urban skyline with the magnificence of medieval cathedrals, while in the countryside rural architecture was enriched with thousands of smaller buildings – signal-boxes, village stations, cottages for employees and small hotels – in a variety of styles. Alongside the railway marched miles of poles and wires bearing the telegraph system, important for the safe running of the railway and for the rapid conveyance of commercial news.

Urban transport

The railways were very efficient over long distances, but they were neither flexible nor cheap enough for journeys of under ten miles. Only London was really large enough to require commuting at this distance. Elsewhere, railway 'dormitory' towns like Altrincham, 12 miles from Manchester, were very much the exception. What the railways did provide was fast communication with neighbouring but independent towns within the general economic hinterland of a major city – Paisley with Glasgow, Wolverhampton with Birmingham, Stockport with Manchester. For shorter distances, and for most journeys even within London, the railway always took second place to pedestrian and road transport.

Urban transport had two main functions: to distribute passengers and goods from railway stations and, in some cases, docks; and to provide delivery and passenger services between city centres and suburbs. Though the railways played some part in the development of the latter, the pricing policy of the railway companies meant that most people chose to travel by road or to walk. In the mid-1850s, when the word 'commuter' came into use, there were fewer than 27,000 of them arriving daily in London by train, compared with 244,000 who walked or came by horse omnibus. With the exception of the Great Eastern Company, which was compelled by Parliament to offer a return fare of 2*d.* (under 1p) in 1864 on its new Edmonton and Chingford branches, the companies running into London were reluctant to offer cheap workmen's fares, finding them uneconomic and likely to drive away a better class of custom. Indeed, public transport in the Victorian city provides an accurate picture of the nature and extent of class divisions. Not only were railway carriages (and station facilities) apportioned strictly to First, Second and Third Class travellers, but fares and the availability of tickets were also used to keep the classes apart. The Great Northern offered quarter-price workmen's tickets from places like Hornsey or Finchley, not cheap at 3*d.* or 4*d.* (about 1p or 2p) return, but only on trains arriving in London before 6.00 a.m.; then came the half-fare tickets for lower-middle-class clerks arriving before 8.00 a.m.; and finally the ordinary third-class fares of between 1*s.* and 1*s.* 2*d.* (5p and 6p) return on which the real profits were made from the middle classes.

It can be no surprise, therefore, to find more people travelling by omnibus than by train. The number of horse omnibuses in use in the cities and towns of Britain expanded rapidly from the 1830s, undoubtedly helped by the increasing numbers of long-distance passengers and goods pouring into the railway termini. The first omnibus route in London, from Paddington to the Bank, was opened in 1829; by the 1850s there were over 800 buses on the streets of the capital, and when the London General Omnibus Company was founded in 1858 it had between 500 and 600 buses, nearly 6,000 horses, and was carrying in the 1860s some 40 million passengers a year. Even so, the omnibus was not – despite its name – for all. Those workers who used public transport were the relatively well-off.

The number of hackney carriages in London grew rapidly after ceasing to be regulated by statute in 1830, and, by mid-century, traffic jams were common in many large cities. In the late 1850s 1,700 vehicles an hour were crossing London Bridge at peak times, and in the 1870s 900 vehicles an hour were using Jamaica Street in Glasgow. Only limited relief was provided by new roads such as Shaftesbury Avenue, Northumberland Avenue, Charing Cross Road and Holborn Viaduct in London, or Victoria Street in Liverpool, or Corporation Street in Manchester. The solution which suggested itself in London was an urban railway system to the heart of the city, running partly underground. The first such line in London was opened by the Metropolitan Railway Company in 1863, and was soon carrying 25 million passengers a year – but the buses continued to carry 40 million. Better transport simply meant more traffic. Gradually further lines were added. The Inner Circle line was completed in 1884, and other parts of what were to become the London Underground were built by the major railway companies, such as the Great Northern, whose lines stretched to Edgware (1867), High Barnet (1871) and Muswell Hill for the newly-opened Alexandra Palace (1873). Urban railways were also developed elsewhere, notably in Glasgow, with the Cathcart circle line of 1887 and the Glasgow District Subway, opened with cable-hauled trains in January 1897. The latter was not a success, though, for within a year it was in competition with a new, more flexible and cheaper form of street transport, the electric tram.

The first tramway was begun in Liverpool in 1868, followed by London a year later. The Tramways Act of 1870 then empowered local authorities to construct municipal tramways, but only for use by private operators. Despite some successful steam-powered trams, the horse remained the main source of traction until the 1890s, when electric trams made their appearance. In London the tram was most important in the inner ring of lower-middle-class suburbs – in the centre, horse buses still held sway – but in many northern cities, where the suburbs were only just passing beyond a reasonable walking distance from the centre, the tram came into its own. Manchester had four times the mileage of tramway per head of population, and Glasgow twice the mileage per head, of London. In the first decade of the twentieth century the total length of track in Britain as a whole grew rapidly, from around 1,000 miles in 1900 to 2,530 in 1911. Electric trams were 40 per cent cheaper to run than horse-trams, and with increasing numbers of complete tramway systems passing under municipal control from the 1890s, cheap fares at last became a possibility – though still not always a reality.

Passenger transport by road in the twentieth century

The triumph of the electric tram was short-lived. Its track was inflexible and expensive, and its fixed routes were economic only in thickly populated areas. By the late 1930s some local authorities were beginning to replace their trams with trolley buses which, although still limited by unsightly overhead wires, made a more flexible use of road space. The number of trams in the country began to fall from 1931, and 30 years later there were fewer than a thousand left. The motor bus revolutionised passenger transport in town and country alike. In the early years there was confusion and chaos. Until 1910 buses were manufactured to meet the London market with little regard for technical reliability or even interchangeability of parts; thereafter the 'standard' London bus appeared. The system of licensing was also slow to evolve. Since 1889 horse buses had been required to register like hackney carriages – that is, the vehicle was licensed, not the route – and the same rule was applied to the first motor buses. As a result, free (and foul) competition reigned uncontrolled in the streets and on the highways, as rival companies jostled for trade. Not until the Road Traffic Act of 1930 was the system of licensing operators on routes introduced. Meanwhile, as with the early railways, the companies were sorting out their own problems, establishing monopolies by mergers and local agreements. Thus, by 1931, 80 per cent of vehicles were controlled by only 18 per cent of all operators. Major provincial companies, like Midland Red, were protected from competition by the licensing policy of Birmingham Corporation, and grew from 92 buses in 1919 to 1224 in 1938. In London, the London Passenger Transport Act of 1933 transferred all the capital's passenger transport, including the Underground, to public ownership.

During the later stages of the First World War buses and lorries played a major part in transporting troops and supplies. After the war, men who had learned to drive as soldiers were able to use their war gratuities to purchase cheap, second-hand vehicles and set up in business. Eighty per cent of bus operators owned fewer than five vehicles. In rural areas, the distinction between the carriage of passengers and goods was slow to evolve, and open lorries with bench seats (literally, *chars à banc*) were a common sight, especially for working-class outings. Buses at first operated mainly on urban routes, but rapid expansion in the 1920s brought regular (though less frequent) services in rural areas, and with the improvement in pneumatic tyres came the first luxury coaches and long-distance routes. In 1925 the railways were challenged for the first time on their own ground when the regular 'Greyhound' service was commenced between Bristol and London. By 1939 there were 53,000 buses and coaches operating in Great Britain.

After the Second World War, which saw a continued growth in the number of buses, two contrary trends emerged. As coaches and roads were improved, long-distance travel passed increasingly into the hands of the coach operators at the expense of the railway companies (British Railways after 1948); while in rural areas the bus companies were themselves put under pressure from the growth in the number of private cars. In 1958 two-thirds of Midland Red services, representing one third of the annual mileage, were said to be uneconomic. Eighty per cent of the Highland Bus Company's routes outside Inverness were also loss-making. Public subsidies were increasingly called for on social grounds, but by the 1960s the ownership of private transport was rapidly becoming the *sine qua non* of a rural existence.

The organisation of public transport was transformed when deregulation of buses, first in the provinces (1986) and then in London (1994), encouraged free competition between companies, with some subsidies for socially necessary but uneconomic routes. Coupled with the fragmentation of railways services into the hands of several private companies after 1996, some of which also had an interest in coach, sea or air travel, this meant that the trend of a century towards greater rationalisation and public ownership was reversed. Between 1986 and 1996 an increase in local bus mileage of 22 per cent was accompanied by a fall of 18 per cent in the number of passenger journeys travelled, while fares increased by half as much again as the retail prices index. How well the reintroduction of competition and private capital will enable public transport to respond to the apparently inexorable growth in private transport is therefore not clear as the century draws to a close.

Goods transport by road in the twentieth century

The history of road haulage follows a similar course to that of public passenger transport, with growth before the First World War from around

4,000 goods vehicles in 1904 to 82,000 by 1914. The demands of the war checked numbers in 1916–18, but thereafter there was rapid expansion from 62,000 vehicles in 1919 to nearly half a million by 1939. The Second World War again checked growth, before the 1950s saw numbers surge towards 1.4 million. The road network was hardly adequate to bear this increasing traffic, but during the next quarter of a century changes occurred not dissimilar to those refinements to the railway network which had taken place in the later nineteenth century. Mileages were cut, with bridges or tunnels across the major estuaries; trunk roads were improved with the construction of dual carriageways; other major roads were widened and straightened; and in 1955 the first motorways were begun. By 1993, 1,951 miles (3,141 kilometres) of motorway had been completed, and there were 404,200 heavy goods vehicles on the roads, controlled by 125,300 haulage operators.

The advantages of road haulage over the railways were cost and flexibility. In 1929, around 80 per cent of lorries were owned by the firms whose goods they conveyed. Most other hauliers were small, one-man or family operators. The main fleet owners at this time were in fact the railways. All four major railway companies had their own lorries, and held a controlling interest in Pickfords and other large firms. The real expansion of major road haulage companies came after nationalisation (1947), which put long-distance haulage in the hands of British Road Services but incidentally stimulated the growth of small local carriers, sometimes funded with their state compensation. Denationalisation (1953) then allowed these companies the scope to develop in competition with both British Road Services and British Railways. The decision to abandon state control in 1953 saw the beginnings of a struggle for survival which the road hauliers won over the railways in the 1960s. In 1952 the roads had carried under half the freight traffic of Britain; by 1958 the positions of road and rail had been reversed; by 1962 the roads had two-thirds of the traffic, and by 1994 they had over 90 per cent, the bulk of which was carried by private haulage firms.

Private road transport

Most people who did not wish to walk were dependent upon public transport until the end of the nineteenth century. Only the well-off could afford to hire – and only the rich could afford to own – private transport. All this was changed by the bicycle, which rapidly became popular after about 1895 among the younger and less wealthy sections of the community. The mass-produced ‘safety’ bicycle, first built in Coventry in 1886, with its pneumatic tyres patented by Dunlop in 1888, worked a revolution in transportation, leisure and engineering. Many of the early motor-car firms started out as manufacturers of bicycles. From the bicycle, those people who wanted mobility rather than exercise moved on to the motor bicycle. Indeed, not until the mid-1920s, when there were over half a million motor cycles in Britain, were their numbers significantly exceeded by those of the motor car. For those working-class families who obtained their own vehicles between the wars, the motor bicycle and side-car was the most likely first choice.

The motor car, though, was the new vehicle of the age, and became fashionable among the well-to-do, especially after the repeal of the Red Flag Act in 1896, followed by the Motor Car Act of 1903, which permitted speeds of 20 m.p.h. Ownership grew rapidly, from 8,000 in 1904 to 132,000 in 1914. In many communities professional men like doctors were the first to have cars. Although Herbert Austin was producing a small car at Longbridge by 1910, the year in which Henry Ford set up his factory at Trafford Park, Manchester, motoring before the First World War was still largely a pleasure of the wealthy few. The revolution in mass-produced, relatively cheap cars did not really begin to make an impact on Britain until after the First World War. The number of cars had fallen during the war, but rose rapidly in the 1920s until, in 1930, there were over a million, and by 1939 more than two million – over a hundred private cars for every mile of classified road in the country. Even so, most people did not have cars or access to them.

Only after the Second World War, which severely depressed numbers by restricting the availability of new models and of petrol, did Britain become a car-owning society. Pre-war numbers, which were again reached in the late 1940s, had doubled by 1958, and then doubled again to nearly 9 million by 1965. The next 30 years saw a further increase to nearly 21 million, with the average daily flow of traffic up 50 per cent on all roads – and double that on motorways – between 1981 and 1995. Car ownership, though, showed a divided society, with the number of households with one car remaining steady at around 45 per cent throughout the last three decades of the century, while the number of households with two or more cars doubled to around 23 per cent. That still left around a third of all households wholly dependent on public transport.

Rail transport in modern Britain

What the roads gained, the railways lost, either directly through the transfer of custom, or indirectly, through the failure to secure a share of new custom. Though railways had never been dominant in the provision of local facilities, they had provided the main long-distance transportation for 100 years. As late as the 1940s it was government policy to encourage an integrated transport system of road and rail. When the railways were nationalised in 1948, the length of track (19,853 miles or 31,950 km) was only 552 miles (888 km) below its peak. Fifteen years later, in

1963, the haemorrhage of custom to the roads led to the Beeching Report which recommended wholesale closure of uneconomic track. By 1994 the mileage had been cut to 10,278 (16,542 km), and the number of railway stations reduced from 4,347 in 1962 to a mere 2,565. Branch lines, rural lines and lines in the extremities of the country had been closed. The Scottish Highlands (never well-provided-for), Central and Western Wales, the South-West of England, East Anglia and Lincolnshire suffered most. Resources were put instead into the replacement of steam with diesel-powered locomotives, and then the electrification of the system, with nearly a third of lines electrified by 1994. Inter-city trains, hauled by electric locomotives travelling at over 100 miles an hour, were provided on some routes by the mid-1990s, but the high-speed passenger services pioneered in Japan and France had not been matched in Britain when the Channel Tunnel linking the railway networks of Britain and France was opened in 1994. The desire of the British government in the 1980s to promote a road link to compete with the railways under the Channel showed the extent to which the railways in Britain had declined in reputation and public policy. Seriously under-capitalised, with the heavily used commuter services around London badly in need of modernisation, British railways seemed in danger of joining the canals and turnpikes as vestiges of a bygone age when the decision was made in 1996 to sell off the track as a private company and to franchise freight and passenger services to several private operators in the hope of attracting fresh management and much-needed investment.

Despite the generally pessimistic figures of decline in public transport in general and the railways in particular, there have been some interesting new developments in the closing decades of the twentieth century, centred on light railways and the revival of the electric tram. The first such development came on Tyneside, where the local authority acquired the under-used suburban railway system, extended it underground through the heart of Newcastle, and opened a new integrated rail and bus urban transport system in 1980, combining the virtues of train, tram and omnibus. Other cities followed, notably Manchester and Sheffield. In each case the initiative was taken by the local authority, but the attempt to provide a subsidised, integrated and efficient public-transport system based on the new trams was hindered, in the short term at least, by the deregulation of bus services in 1986.

Sea and air

Although steamers had been in use in the coastal waters of Britain since the early nineteenth century, the transition from sail to steam in ocean-going vessels came relatively late. Brunel launched his celebrated *Great Western* in 1838, but the technology of sailing ships was also improved in the nineteenth century. They did not reach their maximum tonnage until 1865, and were not overtaken by steam ships (mainly screw-propelled after the 1840s, and built of iron) until 1883. The great steam liners (turbine-driven from the beginning of the twentieth century, and increasingly powered by oil rather than coal) were the pride of their merchant fleets, and for a hundred years vied with one another to achieve the fastest crossing of the Atlantic. The position of Britain as an island meant that sea transport remained essential for all normal freight, carrying 94 per cent by weight (76 per cent by value) of British overseas trade until the opening of the Channel Tunnel in 1994; but in 1958 the first transatlantic air passenger service using a jet-propelled aircraft spelt the end of the great ships for all but luxury cruises.

Aircraft were important for the carriage only of light, high-value freight, including mail, so that even in the 1990s less than one per cent of Britain's overseas trade (by weight) was taken by air. British civil airports in 1995 handled about 1.7 million tonnes of cargoes, over half of it through London Heathrow, but this was only a tenth of what passed through Dover alone. Bulk cargoes remained the monopoly of shipping, and 'super' oil-tankers replaced the great passenger liners as the largest ships afloat. Ferries, though, continued to be important in coastal waters for the conveyance of both people and freight. Nevertheless, in the Scottish Highlands and Islands light aircraft supplemented the sea services, and flights between major mainland cities became competitive with First Class rail travel. In 1965 4.7 million passengers travelled on domestic flights, a figure which was to increase three-fold in the next 30 years. The real significance of the advent of air travel, though, lay in international flights. By the 1960s almost all passenger travel to destinations beyond Western Europe was by air, and Heathrow airport, opened in 1946, grew to be the busiest in the world. By the mid-1990s over 131 million passengers were passing through British airports on international flights, over a third of them through Heathrow. The significance of this expansion of air travel in the jet age can be appreciated if a map of time-distances in the 1990s is imposed on one for the 1780s. Sydney now appears no further from London than was Bristol before John Palmer introduced the first mail coach in 1784.

Towns

Urbanisation – not simply the growth of towns, but the transformation of society into one dominated by the facts of urban existence – needs to be discussed with care, for there is no generally accepted definition of what is meant by 'urban'. Often size is used as a rough guide. In the case of Britain, communities of under 10,000 people are sometimes excluded from the definition, although in other cases a population of 2,000 is regarded as being sufficiently large to define a town. At around this size a community begins to be functionally differentiated from the countryside. If towns are to grow much above this size they need a purpose beyond that of local centres for trading and economic organisation. Thus many of the larger urban communities of Britain in the eighteenth century were ancient administrative centres, the county towns and cathedral cities of an earlier age.

Constraints on the growth of towns were severely practical. Their market-places had to be either within a day's return journey of the villages and farms in their neighbourhood – thus favouring a dispersed pattern of small settlements – or situated on good lines of communication, such as the coast or a river. Once a town exceeded a size of a few thousand, the logistical problems of feeding the population, supplying it with water, and disposing of its waste products became acute. The largest cities of Europe – the administrative capitals – grew despite such constraints, and periodically paid the economic (and political) penalties for failure well into the nineteenth century. To be released from these constraints on urban growth, a society needed good communications and an agricultural sector of the economy sufficiently developed to be able to support an expanding non-agricultural sector, as well as a population wishing (or constrained) to live in towns. These conditions were met in later eighteenth-century Britain, when the process of urbanisation began.

The growth of an urban society

London was unique, not only within Britain, but within Europe. At the beginning of the eighteenth century, it was already as large as its nearest rivals – Constantinople and Paris – were to be a hundred years later. By 1801 its population was around one million, approximately 8 per cent of the inhabitants of Britain. Paris was about half the size of London at this time, and contained only 2 per cent of the population of France. Most urban centres, apart from London, were small. The five largest provincial towns in England in the early eighteenth century – Norwich, York, Bristol, Newcastle and Exeter – all had populations of under 20,000. By the time of the first census in 1801, the five largest towns – Manchester/Salford, Liverpool, Birmingham, Bristol and Leeds – had populations in excess of 50,000, but no town other than London had a population exceeding 100,000. Indeed even at this date there were only 19 towns with populations exceeding 20,000, the combined populations of which added up to slightly less than the population of London. At the other end of the scale, there were over 200 urban communities with populations of between 2,500 and 10,000.

With their smaller populations, Scotland and Wales had far fewer urban communities than England. Scotland in the mid-eighteenth century had four towns with populations of over 10,000 – Edinburgh, Glasgow, Aberdeen and Dundee – but by 1801 only Edinburgh and Glasgow had exceeded 50,000, and only five other towns – Aberdeen, Dundee, Paisley,

Inverness and Greenock – had populations of over 10,000. There were no large towns in Wales. The biggest in 1801 was Merthyr, with 8,000 inhabitants brought together by the rapidly expanding iron industry. Swansea had just under 7,000, but other towns of later importance, such as Cardiff and Newport, were still under 2,000.

At the very beginning of the nineteenth century one-third of the 8.9 million population of England and Wales was already 'urban'; by 1851 approximately half of the 16.9 million inhabitants lived in an urban environment. That is, the number of people living in urban communities of over 10,000 people increased by over 5 million during the first half of the nineteenth century, representing an annual average growth of 0.36 per cent – a rate of urban concentration twice that of any continental European country. Scotland, with 0.3 per cent, experienced a similar increase in its urban population, although not until the 1880s did over half its population live in centres of more than 5,000 population.

The first half of the nineteenth century saw the very largest towns – London, Manchester/Salford, Glasgow, Edinburgh, Liverpool, Birmingham, Bristol and Leeds – continue to grow rapidly, but urbanisation involved also the emergence of increasing numbers of smaller towns, including some which had been scarcely more than villages at the end of the eighteenth century. The urban world of early industrial Britain was essentially one of (by later standards) small communities. This is where definition becomes both important and difficult. In 1831 Halifax was a town of 15,382 people, set in a large moorland parish of 109,899 inhabitants; Bacup was a town of a mere 9,196 people in the parish of Whalley with 97,868 inhabitants. In each case the town was small, but in the 1831 Census Report John Rickman (who was responsible for conducting the early censuses) added together the several populations of the different townships in such heavily populated parishes, and gave the total figure under the separate heading of what he termed the 'aggregate population of connected places'; indeed, he credited the whole of the 123,393 population of the similarly sprawling parish of Leeds to the town of Leeds itself. What we see here is the emergence of a concentration of population which had ceased to be rural, but which was not yet quite urban.

The distribution of such distinct concentrations of over 10,000 people in 1831 shows marked regional variations. There were 155 such places in England, 38 of which – including some of the largest – were in and around London. The City of Westminster alone, with a population of 202,000, was the same size as Glasgow. Of the 117 provincial centres of population, 30 were in the North-West (23 of them in Lancashire) and 24 in Yorkshire (21 in the West Riding); no other region had more than 15 (the South-East, excluding London) and no other county had more than six (Durham, Kent and Staffordshire). East Anglia, with only five centres, had the fewest. If we turn to centres of over 50,000 population then the pattern becomes even more marked. There were eight such places within 'greater' London, and 16 elsewhere in the provinces, of which four were in Yorkshire and seven in the North-West.

Wales had only five centres of over 10,000 population (and only 17 of over 5,000); one of these (Wrexham) was in the North-East, and the other four (Merthyr, the largest; Swansea; Bedwelty parish, including Tredegar; and Trevethin, including Pontypool) were in either Glamorgan or Monmouthshire. Urbanisation in Scotland showed a similar geographical concentration. Though there were 52 places with over 5,000 inhabitants, scattered across 19 counties, there were only 13 of over 10,000, of which only Aberdeen, Inverness and Dumfries lay outside the Central Lowlands.

Most people continued to live in small communities, and even London covered a remarkably small geographical area, while the built-up centres of Birmingham, Manchester or Glasgow were still within easy walking distance of green fields and open country. Although language was changing to meet new perceptions, the word 'urbane', with its connotations of civilisation and culture, still held its own against 'urban'. Jane Austen may not have shared the priorities of social historians, but she accurately reflected the dominant perceptions of her age. Alongside Paisley or Oldham, one must set the similarly sized Bath or Shrewsbury. More typical of its age than spreading Leeds was sleepy York, still confined within its city walls and bearing the marks of past more than present greatness. When the Frenchman, Gustave d'Eichthal, made his way northwards from London in 1828 he commented:

> There is hardly a single mill along the way. The terrain is flat and chiefly agricultural. On this side of England there is not one industrial town; . . . While commercial towns in England have grown enormously in recent years, market towns in agricultural areas have remained unchanged or even been reduced in size. York . . . has not grown at all.[7]

The last point is not strictly accurate, for York had grown; but the impression is useful. Though the years 1750–1830 did see enormous changes in both town and countryside, these must be put in perspective. Whatever the economic indicators suggest about an industrial revolution occurring in the late eighteenth century, the consequences of that revolution are more frequently overstated than understated. The rate of change was quickening, but the overall context of society, even as late as 1830, was one in which traditional influences and attitudes were still tremendously important.

The urban environment, 1750–1830

With such a diversity of towns and cities, no easy generalisations can be made about what constituted the urban environment. London was, on account of its size, unique. During the eighteenth and nineteenth centuries elegant squares filled out the spacious West End, and formerly fashionable housing to the east in Soho and St Giles was turned into tenements. After 1750 the parish of Marylebone grew rapidly, with the building of the New Road (1756–7) between Paddington in the west and Islington in the east, while new bridges across the river at Westminster and Blackfriars opened up the south bank to speculative building. In the City of London itself, the population was probably already falling, with increasing amounts of space being devoted to commercial premises; but on the fringes of the City, beyond the line of the ancient walls, housing densities were increasing to cope with the rapidly expanding population attracted to the metropolis by opportunities of work in its docks and manufacturing industries. The population of Clerkenwell more than doubled during the course of the century, from 9,000 in 1710–11 to 23,396 at the time of the census in 1801, with over seven people on average living in each house. Fourteen London parishes had populations of over 20,000 at the start of the nineteenth century, the largest being Marylebone which, with 64,000, had the same population as Bristol.

London therefore provides us with the first 'modern' urban environment even before the conventionally defined 'industrial revolution' began. There were few characteristics of life in the environment of a nineteenth-century industrial city which had not been anticipated in eighteenth-century London. Social differentiation of the classes was well under way by the mid-eighteenth century, as the settlement pattern of the pre-modern city (still common in the developing world today) was reversed. Instead of suburbs spreading – but hardly built, and certainly not designed – outside the line of the ancient city walls in places like Wapping and Shoreditch, where the poor lived a half-urban and half-rural existence, new suburbs were now being built for the wealthy. City merchants moved away from the heart of their commercial operations, leaving behind a deteriorating housing stock and a rash of cheap, speculative infill building. Dilapidated and overcrowded tenements and lodging-houses became warrens of disease. Life in the countryside was hardly idyllic, but the overcrowding associated with urban living compounded the nuisances of an impure and irregular water supply, inadequate or non-existent sewage disposal and atmospheric pollution. Some improvements were made in the main thoroughfares with successive local Acts of Parliament for paving, draining and lighting, and slum clearances were undertaken, but the rate of London's growth made the task of general improvement seem almost impossible.

It is probably only since 1945 that cities across the world have contrived to look alike. In an earlier age the provincial cities and towns of Britain were marked by an individuality born of differences in history, function and even civic personalities. Nevertheless, there were trends and fashions. Brick or stone, with slate or tile roofing, were now universally used for town buildings. Architects' pattern books spread the latest styles from London, as merchants and gentry built and rebuilt their town houses. Older buildings were refaced in accordance with modern fashion. Public buildings multiplied, as ancient churches were now joined by assembly rooms, newspaper reading rooms, libraries, theatres, hospitals, educational institutions and Dissenting chapels, as well as corn exchanges, cloth halls, customs houses or whatever else the local economy required. All was built in a style which proclaimed the confidence and pride of provincial Britain.

Purpose-built housing for the lower classes was rare before the mid-eighteenth century, but, as urban populations began to expand, so housing of distinct types was provided for the various classes. As in London, the merchant, gentry and professional classes began to move outwards in search of space and fresh air, and new streets, terraces and squares appeared, as in the metropolis. Within Glasgow, the tobacco barons occupied new houses in George Square in the third quarter of the eighteenth century, followed by other streets, appropriately named Virginia, Havannah and Jamaica. But such excursions into town planning were not always a success. David and James Laurie laid out what was to be one of the finest residential areas to the south of the river, with grand names such as Carlton Place, Cavendish Street and Marlborough Street, but by the early nineteenth century Laurieston had become the core of the Gorbals slums.

The greatest success of eighteenth-century urban development was undoubtedly achieved in Edinburgh. To the south, George Square was laid out in 1766 as a suburb for the prosperous who wished to leave the Old Town, where they inhabited respectable floors in the same tenements as tradesmen and artisans; and in the same year plans were invited for a major new development to the north, strictly controlled by the Town Council. Over the next few decades the New Town emerged, at once both a social and political statement, intended to accommodate those who could afford to remove themselves from the stench of the Old Town, and to assert the right of Edinburgh to continue to be regarded as the metropolis of the North even after its loss of status following the Act of Union.

Within England, similar examples could be multiplied. In Bristol, Queen Square had been laid out in the first quarter of the eighteenth century; Bath was remodelled as the most fashionable resort in the middle decades of the century, with squares, crescents and circles in the classical tradition, which found a later echo in Edinburgh. And there were also disasters to match Glasgow's Laurieston. In Liverpool a residential 'new town' was planned on land leased from the Earl of Sefton at Toxteth Park; but the sub-leases were loosely drafted, and builders followed the market in erecting not spacious dwellings for the wealthy but cramped courts and mean streets for the poor.

Historians of the period of the early industrial revolution have invariably been drawn to Manchester and Birmingham as the typical urban products of that era. Certainly the growth of both towns was astonishing, repeating towards the end of the eighteenth century the experience of Liverpool a generation earlier. Manchester (including Salford) grew from around 30,000 in 1775 to 84,000 in 1801. But unlike Liverpool and Edinburgh, where civic corporations tried to influence the development of their cities, neither Manchester nor Birmingham had urban institutions above the level of parish and manor. Their growth was largely undirected. This was also true of many of the 'satellite' towns which grew up in the Black Country, south-eastern Lancashire/north-eastern Cheshire, and the textile districts of the West Riding and East Midlands. Here urban development occurred on an economic and social frontier, beyond the reach of traditional restraints and authority – almost, it seemed, beyond civilisation itself. For this reason, if for no other, contemporaries came to identify in these districts not merely progress and wealth creation, but a social and political threat to the old order.

The deterioration of the environment in the towns and cities of early industrial Britain has frequently been commented upon. No-one can claim that it was pleasant, but developments need to be put into context. Most building was piecemeal, by small speculative builders with little capital, working on sub-leases. They were acutely aware of their market and the limits of what it would bear. Many of the new houses erected were, in fact, superior to what had previously been available. Lath and plaster walls gave way to brick, albeit sometimes only single-brick walls. Back-to-back housing was seen as an improvement, for at least every family had its own front door.

The real problem was not the housing as such, but the total environment. Unregulated infilling produced mazes of courts and alleys, with few or no services. In towns like Leeds, Newcastle and Nottingham the increased populations were accommodated within the existing built-up central areas. Scottish tenements naturally lent themselves to minute subdivision of properties and high population densities, while in England the more typical terraced house was not exempt from the same process. As immigrants from the countryside (and, in the early nineteenth century, from Ireland) crowded into the towns of Britain in search of work, houses were sub-let by the room, and cellars became homes for the poorest families. Above such scenes of human degradation hung palls of smoke and industrial fumes, while everywhere was the inescapable stench of animal and human excrement. Though familiarity with such an atmosphere could lead to acceptance, those who could move out to suburbs did so.

Urban development in the age of the railway

Despite the initial fears of countrymen about what the railway might do to their livestock, the greatest upheaval caused by the railway was in the towns, where the railway companies became owners of hundreds of acres of central building land. Their lines cut through communities, their marshalling yards displacing thousands of the poorest labouring families from their homes and causing the first clearances of urban slums. Some 800 acres (324 hectares) of central land were taken in London for railway purposes during the course of the nineteenth century, entailing the displacement of between 76,000 and 120,000 persons. The homeless packed into what housing remained, or slept underneath the great viaducts which strode across the urban landscape. Carefully avoiding the most expensive land already given over to commercial property, the railway companies frequently ended their lines on the fringes of the developed city centres. The last mile of track into a major city was often by far the most expensive to construct. With their warehousing facilities, the railways transformed the shape of the large towns through which they passed or in which they terminated. Though land values along the railway routes through cities were often depressed, near the terminals and major stations values and rentals were inflated, as industrial and commercial property expanded and extended the old commercial centres with their high densities of building but low densities of population. Where housing did remain, trapped between commercial and industrial developments in areas marked off by intersecting tracks, there was little incentive to improvement. Landlords simply let to a poorer class of tenant and awaited a profitable offer from some commercial concern. But the railways were not a complete environmental disaster in the inner city. They also brought positive gains, with stately buildings and new approach roads which proclaimed the commercial vigour and civic pride of urban Britain.

The social geography of towns was deeply affected by developments in transportation, though railways in the main reinforced existing trends rather than started new ones. Sometimes the railway companies consciously indulged in social as well as civil engineering, exploiting the desire of the prospering to live in suburbs in the hope of increasing a lucrative middle-class commuter trade, but such attempts were rarely successful. More common was the expansion and revitalisation of older centres, like Croydon, Epsom, Kingston and Richmond to the south and west of London. One clear example of the impact of the railways can be seen in the consequences of the Liverpool Street Station Act of 1864, which compelled the Great Eastern Company to offer a return fare of 2*d.* (under 1p) on its new Edmonton and Chingford branches. The north-eastern suburbs along these lines grew dramatically in the second half of the nineteenth century, with twice the rate of immigration and population density of any other sector of the suburbs. The transformation worked here by the railway was graphically described by William Birt, general manager of the Great Eastern, in evidence to the Royal Commission on the Housing of the Working Classes in 1884:

> That used to be a very nice district indeed, occupied by good families, with houses of from £150 to £250 a year, with coach houses and stable, a garden and a few acres of land. But very soon after this obligation was placed on the Great Eastern to run workmen's trains . . . the speculative builders went down into the neighbourhood and, as a consequence, each good house was one after another pulled down, and the district is given up entirely, I may say, now to the working man. I lived down there myself and I waited till most of my neighbours had gone; and then, at last, I was obliged to go.[8]

On the Great Northern, by contrast, which did not offer such cheap workmen's fares, neighbouring Hornsey, Wood Green and Southgate belonged to the commuting clerk.

Such social zoning is a characteristic of the modern city, and in London can be closely related to methods and costs of transportation. Broadly speaking, the poorest were to be found in an inner pedestrian zone; then came the better-off working class and lower-middle class on the omnibus routes, and the middle class in the railway suburbs, graded by the fares structure; while the wealthy carriage trade and first-class rail commuter would be found in the leafiest suburbs or out in the country in the Chilterns, on the Downs or even on the coast at Brighton.

Elsewhere the pattern found in London was not so pronounced. Even at the end of the nineteenth century, many respectable suburbs in the provinces were still within walking distance of town centres, and the nature and availability of public transport were not the sole determinants of where people lived. In general, the better-off areas were upwind and uphill of the most noxious 'down-town' areas, where the poorer classes lived close to the stinking river, canal and railway line. As Maurice Beresford has written of Leeds:

> Any time after 1838 one could catch the omnibus from Paradise Lost to Paradise Regained, with a choice of northbound vehicles, one on the Otley turnpike to Headingley village and the other on the Harrogate turnpike to Potternewton and Chapel Allerton.[9]

And when Headingley was no longer select enough, they moved on to Roundhay. By the mid-twentieth century, they were taking refuge in Harrogate.

It is unwise to seek monocausal explanations for the way in which the urban geography of towns developed. The attitude and policies of the ground landlord could be decisive in initiating developments – men like the Earl of Cardigan, who owned half of Headingley; the Ramsden family, on whose lands most of Huddersfield was built; and Lord Calthorpe, who developed his Edgbaston estate south of Birmingham and did his best to keep it exclusive – but the effectiveness of such control depended upon the length and restrictiveness of the leases granted and the nature of fashionable demand, itself always subject to change. Suburban railways and, more particularly, public road transport, were also important. For those who did not have their own means of conveyance (the vast majority until after the Second World War), where they worked, and how easily and cheaply they could get there, were major factors in determining where they lived. When tram-lines were laid, land values went up along the routes and building mushroomed at the outer termini. Discriminatory fare policies, by private companies and local corporations, determined the social complexion of the suburbs and largely kept the poor within the confines of the inner city. But public transport also united communities, giving provincial municipalities a new coherence and sense of identity.

The built environment

The built environment has largely been the creation of architects working on single or small groups of buildings for clients, and speculative builders putting up houses for sale or for rent. The bulk of working-class housing before the First World War was provided by middle-class entrepreneurial landlords. Occasionally co-operative bodies such as freehold building societies and, more recently, housing associations erected houses for their members, but an alternative approach which has been current in various forms over the past two centuries has been the planned (usually philanthropic) development which, after 1919, included subsidised municipal housing.

The early factory-masters had often, of necessity, to provide housing for their workforces; and rural landlords also on occasions planned or even removed and rebuilt whole villages on their estates. David Dale's New Lanark is an example of the wedding of the Scottish planned village movement with the factory community, even to the extent of rehousing emigrants from Caithness beside the River Clyde. Later in the nineteenth century, factory-masters continued to build colonies of houses through a mixture of philanthropic and self-interested motives, the most famous being Saltaire, built by Titus Salt in the Aire valley above Bradford in the 1850s; and Akroydon, begun in Halifax in 1861 with Gilbert Scott as the first architect. Other employers to provide housing on a large scale for their employees were coal-mining companies – between a quarter and a third of British miners were housed by their employers – and railway companies, especially in the company towns of Crewe, Wolverton and Swindon.

At the end of the nineteenth century came three settlements which were much more in the way of social experiments: W. H. Lever's Port Sunlight, begun in 1888; George Cadbury's Bourneville, started in 1893; and Joseph

Rowntree's New Earswick, commenced in 1901. The aim of all three was to demonstrate that industrial life did not need to be drab, and to bring to town-dwellers the benefits of country living. Port Sunlight was primarily a company village, providing subsidised homes for employees, with rents from 6*s*. (30p) a week at a density of only eight houses per acre (about 20 per hectare). Bourneville and New Earswick, on the other hand, were model villages not primarily intended for company employees, being more of a general statement of what housing should be like and a demonstration that it could be built for economic but realistic rents. Rowntree's scheme derived its inspiration partly from Cadbury's example, but also from his experience (and his son Seebohm's experience) of poverty in York, where the problem was not a shortage of houses but of housing at rentals the poor could afford – not more than 5*s*. (25p) a week. In all three places, the regimented barrack-square approach to housing was abandoned in favour of natural street lines, open spaces and gardens.

In the twentieth century two strands of development can be traced: the garden city or garden suburb movement, and the provision of low-cost municipal housing.

Ebenezer Howard published his celebrated manifesto, *Tomorrow: A Peaceful Path to Real Reform* in 1898, advocating garden cities to provide a fresh environment combining the best of town and country. This work, reissued in 1902 as *Garden Cities of Tomorrow*, influenced Joseph Rowntree, who employed as his architect at New Earswick a strong advocate of the garden city ideal, Raymond Unwin. Howard's ideas were given material form at Letchworth, started shortly after New Earswick, but the ideal never succeeded in the revolutionary way Howard had intended. It inspired not reconstructed cities, but merely garden suburbs such as Hampstead, laid out between 1907 and 1914 with Unwin as one of the architects. Nevertheless, the proponents of the garden city made important contributions to both the planning of housing and the appearance of twentieth-century urban developments. Unwin was a member of the Tudor Walters Committee in 1918, which established the standards for municipal housing between the wars.

The solution of many planners to the inner-city problems of the mid-nineteenth century was to use public transport as a means of alleviating overcrowding; but this remedy was too exclusive to help the poor, who could not afford any kind of public transport and yet needed to be on hand centrally each day to pick up what casual work they could. The demolition of cheap slums by railway companies which did not also demolish their places of employment simply made matters worse. So from the 1840s various philanthropic housing societies were formed in London to provide 'model dwellings' for the labouring classes, the best-known being the Peabody Trust of 1862. They built largely tenement blocks, but by the end of the century had scarcely scratched the problem, housing only 123,000 people, or less than 3 per cent of the city's population.

Following the Artizans' and Labourers' Dwellings Act of 1875, local authorities also began to involve themselves in the provision of housing for the working classes, but only on a modest scale. The main purpose of the Act was to encourage the replacement of unfit houses, not to add to the existing stock. This came only with the Housing of the Working Classes Act of 1890, and between 1890 and 1914 the newly formed London County Council replaced 22,000 houses and built a further 25,000 – a very modest start. The most active local authority for its size was Liverpool, which built 2,895 houses under the Act, providing accommodation for 1.3 per cent of the city's population compared with an average for England and Wales of 0.5 per cent. None of these houses was subsidised. The prevailing view was that wages followed rents, so to keep the one artificially low would merely depress the other. The solution to the housing crisis which confronted Edwardian Britain was not, it was argued, local authority housing, but private developments on cheap suburban sites. The price of building land was the key to economic but low rents. Twentieth-century politicians had therefore to consider two approaches to the housing problem: the garden city model, which developed into the new towns policy; or the provision of subsidised municipal housing.

After the First World War there was a shortage of some 600,000 houses in Great Britain. Rent restrictions imposed in 1915 had discouraged speculative building for rent. Overcrowding was widespread. The 'homes fit for heroes' policy led to Acts of Parliament in 1919 which provided central subsidies for both council and private building, and allowed for council rents to be held artificially low at the pre-war levels pegged by the 1915 Act. Though further Acts were needed in the 1920s to make the new policy work – particularly the first Labour Government's 1924 Act (the Wheatley Act) – considerable progress was made.

The situation in Scotland was far worse. Not only was the existing housing stock of tenements in poorer condition than the working-men's terraces of England, but overcrowding was also more severe. In 1911, one in five Glasgow families was living in one room, over half with three or more people to the room, half as bad again as in the worst London boroughs. Yet of the 126,000 houses built in Britain between 1919 and 1921 only 6,000 were in Scotland. Although by 1939 300,000 new houses had been built, Scotland still lagged far behind the rest of the country. A survey conducted in 1935–6 showed that, whereas 3.8 per cent of English homes were overcrowded, the figure for Scotland was 22.5 per cent. Even where extensive slum clearances and rehousing took place, the quality of what replaced it was not good, and estates like those at Wardieburn and Craigmillar in Edinburgh or Blackhill in Glasgow were a far cry from the ideals of architects like Raymond Unwin.

Nearly 2.5 million new houses were built in England and Wales between 1919 and 1934; 31 per cent of these were council houses, and of the remainder a quarter had received a subsidy. Large new estates were built on green-field sites, linked with town centres by efficient and cheap tram, trolley and bus services. Yet the fundamental problem of housing the poor had still not been solved. The new council estates were, in the main, for the better-off sort of working-class families who could afford the rents and the fare to work. The poor were still trapped in the inner cities, and would remain there until low wages and casual labour were abolished, or until their places of work were moved out to where their new, subsidised homes were to be built.

This was the attraction of the 'new town' policy, one which became fashionable after the Second World War, although its origins can be traced back to Howard in England and Patrick Geddes in Scotland. After 1945 the policy was to try to halt the growth and decay of the big conurbations, and to avoid the multiplication of heartless suburban council estates by creating new (or expanding old) urban communities in the countryside. Urban sprawl was to be limited by 'green belts', designated by Act of Parliament in 1947. This policy produced five 'new towns' in Scotland, two in Wales, and 22 in England. As with previous 'final solutions' to the housing problem, the new towns were only a partial success. They drew not only population and employment from the inner cities, but also the resources needed to redevelop what was left. By the early 1990s, with economic depression intensifying and with the collapse of much of the old industrial structure, the problem of the inner cities remained as acute as at any time in the previous hundred years.

Radical exercises in planning were only part of the post-Second-World-War response to the housing needs of the population. The main thrust of policy was still, as in the inter-war period, the encouragement of house construction in both the public and private sectors, but one major change was the collapse of the privately rented house market. In 1947 58 per cent of the housing stock was rented from private landlords; in 1973 the figure was 14 per cent. Meanwhile the proportion of houses rented from public authorities had doubled to 30 per cent, but with marked differences between England and Scotland, where in 1977 53 per cent of housing was rented from public authorities and still 21 per cent from private landlords. This dependence on the public sector was greater than in any other Western economy, and in the 1980s central policy changed to encourage the transfer of local-authority housing into private ownership. Whereas after the Second World War less than a third of housing was in owner occupation, this had risen to two-thirds 40 years later, and local-authority rented housing had fallen to under a fifth of the housing stock.

The policy of council-house building was partly discredited by its social failure. The idealists of the garden city movement had aimed to recreate whole communities, but many of the suburban housing estates conspicuously failed to do this. Furthermore, in the drive after 1945 to reconcile high land values and high building costs with the need for low rents, architects resorted on a large scale to building high-rise flats constructed of prefabricated materials. The tower block appeared to be the answer to the housing problem, just as the office block satisfied the commercial planner's dream, and both came to dominate the skylines of all the major cities in the 1960s. The flats were little different from tenements, only the new methods of construction enabled them to be bigger and (it was thought) better than ever before. In fact they came to be hated by those who lived in them, and their constructional materials turned out to be less durable than had been hoped. By the 1980s they were being demolished and replaced with conventional housing built by a variety of public-sector and private partnerships. Nevertheless, despite sales and demolition, public housing authorities in Great Britain still owned around 4.6 million houses and flats in the mid-1990s, compared with under a million homes provided by housing associations.

The motor car and the modern city

Few of the houses built for the working classes before the 1950s had a garage. The majority of people used public transport, and this was reflected in both the design and location of housing estates. But as more and more people acquired the use of a private motor car, so they joined the rich, who had always had more freedom over where to live. Within the limits of 'green belt' planning policy, private builders could now look for low-cost sites in the country. As the inner cities decayed, the suburbs became ever more extensive, and villages also were drawn into the residential as well as economic orbit of towns.

The social consequences of this were far-reaching. Areas with dying industries, like the textile communities of the Pennine valleys, became dormitory suburbs for the towns and cities of the West Riding and Greater Manchester and lost their independent identities. In small villages, protected from development or not yet thought desirable by builders, shops, schools and churches lost customers, decayed and closed. Even in growing villages the central pull of the easily accessible town could damage amenities, people often preferring to drive into the larger commercial centres for greater choice and lower prices.

The motor car also reshaped the urban environment. Drivers, impatient at traffic jams, expected bigger roads and more parking places. Like the railways before them, the new roads pushed decaying housing out of their paths and polluted the environment of that which remained. In the better-planned developments, and in the new towns, the garden city principle was reasserted, with the segregation of pedestrians from motor traffic. In the 1960s, for example, the new town of Milton Keynes was built with a traffic-free shopping precinct, but overall the design of the town was still centred on the motor car. Older cities also adopted the pattern of creating traffic-free shopping areas. Coventry, rebuilt after extensive bombing in the Second World War, excluded the motor car from much of the city centre, a policy followed by other older towns such as Leeds and Newcastle, which resorted to urban motorways to secure – at a price – more peaceful and pedestrianised centres. By the 1990s a combination of bypasses and impossible traffic congestion within many ancient town and city centres has made this a common response as, amid continuing social and technical change, man struggles to come to terms with his ability to create, destroy and recreate the environment.

The location of industry

The first industrial revolution

The location of industry was determined by the availability not only of raw materials and markets, but also of a skilled labour force, and for much of the eighteenth century this had a conservative effect on the distribution of industrial activities. The great market of London, for example, with its ready supply of skilled and unskilled labour, and its good communications by sea both with the rest of Britain and with the wider world, ensured that the capital long remained the chief manufacturing centre despite the fact that it had few natural power resources and did not share in that spectacular transference of manufacturing activities from the home and small workshop to the factory and large workshop which has long been identified with the industrial revolution in the north of England.

It would nevertheless be wrong to imply that by 1800 most industry even in the provinces was so organised. At the time of the 1801 Census at least half the populations of many villages in the West Country were engaged in industrial pursuits, and not only textile production. Village craftsmen were as much a part of the scene as village weavers or agricultural workers. Every county produced a wide range of manufactured goods, but certain places were becoming identified with specialised products – straw plaiting in Bedfordshire, Buckinghamshire, Cambridgeshire and Hertfordshire; textiles in the West Riding, Lancashire and the East Midlands; guns, locks and buttons in Birmingham; watches in Coventry; nails in Dudley; files in Warrington; cutlery in Sheffield. All this was still small-scale, often domestic, production. Only in certain industries requiring expensive capital equipment, such as brewing and iron-making, were large works required.

In 1791, Arthur Young observed that 'all the activity and industry of this kingdom is fast concentrating where there are coalpits'.[10] He was exaggerating, but had correctly observed the long-term trend. More accurately, he should have noticed the extent to which industry was concentrating in those places which had both coal and other raw materials to hand. For example, Prestonpans on the Forth, where John Roebuck set up his sulphuric acid works in 1749, had local coal, but more importantly, it was already a major producer of sea-salt. And the coalfields of Britain were also the main iron fields. It was here that major industrial growth occurred. Older centres of iron production, like the Weald, declined; the last furnace there closed down in 1812, and the last forge in 1828. But in South Wales and Monmouthshire, around a hundred furnaces were built in the decade 1796–1806, by which date 90 per cent of British pig iron was being smelted in the five coalfields of South Wales, Shropshire, south Staffordshire, south Yorkshire and Scotland. Within the Scottish field the great Carron works had been built by Roebuck and his partners in the east, but by 1830 easier coal seams and better iron reserves were drawing the centre of the Scottish industry to the west.

Much of this and other, even larger-scale, industry was still located in the countryside. Coal mining was and long remained a village activity. Pits were small and widely scattered within their fields. Rapidly industrialising areas, like the Black Country or the valleys of South Wales, comprised strings of industrial villages, small communities centred on the pit or iron-works. Innovations in textile production initially intensified this trend. The early spinning-factories in the cotton industry were powered by water, and so entrepreneurs turned to the countryside for power: the Derwent valley at Cromford, where Richard Arkwright built his first mills; the Goyt Valley above Stockport, where Samuel Oldknow opened his Mellor factory; Samuel Greg's Styal mill on the River Bollin south of Manchester; New Lanark in the gorge below the celebrated Falls of Clyde. In such isolated places, with no natural advantages except abundant power, labour was hard to find. Houses had to be built to attract workers; child labour was imported from urban workhouses; Oldknow even had to take up farming to employ the menfolk so that he could use their families in his factory. As the output from mechanised spinning increased, so did the search for weavers. Part-time weaver-farmers were tempted to devote themselves more and more to their lucrative industrial trade; yarn was put out to weavers in ever-expanding hinterlands; the countryside became increasingly dependent on manufactures whilst remaining essentially rural.

All this changed as the application of steam power to textile machinery became more common in the early nineteenth century. There was now no limit to the power sources of a small town with good canal links to a nearby coalfield, and the advantages of a central location began to assert themselves. By 1830 the textile factory (especially the cotton textile factory) had entered its second phase of development. The countryside was beginning to experience de-industrialisation, though the process was to be a long-drawn-out one over many decades, and would not be completed before much social hardship had been experienced in village and town alike.

The workshop of the world

The spread of steam power and the establishment of the basic railway network had, by 1850, reinforced the tendency within the British economy towards concentration and specialisation in industrial production. In 1838 Lancashire already had 69 per cent of the cotton workers of England and Wales; by 1850 the figure was 74 per cent. In the worsted industry Yorkshire had acquired a virtual monopoly of the trade by 1830. In 1850, when the former centre of Norfolk had 1,400 employees in 11 mills, Yorkshire had 70,905 in 418 mills. The advance of Yorkshire was almost as clear-cut in the woollen industry. Between 1835 and 1850, the number of mills in Yorkshire rose from 406 to 880 and the number of employees from 23,600 to 40,600; in the West Country, by contrast, the number of mills fell from 205 to 147, and that of employees from 12,600 to 11,100. The only other major region to show growth was Scotland, with an increase of 6,000 employees to 9,500 in 1850. These trends were to continue for the next quarter of a century. Minor areas of production, like Montgomery, lacking coal and adequate transport, were totally eclipsed. When the railway finally reached mid-Wales, it was not to take out Welsh flannel but to bring in Rochdale flannel. The ancient silk-weaving centre of Spitalfields in east London also declined with mechanisation, as the trade moved out to East Anglia, Derbyshire, Lancashire and, especially, Cheshire, which had the largest number of employees in 1838.

A similar regional specialisation occurred in Scotland. Dundee became the centre of the linen industry at the expense of the Angus countryside; cotton production was concentrated around Glasgow, but suffered somewhat from Lancashire competition; and woollens were strongest in the Borders and Clackmannan. However, quality and specialisation enabled Aberdeen to preserve its linen industry, and the demand for high-quality hand-woven woollens kept alive the hosiery trade of Shetland and the tweed industry of the Outer Hebrides. The most important change in Scottish textile production came in the 1850s, with the switch from linen to jute in Dundee.

The early industrial revolution was characterised by textile production, and social historians have rightly concentrated on the consequences of changes in textile processes and location when considering the history of the first half of the nineteenth century. But during the course of the century the front of economic advance became broader and more diversified, affecting different groups of people in different ways. Whereas textiles had a labour force of 883,000 in 1841, rising to 1,310,000 in 1871 and 1,509,000 in 1911 (a majority of whom were women), those involved in metal trades and engineering rose from 410,000 in 1841, to 913,000 in 1871 and 1,923,000 in 1911 (almost all of whom were men). The focus of regional attention therefore moves in the later nineteenth century from the textile areas of Lancashire, Cheshire and West Yorkshire, to the heavy industrial areas of South Wales, West Scotland, the West Midlands, South

Yorkshire and the Tees–Tyne region of the North-East – although, as with textiles, small pockets of specialised production also thrived elsewhere, such as textile machinery in the Leeds and Manchester areas, agricultural machinery in Suffolk, and locomotive and carriage building in the various workshops of railway companies around the country.

The changing locations of iron production were in part governed by the availability of iron ore, either imported or mined in the new Jurassic seams of eastern England. The discovery of iron in the Cleveland Hills of the North Riding in 1850 led to a major change in the location of pig-iron production in England. Whereas Staffordshire had been the leading English county in 1830, with almost a third of the total British production, by 1870 the North Riding was the leading producer, followed by Durham and Northumberland. But most remarkable of all was the expansion which western Scotland enjoyed after 1840, overtaking South Wales as the main British producer around the mid-century and retaining its position, despite its dwindling ore supply and fierce competition from a more innovative North-East of England, until the First World War.

The rise of the North-East is also seen in the steel industry, long the preserve of the Sheffield area of Yorkshire. This was facilitated partly by technological developments – the Gilchrist-Thomas process enabling manufacturers to use phosphoric ores – and partly by the development of iron as a material for building ships. By the end of the nineteenth century the great shipbuilding yards of Britain were to be found on the Clyde and in the North-East. There was also a major relocation of industry in South Wales from the Valleys to the coast, where there was easier access to imported ores. The Guests moved their Dowlais works down to Cardiff in 1891, though they left their rolling works behind to preserve the original community. Other firms did not have the capital to move. That at Ebbw Vale remained and survived; but the great Cyfartha works at Rhymney was closed in 1890, with the company concentrating thereafter on its coal-mining interests. The firms on the coast were, more often than not, new ones moving out of the Midlands. Welshmen went to Middlesbrough, or emigrated.

By the First World War, therefore, regional specialisation had become very marked in Britain. There was far less manufacturing in the countryside than had been the case a hundred years earlier; and the industrial districts were larger and more specialised in their outputs. Some towns, though, were dangerously dependent on a narrow range of products, and their prosperity was maintained only by a buoyant export trade to uncertain and changing world markets.

Decay and renewal

Though it was not immediately apparent after the First World War, many of the basic industries on which British economic success had been based were not merely in depression but decline. Textiles, iron and steel making, shipbuilding and coal mining were all vulnerable to foreign imports or rival commodities. The depression in world trade merely accentuated the decline of these basic industries. The problem for governments was whether to allow them to contract, or to support them artificially. In fact they did both, but without conviction. New industries grew up to replace the old, but not always successfully or where they were most needed.

Scotland, South Wales and the North-East suffered most; the West Midlands and the South-East gained most. Industry came to be concentrated in what was appropriately known as the 'industrial coffin', an area extending from the West Riding, Lancashire and Merseyside through the Midlands to London. Within this coffin-shaped box – and increasingly towards its southern end – lay the economic heart of the country. All the 'Special Development Areas', as defined in 1982, were – with the exception of Merseyside – outside this area.

The key to the location of industry was power, but with the establishment of the National Grid after 1926 the old dependence on the coalfields came to an end. In so far as the former pattern remained, this was largely a product of inertia, the social and economic infrastructure and the presence of a skilled workforce tending to keep manufacturing industry in its traditional locations. West Scotland, the North-East and South Wales in particular were living on borrowed time. With the growth of firms through amalgamation, and the increasing pull of the centre on the periphery after the Second World War, even a new industry like motor-vehicle manufacturing struggled to survive in Scotland. Though Teesside became an important centre of the chemical industry, and all three areas recorded some successes in the 1970s with the manufacture of electrical equipment and components, the necessary fundamental shift in the structure of their economies was slow to take place.

One factor which to some extent aided the North-East was the European Economic Community (later, European Union) which Britain joined in 1973. The wealth of the west coast of Britain was based on the Atlantic trade, and decline had been delayed during the World Wars by the relatively safety of the west coast from enemy attack, but, as the direction of Britain's outlook turned increasingly towards Europe, the east coast began to gain an advantage over the west. Liverpool and Glasgow were among the casualties of this change in emphasis, but the North-East gained when a major Japanese car manufacturer decided to break with previous patterns and establish a plant near Sunderland from which to attack the European market.

The eastern part of Britain also benefited from the changing location of new fuel supplies. As the coalfields of Scotland, Lancashire, South Wales and the western part of Yorkshire became exhausted or less profitable to work, new prospects appeared in the deeper coal seams to the east, in Nottinghamshire, the Selby coal field of Yorkshire and the Vale of Belvoir in Leicestershire. Even more important, the discovery of gas (1965) and oil (1969) beneath the North Sea, though distributed throughout the country mainly by pipeline, did aid the economies of the North-East and, more especially, north-eastern Scotland. Far from being peripheral, Shetland, Orkney and Aberdeen found themselves, temporarily at least, at the centre of economic activity.

This eastwards shift in the 1970s and 1980s overlaid, but did not displace, a much more fundamental change in the location of industry and economic wealth from the north to the south. The years between 1750 and 1914 saw the triumph of provincial Britain. Despite the dominance of London, the provinces of Britain had an independent vitality and strength which gave them a major role in social, political and economic affairs. By the later twentieth century the balance had swung back in favour of the South-East, though there are signs at the very end of the century that this swing might not prove permanent. The depression of the early 1990s hit the South-East of England as hard as other parts of the country, with rising unemployment and depressed housing prices affecting consumer confidence and general prosperity. Moreover, despite the abandonment of Regional Planning Councils in 1979, a policy of regional aid and development survived through the European Union and the willingness of Japanese and other Asian companies to locate their European bases in South Wales and Central Scotland as well as the North-East, provided the government gave suitable financial inducements. Though the economic problems of the west coast, and particularly of Liverpool, continued, there were at last signs that the British economy could be successfully restructured within a European context to take advantage of the advanced electronic technologies of a new industrial revolution.

Notes

1. William Cowper, *The Task* (1785), book 1, l. 749.
2. Thomas Hobbes, *Leviathan* (1651), ch. 13.
3. *Royal Commission on the Agricultural Depression* (1895), quoted by J. T. Coppock, 'The Changing Face of England: 1850–circa 1900', p. 325 in H. C. Darby (ed.), *A New Historical Geography of England after 1600* (Cambridge, 1976), pp. 295–373.
4. Adam Smith, *An Inquiry into the Nature and Causes of the Wealth of Nations* (1776), quoted in W. T. Jackman, *The Development of Transportation in Modern England* (Cambridge, 1916; 3rd edn., 1966), p. 213.
5. John Ruskin, *The Seven Lamps of Architecture* (1849), quoted in H. C. Darby (ed.), *A New Historical Geography of England after 1600*, p. 275.
6. John Ruskin, *Praeterita* (1885–9), quoted in O. S. Nock, *The Railways of Britain* (1947; revised edn., 1962), pp. 164–5.
7. *Gustave d'Eichthal's Journal and Notes*, in B. M. Ratcliffe and W. H. Chaloner (eds.), *A French Sociologist Looks at Britain: Gustave d'Eichthal and British Society in 1828* (Manchester, 1977), pp. 63–4.

8. Quoted in D. J. Olsen, *The Growth of Victorian London* (1976), p. 318.
9. M. Beresford, 'The Face of Leeds, 1780–1914', p. 99 in D. Fraser (ed.), *A History of Modern Leeds* (Manchester, 1980), pp. 72–112.
10. Quoted by E. Pawson, 'The Framework of Industrial Change, 1730–1900', p. 381 in R. A. Dodgshon and R. A. Butlin (eds.), *A Historical Geography of England and Wales* (London and New York, 1978), pp. 267–89.

2

People

The population question

Almost all details about the size, structure and distribution of the population of Britain before 1841, and some of the details even after that date, are uncertain. What information we have is based upon contemporary estimates, census data known to be not wholly accurate or explicit, and sophisticated modern guesswork. Figures and percentages quoted should therefore never be treated with that degree of precision which their outward form would appear to warrant. Nevertheless they have to be used, and there is probably now enough of a consensus among historians about orders of magnitude for the figures to be treated as relatively accurate and sufficient for most purposes.

The first step in assessing the value of statistical information is to understand how it has been acquired. Civil censuses have been conducted in Britain every 10 years since 1801, with the exception of the war year 1941. On first sight these official censuses would appear to provide firm data for the social historian, but this is not the case. The first four censuses, held in 1801–31, were organised by John Rickman, who required local enumerators (usually poor-law overseers in England and Wales, and schoolmasters in Scotland) to visit each household and record certain information on forms. Not only have these early forms not survived for most places, but Rickman himself was aware of the incompleteness and variable quality of the information gathered.

A major change came in England and Wales with the Civil Registration Act of 1836, which created the office of local registrar and made provision for the civil registration of births, marriages and deaths and the central collection of data. (Scotland did not get civil registration until 1855.) The General Registry Office assumed responsibility for the census from 1841 (1861 in Scotland), and thereafter the enumeration forms were given to householders to fill in, the results then being copied into enumerators' books, which have survived – though they and the published data derived from them still need to be treated with caution, especially in making inter-census comparisons. The Registrar General also produced annual reports for England and Wales from 1840, summarising the statistics collated from the civil registers of the preceding year, and these provide a further useful source of information on population trends.

Before 1801 the only extensive record of population trends was kept in parochial baptism, marriage and burial registers. At the time of the 1801 census Rickman asked the parish clergy to supply him with the annual numbers of baptisms and burials at the start of each decade between 1700 and 1780, and for each year thereafter, and the annual number of marriages since 1754, the first full year under Hardwicke's Marriage Act. From these data he calculated the population of England and Wales throughout the eighteenth century.

Until comparatively recently all discussion of population before 1801 was based on Rickman's Parish Register Abstracts, suitably modified by critical scholarship, but the advent of the electronic computer has meant a transformation in the study of historical demography. Calculations undertaken by the Cambridge Group for the History of Population and Social Structure have now provided historians with new estimates for the population of England in the eighteenth and early nineteenth centuries, as well as information about the age structure of the population and patterns of nuptuality (the marriage rate), fertility (number of births per thousand women of child-bearing age) and mortality (the death rate) which are essential to the social historian.[1]

Information on Wales and Scotland is less readily available. As many as 20 per cent of Welsh parishes may have been missing from Rickman's Parish Register Abstracts of 1801, and when he attempted to gather Parish Register Abstracts from Scotland in 1801 he was able to obtain information from only 99 out of 850 parishes. There are, however, three additional – though imperfect – sources available to the historian of Scotland, all of which ultimately derived from the parish clergy. The first is an *Account of the Number of People in Scotland, 1755*, prepared by Alexander Webster, an Edinburgh minister, but his methods are not fully known and his conclusions, however promising, must be used with caution. Then, in the 1790s and again in the 1830s, two statistical accounts of every parish in Scotland were undertaken. The *Old Statistical Account*, produced by Sir John Sinclair between 1791 and 1799, provides information only as good as the local clergyman chose to make it, and is weakest when dealing with the larger towns; but it does provide sex distributions for about 40 per cent of the population, and a rough age distribution for about a quarter of the parishes. The *New Statistical Account*, published in 1845, is more systematic, but its population data is usually derived from the censuses, and so adds little beyond useful local comment in this respect.

Population size and growth, 1750–1830

The most recent estimates for England suggest that a mid-seventeenth-century slump was followed by renewed population growth at the end of the seventeenth century.[2] The population exceeded five million for the first time since the early seventeenth century in 1699; six million in 1757 (after a brief setback in the decade 1727–37); seven million in 1781; eight million in 1794; nine million in 1804; ten million in 1812; eleven million in 1819; twelve million in 1824; and thirteen million in 1830. The accelerating rate of population growth is quite marked, from under 10 per cent in the decade 1781–91 to over 16 per cent in the decade of fastest growth, 1811–21.

In the absence of comparable data for Scotland, estimates have to depend upon older sources. If Webster's estimate of 1755 is accepted the population of Scotland at that date was 1,265,380. According to the 1801 Census the population rose in the second half of the eighteenth century to 1,625,002, an annual average growth rate of 0.62 per cent compared with 1 per cent for England. Scottish growth rates in the early nineteenth century follow the same pattern as those for England, though at a slightly lower level. It is therefore possible either that Webster overestimated the population in 1755, or that the course of Scottish demographic history was different from that of England in the later eighteenth century, with a slower and more prolonged take-off into population growth and heavier losses through emigration.

Data for Wales are even harder to find, and such as exist often exclude Monmouth (which was technically not within the Principality). Wrigley and Schofield estimate a population figure for Wales (including Monmouth) as low as 406,000 in 1750, rising to 606,000 in 1801, compared with a census figure in 1801 of 585,128. Using raw census figures, the population of Wales then rose to 901,200 in 1831, a rate of increase in the first two decades of the nineteenth century which exceeded even that of England.

The reasons for this increase in the population of Britain have caused much historical controversy between those who concentrate on changes in the death rate and those who see the rising birth rate as the most significant factor. The former have argued that changes in nutrition, personal hygiene or medical provision could account for a crucial fall in the death rate. For example, the widespread use of inoculation and, later, vaccination to combat smallpox alone reduced deaths attributable to that disease from 16.5 per cent of all deaths in the middle of the eighteenth century to between 1 and 2 per cent a century later. Some proponents of the birth-rate argument suggested that low agricultural prices in the second quarter of the eighteenth century led to rising living standards and increased fertility in the form of earlier marriages and, possibly, healthier mothers. Yet others have found the connection between this earlier period of low prices and the rapid expansion of population a generation later too tenuous, but argue that the rise in living standards may have stimulated the first stages of economic growth, which in turn may then have caused the population to expand in the later eighteenth century.

The data calculated by Wrigley and Schofield show that, whilst the total numbers of births, marriages and deaths were all increasing (as one might expect with a rising population) in the second half of the eighteenth century, births were increasing at a faster rate than deaths, and this was due less to a fall in the death rate (which became marked only in the first quarter of the nineteenth century) than to a rise in the birth rate (which was a feature of the eighteenth century).[3] The most important cause of this was an increase in the fertility rate, mainly a function of an increasing marriage rate and a fall in the mean age of marriage. Why this should have happened is still very much a matter for conjecture, but it is widely argued that the decision to marry is related to social custom and economic opportunity. In a society in which it was most usually the case that a new marriage meant a separate household, the opportunities for creating and sustaining such a household seem likely to have played a major part in that most crucial of all demographic decisions before the advent of modern methods of family limitation – the decision to marry.

Population trends, 1841–1911

The population of England, which stood at 8.7 million in 1801, had increased to 15 million in 1841, by which time Wales had around 0.9 million inhabitants and Scotland 2.6 million. In 1911 the combined populations of England and Wales totalled 36 million, with a further 4.8 million in Scotland. Within these gross figures significant changes were taking place. Broadly speaking, before 1871, the birth and death rates were steady, having fallen during the first three decades of the century, while the marriage rate was rising slightly. After 1871 all three rates began to fall.

Demographers have long recognised the 1870s as a turning-point in the history of population, but there has been little agreement on the causes of the reversal in trends. It might seem plausible to argue that the increasing age of female marriage was the main reason for the fall in fertility, but research has shown that, whereas this argument might have some validity for most of Ireland and the Highlands of Scotland, the actual contribution of marriage deferment to the reduced fertility rate in England, Wales and the industrial part of Scotland was relatively small.[4] The explanation rather appears to lie with the deliberate limitation of fertility within marriage, through either the adoption of 'natural' methods of birth control or the use of 'artificial' techniques of contraception.

It has frequently been observed that the reversal of the trend in fertility rates coincided exactly with the trial of Annie Besant and Charles

Bradlaugh in 1877 for republishing Dr Charles Knowlton's birth-control work, *The Fruits of Philosophy*, and the conclusion has therefore frequently been asserted that the flood of birth-control information which followed this celebrated trial was the major reason why family limitation came to be practised on an increasing scale over the next 30 years. Certainly it is true that propaganda for birth control did become widespread after 1877. Not only did the national newspapers inadvertently advertise the issue in their reports of the Bradlaugh–Besant trial, but a great impetus was given to the sale of Knowlton's and other publications. In all it has been calculated that around a million pamphlets on birth control were put into circulation between 1877 and 1914, and it is hard to believe that all this literature made no impact at all on popular awareness.[5]

Nevertheless, the argument can be overstated. The evidence for declining family size suggests that, far from hundreds of poor families reading and acting successfully upon the advice given, it was the upper classes who pioneered the limitation of families. The conclusion derived from questions about fertility in the 1911 Census is that the decline was most pronounced among those classified as 'upper professional' within the Registrar General's Class 1, and that this decline was under way before 1861. Indeed, such was the trend that some late Victorians began to fear that birth control would lead to the degeneration of the race if the wealthy (and therefore, it was assumed, intelligent) reduced their numbers while the ignorant poor continued to breed.

Much of the early propaganda about birth control was physiological and/or economic: that is, it explained how procreation occurred (not always entirely accurately) and why it was necessary to limit families. Advice on contraception itself was limited, and the medical profession was almost uniformly hostile to its practice. The most widely practised methods of family limitation among the bulk of the population throughout the nineteenth century were the 'natural' ones – abstinence, *coitus interruptus* (withdrawal), prolonged lactation, and abortion. The technology of contraception – especially of female contraception – was still in its infancy, and although cervical rubber caps and soluble pessaries, along with condoms, were known and used, the cheap availability of reliable devices came only after the birth rate had begun to fall in the last decades of the century. Even so, with condoms costing at least 2*s*. (10p) a dozen, quinine pessaries the same, and sponges 1*s*. (5p) each in the 1890s, few of the poor could afford to limit their families except by time-honoured, unreliable and sometimes downright dangerous methods.

The spread of birth-control practices at different times amongst different social and occupational groups suggests that it is the incentive to limit family sizes which is the key to understanding the decline in fertility in modern Britain. Whereas knowledge, availability and cost were important, these determined the nature and effectiveness of the measures taken rather than the actual attempt to practise some kind of family limitation.

The coincidences of the 1870s can be multiplied, for the decade saw not only the Bradlaugh–Besant trial, but also restrictive legislation on the employment of children and an end to the mid-century economic boom. In 1876 Parliament legislated the beginnings of compulsory education for all children aged 5 to 14 and prohibited employment under the age of 10, while the change in the economic climate brought greater uncertainty for the middle classes. The argument is that children were seen by the lower classes to be an economic asset until the 1870s, but this view is both naïve in its expectation of human economic rationality and untrue. The propaganda of feminism also became more common in the latter decades of the century, and this could have been an important source of pressure for change from within families; but again, the limit on overall numbers despite the lack of spacing between conceptions suggests that contraception was not being seen primarily as a matter of female health and comfort. There are also some contrary trends in the 1870s. The availability of work for women in textile factories seems to have been associated with some of the earliest evidence of birth-control practices among the working classes in the first half of the century, but, so far as one can extract the figures from the census returns, it appears that the overall trend for economic activity among females was downwards from the last third of the century – at the same time as the fertility rate was declining.

Various suggestions have been put forward, notably by J. A. Banks, to locate within the broader trends of social history the reasons why people should have chosen to limit their families.[6] This interpretation plays down feminism and the Bradlaugh–Besant trial, and gives greatest emphasis to the rising economic cost of children and changing social aspirations of parents for their children. Above all, it is the cost of education which seems to have weighed most heavily on many Victorian fathers of the upper and professional classes. In an age when career structures were becoming more clearly defined, and when educational qualifications (examinations, references and 'the old school tie') were replacing older forms of patronage, maintaining or raising the social standing of a son was becoming an increasingly expensive business. This seems persuasive, and appears to explain the early predilection of the professional classes for birth control, but it is an argument framed almost exclusively in terms of boys. Since family limitation rather than family planning seems to have been the norm (i.e. the number of children was more important than the spacing of their births) one needs to know more precisely whether families with girls were regarded as cheaper and therefore could be larger than families of boys.

To explain further the adoption of family-planning practices among the upper and professional classes, Banks also points to the development of what he calls 'future-time perspective' – that is, the habit of planning ahead, which might be engendered by education and necessitated by a career structure, but which affects all aspects of life.[7] The ability to develop such a perspective has been related to intelligence (or, at least, to education) and social class, and may go some way towards explaining the correlation between education and evidence of family planning. It may be this aspect of mass schooling for the lower classes, rather than the removal of children from the labour market, which has done most to help extend attitudes and practices from the upper to the lower classes in the decades since the 1870s. Thus, whilst general labourers who married before 1861 had a mean completed family size of 7.85 children, those marrying in the last decade of the century had only 5.32 – fewer than most Class 1 families who married before 1861.

But in considering the lower class additional factors have to be taken into consideration, especially in the twentieth century: the rapid decline in infant mortality, the provision of basic welfare support for the elderly by the state and a generally rising standard of living. These factors may suggest that the Malthusian argument can be turned on its head. Though poverty was associated with too many children, it was probably not caused by them: large families among the poor were at least as much the product of their parents' poverty, their economic uncertainty, lack of education and absence of realisable alternative social and economic goals. The social history of the twentieth century traces the reversal of these trends, as well as a dramatic fall in family sizes among all social and occupational groups.

Population trends since 1911

The population of England and Wales has risen only slowly in the twentieth century, from 36.1 million in 1911 to 43.8 million in 1951 and 51.1 million in 1991, an increase of 15 million in the 80 years after 1911, compared with one of 22.2 million for the 80 years before 1911. In Scotland the growth has been even slower, from 4.8 million in 1911 to 5.1 million in 1951; between 1921 and 1931, and again from 1961, the population of Scotland actually fell, and in 1991 it was still only 5.1 million.

The trend in the birth rate which became established in the later nineteenth century continued until the Second World War, except for a minor reverse at the end of the First World War. By the 1930s the fertility rate had fallen below the level at which the population replaces itself, even allowing for the considerable improvements that had taken place in the level of infant mortality. After the Second World War the fertility rate was around the replacement level, but subject to cyclical fluctuations following a post-war peak in 1947. In the second half of the twentieth century fluctuations in the birth rate have not corresponded with the number of women of childbearing age in the population, which suggests that by the 1950s the total number of births in the population was being controlled mainly by decisions about birth control, especially after the introduction of hormone contraceptives (the 'Pill') in 1963.

With such a low and decreasing birth rate, population growth in the twentieth century was sustained by an even more dramatic reduction in the death rate. In the nineteenth century improvements in the environment and in health care made scarcely any impression on infant mortality figures. Even allowing for the better registration of infant deaths (children aged under one year), the figures at the end of the nineteenth century were as bad or worse than at any time since registration began – 146 per thousand live births in England and Wales in 1900–02, and 124 in Scotland. Thereafter the Scottish figures moved sluggishly downwards and the figures for England and Wales fell rapidly until, for the first time at the end of the First World War, the Scottish rate was above that for the rest of Britain. By 1940–2 the rates for England and Wales had reached 55 per 1,000, compared with 77 per 1,000 in Scotland. By the 1990s the infant mortality rate for England and Wales was down to only 6.9 per 1,000 for boys and 5.3 per 1,000 for girls. The Scottish rate was a little lower for boys – 6.4 per 1,000 – and a little higher for girls – 6.1 per 1,000. This demographic revolution had resulted from a combination of environmental improvements, better care and nutrition, and – probably least important until the 1940s – changes in medical practice such as active immunization against diphtheria, and inoculation for tuberculosis and poliomyelitis (infantile paralysis). At the same time the number of maternal deaths per thousand live births fell from over four to under one, thanks largely to the development of antibiotics in the 1940s.

These improvements in infant care also helped bring down still further the falling mortality rates for children, young people and adults, as measured by the life expectancy figures. Between 1901 and 1995 the life expectancy at birth for males in the United Kingdom rose from 48 years to 73.9, and for females from 51.6 to 79.2. A 15-year-old boy at the end of the nineteenth century could expect to live to be 61.9 years of age, and a girl 64.5; by 1995 the respective figures were 74.6 and 79.8 years. A 60-year-old man in the 1901 could expect to live to be 73.4 and a woman 74.9; by 1996, the man might live to be 76.9 years old and the woman 80.8. The only modest improvement in the life expectancies of older people is an indication of the extent to which, in previous ages, high infant and child mortality were the major threats to survival. Those who lived to be adults were almost as likely as now to survive until the onset of old age. The main killer diseases of the 1990s, though, were no longer those of infection (with the exception of pneumonia among the elderly) but of physical failure – diseases of the heart and circulatory system, which accounted for nearly half of all deaths, and cancers, which accounted for a quarter. In 1981 only 2,386 people in Britain died of those infectious and parasitic diseases which had been the scourge of the nineteenth century. By 1995, though, this figures had increased to 3,916, largely due to AIDS (acquired immunodeficiency syndrome) and AIDS-related diseases.

Alongside these declining rates for births and deaths, marriage was becoming more frequent and taking place at an earlier age. A turning-point here came at some time between the censuses of 1931 and 1951, and first showed in the 1951 figures. Whereas only a third of women in England and Wales aged 24 or under were or had been married in 1881, and only a quarter in 1931, the proportion in 1951 was almost half and in 1971 had reached over 60 per cent. In Scotland the same trend was apparent, but at a lower level: 26.4 per cent (1881), 22.9 per cent (1931), 39.8 per cent (1951) and 58 per cent (1971). Men tended be a little older than their wives, but the same trend was apparent.

Between 1971 and 1991 a new trend towards late marriage began, so that by 1991 only 28 per cent of women in England and Wales (27 per cent in Scotland) aged 24 or under were or had been married, and even at 34 the figures were still only 71 per cent for each part of Britain. Not until one considers the age cohort of 44 and under do the figures exceed 90 per cent and indicate a similar picture to that of the same age group in 1971. Again, though men were marrying later in 1991, the trend was the same. In the past this would have meant a significant fall in the fertility rate, but late marriage had already by 1971 ceased to be the principal means of limiting fertility. Instead, the significance of the trend towards late marriage can be understood only when set against figures for cohabitation and children born out of wedlock. In the final quarter of the twentieth century, unmarried couples have been redefining the family.

Population structure

Though the size and rate of growth of a population have obvious implications for the history of a society, no less important are the age and sex structures of that population. These have an important bearing not only on the rates of population change, but also on the demands which a population places upon its constituents. A population with a large proportion of dependants – too young or too old to work – will behave differently and have different economic needs and costs from one in which there is a more even age distribution; and a population with a sexual imbalance – either too many men or too many women for all who expect to marry to do so – will exhibit different economic and cultural characteristics from one in which monogamous, heterosexual marriage is likely to be available to all who choose it.

A major consequence of the increase in fertility in the later eighteenth century was a change in the age structure of society towards a younger population. Calculating young 'dependants' as those under 15 years, and aged 'dependants' as those of 60 or over, the number of dependants to every 1,000 of the population aged 15 to 59 rose from around 700 in the middle of the eighteenth century, to around 800 at the end of the century, and to a peak of over 850 in the 1820s. During this period the proportion of aged dependants actually fell. The population was becoming increasingly young: between 1806 and 1836, there were in England more children under 15 than there were adults aged 25 to 59. This had enormous social consequences, not least for the provision of schooling. Of course, it is misleading to describe all such people as 'dependants', for another characteristic of this period was the growth of opportunities for regular child employment, although such child labourers were paid on the assumption that they were dependent upon an adult for their full maintenance.

Figures for the age structure of Scottish population in the mid-eighteenth century have to be derived from Webster's survey which, although a source of dubious accuracy, does yield results not unlike those available for other countries, including those obtained by Wrigley and Schofield for England. The same is true for figures derived from the *Old Statistical Account* in the 1790s, when a sample of 167 parishes suggested that 25 per cent of the population was aged under 10, with a further 20 per cent aged between 10 and 19 years. There is little here to suggest significant differences between Scotland and England which would be likely to shape the social histories of the two countries in different ways.

The youthful age-structure of the population was in part the function of the increasing birth rate; but it was also a product of the pattern of death rates, for many of those recorded as infants did not live to add to the adult population. Indeed, the difficulty was for the infant to survive even into childhood: of all burials recorded in English parish registers between 1813 and 1830, 20 per cent were those of infants under one year old, and 35 per cent were of children under 5. Moreover, there were significant differences between the survival rates of male and female children, which in turn affected the sexual composition of the population. For every thousand boys under 5 in England between 1813 and 1830, 628 survived beyond their fifth birthdays; but for every thousand girls, 676 survived. (Mortality levels in Wales were lower, but the proportions were nearly the same.) Only between the ages of 15 and 40 – the principal years of childbearing – did the mortality figures for women in England exceed those for men, and in old age women were again the survivors. As a result, for every 1,000 women in England in 1831, there were 950 men; in Wales, 970 men; and in Scotland, 890 men. The most likely explanation for these differences, especially between Wales and Scotland, lies in different patterns of emigration to and immigration from England. In industrializing Monmouth, which was attracting English labour at this time, there was actually a surplus of 90 males for every thousand females in the population.

As the large numbers of children who were born and survived in the early decades of the nineteenth century passed into the adult population, so the dependency ratio began to fall, until in 1911 it was only 631 (678 in Scotland), a level not seen since the middle of the seventeenth century. The youthful population of the early nineteenth century had become middle-aged. In the twentieth century two contrary trends are concealed within the figures: between 1851 and 1911 the decline in the number of dependants was caused almost entirely by the falling proportion of children under 15 years old: 35.5 per cent (Scotland 35.6 per cent) in 1851; 30.6 per cent (Scotland 32.3 per cent) in 1911. Thereafter a considerable fall in the number of children masked an even greater rise in the number of aged dependants: between 1911 and 1951 the proportion of children under 15 in England and Wales fell to 22.1 per cent (Scotland 24.6 per cent), while the proportion aged 60 and over almost doubled from 8 per cent (Scotland 8.1 per cent) to 15.9 per cent (Scotland 14.4 per cent). Though the dependency ratio was only 615 (639), the population of Britain was aging. By 1995 the proportion of aged dependants had reached 20.5 per cent in England and Wales and 20.1 per cent in Scotland, nearly three times the level of a century earlier, pushing the dependency ratio up to 662 (Scotland 641).

Just as the youthful population of the nineteenth century had presented great social challenges in such matters as the provision of education, the aging population of the later twentieth century has created other demands on resources, especially since the state has come to accept a large part of the financial costs of old age through health care and pensions. The proportion of the population of Great Britain which was of pensionable age (women over 59 and men over 64) was 13.6 per cent in 1951, rising to 18.3 per cent by 1995, though with an increase in the age of female retirement to 65 being phased in from 2010 the proportion of pensioners in 2011 has been limited to an estimated 19.3 per cent.

This increase in the numbers of old people, two-thirds of whom are women, has concealed another new trend in the population structure of the later twentieth century – that of the altering balance between the sexes. Though the number of male babies has always exceeded that of female, the higher mortality rate among boys usually ensured that females outnumbered males in the population as a whole. Consistently throughout the nineteenth and first half of the twentieth centuries the number of males per 1,000 females in the population of England and Wales fell – from 960 in 1851 to 936 in 1911, and to 924 in 1951. The better survival rate for women, at birth in the nineteenth century, and in old age thereafter, maintained the traditional imbalance. In Scotland the picture was slightly different, with an unusually high loss of males through emigration in the early nineteenth century, and then a lower infant mortality rate which meant that a small surplus of males reached adulthood between 1881 and 1911; but the overall trends thereafter closely followed those of

England and Wales, with 942 males per 1,000 females in 1911 and 916 in 1951. But, as infant mortality rates fell in the twentieth century, so the number of boys surviving to adulthood increased and eventually began to influence trends even against the growing numbers of aged females. By 1995 the number of males per 1,000 females was back at the level of the mid-nineteenth century – 964 (940 in Scotland). More importantly, males in England and Wales were now in the majority in the youthful population: for every 1,000 females aged between 20 and 29 (when most cohabiting partnerships or marriages were begun) there were 1,048 males (1,031 in Scotland). The nineteenth-century 'problems' of spinsters and the deceased wife's sister were being replaced by the potential difficulties of men unable to find brides – and the likelihood of increasing numbers of twice-married women.

Households and families

Household size and composition

There has been broad agreement among historians since the late 1960s that the mean household size in England (and possibly Britain) did not change a great deal between the late sixteenth and early twentieth centuries. This long period of stability poses serious problems for those interpretations of the history of the family which see a transition from an extended 'peasant' household to a nuclear 'proletarian' household resulting from the advance of capitalism in the agricultural and industrial revolutions. By contrast, the mean size of households in the twentieth century has fallen by 40 per cent. So far as the history of the household and the family is concerned, the decisive break between pre-modern and modern comes as late as the middle of the twentieth century.

Although the mean size of households before the twentieth century was around 4.75 persons, there were important differences according to such variables as geography and social class. In a sample of pre-industrial households studied by Peter Laslett, the mean size of gentlemen's households was 6.63, compared with 5.09 for husbandmen and 4.51 for labourers. Alan Armstrong has found a similar gradation between the social classes in York in 1851. Yet when the number of children in households is examined, husbandmen had more children on average (3.10) than gentlemen (2.94), despite having smaller overall households. This suggests that perhaps some gentlemen were already restricting the fertility of their marriages, or that the resident gentry in the sample were of an age when some of their children would have left home or been sent away to be educated in other households or institutions. The higher social groups were, of course, also more likely to have servants, and the higher the social standing, the larger the number of servants of various kinds.[8]

The changing structure of the household in different social contexts in the mid-nineteenth century has been explored by Michael Anderson, combining the results of his own work on Preston and rural Lancashire in 1851 with those of Laslett on pre-industrial England and Armstrong on York in 1851. He finds that, over the period of rapid population growth, the number of households with living-in kin increased significantly in both town and country; that the number of households with lodgers was higher in the town than in the countryside; and that the industrial town had fewer households with servants than other types of community. Compared with rural Lancashire in 1851, Preston householders had in effect replaced their servants with lodgers.[9] The continued presence of kin in urban, industrial households is especially significant in view of the widespread belief that the industrial revolution destroyed the traditional family. Anderson's conclusion is that, far from disrupting the family, the move to the town appears, if anything, to have strengthened it. Whereas in the Lancashire countryside 26 per cent of those without a spouse lived with their married children, the figure for Preston was 41 per cent. In poor rural communities, aged parents could be an economic burden; but in the industrial town (or, at least, the textile town) where there was the opportunity for women to work out of the home, the grandmother had a useful economic role to play.

The life-cycle of the mid-nineteenth-century urban family might look something as follows. On or shortly after marriage (before children were born) a little over half the couples might form a new household, compared with over three-quarters in the countryside; but as many as a quarter would lodge within another household, four times as many as in the countryside. The balance lived with their parents. This urban pattern probably reflects a housing shortage and/or the high level of rents in the town. With the arrival of children, a separate, two-generational household was the norm – three out of every four households were of this type. As the children grew up and the parents aged, over a third of the parents would find themselves in a single-generational household, but nearly half would still have at least one unmarried child living with them, and around a sixth would be living with their married children. On bereavement, however, a much larger proportion of the widowed would find themselves with their married children. A minority of households would also contain unmarried or widowed siblings, nieces or nephews (without their parents) and grandchildren (without their parents). Indeed, 28 per cent of all resident kin in Preston (and 42 per cent in the countryside) were 'parentless' children, most of whom would either be serving a function for their hosts (e.g. looking after an aged relative) or deriving a function from their hosts (e.g. boarding with kin in order to find work not available closer to home).

In this and many other respects, the late-twentieth-century family looks quite different. Not only are there far fewer children around and far more old people, but the conditions for forming a household are different. In the mid-nineteenth century it was as common as not for a grown-up child not to expect to form a separate household. This pattern was very slow to change in the twentieth century for several reasons: more parents survived to provide a home for adult children; with fewer children, there was more room in the parental home; post-Second-World-War housing shortages made it difficult for children to find alternative accommodation. As late as 1960, 40 per cent of young childless couples in Swansea lived with parents, though the practice of lodging had almost died out. After 1951, though, the census shows a dramatic change in the formation and structure of households. The tendency since then has been towards a proliferation of smaller and smaller units, encouraged by a standardised pattern of small house-building. Between 1971 and 1995 the number of households increased by 20 per cent at a time when the population was increasing by less than 5 per cent. Children had come to expect that, on reaching adulthood, they would form a new household in a separate house, whether married or not. Smaller families and increased longevity also meant that a married couple could expect (if they did not divorce) a considerable period of life together after shedding the burdens of parenthood, and with some financial support from pension schemes there was less need for them to live with their children in old age. In 1995 a third of households contained only two people, compared with a sixth in 1911. At the end of the twentieth century two-thirds of aged married couples live on their own, and 12 per cent of all households comprise a single female over the age of 60. Probably more old people live alone than ever before.

Illegitimacy

Studies of illegitimacy have shown little agreement over the reasons for it, but all are agreed on the general outline of its history in England and Wales, with an increase in the proportion of illegitimate births up to the middle of the nineteenth century, a fall until the beginning of the twentieth century, and an accelerating rise thereafter. Between 1750 and 1800 the proportion of illegitimate births may well have doubled to 6 per cent of all births; in the first five years for which registration figures are available (1845–9) the figure was 6.8 per cent, but it had fallen to under 6 per cent by 1871 and under 4 per cent by 1901. This decline was then reversed, rising to nearly 5 per cent in 1951. In Scotland the ratios were much higher and the pattern different, peaking at 9.44 per cent in 1871, and falling to 6.34 per cent in 1901, before rising again in the twentieth century to 7.31 per cent in 1931, and then falling almost to the English level in 1951. The next 40 years then saw a sharp upswing in the proportion of illegitimate births in Britain as a whole, to 5.8 per cent in 1961,

8.4 per cent in 1971, 12.7 per cent in 1981 and 26.7 per cent in 1991. By 1995 over a third of all births were occurring outside marriage, with marked regional variations. In Merseyside, 47 per cent of births occurred outside marriage.

However, illegitimacy figures on their own do not tell the whole story, for they assume a constant relationship in the behaviour of legitimate and illegitimate fertility rates. When the former falls more quickly than the latter the illegitimacy ratio will rise and vice versa, but the cause may be a change in the behaviour of married couples, not in the behaviour of the unmarried. In the second half of the nineteenth century the illegitimate fertility rate fell twice as fast as that for legitimate births; in the first half of the twentieth century the illegitimate fertility rate rose slightly, while the rate of legitimate fertility fell; and in the period 1951–81 it more than doubled, while legitimate fertility continued to decline. In 1981 a married woman was half as likely to have a child as she was in 1901; but an unmarried woman was three times as likely to become a mother. These trends accelerated in the 1980s, so that whereas in 1981 the fertility rate for women aged between 15 and 44 was 88 per 1,000 married women, and 25 for unmarried women, in 1991 the figures were 82.7 for married women and 40.2 for unmarried women. While, therefore, it was twice as likely that a married woman would have a child than that an unmarried one would, the closing of the gap between the two figures indicated the extent to which not only marriage but also the social and legal context for childbearing were redefined in the 1980s.

Explanations for these changing ratios and rates over the centuries are many and varied, and there is probably no single or constant cause. There seems little evidence, though, that illegitimacy rates rose with the age of marriage – if anything, the reverse would appear to have been true before the later twentieth century. The twentieth-century figures might be interpreted as meaning that married couples are more likely to be using contraceptives (or using them more effectively) than the unmarried, but changing sexual customs and social sanctions may also be relevant. Pre-marital intercourse followed by marriage (called 'bundling') was widely practised in many parts of the country well into the nineteenth century, but, if pregnant brides were socially acceptable, failure to marry when in such a condition was not. It could be argued, therefore, that if such rural customs were carried into the towns of the early industrial revolution the absence of sanctions on young men (and women) might have led to increased numbers of bastards. The rise in illegitimacy ratios in early-twentieth-century Scotland can, on the contrary, be attributed to the opposite process. In the towns there was perhaps more knowledge of contraception, and more economic incentive to remain capable of earning at least until a marriage partner was assured, but in the North-East and Borders illegitimacy, however measured, was far in excess of the levels in other areas, while urban areas were below the average for the country as a whole.

The change in trends since 1951 is undoubtedly part of what has been called the 'sexual revolution'. Indeed, there is a sense in which the later nineteenth century did not really end, in demographic terms, until 1951. The discontinuities between the post-Second-World-War period and the previous 70 years are far more marked than any within those 70 years, and the speed of social change from decade to decade since 1951 has made meaningless all attempts to project future trends. One interesting development has been the change in the abortion rate since abortion was legalised in 1967. At first a high proportion of conceptions outside marriage were aborted: in 1971, for every 1,000 live illegitimate births, another 703 were aborted; by 1981, this figure had reached 1083. Over half the conceptions outside marriage in 1981 could therefore be described as unwanted. But with the dramatic increase in illegitimate births after 1981, the abortion rate fell, to only 552 per 1,000 live births. This compared with a legitimate abortion ration which was also falling, but not so steeply – from 90 per thousand births to 79. So, while abortion has continued to be used primarily as a means of late birth control by the unmarried, many more unmarried couples are choosing to have and keep their babies. This is borne out by the figures for the registration of births, with the proportion of illegitimate births registered in the names of both parents rising sharply, from 38 per cent in 1961 to 58 per cent in 1981 and around 75 per cent in 1991. Of these, two-thirds were living at the same address, suggesting that, for an increasing minority of couples, the rise in illegitimacy represents a deliberate rejection of traditional marriage.

Marriage and divorce

The reasons why people married, and what they expected of their conjugal relationships, can only be guessed at in days beyond the reach of oral history. Literature and the visual arts may give some hints, but the field is wide open for fertile historical imaginations, working with shreds of evidence, a 'feel' for the past and a certain amount of common sense. One of the most productive adventurers into the meaning of marriage in past ages has been Lawrence Stone, whose thesis is that between the seventeenth and nineteenth centuries families came to serve fewer practical functions, became more private, came to carry a greater emotional commitment, and invested increasing amounts of emotional capital (and money) in children.[10] Whilst Stone may have underestimated the place of love in family relationships in early-modern England, it is no doubt true that the family had become more limited and private. William Cobbett denounced the wives of the 'new farmers' of the early nineteenth century who no longer wished to share board with the farm workers;[11] even comparatively modest houses in the nineteenth century had back stairs, so that servants could move between their living-quarters in the attics and their working-quarters in the basement without intruding upon the family's privacy. Between the late-eighteenth and mid-nineteenth centuries the majority of households ceased to function as productive economic units. Domestic industry gave way to domesticity. This change in the nature of the household and family came first among the higher social classes, but by the mid-nineteenth century the private, domestic household and the 'sentimental' family were well-established throughout the population.

Critics within the Marxist tradition of writing have argued that relationships within the family reflect the norms of capitalist society, and are based upon the exploitation of women. The cult of domesticity is seen as the means by which male dominance is asserted, and represents the imposition of bourgeois values and interests on the families of those who provide the labour for capitalist enterprises. Most people, as recorded by oral historians, do not seem to have shared this account of their behaviour. The 'bourgeois' family belonged, as one might expect, to the middle classes. Working-class households and families remained a partnership of economic and emotional interest, too near the precipice of poverty into which division might plunge them. A man might love his wife, but he expected and needed her to be 'a good manager'; a woman might love her husband, but she needed him also to be a reliable and sober workman. Roles were divided, but responsibilities were shared within an equal partnership: the man dominant in the outside world; the wife in charge within the home. Marriage was often but not always loving, but it was highly functional.

Such a picture of the working-class home, which in the 1990s still shapes the understanding of many elderly people, has faded in recent years with increasing opportunities for married women to work – the opportunity of years without the burden of repeated pregnancies as well as a widening range of 'women's jobs'. This has led women to question the sexual division of labour which confined them to the 'private' sphere of the home. A hundred and fifty years of increasing state intervention have also taken from families many of their responsibilities for education, mutual welfare and old age. The diminution in the place assigned to procreation and child-rearing, and the greater economic independence of women within marriage, have completed the reduction of the 'sentimental' family to its basic justification – mutual love.

Where love fails, divorce has become readily available to dissolve the union on which the family is based. In 1995 13.1 marriages were dissolved each year in England and Wales (10.8 in Scotland) for every 1,000 married couples. Though the rapid increase in the divorce rate following the Divorce Reform Act (1969), which came into force in 1971, was not sustained into the 1980s, by the last decade of the twentieth century around one-third of all marriages were not expected to run their natural span, giving the United Kingdom the highest divorce rate in the European

Union; and there were almost as many divorces as first-time marriages each year. Out of every 1,000 marital transactions (marriages and divorces) in 1961 there were 802 first-time marriages, 134 marriages in which at least one of the partners had previously been married and 64 divorces. In 1995, there were 394 first-time marriages, 263 second-time marriages and 343 divorces.

Mainly as a consequence of this high divorce rate, in 1995 10 per cent of households were headed by single parents, compared with 7 per cent in 1971, and a fifth of all children under 16 lived with a single parent, most of whom were female. Conversely, the most rapidly growing category of single-person households was that of single males under 65, from just 3 per cent in 1971 to 9 per cent in 1996 and a projected 13 per cent by 2016, by which time this category was expected to exceed even the numbers of women over 65 living alone. Nevertheless, the experience of most people was still that of the 'classic' family household, headed by a married couple, which in 1961 had accounted for 74 per cent of all households containing 82 per cent of the population, and in 1995 still accounted for 58 per cent of all households and 74 per cent of the population.

Migration

The most difficult variable to take into account when determining the size of the population is migration – from parish to parish, between the different parts of Britain, between Britain and Ireland, and wider patterns of emigration and immigration. Before the mid-nineteenth century direct evidence rarely exists from which the numbers of migrants can be calculated, and information has therefore to be inferred from records not intended for that purpose, especially parish registers. The simplest approach is to take the excess of births over deaths and to subtract the actual increase or decrease in population. The difference is assumed to be the loss or gain through migration, though allowance must be made for under-registration. Patterns of migration also can sometimes be established from the parish registers; and from 1851 the census gives birthplace details for all members of a household. But even if a sequence of events can be identified for a particular family, there is still no record of travels between these recorded events.

Data on immigration from and emigration to overseas destinations are similarly elusive. Net movements of population after 1801 can be calculated from the censuses in the same way as local movements can from the parish registers, and with the same problems of under-recording in the early years. Except for a short period between December 1773 and April 1776 there is no record of the level of emigration until 1815, when information was kept of passengers leaving United Kingdom ports (Scotland was recorded separately from England and Wales only after 1825) for non-European destinations; but these figures are known to be incomplete, and the destinations of emigrants are recorded only from 1853. Passenger lists of immigrants were kept – incompletely – from 1855. However, the 1841 Census shows numbers of resident immigrants, with the country of origin being stated from 1851.

Migration within Britain before 1830

Some migration was temporary or seasonal, some represented a permanent shift in the balance of population – from upland to lowland Scotland, from mid- to southern Wales, from the south and east of England to the north and west, and from rural to urban areas, especially London – but most migration within Britain was over short distances, often no more than between adjacent parishes. Transportation for the poor was still rudimentary before 1830, and the economy remained sufficiently diversified for there to be no need to change age-old habits and horizons. Marriage partners were usually found in the same or neighbouring parishes. At Colyton in Devon between 1765 and 1777, 89 per cent of the mothers of infants baptised there came from the parish or from within ten miles of the parish, and the proportion was practically the same in 1851. Similarly, at Easingwold in the North Riding only 12 per cent of marriages in the years 1747–1810 involved a partner who lived more than 10 miles distant.[12] Most towns were small, and grew by local recruitment, though this could mean a shortage of agricultural labour (and higher wages) in the vicinity of towns, drawing in other labourers from slightly farther afield. Populations moved by short steps rather than by long jumps. London is very much the exception to any generalisation about population trends, but even in the vast metropolis, which was highly dependent on immigration from all over the British Isles for its massive population growth throughout the eighteenth century, a quarter of the 3,236 married people who attended the Westminster Dispensary between 1774 and 1781 were born in London, and only 17 per cent came from beyond England and Wales.[13]

The bulk of provincial towns and cities did not share London's cosmopolitanism. The characteristic pattern was for country boys to seek apprenticeships in their local towns, and for country girls to move there in search of work as servants. The textile towns of Yorkshire and the North-West recruited from rural textile workers and their families living in the same or neighbouring counties. Highly skilled workers in the iron industry might be sought from further afield, and agricultural workers might move over considerable distances on a seasonal basis, but the overall evidence suggests that the rate of population mobility increased only slowly, if at all, during the eighteenth century. No English county experienced an absolute fall in population during the period 1751–1831, and only nine – Cheshire, the East Riding of Yorkshire, Durham, Kent, Lancashire, Middlesex, Surrey, Warwickshire and the West Riding of Yorkshire (and also Monmouthshire) – increased their populations by more than their natural increases. Of these, three included parts of London, and all the others – except Durham, where the expansion of coal mining multiplied pit villages – experienced major urban growth within or close to their county boundaries. Similarly, in Scotland there was no actual depopulation in the Highlands in the period 1801–1831, although between half and three-quarters of the parishes there lost some of their natural increase, 62 per cent in the case of the Hebridean parish of Tiree and Coll; but even the population of the county of Sutherland, notorious for its clearances, did not actually fall in these years. Indeed, if any Scottish region at all lost population between 1755 and 1821, it was not the Highlands but the Borders, much nearer to the main centres of urban growth.

What these figures conceal is the scale of local mobility. Some parishes could suffer depopulation while others within the same county might gain – and not necessarily the same people. The general picture, though, is that, in the first stage of industrialization and urbanization, population growth was sufficient overall to support both a growing population in the countryside and an increasing number of town-dwellers. Except in London and, particularly after 1801, the North-West, Yorkshire, Lowland Scotland and south-eastern Wales, urban expansion fed on the excess arising from local population growth rather than distant migration from depopulating rural areas. That development had to wait until the mid-nineteenth century at the earliest.

Migration, 1830–1914

As the pressures of population in agricultural areas grew, as urban industry increased its demand for labour, and as better communications helped link the two, whole counties began to experience population loss for the first time. During the 1840s Wiltshire, and in the 1850s Cambridge, Norfolk, Rutland, Wiltshire and Anglesey all suffered an absolute loss of population. Several other counties were stagnant, and with agricultural wages throughout the second half of the nineteenth century running at around 50 per cent of those to be had in industry and mining, there was little after the collapse of the 'high farming' boom in the 1870s to staunch the flow of people from many rural areas. West and central Wales were particularly hard-hit, but so also were Cornwall, Hereford, Huntingdon, Rutland, Shropshire, Somerset and Westmorland, which all had lower populations in 1911 than in 1871. On the other hand, the industrial counties and those bordering London experienced considerable growth, although depopulation was experienced in the more rural parishes even of some industrial counties.

In Scotland there was a similar pattern of population loss from the more remote upland counties and from those rural areas close to centres of urban growth. Argyll, Dumfries, Peebles, Perth and Sutherland were losers of population in the 1840s, whilst Argyll, Banff, Berwick, Caithness, Dumfries, Kirkcudbright, Moray, Nairn, Orkney, Perth, Ross and Cromarty, Roxburgh, Shetland, Sutherland and Wigton were all smaller in 1911 than they had been in 1871. In 1851 18.1 per cent of those born in the Highlands and 14.5 per cent of those born in the Borders lived in other regions. Whilst the Far North, the Highlands and the North-East recruited less than 10 per cent of their residents from other regions, 30 per cent of people in the Western Lowlands came from elsewhere. The nature of this recruitment from the Highlands to the Western Lowlands can be seen in the case of Greenock. In 1851, one in 26 of those born in Argyll lived in Greenock. Some had travelled only across the water from Dunoon, but one in nine of those born in Jura also had found their way to Greenock. This recruitment over greater distances became more marked during the second half of the century, the smaller towns acting as staging-posts *en route* for the larger towns and cities.

Growth-points in the later nineteenth century can be identified by comparing the populations of the major cities of Britain in 1871 and 1911. The 16 largest cities with over 100,000 population in 1871 were on average three-quarters as big again by 1911: Hull and Stoke more than doubled in size, and Manchester, Bradford and Bristol almost doubled. More significantly for the distribution of population, 22 other towns had populations of over 100,000 by 1911, having grown at an average rate of 126 per cent. Of the nine which grew faster than the average, four were in the Midlands (Coventry, Derby, Leicester and Nottingham), three were in the North East (Gateshead, Middlesbrough and South Shields), one was on Merseyside (Birkenhead), and one in South Wales (Cardiff, which was the fastest growing major city in Britain, having increased from 40,000 to 182,000 in 40 years). The total population of the London area, though, grew by as much as the combined total of all the provincial conurbations, and in 1911 it contained almost as many people (7.3 million) as South-East Lancashire, the West Midlands, West Yorkshire, Merseyside and Tyneside (7.5 million) put together. Glasgow was the largest provincial city at this time, with 784,000 inhabitants.

Migration in the twentieth century

Three contradictory trends are apparent in migration patterns in the twentieth century. First, the nineteenth-century pattern of migration from small settlements to large, from rural communities to urban, and from peripheral areas to central has continued. Second, as some of the older centres of industry have declined people have moved away from places which were attracting migrants in the nineteenth century. Third, with improvements in transportation, especially with the coming of the private motor car, there has been some movement from the towns back to the countryside in the vicinity of centres of employment and economic growth.

The decline of small rural communities has become increasingly marked, especially in the uplands of northern and western Britain. In England only six counties actually lost population between the inter-war censuses of 1921 and 1931 – Cornwall, Cumberland and Westmorland (all peripheral and upland), Hereford and Rutland (rural) and London. But in Wales the only counties to gain population (and then only marginally) were Carmarthen and Flint. Similarly, in Scotland only Lanarkshire, Midlothian, Stirling and (marginally) Roxburgh gained in population. Population growth after the Second World War reversed this trend in England, but not elsewhere. Cornwall was the only English county still losing people between 1951 and 1961, but the populations in six of the 13 Welsh counties were still in decline, offset by some significant growth in the industrial counties of Monmouth and Glamorgan. Scotland, however, was still losing population in 19 of her 33 counties. Between 1871 and 1971 the population of the Islands fell by 37.1 per cent, of the Highlands by 18 per cent, of the Borders by 17.3 per cent and of Dumfries and Galloway by 7.9 per cent. Despite some growth in the Grampian and Tayside regions, overall the outer regions of Scotland had no more population in 1971 than a hundred years earlier, while the population of the Central Belt had nearly doubled. In all cases, the smallest communities lost population most heavily, and the largest settlements gained most; those of 5,000 population and over grew, even in the outer regions, by around 80 per cent.

The decline in the basic industries of the Industrial Revolution also affected the distribution of population. Between 1921 and 1937 Lancashire was losing part of its natural increase in population at the rate of 20,000 a year – not far short of the losses experienced by Wales and Scotland. The drift to the South was a pronounced feature of population movements from the end of the First World War onwards. While Scotland, Wales, Lancashire, the North-East and the West Riding/Nottingham/Derby region were all, relatively speaking, losing population, the rest of the Midlands and the London/Home Counties region were gaining. After the Second World War the pattern became even clearer, with massive losses from Scotland being offset by increases in population not only in the Midlands and South-East, but also in East Anglia and the South-West (excepting Cornwall, which continued to experience an absolute fall in population). In 1960–1 the northern regions and Scotland lost about 150,000 people to the South, and received about 100,000 from the South, but no English region showed an absolute fall in numbers until the 1970s.

A pattern then emerged whereby Scotland and the northernmost regions of England lost population – mainly young adults and children – while the South-East, which sustained the heaviest losses, did so in all age groups except those of young adults and children. With the recession in the economy in the early 1990s, though, the economy of the South was hit as badly as that of the North. With an equalisation of misery came a more even flow of population between the regions and, indeed, in 1989 there was a small net flow of population from the South to the North, reversed again in 1992. Taking the years 1991–5 overall, no English region, and neither Scotland nor Wales, actually lost population. By 1995, as the economy recovered, regional patterns of internal migration were changing. While the South-West saw an outflow of 108,000 people, half of them to the South-East, it received 132,000, half of them from the South-East, and the net inflow to the South-West was nearly three times that into any other region. The worst-hit region for outflow was the North-West, which lost population to the East Midlands, the South-East and, particularly, the South-West. The attractiveness of the South-West appears to have been its climate, as older people in search of a comfortable retirement settled in the region. The 'drift to the South', therefore, did not mean that London was feeding on the population of the provinces as it had in earlier centuries. Rather, it was a drift from the northern and western provinces and London to East Anglia, the East Midlands and the south coast. If such a statistical abstraction as the 'typical' migrant could exist, it might be an elderly Liverpudlian woman retiring to Bournemouth, or a young man from Glasgow working in Milton Keynes.

Within these regional trends the cities form a special case, and until the 1980s the apparent paradox that a drift to the South coincided with a fall in the population of the South-East was largely due to the anomalous position of London, which was contracting sharply, losing over half a million people in the years 1971–81 alone. This decline was a continuation of a general drift from the centres of the largest cities that had begun in the first half of the nineteenth century. All the major cities, except Aberdeen, Bradford, Leeds and Sheffield, were losing population in the 1970s: Liverpool had declined by 35 per cent and Glasgow by 30 per cent of their 1951 populations by 1981. Though some of this loss was to outer suburbs, which led the 1951 Census to employ the concept of the conurbation, all the conurbations too were in decline by the 1970s, in marked contrast to the situation at the beginning of the twentieth century – Merseyside declined by 11 per cent and London by 10 per cent in the period 1971–81. This decline was halted, however, by the recession of the early 1990s, with only Manchester, Glasgow and Liverpool among the major cities losing population between 1991 and 1995. London, Leeds, Leicester, Nottingham, Plymouth, Stoke, Cardiff and Edinburgh were all larger in 1995 than they had been in 1981, though only Leicester, Plymouth and Cardiff were larger than in 1971.

Emigration before the mid-nineteenth century

The net loss of population through emigration from England before the 1820s was probably negligible – as low as 4,000 a year in the 1780s – though this was due in part to a compensating inflow of population from other parts of the British Isles. The vast majority of emigrants in the eighteenth century were bound for the Americas. Some of the earliest settlers went as convicts, but the majority were indentured servants. Rates of emigration fluctuated with external factors. Depression in the early 1770s produced an upsurge which was particularly noted in Scotland. In all, some 25,000 may have left for America in the years 1763–75, before the American war halted the flow. A second quickening in the scale of emigration ended with the French Wars (which disrupted travel and offered in the armed forces an alternative to settlement abroad); but depression and the hope of peace produced a further peak around 1801, when hundreds of Welsh families, struck with 'Madoc fever', went in search of Beulah Land.[14] Peace and renewed depression lay behind a further surge in emigration figures after 1815, which almost trebled for the whole United Kingdom from 13,000 in 1816 to 35,000 in 1819; then, after a further lull, numbers rose from the late 1820s to a new peak in 1832 of 103,000, of whom 9,099 came from Scotland. Though the United States continued to attract the most emigrants overall, the preference of Scotsmen for Canada was marked, with three-quarters of those leaving Scotland between 1825 and 1829 destined for that country.

Emigration from the mid-nineteenth century

The period between the middle of the nineteenth century and the outbreak of the First World War saw a massive increase in the flow of emigrants from Britain, and though the figures are complicated by the emigration of Irish-born people from British ports – especially, but not exclusively, in the years 1847–54 – it is clear that the Irish exodus was only a part of a much wider movement of peoples from the whole of the United Kingdom. Indeed, it has been suggested that Scotland may come second to Ireland in the whole of Europe as an exporter of population, losing over half of its natural increase in population through emigration, four-fifths of them going overseas. The bulk of emigrants went, as in the eighteenth century, to the United States, but Canada continued to attract between 10 and 20 per cent of the United States' figure in most years before 1900, while Australia became popular at around the same level in the 1850s, 1870s and 1880s. After 1900, when total levels of emigration reached their highest ever, there was a marked increase in numbers going to the Empire – especially to Canada, Australia and South Africa – and, for the first time, more people emigrated to British North America than to the United States. In 1911, when 455,000 left United Kingdom ports for extra-European countries, 29 per cent went to the USA, 41 per cent to Canada, 18 per cent to Australia and 7 per cent to South Africa.

After the First World War the volume of emigration fell sharply to levels not experienced since the 1870s, the most favoured destinations being Australia and Canada, and in the 1930s there were actually more people coming into Britain from America and what was later to be called the 'white Commonwealth' than were leaving for those countries. The flow was again reversed in the 1960s – excepting 1978 – until 1983, after which there was again a net inflow in most years, of whom about a third were British citizens, a third Commonwealth citizens (mainly families of earlier immigrants from the New Commonwealth) and a third foreign citizens from Europe, the United States and elsewhere.

Migrants and their motives

The decision to move from one's native parish or country was not lightly taken, and one should never forget that figures which give a net flow of population conceal a whole variety of hidden and contradictory motives. What needs to be asked of a depopulating area is not why people wanted to leave it, but why more people wished to leave than to enter it.

Free-market economists might suggest that population will always flow from areas of low demand/wages to areas of high demand/wages, and in this context much is often made of the relation of the Settlement Laws to the development of a capitalist economy in the early nineteenth century. The Settlement Act of 1662 (modified in 1691 and subsequently) restricted the right of poor relief in England and Wales to those born in a parish, married to someone born in the parish, or who had otherwise acquired a right of settlement by residence or employment. Any person who might become a burden upon the rates could be removed within 40 days from any parish in which he or she did not have a 'settlement'. In Scotland the poor could not be removed until they had become paupers, and they could acquire a settlement by three years' residence. Undoubtedly these laws could restrict the mobility of labour and did lead to much hardship and inhumane treatment of paupers and would-be paupers, but they do not seem to have been a major obstacle to migration. Few parishes with labour surpluses were going to prevent their poor from migrating, and few with labour shortages were going to refuse to receive them. Removal of paupers was expensive, and it appears to have been a common alternative for mutual arrangements to be made between the parish of settlement and the parish of residence for the payment of costs incurred in the temporary relief of a family during a trade recession. The practice of giving a pauper a ticket to enable him to pass freely through other parishes on his way back to his parish of settlement may well have meant that the poor rates were unwittingly used to subsidise labourers 'on the tramp'.

Another source of friction in the smooth working of a free labour market might be the reluctance of people to move for personal, family or community reasons. For example, Weardale lead miners in 1842 would not go to the coal mines, where they could double their wages, unless forced to by unemployment. The issue was not whether things were bad in an area, but how bad they were.

Undoubtedly a major reason why people migrated was the search for better things following the collapse of a local source of employment, changes in landholding or often simply the pressure of population on resources. In some Scottish parishes landlords evicted tenants in order to preserve peat supplies before the removal of the duty on coal in 1793, and the conversion of estates to sheep-farming led to widespread evictions. Where enclosures had resulted in the loss of rights to commons, poor people were driven to travel in search of work, and some parishes experienced absolute decline in the 1820s. The decay of rural industry could also affect local opportunities in the countryside, which may account for the fact that Wiltshire lost nearly half its natural increase in population between 1801 and 1831. In parts of northern Scotland the suppression of illicit distilling after 1821 figured prominently in the *New Statistical Account* as an explanation for the loss of population. Employment seems to have been a key factor in determining who went where, though a shortage of cottages and the lack of freedom to marry in agricultural districts may well have been additional reasons why some young people went to the towns. But the push from the countryside was only part of the story. The attraction of higher wages in industry played some part in the movement of population, especially of young people, who saw – or thought they saw – endless opportunities amidst the bright lights of the city.

Internal migration in the mature industrial and urban society of Britain in the late nineteenth century and after was, not unnaturally, governed less by the problems of the countryside than by the changing distribution of industry, with net flows of population between, as well as into, towns and cities. But, as in the countryside, the free-market model of labour mobility was not always judged appropriate either by potential migrants or, indeed, by economic planners. Though Scots steelworkers might move to Northamptonshire to work in the same industry, skills were not always easily transferable between 'old' industries in areas of high unemployment and 'new' industries in areas of relatively low unemployment. Furthermore, with infrastructures of houses, roads, hospitals and schools in depressed areas there was little economic reason for internal migration to be encouraged. The loss of population in an area of economic depression merely multiplied the economic problems of such areas. Thus, despite the drift to the south, governments in the twentieth century initiated regional policies to work in the opposite direction, encouraging the creation of new jobs in existing communities and areas of high unemployment.

Overseas emigration was the reluctant resort of the desperate, for to uproot oneself from one's homeland was both dangerous and expensive. Many of the poorest could not afford to go. With this in mind, organised emigration became a philanthropic business in the nineteenth century. Scottish landlords sent their unwanted tenants to America, Canada and Australia at their own expense, and in 1851 the Highland Emigration Society was set up to subsidise the emigration of whole families to Australia, shipping 4,709 people out from Glasgow to the Australian colonies in the early 1850s. Similar societies were organised in England, but public funds were also used. Under the Poor Law Amendment Act of 1834 over 25,000 paupers had been helped to emigrate by 1860, and the Colonial Land and Emigration Commissioners used funds from the sale of colonial land to help over 370,000 emigrate to Australia between 1840 and 1869. The Colonial Office also became involved in the 1830s, shipping over 3,000 unmarried women to Australia, where there were 2.6 males to every female. Several hundred surplus children also were exported in the 1830s to the Canadian and Australian colonies and the Cape of Good Hope through the agency of the Children's Friend Society for the Prevention of Juvenile Vagrancy, and the 'philanthropic abduction' and 'pre-emptive rescue' of working-class children by men like Dr Barnardo provided a ready supply of child labour for the colonies throughout the nineteenth century.

Emigration from Britain in the first half of the nineteenth century was therefore associated with paupers and criminals, and was not readily resorted to by free labour except when faced with abnormal hardship. America, however, was regarded by some of the more articulate leaders of working-class opinion in a more favourable light. It promised political freedom and access to land. Emigration societies were formed among Owenites and Chartists in the 1830s and 1840s. By the 1850s many a disillusioned radical had found his way to the land of freedom and opportunity, and this positive attitude became much more common among emigrants in the later nineteenth century. The discovery of gold in Victoria in 1854 also brought a sudden rush of emigrants to what had hitherto been an unpopular destination at the end of a much longer and more hazardous journey than that across the Atlantic. The great upsurge in emigration in the later nineteenth century, helped by better sea and land communications, was based more on hope than on despair, though by the 1880s the openings for skilled British workmen in America were contracting, leading to the need for more accurate advice about opportunities abroad, and greater consular guidance for would-be emigrants. There were also, as in the seventeenth century, religious reasons for emigration. A new twist was given to this in the 1840s, when a sect of American origin, the

Mormons, recruited 40,000 converts in Britain who then sailed for the Promised Land.

Personal information about internal migrants can be taken from the Census enumerators' books after 1851, and further demographic details can be derived from the overall population structure of areas of net population increase and decrease. Broadly speaking, mining districts and areas with heavy industry attracted male labour; conversely, the declining mining area of Cornwall lost more men than women, while the outflow from the rural areas was greater among women than men. Thus both mining/heavy-industrial counties like Glamorgan and Durham, and purely agricultural counties like Rutland and the Isle of Ely, figured largely among those counties with a predominance of males in their populations. Towns with opportunities for female service drew a disproportionate number of young females. London, for example, shows an excess of girls aged between 12 and 30 years which corresponds to a deficiency of the same age-group in Essex. The young (under 20 years) and the lowest social classes were likely to migrate the shortest distances, and the most common age group among all migrants was that of 'young adults', aged between 20 and 35.

Many of those who went overseas were men in early manhood, or young families without children who could no longer find a future in the changing rural economy. However, only about 18 per cent of those emigrating from Britain to all destinations in the last quarter of the nineteenth century were farm labourers, and a study of English and Scots emigrants to the United States shows that rural workers were moving first to the larger towns, and then emigrating as general labourers already accustomed to urban living. Building workers also figured more prominently in the New York shipping lists of both the 1850s and the 1880s than their proportion of the total population would warrant, and there is some connection here between the level of emigration and the state of the building market in Britain. About half the emigrants to New York in the late 1880s were classed as either general labourers or workers in the building trades. Miners were another prominent group much influenced by economic opportunities, constituting 8 per cent of men emigrating to New York in the 1880s, but in the 1890s they switched to Australia and South Africa, where the prospects were better. There were also a number of 'mechanics' – around 10 per cent of the total – but workers in textiles, steel and engineering – the 'new' industries of the industrial revolution – were under-represented among emigrants. When the smaller numbers of women are added to the passenger lists the result, as expected, is to increase the category of servants from less than 1 per cent to over 11 per cent, making it second only to general labourers as a proportion of all British emigrants to New York in the later 1880s.

Not all emigrants came from the lower social classes. Farmers looking for more land and the opportunity to expand their activities for themselves and their children were attracted to the prairies of the United States and Canada. Clerical and commercial occupations were also over-represented in the passenger lists, which also included 753 gentlemen – 8 per cent of the total number of male passengers – but many of these were visitors rather than emigrants. Indeed, around 14 per cent of those designated temporary visitors were tradesmen and skilled workers, reflecting in part a continuance on an international scale of the ancient tradition of the tramping artisan.[15]

Immigration

The population of Britain in the eighteenth century was at its most cosmopolitan in the major seaports – notably London, but also increasingly Bristol, Liverpool and Glasgow. Most of these foreigners would have been seafarers whose stay in Britain was temporary, but some were refugees. London in the eighteenth century, even more so than the American colonies, was the place of refuge for those fleeing religious persecution on the Continent. Apart from the French community of Huguenots in Spitalfields there were many artisans of European origin in central London (around Soho), and labourers in the expanding sugar-refining industry in the East End were chiefly Germans. Estimates of the origin and extent of London's foreign population are not easy to obtain. The records at the Westminster General Dispensary between 1774 and 1781 show that, of 3,236 married people treated, only 40 men and 13 women (1.64 per cent) were foreign born, compared with 162 men and 119 women (8.68 per cent) from Ireland and 135 men and 74 women (6.46 per cent) from Scotland.[16]

Revolution and counter-revolution after 1789 brought further successive waves of refugees to Britain, chiefly to London: French Catholics and Royalists in the 1790s; Poles after 1830; Germans, Czechs, French and Italians after 1848. Many passed on to America; some stayed, and to their numbers were added seamen and other miscellaneous characters from every corner of the globe. Southampton had a strong Polish community from the 1830s, and Liverpool saw the influx of many Chinese after the Blue Funnel Line began to trade directly with China in 1865.

Despite the Aliens Act of 1905 and the Aliens Restriction Act of 1919, which made Britain a far less open country than it had been in the nineteenth century, wars and political upheavals in Europe ensured a continuing supply of refugees – not only Jews but also Poles, Ukrainians and Hungarians – fleeing German advances in the 1930s and Russian advances in the 1940s and 1950s.

Rich though this variety of immigrants was, their numbers were small and their impact less than in the United States, where their presence contributed significantly to economic and social life. In Britain, though, there are four other groups of immigrants whose numbers were such as to make a major impact on the social history of the country: the Irish from both Ulster and the South; Jews, mainly from Eastern Europe; Africans and Afro-Caribbeans from the British West Indies, Guyana and Honduras; and Indians, Pakistanis and Bangladeshis from the Indian subcontinent.

Irish immigrants

The Irish in Britain were technically not immigrants in the sense of being foreigners, and they should perhaps be seen rather as migrants within the United Kingdom, no different from the Scots, Welsh or English. It would also not be accurate to regard them as alien in religion, politics or culture, for many of the Irish who travelled to Scotland in particular were Ulster Protestants who had rather more in common with the lowland Scots than the latter had with the Gaelic-speaking Highlanders of the Western Isles. Nevertheless the Irish were seen as different, especially by the English, and their migrations and settlements had many of the characteristics associated with immigrants.

The Irish were already well-established in Britain by the end of the eighteenth century. Indeed, the London community, which was the largest and oldest, had been established during the seventeenth century, and Liverpool also had about 1,800 Irish manual workers at this time. By the mid-eighteenth century the Irish were providing the metropolis with many of its unskilled workers – builders' and dock labourers, street hawkers, milk-sellers, coal-heavers, porters and sedan chairmen, as well as weavers who came from the Dublin linen industry to work in London silk; while Irish women often found a necessary employment in prostitution. Though there were also upper-class Irish in London – lawyers, politicians, landlords, actors – the bulk of their countrymen settled at the very bottom of English society, despised by the natives with whom they were sometimes in conflict.

Heavy immigration, though, began only at the very end of the eighteenth century, possibly as a consequence of the 1798 Rebellion. The famine of 1801 and the decline in domestic textile manufacture in the early nineteenth century continued the process and, although the scale of the influx from Ireland nowhere near reached that of the Famine years of the 1840s, there were already sizable Irish communities in London, Lancashire and south-western Scotland by the 1830s. In 1818 the first steam ferry ran between Glasgow and Belfast, and by the mid-1830s fares were as low as 3*d.* (1.25p) a head. A private census of Glasgow in 1819–20 showed that 10.3 per cent of the city's population was Irish-born, just over half of whom were Catholic, and in some of the smaller parishes of Wigtown and Ayrshire the percentage was much larger.

Numbers of Lancashire Irish were similarly building up from the 1790s, with around 100,000 in 1825, 35,000 of whom were in Manchester and 24,000 in Liverpool. By 1841 there may have been as many as 80,000 Irish-born in London alone, and around 400,000 in the whole of Britain.

Many more Irish came to Britain not to settle, but to seek casual and seasonal work. The spread of threshing machines in the early nineteenth century increased the gap between the regular labour requirements of farmers, and those needed only at harvest time. The Settlement Acts may also have made casual Irish labour more attractive to farmers than English: in 1841, at least 57,000 seasonal immigrants were recorded, most of them men whose families remained in Ireland to till plots of land which tied them to their home country without supplying them with the means of adequate subsistence. Though such casual labour continued to visit Britain throughout the nineteenth century and into the twentieth, with other seasonal trades such as building and constructional work (including railways) also drawing heavily on Irish labour, the Famine of the late 1840s broke the links of many with the land and home, and produced unprecedented numbers of permanent settlers. Between 1846 and 1851 at least 1.4 million Irishmen, women and children came to Britain, and about 1 million of them later emigrated to the United States. Some died, but at the 1851 Census the number of Irish-born living in Britain had increased from 415,725 to 730,335. In 1841 1.8 per cent of the population of England and Wales, and 4.8 per cent of the population of Scotland were Irish-born; 10 years later the proportions were 2.9 per cent and 7.2 per cent respectively.

Places of settlement were geographically concentrated in traditional Irish areas. Those counties with more than 5 per cent Irish in 1851 were Lancashire, Wigtown, Ayr, Lanark, Renfrew, Dunbarton and Stirling. By 1861 some dispersal had occurred, with Cumberland, Cheshire and Durham joining Lancashire in England, and Angus (i.e. Dundee with its linen industry) being added to the Scottish list. By 1891 there were no English counties with more than 5 per cent Irish-born, and the national average was only 1.6 per cent, though Glamorgan had joined Lancashire and the others as a relatively important centre for Irish settlement. Clydeside remained the most heavily Irish part of Britain, with over 5 per cent, though by this date the proportion for the whole of Scotland had fallen below 5 per cent for the first time since the 1840s. This does not fully measure the population of the Irish communities, though, for increasing numbers of Irish children were being born within Britain itself. In London, for example, it has been calculated that, although the number of Irish-born was 109,000 (4.6 per cent) in 1851, the Irish community actually contained 156,000 people; and, although the proportion of Irish-born had fallen to 3.8 per cent in 1861, the size of the community had risen to 178,000. Immediately after the Famine the Irish migration was unusual in that whole families took part, although the father might precede the others to earn the passage money for the rest. Only as the flood died down to a gentle trickle of a few thousand a year did the immigrant population assume the characteristic structure for migrants – that is, weighted towards young adults and the unmarried. Immigration never completely ceased, though it fell below 10,000 a year in 1884, far fewer than the number of migratory workers in England alone, which did not fall below 10,000 until 1911. The condition of Ireland remained such that its economically powerful neighbour could continue to attract and employ immigrant and migrant Irish, but it was not until the Second World War that Ireland – in spite of the South's neutrality in the War – again provided labour on a massive scale for the British economy. Between 1943 and 1950 116,304 men and 113,621 women received travel permits to go to employment in Britain. In 1951 there were 716,028 Irish-born in Britain, almost as many as a hundred years earlier at the height of the Famine. Three-quarters of those living in England and Wales, and half of those living in Scotland, were from the South.

Most of the Irish immigrants, especially in the early post-Famine years, came from the countryside, but settled in cities, where they did largely unskilled work. Although the contemporary fear was that the Irish were taking jobs from English, Scots and Welsh urban workers and depressing their wages, it is likely that the natives with whom they were most in competition were agricultural labourers, both in the countryside and in the towns to which they, like the Irish, were recent migrants. In Liverpool in 1851, unskilled work made up 49 per cent of all labour, but 60 per cent of the Irish were unskilled, and they constituted between half and three-quarters of all dock workers. In London 30.8 per cent of the Irish worked as general labourers compared with 10.1 per cent of the population as a whole; 20.8 per cent were transport workers, compared with 11.2 per cent; and 12.8 per cent were construction workers, compared with 10.2 per cent. Irish women were less likely than the population as a whole to work in service (42.7 per cent compared with 55.7 per cent), but more likely to work in clothing and food manufacture. In York, where there was a relatively large Irish community (5.4 per cent Irish-born; 7.2 per cent total community), half the male farm-workers and a quarter of the male labourers were Irish, together with all the female farm-labourers, three-quarters of the general female labourers and 41 per cent of the hawkers. Gradually one can see the process of assimilation and diversification. In 1861 the proportion of general labourers among London male Irish had fallen to 17.8 per cent and that of transport workers had risen to 32.1 per cent, but there had been little change in the occupations of the women. In York also there was a slow diversification of employment, but agricultural workers and labourers continued to be strongly Irish in complexion.[17]

During this early period of Irish settlement the image of the 'Paddy' became fixed in the mind of host communities. Friedrich Engels, himself an immigrant, gave a celebrated description of 'Little Ireland' in Manchester, even before the Famine hordes appeared:

> These Irishmen . . . insinuate themselves everywhere. The worst dwellings are good enough for them; their clothing causes them little trouble, so long as it holds together by a single thread; shoes they know not; their food consists of potatoes and potatoes only; whatever they earn beyond these needs they spend upon drink. What does such a race want with high wages? The worst quarters of all the large towns are inhabited by Irishmen.[18]

What is in contention about this widely accepted picture is not its truth but its explanation. Undoubtedly the Irish did contribute to their own conditions by bringing their rural ways straight into the towns. As Engels went on to observe, the Irish brought their pigs with them, and if they could not construct a sty outside their dwellings they brought the pigs inside, and they stored their manure and human refuse as though they were still back in Ireland conserving goodness for the land. It is also true that the funeral customs of the Irish, involving keeping the corpse for days, and celebrating death (and other rites of passage) with excessive drinking, horrified many of the more puritanical and increasingly health-conscious respectable classes in the host communities. There was clearly a clash of cultures.

Yet it is also true that the Irish had little choice. It may be that the cellars of Manchester had been built intentionally damp for cotton handloom weaving, and had been regarded as uninhabitable before, through pressure of numbers, they were opened up for the Irish; but the general conditions endured by the Irish were no different from those experienced by the lowest classes of native English and Scots. The only difference was that a visible majority of Irish endured what only an invisible minority of natives suffered. It may also be true that the Irish deserved their reputation for fighting and drunkenness, but a study of the community in York has shown that their crimes – 26.3 per cent of total convictions in the city in 1851, falling to 16.5 per cent in 1871 – were usually minor assault, petty theft, disorderly conduct and drunkenness. They were less likely to contribute to major crimes, and their petty crimes were largely confined to their own areas of the city.

As with any national stereotype, 'Paddy' was founded on an element of truth, grossly distorted by observers who wrenched his behaviour out of context. Despite their reputation the Irish retained a low profile and, after the 1860s, they were not generally regarded with hostility by the wider population. There is little evidence of outright racism in British attitudes to the Irish. Major conflict arose over religious issues, or at times of political tension; and the most severe disturbances were experienced where both Orange and Catholic communities existed, in Lancashire and on

Clydeside, where the divided Irish society of Ulster was more closely replicated. What was true in the later nineteenth century remained so in the twentieth, and the further influx of Irish after the Second World War did not, despite renewed troubles in Ulster from the late 1960s, result in the arousal of noticeable anti-Irish feeling within Great Britain.

Jewish immigrants

The Jewish community was, like the Irish, well established in Britain by the eighteenth century and constituted the largest single group of resident aliens from continental Europe. Rich Jews of the Sephardim had come to Britain from Spain and Portugal in the second half of the seventeenth century, but, following the establishment of a synagogue of the Ashkenazim Jews in Aldgate in 1722, poor Jews came to predominate, fleeing Bohemia in 1744, Poland in 1772 and Gibraltar in 1781. It has been estimated that there were around 5,000 Jews in England in 1750. By 1800 there were 15,000–20,000 in London alone (and a further 5,000 or 6,000 elsewhere in the country), of whom approaching three-quarters were poor Jews from Poland, Russia and the Ottoman Empire. These were welcomed in such numbers neither by the rich Jews of the Sephardim, nor by the native population. Repeal of the Jewish Naturalization Act in 1753 was one result of this prejudice, and largely fruitless attempts were later made to restrict the free immigration of Jews through Holland. In 1792, the Alien Act – intended chiefly to supervise the flow of French refugees after the Revolution – was used to remove some poor Jews back to the Continent.

The Jewish community for much of the nineteenth century continued small, divided and introspective. At the top an élite of families – Montefiore, Samuel, Mocatta, Goldsmid, Franklin, Henriques, Lucas and Rothschild – dominated Jewish life; at the bottom, street traders eked a living on the fringes of legality. Charity was administered through the synagogue, but not all Jews were so attached, and in 1859 the Jewish Board of Guardians was founded in London – to be later copied elsewhere – to superintend the distribution of Jewish charity to their community as a whole. Apart from London, respectable communities existed in places like Manchester, but numbers generally were small. In Leeds in 1841 the community was reported to comprise only 10 families. They were little prepared for the shock of mass Jewish immigration which was to hit them in the later 1880s.

Between 1870 and 1914 around 120,000 Jews emigrated from Russia and Eastern Europe to Britain (all but about 10,000, in fact, came to England). This was not a large number – over 200,000 Irish entered Britain during these same years – but their presence was rapidly felt, and they were joined by many others who, like the Irish before them, were in transit for the United States. The initial reaction of the British Jews to the first wave of mass immigration in 1881–2 was to discourage permanent settlement in Britain, but this could not be avoided as successive expulsions and pogroms sent Jewish traders, shopkeepers and artisans fleeing westwards in destitution. In Britain they attempted to revive their old ways, as pedlars and street traders, arousing the resentment of the London costermongers. Only a few managed to establish shops, chiefly in the major areas of Jewish immigration in the East End of London, the Strangeways and Red Bank districts of Manchester and Salford and the Leylands district of Leeds. Here some streets were over 80 per cent Jewish. The ghetto had been recreated. Displaced or embattled English shopkeepers resented the alien intrusion.

Like the Irish, the poor Jews sank to the bottom of the labour market, and found themselves, like the Irish womenfolk, working in the sweated trades, particularly clothing. But, unlike the Irish, they already had skills and were accustomed to urban life. Beatrice Potter concluded in the 1890s that the Jew:

> is unique in possessing neither a minimum nor a maximum; he will accept the lowest terms rather than remain out of employment; as he rises in the world new wants stimulate him to increased intensity of effort, and no amount of effort causes him to slacken his indefatigable activity.[19]

This was not a characteristic which Engels had noted among the Irish in the 1840s, and it was not one which endeared the Jew to English trade unionists. Jews were particularly prominent in the tobacco trade, and it was an Austrian Jew who introduced cigarette manufacture to Britain, helping set up Player's factory at Nottingham in 1882 and Imperial Tobacco at Glasgow in 1888. But it was tailoring which was *par excellence* the Jewish immigrant trade, and Jews were largely responsible for the creation of the cheap, ready-made clothing industry, aided by the Singer sewing machine and a rising standard of living among the working classes who had previously been satisfied with second-hand garments or cheap 'slop' products. Some 29 per cent of the new wave of Jewish immigrants were in tailoring, joining an industry in which German Jews had been prominent since the mid-nineteenth century. By 1911 12,344 men and 2,939 women of Russian and Polish origin (i.e. Jewish immigrants) were working as tailors in London; there were 1,015 workshops in Whitechapel alone, according to Beatrice Potter in the late 1880s. Sweating was less bad in Leeds, where the workshops were larger and had some steam power. Though all but one of the 51 clothing factories in Leeds were Gentile, nearly all the 101 workshops were Jewish, employing possibly a third of the Jewish community, which in the late 1880s numbered around 6,000.

Like other immigrant groups, the Jews first settled in cramped conditions engendered by high rents and low wages, but their ghettos never resembled the worst quarters of the Irish or the poor English and Scots. Sometimes, as in Spitalfields, Jewish settlement could actually lead to improvement, and, despite complaints of dirtiness and alien habits, the mortality statistics suggest that Jewish children were healthier and better-fed than their equivalents in the host population. The richer Jews, like the rest of their class, could afford to move out of the central, overcrowded areas, but many poor Jews found security and protection for themselves and sound influences with which to surround their children in their own inner-city ghettoes. The result was a rejection of the policy of dispersal, such as was advocated by Sir Samuel Montagu in 1903, and a steady expansion in the ghettoes instead. Of 95,245 Russian and Polish aliens in Britain in 1901, 56 per cent lived in London, of whom 79 per cent lived in Stepney. 'It is like the waves of the sea,' complained an English carpenter in 1903, ' – they simply keep spreading, but they do not retreat like the waves of the sea do.'[20] The Aliens Act of 1905 was in part a response to this kind of alarmism, and it brought to an end the great period of Jewish immigration. The next wave of refugees, who came from Germany and Austria between the wars, was socially quite different, but its members found in Britain disturbing echoes of anti-Jewish feeling. Nevertheless, the community prospered. In 1900 there were 80 synagogues in Great Britain: 50 years later there were around 240, and in the 1990s the total Jewish community was reckoned to be about 300,000, two-thirds of whom lived in London. Dispersal had occurred, aided partly by slum clearance but also partly following a usual trend. Leylands had been home to the Leeds Irish before the Jews arrived, and Spitalfields had housed French Huguenots. The Huguenot church at the corner of Brick Lane and Fournier Street became successively a Methodist Chapel in the late eighteenth century, a synagogue in the late nineteenth century, and a mosque for Bangladeshis in the late twentieth century.

Coloured immigrants

Most coloured people in eighteenth-century Britain were originally the servants of merchants from the Americas and the East and West Indies. Estimates as to their numbers vary, but there were probably no more than 10,000 for much of the eighteenth century. To have a black or Indian as a servant was highly fashionable, as well as allowing the rich planter or nabob to maintain in the home country the standard of living which he had enjoyed overseas without the cost of English servants. But there was also a residuum who had lost, fled or been discarded by their masters. To these were added after 1783 blacks who had fought on the British side in America. The philanthropic campaigner Granville Sharp felt himself responsible for some 400 of these black pensioners from the army, whose plight led to the disastrous settlement of Sierra Leone in 1787. Other blacks returned to the West Indies, but such repatriation still left many to settle permanently in Britain.

The main sources of coloured immigration into Britain during much of the nineteenth century remained the armed forces and the merchant navies of the world. Their numbers were relatively small, and even fewer settled permanently. A native of Britain would be likely to encounter a coloured face only in the major seaports, especially London. The process of settlement is illustrated by developments in South Wales, where the coal trade expanded rapidly in the last third of the nineteenth century. Seamen were signed off at the end of the voyage, or alternatively jumped ship, attracted by the prospect of a spell ashore and the casual work which was readily available in the expanding economy of the port and its hinterland. By the end of the century Cardiff had about 700 Africans and West Indians in its population. Once they had left their ships blacks often found it harder than whites to find new berths, white crews often refusing to accept them. White dockers also proved reluctant to work alongside blacks. Like other immigrant groups, they found themselves at the bottom of the social pile.

The demand for labour and fighting men in the First World War transformed their economic situation, but not the prejudice against them. Unlike the Irish – and even the Jews – who were disliked for particular economic and social characteristics associated with them rather than for their race as such, the blacks suffered outright racial prejudice. Demobilisation increased Liverpool's coloured population from 2,000 to 5,000, and Cardiff's from 700 to 3,000, many of whom were unemployed. In the summer of 1919 serious race-riots broke out in Liverpool, Newport and Cardiff, after which about 600 coloured men accepted voluntary repatriation. The complaint everywhere emphasised sexual relations between coloureds and whites, for the coloured community was overwhelmingly male.

Prejudice in employment was made worse by the depression. Despite the fact that many coloureds were British citizens (a status they retained until 1962), they were treated as aliens. Two investigators for the League of Coloured Peoples reported of Cardiff in 1935:

> We found a canvas crowded with strange figures: shipowners, aldermen, police, trade unionists, pulling from various angles a net which has entangled people from all over the British Empire. We lived in a compact community of West Indians, West Africans, Arabs, Malays, Somalis, men from Singapore, East Africa and every land where the Union Jack has planted itself; a settled, orderly community, trying with desperate success to keep respectable homes under depressing conditions . . . We met men as British as any Englishman, forced by fraud to register as aliens, after living here since the war;

> charges and counter-charges; misleading newspaper reports; men in authority bellowing 'repatriation'; muttered resentments against British children called 'half-castes'; and dominating everything, an imminent danger that deliberate trickery would mean for these men and their families expulsion from British shipping and ultimately from Britain.[21]

Against this background came the Second World War, followed by a period of intense labour shortages, during which a massive immigration from the West Indies and India was promoted with scarce regard for the social consequences.

Inflation and unemployment in the Caribbean drove British West Indians to seek better prospects in their 'mother country' which had guaranteed them United Kingdom citizenship by the Nationality Act of 1948. The first boatload of 492 Jamaicans arrived in 1948, and in the mid-1950s the annual flow exceeded 20,000 a year. By 1958 some 125,000 West Indians had settled in Britain since the war. Many of them (87 per cent of the men and 95 per cent of the women) had skills to offer; indeed, a quarter of the men and half the women were non-manual workers. Yet in general they found work that was beneath their abilities, doing tasks which white employees preferred to avoid – cleaning and hospital work for the women; street-sweeping, shift-work and general labouring for the men. At the same time, immigrants also came in increasing numbers from the politically and economically uncertain Indian subcontinent. Textile firms, unable to employ women on night-shifts yet needing to work expensive machinery round the clock, were glad to take on Indian and Pakistani labour. Bradford became a major Pakistani city. In the East End of London and elsewhere, Asian workers and petty capitalists produced cheap, ready-made clothing in sweated workshops. Around many transport depots in the leading industrial cities streets of houses passed into immigrant hands. London Transport deliberately sought staff in the West Indies, recruiting 3,787 Barbadians between 1956 and 1968, but in the Midlands members of the Transport Workers' Union objected to the employment of all but a few coloureds on the buses. Nevertheless, in many places both public transport and hospital services would have been adversely affected without immigrant labour.

The appearance of coloured immigrant communities in many of the major cities of Britain over the space of a decade caused growing unease in the host community. In the later 1950s the balance of population flow was inwards, at around 50,000 a year, rising to over 100,000 in 1961, as the government prepared to close the doors in response to public pressure. The Commonwealth Immigrants Act of 1962 restricted entry to those with employment vouchers, and in 1965 the number of such vouchers was limited to 8,500 a year as the Labour government adopted a policy of squeezing excess employment out of the economy. Then, in 1968, events

Table 2.1 Population of Great Britain by age and ethnic group, Spring 1996

	Under 16	16–34	35–54	55 and over	Numbers
	%	%	%	%	
White	20	27	27	26	52,942,000
Black Caribbean	23	36	24	17	477,000
Black African	28	43	23	6	281,000
Other Black	49	38	12	–	117,000
Indian	27	32	29	12	877,000
Pakistani	40	33	19	8	579,000
Bangladeshi	40	35	17	8	183,000
Chinese	16	40	30	15	126,000
Other Asian	27	31	36	6	161,000
Others/mixed	51	30	15	5	506,000
All ethnic groups	21	27	27	25	56,267,000

Source: Social Trends, 27 (1997), Table 1.8, p. 31.

in Kenya (and later in Uganda also) forced many Asian holders of British passports to flee to Britain, leading to further controls on immigration. Finally, the 1971 Immigration Act was introduced to end primary immigration and to restrict future entries to dependent kin, a category needing further restrictive definition by the British Nationality Act of 1981. Even so, British politicians continued to fear a resurgence of immigration, especially from Hong Kong as the date (30 June 1997) approached for the return of the colony to China, and further legislation was introduced in 1993 to deter 'economic migrants' from developing and war-torn countries from seeking refuge in Britain.

A question about ethnic grouping was included for the first time in the 1991 census. It revealed that 5.5 per cent of the population – just over 3 million people – was non-white, of whom just over half had been born in Britain. The population structure of these immigrant groups reflected their history, with the older-established Chinese group having fewer young and old people than the white majority population, while the Pakistani and Bangladeshi groups were predominantly young (see Table 2.1).

This age structure to some extent was reflected in some of the major social concerns of these communities: the high unemployment rate among young blacks and the problems of multi-ethnic education for Moslem children. Like all immigrant groups, the coloured communities were concentrated in inner-city areas, where their presence and difficulties became associated with the quite separate problems of the inner cities. Three-fifths of the black community and two-fifths of the Indian community lived in London, with nearly 45 per cent of the population of the north London borough of Brent being made up of ethnic minorities, and over a third of the populations of Newham, Tower Hamlets and Hackney in east London. West Yorkshire and the Midlands were major areas of settlement for the Pakistani community, but even so 18 per cent of the latter lived in London.

The tensions generated in British society by the presence of these relatively small but (on account of their colour) highly visible minorities were and remain complex. Moslems, Sikhs and Hindus are divided and, like the Irish, have brought their own quarrels with them, Indians from the north of the sub-continent despise Indians from the south; middle-class Kenyan Asians wish to distance themselves from their socially inferior brethren direct from India; West Indians and Africans mistrust Indian shopkeepers – 'the Jews of Africa' – who seemed to have an access to capital denied to themselves. As diverse from each other as from the majority whites, they presented an opportunity for the mutual enrichment of British culture; but, with relatively high levels of structural unemployment in Britain in the 1980s and 1990s, which hit young black and Asian school-leavers in particular, the potential for resentment, racial violence and community unrest is never far below the surface in parts of London and other major cities as the twentieth century draws to a close.

Notes

1. E. A. Wrigley and R. S. Schofield, *The Population History of England, 1541–1871: A Reconstruction* (1981).
2. Wrigley and Schofield, *Population History*, pp. 531–5.
3. Wrigley and Schofield, *Population History*, p. 529.
4. M. S. Teitelbaum, *The British Fertility Decline* (Princeton, 1984), especially chs. 5–6.
5. This argument was first put forward in N. Himes, *Medical History of Contraception* (1936).
6. See, in particular, J. A. Banks, *Victorian Values: Secularism and the Size of Families* (1981) which refines the interpretation first set out in *Prosperity and Parenthood: A Study of Family Planning among the Victorian Middle Classes* (1954).
7. Banks, *Victorian Values*, pp. 57–8, 103.
8. P. Laslett with R. Wall (eds.), *Household and Family in Past Time* (Cambridge, 1972), especially ch. 4, P. Laslett, 'Mean Household Size in England since the Sixteenth Century' and ch. 6, W. A. Armstrong, 'A Note on the Household Structure of Mid-Nineteenth-Century York in Comparative Perspective'.
9. Laslett and Wall, *Household*, ch. 7, M. Anderson, 'Household Structure and the Industrial Revolution; Mid-Nineteenth-Century Preston in Comparative Perspective'. See also his *Family Structure in Nineteenth Century Lancashire* (Cambridge, 1971).
10. L. Stone, *The Family, Sex and Marriage in England, 1500–1800* (1979).
11. W. Cobbett, *Rural Rides* (1830; new edn., Harmondsworth, 1967), p. 229.
12. See articles from *Local Population Studies* by B. Maltby and E. A. Wrigley, reprinted in M. Drake (ed.), *Population Studies from Parish Registers* (Matlock, 1982), pp. 113–16 and 117–24.

13. M. D. George, *London Life in the XVIIIth Century* (1925; 2nd edn., 1930), pp. 111–12.
14. G. A. Williams, *The Search for Beulah Land: The Welsh and the Atlantic Revolution* (1980).
15. C. J. Erickson, 'Who were the English and Scottish Emigrants in the 1880s?', in D. V. Glass and R. Revelle (eds.), *Population and Social Structure* (1972), pp. 347–81.
16. M. D. George, *London Life in the XVIIIth Century*, pp. 111–12.
17. F. Finnegan, *Poverty and Prejudice: A Study of Irish Immigrants in York, 1840–1875* (Cork, 1982).
18. F. Engels, *Condition of the Working Class in England* (1845), new edn., V. Kiernan, ed. (Harmondsworth, 1987), p. 124.
19. Quoted in L. P. Gartner, *The Jewish Immigrant in England, 1870–1914* (1960), pp. 64–5.
20. Quoted by C. Holmes, 'The Impact of Immigration on British Society, 1870–1980', p. 178, in T. Barker and M. Drake (eds.), *Population and Society in Britain, 1850–1980* (1982).
21. Quoted in P. Fryer, *Staying Power* (1984), p. 357.

3

Class

Social and occupational structures

The old order

Society in the eighteenth century has often been portrayed as a pyramid, with the monarch at the apex and the great masses of the labouring poor at the base, though it would probably be more accurate to think of 'societies' rather than 'society', since the experience of the bulk of the population was not national but local and parochial. Relationships were vertically structured, bound together by the local ties of deference from below and paternalism from above. This picture was somewhat embellished by conservatives in the early nineteenth century, but it does express the essence of social relationships in the countryside before that transformation which accompanied the industrial revolution.

At the top of society in the eighteenth century, locally and nationally, came the peerage. This was a small group – fewer than 200 before 1784. Next to these came the substantial landed gentry, often related to the peerage and as rich as or richer than the lesser peers, together with junior members of aristocratic families who might expect to have to seek fortunes through marriage, political office or the professions. These men belonged to a relatively closed society. John Cannon has calculated that in 1750 the British social élite contained no more than 1096 peers, baronets and knights and, despite a flurry of new creations after 1784, there were still only 1386 in the élite in 1800. Most promotions came from internal recruitment. Only 10 per cent of newly created peers in the eighteenth century were men without direct peerage connections, and of 113 recent creations (out of a total of 257 English peers in 1800), only seven had no previous connection with the peerage.[1]

Scotland, like England, was ruled by a small élite – a handful of magnates (most of whom had been elevated to dukedoms by the end of the eighteenth century) and about 40 earls. No new Scottish peers were created after 1707 and their numbers had fallen to only 68 by 1800. These were not entitled to sit in the House of Lords, except through 12 of their number whom they elected, and their prestige fell further after 1782 when Scotsmen raised to the British peerage were allowed to take personal seats in the Lords. But despite an exclusiveness at the top greater even than that to be found in England, land-ownership extended more widely in the middle ranks of society. Highland 'tackmen' (in many cases the relatives of clan chiefs) held land on leases, but often secured ownership through the 'wadset', a loan to their impecunious lords on the security of their property. In the south, especially, lairds established themselves as a landowning gentry (heritors) much as in England.

In Wales the picture was somewhat different. Here the social pyramid was much truncated. The aristocratic élite was small and English-speaking: of the 25 greatest families in 1760, 12 had no recent Welsh connections. In the nineteenth century 60 per cent of Wales (compared with 53.5 per cent of England) comprised estates of over 1,000 acres (400 hectares); 44 per cent of the cultivable land was in the hands of 31 peers and 148 great landowners. At the other end of the social scale there were many impoverished Welsh-speaking minor gentry and lesser landholders, with tenant farmers and labourers often barely distinguishable from one another. To differences of economic position and social status in the countryside were added divisions of culture, language, religion and history.

This view of society as a hierarchy of ranks and orders was set out in tabular form by Gregory King in his famous survey of income in 1696. Just over a hundred years later Patrick Colquhoun repeated the exercise and reached strikingly similar conclusions (see Table 3.1).

Table 3.1 Distribution of national income by families, England and Wales, 1803 (with percentage distribution of families and total wealth)

	Families		**Income per family** £	
Aristocracy:				
Monarch	1		200,000	
Peerage	313		7,668	
Lesser titled ranks and gentlemen	26,890		935	
Total	27,204	(14%)	1,206	(15.7%)
Middle ranks:				
Industry and commerce	230,300		288	
Professions	84,340		240	
Agriculture	284,000		134	
Total	634,000	(31.6%)	196	(59.4%)
Lower orders:	1,346,479	(67.0%)	39	(24.9%)

Source: derived from P. Colquhoun, *A Treatise on Indigence* (1806), as summarised in H. Perkin, *Origins of Modern English Society* (1969), pp. 20–1.

These figures almost certainly understate the size of the lowest group in society. Two generations later, in 1867, the Victorian statistician, R. Dudley Baxter, calculated from national income and occupation figures that 77 per cent of the employed population of the United Kingdom belonged to what he called the 'manual labour class'.

The language of class

In the eighteenth and early nineteenth centuries most writers assumed that people were bound together according to broad occupational interests which were vertically structured, and within which people had a recognised status. Thus the landed interest embraced all those whose livelihood was linked to the land, from the largest proprietor to the lowest farm worker. Accordingly in the very earliest census reports John Rickman divided the population into three groups by source of employment – in agriculture; trade, manufacture and handicraft; and 'other'. Only in 1831 did he move towards some kind of horizontal classification, when he employed occupational status to divide his agricultural group into those occupiers employing labour, those not employing labour, and labourers, in recognition of the fact that the population was structured in a more complex fashion than was suggested in the simple interest-based model, with different and possibly conflicting vertical and horizontal dimensions. After 1841, though, the Registrar General took occupation as his principal category of analysis, attributing importance to the nature of the materials with which a person worked rather than his (or, less commonly, her) occupational status, and no attempt was made to put occupations into any social order until the census of 1911. When contemporaries did attempt to classify occupations, this was usually in a fragmentary way according to the social status given to their occupations, not the broader class positions within which their occupational status placed them. Nevertheless, nineteenth-century social commentators were all too well aware that their society was stratified along class lines. Colquhoun's work, for example, embodied the idea that the vertically structured social pyramid could also be sliced horizontally according to the class position of people in society – that is, according to the distribution of economic resources and power, with all that these entail for human experience. Thus his aristocracy was distinguished by the absence of any need to work, and his lower orders by their lack of property.

The actual language of 'class' began to be applied to social structures in the second half of the eighteenth century. The phrase 'middle class' has been dated from 1766 as a purely descriptive term for those neither high nor low in society; the phrase 'working class' is slightly newer, being dated from 1789. The existence of the words, though, is only a rough guide to the evolution of meaning, for they were not used consistently and were often interchanged with the language of ranks and orders. A distinction of meaning only gradually emerged. Not until 1836 was the adjectival phrase 'middle-class' used to describe certain attributes characteristic of the middling section of society, and it was 1839 at the start of the Chartist movement before 'working-class' gathered this extra meaning. The older terms of rank and order implied hierarchy and a division of society according to legal and social status, but with the language of 'class' the economic dimension also became important. Instead of a multiplicity of status groups within the social hierarchy, bonded together by community, deference and paternalism, by the 1830s horizontal classes were being commented upon and distinguished according to their access to and control over economic resources, and in their partisan literature they were presented as being in conflict with one another about the distribution not only of economic but also of political, social and ideological power.

An early attempt to understand how class positions relate to economic experience is to be found in the writings of the political economist David Ricardo who, in his *Principles of Political Economy and Taxation* (1817), outlined three social classes defined by their sources of income: landlords, whose wealth came from rents; capitalists, whose income arose from profits; and labourers, dependent upon wages. This tripartite division accurately points to some of the major elements in nineteenth-century class conflict, between industrialists and landed aristocrats, and between employees and employers. Radicals of both middle and working classes looked to Ricardo for a theoretical justification of their class positions. The theory of rent, which shows how all profits accrue to the landlord, was seized upon by the middle classes to explain why their economic interests were at odds with those of the aristocracy who controlled the land; and the labour theory of value, which explained how value is added to raw materials by human labour, was developed by working-class spokesmen to show that they alone were the producers of wealth which was then unjustly taken from them by parasitic middlemen. This model may well have described the essence of eighteenth-century rural society, divided into landlords, farmers and labourers, but it is too simple to describe British society as it actually was during the early industrial revolution. It ignored those landlords who were also capitalists, and those capitalists who were or aspired to be landlords; it passed over those many men of small capital who were not wholly reduced to wage labour; and it omitted the small professional class whose income was derived from fees.

By the mid-nineteenth century the occupational structure of society had become extremely complex, and not everyone was satisfied with the system employed by the Registrar General. One such person was Henry Mayhew, a journalist. In his study, *London Labour and the London Poor*, he began by dividing the population into four broad groups according to their relationship to work, several sub-groups according to economic function, and a multiplicity of precise occupations.[2] The detail is too great for Mayhew's classification to be of much use in broad social analysis, but from his knowledge of the complexities of life on the streets of London he did point to important social facts about class positions to which contemporaries repeatedly returned; namely the existence of

1. a leisured class from which the leaders of society were drawn, able to enjoy the benefits of a liberal education, and characterised by the quality of gentility;
2. a broad mass of respectable people who had to work for a living and were dependent on the vagaries of personal health and the national economy to maintain their positions in society;
3. the deserving poor, dependent upon private and public charity;
4. social outcasts.

He was thus able to superimpose on his occupational classification a much broader pattern based on the social attributes of economic power, though it is interesting in this context to note that Mayhew chose to include employers and employees in the same social class, defined by the necessity of work. In this he was echoing the views of political economists as well as of employers, who frequently saw themselves as leaders of the industrious against the idle classes. Much of the debate about the meaning and significance of class for an understanding of nineteenth-century society centres on the accuracy of this observation. Was there an irreconcilable economic division between employers and employees, based on those who received the profits and those who received only wages; or were the two sides of industry united in a common bond of interest against the landlord class? In Mayhew's day his approach was not unreasonable. Much social and political power still remained the preserve of the aristocracy, and the divorce between ownership (i.e. capital) and management (a form of non-manual labour), which was first experienced on a large scale in railway companies, was spreading only slowly throughout the economy as a whole. Until a clear division of economic interest occurred, many industrialists were able – despite differences of status – to regard their profits as earned income analogous to wages, and to maintain through daily personal involvement in their works and the welfare of their employees some sense of identity of interest with their workers in a business on which the prosperity of both depended.

Generally speaking, though, the social realities of nineteenth-century life made this view of the 'industrious classes' seem rather old-fashioned, or made it look like special pleading. Socialist writers in particular saw the major cleavage in society as occurring not between the idle and the industrious, but between the 'working classes' and the rest. Yet there were many ambiguities in the ways in which the phrase 'working classes' was used, most contemporaries being impressed both by the fact of a working-class presence and by the multitude of occupational and status divisions which were to be found within that working class. There was widespread agreement, for example, with the view that a distinction should be made between the working class proper and the poor. As the *Quarterly Review* recognised in 1863, 'The mechanic and artisan class did not readily mix with the poor, nor even with the lower orders of the unskilled workers.' In a book written in 1867 by the middle-class lawyer and Christian Socialist J. M. Ludlow, and the Irish ex-fustian cutter and former Owenite Socialist, Lloyd Jones, entitled *Progress of the Working Class*, the authors defined 'the true working class' as follows:

> The terms 'working class', 'working men', will, in this volume, be taken in their everyday acceptation, as meaning those who work, chiefly with their muscles, for wages, and maintain themselves thereby. . . . It is not, indeed, intended to deal with 'the poor', – i.e. those who may work, but cannot thereby habitually maintain themselves.[3]

The theme of their book was unashamedly masculine and urban, discussing agricultural workers in a single, contemptuous paragraph:

> Farm labourers have few political thinkers among them. Ideas of social reform do not easily penetrate, or rapidly spread, among the solitary workers in the fields. They are not given to association; and in no way are under the influence of 'demagogues'.[4]

Their working class in effect was a very restricted concept. In excluding the poor, Ludlow and Jones left out the bottom third of society; in omitting female domestic servants and agricultural workers, they ignored the two largest occupational groups. Yet despite these limitations, their working class was no mere élite or aristocracy of labour. According to figures based on Dudley Baxter's analysis of 1867, skilled workers comprised 37 per cent of the total workforce, and 48 per cent of the manual working class. More important than what they left out of their definition is what they put in. Ludlow and Jones identified two central issues. First, the characteristic of manual labour: as Robert Roberts was later to put it in *The Classic Slum*, 'a real social divide existed between those who, in earning daily bread, dirtied hands and face and those who did not'.[5] And, second, they introduced the idea of political consciousness and organisation into their definition. They were interested not so much in a socio-economic working class as in the politically organised working class of the labour movement. In this they have frequently been followed by historians who have not always been so explicit as to what they mean, or do not mean, by 'the working class'.

The most sophisticated attempt to move from social analysis to the meaning of class was made by Charles Booth in his *Life and Labour of the People of London*, published between 1889 and 1903.[6] Unlike Mayhew, he took the level of income as the basis for his division of the population into eight categories, arranged in inverted order of prosperity as follows:

A. the lowest class: occasional labourers, loafers, semi-criminals
B. those with irregular work: the very poor
C. those with intermittent earnings
D. those with small, regular earnings, requiring little skill or intelligence
E. those with standard earnings: artisans
F. the best-paid artisans and foremen
G. the lower-middle class: shopkeepers and clerks
H. the upper-middle class: those who keep servants.

Groups C and D he defined as 'the poor', earning between 18*s.* and 21*s.* (80p – £1.05) a week. According to the cost-of-living table worked out by Seebohm Rowntree for York a few years later, such people would not be able to support themselves at even the most basic level unless their income were supplemented by other members of the family. The society which Booth described, though, was not a social pyramid, even in the East End of London, but a social pear. The lowest four classes (A–D) constituted 35 per cent of the population of East London and Hackney, compared with 42 per cent in class E alone.

Booth recognised, however, that income alone was an insufficient guide to social class, and he made some perceptive comments on social behaviour which reach to the heart of the historian's problem:

> It will be seen how large a part the lower middle class plays in East London club life, but it is not easy to draw a line between this class and the so-called working men. 'What is a working man?' is a question to which no very clear answer can be given. In theory, dealers and small master men would be excluded, but in practice my classes E, F, and G, the central mass of the English people, consort together in a free and friendly way. Some of the clubs also draw from classes C and D. Class H has its own clubs apart, class B has only those provided for it philanthropically.[7]

Social class is based on a variety of criteria, of which occupation is but one. Access to economic power and the level of economic reward are important aspects of class, but the meaning of class is grounded also in the values, expectations, beliefs and experiences of a social group. This must be borne in mind when one turns to the impersonal categories employed in the Census Reports.

The Census and social structure

In the Census of 1911 the various occupational groups were assigned to five broad social classes. These were:

I professional occupations
II intermediate occupations
III skilled occupations
IV partly skilled occupations
V unskilled occupations.

Thus social class was derived from the assumed social status of each occupation – that is, its general standing in the community, irrespective of the rate of remuneration. The major assumptions behind this approach were that 'white-collar' or mental labour is of higher status than 'blue-collar' or manual labour, and that skilled work is of higher status than unskilled.

Despite the fact that these categories were not employed before 1911, and although thereafter they were not applied to all occupations in a consistent manner, historians have attempted to use the Census Reports to analyse the changing social as well as occupational structure of the employed workforce. Professor J. A. Banks has studied the Census Reports for 1841 and 1851 and has concluded very roughly that around 81 per cent of adult males belonged to the working class – a figure not out of line with Dudley Baxter's estimate of 77 per cent for 1867 – while 12 per cent were employers of labour and 7 per cent self-employed. Class here is being defined as occupational status, extending Rickman's approach in the 1831 Census to later figures not collected with this method of analysis in mind. For the years 1841–81 Banks has also felt able to arrange the data for males aged 20 and over in accordance with the five-class division introduced in 1911, thus producing an outline (shown in Table 3.2) of the social structure of England and Wales in the mid-Victorian years.

These figures suggest that there was a slight growth in the higher classes and some consequent upward mobility from Class IV in the mid-Victorian years, and that there was also some redistribution – possibly due to reclassification – between the bottom two classes. Overall, though, the picture

Table 3.2 Social structure of England and Wales, 1841–1881

Males aged over 20 (percentages); 1911 classification

Class	1841	1851	1861	1871	1881
I	9.4	8.5	9.1	9.9	10.9
II	12.3	14.0	13.8	13.5	12.8
III	20.0	20.1	21.0	20.7	21.5
IV	44.1	43.2	41.8	38.4	36.3
V	14.2	14.2	14.3	17.5	18.4

Source: J.A. Banks, in R. Lawton (ed.), *The Census and Social Structure* (1978), p. 194.

Table 3.3 Social structure of England and Wales, 1881–1961

Males aged over 20 (percentages); 1951 classification				
Class	1881	1911	1951	1961
I	2.1	2.7	3.2	4.5
II	14.6	15.3	14.3	16.4
III	39.8	43.1	53.4	53.5
IV	30.5	29.2	16.2	13.4
V	13.1	9.7	12.9	12.1

Source: J.A. Banks, in R. Lawton (ed.), *The Census and Social Structure* (1978), p. 197, and *Census Report* (1961).

over the period of the first industrial revolution, from the late eighteenth to the late nineteenth centuries, is one of relatively little change in the general social structure – though of course this says nothing of those individuals who comprised the different classes. The main shifts occurred, in fact, within rather than between the classes, as old skills declined and new skills emerged to assume an increasing importance within the workforce.

The pace of change quickened after 1881, with the decline in the relative importance of the lower social classes becoming more pronounced as employment in agriculture and then mining contracted. At the same time a lower-middle class was emerging, clearly distinguishable from the upper reaches of the working class, and there was also some expansion among the higher social classes, attributed in the 1961 Census Report to growing numbers of managers, teachers and draughtsmen (Class II), and of engineers (Class I) (see Table 3.3).

These changes exposed the limitations of the 1911 system of five-fold classification, and in 1951 – by which time the middle ground of the social structure had grown to include over half the adult male occupations – the population was additionally divided into thirteen socio-economic groups which tried to take account of both occupation and social status. Additionally, in 1971, Class III was abandoned in favour of two new classes – Class IIIN for skilled non-manual occupations, and Class IIIM for skilled manual occupations. For this and other reasons (the creation of a residual category, including members of the armed forces and students) the 1971 categories are not wholly comparable with those for earlier years. Further modifications in 1981 and 1991, though, were only slight, so it is possible to give some indication of trends towards the end of the twentieth century (see Table 3.4).

The figures given here, in line with Professor Lawton's calculations, are for males only as, even in 1995, in only about 14 per cent of households was the female partner the major earner. In facts the profile for economically active women in 1991 was not very dissimilar from that for men,

Table 3.4 Social structure of Great Britain, 1971–1991

Economically active males over 15 (percentages), Great Britain

Class	1971	1981	1991
I	4.7	5.4	6.7
II	17.1	21.3	27.0
IIIN	11.3	11.2	10.7
IIIM	36.6	35.3	31.6
IV	17.2	16.1	15.1
V	8.2	6.0	5.3
Other	5.0	4.6	3.6

Source: Census Reports (1971–91).

except in two very important respects: women were under-represented in the highest category, and the skilled manual and non-manual proportions were reversed. Within Great Britain Scots men were also under-represented at the top, with 29.1 per cent in social classes I and II compared with 34 per cent in England and Wales. One explanation for this difference probably lies in the concentration in London of the higher levels of both national government and commercial administration.

The structure of employment

The nineteenth-century census gives surprisingly little accurate information about the composition of the workforce. One major weakness in the figures is that they often refer only to adult males, or (as in 1811–31) to households, of which adult males were commonly the head. Even though women and children were supposed to be listed according to their separate occupations this was not always done; the requirements of the census returns varied from decade to decade, and much part-time, seasonal and domestic work must have gone unrecorded.

For the great majority of the population of all ages and both sexes before the twentieth century work was a necessity. Children were pressed into menial tasks from the age of 3 or 4, scaring birds in the fields, running errands, assisting in domestic industry or – less common but more highly publicised – working in the early textile mills or opening ventilation traps in coal mines. At the other end of their lives, often shorter than in the twentieth century, retirement was virtually unheard-of until physical or mental incapacity threw the worn-out labourer upon family, private charity or the poor law. Gradually legislation began to enforce the withdrawal of various groups from the labour force and to restrict the hours of others. Despite the rising population, the number of children under 15 years old recorded as employed fell, from 423,000 boys and 237,000 girls in 1851 to 346,000 boys and 200,000 girls in 1911. The single most important measure to reduce the participation of children in the labour force was the extension of schooling in the last quarter of the nineteenth century.

The figures for women's work are difficult to extract from the nineteenth-century censuses which concealed much of the part-time and casual work traditionally undertaken by women – not to mention the important but unrecorded contribution which women made to the household economy. In the eighteenth century this latter was more than just the unpaid domestic service of a later generation, for women took a full part in both farming and domestic industry.

Farmers' wives were expected to manage a household which might include a number of living-in farm servants, as well as take charge of the poultry and the dairy, orchard and kitchen garden; and, while they might aspire to more genteel pursuits in a minority of cases, many small farms relied heavily upon the labour of the whole family, both male and female. If a farmer died and left no sons, his wife might succeed to the farm. In 1851 about 10 per cent of the farmers and graziers listed in the census were female. Women were also important as farm labourers. They were employed chiefly as milkmaids, additional workers at harvest-time, and to hoe long rows of turnips, gather stones and perform other monotonous and back-breaking tasks. This kind of work probably became more common in the later eighteenth century, as the new methods of agriculture found favour with farmers eager to cut costs. It also became necessary for the workers themselves in areas where agricultural wages were below subsistence level. In south-eastern Scotland and also Northumberland, it was the custom for a male tenant to provide a woman's labour as part of his rent, especially at harvest-time when labour was in short supply. As late as 1867, some Dorset farmers were reported to be refusing to employ men unless their wives were willing to work when required.

By this date, though, women's work in the fields was in decline. Victorian sensibilities were aroused at the prospect of women and children working in labour gangs under harsh gang-masters, which was common in the eastern counties and survived parliamentary condemnation in 1843; male farm workers were organising to demand a living wage and an end to competition from female labour; and women themselves were increasingly reluctant to be so employed. The flight from the land in the second half of the nineteenth century was, not surprisingly, led by the womenfolk. In 1851 144,000 females (other than farmers' wives and daughters) were employed in agriculture, of whom 99,000 were indoor servants (mainly domestic and dairy). Their numbers fell sharply in the later nineteenth century until in 1911 there were only 13,600 left.

Women also worked alongside their husbands as artisans and in the domestic textile industry. Straw-plaiting, lace-making and a whole variety of sweated handicraft trades were the lot of many women in the home. During the course of the nineteenth century the trend was towards the exclusion of women from the labour force, partly through the determination of men to reduce the challenge of cheap female labour, but also because many working men and women thought it proper for the man to be able to keep his wife and family without the necessity of their obtaining paid employment. Technological change also contributed to the reduction in opportunities for women's paid employment, with the separation of home and work. This occurred not only in the heavy metal trades but also in textile production, for the demands of child-rearing and domestic duties meant that married women were reluctant to work long hours in factories. Nevertheless, there were many women whose husbands could not support them, or who had no husbands. Work remained a necessity for them, and they took it wherever they could find it. In the major textile-producing areas this could mean factory work, increasingly supervised and protected by legislation; but more often it meant repetitive, labour-intensive work in appalling conditions at home or in clothing sweatshops.

For many unmarried women, domestic service was the best source of employment. In 1851 1,027,000 (37 per cent) of the female workforce over the age of 15 was in domestic service, slightly more than were employed in textile manufacture and dressmaking. Even as late as 1911 domestic service remained by far the largest single category of female employment, having almost doubled in size during the period 1851–1911 to 2,127,000 (39 per cent of the total occupied female population). Textiles and clothing industries came next, together employing 1,695,000 (31 per cent). There was little choice for most women until changes in the structure of employment brought new opportunities at the beginning of the twentieth century.

At the beginning of the nineteenth century an estimate based on imperfect census returns suggests that slightly under 40 per cent of families were connected with agriculture, and slightly over 40 per cent were connected with trade, manufacture or handicraft. The gap between the two sectors of the economy widened each decade, until in 1841 little more than a quarter of adult males (26 per cent in England and Wales, 28 per cent in Scotland) were engaged in agriculture compared with approaching half (43 per cent in England and Wales, 47 per cent in Scotland) who were occupied in trade, manufacture or handicraft. These were national averages. A regional analysis shows great diversity. The most agricultural county in England in 1841 was Lincolnshire, with 40 per cent engaged in agriculture compared with only 24 per cent engaged in industry; whereas in Lancashire, the most industrialised county, 63 per cent were occupied in industry and only 7 per cent in agriculture. In Middlesex, the most urbanised county, the agricultural proportion was only 2.5 per cent. The trend in the nineteenth century was for agricultural employment to continue to contract, both as a percentage and absolutely, until by the end of the century it accounted for only 10 per cent of the labour force. The industrial proportion also fell relatively, though absolute numbers continued to rise. The most rapid growth occurred in the residual category, which in 1841 included members of the armed forces and merchant navy, persons of independent means, members of the professions and (the largest categories) domestic servants and general labourers.

In 1851 the largest male employment groups were in agriculture (1,788,000), textiles (661,000) and metal manufacture (536,000). Sixty years later metal manufacture had risen to 1,795,000, transport workers had almost quadrupled to 1,571,000 and agriculture had fallen back to 1,436,000. Most striking, though, was the expansion in the professional, administrative and commercial categories, which accounted for only 351,000 males in 1851 but 1,423,000 in 1911. The twentieth century saw a continuation of these trends. Between 1911 and 1961 the total number of white-collar workers increased by 147 per cent (and those in clerical occupations by 260 per cent), whilst the number of manual workers increased by only 2 per cent and those engaged in agriculture fell by 45 per cent. Between 1961 and 1991 the total number of employees in manufacturing industry also passed its peak. Those engaged in engineering and allied trades declined from 3.7 million in 1971 to 2.1 million in 1991, and employment in other manufacturing industries fell from 3.1 million to 2 million. But during the same period employment in the distributive industries increased from 3 million to 4.8 million. There could be no greater indication of the change in the structure of employment since the eighteenth century than the fact that in 1991 national and local government services accounted for 854,000 employees, compared with the 456,000 who worked in agriculture, forestry or fisheries (less than half of whom were full-time employees), and the mere 174,000 who worked in textiles.

The proportion of the female population in employment, which had been falling in the second half of the nineteenth century, began to rise again after the First World War, though it was not until 1966 that it reached 42 per cent – half the equivalent figure for men. Between 1911 and 1966 women made up a steady 30 per cent of all manual workers, but they were disproportionately represented among the semi-skilled (around 40 per cent) and did not share in the general trend away from unskilled to skilled work. On the other hand, they were increasingly important in the white-collar sector. The expansion in the service industries brought new opportunities for women in the later nineteenth century, as those with a little basic education were able to find employment such as teaching in the new elementary schools, or shop-work in the expanding consumer economy, while minor clerical and administrative positions were opening up in such businesses as the Post Office. The typewriter, no less than the sewing machine, was an invention which reshaped the employment of women. Administrative, professional and commercial employments accounted for 590,000 jobs for women in 1911, compared with only 164,000 40 years earlier.

In 1911 women constituted 30 per cent of white-collar workers – mainly lower professionals and technicians (teachers and nurses), of whom 63 per cent were women. By 1951 there were two other categories of employment in which women were in a majority – clerks (70 per cent of whom were women in 1966) and shop assistants (59 per cent in 1966). These included many jobs for which women were felt to offer a more pleasing image to the public, but they were also ones in which casual working and low pay were common, and in which women were not thought to pose a threat to the career prospects of men. The change in the structure of employment from the 1970s worked to women's advantage in that the expansion of the service industries was principally in those areas in which women's work was becoming concentrated, while the declining industries were those traditionally dominated by men. Between 1971 and 1996 the size of the male labour force remained unchanged at 15.6 million, while the female labour force increased from 9.4 million (33 per cent) to 12.3 million (44 per cent); but, whereas only 8 per cent of employed men were working part-time, this was the case with 45 per cent of employed women.

The making of a class society

The breakdown of the old order

The bonds of community were difficult to maintain in the rapidly growing urban centres of the late eighteenth and early nineteenth centuries. Cities had always been solvents of ancient ties, and radicals looked upon them as centres of enlightenment and progress, but they were regarded by conservatives as dangerously subversive places. London in the eighteenth century already embodied many aspects of the new society which were to undermine the old order. Though the aristocratic landlords of London derived great incomes from their properties, the commercial wealth of the City of London provided an alternative base for political power and a challenge to aristocratic monopoly. Furthermore, even lesser freeholders in Middlesex were claiming extended rights in the later eighteenth century, calling into question the whole idea of a deferential society.

In the countryside relationships were changing more slowly. It would be wrong to imply that there were no tensions in the eighteenth-century countryside or resentment against the rich on the part of the poor. Tithes and the Game Laws were a source of perpetual friction, and the accumulation of savage penal legislation is witness to the strong element of compulsion which underlay the bonds of deference. Where there was a single, resident landlord in a 'closed' village the social ideal of paternalism helped reinforce or even revive the old order well into the nineteenth century. But in 'open' villages where there were many lesser or absentee landlords the social order was already disappearing at the end of the eighteenth century. Instead of supervision from above, with neatly rebuilt cottages, a church and a school, there was speculative building of inferior dwellings to house the swarms of labourers without parish settlements who were excluded on that account from the tidy closed villages. Here the spirit of unregulated independence was expressed through nonconformity in religion and even, on occasions, through radicalism in politics. In some such parishes where industrial pursuits developed, perhaps in the vicinity of a town, a no-man's land could be created with a reputation for crime, immorality and social unrest.

Throughout the Victorian period one can find examples of the old values being preached to buttress the traditional view of society. Indeed, the fact that the old order was passing away lent a new urgency to the need to restore not only deference but also paternalism. The social disorders of the newly growing towns and the widespread unrest of the early nineteenth century called forth a revival of traditional values precisely because social harmony had been undermined both from below and by what Thomas Carlyle called the '*abdication* on the part of the governors'.[8]

Why this should have happened in the first place is unclear. Conservatives like Disraeli and Carlyle blamed the new rich for failing to appreciate that power carried with it social responsibilities. Though some industrialists – especially men of the first generation, like Sir Robert Peel (the elder) and Robert Owen – attempted to continue the paternalist role, many others did not. Especially in the towns, where the unit of employment was no longer coterminous with the community at large, employers saw their responsibilities as starting and ending with the working day. Obligations were discharged when the wages were paid. As Carlyle again put it, in a phrase which has long survived its original context, the old personal relationships of master and servant were being replaced by 'cash payment the sole nexus'.[9] If workers were beginning to think of themselves as 'wage slaves', that was because their masters often treated them as such.

Less easy to understand is the decline of paternalism in the countryside. The growing wealth of gentlemen benefiting from the effects of agricultural improvement may have distanced them from their lesser neighbours and employees as they aspired to more aristocratic lifestyles. Though the practice of 'living in' survived well into the nineteenth century, especially in the northern parts of the country, William Cobbett felt strongly that in the south of England 'bullfrog' farmers who had done well out of the wars of the 1790s were abandoning their proper roles, as they (and especially their wives) sought a higher standard of living and gentry status. Then, as agricultural depression set in after the wars, matters were made even worse as farmers tried to economise by cutting their labour costs and crying poverty to their landlords. The 'Swing' riots which swept southern and eastern counties in 1830 and 1831 completed, for many, the destruction of the old ties, as the latent antagonisms of rural society erupted into open violence, breaking the charms of deference from below and undermining the claims to paternal concern from above. The Poor Law Amendment Act of 1834, cast in accordance with the dictates of political economy, was the response, and it earned the condemnation of defenders of the old order as different as William Cobbett and Benjamin Disraeli.

Nevertheless, the ideal of a vertically integrated interest-group did not die easily. Only slowly and with some reluctance did Cobbett abandon the theory that farmers and agricultural workers shared a common interest in the land against the 'Old Corruption' of aristocracy and fundholders; and in the 1840s the Anti-Corn Law League was unsuccessful in its efforts to drive a wedge between the farmers and their landlords. The land as a vertical interest-group remained a powerful symbol of the old society until the agricultural depression of the 1870s. Similarly the new industrialists also thought of themselves as a vertical interest-group, and were eventually accepted by the aristocracy as representatives of the whole manufacturing interest in the parliamentary Reform Act of 1832. Some large industrialists continued throughout the nineteenth century to appreciate the advantages of paternalism in the management of their works and to enjoy playing the role of industrial squire.

Class and social theory

The most influential contemporary observer of the development of class society in nineteenth-century Britain was the German philosopher and political refugee, Karl Marx; and his ideas have continued to shape the thinking of more recent historians on the subject. Even as Marxist theory has fallen out of fashion since the political demise of Marxist-Leninism in Europe in 1989, historical debate has still largely been expressed as a reaction to Marxism. Marx's theory, as expressed in the *Manifesto of the German Communist Party* (1848), presents a dynamic view of how society was evolving under the capitalist system during the period of the industrial revolution. Gradually, he believed, the many social groups of Victorian Britain would be reduced to two classes: the owners of the means of production, and those who owned nothing but their own labour – the expropriators and the expropriated. In *The 18th Brumaire of Louis Bonaparte* (1851), Marx further explained what he understood by the word 'class' as he distinguished between the French peasantry as a class, lumped together like potatoes in a sack, and their lack of any consciousness of themselves as a class:

> In so far as millions of families live under economic conditions of existence that separate their mode of life, their interests and their culture from those of the other classes, and put them in hostile

> opposition to the latter, they form a class. In so far as there is merely a local interconnection amongst these small-holding peasants, and their identity of interests begets no community, no national bond and no political organisation among them, they do not form a class.[10]

Thus, for Marx, there are two stages in the development of class. In the first stage there is simply a social aggregate, such as might be measured in the occupational categories of the Census Reports. Class in this descriptive sense is what Marx called 'a class in itself'. The second stage comes only when such a social aggregate begins to act, uniting in communities, forming national bonds, creating political organisations and developing a class consciousness – what Marx called 'a class for itself'. The dynamic link between the two stages is forged by conflict and struggle.

Many historians working from both inside and outside the Marxist tradition are agreed that eighteenth-century society was not a class society in the second sense, but that class consciousness was latent within the social tensions of that society. There is also widespread agreement that class was born in the generation after the French Revolution of 1789, when conflict became explicit and there is a great deal of evidence for the creation of national bonds and political organisations. In one non-Marxist view – that of Professor H. J. Perkin in *The Origins of Modern English Society* – the eighteenth century was 'a one-class society'. That is, only the aristocracy had those national characteristics which are the hallmark of class. Other classes – the middle class and the working class – were born in the half-century after 1780, and a period of struggle ensued which was resolved in the mid-Victorian years with the ideological victory of the middle class over both the aristocracy and the working class, and the institutionalisation of working-class antagonism in the organised labour movement. Thus, by 1880, a 'viable class society' had been established in place of the old aristocratic society.[11] For Marxists such an interpretation does not place sufficient emphasis on the importance of continuing class conflict in the making and remaking of class. There has consequently been much debate over the reasons for the stability of class society in Britain since the mid-nineteenth century and the failure of British society to develop in accordance with Marx's predictions.

The most influential historian writing about the origins of class from within the Marxist tradition was E. P. Thompson, whose *Making of the English Working Class* shaped the terms of the debate following its publication in 1963. Thompson pointed to two separate strands in the formation of class: conditioning and agency. That is, class is in part determined by changes in society – principally changes in the economy – which produce class as a social aggregate; but class is also its own creator through the experience of class struggle, as social groups dissimilar in many ways find a common identity in their opposition to other groups, and in turn are reinforced by their experience of opposition from other groups.[12] This interpretation has drawn fire both from economic determinists in the Marxist camp, who argue only for conditioning, human agency being a reaction dependent upon the material environment, and from empirical non-Marxists, who see little evidence that the many different groups within the same class situation ever showed themselves capable of acting as a united class.

Unhappiness with the Marxist approach to class in the period of the industrial revolution had led some historians to challenge its whole basis. All understandings of the past are constructed by historians through concepts developed in their own day. The popular Marxist concept, it is argued, which can help illuminate our understanding of social structure and conflict, can also limit our approach by substituting its own 'reality' for that of the past. By concentrating on 'class', the historian may miss more significant ways of seeing the past.

Some historians, of whom Patrick Joyce has been the most influential, have borrowed the tools of linguistic analysis from literary criticism to raise questions about the ways in which we represent the past and read its language. His argument is that a study of how contemporaries actually saw themselves and their society reveals not only class but also other concepts, based not on conflict and exclusion but on positive identities and inclusion.[13] A continuing belief, for example, in the rights, wisdom or virtues of the 'common people' runs throughout the nineteenth century, identifying opposition not to capitalists or employers, but to sectional interests – typically in government, the law, the church or the medical profession – that were judged hostile to the common or popular interest, dignified by such self-descriptions as 'ordinary folk'.

In the mid-century, in the language of radicalism, this was known as 'patriotism'. A 'true patriot' was one who had at heart the well-being of 'the people'. By the end of the century, patriotism had been broadened to embrace the entire national interest and, linked with imperialism, was associated with the mission to confer the rights, wisdom or virtues of the British (or, more particularly, the English) on the rest of the world. This was a powerful language which transcended class and party alike. It meant that, although the Liberal Party could lay claim to much 'popular' support, the Conservative working man was always a historical reality whose presence troubled Radicals, Liberals and Socialists at the time as much as he has challenged historians since.

Other manifestations of identities among 'the people', before and beyond class, included the community, in town, village or suburb, expressed in church, public house or – in the later nineteenth century – the local football team. More widely in England, an identification with Protestantism in general and the Church of England in particular summed up for many what it meant to be English, especially in areas of Irish settlement such as the North-West of England. The language of the patriotic 'free-born Englishman' has been widely recognised by historians as significant in the later eighteenth century, but its appearance in the nineteenth century has too often been dismissed as backward-looking, anachronistic or typical only of the drunken, ignorant and unthinking mob. This has been to impoverish our understanding of past society. Nevertheless, to recognise such alternative ways of seeing and to reject the universality of class is not to deny the reality of class as one of the ways of understanding important aspects of social relationships in the nineteenth century.

Other writers, influenced by feminist history, have been unhappy at the extent to which the masculine nature of much writing about class has taken the formative part played by men for granted, without exploring how and why men became so dominant in the work place and the public sphere, why domestic ideology became so powerful a constraint on actions and perceptions in the past, and what part women emerge as playing in history once one starts looking at their actions through female rather than male concepts of the past.[14]

Such alternative views are important to the historian, who needs to be aware of the tyranny of all concepts. However, it would appear to be a counsel of despair to follow the most extreme of literary critics in denying all reality to the world outside the head of the interpreter. Most historians work on the assumption that the past happened, and that the 'reality' of that happening can be glimpsed – albeit in different ways – by historians wrestling imperfectly with the evidences of the past. Such evidence cannot be read uncritically, but taken in context it can be interpreted. The meaning of class is ambiguous and changing, but its existence appears firmly stamped in the evidence. Different people in the past may have used their language of class in different ways, for their own purposes, to assert or deny as well as to describe features of their world, but there is something there to be identified, and then accounted for. The language of class is unavoidable in historical accounts, but it should be used with care. In subsequent chapters, issues of leisure, religion and education are discussed apart from, as well as in relation to, class. In this chapter class analysis is seen as a useful way of understanding the past, so long as the word 'class' is taken to refer to that active element within a wider social stratum, which was specifically rooted in political, economic or social movements for protest, recognition or change.

Economic change and the origins of class society

During the century of the first industrial revolution – approximately 1780–1880 – there were many changes in British society which were instrumental in the creation of class. Of these, urbanisation and the development of communications have already been discussed (pages 27–8). Both brought people together, broadening horizons and facilitating the spread of new ideas and forms of social organisation. In the developing urban cultures of eighteenth-century towns, manufacturing and trading élites emerged to express their identities in attitudes, language and associations for work and leisure. Young Robert Owen, for example, found himself incorporated into this middle-class culture in Manchester in the 1790s, when he was invited to join the Literary and Philosophical Society. But the changes which were gathering pace from the later eighteenth century affected more than just the aspiring new urban élite. A transformation was occurring also among the lower classes as a result of economic and technological change. As Owen observed in 1815, 'The general diffusion of manufactures throughout a country generates a new character in its inhabitants.'[15] Engels echoed these sentiments a generation later in the opening words of his *Condition of the Working Class in England* (1845):

> The history of the proletariat in England begins with the second half of the last century, with the invention of the steam engine and of machinery for working cotton. These inventions gave rise, as is well-known, to an industrial revolution, a revolution which altered the whole civil society.[16]

As a description of what actually happened, this is, broadly speaking, accurate. The new society was born amid the textile mills of Lancashire, Yorkshire and the West of Scotland. But as an explanation it is deficient. Marx more correctly saw that behind the technological innovations and factory system lay a much more profound development, the growth of capitalism, which led to the emergence of the two new classes of modern society. In Ricardo's terms, these may be described as those who derived their income from profits accruing from capital invested in trade and manufacture, and those dependent upon wages.

Capitalists were not, of course, new in the later eighteenth century. Merchants had ventured capital in trading expeditions for centuries, and the West Country trade in woollen goods had long been organised by merchant capitalists. What was new was the pervasive influence of capitalism as a system, the extension of the capitalists' control over production, and the acceptance of marketplace economics as the reason for and guide to all forms of human activity.

The making of the working class

Industrial growth throughout much of the eighteenth century rested not on steam engines and factories but on merchant capitalism and small-scale domestic and workshop production, with workers in the countryside frequently enjoying additional sources of income from agriculture. Though the work was hard, the domestic worker and his (and her) family retained a measure of independence in the organisation of their labour, while in the workshop skill conferred status on the artisan and there was often no clear separation of function locally between production and distribution. Though he would probably be dependent on a merchant capitalist for his raw materials, working on a small scale he might well be his own retailer. The village blacksmith, cobbler or tailor was often in this position, as was the weaver-clothier of the West Riding domestic woollen industry. The ambiguous double meaning of the word 'tradesman' is important, meaning both one who was 'in trade' – that is, an intermediary or shopkeeper, dealing in finished products – and one who had a trade, that is, an independent or semi-independent skilled craftsman, who had served an apprenticeship to learn his trade, and who often combined with others to protect his skill in a society or union. The language of class is inappropriate to describe such a person. He was not a labourer, because he had skill and was not directly or wholly employed for wages, but he was quite clearly a manual worker.

Gradually his position began to change. As markets grew, or became more international, the craftsman would be likely to sell his goods through an intermediary – perhaps the merchant from whom he had purchased his raw materials. Then, if new machinery were introduced to improve output or quality, the merchant might provide the capital to purchase it, and it was from here but a short step towards the total control of the industry by the capitalist. At a time of expanding trade the best way for craftsmen to maintain their bargaining power lay in their control of apprenticeship to preserve the scarcity of their skilled labour, but new machinery often devalued their skills and, even when this was not so, many people were eager to respond to the calls of capitalists who were willing and able to employ them whilst ignoring the apprenticeship regulations. This had happened in the textile industries of the West Country, East Anglia and the East Midlands by the mid-eighteenth century, whilst in Yorkshire the wealthier clothiers were taking control of woollen manufacture from the hosts of smaller independent weavers by the beginning of the nineteenth. The cotton industry was led from the start by merchants from London, Liverpool and Glasgow, but the same process of control was also becoming common right across the industrial scene: metalworkers in the Black Country, craftsmen in Birmingham and cutlers around Sheffield were all losing their independence. In London, the centre of the manufacturing trades, only a minority of 'honourable' craftsmen with exclusive skills catering for the luxury market were able to hold out against the erosion of status and skill in the 'dishonourable' sweatshops of the metropolis.

All this could and frequently did take place outside the 'factory system', which developed only slowly with the desire of entrepreneurs to control production by concentrating their workforces in 'manufacturies' and to take advantage of water or steam power to work the new machines. Not until well into the nineteenth century did the home and small workshop

Table 3.5 Employment in textile factories in Great Britain by age and sex, 1839

	cotton	worsted	woollen	silk	flax
number of factories	1,795	416	1,291	268	352
average size of workforce per factory	142	76	41	128	98
males under 10	1,108	321	869	1,031	152
females under 10	731	417	649	1,461	114
males 10–12	5,963	1,595	2,628	2,343	761
females 10–12	4,475	2,201	2,052	3,769	636
males 13–17	40,610	3,573	10,906	3,185	4,560
females 13–17	55,688	10,129	9,159	8,410	10,097
males over 18	63,495	3,024	18,236	4,304	4,643
females over 18	82,656	10,192	9,050	9,730	13,517
total workforce	254,726	31,632	53,549	34,233	34,480
males	111,176	8,693	32,639	10,863	10,116
females	143,550	22,939	20,910	23,370	24,364
per cent adult males	24.9	9.6	34.0	12.6	13.5

Source: calculated from G. R. Porter, *Progress of the Nation* (1851), pp. 172, 193, 221, 230.

cease being the usual environment within which the worker practised his and her trade. Of the 618,508 people employed in textiles in England and Wales in 1841, only 349,545 (56.8 per cent) worked in factories, and in Scotland the figure was lower still – 59,312 out of 181,738 (32.6 per cent). Moreover, the vast majority of factories were small, and they relied heavily on female and child labour.

In 1803, when the largest cotton factories in Scotland were those at New Lanark, employing 2,000 people, the largest employer in the Scottish textile industry was Andrew Milne of Aberdeen, with a workforce of between 3,000 and 4,000 scattered over many miles. As late as 1841, only 39 per cent of the adult male labour force employed in cotton textile manufacture worked in factories. Even in the most highly developed sector of the economy, the typical worker was not a factory worker: the working class, even in industrial south-east Lancashire, was not a working class of the factory floor.

Yet the factory did dominate the textile districts. Men who worked in domestic industry or in other trades would have worked in the factories as children, and members of their families would probably be working in the factories. Adult male handloom weavers resented their loss of independence as domestic producers, and sought to weaken the competitiveness of the factories by reducing the amount of cheap child and female labour available. At the same time they were dependent upon the wages paid to their wives and children in the factories. Above all they resented the undermining of their skills, and this applied even to those like the early cotton spinners, who had once held the best jobs in the factories before the development of the self-acting mule in the 1830s. But, if textile workers felt threatened by machines, someone had to make those machines. New skills were created in engineering. As the independent skilled artisan fell before the advance of capitalist production and technology, a new class of skilled workman was being born, secure within the increasing demands of the expanding capitalist economy.

In so far as increasing numbers of workmen were finding themselves dependent upon wages and without direct control over production, the objective conditions for the birth of a working class were present by the mid-nineteenth century. Marx's 'class in itself' had been created. The Manchester Statistical Society estimated in 1836 that 64 per cent of the population of commercial Manchester belonged to the 'working class'; but in the neighbouring textile towns the proportion was much higher – 81 per cent in Ashton, and 95 per cent in tiny Dukinfield. But concern with status or the loss of it helped keep the working class fragmented. Any analysis of its composition shows up a wide variety of incomes and employment experiences which defy generalisation. The Wiltshire agricultural labourer earning below 10*s*. (50p) a week was far removed from the London compositor working on the morning papers for 48*s*. (£2.40) a week. At a typical ironworks in South Wales in 1845, labourers earned 12*s*. (60p) a week, while the best-paid skilled men earned nearly four times that amount. Handloom weavers in Arbroath in 1830 earned 12*s*. 6d. (62½p), twice as much as in Angus as a whole. When an Oldham handloom weaver was earning 7*s*. (35p) a week, a young female spinner in Manchester could earn 9*s*. (45p) and a male spinner 27*s*. (£1.35). Income reflected skill and the supply of and demand for labour. London rates were generally twice those in Glasgow. A carpenter working on the Greenwich hospital in 1825 was paid 30*s*. (£1.50) a week; but in Manchester he could have earned only 24*s*. (£1.20) and in Glasgow as little as 17*s*. (85p).

Income was often taken as a measure of status. A man felt he ought to be paid what he was worth: if paid less than a woman, he felt degraded. Income to a large extent determined lifestyle, which in turn could become more important than class position in shaping attitudes. One could therefore argue that the working class existed only at its most basic level of wage labour, which had little consequence for social relations, attitudes and conduct. It is for this reason that proponents of the reality of class in the early nineteenth century, like Edward Thompson, have agreed with non-Marxists that the concept of a single class created solely by economic conditions has little meaning for the historian, and have instead turned to evidence of class organisation and political struggle – not 'class in itself' but 'class for itself'. These features of class formation will be examined below (pages 122–8).

The middle classes

If the nature of the working class causes the historian concern, then the concept of the middle class threatens complete confusion. In a literal sense the middle class may be defined negatively as that part of society which came between the aristocracy and the manual labouring class. Positively, the middle classes may be distinguished by a number of different functions: some were tenant farmers with interests different from those of their landlords and labourers; others were intermediaries between producers and consumers, in either commerce or industry; yet others provided services in the professions or public administration. At the lower end of the social scale they almost merged with the working class, as smallholders, petty masters, clerks and corner-shop keepers. At the upper end they aspired to, and increasingly achieved, acceptance into the aristocracy, their wealth being made socially acceptable through the acquisition of land, well-chosen marriages and education at the right kind of school. Unlike the aristocracy, they were a numerically significant sector of society, making up between one-fifth and one-third of the whole. During the nineteenth century they became increasingly important in power and influence, though the translation of their economic ascendancy into political strength was a slow and much-delayed process, not fully achieved until the twentieth century.

Most prominent among the middle classes were those engaged in finance and commerce. These men were already organised in the eighteenth century in well-established interest-groups with representation in Parliament: the East and West India lobbies, for example, and the City. In terms of wealth, this was the most important element in the middle class: of 154 men who died between 1809 and 1829 worth between £160,000 and £500,000, 85 (55.2 per cent) belonged to this category, including 48 merchants and 24 bankers. The next-largest category comprised those in the professions (including 12 lawyers) and public administration, who together made up 22.7 per cent of these moderately wealthy men. Manufacturers, including 4 cotton spinners and 3 iron-masters, accounted for only 14.3 per cent. As W. D. Rubinstein has concluded, 'the wealthy in Britain have disproportionately earned their fortunes in commerce and finance . . . rather than in manufacturing or industry'. He has also added an important *caveat*:

> During the first half of the nineteenth century . . . the non-landed wealth owners were a virtually insignificant percentage of the entire wealthy class. An observer entering a room full of Britain's two

> hundred wealthiest men in 1825 might be forgiven for thinking that the industrial revolution had not occurred.[17]

This is not to argue that landowners were not supplementing their wealth from the exploitation of mineral reserves on their estates, or that merchants and landowners were not investing in manufacturing industry. What these figures do show is that the bulk of manufacturers were not exaggerating when they thought their own economic position precarious and saw their interests to be aligned with those of the 'industrious' classes against the 'idlers' who dominated Parliament, controlled commercial policy, benefited from mining royalties and industrial rents without themselves having to work, and drew unearned incomes from investments in government funds paid for out of taxes on the industrious.

It is not surprising, therefore, that the roots of middle-class consciousness in the first half of the nineteenth century are to be found among such people. Like their workpeople in whom a working-class consciousness was developing, they were not typical of the whole of their class, but through the eyes of their contemporaries and in their own propaganda they were the embodiment of the middle class. Feeling resentment against those above them, and hostility to those below who rejected their claim to lead and know what was best for the industrial interest, the middle class developed alongside the working class, each feeding its own identity on its sense of difference from the other. When Disraeli wrote of 'the two nations', he meant the rich and the poor; but he went to the manufacturing districts to find them in the world of the industrial revolution. In vain industrialists pointed out that the rich and the poor existed in the countryside, where class differences and exploitation were acute. That looked like special pleading. Contemporaries were quite clear (even if historians since have shown scholarly doubt) what it meant in the early nineteenth century to speak of working-class and middle-class.

People in the professions were another matter: three professions were ancient and honourable – the Church, the Armed Forces, and the Law – such that gentlemen and lesser sons of the nobility regarded them as part of their aristocratic world. Recruitment to the higher professions, in the words of W. J. Reader, meant 'admitting educated gentlemen to small, self-governing groups of their social equals to whom they would be personally known and by whom their fitness would be judged'.[18] Other professions – surgeons, writers, lesser (including Dissenting) clergy, schoolmasters and attorneys – were less well-thought-of in the eighteenth century, but during the course of the nineteenth century they too acquired status through formal qualifications and professional organisations. This professional middle class – the *bourgeoisie* of the *ancien régime*, as opposed to that of Marxist terminology – was quite separate from the middle class of industry and commerce. They derived their income not from profits but from fees and salaries, and their interests were often associated with those of their patrons, who included the aristocracy –

though through their contacts with the poor some came to sympathise with and even to articulate the demands of the working class.

The earliest method of training for a number of the lesser professions was apprenticeship, and in this they were not far removed from artisan-craftsmen. Such qualifications as were obtained were recognised by the relevant professional body, which sought control rather like a trade society. In about 1739 the attorneys organised themselves into the Society of Gentlemen Practisers in the Courts of Law and Equity (the first Law Society), the function of which was to control malpractice and to promote professional education. The medical profession in England and Wales had professional bodies for each of its constituent parts, with their equivalents in Scotland – the Royal College of Physicians, the Company (from 1800, Royal College) of Surgeons and the Society of Apothecaries. Physicians were socially the most prestigious; then came the surgeons, who had been formally separated from the barbers in 1745; and at the bottom of the ladder were the apothecaries who, although they had parted from the grocers in 1617, did not fully shake off shopkeeping until the Pharmaceutical Society was set up in 1841. The modern 'doctor' in general practice dates only from the Apothecaries Act of 1815. Thereafter it became usual for medical men wishing to enter general practice to acquire a licence from the Society of Apothecaries and a diploma of membership from the Royal College of Surgeons.

A university degree – or, at least, attendance at a university – was one route into the higher professions, and had always been a channel of upward mobility for a small number of intelligent boys able to attract appropriate patronage. Nevertheless, the teaching offered at Oxford and Cambridge was not directed towards any particular profession, except possibly the Established Church or the Civil Law. Not until the 1820s was it necessary to study medicine to obtain an MB from Cambridge, and at St Andrews medical degrees were openly sold for profit (the French revolutionary, Marat, acquired one). In Scotland there were close links between the legal and medical professions and the university of Edinburgh, which put Edinburgh in the eighteenth century at the centre of middle-class Scottish professional life.

The creation of professional bodies to raise status, and the introduction of formal training and qualifications, were the hallmarks of professionalisation in the nineteenth century. A new Law Society was created in 1825 for 'Attorneys, Solicitors, Proctors and others not being Barristers', which arranged lectures at the Inns of Court and, from 1852, voluntary professional qualifying examinations. In 1832 the Provident Medical and Surgical Association (later, the British Medical Association) was set up, with a *Journal* from 1840, to maintain 'the Honour and Respectability of the Profession' of general practitioner. Civil Engineers founded their Institution in 1818, and the more lowly Mechanical Engineers followed in 1847; but apprenticeship remained the predominant method of training for both branches of engineering until the end of the nineteenth century. Gradually but imperfectly, the Census records the arrival of the professions: civil engineers, teachers and journalists were first recognised as occupational categories in 1861; architects and surveyors in 1881; accountants, whose professional body was founded in 1880, not until 1921. Yet the three ancient professions still predominated: in 1881 there were as many Church of England clergy (21,700) as there were architects, civil engineers and surveyors put together. Many of the two largest groups – civil servants (97,000) and teachers (168,000) – had hardly achieved professional status, except at the very top, where successful applicants were largely those who already enjoyed high personal status. Overall the numbers in the 16 leading professions (excluding teachers and commercial clerks) doubled between 1841 and 1881 to just under 150,000, and had increased by a further 50 per cent by 1911.

The importance of this development and growth is twofold. First, the rise of professional organisations – what might be called the trade unionism of the middle classes – marks a growing consciousness on the part of these middle classes of interests which separated them from those beneath them in society, and proclaimed their independence from those above. Second, their increase in numbers established a significant and stable sector within British society which had no commitment directly to either side of the economic struggle between capital and labour.

A viable class society, 1850–1900

Mid-Victorians thought of themselves as living in a structured class society in which class positions were clearly recognised. They also prided themselves on the social stability which they enjoyed, and believed that within the class system individuals could rise by hard work. Such complacency would have been unthinkable in the 1830s and early 1840s, when socialist predictions that capitalism as a system was destroying itself through reckless competition, over-production and domestic under-consumption seemed all too plausible, and revolutionary conflict posed a very real threat. How was this stability achieved?

For some historians, the key concept is that of 'the aristocracy of labour'. From the 1840s the Victorian economy expanded, and the deflationary years which had followed 1815 were succeeded by three decades of mild inflation. Profits rose, and the monetary rewards of capitalism began to reach a wider sector of the working class than ever before. Skilled men, organised in trade unions, were able to negotiate successfully for a share in an economic system which was looking increasingly invulnerable to decay from within or attack from without. Labour became fragmented in the maturing capitalist system, and that minority of workers which did well out of it – the labour aristocrats – ceased to criticise it.

This theory has been challenged from two points of view. First, the existence of a labour aristocracy in all trades has been questioned. In certain industries, such as printing and engineering, a strong apprenticeship system did preserve an élite of skilled workmen who could normally expect their sons to follow in their footsteps: these may well be described as an open aristocracy. But in other industries, such as mining or textiles, differences were variously those of seniority, physical strength or sex rather than apprentice-trained skill as such. Second, there is little evidence in the contemporary literature that skilled workers were necessarily politically or industrially quiescent; rather, the reverse would more frequently seem to be the case.

Dissatisfaction with a theory which seeks to connect economic circumstances with political and social ideas has led some historians to turn instead to the theory of 'hegemony', derived from the writings of the Euro-Communist Antonio Gramsci. This involves:

> a socio-political situation . . . in which the philosophy and practice of a society fuse or are in equilibrium; an order in which a certain way of life and thought is dominant, in which one concept of reality is diffused throughout society in all its institutional and private manifestations, informing with its spirit all taste, morality, customs, religious and political principles, and all social relationships, particularly in their intellectual and moral connotations. An element of direction and control, not necessarily conscious, is implied.[19]

Though total middle-class hegemony in this sense was never established, there is widespread agreement among historians that something like it is to be found in mid-Victorian Britain. Harold Perkin's thesis is that 'a viable class society' was created with the triumph of the middle-class 'entrepreneurial ideal' over its rival aristocratic and working-class ideals. Ideals are for Perkin the only real embodiments of class, and class struggle is therefore to be understood as a struggle between ideals. The mid-Victorian period saw the triumph of faith in the enterprise of active capitalism enabling wealth to be created for the good of all; the virtues of competition and the free-market economy; the morality of individual effort and hard work; the philosophy of Utility; the religion of the evangelical; and the politics of the professional and expert.[20]

There is also widespread agreement among historians as to how this hegemony was achieved. Contemporaries quite openly admitted that the socialisation of the lower classes was their major task, and they achieved their desired end through an increasing concern for social welfare, control of leisure, religious institutions and doctrine and popular education: see below, Chapters 4–7. Nevertheless, it would be a gross distortion to imply that the middle classes saw their actions as anything other than beneficent, or that many of the working classes did not welcome what was offered to them. They were hardly reluctant pupils, and the ideals they seized upon – which can be summed up crudely in the word 'respectability' – arose as much out of working-class pride and traditions as out of the indoctrinating efforts of another class. The leaders of working-class opinion did not accept uncritically the ideals of their economic masters, but found there much with which they could agree: co-operative economics survived within a capitalist framework, mutual improvement served for self-help. Their pride and independence kept them separate from the middle class, and at the same time distinguished them from the labouring poor beneath them. Once granted the franchise, such men were natural Liberals. Conflict was largely restricted to the workshop and factory, because that was where class interests were most visible in the struggle to apportion more equally the economic cake. The stable class society of the later nineteenth century was based on the institutionalisation of labour and the radical appeal of popular Liberalism beyond the language of class.

Much of the debate about class stability has in fact been focused on the upper sections of the working class. What of the rest? During the first half of the nineteenth century many people believed that the lower classes were incapable of political thought, but were dangerous because they were open to corruption by unscrupulous demagogues eager to upset the social order. Edward Thompson's thesis in *The Making of the English Working Class* rests on a rejection of this familiar upper-class view and asserts that, through the common experiences of struggle and organisation, the whole working class had discovered a unity even in the midst of diversity. Many historians would argue that both interpretations are wrong. The bulk of the lower classes was neither a threat to the social order, nor a part of the working class other than in a strictly economic sense. Politically conscious activists were for rather than of their class, and the mass was rarely ready to follow where they led. Most people were inherently pragmatic and conservative. Those at the bottom of society with least to lose could, paradoxically, least afford to challenge the established order: they had so little that they clung all the more tenaciously to what they had. As Robert Roberts recalled of the early twentieth century,

> The class struggle, as manual workers in general knew it, was apolitical and had place entirely within their own society. They looked upon it not in any way as a war against the employers, but as a perpetual series of engagements in the battle of life itself. . . . All in all it was a struggle against the fates, and each family fought it out as best it could. . . . Marxist 'ranters' from the Hall who paid fleeting visits to our street end insisted that we, the proletariat, stood locked in titanic struggle with some wicked master class. . . . Most people passed by; a few stood to listen, but not for long: the problems of the 'proletariat', they felt, had little to do with them.[21]

In a study of London in the late nineteenth century, Gareth Stedman Jones has suggested some reasons for these attitudes. In his opinion the last third of the nineteenth century saw the remaking of the working class along more passive and introverted lines than was true of earlier in the century. The 'first' working class, described by Thompson, had been based upon the individual political activism of the artisan, centred on his place of work. But, with the decline of the artisan world a new working-class culture took hold, centred not on work but on leisure. The business of class struggle was left to the organised labour movement.[22] This thesis, however, begs the question as to how extensive was the 'first' working class. Roberts's recollections of the end of the nineteenth century echo those expressed by various observers of the working class throughout the century. The politically conscious working class and the working class of organised labour alike were but fractions of the working class of wage labourers as a whole.

Class in modern Britain

During the past hundred years several important changes have occurred within the broad social structure. First, with the erosion – but never elimination – of differentials between skilled workers and the rest, those marked social divisions on which the Victorians so frequently commented have been reduced in importance. Though concern for status remains, the labour movement as a whole from the 1890s has incorporated labourers as well as aristocrats of labour within its ranks. Second, there has been a similar consolidation within the middle class. With the rise in social status and expansion of the lesser professions, the professional classes have acquired a greater unity and merged with the commercial and financial classes and the lesser aristocracy to produce an upper-middle class which, in the twentieth century, has become the new governing élite. Furthermore, in the late nineteenth century the industrial middle class also began to be drawn into this consolidating group of substantial property-owners, especially through shared educational experience in the public schools. With changes in the structure of industry, the replacement of the active capitalist by the salaried manager and the consequent divorce between management and ownership, the different sections of the middle class have become defined less by function than by income and all that income can mean in terms of lifestyle.

The consolidation of labour and property, though, has not led to that polarisation envisaged in Marxist theory, for the most striking social feature since the later nineteenth century has been the growth of the lower-middle class. Like the middle class proper, the lower-middle class initially contained various branches – administrative (clerks), commercial (shopkeepers), professional (teachers) – which shared, in part, the values of those above them, and yet were little removed from the upper reaches of the working class.

Clerks, with their black coats worn shiny with age, and frayed white collars, were but a mechanics'-institute evening class away from the working class to which their families might still belong. Frequently paid less than artisans, they had – in George Orwell's later, celebrated phrase – 'nothing to lose but their aitches'. Society did not acknowledge their claim to superior status in the wages it paid them, and in the last quarter of the nineteenth century their relative position probably declined as their numbers increased. Though with expanding career opportunities in the twentieth century some clerks did become firmly established in the middle class, the position of the 'black-coated worker' remains an anomalous one, complicated still further by the presence of large numbers of low-paid female secretaries of working-class backgrounds within their ranks.

Like clerks, shopkeepers are also hard to place socially. As self-employed persons they are middle-class, and yet their daily work might be no different from that of a shop assistant. Small shopkeepers at the beginning of the twentieth century can almost be said to have belonged to the social class of their customers: those dependent on the corner-shop custom of a working-class street, like Robert Roberts's father in Edwardian Salford, were ambiguously part of and yet apart from the working class. Roberts recalled the fine social divisions between working class, lower-middle class and middle class with great sensitivity:

> Class divisions were of great consequence, though their implications remained unrealised: the many looked upon social and economic inequality as a law of nature. Division in our society ranged from an élite at the peak, composed of the leading families, through recognised strata to a social base whose members one damned as the 'lowest of the low', or simply 'no class'. Shopkeepers, publicans and skilled tradesmen occupied the premier positions, each family having its own sphere of influence. A few of these aristocrats, while sharing working-class culture, had aspirations. From their ranks the lower middle class, then clearly defined, drew most of its recruits – clerks and, in particular, schoolteachers . . . But despite all endeavour, mobility between manual workers, small tradesmen and the genuine middle class remained slight, and no one needed to wonder why; before the masses rose an economic barrier that few men could hope to scale. At the end of the Edwardian period an adult male industrial worker earned £75 a year; the average annual salary of a man in the middle classes proper was £340.[23]

That wide section of families beyond the purely manual class, where incomes ranged between the two norms mentioned, was considered by many no more than 'jumped-up working class'.[24] The best way out of the working class for those who wished it for their children lay in education. Once elementary education was widely available, both the means and the end were provided, as intelligent children aspired themselves to become schoolteachers. But individual social mobility was no solvent of class barriers, based on the enormous inequalities of wealth referred to by Roberts, and even the lower-middle-class teacher was little regarded in the social scale, except by the working-class community among whom he or she represented the source of that great mystery, 'book learning'. There was a gulf fixed between the mere schoolteacher and the schoolmaster or mistress. The latter taught middle-class children in middle-class schools. Stratification in the provision of education throughout the nineteenth, and for much – some would say all – of the twentieth century, remains one of the most sensitive indicators of class in British society.

The governing class

Britain was governed until late in the nineteenth century by its landed aristocracy, men of substantial wealth drawn from among those whose fortunes were primarily derived from or invested in land and real estate. The ownership of land brought a power and status which merely being 'in trade' could never do, however lucrative the trade. From the late nineteenth century, the aristocratic system began to give way to a plutocracy – the rule of the rich – as men of wealth were recruited from non-landed backgrounds. Relatively few men managed to penetrate the élite by virtue of ability alone, without the aid of family and fortune, until the combined wealth of organised labour thrust some of its leaders into powerful positions in politics during the course of the twentieth century.

The aristocracy

Though social leadership and political power were concentrated in relatively few hands in the eighteenth century, authority was not centralised, and locally all property conveyed some status. Society was made up of hundreds of local pyramids of power. At the head of county society was the Lord Lieutenant, the monarch's representative, usually drawn from a major aristocratic family. At the lowest level, ordinary freeholders in England could express their opinions at the County Meeting, and those with a 40-shilling freehold could vote in the infrequent parliamentary elections for their County members.

The daily business of ruling was left to the landed gentry, from whose ranks came the Justices of the Peace. This office was not always popular, and was often sought more to confer prestige and confirm local influence than in a desire to serve the community. The Justice of the Peace might be more interested in protecting his own interests and property than in his other duties. Yet he had considerable responsibilities touching on all aspects of life, from fixing wages and prices, regulating apprenticeships and making settlements under the poor law, to overseeing markets and regulating popular entertainments, quite apart from his judicial role as a magistrate responsible for the maintenance of law and order day by day and at the Quarter Sessions. Taken seriously, this could be a very time-consuming business, and increasingly the most active magistrates were clergymen, whose dual role of praying for the forgiveness of sinners on Sundays and sitting in judgement over them on weekdays generated much tension between the Church and its lesser parishioners.

The country gentlemen also provided about two-fifths of the eighteenth-century House of Commons, though only around 60 to 80 of these were from the lesser squirearchy. Most sat as borough representatives, but the most senior and socially important sought the honour of sitting for the county itself. They prided themselves on their independence, and considered themselves to be the guardians of English liberties, of the Revolution Settlement of 1688 and of the Established Church, as well as the staunchest defenders of private – especially landed – property. No aristocratic ministry could afford to ignore their prejudices.

In Scotland the lesser landowners had little power, and political life between 1707 and 1832 was even more restricted than in England. In the counties only about one-third of landowners qualified for a vote. Locally, authority was exercised by the heritors, acting (especially after the abolition of heritable jurisdictions in 1747) as justices of the peace, while the greater heritors held county office as Commissioners of Supply, responsible for apportioning the land tax, and as Lords Lieutenant after the Militia Act of 1797. The main difference from England lay in the political and social importance of the Presbyterian Kirk, through which the heritors exercised an authority over their local communities which many an English squire might have envied.

The aristocratic élite monopolised public office, holding the major places for themselves and exercising rights of patronage over lesser positions. They dominated Parliament not simply through the House of Lords, but also through their membership in and control of the Commons. In John Cannon's opinion: 'The cohesiveness of the eighteenth-century House of Commons, from which sprang a sense of common values and a sense of confidence, made it one of the most exclusive ruling élites in human history.'[25] In the Parliament of 1784 the House of Commons contained 107 peers' sons and Irish peers, 68 other close relatives of peers and 129 baronets and close relatives of baronets, making a total of 304 members of the élite in a House of 558 (54 per cent). Many of these men, and others, sat in the House for seats where the aristocracy had influence. Cannon estimates that in 1747 the number of seats controlled or influenced by the peerage was 167, rising to 207 by the end of 1784. The number of seats influenced by any one peer was not large – 70 peers controlled 169 seats in 1784, and the 13 seats under the patronage of the Duke of Newcastle in the mid-century was rather unusual – but half a dozen was not uncommon. Of the Scottish seats, 26 were controlled by 20 Scottish peers.

This state of affairs was typical of the eighteenth century, during which the élite was tightening its grip on national politics. Indeed, the trend was not significantly reversed until the Reform Bill crisis of 1831–32, which may truly be said to have made the first inroads on the British political *ancien régime*. This is what the radicals meant by 'the boroughmongers', and why a majority in the House of Lords in 1831–2 was so opposed to the Reform Bills.

Quite naturally, high political office was even more securely in the hands of the élite in the eighteenth century. In Pelham's Cabinet at the end of 1744, half the members were Dukes. In George Grenville's Cabinet of 1763–5 he was the only commoner. Of the 65 men who held Cabinet office between 1782 and 1820, 43 were peers, 22 were the sons of peers and of the remainder only six were non-aristocratic – of whom three eventually became peers. One of those who did not – George Canning, whose mother was an actress – can therefore hardly be cited as evidence that the political system was one open to talent in the early nineteenth century. The same might be said of Canning's political heir, Robert Peel, who always felt himself an outsider even though his father's textile fortune had been 'laundered' through Harrow, Oxford and a country estate in the West Midlands.

Urban government

In the smaller towns, many of which were unincorporated, local government differed little from that in the county as a whole; but in the corporate boroughs and expanding unincorporated urban areas power was shared between the gentry and the merchant élite. In Leeds, for example, 71 per cent of aldermen and 73 per cent of mayors between 1710 and 1835 were merchants from families and business partnerships which dominated the economic and social life of the town. Local mercantile élites and the leading livery companies likewise controlled politics in most other major cities. The Scottish burghs were particularly exclusive. Edinburgh was ruled by a self-electing council of 33 merchants and members of the incorporated trades. Nottingham was unusual in that there were 13 hosiers, three lace manufacturers and two cotton manufacturers among the 34 men who became Senior Councillors between 1785 and 1835.

Whatever their immediate economic background, such men were drawn from a select group of wealthy and influential citizens. Political activity was a matter not of class conflict but of personal and family struggles within the urban propertied élite. Many corporations were self-perpetuating oligarchies, and their opponents demanded reform not for social or economic reasons but because they saw elections as the means by which the closed corporations could be opened up to themselves. Sometimes, as in Edinburgh, the outsiders mounted their challenge to the corporation through separate commissions for such matters as lighting, paving and policing the city. The picture was very little different in the larger unincorporated towns like Birmingham and Manchester, where leading tradesmen and professional men acquired private Acts of Parliament for paving, lighting, policing and otherwise improving their towns, and sat on the various committees set up to provide such amenities as hospitals, almshouses and schools.

Church and State

Within the eighteenth-century view, Divine Providence was a loyal subject of the Hanoverian monarch who, through his Established Churches (Episcopalian in England and Wales, Presbyterian in Scotland), preserved godliness and good order. Assize sermons, parish homilies and the Prayer Book all commanded obedience to and acceptance of the established order. 'Christianity is parcel of the laws of England, and, therefore, to reproach the Christian religion is to speak in subversion of the law,' proclaimed the Common Law of England, while statute law in both England and Scotland made blasphemy a criminal offence subject to the death penalty in Scotland. The maintenance of orthodox religious beliefs through the 'Church by Law Established' was therefore an essential characteristic of the old political order, and membership of the political élite was open only to those who subscribed also to the Established Church. Protestant Dissenters were tolerated, but no more, and any who wished to progress in society were advised to discover the merits of Conformity. The alliance of State and Church in England and Wales was cemented in Parliament, where 26 bishops and two archbishops performed the political duties expected of them by those who had furthered their ecclesiastical careers. In Britain as a whole the Church of Scotland did not enjoy the same privileges, but within Scotland it effectively provided the framework for local government through the Kirk Sessions, while the enlightened professional classes found a substitute for a national parliament in the annual sessions in Edinburgh of the General Assembly.

The survival of the élite, 1832–1886

During the course of the nineteenth century the élite was gradually transformed, as new people and practices were absorbed and conditioned into its ways. Slowly the urban élites were incorporated within the national ones. Merchants, who had been no more than one-ninth of the membership of the Commons in the mid-eighteenth century constituted as much as a quarter by the early nineteenth.

Nevertheless, in the Parliament of 1841–7, there were still only 157 MPs out of 815 (19 per cent) for whom no aristocratic or landed gentry connections have been discovered; and of these only 73 (9 per cent) could be described as businessmen.[26] Thereafter the social background of MPs began to broaden, though as late as 1874 the landed interest was still the largest group, accounting for 32 per cent compared with 24 per cent each from the professions, commerce and industry. Entry to the Commons was an expensive business. Not only was there the cost of elections – about £3,000 for a county seat and over £1,000 for a borough seat as late as 1880 – there was also the expense of being an MP. It has been estimated that in 1880 a borough Member might spend £500 a year on such matters as keeping up the electoral register, paying towards the expenses of his local political association and making donations to local causes; a county Member could expect to pay out over twice as much. Additionally, the man whose wealth was not derived from unearned sources could not afford to neglect his business in pursuit of what was in fact a leisure-time activity for gentlemen. Not surprisingly, therefore, holders of Cabinet office in the nineteenth century continued to be drawn largely from the landed élite. Of 29 men who became Cabinet ministers for the first time in the period 1868–86, nine were from landowning families, and only six were from manufacturing and commercial families. According to W. L. Guttsman, the 'traditional ruling class' (defined as those from aristocratic and landowning families, and those who had attended one of the seven principal public schools) still provided 80 per cent of Cabinet Minsters in the period 1868–86.[27]

The social consequences of reform were remarkably few, despite the legislation of 1828–35 which abolished most religious tests, extended parliamentary representation, reformed the poor law and opened up municipal corporations. The middle classes were able to dominate politics only at the local level, where the power they had long enjoyed was now more widely distributed among merchants, tradesmen, the professional classes and manufacturers. Nationally the aristocracy exhibited a remarkable resilience, and not until after 1886 are there signs of 'new men' making significant inroads. Only when looking at the period from the Second Reform Act until the First World War as a whole can one at last detect clear evidence of social change at the top: over half the Liberal Cabinet Ministers (28 out of 53) between 1868 and 1914 were from the middle class, with a further two from the working class; and as many as 21 out of 47 Conservative Ministers were also from the middle class in these years.

Class and party, 1886–1951

Despite the propaganda of party politics, neither the Liberals nor the Conservatives were single-class parties in the later nineteenth century. By the time the middle class had achieved high office in significant numbers it was a very different middle class from that which Tories had feared in 1832. Gone was the assertiveness of the outsider, tainted with trade and religious Dissent, lacking the true breeding of a gentleman. The 'new man' of the late nineteenth century had been incorporated into a new governing class within which middle-class and aristocratic elements were combined, united in wealth and shared cultural values imparted through the public schools. The parties differed in degree rather than in kind: Conservatives were more likely to be landowning than Liberals; Liberals were more likely to be drawn from commerce, industry and the professions, especially after the loss of the Liberal Unionists in 1885. In the Parliament of January 1910 approximately half the Conservatives came from backgrounds in commerce and industry and a quarter in land, compared with the Liberals' two-thirds in commerce and industry and a quarter in the professions.

The Labour Party was quite different. An analysis of the class backgrounds of Labour MPs between 1918 and 1935 shows the extent to which the advent of Labour broke the social mould of British politics. Of the 57 MPs elected in 1918, all were working-class in origin and 49 were sponsored by trade unions. As the Party grew its social base became wider, but never fewer than two-thirds of its Members in the inter-war years were trade-union sponsored – most of them working men – and of the rest, around a third were also working men. Three-quarters of Labour MPs elected between 1918 and 1935 had received an elementary schooling only; 15.5 per cent had been to grammar school and 9 per cent to public school. Conservative MPs in the same period divided into 2.5 per cent elementary, 19 per cent grammar and 78.5 per cent public school. The contrast between the two parties is also marked in the composition of their Cabinets: MacDonald's second Labour Cabinet in 1929 contained 12 working men, four middle class and two aristocrats. Baldwin's Conservative Cabinet of 1925–9 had contained nine aristocrats, 12 middle class and no working men.

After the Second World War the proportion of the Parliamentary Labour Party which had been to grammar school and public school rose at the expense of those who had received only an elementary education, an indication of changes in the educational system, increasing social mobility and the widening social appeal of the Labour Party. At the same time the grammar-schooled proportion of Conservatives fell in favour of the public schools. Thus in the Parliament of 1951, 51 per cent of Labour Members had received only elementary schooling compared with 3 per cent of Conservatives; 26 per cent had been to grammar school compared with 14.5 per cent of Conservatives; and 23 per cent of Labour had been to public school compared with 82.5 per cent of Conservatives (25 per cent at Eton alone). The gap between the parties was still colossal in 1951, and such slight narrowing as had occurred represented not a decline in élite politics, but its advance into the party of the working class.

The challenge of radicalism

The beginnings of radicalism, 1760–1800

The language of opposition in the eighteenth century was that of independent country gentlemen, opposed to expensive continental wars which threatened to increase government indebtedness and taxation; and against ministerial corruption exercised through Royal patronage, placemen, pensions and seven-year Parliaments. Rarely did the mass of the people have any say in affairs, except as vocal, riotous and ultimately ineffective bystanders at election time. The Houses of Parliament were regarded as private gentlemen's clubs, the proceedings of which were not for discussion or even scrutiny by the public at large. But with the growth of news-sheets and coffee-house discussion societies, an informed public outside Parliament began to emerge. By 1760 there were around 40 provincial newspapers in existence, and with the dissemination of information came the formation of public opinion and the politics of the extra-parliamentary pressure group. Once this had happened, politics could never again be exclusive.

The man whose career personified this important development is John Wilkes. During his stormy career as a champion of popular opinion he vindicated the freedom of the press against ministerial 'despotism' – the use of General Warrants for the arrest of the (unnamed) 'authors, printers and publishers' of his *North Briton* no. 45 in which he had criticised the King's Speech at the proroguing of Parliament in 1763; he championed the right of the electors of Middlesex to decide whom they wanted as their MP without interference from the Commons – the Middlesex elections of 1768–74; he supported the reporting of parliamentary debates by giving legal sanctuary to reporters in his capacity as a City magistrate in 1771; and he argued in the Commons in 1776 that the 'meanest mechanic, the poorest peasant and the day-labourer' should have some share 'in the power of making those laws, which deeply interest them, and to which they are expected to pay obedience'.

Wilkes was but the symptom of a groundswell of radical opinion in the second half of the eighteenth century, based on the intellectual challenge of religious Dissent, Utilitarian philosophy, Scottish Political Economy and the activities of a group of radical organisers in London. Though Dissent as a whole had been politically quiescent since the early eighteenth century, it had nurtured in its Academies the leading radical intellectuals of the English Enlightenment – men such as Richard Price, Joseph Priestley, James Burgh and William Godwin. The latter's *Political Justice* (1793) was one of the most important radical political treatises of the time, and an major influence on nineteenth-century radicals as different as Francis Place and Robert Owen. Just as the Church in the eighteenth century was allied to the political establishment, so the Dissenting Meeting House belonged to its critics.

These Dissenting philosophers were rationalists and utilitarians, whose criticisms of the contemporary social and political system had much in common with those of Jeremy Bentham. The latter was essentially a legal reformer, but the logic of his arguments, especially when developed by James Mill, led in the early nineteenth century to a demand for universal suffrage as the only safeguard of 'the greatest happiness of the greatest number' against the naturally selfish pretensions of 'sinister interests'. Thus the Benthamites, or Philosophic Radicals, became one of the most influential of ideologically committed pressure groups working for reform, and had a major impact on government in the 1830s.

Many of those influenced by Bentham, including James Mill, Joseph Hume, Henry Brougham and Joseph Parkes, were Scotsmen or had attended one of the Scottish universities. In the late eighteenth and early nineteenth centuries, Glasgow and Edinburgh were breeding-grounds for intellectual radicalism and Whiggery. Classical Political Economy ruled supreme, with its corrosive criticisms of traditional aristocratic values and policies. With the political triumph of the Whigs in the 1830s, Utility and Political Economy were to become the twin supports of a reforming ideology – what William Cobbett contemptuously dismissed as 'Scotch feelosophy'.

More immediately, radicals were active, especially in London and Middlesex, forging the beginnings of radical organisation. In the City of London the tradition of opposition to ministries that had intermittently been present since 1725 was continued in the 1760s by William Beckford (MP for the City and twice Lord Mayor) in association with James Townsend and John Sawbridge. These men linked parliamentary and extra-parliamentary opposition to such ministerial policies as the Peace of Paris (1763) and the policy towards America. In 1769 Sawbridge and Townsend joined with John Horne (later Horne Tooke) and other Wilkites to form the Society of the Supporters of the Bill of Rights, which organised a petitioning movement to extend the Middlesex agitation to the rest of the country. Although Wilkes received support from across the social spectrum, this appeal to the middle ranks of society was most important, for their support was founded on sound commercial and economic interests which were ill-represented under the existing political system.

The seeds of radicalism sown in the 1760s germinated in the late 1770s, as merchants and taxpayers in the American colonies rose in defence of their 'liberties' against the heavy-handed exactions of George III's ministers, and elevated their struggle into one for the natural rights of man (excluding women and slaves). In Britain, as in America, the opposition to the king had its moderate and radical wings. Leading the moderates was a Yorkshire gentleman and clergyman, Christopher Wyvill, who attempted to stir the country gentlemen of his own and other counties to demand reform. After some initial success in 1780 his impact was limited outside Yorkshire and Middlesex, and he pinned his hopes after 1784 on a reforming ministry under the younger William Pitt. Not only did Pitt prove a disappointment, but the spread of political extremism after the French Revolution effectively put an end to Wyvill's efforts, and the desire of country gentlemen for reform was not rekindled until the 1820s. The radicals, including former Wilkites, organised the Society for Constitutional Information (SCI) in 1780 to publish the radical message 'throughout the realm, to circulate it through every village and hamlet and even to introduce it into the humble dwelling of the cottager'. The most active propagandist was Major John Cartwright, brother of the inventor of the power loom, whose *Take Your Choice* (1776) stated the radical case for manhood suffrage and annual parliaments.

Despite their initial enthusiasm and the extreme nature of their radical programme, those who challenged the political system in the 1780s were still drawn largely from the 'respectable classes' – professional men, merchants and gentry – and they even enjoyed some aristocratic support. The radical message had not yet become identified as the ideology of an emerging political class. This began to change in the 1790s as the Revolution in France inspired reformers to hope for an extension of civil and religious liberties in Britain also. At the time of the second anniversary celebrations of the Fall of the Bastille in July 1791, radical merchants, manufacturers and professional men were organising themselves in Manchester, Birmingham and other leading provincial towns, with Dissenters frequently playing a leading part. Against them, loyalist 'Church and King' mobs were stirred to riot and to support the established political and religious order. But as the social dimension to the French Revolution became more pronounced, the *ancien régime* in Britain closed its ranks. During the winter of 1791–2 a new element entered the contest, as artisans in Sheffield, Norwich and London formed societies to demand reform along the lines spelt out in Thomas Paine's *Rights of Man* (published in February 1791, with a second part a year later). Similarly, in Scotland during 1792 constitutional societies organised by radical lairds and professional men were joined by shopkeepers and artisans. The propertied classes were becoming alarmed as men who had previously had no recognised political existence followed Paine in asserting their right to be directly represented in Parliament, and demanded an equalisation of property through redistributive taxation.

Even so, at this stage in the development of radicalism the language of class remains inappropriate. Paine's radicalism was essentially the politics of the excluded, and his target was the aristocratic system of government. He championed 'the people', by whom he meant all worthwhile citizens, against what he called the 'no ability'; his democracy was one of small and roughly equal property owners, and the 'popular' societies contained few day-labourers. In economics Paine followed the *laissez-faire* ideas of the political economists, accepting the existence of natural laws governing trade and commerce without the need for government intervention; and he wanted workmen to be free to negotiate their own wages without interference. The major conflict of interests for Paine came not between capital and labour, but between the productive and the unproductive sections of society. Nevertheless, Paine's radical ideology was far too dangerous for moderate parliamentary reformers, because it was taken up by artisans who avidly discussed and spread his ideas in their clubs and trade societies at a time when revolutionaries in Paris were filling the propertied classes of Europe with alarm. The government prosecuted Paine for sedition and then used the popularity of his publications to discredit the cause of parliamentary reform throughout the period of the long war with France.

Radicalism and class conflict, 1800–1850

In the early nineteenth century assumptions about the unity of the productive classes became increasingly difficult to maintain. Small producers were finding themselves excluded not only by the upper class from political power but also by the capitalist middle class from economic power; while for their part middle-class radicals were beginning to doubt the wisdom of extending political power to those who had no substantial property to guarantee their social moderation, and were finding it expedient to distinguish their own position from that of the lower classes. So, while both sections of the excluded employed the language of 'the people', demanding 'reform' to destroy the aristocratic system and needing each other's help to do so, they were also themselves divided by class as their economic interests diverged.

The industrial middle class did not at first seek to challenge the political power of the aristocracy. Their main concern was the prosperity of their businesses, and they came to politics when their economic interests appeared threatened by government policy. Though there were some early signs of this in protests at the ending of the lucrative commercial war in 1763, the first real evidence of a new spirit among the urban manufacturers of the provinces came in 1785 when the General Chamber of Manufactures was formed to protest at Pitt's Irish trade policy. One of the first things the Chamber did was to point out the lack of representatives of the manufacturing interest in Parliament. Similar grumblings were heard over the cost of the French War and the imposition of an Income Tax in 1798, but only towards the end of the long wars in 1811–12 did the extra-parliamentary opposition experience success with its campaigns to end the East India Company's monopoly of the India and China trades, and to secure the abolition of the Orders in Council which were damaging British industry and commerce, particularly in the American market. There was always a suspicion, though, that opposition to the government during wartime was unpatriotic – that is, the language of 'patriotism' was not available to 'the people' because it had been appropriated by the government – and so the full force of organised middle-class opinion was not felt until 1815, when a campaign was launched against the Income Tax (abolished 1816) and the new Corn Law of 1815, which seemed to guarantee high returns to the landed interest at the expense of the rest of the community.

By this time middle-class opinion was sufficiently well-organised to demand representation in the Commons for major manufacturing cities such as Manchester, Leeds and Birmingham which did not have their own borough members. In the West Riding the *Leeds Mercury* was acquired by Edward Baines in 1801, and became the mouthpiece of the manufacturing interest; across the Pennines, the *Manchester Guardian* was founded with a similar function in 1821. In London the Benthamite radicals, especially James Mill and the radical master tailor Francis Place, were urging the necessity of an extension of the suffrage. Likewise, in most major centres of population a vocal party was formed to demand an end to the old, closed, oligarchic and aristocratic system of government. But the opportunity for a radical reform of Parliament did not come until 1830, following the temporary division of the governing Tories over the legal emancipation of Roman Catholics which was carried in 1829 against the force of British Protestant opinion. This attack on one of the pillars of the Constitution signalled the end of an era and the beginning of a decade of intense reform. The reforms of the 1830s, though, were carried by aristocratic ministries, not by revolutionaries as in France.

The politicisation of the emergent working class also occurred during the period of the Revolutionary and Napoleonic Wars. Here the main issue was the plight of domestic manufacturers in the textile industry, especially during the great economic depression associated with the Orders in Council and the American blockade in 1811–12. There was a long tradition of legislative protection for workers going back to the reigns of Edward VI and Elizabeth I, but much of this had fallen into neglect. In response to the demand that the law should be enforced on such matters as the ban on gig mills (used to raise the nap on cloth) in the woollen industry, and the apprenticeship clauses of the Statute of Artificers, Parliament proceeded to remove the protective legislation, denied further legislation to protect such groups as the framework knitters who were petitioning Parliament for relief, and made frame-breaking a capital offence. It was quite clear to the leaders of the workers that the law existed to protect the property of the capitalists but not their own sole property – their labour. This was an aspect of that 'abdication on the part of the governors' of which Thomas Carlyle was later to write. Thus, in the dreadful winter of 1811–12, when bread prices reached record levels, economic hardships and industrial grievances merged with the remnants of 'Jacobin' radicalism from the 1790s, and burst out in the angry name of 'Ned Ludd'.

Of course, class identity was not forged by one episode, but by cumulative reactions to events, especially in the years 1815–20, which culminated in the so-called 'Peterloo' massacre of 16 August 1819. This infamous event, when 11 people were killed and hundreds injured at a peaceful reform demonstration, epitomised all the social tensions of the post-war years. The victims were largely domestic textile workers and their families who had marched into Manchester to hear that great exponent of the radical platform, Henry Hunt, advocate the cause of universal suffrage; the assailants were the Yeomanry Cavalry, drawn from a local middle class. Although some leading middle-class Manchester radicals were quick to condemn the authorities for their action, central government made haste to congratulate the magistrates on their good work. The Manchester massacre entered the mythology of working-class identity, a symbol of class pride and class hatred.

A further development in the 1820s which emphasised the growing difference between leaders of middle- and working-class opinion was the adoption of anti-capitalist economics by artisans influenced by such lecturers and writers as Thomas Hodgskin, William Thompson and – above all – Robert Owen. Though some followers of the latter were persuaded to seek the cooperative commonwealth by means other than political, the overall effect of the new ideas in the 1820s was to strengthen the identity of a separate working-class radicalism, denouncing not only aristocratic corruption, jobbery and boroughmongering but also dehumanising, greedy and oppressive capitalism. At the same time, middle-class radicalism was consolidating around the ideology of Utility and Political Economy. During the Reform Bill crisis in 1831–2 working men in London, Leeds and Manchester formed their own Political Unions to rival those of the middle classes, and when the Whig Reform Bill was finally carried in 1832 the measure was regarded at best with suspicion and at worst with downright hostility.

The Reform Act of 1832 achieved much in principle, but little in practice. The major new centres of population received separate representation in the Commons, the manufacturing interest was given political recognition, the wealthier middle-class householders were given the vote, and some of the worst features of boroughmongering were removed. By uniting the propertied classes behind the modified constitution it thus ensured the continued political dominance of the aristocracy, and those middle-class radicals who had hoped for more found themselves outmanœuvred.

The policy which united property against poverty appeared vindicated over the next 20 years. Whereas on the Continent middle-class liberals, still excluded from political power, provided the leadership for a revolutionary upsurge which experienced partial success in 1848, in Britain the governing class was immeasurably strengthened to withstand the demands of radical reformers. Meanwhile, in the reformed Parliament, Whig legislation inspired by principles of Utility and Political Economy looked to working-class leaders suspiciously like 'class legislation', the first-fruits of the middle class's newly found political power. The most frequently cited examples of this 'class legislation' were the dismissal by Parliament of the Ten Hours' factory movement in 1833 and the passing of the Poor Law Amendment Act in 1834.

The factory movement had gathered new pace from 1830, when Richard Oastler took up the cause of the children working in the Bradford worsted mills. During 1831 and 1832 a massive campaign was mounted in the West Riding in which working-class Short Time Committees joined with Tory reformers to condemn their common adversaries, the Whig-Liberal manufacturers led by Edward Baines and the *Leeds Mercury*. Evidence of conditions in the factories was gathered by the working men and presented to a parliamentary Select Committee led by Oastler's friend, Michael Sadler. But the work of the Committee was disrupted by the dissolution of Parliament in 1832, and meanwhile the manufacturers rallied and persuaded a Royal Commission that the laws of sound Political Economy would not permit the working hours of adults as well as of children to be reduced. The division of opinion was a stark matter of class. On the one side were manufacturers and political economists wedded to the doctrines of free enterprise and *laissez-faire*, abetted by Philosophic Radicals with their coldly rationalised view of humanity and efficiency; on the other were old-fashioned Tory paternalists, suspicious of upstart manufacturers, and working men looking to government to protect them from the cruelties of the 'free' market.

This social division was repeated when in 1834 the main recommendations of the Royal Commission on the Poor Laws were implemented in the Poor Law Amendment Act. What looked to Philosophic Radicals like a sensible reform, and to political economists like a necessary withdrawal from interference in the labour market, was denounced as the 'poor man's robbery bill' by working men who feared brutal imprisonment in the proposed new 'bastilles' (workhouses) for the crime of poverty, and resented the removal of the traditional right of the poor to parish assistance in their own homes in time of need. Local communities throughout England responded to the new law with violent protest. In the textile districts, already seething with discontent over the failure of the Ten Hours movement, the new law was openly defied – in some cases for over a year.

The Poor Law Amendment Act illustrates clearly how far the common ground of radicalism had been divided between opposing economic classes, because the Act was in fact one of the most radical administrative measures of the nineteenth century. Taken with the repeal of the Test and Corporation Acts (1828), the Parliamentary Reform Act (1832) and the Municipal Corporations Act (1835), it revolutionised local government in England and Wales. Together these measures effectively broke the power of ancient local oligarchies and extended the elective principle in local government. And yet, far from being hailed as welcome breaches of the aristocratic system, these measures were seen as new forms of oppression because they did not fundamentally alter the social base of local political control: on the contrary, they helped place it even more firmly in the hands of the urban élites which, in the manufacturing districts, meant the industrial middle classes.

Seen from the point of view of certain Tories, such as Oastler, Carlyle and Disraeli, the Whig reforms signalled the death of the old, paternalist, aristocratic system of government. Seen through the pages of periodicals aimed at working-class audiences, it was not the Tories but the working classes who were the victims of change. The so-called 'Great Betrayal' of the Whig legislators was powerfully felt; Whigs, Philosophic Radicals, Political Economists and middle-class reformers who in the 1820s had seemed to be supporters of 'the people' in their attack on the aristocratic system, were now reckoned among the bitterest enemies of the working class.

Working-class hatred was reciprocated by middle-class distrust. Since the first decade of the nineteenth century class positions had been expressed through radical political agitation in a fitful kind of way, but between 1830 and 1850 both the middle and working classes achieved a new sense of identity through separate and conflicting radical organisations: the Anti-Corn-Law League was the essence of a middle-class pressure group; Chartism was the voice of the working class, excluded from political and economic power. It was not differences in immediate aims that divided the two organisations: most Chartists wanted the cheap bread and more plentiful employment which repeal of the Corn Laws promised; and the leaders of the Anti-Corn-Law League wanted to destroy the aristocratic system and to extend the franchise. The difference between them was one of class. To the *Charter* newspaper (not an extreme publication) in 1839, the League was 'a party comprised of avaricious, grasping, money-mongers, great capitalists, and rich manufacturers'. To the *Leeds Mercury* the Chartist leadership of the great strike against manufacturers in the summer of 1842 comprised 'wicked and designing men' who were 'deplorably ignorant' of sound Political Economy.

Consensus and compromise, 1850–1900

Such words were heard less frequently in the calmer 1850s; but that does not mean that class had withered away, only that radicals from the working and middle classes had learnt to live and work together, allowing other ways of seeing social experience to override or coexist with class. In the bitter struggles of the first half of the nineteenth century politics and economics had frequently coalesced, a development which had reached its climax in Chartism. The form of the movement was radical – its platform and methods dated back to the days of Major Cartwright – but its focus was new. As the *Annual Register* noted with some surprise in 1839:

> Another remarkable feature in the Chartist agitation was the hostility declared by them, not so much against the privileged orders of the state, who have hitherto been the especial objects of democratic indignation, as against the capitalists in general. It was, in fact, an insurrection directed avowedly against the middle classes.[28]

In the mid-Victorian years the pattern of popular agitation reverted to that established before 1830 as the political battle was renewed against 'the privileged orders of the state' – the aristocracy. Despite the 1832 Reform Act, the middle classes had not taken the House of Commons by storm; and despite the 1846 repeal of the Corn Law the economic basis of the landed interest had not instantly collapsed. Middle-class radicals needed the implied threat of working-class support. Similarly, working-class radicals had learnt in the defeats of Chartism that the constitution could not be changed solely by extra-parliamentary pressure. Ex-Chartists needed the support of middle-class voters and sympathetic Members of Parliament. The Liberal consensus of the mid-Victorian years was therefore not a substitute for the politics of class, but a consciously contrived compromise which avoided the politics of class conflict in the common name of radical progress. Especially after 1867, when the borough franchise was extended to approximately one adult male in three (thereby including within the political nation for the first time most urban working-class heads of households in steady jobs), the emphasis switched away from the violent campaigns of the first half of the century to a concerted attack on the aristocracy. The major socio-political issue of the 1870s and 1880s was not capitalism, but the land. This does not mean that the anti-capitalist grievances of the Chartists were submerged beneath a tide of popular Liberalism in the mid-Victorian years. Rather, they were institutionalised within the labour movement and confined to the immediate economic battlefield of the workplace.

The policies of the Liberal Party between 1868 and 1914 fulfilled some of the hopes of the radicals, but it would be a mistake to imply that the Liberal Party was therefore the party of the middle classes, still less of the working classes. The fact is that there was no complete match between social class and political allegiance. Middle-class men of a liberal outlook supported the Liberals; conservatively minded men from the middle classes supported the Conservatives – and did so in increasing numbers after 1885. The disposition to favour one or the other party was determined more by religious affiliation than class: Dissenters identified with the Liberals, even though most Liberals were probably not Dissenters; Conservatives felt a special commitment to the Established Church. Working men were similarly divided and, although a majority of politically active working men were probably radical and thus supporters of the Liberals, there were also many conservative working men, especially in parts of the country such as south-west Lancashire, where Evangelical anti-Irish Protestantism was strong; and after 1867 the Conservative Party proved particularly adept at moving into the new experience of mass political activity to exploit the conservatism, patriotism, Protestantism and imperialism of working-class sentiments and interests.

By the end of the nineteenth century few aristocrats had failed to be influenced by the values and philosophy of the middle class – what Perkin has called 'the entrepreneurial ideal'; and few of the middle class had resisted the charms of aristocracy. The question of the day was ceasing to be whether the Liberals could defeat the landed interest – the agricultural depression was undermining it more effectively than any politician could. The new issue was whether the Liberals would be able to continue to face two ways at once, retaining moneyed support as well as that of organised labour at a time when the economic problems of labour were again calling for political solutions which Liberal capitalists were unwilling to accept. The challenge of radicalism, which had always been more than the challenge of a single class, was about to be replaced by the class challenge of politically organised labour.

The organisation of labour

Trade societies in the eighteenth century

Wage labour emerged slowly and patchily in the economy of early modern Britain, but on the eve of industrialisation it was the dominant form of employment. The ancient guilds, which had once united the masters, journeymen and apprentices in a trade, were largely moribund or now represented only their most powerful members. New societies had been created, performing many of the former functions of guilds – such as the regulation of apprenticeship and wages – but devoted explicitly to the needs of journeymen. Combinations in restraint of trade were illegal but frequently practised, sometimes with violence. The trade societies also existed for the benefit of their members 'on tramp', arranging for members in search of work documentation which would be acceptable by those in the trade in other towns. The centre for local organisation was usually a public house – 'the house of call' – where journeymen would gather for conviviality, mutual support and, despite an Act of 1719 which threatened licensees who allowed their houses to be used for illegal purposes, organisation. Masters in search of tradesmen would know to go the house of call, as would tradesmen in search of work. The publican might act as treasurer for the society, for without legal protection of funds it was well to trust the money to someone least likely to disappear overnight (though this was not unknown). He might also help organise a benefit club to assist the members when unemployed or sick, and their families should they die. Though the Friendly Societies Act of 1794 tried to distinguish between benefit societies and trade societies, no such division was possible in practice: artisan life in all its aspects was organised through the trade society and its place of meeting.

These functions were basic to most trade societies not only in the eighteenth century but also throughout the first half of the nineteenth and even beyond, although changing circumstances brought pressures which gradually modified attitudes and reshaped the aims and objectives of the societies. The first pressure came through the decay of formal apprenticeship, the decline of small masters, and the growing economic power of capitalist employers. This caused the societies to organise more effectively to bargain over rates of pay and to conduct strikes, seeking additional funds and striving to limit the importation of 'blackleg' labour by extending their geographical horizons. The second pressure was political, as the public events of the day and the writings of Paine and other radicals were discussed over a pot of ale at the house of call. Artisans in London flocked to hear the popular orator, John Thelwall, and to join the London Corresponding Society. Weavers in Lancashire were also organising on a wide scale in the late 1790s, amid anti-war feeling and rumours of Irish and 'Jacobin' plots. The government grew alarmed and not only prosecuted publishers of radical literature and legislated against the popular societies, but also passed the Combination Acts (of 1799 and 1800) which codified and simplified the prosecution of organisations in restraint of trade. In practice, the Acts were little used – and were a dead letter in Scotland – but their importance was symbolic: the legal system, which had hitherto in theory been regarded as the arbiter in wage disputes, now appeared in practice to be the defender of capitalist interests.

The function of many of these early trade societies – the word 'union' was used chiefly for political organisations in the early nineteenth century, and was not widely applied to trade societies until the early 1830s – was to protect skilled labour against both masters and unskilled labour. They were usually small and highly localised, and contributed not to the unity of the working class but to its division. Most wage labour did not belong to a labour organisation: scattered agricultural workers and domestic servants were not easily organised; paternalist masters frequently made combinations of workers appear unnecessary; little room was found for women and children; and the unskilled majority had no power or opportunity to organise. Even among that minority of labour which was organised there was a great deal of variety from area to area and industry to industry. As the scale of production grew, new and less localised societies were formed to represent skilled sections of the workforce, such as the Friendly Society of Ironfounders (1809), the Potters, or the Operative Cotton Spinners, who in 1810 were the strongest trade society in Scotland, able to impose what was virtually a closed shop in the Glasgow area. Where there was a genuine and scarce craft skill, expanding demand could mean a strong union. This was the case with the Journeymen Steam Engine Makers (the 'Old Mechanics') founded in Manchester in 1826. But, where this was not so, expansion brought a flood of new recruits (including many Irish) whose presence undermined effective union action.

Trade unions in the early nineteenth century

It is no coincidence that trade unionism came of age in the 1820s, as the spread of capitalism, industrialism, political radicalism and labour ideology were giving new meaning to the word 'class'. The celebrated repeal of the symbolic Combination Acts in 1824 was thanks to the efforts of Francis Place and Joseph Hume, and was more a triumph for *laissez-faire* economics than for the labour movement; but, coinciding with a brief trade boom, it was the occasion for a great flowering of workers' organisations. As the *Sheffield Mercury* observed in the autumn of 1825:

> It is no longer a particular class of journeymen at some single point that have been induced to commence a strike for an advance of wages, but almost the whole body of the mechanics in the kingdom are combined in the general resolution to impose terms on their employers.[29]

One of the most bitter conflicts occurred in the West Yorkshire textile industry, centred on Bradford, where the wool combers had had their trade clubs since the 1740s, maintaining wage rates and seven-year apprenticeships throughout the eighteenth century. Combing machinery was not successfully introduced until the 1840s, but the expansion of the trade with the application of machinery to worsted spinning at the beginning of the nineteenth century, together with the abolition of apprenticeship in 1809, undermined the exclusiveness of the combers. Instead of working for small masters in workshops they were employed by master manufacturers on the 'putting-out' system in their own homes, with many formerly independent master craftsmen being reduced to the position of wage-labourers. At the same time, weavers were feeling the first impact of power-looms on their already overmanned trade, as mechanised production forced down the piece rates for woven cloth. The newly formed Combers' and Weavers' Union went out on strike to force the large manufacturers to pay handloom piece rates for power-woven cloth. They attracted support from many small masters in the domestic industry as well as wage-labourers. Significantly, this local dispute, exemplifying the new conflict between capital and labour which was becoming common in the experiences of labour everywhere, attracted national attention. As the London *Trades Newspaper* said, 'The people of Bradford are . . . the champions of a common interest.' The strike failed after 23 weeks, but not before the union had been recognised by the manufacturers and over £15,000 had been subscribed to the strike fund from supporters as far away as the south of England and the west of Scotland.[30]

The domestic weavers and combers had much in common with artisans in London and elsewhere, although their skills were less easy to defend. The cotton spinners were rather different. Their industry was the subject of new legislation in 1819 and 1825, restricting the hours of child labour, and so, apart from wages, a principal concern of the union in the 1820s and early 1830s was to secure the enforcement and extension of this legislation in collaboration with sympathetic masters such as John Fielden of Todmorden (MP for Oldham after 1832), Joseph Brotherton (MP for Salford) and Robert Owen (who with Robert Peel the elder had been responsible for the 1819 legislation). The leader of the Lancashire spinners was an Irishman, John Doherty, who realised that the main threat to strike action lay in the importation of blackleg labour, and that national organisation was therefore necessary to secure the bargaining power of labour in the industry. This was the pragmatic origin of his ambitious Grand General Union of the Operative Spinners of Great Britain and Ireland, launched in 1829, and his National Association for the Protection of Labour of the following year. The latter was not the first such attempt at a union of different trades; in 1818 a federal Philanthropic Society had been started in Lancashire, and in the same year John Gast had tried to link the London trades in the 'Philanthropic Hercules', but neither had lasted long. Nor did Doherty's attempts. The Cotton Spinners were defeated in a strike in 1831, with Scotland and Ireland failing to support Lancashire; and the National Association disappeared in 1832 after the secretary had absconded with the funds.

In direct confrontation with employers, none of these early unions enjoyed lasting success. Combinations of capitalists – illegal under the Combination Acts, but never prosecuted – were always more powerful than combinations of workers. Labour theorists, however, suggested in the 1820s an alternative to strike action: the workers should opt out of the capitalist system and employ themselves.

Co-operative organisations had three distinct roots: first, consumers' co-operation, chiefly for the purchase and milling of flour, which had existed in the eighteenth century in such places as dockyards, where there were large concentrations of labour; second, co-operation in production, to provide employment during strikes; and third, co-operation in isolated communities, where the socialist utopia could be built untainted by the capitalist system. All three forms of co-operation expanded and interacted after the failure of the strikes of 1825, and by 1830 there were over 300 co-operative trading associations in Britain, concentrated particularly in the textile districts and London. One group of London artisans led by William Lovett and James Watson, whose store had originally been intended to raise funds for a community, also began a propagandist journal, the *Co-operative Magazine*, and a Union Exchange Society through which artisans could directly exchange their products without selling first to a middleman. The inspiration for much of this activity was Robert Owen of New Lanark, whose Scottish followers ran a short-lived community at Orbiston near Motherwell between 1825 and 1827, while Owen himself was in the United States attempting to create his socialist dream at New Harmony. As artisans turned from politics after 1832, disillusioned with the Reform Act, Owen and his followers offered them an alternative route straight to the 'new moral world', and as trade expanded after a sharp recession in 1829–32 many artisans accepted their lead. A National Equitable Labour Exchange was set up in London in 1832, using labour-value notes instead of conventional currency; and the following year the London trades took over its organisation. A similar body was set up in Birmingham in 1833. Neither lasted long. They are mainly important to the historian as evidence of the fact that capitalism was not automatically accepted at this date by artisans who still cherished their independence as small producers.

Trade unionism also revived in the early 1830s among weavers in Yorkshire, spinners in Lancashire, miners in Durham, tailors in London, potters in Staffordshire and builders in Birmingham; but one by one they failed before the organised strength of employers. The most spectacular effort was the Grand National Consolidated Trades Union. It was organised by trades delegates to support the Derby trades who had been 'locked out' by their employers, and may for a time have linked as many as a million unionists up and down the country; but its nucleus of paid-up members was only about 16,000, being mainly London tailors and shoemakers. Its chief claim to fame is the fact that six agricultural labourers in Tolpuddle (Dorset) took illegal oaths to the union and were sentenced to transportation to Australia. The Grand National took up the case in London and made great propaganda out of it, as the labour movement has ever since. The real significance of this incident is not its misleading implication that trade unionism was about to sweep the countryside, but that urban workers throughout the country were made to feel a sense of identity with six agricultural workers in an obscure Dorset village.

The celebrity of the 'Tolpuddle martyrs' has tended to obscure the fate of the five Glasgow cotton spinners. These were leaders of the Glasgow cotton spinners' union, sentenced to transportation in 1838 for violence shown by their union towards 'blacklegs' which resulted in murder. Glasgow employers had a reputation for harshness, having a ready supply of alternative labour among immigrant Irish, and the Glasgow unions had a corresponding reputation for violence. Matters rose to a pitch in the late 1830s as the master manufacturers began to introduce Lancashire machinery, and a bitter strike resulted. The union was broken and, with the deep trade depression of 1837–42, trade unionism in Scotland was set back by more than a decade. The significance of the Glasgow struggle lay in its contribution to Chartism. Scotland had not had the 1834 Poor Law Amendment Act to rouse the bitter hatred felt in England, so, more than in most English towns, political radicalism in Glasgow in the late 1830s was founded on the trade societies. It is no coincidence that the beginning of the Chartist movement is usually dated from a meeting held on Glasgow Green on 21 May 1838 at which 70 trade societies were represented.

In England the heart of the Chartist movement lay in the textile districts, where working-class organisations already existed in the form of Short Time Committees and anti-Poor-Law organisations, and where the radicals already had their own newspaper, the *Northern Star*. Links with trade societies were of secondary importance. Only in the summer of 1842, during the 'Great Strike', did the Manchester Trades take the lead in proclaiming the Charter. Although many local activists in the labour movement were also noted local Chartists, they seldom identified the two roles. This was less so in Birmingham, where small trades predominated, and least so in London where the situation was closest to that found in Glasgow. In fact, in London Chartism only really became firmly established once it had been taken out of the hands of political radicals like William Lovett, who had drafted the Charter, and placed firmly in those of the trade societies, some of which formed trade localities of the National Charter Association in the 1840s. The larger unions stayed aloof. When Tommy Hepburn, the radical leader of the Durham Miners, brought his men out in support of the Charter in answer to the call of the National Convention in 1839 they found themselves alone, and resolved not to involve themselves in political strikes again. Only when trade unionists felt themselves politically threatened did they turn to political action. This occurred briefly in 1844 over proposed changes to the Master and Servant law, but the consequent National Association of United Trades for the Protection of Labour soon became more of a London-based pressure group than a representative body of trade unionism in the country.

Labour, radicalism and class in the mid-nineteenth century

The labour movement had contributed little by mid-century to the making of the working class. The social fact of class as wage-labour – 'class in itself' – was created by the growth of capitalism. Only a small proportion of wage labourers constituted organised labour. The majority of workers were class-conscious only in the sense that they identified with their own kind, in their trade societies or elsewhere. As one leading costermonger told Henry Mayhew in the 1850s, 'The costers think that working-men know best, and so they have confidence in us.' If their horizons were extended, it was not by trade unionism but by politics, which were all-pervasive. A superficial acquaintance with politics was unavoidable, except possibly in the remotest corners of the countryside. 'I am assured,' reported Mayhew, 'that in every district where the costermongers are congregated, one or two of the body, more intelligent than the others, have great influence over them; and these leading men are all Chartists,' though he went on to report that many costermongers were 'keen Chartists without understanding anything about the six points' of the Charter.[31] Political organisations gave expression to class and provided leadership in times of crisis without necessarily transforming all working people into a working class conscious of itself. The message of Chartism was that a majority of the working class (in the industrial districts, at least) could be roused to sign a petition or attend a meeting, but that deep commitment to any form of political or labour organisation could not be sustained. Distinctions therefore have to be drawn between the emergence of the working class as wage labour, the making of the politicised working class and the organisation of class as labour. As Ludlow and Jones perceived in their *Progress of the Working Class, 1832–1867*, the historian of the working class is concerned only with the political working class and with organised labour, not the whole working-class world of work.

Until the 1840s, class expression had been dominated by the political radicals who succeeded in creating a degree of political consciousness among the ranks of labour, but in the 1840s the relationship between radicalism and the labour movement began to change. The Chartists represented the culmination and collapse of the strategy of the mass platform which promised radical change for labour through universal suffrage and the ballot box. Their inability to marshal the forces of organised labour to support their strategy of the general strike was a major reason for their political failure. Radicalism in the first half of the nineteenth century was essentially the voice of the artisan in his small trade society and the protest of the vulnerable domestic worker. From the 1840s, the labour movement took the initiative. As unions became larger and better organised, Radicalism was supplanted by the political voice of organised labour. The political leader of the modern labour movement was therefore to need roots deep in trade unionism; an old-style radical like Charles Bradlaugh, who was a great popular leader in the plebeian style of the 1790s, was by the 1880s completely out of touch with the aspirations of the labour movement in a way which would have been unthinkable in his youth.

Acceptance and consolidation

In their *History of Trade Unionism* (1894), Sidney and Beatrice Webb gave prominence to the so-called 'new model' unions in the 1850s, especially the Amalgamated Society of Engineers.[32] Based on the Journeymen Steam Engine Makers, this union brought together in 1851 machinists, millwrights, smiths and pattern-makers from across the country, each paying a weekly subscription of one shilling under the general secretaryship of William Allan. This was indeed an important development and, having survived a bitter strike in 1851–2, the union gradually won recognition from employers and became a model for other craft unions. But it was hardly typical. The largest unions at the time were in coal and cotton, though these had low subscriptions, were principally strike organisations and had an intermittent existence. The Miners' Association of Great Britain, led by Martin Jude, was formed in 1842 with 70,000 members drawn from all the coalfields of Britain; but after a bitter strike in the North-East in 1844 it was considerably weakened, and it collapsed in the depression of 1847–48. It was revived in 1858 as the National Miners' Association by Alexander McDonald, the Scottish leader. Like the Spinners' Union, it worked for legislation to improve safety in the pits, and achieved the Mines Regulation Act of 1860. In the cotton industry various local spinners' unions were brought together in 1853 as the Amalgamated Association of Cotton Operative Spinners. In the same year a strike in Preston – a notoriously low-wage town – proved something of a test case, drawing national attention including that of Charles Dickens, who wrote *Hard Times* on the strength of a brief visit. The strike lasted from October 1853 until May 1854, involving 18,000 workers and a strike fund which raised £100,000. Though eventually defeated, the strike was in fact a triumph for the workers. Not only did the Chartist leader, Ernest Jones, belatedly learn not to underestimate the power of organised labour, but so too did the masters; and in 1859 the East Lancashire Power Loom Weavers' Association was successful in raising Padiham rates to those paid in nearby Blackburn. Furthermore, the law on molesting and obstructing which was used against the Preston strike leaders was modified in 1859 by the Molestation of Workmen Act.

These strikes of the 1850s are sufficient to indicate that, whatever the supposed new mood of labour and spirit of political compromise, the class struggle over wages and conditions had not abated at the place of work after 1848. What was happening was a natural response to changing conditions. As the national economy became more unified and large employers emerged who were willing to collaborate with one another to determine conditions of employment, and as the state became more involved in both protective and enabling legislation, so it was natural for organisations of labour also to acquire national perspectives. With larger unions came greater professionalisation; with professionalisation came circumspection –

an unwillingness to risk union funds on strikes except as a last resort – and respectability. In achieving the latter the union leaders were helped by the Christian Socialists, led by F. D. Maurice, J. M. Ludlow, Charles Kingsley and E. V. Neale. Their aim was to neutralise Chartism after 1848 by promoting 'sensible' labour organisations, particularly co-operative production. Ludlow was a lawyer, and worked hard to improve the legislation relating to workers' organisations, notably the Industrial and Provident Societies' Act of 1852, which gave protection to all forms of voluntary association and which constituted what Ludlow called the 'Magna Charta' of co-operative trade and industry; and the Friendly Societies' Act of 1855, which gave legislative protection to both Benefit Societies and Trade Societies formed 'for any purpose which is not illegal'.

Another important development in the mid-century labour movement was the formation of trades councils. These were central to the organisation of Scottish labour, where the trade-union movement was relatively weak. The problem in Scotland was the overwhelming might of the Glasgow trades, which resented interference either from Scottish unions in which other towns had some say, or from English-based national unions. The fragmentary nature of Scottish unions made blacklegging easy; and matters were compounded by the refusal of many Scots to pay high union dues. As a consequence the ablest labour leaders devoted themselves to the trades councils instead. Although Liverpool and Edinburgh might claim precedence, the first effective trades council was set up in Glasgow in 1858. If one man can be called its founder it was Alexander Campbell, an old Owenite who had been a leader at the Orbiston community in the 1820s, secretary of the Glasgow Carpenters' Union in the 1830s, and was editor of the Scottish miners' newspaper in the 1860s. Although open to all trades, the Glasgow Trades Council attracted chiefly the smaller unions – McDonald affiliated the Scottish Miners Association and occasionally attended meetings, but the engineers and spinners generally remained aloof. Membership fluctuated, from around 30 in 1861 (representing two-thirds of the organised trades), to 10 in 1866 and 41 in 1875. Their principal achievement in the early years was the successful agitation for a change in the Master and Servant Law, achieved in 1867. Other cities soon followed Glasgow's lead: Edinburgh and Greenock in 1859, Dundee in 1867, Aberdeen in 1868. Delegates sent to the Trades Union Congress in 1875 claimed to represent 4,000 trade unionists from Dundee, 10,000 from Edinburgh and 140,000 from Glasgow.

Trades councils also developed in the rest of Britain. Most important was the London Trades Council, formed in 1860, because not only was London the centre for a large number of the smaller organised trades, but it was also the headquarters of the larger, national unions whose leaders were, through the council, able to offer some kind of national leadership to the whole union movement. The Webbs dubbed these leaders the 'Junta' – George Odger, secretary of the Trades Council, William Allan of the

Engineers, Robert Applegarth of the Carpenters, Edwin Coulson of the Bricklayers and (from 1867) Daniel Guile of the Ironfounders. As with many of the Webbs' statements, the picture of a 'Junta' is somewhat misleading, though they were right to note the significance of this group of men who not only spoke powerfully for labour but had emerged from *within* the ranks of labour. However, they did not always act in concert – Allan's union, for example, forbade him to become involved in politics – and they did not always represent the views of the smaller London trades. This role passed to George Potter, who had taken a prominent part in the great London builders' strike of 1859–60 which was responsible for reviving the traditional radicalism of the labour movement in London.

Labour advanced on two fronts in the 1860s. First, aspiring politicians among the unionists – including Potter, Applegarth, Odger, W. Randal Cremer and George Howell – became involved in the agitation to extend the franchise, forming the Reform League in 1865 which organised mass meetings in Hyde Park and elsewhere in 1866 and 1867 while Parliament debated what was eventually to become the Second Reform Act of 1867. Second, the unions rallied to secure legislative protection following a legal decision (*Hornby* v. *Close*) which took away the benefits which unionists had thought had been granted by the Friendly Societies' Act of 1855. At the same time a scandal broke over the violent methods used by unionists against non-unionists in the Sheffield cutlery trades. A Royal Commission was appointed to investigate trade unions in general and, although the Commissioners thought unions ought to be recognised in law, the majority argued that the Registrar of Friendly Societies should exercise some control over union rules, including those restricting the numbers of apprentices. Though the unions did not like the majority's reservations, the overall favourable tone of a report which distinguished between legitimate unionism and the 'Sheffield outrages' represented a triumph for organised labour. Meanwhile several attempts were made in the 1860s to bring unions together in common action. In London the 'Junta' held a Conference of United Trades, and Potter organised a rival Conference of Trades in 1867. But the measure which succeeded was initiated in the provinces when Sam Nicholson, a Manchester printer and member of the Manchester Trades Council, called a Congress in Manchester at Whitsuntide, 1868. Thirty-four delegates attended, and a year later, at the next of what was to become a regular series of Trade Union Congresses, 40 delegates took part representing around a quarter of a million members.

The main concern of the Congress was the legislation arising out of the Royal Commission, and a committee was formed to watch over parliamentary affairs. This Parliamentary Committee was renewed annually and became that permanent feature of trade union life usually referred to as the TUC. The legislation introduced by the Liberal government was disappointing for, while giving legal protection to the unions, it left the liability for criminal damages which had been imposed in 1825 after the repeal of the Combination Acts. All the TUC could do was to persuade ministers to divide the proposed legislation into two Acts: the Trade Union Act, of which they approved; and the Criminal Law Amendment Act, against which they were resolved to fight. This disappointment with Gladstone's First Ministry came on top of the frustration felt by many Reform League members at George Howell's deal with the Liberal Party not to run working-class radicals against Liberals in the 1868 General Election. Working-class leaders – both radicals and trade unionists – saw the need for separate working-class representation. This was theoretically possible after the 1867 Reform Act and the Ballot Act of 1871, but in practice working men had neither the time nor money to stand for Parliament. Only the trade unions had the resources, and in 1874 two of their members – both miners, Alexander McDonald at Stafford and Thomas Burt at Morpeth – were elected with Liberal support.

The early 1870s saw a period of remarkable growth in the trade union movement at a time of unprecedented prosperity. The craft unions expanded their memberships nationally, and won an important struggle in the North-East. Here the Engineers, led by John Burnett, extracted a nine-hour day out of Sir William Armstrong and other employers in the region's engineering works, and established the claim of unions to exercise some restraint on capitalists in the way they managed their businesses. The example set by the engineers in restricting hours was followed elsewhere, not least in the pit-head engineering workshops. The early 1870s also saw new unions among workers not previously unionised – gas workers, dockers, railway workers, boot and shoe operatives, agricultural workers, women and white-collar workers. Some of these reflected changes in the structure of employment; not all survived. Joseph Arch's National Agricultural Workers Union had a thousand branches and over 72,000 members by the end of 1873, but was severely weakened by the ensuing agricultural depression, when thousands of labourers emigrated. The National Union of Elementary Teachers, on the contrary, thrived, with over 14,000 members by 1888.

Female artisans had long had their own trade societies: in the early 1830s there had been organisations such as the Lodge of Female Tailors, and in the textile trades women were admitted to the Lancashire weavers' union on equal terms with men; but many of the old craft unions were exclusive, and the TUC in general showed little interest in women. To many male craftsmen female labour presented the threat of cheap labour and the dilution of skills. Inspired by the example of Joseph Arch's union and also the Female Umbrella Makers Union of New York, Emma Paterson, a female bookbinder, set about challenging this male dominance in the British labour movement. In 1874 she organised a general union for women, the Women's Protective and Provident League 'for the formation of protective and benefit societies among women earning their own living' (called the Women's Trade Union League after 1891). Through the

League's propaganda the National Union of Working Women, the Society of Glasgow Tailoresses and several other women's unions were formed, as well as women's sections in some male-dominated unions. In 1875 Emma Paterson and Edith Simcox of Bristol became the first two women delegates to attend the annual TUC. But in arguing for the protection of working women through unions, not special legislation as in the factory acts, she was fighting an uphill battle against entrenched ideas within both the labour movement and the parliamentary world.

The economic boom of the early 1870s did not last beyond 1873, and with intermittent depression in the late 1870s and 1880s union membership fell from over 1,000,000 in 1874 to around 750,000 in 1888. Not all unions suffered equally. The engineers survived a bad year in 1879 and increased their membership overall. The federal National Miners' Association (based on Scotland and the North-East) proved flexible; its rival Amalgamated Association of Miners (with members mainly in the west and South Wales) did not. The Northumberland and Durham miners were among the strongest. Not only did they survive, but they and the North-East ironworkers evolved new forms of labour relations appropriate to hard times. By accepting conciliation, arbitration and wage/price sliding scales they avoided costly strikes and lock-outs, and were in a strong position to bargain for their members when economic recovery came.

The Webbs looked upon the years 1875–88 – during which the staunch Liberal, Henry Broadhurst, was secretary of the Parliamentary Committee of the TUC – as a time of sterile compromise, in marked contrast with the years after 1888 when union membership expanded and socialism revitalised the labour movement. This view does less than justice to a period in which unions established themselves as permanent features on the industrial relations scene. What was relatively new in 1889 was a revival of general unions among the unskilled. Only about 10 per cent of the workforce was unionised in 1888, and many unions still saw their function to be exclusive rather than inclusive. Socialists had a wider vision, which they sought to spread among the working class. The paradox is that they enjoyed their greatest success defending privilege in the smaller craft unions, whose members were increasingly feeling the pressures of new labour processes and loss of status which had been the experience of their less-skilled brothers for most of the century. Socialists were therefore better represented on the trades councils than in the unions themselves, though the councils overall were more labour than socialist on account of their co-operative and friendly-society representatives.

The extension of unionism to the unskilled was nevertheless significant, even if the unionisation of the unskilled was not entirely new and although the members of the new general unions accounted for less than 200,000 out of 1,500,000 members in 1892. In Scotland the Trades Councils had always been more open to unskilled workers, but in England and Wales, even where the unskilled were not specifically excluded, high union dues kept them out in all but the most prosperous years. The spread of socialist ideas in the 1880s, particularly through the Fabian Society and the Social Democratic Federation in London, produced a new generation of labour leaders who made headway in the depressed years of 1886–7 and then took the initiative when trade revived in 1889. The best-known were Tom Mann, president of the Dockers' Union which arose out of the successful dock strike of 1889, and Will Thorne of the Gasworkers and General Labourers' Union. Neither union was able to keep its membership at the heights achieved in the early days, but both survived. Moreover, attitudes also began to change in the older unions. The engineers changed their rules to become less exclusive, and the new Miners' Federation of Great Britain took up the new unionists' call for an eight-hour day.

There was to be no easy victory for the socialists, though. When Broadhurst retired in 1890 he was replaced by another Liberal, Charles Fenwick, whose power-base was with the Liberal miners of the North East. Above all, in 1895 the constitution of the TUC was changed to replace voting by head with block voting, and to restrict delegates to workers at their trade and union officials. Not only did this exclude the retired Henry Broadhurst and middle-class women supporters of women's trade unionism, but also the delegates of trades councils. This precipitated the decision of the Scottish trade councils to set up their own separate Scottish TUC in 1889 – a reminder that within the labour movement the Scots always occupied an ambiguous position with dual and sometimes conflicting loyalties to British labour and to Scotland. Above all, the new standing orders placed the power of the TUC firmly in the non-socialist hands of the big unions in coal, engineering and textiles which between them accounted for half the trade union membership in the country.

Labour representation

Socialism entered the labour movement not so much through the unions as through the demand for separate labour representation. Frustration at the failure of Gladstone's Liberal Ministries to pay rather more attention to British social conditions and rather less to Ireland was compounded by the refusal of local Liberals in many constituencies to select working men as parliamentary candidates. One such Lib–Lab aspirant, Keir Hardie, failed to be selected for Mid-Lanark in 1888, fought as an independent, came bottom of the poll and founded the Scottish Labour Party, but not yet with a specifically socialist programme.

Conditions for the spread of socialism were most favourable in the West Riding. Here the unions were weak, and the employers – personified by Alfred Illingworth of Bradford – strong Liberals of the old *laissez-faire* school. In 1890 the imposition of the McKinley tariff by the United States devastated the Yorkshire trade. Wages were cut, and a great strike took place at Manningham Mills in Bradford. Socialist organisations thrived, and in January 1893 the Independent Labour Party (ILP) was founded at a conference held in Bradford.

Organisation scarcely meant instant success. At the 1895 general election all 28 ILP candidates were defeated, including Hardie, who had won West Ham in 1892. There were a dozen Lib–Lab Members, mainly miners and including the erstwhile socialist, John Burns. Socialism seemed doomed and the cause of independent labour representation with it. What changed matters was a renewed threat to the legal position of the trade unions. In 1875 the Conservative government had restored the right of peaceful picketing taken away by the Liberals in 1871; but increasing employer militancy in the later 1890s was supported by the courts, culminating in *Lyons* v. *Wilkins* (1897–8), in which an injunction was granted to an employer preventing picketing by union members at his premises. Then, from July 1897 until January 1898, the Engineers, demanding an eight-hour day, were locked out nationally by the employers' Federation of Engineering Associations. The need for independent labour representation was again apparent, and in February 1900 the TUC called a conference in London at which the Labour Representation Committee (LRC) was set up.

Independent Labour candidates had hitherto eroded both Liberal and Conservative support without turning votes into seats; but they were able to affect the local balance of power. At West Bradford, for example, where Ben Tillett had fought in 1892 and 1895, he had come bottom of the poll on each occasion. But in 1895 what had been Alfred Illingworth's old seat fell to the Tories and in 1900 the Liberals withdrew their candidate, enabling Fred Jowett to win it for the ILP – and causing Illingworth to withdraw financial support from the Liberals for a couple of years. Jowett held the seat in 1906, forcing the Liberal to the bottom of the poll – the only socialist to win an English constituency in 1906 against official Liberal opposition. (There were two others in Scotland, and two further victories against unofficial Liberals.) The Liberal dilemma was how to satisfy the demands of Labour and at the same time keep the support of the party's local capitalist financiers. In the event, Labour made its electoral breakthrough in 1906 in seats which the Liberals were resigned to losing to the Conservatives after their own disastrous showing in the 1900 election. In 1903 the Liberal Chief Whip, Herbert Gladstone, and the secretary of the LRC, Ramsay MacDonald, made an informal electoral pact which in effect gave LRC candidates a free run in about 30 seats. A further pact in 1905 between the LRC and the TUC ensured that LRC candidates did not run against TUC-sponsored Lib–Lab candidates and vice versa. As a result, 56 representatives of labour were elected to the House of Commons in 1906, 29 of them LRC men. Labour had arrived.

This achievement cannot be understood without reference to the changing attitude of the trade unions, for although many of these Labour men were socialists their party was overwhelmingly a trade union party. When the LRC was set up affiliated unions provided it with 353,070 members; by 1906–7 membership had reached a million and all the large unions except the miners (who had their own Lib–Lab representatives) had joined. What brought this about was the decision of the House of Lords in 1901 that the Taff Vale Railway Company could claim £23,000 damages from the railwaymen's union for losses incurred during a strike. The basic weapon of organised labour – the withdrawal of that labour – was in effect neutralised by this decision. The infant LRC suddenly had a new relevance for all trade unionists which ensured that it did not, like earlier organisations to promote labour representation, fade away. And with union support came money, to fight elections and to pay MPs. MacDonald was able to enter negotiations with the hard-up Liberal Party in 1903 with an electoral fund of his own.

The year 1906 has therefore rightly been seen as a turning-point in the history of élite politics in Britain. All but one of the 50 LRC candidates in 1906 were working men; all the 29 elected were working men. The Labour Party was a class party and its arrival represented a triumph for the working class, 40 years after the extension of the urban franchise to working men. With the conversion of the miners in 1909 Labour held 40 seats in the Parliament of January 1910. Nevertheless, this was hardly victory. Labour fought only 78 seats in January 1910, taking 38.4 per cent of the votes in those constituencies but only 5.9 per cent of the total votes cast. The power base of Labour was narrow and sectional. Many adult working men did not possess the vote, and the unions represented only 17.7 per cent of the total workforce. Also, many working men, if they were not Conservative, still thought of themselves as Lib–Lab rather than socialist. Moreover, in 1909 the House of Lords had ruled (in the Osborne Judgment) that the compulsory union levy for the support of MPs was illegal, yet in January 1910 each contest cost Labour £881 – though this was less than either of the other parties. The future was by no means assured.

The real strength of labour as a political force before the First World War lay in local government. Just as in the early years of the nineteenth century the middle classes had made their initial impact locally while the bastions of Parliament remained unconquered, so after 1867 working men began to make their impact on local representation, firstly on School Boards (created under the 1870 Education Act) where a system of cumulative voting favoured 'minority' candidates, and then on local councils, chiefly as Liberals or (in London) Progressives. This process accelerated in the late 1880s as socialist activists became involved, especially in London, which gained its own County Council in 1889. The electoral power of the Liberals, which appeared undiminished at Westminster with the massive landslide victory of 1906, was being rapidly eroded in many of the major urban centres of population. In Leeds, for example, the first Labour councillor was not elected until 1903, but by 1913 there were 14 Labour councillors, and their presence pushed the Liberals from being the largest to being the smallest of the three parties. The 10 Labour members in Bradford in 1905 held the balance of power which enabled them to gain places on a number of important committees. In 1906 there were in all only 56 Labour representatives on local councils; in 1913 this figure had risen to 184. The increase in local influence can also be measured by the number of trades councils and local Labour parties affiliating to the national party: 73 in 1905–6, and 177 in 1914.

The conditions for Labour to register considerable gains nationally were created between 1916 and 1918: the Liberals split, the franchise was extended to all males over 21 (and women over 30), and the Labour Party adopted a new constitution, admitting individual members for the first time and taking socialism as the basis of its reform programme. During the war organised labour had been involved in the national effort and incorporated into the machinery of state through representation on public bodies and arbitration tribunals. At the same time the state had been more involved in controlling the economy, fixing wages and profits and assuming responsibility for the railways and coal industry. The demand of the Welsh miners in 1907 for nationalisation of the mines no longer seemed utopian. Labour in 1914 had still been a political pressure group fighting to maintain a separate identity. In 1918 it looked like a credible political party.

In 1918 Labour fought 388 seats and, although only 63 seats were won, the popular vote was 2,385,477 (22.2 per cent of the total). Apart from Sinn Fein (whose members did not take their seats) Labour was the largest party in opposition to Lloyd George's ruling coalition. In 1922, with 142 seats and 29.5 per cent of the vote, Labour was larger than the two wings of the Liberal Party combined. In 1924, with 191 seats and 30.5 per cent of the vote, Labour formed its first administration, albeit a minority one which lasted less than a year. Throughout the 1920s Labour's electoral strength increased while that of the Liberals waned, and in 1929 Labour became the largest single party. Not until 1945, though, did Labour capture the largest proportion of votes (47.8 per cent) and form a majority administration.

Trade unions in the twentieth century

Between 1910 and 1920, with an intermission during the war, trade unions in Britain underwent a period of militancy and growth. In a period of rising prices and buoyant employment, many workers who had not benefited from the collective bargaining strengths of the established unions sought to make good their claims. In addition the major unions were growing dissatisfied with wage-bargaining procedures which meant that in bad years, such as 1908, wages fell. Miners in South Wales rejected the new rates offered by their Conciliation Board in 1910, and went on strike for eight months, during which time troops were sent to quell disturbances and one man was killed in Tonypandy. In 1911 dockers and seamen struck. Two men were killed in clashes between strikers and troops in Liverpool. In the same year the first national rail strike occurred. In all over 10 million working days were lost through strikes, but the following year the total was four times as great, making 1912 the third-worst year ever for strikes as the Miners' Federation brought out a million men to claim a national minimum wage of five shillings a shift. Though anti-parliamentary syndicalist theory has sometimes been credited with causing this massive unrest of the pre-war years, adequate industrial explanations can be found for all the disputes. The theorists were in a minority; the majority of workers struck because they believed they deserved and could extract better terms and conditions of employment from their employers. The same trend continued in the short-lived boom after the war, with major national strikes among cotton workers and railwaymen in 1919, miners in 1920 and again in 1921 and engineers in 1922. In 1921 85.9 million working days were lost through strikes – by far the worst year ever, excepting 1926. Then depression began to bite, and disputes subsided until the General Strike and the miners' strike of 1926, when 162.3 millions days were lost.

The General Strike of 4–12 May 1926 arose out of the bitter conflict on the coalfields between the miners and the coal owners, who had imposed a wage cut in 1925 when exports were hit as a consequence of the government's deflationary economic policy. It was not a general strike in the nineteenth-century sense of the phrase, but a selective strike by around 4 million workers out of a total labour force of nearly 12 million. The strike was general in that it was nationally organised by the General Council of the TUC. After nine days the TUC drew back from the political implications of the strike, called it off, and left the miners to fight (and lose) their battle on their own. Organised labour, however committed, was a minority force in the country as a whole, and in the end drew back from a prolonged confrontation with public opinion and the government.

During the first two decades of the twentieth century the membership of trade unions increased from around 2 million in 1900–05 to 4.1 million in 1913. As a result of labour organisation and responsibility during the war, membership then rose to 6.5 million and reached a peak of 8.3 million in 1920 before falling steadily to a low of 4.4 million in 1932 and 1933. Expressed as a proportion of the employed population, around a quarter of males were in unions in 1912 and 1932; over half in 1920. Far fewer women joined unions: around 8 per cent before the First World

War, 24 per cent in 1920, and 12.4 per cent in 1932. Concealed within these totals were two major trends. First, the actual number of unions fell by over a quarter between 1920 and 1939, as smaller unions consolidated into industrial unions to achieve greater bargaining strength, and general workers' unions came together into huge national conglomerates with workers, some of them previously unorganised, in practically every industry. Second, for the first time white-collar trade unionism became a significant force in the ranks of organised labour.

In 1913 the various railway unions, except for the locomotive footplate men, joined together as the National Union of Railwaymen; and the dockers, miners and railway workers formed the so-called 'Triple Alliance' to ensure unity of action in three industries which were mutually dependent. After the war in 1920 the Amalgamated Society of Engineers merged with other engineering unions to form the Amalgamated Engineering Union; in 1922 the dock and transport workers united as the Transport and General Workers Union; and the Gasworkers and other general unions, including the 40,000 members of Mary Macarthur's and Margaret Bondfield's National Federation of Women Workers, became the National Union of General and Municipal Workers in 1924. These four unions, together with the Miners Federation, were the largest unions throughout the inter-war period.

As the economy recovered in the 1930s union membership also increased, so that by 1939 it was back to 6.3 million – approximately the level of 20 years earlier. During the Second World War organised labour once more benefited from its close involvement in government at both union and Labour Party levels. Trade unions were becoming an integral part not only of British industrial relations but also of wider economic planning. This was a natural development when Labour formed its first majority government in 1945, with a union leader like Ernest Bevin a prominent member of the Cabinet, but it was continued in the 1950s under Conservative governments. The state was becoming directly or indirectly responsible for an increasing amount of employment, in the public service and in nationalised industries such as the mines and the railways. But with public responsibility and increasing bureaucratisation in the union movement, the danger was that its leaders might lose touch with their members. This had already become evident in the shop stewards' movement in the engineering industry during the First World War, and again in 1937 when there was an unofficial London bus strike which led to expulsions from the Transport and General Workers Union.

After the Second World War union leaders walked a tightrope between the demands of their more extreme members and the needs of industrial statesmanship. Despite their political links with Labour, they remained first and foremost pragmatic industrial negotiators, their aim being to secure the best deal for their members. In the 1950s they rejected overtures from the Conservative Chancellor of the Exchequer, R. A. Butler, for a link between wages and productivity, but they also ensured the regular defeat of motions at the TUC against all wage restraint. Rank-and-file members sometimes grew restive. Mindful of a public opinion hostile to disruptive strikes such as had occurred in the London docks in 1950, Tom Williamson, General Secretary of the General and Municipal Workers, lectured his members:

> The right to strike is a fundamental principle of democratic trade unionism, and any attempt to interfere with the right of a workman or workmen to withdraw his or their labour, subject to authority of proper notice in accordance with contract or agreement, would be met with the fierce opposition such a move would deserve.
>
> But there are some who do not know, or who seem to forget, that the rights of democratic trade unionism, which do not exist in some parts of the world, carry with them certain responsibilities, and that in the long run we cannot have the rights without the responsibilities.[33]

The warning was not heeded. The inability of the unions to reform themselves, and the failure of either Conservative or Labour governments to work out an incomes policy acceptable to the trade union movement, meant that, when in 1966 a Labour government was returned with a comfortable majority for only the second time, organised industrial labour found itself at odds with organised political Labour. Between 1964 and 1966, when a Labour government narrowly held power after what was dubbed 'thirteen years of Tory misrule', 1,697,000 working days were lost through unofficial strikes, compared with only 733,000 through official strikes. In 1969 the Labour Government of Harold Wilson set out what proved to be its abortive policy for trade union reform, *In Place of Strife*. To many trade unionists it seemed as though Labour had forgotten its roots and had become a governing party just like any other.

The changing structure of employment in the twentieth century is clearly reflected in union membership figures, with the balance moving away from traditional industrial unions towards general and 'white-collar' unions (see Table 3.6). Between 1948 and 1974 union membership among manual workers fell by 6.8 per cent, while that among white-collar workers rose by 104.7 per cent. In 1974 38 per cent of all full-time white-collar workers were in unions, compared with 53 per cent of manual workers. A decade later these proportions had been reversed (see Table 3.7).

The year 1991 was the last year for which the figures can be presented in this way as, with declining memberships, several major unions then amalgamated to retrieve their economies of scale. Following the formation of UNISON (incorporating the health workers, local government officers and public employees) in 1993, these white-collar workers now constituted the largest single union of organised labour, with about 1.5 million members in 1995.

Table 3.6 Membership of the eight largest trade unions of 1960, selected years between 1924 and 1991 (thousands)

	1924	1960	1980	1991
Transport and General Workers	300	1,302	1,887	1,127
Amalgamated Engineers	206	973	1,381	702
General and Municipal Workers	327	769	916	860*
National Union of Mineworkers	800	586	257	44
Shop, Distributive and Allied Workers	93	355	450	341
National Union of Railwaymen	327	334	170	110
National and Local Government Officers	34	274	782	760
Electricians	28	243	405	357

Source: D. and G. Butler, *British Political Facts* (1994), pp. 368–9.
*includes the Amalgamated Society of Boilermakers from 1982.

Many of these newly-unionised white-collar workers were women. In 1979, the last year for which separate figures were kept, 37 per cent of all employed females were members of trade unions compared with 58 per cent of all males. The 1983 General Household Survey found that half of all women in full-time employment (and 57 per cent of men) were in unions, and they were well-represented in all groups except the 'professional' and 'unskilled manual' categories. This survey also showed that the most highly unionised sector of the labour force for both men and women was the 'intermediate non-manual' class, followed closely by 'skilled manual'. Despite the growth in unionisation amongst all groups of workers, over 40 per cent of unskilled workers still remained outside the ranks of the organised working class, while large numbers of workers who were not part of the traditional working class had become unionised. These trends were borne out by a differently calculated Labour Force Survey in 1995, which found that the most unionised sectors of employment were Energy and Water Supply (56 per cent of men and 36 per cent of women) followed by Public Administration, Education and Health (54

Table 3.7 Membership of 'white-collar' unions, 1950–1991 (thousands)

	1950	1980	1991
National and Local Government Officers	197	782	760
Shop, Distributive and Allied Workers	343	450	341
Scientific, Technical and Managerial Staffs	120	491	653
National Union of Teachers	192	249	169
Civil and Public Service Association	134	224	123

Source: D. and G. Butler, *British Political Facts* (1994), pp. 368–9.

per cent of men and 46 per cent of women). Manufacturing employment, on the other hand, had a much lower level of unionised workforce – 33 per cent of men and 21 per cent of women. Overall, by 1994, trade union membership had fallen from the 1980 peak of 53 per cent of the workforce to only 32 per cent, with practically no difference between male and female participation. The working class, in the sense of organised male labour, was by the mid-1990s both shrinking in size and bearing instead a distinctly white-collar (and, indeed, white-blouse) appearance.

Towards a classless society?

With the election of the first majority Labour Government in 1945, followed by extensive welfare legislation and then in the 1950s a gradual relaxation of wartime austerity without a return to the unemployment levels of the inter-war period, many people looked forward to the establishment of a more egalitarian society in Britain. If by this was meant some further reduction in inequalities of wealth, progress was made. In 1938 those in receipt of the top 100,000 incomes in the United Kingdom (that is, incomes of over £2,070 p.a.) accounted for 11.7 per cent of all personal income before tax; in 1955 the top 100,000 accounted for only 5.3 per cent, and the share of the top million fell from 21.5 per cent to 12.3 per cent. But the main beneficiaries were the middling groups, the second 5 million, not the poor. The bottom 12 million out of a total occupied population of around 22 million were earning under £123 a year in 1938 and under £510 a year in 1955, and their share of personal income barely increased. Even so, there were some improvements in their relative position after the Second World War, as their real incomes (before tax) rose by 24 per cent between 1949 and 1955 compared with only 14 per cent for the top 10 million incomes.

In this sense, the 1950s saw the advent of the affluent worker, leading to the so-called 'never-had-it-so-good' years of the late 1950s and 1960s. Against a background of Conservative political success, sociologists began to debate whether affluence had now undermined the labour movement and brought an end to the old class society. The arguments put forward were threefold: first, that the changing structure of the national economy had facilitated social mobility, thus weakening class barriers; second, that the working class as workers were achieving levels of consumption previously regarded as attainable only by the middle class, leading to a merging of the classes through the progressive *embourgeoisement* of the workers; and third, that the sharp edge of class had been removed from politics as the two main parties adopted similar, moderate policies, with the Conservatives capturing political support from working people and undermining the ability of the Labour Party to win elections. Against these arguments others maintained that Britain had remained a class society throughout the years of affluence, and that the failure of the Labour Party had more to do with political ineptitude and the inadequacy of its response to a changing but still relevant class structure.

Social change and social mobility

The social-mobility thesis states that the class position of the working class is consolidated by shared experiences, but is disrupted by possibilities of mobility which turn individuals away from traditional family and community values towards individual aspiration and effort. So, increased opportunities for social mobility should undermine inherited class positions.

Britain in the 1950s and 1960s experienced a sustained period of economic growth. At the same time, with the decline of the old, basic industries the rise of new high-technology industries, and the expansion of the tertiary sector of the economy, the nature of the workforce was changing. Whereas in 1946 almost half of net national income was in the form of wages and a little under a quarter in the form of salaries, in 1968 wages accounted for two-fifths while salaries had risen to a third. With increased educational provision and more 'room at the top', individuals – especially men – were able to progress to higher-status jobs than those held by their parents. In the early 1960s recruitment to non-manual occupations was fairly evenly divided between those from non-manual backgrounds and those from manual backgrounds. Britain seemed to have become a meritocracy, with careers open to talent. A generation later, the 1984 British Social Attitudes Survey showed that 29 per cent of those asked thought they were of a higher social class than their parents; 40 per cent of those who said they were middle-class thought their parents were working-class.

However, seen from another point of view the picture looks rather different. Over 80 per cent of manual workers came from manual backgrounds, and three-quarters of the sons of manual workers went into manual work themselves. Similarly, around two-thirds of the sons of non-manual fathers themselves found non-manual work. Public perceptions tended to be influenced by the experiences of a minority, but the odds remained heavily in favour of sons finding employment in the same category as their fathers. Where opportunities for upward mobility are limited by the disadvantages inherent in a class position, the effect of new opportunities that are not targeted towards the poor can be the reverse of what might be expected. The middle class has, for example, shown itself far more adept than the working class at exploiting the greater educational opportunities made available to all since 1944. Thus a policy of creating social mobility through education can result in the reverse of what is intended unless equality of condition is also established. This was argued by David Glass in the early 1950s, and its consequences were confirmed by John Goldthorpe at the end of the 1970s.[34] In so far as social mobility can be assumed from occupational mobility, the evidence would appear to suggest that the economic opportunities and social legislation of the post-Second-World-War period did not move Britain significantly nearer the goal of a classless society.

Nevertheless, if social mobility has not narrowed the gap between the classes, it is possible to argue that the changing structure of employment has done so, as 'producers by hand and brain' have recognised a common class position. One of the earliest and most scathing critics of this interpretation was the economist J. K. Galbraith. In *The Affluent Society*, published in 1958, he firmly rejected 'the grand homogeneity of work', and distinguished two clear class positions. The first corresponded to the working class:

> For some, and probably a majority, it [work] remains a stint to be performed. It may be preferable, especially in the context of social attitudes towards production, to doing nothing. Nevertheless it is fatiguing or monotonous or, at a minimum, a source of no particular pleasure. The reward rests not in the task but in the pay.[35]

The second which, for want of a better title, he called 'the New Class' – by which he meant the educated middle class – had quite a different attitude:

> It is taken for granted that it [work] will be enjoyable. If it is not, this is a source of deep dissatisfaction or frustration. . . . One insults the business executive or the scientist by suggesting that his principal motivation in life is the pay he receives. Pay is not unimportant. Among other things it is a prime index of prestige. Prestige – the respect, regard and esteem of others – is in turn one of the more important sources of satisfaction associated with this kind of work. But, in general, those who do this kind of work expect to contribute their best regardless of compensation.[36]

Galbraith's two classes in fact represented the two extremes of the census classification: his working class corresponded to social classes IV and V, the semi-skilled and unskilled, who were shrinking as a proportion of the working population; and his 'new class' was social classes I and II, those in professional and intermediate occupations, which were expanding. The division between these two extremes was real enough in the 1950s, and recruitment figures into higher education since then might suggest that opportunities for upward social mobility into the 'new class' – which constitutes the new élite – have remained unequal. In 1955 around 60 per cent of male and 70 per cent of female admissions to university from England and Scotland (the figures were about 10 per cent lower for

Wales) came from social classes I and II, which in 1951 constituted under 20 per cent of the general population. In 1984, using the different social categories employed by the Universities Central Council on Admissions, 66.8 per cent of applicants and 70.3 per cent of acceptances at British universities came from the professional and intermediate classes, and these figures were also representative of A-Level performances at school. Despite an expansion in higher education in the 1980s and early 1990s, the proportion from the higher social classes applying to the traditional universities in 1992–3 had fallen only to 61.2 per cent, and in the less élitist former-polytechnic/new-university sector the figure was still 55.6 per cent – around twice what one would have expected if opportunities had been equal. At the same time, examination achievements at school continued to follow the same rank order as the social class of the student. Far from creating an open meritocracy, education appeared to have ensured the consolidation of the new élite through the admission of only limited numbers of the lower classes into the traditional preserves of the higher.

Though Galbraith's view of the 'new class' has much to commend it, it could be argued, on the contrary, that the changing nature of work since the 1950s has blurred some of the distinctions he made between the waged and the salaried, especially in the middle ground of skilled white- and blue-collar workers in social class III. Since the Second World War increasing numbers of 'middle-class' workers have joined trade unions affiliated to the TUC: the Scientific Workers joined during the war; the Civil Servants in 1946; NALGO (National and Local Government Officers) followed in 1965; and the National Union of Teachers in 1970. Even a once-professional body like the Association of University Teachers began to adopt 'trade union attitudes' in the 1970s, and joined the TUC in 1976 to defend its members' interests.

The rise of this 'white-collar' militancy has confused the definition of class in modern Britain. It can be seen, in part, as a response to the narrowing of differentials between skilled manual and some groups of white-collar workers brought about by the success of industrial action on behalf of manual workers in the 1950s and 1960s, and in part as a product of the changing role of the state in the economy. With a steady expansion in the state's activities, not only indirectly through nationalisation of the basic industries, but also directly through the growth of the education, health and civil services, the government became in the post-war years paymaster to an increasing proportion of the workforce. Throughout the 1960s and 1970s governments sought a means of controlling wage-settlements, and what they failed to achieve as governments they attempted to do as employers. White-collar workers grew correspondingly militant in defence of their salaries and status, as non-manual and manual workers found themselves moving into a common employment position.

Perhaps the strongest indication of this consolidation of a new working class of producers by hand and brain has been the appearance of employment schemes which do not recognise traditional boundaries between blue- and white-collar work. The first major example of this came with the adoption of Japanese working practices at the new Sunderland plant of the motor car manufacturer, Nissan, where traditional 'staff'/'worker' status differences of dress and canteen facilities were abandoned in 1986; but more significant was the adoption in 1997 of a single employment scheme for all workers in local government.

Nevertheless, to argue that manual work no longer provides an adequate marker for what might be termed the 'working class' is not to assert the absence of all differences of class in British society. The distinctions made by Galbraith were related to work, but were expressed also in cultural form. In this respect his argument is reinforced by the critique offered by Goldthorpe and his associates of the *embourgeoisement* thesis.

The embourgeoisement *thesis*

The *embourgeoisement* thesis argues that class divisions have been diminished in the second half of the twentieth century not so much by the promotion of individual members of the working class into the middle class as by the transformation of the working class into a part of the middle class – the reverse of the 'by hand and brain' thesis. Much of the evidence for this is subjective, or concentrates on levels of conspicuous consumption. It was calculated in 1959 that, among the more prosperous half of the working class, 85 per cent of households had a television set, 44 per cent a washing machine, 16 per cent a refrigerator and 32 per cent a car. Research, largely conducted on new housing estates and in new towns, lent support to this picture of affluence and middle-class aspirations among the upper sections of the working class, but this fashionable interpretation did not go entirely unchallenged. An investigation conducted by Goldthorpe and others in the 1960s concluded that if class is studied as a pattern of relationships and attitudes, and not merely a matter of income and consumption, class positions are still clearly observable in modern British society.[37] Their findings may be summarised as follows:

> 1. The industrial worker 'remains a man who gains his livelihood through placing his labour at the disposal of an employer in return for wages, usually paid by the piece, hour or day'; his work may well be unpleasant and experienced only as labour; and his affluence may be highly dependent on overtime (and the earnings of his wife).[38]

This emphasises the continuing importance of the nature of the work experience in determining class. It also draws attention to one of the most common differences between the waged and the salaried, the latter frequently being expected to complete a task for a fixed remuneration without fixed hours or expectation of overtime pay. Thus the salaried person's working time may be unpredictable, but his or her income is not.

> 2. Although behavioural patterns may be modified on new housing estates and in new towns, 'affluence, and even residence in localities of a "middle-class" character, do not lead on, in any automatic way, to the integration of manual workers and their families into middle-class society'.[39]

Such behavioural patterns, it was argued, involve both norms and relationships. Working-class social norms include such things as a fatalistic acceptance of inequality, a belief in luck, a willingness to enjoy oneself while one can, and a sense of safety through group loyalty. By contrast, middle-class social norms include an acceptance of hierarchy coupled with a belief that the individual can and should climb it, a willingness to make long-term plans for one's children, a preparedness to make present sacrifices to achieve long-term goals, and a trust in self-reliance. Working-class relationships put great emphasis on kinship and neighbourhood; socialising takes place mainly outside the home in public house or working-men's club and there are often separate male and female networks of conviviality. Middle-class relationships are more privatised and emphasise the centrality of the nuclear family; entertaining (including drinking) takes place within the home, though leisure may take the form of subscriptions to certain kinds of societies which are commonly regarded (sometimes mistakenly) as belonging exclusively to the middle class, such as golf and tennis clubs. Such descriptions of class behaviour are, of course, abstractions, but the contention is that they state the essence of their respective classes more clearly than the outward signs of pay-packet and conspicuous consumption.

> 3. Despite aspirations to greater material consumption, 'our respondents' orientations to the future were still conditioned by their unchanged class situation as producers'.[40]

In other words, the values and norms of each class are not matters for moralising, but arise out of the fundamental conditions of labour. For example, the lack of a 'future-time perspective' among the working classes arises directly out of the uncertainty of employment and earning capacity. The middle-class observer can lament the illogicality of such uncertainty not leading to frugality, but he does this from the fortunate position of having a regular (perhaps incremental) salary, generous sick-pay arrangements and an assured (index-linked) pension.

Since the late 1960s, when Goldthorpe's team published their findings, events have borne out their conclusions. In 1970 the average weekly income of a male manual worker was 75.5 per cent of that of the male non-manual worker; in 1984 it had fallen to 73.1 per cent and was down to 69.7 per cent a decade later. Doctors who earned three times as much as cleaners in 1981 were earning four times as much in 1996. Given that unemployment, which has risen sharply, though cyclically, from the 1960s has affected the lowest social classes most severely, the picture of Britain by the mid-1990s is one of widening rather than narrowing social divisions. In the 1970s the Labour government attempted through the introduction of comprehensive schools to eliminate those social class distinctions in education which appeared to limit the opportunities for working-class children to achieve social mobility; and in the 1980s the Conservative government attempted to spread more widely both house and share ownership to promote *embourgeoisement* and middle-class values; but neither made any significant impact on the fundamental inequalities of wealth and income. In 1976 the top 20 per cent of households enjoyed 38.1 per cent of disposable income, the top 40 per cent enjoyed 62.1 per cent, and the bottom 40 per cent only 19.6 per cent. In 1994–5 the comparable figures were: top 20 per cent – 39.8 per cent; top 40 per cent – 64.2 per cent; and bottom 40 per cent – 18.6 per cent. The distribution of wealth was virtually unchanged, with the top 50 per cent of people owning over 90 per cent of marketable wealth. Though those male workers who were in work were better off in real terms than ever before, their relative positions – except in relation to the unemployed – had not advanced, and the traditional boundaries of class were showing little evidence of withering away.

The conclusion to this debate about whether Britain has become a classless society would therefore appear to be that it has not. The structure of society and the meaning of class have retained a familiar appearance whilst changing in outward appearance. The class structure of modern Britain would appear to have two, partly contradictory, aspects. One, in classic Marxist fashion, shows 'producers by hand and brain' sharing a common class position when at work, dependent on wages and salaries, and in potential conflict with their employers (including the state). The other rests on older distinctions of status, between non-manual and manual labour and the culture which this distinction still generates. Above this 'working-class' section of society sits an educated élite. Beneath it lies an underclass of the poor. This could describe society in any period covered in this book. The idea of a working class united as wage labour but divided by status and culture is a very familiar one; only its details are different.

Class, party and the governing élite since 1951

This interpretation of the structure of British society in the second half of the twentieth century has implications for class-based accounts of party politics. In the first half of the century the Labour Party was, in its support and composition, overwhelmingly the party of the working class, but never the party of the whole working class. So, although the majority of voters belonged to social classes III, IV and V, Labour was barely able to retain power in the general election of 1950, and lost it a year later, despite taking its largest ever share of the vote (48.8 per cent). Thereafter support for Labour gradually declined, down to 43.8 per cent in 1959. A brief recovery to 47.9 per cent in 1966 was then followed by a new fall, to 36.9 per cent in 1979 and only 27.6 per cent in 1983 – the lowest level of support for Labour since 1918. Individual membership of the Party fell from over a million in 1952 to under 300,000 in 1993. Three explanations – not mutually exclusive – could be offered for this decline in support for the party of Labour: it was losing its appeal to working people; the number of people who regarded themselves as working-class and identified with Labour was shrinking; or class was ceasing to be relevant in modern British society.

In the 1960s the debate about class and politics focused on the three successive Conservative victories at the polls, in 1951, 1955 and 1959, each with increasing majorities, followed by a narrow Labour victory in 1964 due more to a revival in Liberal than in Labour fortunes. It was argued that class politics had been replaced by the politics of consensus – what was known as 'Butskellism' after the leading liberal Tory, R. A. Butler, and the leader of the Labour Party until his death in 1963, Hugh Gaitskell. The Conservatives had accepted the Welfare State and had successfully cultivated the moderate middle ground of politics. With the working class in apparent decline, the Labour Party seemed redundant, and analysts prepared to write its obituary notices.

In fact, they were acting somewhat prematurely. For a start, fluctuations in the total Labour vote over the period were far less than changes in the numbers of MPs suggest, so the parliamentary decline of Labour did not necessarily reflect major social change in the country. Second, during the years of apparent Labour decline the level of support for trade unionism was rising, reaching a peak of 49.94 per cent of the total full-time employed population in 1979, so the size of organised labour was not at this time declining either. Only after 1979 did the proportion of union members fall, and this can probably be attributed as much or more to unemployment and the declining male labour force as it can to *embourgeoisement*. Indeed, the level of trade-union membership continued to fall throughout the 1980s even when electoral support for Labour was recovering – to 30.8 per cent at the 1987 general election and 35.2 per cent in 1992. This would appear to suggest a weak and declining connection between organised labour as expressed in the trade union movement and the Labour Party – not so much a decline of class as a decline of Labour as a class party. In 1974 only 55 per cent of trade unionists voted Labour, and this was down to 46 per cent in 1992.

Despite this, when Goldthorpe and his colleagues made their study of affluent workers in the 1960s they found support for the Labour Party as the party of the 'ordinary working man' surprisingly strong.[41] This was particularly marked in traditional Labour areas – mining villages and centres of heavy industry. At no time after the Second World War did Labour fail to win a clear majority of seats in the North of England, Wales and (after 1955) Scotland. But Labour was contracting to its heartlands, losing ground in London, the Midlands and – above all – in the South of England. This made it more, not less, of a class party in the 1980s.

An analysis of party support shows the extent to which party politics retained their class bias in post-war Britain. In 1966 a National Opinion Poll found that, whereas Conservative support rose with the social order, Labour support fell: 72 per cent of middle-class voters were Conservatives compared with 15.5 per cent Labour and 11.4 per cent Liberal; but 65.2 per cent of the unskilled voted Labour, compared with 26.6 per cent Conservative and 6.6 per cent Liberal. Labour took approximately two voters for every one Conservative voter among the skilled working class, and vice versa among the lower-middle class. Though Labour was never, therefore, the sole political party of the working class, it was the predominant party of that class with a leaven from the higher classes. The Conservatives were overwhelmingly the party of the smaller upper-middle class, but their electoral success rested on their ability to hold the majority of lower-middle-class votes and to take also a substantial minority of working-class votes, including, in 1992, 30 per cent of unskilled and casual workers.

The electoral failures of the Labour Party between 1979 and 1992 were due therefore in part to its failure to appeal to a section of traditional labour, but more to the decline of that constituency and the failure of Labour to win a compensating increase in support from the higher social classes. If Labour could project itself only as the party of manual labour at a time when 'white-collar' employment was expanding and 'blue-collar' employment contracting, then it would be unlikely ever to rival the broader appeal of the Conservative Party, projected not as a party of class but as the party of the nation. After 1992, therefore, the Labour Party came to the conclusion that, like the Democratic Party in the United States, it would have to abandon its crumbling and ambiguous basis in organised manual male labour, and seek support from those voters who, in the 1950s and even more emphatically in the 1980s, had asserted their desire for individual affluence uninhibited by collectivist political dogma. Whereas in the 1980s Labour had yielded the 'middle ground' of politics to the Conservatives, in the 1990s it made an effort to regain it by adopting policies and positions not radically different in appearance from those of the Conservatives on sensitive issues such as the economy, taxation and law and order. Taking its diminishing class support in organised labour for granted, and hoping to pick up working-class Conservative support, it made an unashamed bid to shed its image as a class party in order to achieve political power. In 1997 it finally succeeded, taking 44 per cent of the vote and re-establishing itself as the party of urban areas in southern England as well as in its traditional strongholds in industrial Wales, Scotland, the English Midlands and the North.

However, this appeal beyond class to what was termed 'middle England' (in both the geographical and class sense) did not mean that socially the Labour Party had become indistinguishable from the Conservative Party. The paradox is that, whilst Labour was most successful, in both 1966 and 1997, when it presented itself as a modern, broadly based party, it nevertheless still remained a socially distinct party. In 1997, though Labour won support from all social groups, the Conservatives retained the confidence of a majority of voters in the top two social groups, with Labour gaining an increasing lead further down the social order.

The trend for the Parliamentary Labour Party to become more like a traditional élite party, though, continued through the second half of the twentieth century, although significant differences still existed between the social identities of the parties as suggested by the educational and occupational backgrounds of their Members of Parliament. Though the largest occupational groups in each party were the professions (around 45 per cent of Conservatives and 40 per cent of Labour in the Parliaments of 1951–70), about a third of Conservatives were businessmen and a third of Labour were manual workers in origin. This pattern was only slowly changing. By the election of 1992, when professionals accounted for 39 per cent of Conservatives and 42 per cent of Labour, the Conservatives were still 38 per cent business and Labour still 22 per cent manual workers; but with the MPs first elected to support Labour in 1997, the professional middle-class complexion of the party was firmly established. Of 230 new MPs, only 10 came from what might be called the 'old' working class of skilled and unskilled manual workers, and only 28 had a background in trade-union bureaucracy, compared with 104 who had previously been lecturers and teachers. Over all, 30 per cent of the Parliamentary Labour Party in 1997 had a background in education. On the other hand, only 16 of the new MPs were company directors, although a third of all Labour MPs in the 1997 Parliament had experience in the world of business.[42]

If the parties could no longer be said to be entirely rooted in class, they still reflected it; and in their leaderships they represented old and new élites. The Conservative Party profile remained very traditional, recruiting its Members of Parliament from a very narrow base in the public schools and the universities of Oxford and Cambridge. In October 1974 74.6 per cent of Conservative MPs had attended public school and 55.1 per cent had attended the ancient English universities. In 1983 this had fallen to 64.1 per cent educated at public schools and 45.7 per cent at Oxford or Cambridge, although the university-educated level had increased overall to 71.7 per cent. By 1992 the proportions had scarcely changed. Conservative Cabinets which, between 1916 and 1955, were divided into 31.6 per cent aristocratic and 65.3 per cent middle-class became more middle class (74 per cent) between 1955 and 1984, but still retained an aristocratic element (18.1 per cent).

Labour during the same period gave some appearance of a party shaking off its working-class roots and also becoming more firmly a party of the middle class, with 55.7 per cent university-educated – but only 20.8 per cent at Oxbridge – in October 1974. The 1983 election suggested some reversal in this trend, largely the result of the disastrous electoral showing of the party in that year, and in subsequent elections the trend was resumed. In 1992 61 per cent of successful Labour candidates had been to university (16.2 per cent to Oxbridge) and 14 per cent had been to public school. In 1997, 57 per cent were university-educated (16.2 per cent at Oxbridge). Labour Cabinets were also becoming more middle-class. Whereas between 1916 and 1955 55.3 per cent of Cabinet ministers were working-class and only 38.4 per cent middle-class, between 1955 and 1979 the middle class was in a small majority – 44.6 per cent to 41 per cent.

The difference between the parties in Parliament by the 1990s was not so obviously a matter of class as it had been earlier in the century, but the educational experience of their members still suggested a significant difference. Conservative MPs in 1992 were characterised by public school and Oxbridge (49 per cent) while Labour MPs had attended state secondary schools and then other universities (47 per cent). This difference was important, and reflected changes in the education system rather than in the social origins of Labour. The Labour Party by 1992 was led by a new meritocracy, promoted through the system of selective grammar schools established after the Second World War followed by university expansion in the 1960s. The Conservative Party, by contrast, was still dominated by an older élite educated in traditional institutions. Moreover, the old élite was male; the new élite in 1997 contained a significant number of women – 119 out of 659. All but 18 of these represented Labour.

This picture of contrasting élites is confirmed by a comparison of the educational background of the Conservative and Labour Cabinets of 1997. Despite the fact that the leader of each party conformed to the social profile expected of the other, those profiles were distinct in that the routes by which their leading members had ascended to the highest positions in British politics were very different. Though the fathers of Conservative Cabinet members ranged from a railway man (Lord Mackay, the Lord Chancellor) to the 12th Earl of Waldegrave (William Waldegrave, Chief Secretary to the Treasury), their educational experiences were remarkably similar. Of the five Cabinet members who had not been to a public or independent school (as defined by the schools' status in 1996), only two had not gone on to Oxbridge. One of these was the Scottish Secretary, who had attended St Andrews; the other was the Prime Minister, John

Major, who had left school at 16. In addition to these latter, only four others in the Cabinet had not been to Oxbridge: two Scots who went to Scottish universities, one Ulsterman who attended Queen's, Belfast, and one English woman who went from her independent girls' school to the new University of Essex.

By contrast, of the 22 Labour men and women holding Cabinet positions in 1997 only nine had attended independent schools, four of them in Scotland. Of these, only three had gone on to Oxbridge as undergraduates, one of them the party leader, Tony Blair. The pattern of higher education was as diverse as the Conservatives' was uniform, with only Edinburgh (three graduates) and Durham, Glasgow and Oxford (two each) appearing more than once. Of the three who had not gone into higher education on or shortly after leaving school, two had graduated subsequently as mature students. In their previous occupations, seven had been in the legal profession, seven in education, and only two came from a trade union background. Five were women, compared with two in the previous Conservative Cabinet, but none in either party came from the ethnic minority groups which registered a small but enlarged presence in the 1997 Parliament.

Educational differences in part reflect social differences in an earlier generation, and a study of the parental occupations of Cabinet members would show a wider gap between the parties than their own occupations do, with several Labour Cabinet ministers coming from skilled working-class and lower-middle-class homes. But this suggests that social mobility through education is likely in the longer term to weaken still further the distinction between the parties in Parliament until, perhaps, as in the nineteenth century, both will be drawn from a common social élite, Galbraith's 'new class', the richer of Disraeli's Two Nations. Though party-identification surveys suggest that the two main British parties still correspond to perceptions of class, neither party can afford to identify itself solely with those supporters alone. But the claim that Britain is therefore moving towards a classless society at the end of the twentieth century must be viewed with caution. Class is still a social reality, although by no means the only one. Britain remains a society divided in the distribution of wealth, patterns of consumption and access to education, but it is a division only partly reflected in the party allegiances of those who choose to participate in the electoral system, and it is ceasing to form the basis for division between those of different parties who are elected to Parliament, and between those who lead them in government.

Notes

1. J. Cannon, *Aristocratic Century: The Peerage in Eighteenth-Century England* (Cambridge, 1984).

2. H. Mayhew, *London Labour and the London Poor* (4 vols., 1861–2, repr. New York, 1968), iv, p. 12.
3. J. M. Ludlow and L. Jones, *Progress of the Working Class, 1832–1867* (1867; reprinted Clifton, NJ, 1968), p. 3.
4. Ludlow and Jones, *Progress*, pp. 4–5.
5. R. Roberts, *The Classic Slum* (Manchester, 1971; republished Harmondsworth, 1973), p. 19.
6. C. Booth, *Life and Labour of the People of London*, vol. i: *East, Central and South London* (1892), p. 33.
7. Booth, *Life and Labour*, p. 99.
8. T. Carlyle, *Chartism* (1839) in *Selected Writings* (Harmondsworth, 1971), p. 188.
9. Carlyle, *Chartism*, p. 199.
10. K. Marx, *The 18th Brumaire of Louis Bonaparte* (1852), p. 334 in K. Marx and F. Engels, *Selected Works* (2 vols., Moscow, 1962), i, pp. 243–344.
11. H. Perkin, *The Origins of Modern English Society, 1780–1880* (1969).
12. For a brief exposition of this thesis, see E. P. Thompson, 'Class Conflict without Class', *Social History*, 3(1) (May 1978), pp. 133–65.
13. P. Joyce, *Visions of the People: Industrial England and the Question of Class, 1840–1914* (Cambridge, 1991).
14. For a discussion of these issues, see Anna Clark, *The Struggle for the Breeches: Gender and the Making of the British Working Class* (1995).
15. R. Owen, *Observations on the Effect of The Manufacturing System* (1815).
16. F. Engels, *Condition of the Working Class in England* (1845), new edn., ed. V. Kiernan (Harmondsworth, 1987), p. 50.
17. W. D. Rubinstein, *Men of Property: The Very Wealthy in Britain since the Industrial Revolution* (1981), p. 61.
18. W. J. Reader, *Professional Men: The Rise of the Professional Classes in Nineteenth-Century England* (1966), p. 47.
19. G. A. Williams, 'The Concept of "Egemonia" in the Thought of Antonio Gramsci: Some Notes on Interpretation', *Journal of the History of Ideas*, 21 (1960), pp. 586–99.
20. H. J. Perkin, *The Origins of Modern English Society*, ch. ix.
21. Roberts, *The Classic Slum*, p. 28.
22. G. Stedman Jones, 'Working-Class Culture and Working-Class Politics in London, 1870–1900: Notes on the Remaking of a Working Class', in *Languages of Class* (Cambridge, 1983), pp. 179–238.
23. Roberts, *The Classic Slum*, p. 18.
24. Roberts, *The Classic Slum*, p. 19.
25. John Cannon, *Aristocratic Century*, p. 114.
26. W. O. Aydelotte, 'The Business Interests of the Gentry in the Parliament of 1841–47', in G. Kitson Clark, *Making of Victorian England* (1962), Appendix, pp. 290–305.
27. W. L. Guttsman, *The British Political Élite* (1965), p. 83.
28. *Annual Register* (1839), p. 304.
29. *Sheffield Mercury*, 8 October 1825, quoted in S. and B. Webb, *The History of Trade Unionism* (1894; new edn., 1920), p. 105.
30. J. Smith, 'The Strike of 1825', in D. G. Wright and J. A. Jowitt, *Victorian Bradford* (Bradford, 1981), pp. 63–79.
31. Mayhew, *London Labour*, i, p. 20.
32. S. and B. Webb, *History of Trade Unionism*, ch. 4.
33. National Union of General and Municipal Workers, *Journal* (June 1955), as given in J. T. Ward and W. H. Fraser (eds.), *Workers and Employers: Documents on Trade Unions and Industrial Relations in Britain since the Eighteenth Century* (1980), p. 303.

34. D. Glass (ed.), *Social Mobility in Britain* (1954); J. Goldthorpe, *Social Mobility and Class Structure in Modern Britain* (Oxford, 1980, 2nd edn., 1987).
35. J. K. Galbraith, *The Affluent Society* (1958; republished Harmondsworth, 1962), p. 274.
36. Galbraith, *The Affluent Society*, p. 275.
37. J. H. Goldthorpe, D. Lockwood, F. Bechhofer and J. Platt, *The Affluent Worker* (3 vols., Cambridge, 1968–9).
38. Goldthorpe *et al.*, *The Affluent Worker*, vol. iii, pp. 157–8.
39. Goldthorpe *et al.*, *The Affluent Worker*, vol. iii, pp. 158–9.
40. Goldthorpe *et al.*, *The Affluent Worker*, vol. iii, p. 159.
41. Goldthorpe *et al.*, *The Affluent Worker*, vol. iii, p. 172.
42. D. Butler and D. Kavanagh, *The British General Election of 1992* (1992), p. 226. As a full analysis of the 1997 results is not available at the time of writing, details have been taken from the *Observer*, 4 May 1997.

4

Poverty and welfare

Poverty

In a universe conceived of as a hierarchy dependent on the sublime Creator, equality was intellectually and emotionally inconceivable. Within the social order there had to be poor people, for poverty was part of the permanent condition of mankind. God – or Fate – was the origin of poverty and most poor people appeared to accept their lot with resignation. Poverty was so much a part of their everyday experience. The families of manual workers were always vulnerable to unemployment, sickness, old age or the death of a breadwinner, which reduced them to pauperism and made them temporarily dependent upon the Christian charity of their superiors. Indeed, how could Christians exercise a proper charity without the poor? So each depended upon each within the natural order.

Sometimes contemporaries suspected that the poor brought hardship on themselves through unnecessary human weakness and a moral failure which would only be aggravated by charitable support. These people were not the 'deserving poor', and their treatment was very different. Only towards the end of the nineteenth century was a serious attempt made to understand the true nature of poverty in other than in religious and moral terms. As Seebohm Rowntree pointed out in his study of York, many – possibly most – members of the manual working class were liable to descend into pauperism at particular times in the life cycle: as young children, when they in turn had families of young children, and in old age.[1] Extreme poverty was to this extent foreseeable, and could therefore in theory be guarded against by the prudent – except that the most common cause of chronic poverty was low wages, which made prudence impossible. For most men and women before the early twentieth century the war against poverty was one of long attrition, often successfully fought in the prime of life but ending in the defeat of an early death or pauperism in old age. Interludes of relative prosperity were seized upon by families as unexpected gifts, to be enjoyed while they lasted.

The experiences of those poor men and women who lived in days beyond the reach of oral history are difficult to recapture, and varied widely according to age, occupation, sex, time and place. Nevertheless, generalisations must be made. In the later eighteenth and nineteenth centuries the broad picture is of a large mass of people – possibly between a third and a half of the total population at any one time – struggling to survive on less than adequate incomes, malnourished, badly housed and ill-clothed, always liable to the ravages of sickness and disease. Nevertheless, although some were worse off than their parents' generation had been, most were experiencing improvement by the 1840s, if not before – or, at least, the residuum in the direst poverty was shrinking as the benefits of economic growth and, in the twentieth century, state welfare reached them for the first time.

The rural poor

In the countryside, where the majority of people lived until the second half of the nineteenth century, life was hard and, for the agricultural worker, was probably getting harder between the 1780s and the 1840s. The agricultural worker existed not only in a low-wage economy, but family incomes were further depressed by under-employment and seasonal unemployment. Chronic poverty in good times meant there was no slack to be taken up in hard times during prolonged periods of bad weather or high food prices.

The labourer's real wages were probably rising in many parts of the country during the second half of the eighteenth century, but the inflationary years at the end of the century and in the first two decades of the nineteenth saw wages fall rapidly behind prices, particularly in the Midlands and South. During the crisis years of 1795, 1800–01 and 1811–12 the agencies of relief were strained almost to breaking-point. Only after 1820 did prices fall appreciably, with corn reaching 43*s*. (£2.15) a quarter in 1822, the lowest since the start of the French Wars in 1793. Then for a brief time wages ran ahead of inflation as conditions generally improved, but in the countryside the relationship between wages, prices and conditions was never as simple as in the towns. High prices meant agricultural prosperity and increased employment opportunities; low prices meant depression which soon filtered through from the farmers to their labourers. Consequently, real wages in the 1820s did not recover to the levels which been common before the war. However, wages were only one ingredient in the agricultural worker's standard of living, and there is much evidence to suggest that, particularly in the south of England, overall conditions were deteriorating in the first half of the nineteenth century, pauperising the agricultural labourer.

This is not to say that conditions in the eighteenth century, or elsewhere in the country, were good. In lowland Scotland, Alexander Somerville's grandparents in the mid-eighteenth century lived in a series of windowless hovels to which they carried their own window as they moved from place to place. Things had not changed much when Somerville himself was born in 1811 in circumstances common among the agricultural poor, in one of

> a row of shabby-looking tile sheds . . . about twelve feet by fourteen, and not so high in the walls as will allow a man to get in without stooping. . . . without ceiling, or anything beneath the bare tiles of the roof; without a floor save the common clay; without a cupboard or recess of any kind; no grate but the iron bars which the tenants carried to it, built up and took away when they left it; with no partition of any kind save what the beds made; with no window save four small panes on one side.[2]

The rent for this dwelling was his mother's labour, reaping the crops at harvest time and carrying the sheaves from the stackyard to the barn during the winter – a task of heavy labour which she performed whilst at an advanced stage of pregnancy (Somerville was born in March). Elsewhere the roofs might be of thatch or turf, and the walls of unbound stone, or wattle and mud, depending on the availability of local building materials. Edwin Chadwick described one such mud house in the Vale of Aylesbury in 1842:

> The vegetable substances mixed with the mud to make it bind, rapidly decompose, leaving the walls porous. The earth of the floor is full of vegetable matter, and from there being nothing to cut off its contact from the surrounding mould, it is peculiarly liable to damp.[3]

Such conditions, however repugnant to modern taste, were all too familiar in the eighteenth and nineteenth centuries.

Evidence suggests that a general deterioration took place in the standard of living of the agricultural worker from the 1780s. Not only did the benefits of high prices not pass to the workers, but enclosure, changes in terms of employment and a decline in alternative sources of income all contributed to the worsening plight of many of the rural poor. Enclosure of commons and wastes (see above, pages 1–3) deprived many of access to free pasturage for a cow or a pig, free kindling and possibly a vegetable patch, while the decline in domestic handicrafts, to which growing numbers had turned in the later eighteenth century, made the poor increasingly dependent on agricultural work. At the same time, annual hirings began to give way in the southern counties to hirings for shorter periods of a few months or even a few weeks: in the south-eastern counties in the early nineteenth century as many as 40 per cent of male hirings were for less than a full year compared with less than 10 per cent a generation earlier. With population growth and agricultural depression the problems of under-employment and seasonal unemployment were exacerbated. General labourers and women suffered most; specialist stockmen and rural craftsmen least. The north invariably fared better than the south.

Conditions eased only slowly and patchily from the 1840s, much depending upon the character of the local landlord, the prosperity of the area and the availability of alternative employment in neighbouring towns or on the railways. Gradually picturesque, damp and insanitary hovels gave way to brick or stone cottages, with the removal of the brick tax in 1850 and improved transportation of building materials along the railways, but boarded roofs and floors were still a novelty towards the end of the nineteenth century. Even when conditions did improve, they did not do so at the rate experienced in the towns, and those workers who could leave the villages did so. The flow became a torrent in the depression after 1879, and when Seebohm Rowntree turned his attention from the urban to the rural scene in 1913 he found the plight of the agricultural labourer far worse than that of his urban counterpart. Taking a weekly wage of £1 0*s.* 6*d.* (£1.02½) as the minimum necessary to maintain a family of five above the poverty line, Rowntree and Kendall found this average actually achieved in only five counties in England and Wales – Westmorland, Durham, Northumberland, Lancashire and Derbyshire. Even allowing for the higher level of family wages, the generally low level of cottage rents and the value of the produce of an allotment or garden, they were driven to the conclusion that 'the wage paid by farmers to agricultural labourers is, in the vast majority of cases, insufficient to maintain a family of average size in a state of mere physical efficiency'.[4] As George Bourne wrote around the same time from personal experience:

> Of poverty, with its attendant sicknesses and neglects, there has never been any end to the tales, while the desolations due to accidents in the day's work . . . have become almost commonplace. In short, there is no sentimentality about the village life. Could its annals be written they would make no idyll; they would be too much stained by tragedy, vice and misery.[5]

Such conditions were only slowly ended in the twentieth century, with the transformation of the countryside and of agriculture as an industry. Even so, agricultural workers have remained among the lowest-paid and most disadvantaged of skilled workers.

Low pay was reflected not only in poor housing but also in the diet of the rural poor. For the ideal countryman's diet of home-baked bread, meat and beer William Cobbett calculated in the 1820s that a man needed nearly £1 4*s*. 0*d*. (£1.20) a week to feed a family of five; actual earnings were less than half this figure. So the labourer was reduced to white baker's bread or potatoes, fat bacon and weak tea. There were marked regional differences. In Scotland and the North of England oats, barley, peas and potatoes were more common than in the south and more acceptable than to the southern labourer and the traditionalist Cobbett. The labourer's family must frequently have been saved from starvation by the cottage pig, the vegetable garden and a great deal of ingenuity. The supply of animal protein was low, especially in the south and east, where cheese was the main protein source. To have meat was a sign of prosperity, and to experience it twice a week was a rare luxury. 'Lor', bless you, we shouldn't know ourselves if we got meat,' one East Anglian told the *Morning Chronicle* reporter in 1849.[6] Bread and potatoes were the staple diet. Poaching was, not surprisingly, a common pastime, increasingly frequent in the years of distress after 1815.

In 1863 Dr Edward Smith conducted the first national food inquiry in Britain. He found that, despite the so-called period of mid-Victorian prosperity and the repeal of the Corn Laws, the agricultural worker was scarcely better off than he had been in the depression of the early nineteenth century. One contemporary recorded the plight of the labourer in the depressed South-West in 1872 as follows.

> The labourer breakfasts on tea-kettle broth, hot water poured on bread and flavoured with onions; dines on bread and hard cheese at 2*d*. a pound, with cider very washy and sour, and sups on potatoes or cabbage greased with a tiny bit of fat bacon. He seldom more than sees or smells butcher's meat. He is long-lived, but in the prime of life 'crippled up', i.e. disabled with rheumatism, the result of wet clothes with no fire to dry them by for use next morning, poor living and sour cider. Then he has to work for 4*s*. or 5*s*. per week, supplemented scantily from the rates, and, at last, to come for the rest of his life on the rates entirely. Such is, I will not call it the life, but the existence or vegetation of the Devon peasant.[7]

Thereafter things improved as real wages rose and the variety of diet improved, so that at the time of the Rowntree and Kendall survey bitter hunger had given way to mere malnourishment.

One example drawn from the 42 given in Rowntree and Kendall will serve to illustrate the life of a poor labourer's family in the countryside at the beginning of the twentieth century. It concerns a Bedfordshire family, the Barringtons, comprising a man, his wife, three sons aged 10, 8 and 7, and three daughters aged 13, 5 and 2. Mr Barrington worked at a rural lime-kiln and not on the land, but with earnings of 14*s*. (70p) a week he received 'the normal rural labourer's wage, even to the extent of being docked in wet weather'. His only source of additional income was his allotment which he rented for 6*s.* 6*d.* (32½p) a year. This yielded him about a seventh of his family's total food consumption. The family ate mainly bread and home-grown vegetables, especially potatoes, but in a typical week in October 1912 they did buy 4lbs. of flank beef which provided a little meat for Friday, Saturday and Sunday dinners, and for the man's breakfast each working day. 'In spite of this the nourishment is terribly inadequate.' There was a deficiency of 49 per cent of protein in the family's diet, and of 42 per cent of energy value.[8]

This case was typical of the 42 case-studies set out by Rowntree and Kendall. What was remarkable about these country diets was the low level of nutriment obtained from animal sources. Though meat appeared more widely on menus than it would have two generations earlier, it was often only a token amount, chiefly consumed by the man in the family; only 26 of the families in the study had fresh, full-cream milk, and they had less than a pint per day per family; 20 families consumed no butter, but only margarine or dripping; only 15 families bought cheese, the one-time staple food of the poor; and only two families consumed eggs as a meal. The lists of weekly expenditure also included little or nothing for clothing. Poor families were hard pressed to find the money for a new pair of working boots for the breadwinner, or shoes for the children. Many clothes were cast-offs handed on by richer neighbours, or sent by grown-up children in service or by relations in better circumstances.[9]

Urban poverty

Poverty in the towns has always attracted more attention than that scattered in the countryside, half-concealed from the untutored eye by rustic quaintness. In the towns the problems of the countryside were collected and compounded, yet poverty was not as widespread as in the villages. The cost of living, particularly of housing, was higher and all food had to be bought, but wages were on average double those of the rural worker throughout the nineteenth century. The urban worker had more money to spend, and more to spend it on.

Nevertheless, there were many extremely poor people who, like their counterparts in the countryside, were ill-paid, badly housed and under-nourished. Whether they were better or worse off is hard to judge. Town diets differed little from country diets before the mid-nineteenth century, though the food might not be as fresh. Housing, though bad, may not have been as bad as in the countryside: J. R. Wood of the Manchester Statistical Society informed Edwin Chadwick that he considered 50 per cent of the houses in Branston (Rutland) as 'comfortable' (i.e. not damp, or with bad flooring or ill-conditioned walls), compared with 72 per cent

Table 4.1 Average ages of death among the different classes, 1842

	Rutland	Wiltshire	Kendal	Bethnal Green
Gentry, professional	52	50	45	45
Tradesmen, farmers	41	48	39	26
Mechanics, labourers	38	33	34	16
	Leeds	**Liverpool**	**Bolton**	**Manchester**
Gentry, professional	44	35	34	38
Tradesmen, farmers	27	22	23	20
Mechanics, labourers	19	15	18	17

Source: E. Chadwick, *Report* (1842), pp. 223–7.

in Manchester and 95 per cent in the small cotton town of Dukinfield.[10] But public health was a greater problem in the towns, and life expectancy was consequently lower. The figures cited by Chadwick in 1842 are well-known but nonetheless striking, as given in Table 4.1.

The chances of survival varied not only between classes but between localities, the country town of Kendal lying between the extremes of the poor rural county and the large town and city. A member of the lower classes in the larger urban centre of the 1830s had the lowest life-chances of all, and there was a clear correlation between death rates and life in the worst districts of a large town. Chadwick attributed this largely to the prevalence of disease, but in ignorance of the many indirect as well as direct causes of disease he was not fully able to appreciate the wide range of factors which put the poorest families in the community 'at risk'.

The causes of poverty were cumulative. The low-wage-earner in the town as in the countryside might just survive if work were plentiful, if there were not too many young mouths to feed, and if health were good. Such conditions were seldom maintained for long. Rowntree found at the end of the nineteenth century that about half (52 per cent) of what he termed 'primary poverty' in York resulted from low wages, and approaching a quarter (22 per cent) from the largeness of the labourer's family. Less importance was attributed to the death of the chief wage-earner (16 per cent), illness or old age of the chief wage-earner (5 per cent), irregularity of work (3 per cent) and unemployment (2 per cent), reflecting the availability of low-paid but regular labouring work in York. Charles Booth's conclusions, derived from London and calculated differently, placed more emphasis on casual work and irregular earnings (43 per cent), highlighting the structure of employment in a large city and port, with a great deal of casual labour, employed by the hour or the day.[11]

Though the great majority of the lower classes could expect to experience poverty at some stage in their lives, how many such people were very poor at any one time is difficult to tell. Most historians who have attempted calculations in local studies have employed the definitions used in the classic studies of poverty undertaken by Booth, Rowntree and Bowley in the late nineteenth and early twentieth centuries. John Foster has concluded that in 1849 (a good year) 15 per cent of families in Oldham were below the poverty line, 28 per cent in Northampton and 23 per cent in South Shields; but in 1847 (a poor year) the level of poverty in Oldham had been as high as 41 per cent.[12] Michael Anderson's estimate for Preston in 1851 is that 9 per cent of families were 4*s.* (20p) a week or more below the poverty line, and that a further 22 per cent enjoyed an income which was less than 4*s.* above the poverty line. Moreover, half the families with children at home and not in employment fell into the category of under or only just above the poverty line.[13]

The daily routine of such people in the cotton towns of the early industrial revolution was described by Dr James Phillips Kay of the Ardwick and Ancoats Dispensary (better known by his later name of Sir James Kay-Shuttleworth) in a pamphlet entitled *The Moral and Physical Condition of the Working Classes*, published in 1832. Kay described the cotton worker, rising at five o'clock in the morning and breakfasting on tea or coffee with oatmeal porridge or bread before hastening to 12 hours of labour in the heated, enervating, dusty atmosphere of a cotton factory. The midday meal consisted of a mess of potatoes with lard or butter and a little fried fat bacon; and in the evening the last meal of the day similarly comprised potatoes, bread or oatmeal, eaten with weak tea with little or no milk. The workers' homes were frequently overcrowded, ill-ventilated, damp and dirty. Unlike the fine spinners, whose higher wages enabled them to maintain a higher standard of living, many of these poor factory workers were prone to disease, mental depression and moral and physical degeneration. Moralists from the higher classes were apt to point out the untypical few who rose above their surroundings, and to condemn with rather less sympathy than Kay those for whom the burdens of life could be lost only in the counter-productive consolations of drink.[14]

Observers of the industrial poor were attracted by Manchester in the first half of the nineteenth century, but for the sheer magnitude of its urban problems there was no escaping London with its 'vast, miserable, unmanageable masses of sunken people'.[15] Henry Mayhew in 1849–50 and Charles Booth in the 1880s were but two of a large number of observers who made expeditions into 'Darkest London' and publicised the scale of the city's problems. In fact, so shocking were their findings that it can be difficult to keep them in proportion when studying them. According to Stedman Jones's calculations based on Booth, around 10 per cent of the population of London in 1891 – 400,000 people – belonged to families with only casual or irregular earnings. Some of these were dock workers, but many were general labourers. Among the casual workers a labour surplus was constantly maintained for times when work was brisk.

Mayhew estimated in mid-century that about a quarter of coal whippers fell into this category, and in the 1890s the figures were no different. Casual working was endemic among a wide range of occupations, both skilled and unskilled, and with the decline of shipbuilding on the Thames and the growing importance of repair work, casual labour was in fact spreading in the later nineteenth century.[16]

The rapid growth of London's population, the decline of its industrial base and the deterioration of its oldest housing stock made life in the slums of the late nineteenth century as bad as if not worse than it had been earlier in the century. Though impressions are difficult to quantify and compare, there is a timelessness about A. S. Jasper's childhood recollection of visiting 'a block of broken-down tenement dwellings' in London in 1910:

> These tenements were set back well away from the road and they were rat-infested. To get to the front entrance, one had to cross a vast square of waste ground. In the summer, this was just a dust and rubbish heap. In the winter, it was a sea of mud and filth. The front doors of the tenements, or what was left of them, were always open. Dirty and half-starved children were playing in the filth and garbage that had collected outside. To get to the flat of my father's workmate we had to climb a flight of rickety stairs. As we passed the other flats on the way up, I could smell the nauseating odours that came from the rooms. I could hear some of the occupants swearing and rowing and children crying.[17]

Unlike the many middle-class visitors whose records of life in the slums betray their own prejudices and assumptions, Jasper was of the working class; his family was a little – but only a little – more respectable than those who inhabited the slum tenements. His experience could be replicated for any town in Britain, but the great ports of Liverpool and Glasgow were probably worse than most. Though the very poor were a small minority of the total population, the dividing line between the poor and the very poor was always and everywhere a narrow one, too easily crossed downwards and into pauperism. In varying degrees the majority of working people and their families faced the same problems: low wages, a shortage of good, cheap housing and under-employment or unemployment. These were to be prominent on the agenda of successive governments as they came to assume increasing responsibility for the welfare of the people in the twentieth century.

The standard of living debate

Faced with a description of the plight of the very poor at the end of the nineteenth century, the historian has difficulty in assessing overall trends in the standard of living. To begin with, though all the lower classes were potentially of the very poor, only a minority at any one time actually fell into that category. Despite the temptation to present vividly reported slum scenes as representing the experiences of the whole of the working class, and to assume that all slum-dwellers were alike, life was not as bleak as the worst scenes might suggest. The historian is concerned with those who benefited by as well as those who suffered from the twin processes of industrialisation and urbanisation. Furthermore, to trace a trend one needs comparable material over a period of time. Despite generalisations which have been made about wages and prices, data on which to base an analysis of changes in the standard of living are scarce, uneven and difficult to interpret. As a consequence historians have been much divided on the subject of whether life was getting better or worse for the people of a country which, as a whole, was undoubtedly getting richer.

In general, economic historians dealing in national statistics have been optimistic about rising standards before 1850, and in the long run their arguments have proved correct. Social historians have been more pessimistic, especially in the short run, emphasising the uneven distribution of the new wealth and the plight of the casualties of industrial change.

The argument for an increase in the standard of living of the majority of people in Britain between 1750 and 1850 has been put most influentially by R. M. Hartwell. His case is

> that, since average per capita income increased, since there was no trend in distribution against the workers, since (after 1815) prices fell while money wages remained constant, since per capita consumption of food and other consumer goods increased, and since government increasingly intervened in economic life to protect or raise living standards, then the real wages of the majority of English workers were rising in the years 1800 to 1850.[18]

All available economic models suggesting the contrary, he argues, fail to reconcile the facts of economic growth with the alleged immiseration of the workers. Furthermore, given the pressures of population growth the historian must also consider what would have happened to living standards had there not been an industrial revolution, however painful the social dislocation of its early years.

The pessimists, whose case has been cogently put by E. J. Hobsbawm, have not been convinced by this economic argument. Much of the evidence for prices and wage trends is of dubious value, given the extent of regional and industrial variations and imponderables such as the extent of unemployment, and the assertion that money wages remained constant after 1815 is open to dispute. Whether the material position of the population as a whole was worse or better before the industrial revolution is impossible to tell. The indications are that, except possibly in London, the physical environment was probably worse in the nineteenth century than in the eighteenth. Real wages were subject to considerable fluctuations. R. S. Neale's calculations for Bath suggest that the upward trend became marked only in the 1840s.[19] Evidence from diet supports this chronology, with tea and sugar consumption rising only in the later 1840s. Indeed, sugar consumption, which the contemporary statistician, G. R. Porter, regarded as 'a very useful test of the comparative conditions at different periods of the labouring classes', was lower in 1839–45 than at any time during the first half of the nineteenth century.[20]

The strongest evidence for accepting the pessimists' argument, though, is qualitative rather than quantitative, and the debate over the standard of living has remained inconclusive not only on account of the shortage of firm statistical evidence but also because the two sides have thought it relevant to ask and answer different questions about the period, the pessimists being far more interested in what the total qualitative experience of industrialisation meant to those who lived between about 1780 and 1850.

There has plainly been much to argue on both sides. On the one hand, it is undoubtedly true that for an increasing minority of the working population engaged in the new industrial processes real wages were rising, especially from the 1820s; and it is probably true that real wages overall were also rising, despite a setback between 1793 and 1820.[21] Britain was a richer country in 1850 than it had been in 1750, and output was increasing even faster than the population. The long series of data calculated by Wrigley and Schofield for life expectancy and death rates also suggest an unsteady but unmistakable improvement. On the other hand, there is plenty of contrary evidence of decline. Compared with the halcyon days of the late eighteenth century, when trade had been brisk and wages over 20*s.* (£1.00) a week, the standard of living of cotton handloom weavers in 1830 earning around 6*s.* (30p) a week had certainly fallen. And their numbers were hardly negligible or declining in 1830, when there were about a quarter of a million of them competing in a depressed and overstocked trade. Similarly, the plight of agricultural labourers, whose family incomes fell by as much as 30 per cent in many parts of southern England between the 1780s and the 1840s, cannot be ignored, however much their standard of living is concealed within an overall trend.

The temptation is for each side to select that evidence which best supports its case. The expansion of manufacturing employment contributed to an improvement in the standard of living, but the associated urbanisation led to some deterioration in living conditions as measured by mortality figures. Different points in the trade cycle tell a different story: in 1833–4 real wages were at their highest to date; in 1839–40 they were lower than in the early 1790s. With 60 per cent unemployment in the mills of Bolton in 1842, the pessimistic reports and accounts of that year, including Engels's *Condition of the Working Class in England* (1845), which draws on evidence from the depression years, are as unsurprising and untypical as the largely optimistic statistical surveys of G. R. Porter's *Progress of the Nation* (1836).

There is also the problem of what to compare with what and when. Pessimistic accounts sometime appear to assume a 'golden age' in the eighteenth century, from which early nineteenth-century standards had declined. This was not entirely myth, for times had been better in the eighteenth century for agricultural labourers and domestic textile workers, but for London artisans in the building trades it was the eighteenth century which saw a fall in their real wages – halved between the 1730s and the early 1800s – and the nineteenth century which saw their gradual recovery. In expanding sectors of the economy there is sometimes no comparison: workers on the railways, for example, received steady if not high wages, and the casual labourer who obtained employment as a railway porter would certainly have been better off, as would the engineer who helped build the power loom which threatened the livelihood of the handloom weaver.

Wage and price series, however, cannot say everything about the living standards of the labouring classes. Money was important for what it could buy, but when the discussion is broadened to one of standards of life, then other dimensions – even more unquantifiable, because intrinsically subjective – have to be introduced. Put bluntly, the question is, 'Were people any happier in the early nineteenth century than they had been fifty or a hundred years earlier?' One suspects the question would have been meaningless to the very poor. For the rest, there is an immediate problem of evidence. In an era of unprecedented social change it is likely that contemporaries among the labouring classes, along with traditionalists of the higher classes, would be predisposed to lament the passing of the good old days, while progressives would be equally likely to stress past evils and present improvements. Thus William Cobbett vividly captures the mood of decline in the countryside, while Francis Place expresses in his *Autobiography* the sense of improvement and achievement among London artisans. Both interpretations are correct, for the two men inhabited different worlds and were describing different experiences.

The debate over the standard of living is therefore likely to continue so long as historians differ over their priorities and the meaning of the evidence on which they choose to rely. The most recent contribution has come from Floud, Wachter and Gregory.[22] They argue that physical height measures the conditions, and especially the nutritional standards, experienced by children and adolescents, and therefore data from military and other sources about the changing height of the mature male population can indicate a great deal about the changing standard of living. Their conclusions cause some problems for what was becoming an accepted chronology. They support the general picture of an improvement in the later eighteenth century, but the height data suggests that the war years,

1793–1815, though undoubtedly difficult, with problems arising from wartime inflation and high taxation as well as the social impact of early industrial change, were nevertheless also a time when many children were still sufficiently well-fed to lay the foundations for a healthy growth into adulthood. By the 1820s, on the contrary, despite some improvement in industry after the post-war depression, the conditions of childhood began to deteriorate. This can be associated with continuing agricultural depression, the presence of large numbers of depressed outworkers in the textile industries, the instability of trade which brought severe cyclical depressions – not least those which caused such misery and unrest between late 1836 and the summer of 1842 – and, above all, the growing size of an urban population living in depressing conditions of squalor and disease. This state of affairs, often held to come to an end in the 1840s, may well, on the height data, have continued until the 1860s.

This latter point provides a welcome extension of the standard of living debate beyond its traditional finishing-point of 1850, for the assumption about general improvement from the 1840s needs to be challenged. Urban conditions remained bad; average real wages were no higher in 1850 than in 1840, and only 18 per cent higher in 1870. Given that historians are agreed that some improvement did occur during these years, it seems likely that only some workers actually gained. The trade cycle and food prices exercised a major influence on fluctuations in living standards throughout the nineteenth century. Such improvements as there were in the 1860s were sustained only with the economic gains of the great economic boom of the early 1870s, followed by the dramatic fall in the prices of basic foodstuffs from the later 1870s as increasing amounts of cheap food were brought in from abroad. Despite higher levels of unemployment during the 1880s, real wages probably rose on average by about 45 per cent between 1870 and 1895, though no further lasting gains were then made before the First World War. This improvement in living standards in the final quarter of the nineteenth century significantly reduced the proportion of the population living in severe poverty, but at the beginning of the twentieth century Rowntree still found 13 per cent of families in York existing below his stringently defined poverty line.

The overall view – *subject to regional and occupational variations* – would now appear to be that living standards were rising to about 1820, reflecting agricultural prosperity and the relatively small adverse impact made by industrialisation, or urbanisation outside London. Decline between the 1820s and 1860s then resulted from the deterioration in the urban environment at a time when an increasing proportion of the people were living in towns. In turn, the improvement detected from the 1860s reflects improvements in urban standards, aided by a fall in food-prices at a time when the bulk of the population was no longer dependent primarily on agriculture. However, such an improvement was only relative, as contemporaries became aware at the close of the nineteenth century.

Poverty in the twentieth century

During the First World War prices rose, but wages, especially among the less skilled, rose even faster and unemployment fell. Those who survived were likely to have been better off after the war than they had been before it, but by the early 1920s all these trends were reversed as real wages fell and unemployment soared. Between 1920 and 1922 wages fell by more than half, prices by nearly half, and unemployment reached 1.5 million. The story of the inter-war years is one of two societies, the employed and the unemployed. For the employed, life was improving as real wages rose by around one-fifth. For the unemployed, life remained harsh. The height data suggest a slowing-down in the improvement in nutritional standards, though poverty was still in decline. In a second survey of York, undertaken by Rowntree in 1936, the proportion of the working class living in extreme poverty was found to have fallen from 15.46 per cent (7,230 persons) in 1899 to 6.8 per cent (3,767 persons) in 1936, despite a considerable increase in unemployment in the city.[23]

The difficulty with any comparative discussion of poverty is the definition of the concept itself. In the Rowntree figures quoted above the 1899 standard is applied to 1936, but Rowntree himself in 1936 worked to a more generous – though still stringent – standard which showed that 17.8 per cent of the population (31.1 per cent of the working class) could not afford adequate nutrition and basic housing, clothing, heating and lighting. The three major causes of this situation in 1936 were low wages (32.8 per cent), unemployment (28.6 per cent) and old age (14.7 per cent), followed by casual work (9.5 per cent), death of husband (7.8 per cent) and illness (4.1 per cent). Nevertheless he believed that the standard of living available to the working class in York had risen by a third since 1899.[24]

By 1936 unemployment nationally was falling from a peak of 2.7 million in 1932, and the late 1930s saw a recovery in the economy which was sustained by the Second World War. After 1945 labour shortages ensured that unemployment remained well under half a million until the later 1960s and, while the cost of living doubled, wages more than trebled between 1950 and 1968. It was widely believed that poverty had at last been conquered. Rowntree's third survey of York, conducted in 1950, showed that only 2.8 per cent of the working class (1.7 per cent of the total population) were living in poverty, and that the major causes were now old age (68.1 per cent) and sickness (21.3 per cent).[25]

In a sense, Rowntree was right: poverty, as known in the eighteenth and nineteenth centuries, has virtually disappeared. The height of working-class men improved as they almost closed the gap with the higher classes. In the later twentieth century, Britain had no poverty to compare with that in the Third World. But poverty in a poor country is different from poverty in a rich country. As the general standard of living rises, so too do expectations and the sense of what is tolerable. In each of his later surveys, Rowntree employed a poverty level higher than that used in the previous one. After 1948 the poverty line was defined as that below which basic National Assistance (Supplementary Benefit from 1966; Income Support from 1988) allowances were paid. If Rowntree's data are recalculated according to the basic National Assistance level, poverty in York in 1950 is shown to have been much higher than he himself thought – 5.8 per cent of all individuals and 8.6 per cent of all families (9.7 per cent of the working-class population and 14.4 per cent of working-class families). Though this still represents a considerable improvement on estimates of poverty in previous generations, it indicates the continuance of a considerable body of poverty in an age of supposed affluence.[26]

Between 1953 and 1973 the real income of the poorest 5 per cent and 10 per cent in the community increased by nearly three-quarters; only a fortieth of the population in 1973 was living at the level experienced by a fifth of the population 20 years earlier. This improvement was due to a general increase in wealth, not a redistribution in favour of the poor. The relative position of the poor had changed little. In 1971, 4.9 per cent of the population and 7.1 per cent of households were judged to have a net income below the Supplementary Benefit level. Those most at risk were the elderly and the retired, who accounted for about half the poor people and two-thirds of the poor households in 1971; next came single-parent families, households with unemployed heads, those with more than four children and women living alone.[27] Twenty years later, a survey of *Winners and Losers* in the 1980s found that between 1979 and 1990–1, real incomes rose for the better-off, but fell for the bottom twentieth of the population (or bottom sixth if housing costs are included). Moreover, those who were the better-off in 1979 did best in the following decade, while middle-income levels began to polarise between high and low incomes.[28]

This was due in large measure to changes in the labour market. In 1971 just over half of the poorest 20 per cent of the population were old people but, despite an increase in their absolute numbers, as a fraction of the bottom 20 per cent they had fallen to a fifth by 1995. In contrast, the proportion of the poorest who were working-age couples with children was up from 17 per cent to 38 per cent. Behind these figures lay a dramatic increase in unemployment, which rose from 751,000 (3.3 per cent of those employed or seeking work) in 1971, to cyclical peaks of 3.1 million (10.7 per cent) in 1985 and 2.8 million (10.2 per cent) in 1993. Even in 1996, when numbers in receipt of unemployment benefit had fallen to 2.1 million, this still exceeded either the number of pensioners (1.6 million) or single parents (1 million) in receipt of Income Support.

In his discussion of poverty in *The Affluent Society*, J. K. Galbraith distinguished between 'case poverty' and 'insular poverty'. The former he described as those who had failed to master their environment through

> some quality peculiar to the individual or family involved – mental deficiency, bad health, inability to adapt to the discipline of modern economic life, excessive procreation, alcohol, insufficient education, or perhaps a combination of several of these handicaps.[29]

The socially inadequate and casualties of modern living are part of the story of the poor in every generation; but of more significance is 'insular poverty', the poverty of the community in the declining industrial area or inner city where the physical and economic environment is hostile even to those who do try to master it. Unemployment – and poverty – are regional or even local characteristics. In the early 1930s as many as three-quarters of all male workers were unemployed in the Valleys of South Wales; the rate in Glasgow was four times that of Birmingham; Jarrow had 67.8 per cent unemployed in 1934, compared to 3.9 per cent in St Albans. The same characteristics can be seen in the unemployment of the 1980s, though the total rates were well below those of the 1930s; but in the 1990s this regional pattern was broken. In the peak year of 1993 only two regions differed by more than one percentage point of the Great Britain mean of 10.2 per cent – the North, with 11.9 per cent, and East Anglia, with 8.1 per cent. What was marked, though, was the persistence in every region of pockets of severe unemployment on certain housing estates, in the most depressed areas of the inner cities, among young people, and among blacks and other immigrant groups of comparatively recent arrival.

Those most vulnerable to poverty are likely to congregate in, or fail to escape, those areas in which poverty is greatest: slum housing areas with multiple occupancy and low rents. A study of part of the St Ann's area of Nottingham in the late 1960s showed the extent of poverty amidst affluence in a 'twilight' area of a typical British city: small terraced housing at over 40 dwellings to the acre, 91 per cent with only an outside lavatory, 85 per cent without a bathroom, and 54.5 per cent without a hot-water system. The fabric of many of the houses was in bad repair, or past repair; 156 out of 413 households in a sample survey of one of the worst areas were judged to be in poverty; a tenth of the population (and a fifth of the children) lived in overcrowded conditions of more than 1½ per room. Though conspicuous expenditure was evident among households with two or more wages and few responsibilities, the wheel of fortune soon turned momentary affluence into poverty, with the birth of children, sickness, widowhood or desertion and old age. Then household goods had to be pawned or sold, and clothing handed down or bought second-hand on the street market or at jumble sales. Within this particular area it was the children who appeared to suffer most, often being physically stunted, frequently ill, and in many cases emotionally or mentally retarded.[30]

Despite the extent of welfare benefits and programmes for housing renewal and replacement, ghettoes of poverty in parts of major cities proved difficult to eliminate in succeeding decades. With a shortage of low-cost housing the number of households officially accepted as 'homeless' continued to rise in the 1980s, reaching a peak of nearly 145,000 in 1991. Most of these were placed in temporary accommodation, but a highly visible minority of individuals, many of them examples of Galbraith's 'case poverty', were to be found literally homeless on the streets of London and other towns and cities throughout the country.

Responses to poverty

Defences against the worst effects of poverty were many and varied. Mutual aid – from family, friends and neighbours – was the first resort of the poor. The better-off might have some friendly-society aid; the worse-off from the early nineteenth century could turn to the pawn shop. Then came private charity, often channelled through religious organisations. Only as a last resort did the poor turn to public relief administered according to the poor law. That so many did depend upon the poor law is a measure of the extensive nature of poverty in Britain throughout the eighteenth and nineteenth centuries.

The old poor law

In England and Wales, the system of state welfare known as the poor law dated back to the sixteenth century, especially Acts of Parliament in 1572, 1597 and 1601, which set out the principal features of a system of relief which was to last until 1834. The parish (or township in the larger parishes of the North of England) was the basic unit of administration, rates were levied on occupiers of land in the parish, and relief was administered by locally chosen overseers under the supervision of the Justices of the Peace. The 1572 Act laid down that beggars should be punished and the able-bodied poor should be set to work, while the impotent poor could be cared for in almshouses. A further principle of the old poor law was that each parish should be responsible only for its own poor. The law was intended to be used as an instrument of control in an age of population growth and increasing vagrancy, and was initially subject to some central direction from the Privy Council through the magistrates. This was brought to an end in the early seventeenth century with the collapse of Charles I's government, and thereafter local officials developed their own practices in accordance with local needs and wishes. At the Restoration, the Poor Law Amendment Act of 1662 codified the law, particularly with regard to Settlement – the right of the overseers to remove incomers to the parish of their birth – but did not alter its basis. (For a fuller definition of Settlement, see above, page 65.)

The law was seen first as a means of coercing and punishing the idle and dangerous poor, and only second as a supplement to existing parochial charities. In 1722 Knatchbull's Act reiterated the determination of the 1572 Act to compel the poor to work, and accordingly parishes were permitted to build workhouses in which to house their able-bodied paupers; but only 200 of the 15,535 parishes took advantage of the Act. It was cheaper to provide outdoor relief, reserving indoor accommodation in almshouses for those too old or sick to look after themselves. A change in the official attitude came with Gilbert's Act of 1782, which reasserted the principle of outdoor relief to the able-bodied, and permitted groups of parishes to form themselves into unions for the more efficient administration of poor relief, though only about a thousand parishes took the opportunity to do so.

Outdoor relief to the poor was administered in individual ways according to local circumstances. In some small parishes local farmers would act informally among themselves to provide relief, or would agree to send the unemployed round the farms to seek work on low wages which would be made up out of the rates. Temporary relief could be given in cash handouts or in kind. Where there was a workhouse, it and its inmates might be let out to a private contractor to make what profit he could out of the labour of the poor. The rates were also used to provide tools to set the unemployed up in business, or to subsidise emigration to America. Though the 1601 Act made no provision for the sick, by the eighteenth century there are examples of parishes engaging a surgeon-apothecary or paying doctors' bills, providing nurses for the blind, and even sending a pauper to the coast to try the newly fashionable cure of sea bathing.

The two most notorious features of the old poor law were its treatment of children and of those without a Settlement. Pauper children, many of whom had lost one or both parents, were supposed to be cared for at the expense of their parish until they were old enough to be apprenticed to a trade. Some overseers conscientiously did this: workhouse schoolmasters were appointed, parents or foster parents were paid to look after children at home and legitimate apprenticeships were found. But the temptation was for pauper children to be sent out to the farms as cheap labour or, with the growth of textile mills hungry for workers, to dispatch them to Lancashire or elsewhere in the industrialising North as cheap factory labour. Paupers without a Settlement also suffered. Though most were probably relieved without enforced removals, overseers were very wary of pregnant female paupers whose babies would acquire a Settlement in the parish in which the birth occurred. With increasing bastardy rates in the later eighteenth century, pregnant women could be mercilessly pushed around from parish to parish, while unmarried mothers might find themselves forcibly separated from their children born in different parishes.

Until the late eighteenth century there was no great controversy over the poor laws. Stories of abuses are probably of only marginal significance. Overseers were no more or less corrupt and greedy than the population at large, while the life of a pauper could scarcely be harsher than that of the poor as a whole. But with mounting population pressure and rising costs towards the end of the eighteenth century, complaints began to be heard from ratepayers about waste, extravagance and maladministration as overseers struggled to harmonise humanity with thrift. The initial crisis was related to the price of bread, the staple diet of the poor. Whereas the average price of a quarter of wheat stood at 47*s.* (£2.35) in the early 1790s, it rose to 76*s.* (£3.80) in 1795–6, fell to 57*s.* (£2.85) in the later 1790s, then rose again to 106*s.* (£5.30) in 1800–1 with a peak of 119*s.* (£5.95) in 1801. 'The people are suffering not from the difficulty of getting at Provisions alone, but from likewise of earning the means of obtaining them,' noted Earl Fitzwilliam, the Lord Lieutenant of Yorkshire.[31] Prices then fell back to 72*s.* (£3.60) a quarter before rising to 106*s.* (£5.30) in 1809–13, with a new peak of 125*s.* (£6.25) in 1812. After the war prices began to fall, despite a temporary rise to 95*s.* (£4.75) in 1817, until in 1822 they briefly reached the pre-war level. Over the decade of the 1820s they averaged 58*s.* (£2.90). The poor rates, which nationally had raised £2 million in 1784, had more than doubled to £5.3 million in 1802–3, and by 1817–18 stood at £9.3 million. Something clearly had to be done.

One expedient in times of high food prices was to make a 'bread-scale' allowance to the poor. This was done during the first wartime crisis of 1795 by the Berkshire magistrates meeting at Speenhamland, thus giving name to the 'Speenhamland system', by which is meant the awarding of outdoor relief in money, according to the price of bread and the size of the family to be relieved. It was not new, it was never a 'system', and as a long-term practice it was never so widespread as was later alleged. But the giving of relief in proportion to the number of children at a time when, in the south of England, pauper mouths seemed to be multiplying uncontrollably, caused great alarm among free-market economists worried at mounting costs and increasing pauperisation. Thomas Robert Malthus, the first version of whose *Essay on the Principle of Population* was published in 1798, was but the most influential of those economists whose ideas shaped the intellectual response to the crisis and the eventual formulation of an alternative policy – to do as little as possible, preferably nothing at all.

It is not surprising that many of these political economists were educated in or influenced by Scotland, for the Scots, in effect, had no poor law. The principle that every parish should be responsible for its own poor had been laid down before the Reformation in 1535, but the intention of the reformers to base poor relief on income from tithes came to nothing. A Statute of 1579, following earlier Scottish practice and the English Act of 1572, categorised paupers into sturdy beggars who were to be scourged, and the impotent poor who were to be accommodated in almshouses or licensed to beg within their own parishes. A parochial poor rate was to be levied, and in 1597 the supervision of relief was transferred to the Kirk Sessions. But local people successfully resisted attempts to compel them to accept a rating assessment, despite an Act of 1617 which gave local justices the duty of assessing the parish; and nationally the Scottish poor law withered away. Sturdy beggars received nothing, though they could be sentenced to their local House of Correction, which came to be regarded as an institution for housing those poor who could not manage on outdoor relief. The destitute and disabled – the aged, sick, widowed, orphaned and, sometimes, the worthy able-bodied poor – received a pittance from church collections, occasionally supplemented by a voluntary assessment among the heritors of the parish, who also helped administer relief to the poor after their cases had been carefully scrutinised by the Minister and the Elders of the Kirk.

The ideal of no help for the able-bodied and Christian charity for the worthy poor was to prove unattainable in England and Wales, and increasingly unworkable in Scotland. The principle of parochial relief both north and south of the border assumed a rural parish and a face-to-face community. As the major cities of Britain grew, the parish as a unit of administration became inadequate and the principle of moral supervision totally unworkable. Furthermore, as the population expanded, the dubious assumption that there was indeed work for all the able-bodied became patently unrealistic. Though no figures are available for levels of underemployment and unemployment, it is clear that by the early nineteenth century trends in poor relief were conditioned less by prices than by the increasing amount of unemployment.

Piecemeal attempts at reform were made as the subject of poor relief became a major topic of public discussion. The philanthropic factory master of New Lanark, Robert Owen, turned to late-seventeenth-century ideas for 'colledges of industry', or self-supporting pauper colonies; but he was ignored by politicians, scorned by economists and denounced by leading popular radicals in England and Scotland alike as a hopeless and dangerous visionary. In 1819 the Sturges Bourne Act permitted what was already an increasing practice, namely the appointment of a small Select Vestry to take the running of poor relief out of the hands of the Open Vestry and make it more professional. Everyone knew that the existing situation could not continue, and when the reformed Parliament in 1832 appointed a Royal Commission, the Commissioners – heavily influenced by their Malthusian economist member, Nassau Senior and the Benthamite, Edwin Chadwick – thought that they also knew the solution to the problem, and found confirmation of their prejudices in the information collected by Chadwick and 25 other Assistant Commissioners about the working of the old poor law.

They rejected the abolitionist stance of Malthus and other extremists, but recommended an end to all outdoor relief (except medical) for the able-bodied and their families. Workhouses were to be built for each category of pauper, in which conditions were to be deliberately made worse than in the outside world so as to discourage all but the desperate from entering them (the principle of 'less eligibility'). Parishes were to be brought together in unions under the superintendence of a new Central Board. The law relating to Settlement was to be simplified, and women were to be made wholly responsible for their bastards, without any claim as hitherto on the putative father. Most of these ideas were incorporated in the Poor Law Amendment Act of 1834, which revised the system of poor relief in England and Wales and laid the foundations for developments during the next hundred years.

The new poor law

An Act for the Amendment and better Administration of the Laws relating to the Poor in England and Wales passed onto the statute book on 14 August 1834 with very little opposition in Parliament. This is surprising, in view of the quite revolutionary nature of the provisions concealed behind the humble word 'amendment'. A Central Board of three Commissioners was established to supervise the enforcement of the law, with no direct responsibility to Parliament; locally, parishes were to be grouped in Unions, superintended by Guardians elected by the ratepayers of each parish or township. Thus, at a stroke, the old Tudor system of local government was bypassed and the basis of a modern elective system laid in its place. Most of the major recommendations of the Royal Commission were embodied in the law, the two most important exceptions being the law of Settlement, about which nothing significant was done, and the recommendation for separate workhouses for different categories of pauper, which proved financially impracticable.

The new law was greeted by the poor with widespread hostility. They were supported by local paternalists who resented the bureaucratic intrusion of central government into local affairs. Most hated of all was the 'workhouse test' and the prohibition on outdoor relief for the able-bodied. Local officials felt best able to judge how to manage their own poor and knew that outdoor relief was cheaper than indoor, while the poor themselves feared the prospect of families being split up in the regimented regimes of the proposed new prison-like workhouses, in which poverty was more than ever to be treated as a crime.

In practice, the 1834 Act produced few immediate changes. Unions of parishes were formed (except where unions already existed under Gilbert's Act), but the same people continued to administer the law on behalf of the same ratepayers in the same sort of way. Where there were prospects of change, local opposition forced the Poor Law Commission to modify its directives, even to the extent of permitting the continuance of outdoor relief. But above all, the new law was blunted because it was based on a misunderstanding of the nature of poverty and the problems of the poor. The Royal Commission had believed that outdoor relief subsidised wages, bringing down wage rates and thus pauperising the labour force. If the subsidy were withdrawn, wage rates would be forced up and the vicious downward spiral of poverty would be reversed. In fact, outdoor relief operated not as a subsidy on wages but on income, enabling the poor to survive on wages depressed by the overstocked nature of the rural labour market. The Commissioners failed to appreciate that the basic problem in the countryside was not the old poor law, but under-employment. Similarly, the major problem in the growing towns was not a lazy workforce, but a mixture of chronic under-employment and cyclical unemployment.

The Poor Law Commission, represented regionally by Assistant Commissioners, did not have full powers over the new local authorities, the Boards of Guardians. The Guardians could be ordered to modify or even close an old and inadequate workhouse, but they could not be compelled to build a new one. Even so, about 350 new workhouses were built in the first five years of the Act, chiefly in the South of England. These were mixed institutions, not the specialised ones for which Chadwick had hoped. The problem was money. The new law had been welcomed as a device to keep the rates down, and the Commissioners had limited powers to compel the spending of money. With local control over finance came a reluctance to spend more than was absolutely necessary. Despite the union of parishes, each parish could influence policy through its Guardians, and so a majority of parishes with few poor could hold back a minority of parishes with many poor. This happened in Bradford in Yorkshire, where the outer townships effectively vetoed proposals by the inner townships to build a workhouse.

The new law was put to the test in the North of England almost immediately after the Assistant Commissioners had introduced it, for in the depression years of the late 1830s and early 1840s more people were thrown upon parochial relief than could possibly be accommodated in such workhouses as were provided. The General Rules of the Commissioners prohibiting outdoor relief could not have been followed, even if the Guardians had been prepared to try – which most were not – and in 1842 some unions were temporarily allowed to administer an outdoor-relief Labour Test instead. With or without permission, the Guardians continued to allow outdoor relief, and as late as 1849–50 all but 12 per cent of the 1 million paupers being relieved in England and Wales were in receipt of outdoor relief.

The cruelties of the new poor law were widely advertised by its opponents in the early years. Women and children were allegedly flogged by sadistic workhouse masters; in the quest for 'less eligibility' paupers were starved. Some of these stories were exaggerated; some contained an element of truth. Much of the cruelty was local and unofficial, as under the old law; but it was encouraged by the official ethos, if not by the actual regulations, of the new law. As a result of a parliamentary investigation into one such scandal at the Andover workhouse, where paupers had been reportedly eating the bones they had been given to grind, the Poor Law Commission was dissolved in 1847 and replaced by a Poor Law Board under the presidency of a Member of Parliament. In fact, the principle of 'less eligibility' was very hard to maintain, given the depths of poverty outside the workhouses. The model dietaries issued by the Commission were rather more nutritious and contained more meat than the meals which were actually consumed by the poorest labourers in their own homes.

The real cruelty of the new workhouse lay in its psychological harshness. The old poorhouses had often been slackly and carelessly administered. In the small, local poorhouses the inmates, chiefly old people, widows and children, had enjoyed considerable freedom. Under the new regime in larger, impersonal institutions, families were divided by age and sex; inmates were depersonalised, with the loss of personal possessions and the issue of pauper uniforms; life was regimented and tedious; personal freedom was minimal. Concessions, at the discretion of the local Guardians, were few. The principles of 1834 in this respect were triumphant, and even when, later in the nineteenth century, some Guardians were willing and able to modify conditions for the elderly, the workhouse continued to be regarded with dread by the poor.

Nevertheless, at no time did the number of paupers receiving relief indoors exceed the number who continued to receive relief out of doors. In 1870, the last year of the Poor Law Board, 15 per cent of paupers relieved were in the workhouse, but then the new Local Government Board, which assumed responsibility for the administration of the law in 1871, began to tighten up procedures. Between 1870 and 1914 the number of indoor paupers rose from 156,800 to 254,644 (excluding casual and insane paupers), while the numbers relieved outside fell from 876,000 to 387,208. This 'improvement' was partly a consequence of a more rigorous administration of relief, and partly a result of a decline in real poverty. Though the total number of paupers being relieved in 1900 was only 10 per cent below that in 1850, as a proportion of the population the number had been more than halved, from 5.7 per cent to 2.5 per cent. In 1914 the figure was a mere 2 per cent, compared with 8.8 per cent in 1834. Only when these figures are set beside those published by Booth and Rowntree can the true extent of poverty be seen. The poor law did not relieve the main body of poverty in nineteenth-century Britain; it merely provided a harsh and undesirable safety-net for the absolutely destitute.

Poor relief in Scotland after 1845

The crisis in the administration of relief to the poor in Scotland was brought to a head in the division of the Presbyterian Kirk by the Disruption of 1843 (see below, pages 313–16). As a result a Royal Commission was appointed, which led in 1845 to the Poor Law Act. This Act created in Edinburgh a Board of Supervision comprising nine nominated members to represent the regions of Scotland and the Crown. It had few powers of compulsion, but gradually exerted its influence to determine the general standards of poor relief in the country. Relief continued to be administered at the parochial level, where parishes remained free to operate the old voluntary system under the Kirk Sessions and heritors. Initially, 75 per cent of parishes took this option, but as the Board of Supervision required increasing standards of provision more and more parishes opted for the alternative of a compulsory assessment administered by an elected parochial board. By 1894, when the Board of Supervision was replaced by the Local Government Board, 95 per cent of parishes had a compulsory assessment. Though the Act permitted the combining of parishes to build Poor Houses, the workhouse principle was not central to policy as in England. The able-bodied poor continued to be denied relief although, until a court decision in 1859, relief was sometimes given to those in temporary need. Relief was often dispensed according to the cheapest method, and there were great variations between, for example, Edinburgh, with a rate income of £25,000 a year, and Elgin, with only £50.

The poor law made no provision for a work test. The Scottish poor houses were not workhouses and the inmates could not be compelled to work, although work was provided. The aim of the poor houses was to provide accommodation for those incapable of looking after themselves (the major category in England and Wales also) and for those dissolute paupers who misspent their outdoor allowances. By 1868 there were 66 poor houses in Scotland, housing 8,794 of the total of 136,444 in receipt of relief (4.2 per cent of the population compared with 4.6 per cent of the population in England and Wales in 1870). By 1898 the number of inmates had increased to 9,212 while those receiving outdoor relief had fallen to 72,891. In that year the parochial boards were replaced by elected parish councils, and administration became more uniform and more like the English. But, as a new welfare system emerged from the old, Scotland remained free from the taint of the English workhouse.

Private charity

Private charity in the eighteenth and nineteenth centuries was far more important than the poor law in the day-to-day relief of poverty. Eighteenth-century Britain inherited from previous centuries a host of diverse charities devoted to the education of poor children, the care of the sick, the support of the widowed and many other worthy causes. Some funds were misapplied, others were not, but their existence was haphazard and bore no relation to the changing pattern of needs which industrialisation and urbanisation brought in the nineteenth century. Nevertheless hospitals and almshouses were built from which a minority of poor people benefited greatly, and many small amounts of money were annually disbursed in parochial charities to individuals in need at the discretion of trustees or local clergymen. An accumulation of bequests in such ancient cities as Coventry, Norwich, Exeter and York – as well as the City of London – did much to take the edge off the poor law and at the same time placed a useful means of social control in the hands of the clergy and local dignitaries.

Though some scholars have detected a slackening of charitable endowment in the mid-eighteenth century, benevolence continued to be expressed, and quickened under the impact of the evangelical revival in the later eighteenth and early nineteenth centuries. At the same time rising rentals increased the income of many charities whose endowments were invested in land. Next to charitable endowments came donations for every imaginable cause. The Evangelical leader, William Wilberforce, regularly gave away a quarter of his income and supported some 70 philanthropic organisations. The crisis years of the French and Napoleonic Wars produced soup kitchens financed by public subscriptions in many centres of population, and in 1811 the Society for Bettering the Condition of the Poor raised over £15,000. Patrick Colquhoun estimated in 1806 that the total funds disbursed by private charity amounted to approaching £4 million a year.[32]

Concern began to be expressed that this money was being misapplied or not used to best effect. Local committees were set up to ensure that funds reached the deserving poor, and Henry Brougham pressed in Parliament for an investigation into charitable endowments. Beginning in 1816 with a Select Committee on the Education of the Poor in the Metropolis, Brougham had by 1819 secured a semi-permanent board of 20 Commissioners with powers to investigate some non-educational charities as well. Their powers were periodically renewed and extended, until by 1840 they had produced 32 reports at a cost of over £200,000. They found that total annual income from charitable endowments amounted to over £1.2 million. From their reports stemmed the beginnings of modern charity administration, with the setting up in 1853 of the permanent Charity Commission.

The total scale of organised charitable endeavour in the mid-nineteenth century can be gauged from Sampson Low's summary of London charities in 1862. He found 640 institutions in all, ranging from 124 colleges, hospitals, almshouses and other asylums for the aged, 80 medical hospitals and infirmaries, 72 professional and trade provident and benevolent funds, and 56 Bible and home missionary societies and funds, 16 charities for the blind, deaf, dumb and crippled, 14 asylums for 1986 orphaned children, and four Indian famine funds. Of these 640 institutions, 144 had been founded between 1850 and 1860, 279 between 1800 and 1850, 114 in the eighteenth century, and 103 before 1700. All together they derived an annual income from property or trade amounting to £841,373, and in 1860 received a further £1,600,594 from voluntary contributions, compared with an estimated £1,425,063 spent by the metropolitan poor law authorities in 1857. Additionally, there were the many non-institutional charitable donations being made by private individuals, from the small offerings put into the 'poor box' at Marylebone Police Court amounting to £306 which was used to provide 2,000 applicants with coal, soup and bread, to the £81,838 19*s.* 5*d.* collected after the Hartley mining disaster of 1862.[33]

By the late 1860s total charitable expenditure in London may have amounted to something between £5.5 million and £7 million annually. With such sums at stake there was a further move to organise philanthropy on a more 'scientific' basis, and in April 1869 the Society for Organising Charitable Relief and Repressing Mendicity was formed, usually known as the Charity Organisation Society (COS). The object of the Society was to establish the worthiness of those seeking help so that private charity would not be wasted or duplicated. This would clear the way for the poor law authorities to threaten the unworthy with the full rigours of the 1834 Act. From 1875 its organising genius was C. S. Loch, a young Scotsman inspired by the example of Thomas Chalmers, who between 1819 and 1823 had, as a minister at St John's, Glasgow, attempted to make the old Scottish system of private benevolence work in an urban context.

The reputation of the COS spread beyond the metropolis, so that by 1891 Loch was in touch with 75 similar bodies in England and nine in Scotland. The Society's view of poverty was harsh and its approach was resented among the poor, but it made two very important contributions to the long-term response to poverty. First, through its publications it expanded public awareness of the extent and nature of the problem – and not only of poverty itself, but also of the plight of the blind, the deaf and the mentally defective. Second, through its emphasis on the individual causes of poverty it came to pioneer case work, and in this sense can be regarded as the parent of modern social work. Loch and the Society were, however, slow to change as modern social work emerged; they were opposed to the increasingly interventionist policies of a collectivist state. By the time Loch retired in 1912 the Society's attitudes had ossified in their mid-Victorian form, and the advent of the twentieth century was not recognised until the 1930s. Finally, in 1946, the modern role of the Society in family case work was acknowledged, when it was renamed the Family Welfare Association.

Changing needs and perceptions brought into being new organisations to meet specific needs. Most religious denominations established bodies for the care of children. The Wesleyan National Children's Home and Orphanage, founded in 1871, and the Waifs and Strays, founded in 1881 (later the Church of England Children's Society), have proved to be among the most enduring, along with Dr Barnardo's, begun as the East End Juvenile Mission with its first 'home' in Stepney in 1867. Rather different was the National Society for the Prevention of Cruelty to Children (1884), whose primary purpose was not to help children directly but to attack cruelty through inspection, legislation and the encouragement of parental responsibility. In this sense the NSPCC was a fore-runner of modern pressure-group charities such as Shelter (1966), which campaigns on behalf of the homeless, and the Child Poverty Action Group (1965), although the model for the NSPCC itself was the much older Society for the Prevention of Cruelty to Animals, founded in 1824.

Organised charity in the twentieth century responded to the changing role of the state. Instead of being the first support of the poor and unfortunate, with the state playing a supporting part, the roles were reversed. With increasing direct taxation both in life and at death, and an expectation (foreign to the nineteenth century) that the state should play a leading part in social welfare, private donations to charitable causes failed to keep pace with rising costs. Throughout the inter-war years charities were forced to rely increasingly on special appeals rather than regular subscriptions and donations; and by 1934 it was estimated that 37 per cent of the income of charities in England was being derived from public authorities. This trend continued after the Second World War as some writers argued that, with the creation of the Welfare State, voluntary charitable effort as such would no longer be needed. William Beveridge, who is often regarded as the architect of post-war welfare policy, and the Nathan Committee on Charitable Trusts (1952) disagreed, and voluntary effort remained an essential arm of the welfare services.

Indeed, the 1960s saw something of a revival in charitable endeavour at home and abroad, led by the Save the Children Fund, founded in 1919 to provide relief to famine-stricken children in Europe after the First World War but later enlarged to work with children everywhere, with a voluntary income of £65.2 million in 1992–3; and Oxfam (the Oxford Committee for Famine Relief), founded in 1942 to help refugees in Greece. After the Second World War its operations were extended to Europe at large and, from the 1960s, to relief work and economic development in the poorest parts of the world. In 1992–3, its voluntary income was £53.3 million. Between 1979 and 1995 the number of registered charities in Britain increased by 38,000 to 171,000, and in 1995 the average giving per household amounted to about £60 a year, double what it had been a decade earlier and rising at twice the rate of inflation over that period. The relationship between these charities and the state was also changing as ministers appreciated that the charities had often become more expert and more effective in providing social care and welfare than direct action by government. The charities were now known as NGOs (Non-Governmental Organisations) which to some extent operated on behalf of government. Oxfam, the leading charity after the National Trust, with a voluntary income of £53.7 million in 1994–5 received a further £30.3 million in fees and grants from central and local government; Save the Children received an extra £50.6 million and the Red Cross £46 million.

In addition to these grants, and tax relief on donations, another major source of supplementary funding was created in 1994 with the creation of a National Lottery for the first time since 1826. Of £5,200 million raised in the first year, £159.1 million was given to the National Charities Board for distribution to over 2,000 charities. Not all this was 'new' money, however. Much giving at all levels continued to rely, as it had in the nineteenth century, on small sums raised through bazaars and jumble sales, local appeals, and other often unrecorded 'special efforts' whose organisers feared the competition of the highly professional lottery organisation.

Health care

Hospitals as specialised institutions for the sick developed only in the eighteenth century. Before that date, almshouses were commonly the only institution offering accommodation for the aged poor. The two exceptions were the great Reformation foundations in London of St Bartholomew's and St Thomas's, which saw their responsibility to be that of catering for the sick poor. Both institutions were expanded in the early eighteenth century, but neither was able to cope with the great growth in London's population, and between 1719 and 1756 five new hospitals were founded. Four of these – the Westminster, St George's, the London and the Middlesex – were funded by annual subscription; the fifth, Guy's, through the single bequest of Thomas Guy, a prosperous London bookseller. In the provinces and in Scotland similar developments occurred. The Edinburgh Royal Infirmary with 228 beds replaced the town's first infirmary (opened in 1729 with only six beds) in 1741; the Aberdeen Infirmary dates from 1742; while, in Glasgow, the Town Hospital of 1733 was replaced by the Glasgow Royal Infirmary in 1794.

These hospitals, and others of a similar kind opened during the course of the nineteenth century, were the backbone of hospital provision in eighteenth- and nineteenth-century Britain and form the basis of the modern hospital health service. Though founded as charities, often by local committees of doctors, clergy and other leading citizens, they were not always easily available to the poor who had first to seek a note from one of the governors (i.e. the principal subscribers) to secure admission.

Though hundreds were admitted annually to the largest hospitals, far more obtained treatment as out-patients – but in the absence of records it is difficult to know how many. Guy's were claiming over 50,000 a year in the 1830s. In 1871 almost 550,000 outpatients were estimated to have been treated at the 16 general London hospitals, which the COS suspected of competing with one another to impress their subscribers.

Also important in the treatment of the poor were public dispensaries. By the end of the eighteenth century 50,000 patients were being treated annually by dispensaries, a third of them in their own homes, at a cost of £5,000. The dispensary movement is usually dated from the foundation of the General Dispensary in Aldersgate, London, in 1770. By 1820 there were around 25 dispensaries in the metropolis and a further 35 in the provinces, and many more were founded over the next half-century. Nevertheless, pressure of population, especially in large and rapidly growing towns, meant that the many of the poorest were still inadequately provided for, and public health care in the nineteenth century increasingly became a concern for the poor law authorities.

The Scottish Poor Law of 1845 contained a statutory requirement that medical attention should be made available to physically or mentally ill paupers. In this respect the Act was more advanced than that passed in 1834 for England and Wales, which merely gave magistrates the power to order medical relief in cases of sudden sickness. Nevertheless, under both systems a rudimentary health service rapidly developed for the relief of the poor. In Scotland after 1848 the authorities received government grants to help provide for the physically ill, and after 1875 for the mentally ill. Hospital accommodation was provided either in the sick wards of poor houses, or beds were paid for in local charity infirmaries. In England and Wales, most Boards of Guardians appointed medical officers, and provided sick wards in the new workhouses. In doing so they were merely following with greater efficiency and resources the practice of the old poor law, under which one of the largest parishes, Marylebone, had already built and staffed its own infirmary in the 1790s. A General Medical Order was issue by the Poor Law Commission in 1842, under which district medical officers were to be appointed. Within two years there were 2,800 of them in England and Wales. Their duties were to treat such sick paupers as were referred to them by the relieving officer, for which they were paid either *per capita* or by annual stipend. The aim of the Guardians was to keep expenditure at a minimum, and the duties of medical officers were frequently put out to private tender. Some Guardians preferred instead to contribute to a local dispensary for the use of its services. The medical officer might also be appointed to attend paupers in the workhouse, and he would be paid extra if called to attend a childbirth. The service was very rudimentary and depended much on the character and generosity of the doctors themselves, whose main incomes came from private patients. As late as 1870 only £300,000 of the £8 million poor-law expenditure went on medical services.

The sick wards of the workhouses showed further evidence of parsimony. Beds, sometimes containing two or three patients each, were crowded together at twice the density permitted in prison infirmaries. Old buildings, damp and ill-ventilated, were frequently pressed into service. Able-bodied female paupers continued to act as nurses long after professional nursing had been introduced elsewhere, despite an order of 1865 requiring the practice to be discontinued. Conditions in the lying-in wards were appalling, even by contemporary standards. Nowhere within the administration of the poor law were the needs of the poor so clearly contrary to the wishes of ratepayers. Not until 1867 did the State acknowledge for England and Wales its obligation to provide hospitals for the poor, and not until 1885 was sickness separated from pauperism, when receipt of medical relief ceased to be a ground for disqualification from the franchise.

Yet, despite this dismal story, even before 1867 the character of the workhouse was changing. The very nature of the pauper community, comprising large numbers of sick and elderly people, was undermining the principles of 1834, as workhouses became *de facto* hospitals for the sick and aged. This process was aided by the medical officers themselves, whose professional standards put them at variance with the principle of 'less eligibility'. From the 1870s conditions did begin to improve, but only slowly and patchily. Liverpool pioneered a new attitude towards workhouse nursing in the 1860s, thanks largely to the efforts of William Rathbone, but as late as the 1890s the Bethnal Green infirmary female section had only one person – a 'labour mistress', whose duty was 'the elimination of that perennial presence, the sturdy beggar' – in charge of 335 female inmates. Though the poor law did indeed lay the foundations for a system of State welfare, it also bequeathed attitudes and fears which were long to hinder the acceptance of a truly open national health service. It can be no surprise that the poor were determined to do all they could to avoid the stigma and experience of pauperism.

Self-help

The mutual aid of neighbours in working-class communities was silently given and received without troubling the historical record, but it is probable that, as a percentage of their resources, the poor were their own greatest benefactors. Friends, family and neighbours could be relied upon to rally round in times of sickness and need. Only a few took unwarranted advantage of such kindness, and they rapidly became 'known' in the neighbourhood.

Within the harsh world of poverty, the recipient of charity shared little of the idealism of the giver. Survival was the most important thing, and the poor helped themselves to charity with a hunger which confirmed every suspicion of the COS. 'We belonged to Clubs, the children went to Sunday school, if possible to several Sunday schools to ensure Treats in summer and at Xmas,' recalled one Stepney resident.[34] The clergy were well aware that this was the price of denominational competition: 'The people have become hardened against all forms of religion,' noted one York rector, 'and that only is acceptable which can supply the best loaves and fishes.'[35]

When family, friends, clergy and others had been exhausted, and the local shopkeeper had refused to put any more purchases 'on the slate', the next resort was to the pawn shop. This was a natural response on the part of those with irregular wages, and pawn shops were to be found mainly in urban working-class districts where casual working was common. The origins of pledging – the practice of obtaining small loans on the security of some item of personal property – are obscure, but the practice was certainly well-established in the eighteenth century, long before the system of licensing pawnbrokers was introduced in 1785. Attempts to control and legitimise the trade were unsuccessful. It was estimated that London in 1830 had between 500 and 600 unlicensed pawnbrokers compared with some 342 legitimate traders. The pawn-shop became a central institution in the poorer working-class urban communities during the course of the nineteenth century. Though there was a number of large and wealthy brokers, most shops were small, and in hard times the broker could find himself almost as badly off as his customers. It was not the very poorest who used the pawn shops most, for they had precious little to pledge, except for a few hours. As Rowntree observed at the end of the century, it was the next group up, his Class B earning between 18*s.* (90p) and 21*s.* (£1.05) a week, who followed the classic weekly pattern of pledging and redeeming their Sunday clothes.[36] Pawning assumed a pattern of poverty relieved by periods of relative plenty during which pawnable goods could be acquired, and families often made their first resort to the pawn shop in hard times, brought on by sickness or unemployment. Once in debt, though, the cycle became hard to break.

Those with higher and more regular earnings were able to make more secure provisions against unexpected loss of earnings, and they were among the greatest supporters of savings schemes and friendly societies. The number of friendly societies and local benefit or box clubs grew rapidly in the later eighteenth century, until by 1801 there were probably several thousand in existence. One estimate in 1818 put their membership at nearly 8.5 per cent of the resident population of England and Wales – about the same as the pauper population in 1834. Their principle was to collect entrance fees and weekly subscriptions from their members, in return for which they made sickness, death and sometimes unemployment payments. In Scotland, the societies were rather different, making payments only to members whose own resources were exhausted.

Some friendly societies were set up by philanthropists, but most were organised by the class which they were intended to benefit. They were mainly small, local and financially unstable, but gradually, during the first half of the nineteenth century, the larger Affiliated Orders – the Independent Order of Oddfellows (1810), the Manchester Unity (1816), and the Ancient Order of Foresters (*c.* 1813) – came to dominate the scene. In 1838 the Manchester Unity had 1,200 lodges and 90,000 members; by the end of the century the membership had reached three quarters of a million. The vast majority of friendly society members were men, but some catered specially for women.

One important benefit which the larger societies came to offer in the second half of the nineteenth century was the provision of medical attention during sickness. The society would pay a small yearly subscription of about 3*s.* (15p) per member which would entitle each member to the free services of a doctor. For those who could not afford membership of a friendly society, the most important concern was to insure against the ignominy of a pauper's funeral. This could be done most cheaply through one of the large collecting societies, and was especially favoured for women and children. The largest of these societies, the Royal Liver based in Liverpool, was founded in 1850, and by 1872 had around 550,000 members and funds of £264,795. Alternatively there was the Prudential Insurance Company, founded in 1847, which provided life cover for 1*d.* or 2*d.* (under 1p) a week. By 1872 the company had issued over a million life policies, and the weekly visit from 'the man from the Pru' was an established feature of many working-class homes. Even the hard-pressed Barrington family (see above, page 166) found 3*d.* (just over 1p) a week insurance money out of the family income of 14*s.* (70p).[37]

Lastly, there was the possibility of saving to meet future contingencies – though this option was open only to those with an adequate income. The rapid expansion of penny savings-banks and building societies in the nineteenth century is clear evidence of rising prosperity among those above the ranks of the very poor. Some of the earliest building societies really did build for their members, and they formed a popular outlet for radical energies which had been channelled in the 1840s into Chartist and Owenite land schemes; but by 1870 the majority had become what they remained until the Building Societies Act of 1986, permanent investment associations which lent money to their members on the security of real estate. Thereafter they became more like banks in the range of services they could offer, and in the 1990s a number of them formally became banks.

Penny banks can be traced back to the eighteenth century, but they were placed on a regular footing with trustees in 1817 (1836 in Scotland). In their origins they were designed to encourage thrift among the lower classes, and they appealed largely to apprentices and domestic servants, whose expenditure was likely to be lower than their income. At the Manchester and Salford Savings Bank in the year ending November 1842

– a year of deep depression and unemployment – the three largest depositing groups were: 3,063 (21 per cent) domestic servants (nearly all female) with 20 per cent of deposits; 3,033 (20 per cent) minors with 11 per cent of deposits; and 1,511 (10 per cent) clerks, shopmen, warehousemen and porters with 10 per cent of deposits. But the next three groups are also of interest – 911 cotton spinners, weavers and their assistants with 6 per cent of deposits; 816 mechanics and handicraftsmen with 6 per cent of deposits; and 538 tradesmen and small shopkeepers with 5 per cent of deposits. The average deposit was around £27.[38]

This was the face of the prospering working and lower-middle classes to whom Mr Gladstone appealed both politically and through the Post Office Savings Bank which he initiated as Chancellor of the Exchequer in 1861. Through this medium in particular, the late Victorian working class and its successors were able to become full members of capitalist society. In his debate on the merits of Socialism with H. M. Hyndman of the Social Democratic Federation in 1884, the staunch Radical, Charles Bradlaugh, felt able to ask:

> What is a property-owner? A property-owner is that person who has anything whatever beyond what is necessary for the actual existence of the moment. All savings in the Savings Bank, the Co-operative Store, the Building Society, the Friendly Society and the Assurance Society are property; and I will show you that there are millions of working men in this country who are in that condition. It is not true that the majority are starving. . . . Property-owners belong to all classes – the wage-earning class are the largest property-owners.[39]

Voices in the audience dissented, and by his last statement Bradlaugh can only have been referring to numbers, not wealth; but he knew his working class from inside, and his point is an important one. Though the poverty-stricken and pauperised were a larger minority than Bradlaugh probably knew on the eve of Charles Booth's investigations, they were nevertheless a minority. Poverty, if not defeated, was on the retreat in later Victorian Britain.

Welfare and the State

The main purpose of government in the eighteenth century was administration, not legislation. Governments did not expect to have legislative programmes, and the principal function of Parliament was to check the Executive (the King and his ministers), not to pass laws. The majority of Acts passed by Parliament were consequently local and private. The function of the State was to defend its people, both externally and internally, from their enemies. Its concerns were therefore the conduct of foreign affairs, the maintenance of law and order, and the raising of sufficient funds from taxation to pay for these. Enforcement of the State's will was ensured by a small professional army, the Royal Navy, and part-time forces under the command of the Lords Lieutenant.

The key to local administration had since Tudor times been the Justice of the Peace, and upon him devolved the enforcement of such social legislation as the poor laws, and the Statute of Artificers (1563) which enforced the obligation to work, laid down conditions of labour, including apprenticeship regulations, and required justices to assess wage rates locally. This legislation was restrictive and conservative in intent, and was rarely enforced in the expanding economy of the later eighteenth century, when it was regarded selectively in the popular mind as a paternalistic safeguard for the labourers' welfare. The prevailing intellectual climate in the later eighteenth century was against such state interference. *Laissez-faire* was becoming the order of the day. The last legislative intervention in the conditions of adult labour came with the Spitalfields Act of 1773, which fixed wages in the London silk industry. An attempt by Samuel Whitbread and other Whigs to secure minimum wages related to the cost of living in the crisis of 1795 was rejected by the government, and in 1813 state regulation of wages was brought to an end. With the repeal of the law governing apprenticeship the following year, only the Settlement Acts remained to control the supply of adult labour. Yet even as the Tudor legislation was being repealed, Parliament was giving its approval to the first Factory Acts which, in time, were to lead to a renewed involvement by the state in the lives of the people of Britain.

The growth of the administrative state

The latter decades of the eighteenth century saw a revolution in the scope of government, as hopes that the size of the Executive could be reduced were shattered by prolonged periods of war. During the long wars against the French between 1793 and 1815 government expenditure and indebtedness rose to what seemed like catastrophic levels, a dangerous new tax on income was introduced, and ministries proliferated to deal with extra administrative business generated by the war. But though expenditure trends are largely explained by the war, other trends indicate that this was not the whole story. The average size of Cabinets continued to rise after 1815; the eighteenth-century device of the 'Secret Committee' of the House of Commons or Lords grew into the Select Committee procedure, and was increasingly used to investigated problems needing legislation; and Royal Commissions – those hated devices of Stuart absolutism – were revived in 1780 to conduct wider enquiries. Sixty were appointed between 1800 and 1831 alone. The volume of Parliamentary Papers doubled in the 1830s, and Parliamentary Sessions became longer – 1,434 hours in 1836, compared with a norm of under a thousand before 1832. Everywhere there was an appetite for information. The Statistical Office of the Board of Trade was established in 1832, the Statistical Section of the British Association followed in 1833, and local statistical societies were set up in a number of provincial towns beginning with Manchester in 1833. Contemporary society and its problems were subjected to the most detailed scrutiny. Yet the Home Office in 1832 had a permanent staff of just 29 officials, and all but £13 million of the government's annual income of £53 million went on the armed forces and servicing the national debt.

This reluctant and under-financed expansion in governmental activity was prompted by the great social changes of the period: population growth, increasing urbanisation, and the transformation of industry in the factory districts. The initiators of the changing attitude were a new breed of experts who, in the informality of a half-formed bureaucracy, were able to formulate policy and persuade reluctant politicians. The first of these experts were amateurs – doctors, clergymen and philanthropists whose work took them among the poor and brought them face-to-face with the conditions in which the lower orders were forced to live and work. Consciences made tender by evangelical religion and Enlightenment humanitarianism were appalled. Men and women began to call for change.

Historians have disagreed over the extent to which change was brought about through the ideas and influence of Jeremy Bentham. He was a man of the Enlightenment who believed that man's best interests lay in accordance with the laws of nature, and that the laws of man were invariably bad. This put him firmly on the side of *laissez-faire*. But, unlike many Enlightenment thinkers, he did not believe in the inherent goodness of man or natural rights. Man was a selfish animal, and the principle of Utility – that which promotes the greatest happiness of the greatest number – could be fulfilled only if man's actions were guided by law in accordance with self-interest. Bentham was a legal reformer, and for him law had a creative role to play in the improvement of human society. Whilst accepting *laissez-faire* in economic policy, therefore, he provided the ideological basis for state intervention in social affairs.

Evidence for direct Benthamite Utilitarian influence is circumstantial, but persuasive. Though the pressure for change was not of the Benthamites' making, they were influential in determining the actual course of change. The Poor Law Amendment Act of 1834 is a good example of this. The demand for change was almost universal; but the particular form that change took was ideological, and that ideology was provided by two men – Nassau Senior and Edwin Chadwick – on whom Bentham had been an important influence. From Bentham also the reformers took two important principles which were at variance with much contemporary feeling: those of centralised administration and inspection.

The rise of the inspectorate – numbers of whom were still doctors and clergymen – marks the transition from the amateur to the professional.

Furnished with limited powers, they were able to observe the contrast between the tentative and reluctantly conceded law and what the situation really demanded. Armed with this experience, they were able to argue for further and more effective legislation. The task was a hard one, and progress slow. Much of the activity of the 1830s, in factory and educational reform, did not bear full fruit until the 1870s. Each case had to be more than made on its merits against a prevailing philosophy of freedom for the individual and low public expenditure. Much legislation was optional, every concession was made to local susceptibilities and vested interests, and as a percentage of the gross national product, government expenditure actually fell throughout the nineteenth century. Nevertheless, as many contemporaries feared, the administrative state continued to grow in response to the increasing complexities of modern society.

Factory reform

The tentative beginnings of factory legislation were paternalistic, affecting only pauper children in cotton factories. The initiative came from a group of Lancashire doctors led by Thomas Percival of Manchester, whom the local magistrates invited to report on an epidemic at one of Sir Robert Peel's mills in 1784. As a result of Percival's report the magistrates agreed to send pauper children to the factories in their area only if the masters accepted limitations on their hours of employment. The resolution was not adhered to for long, but Peel, the richest man on the Manchester cotton exchange, had been alerted to a problem. In 1796 Percival and his friends formed themselves into the 'Manchester Board of Health' to continue to agitate for better conditions. One of their number was a young Welsh factory manager, Robert Owen. About the same time, David Dale of the New Lanark mills in Scotland was in correspondence with James Currie, a Liverpool doctor and member of Percival's circle, expressing anxiety about the welfare of his pauper apprentices if he sold his mills. He was therefore delighted when Owen became his son-in-law and owner-manager of New Lanark in 1800.

This concern for pauper children led Peel to sponsor the first factory act, the Health and Morals of Apprentices Act of 1802. It did not affect 'free' children, whose parents could look after them, it provided for no effective inspection and it rapidly fell out of date. Benevolent factory masters such as Peel and Owen, who had made their fortunes relatively early in the industrial revolution, became increasingly concerned about the exploitation of all children and their lack of education. Owen led the propaganda campaign and the House of Commons set up a Select Committee in 1816 to take evidence, but by the time Peel's second Factory Act came on to the statute book in 1819 its clauses had been emasculated after intensive propaganda from employers. Owen began to lose patience with gradualist reform. Two further Acts were introduced by J. C. Hobhouse in 1825 and 1831, but these made only minor modifications to hours of work, applied only to cotton factories, and still contained no effective provision for enforcement. The cotton-spinners' union led by John Doherty tried to bring prosecutions against offending masters, but secured only 27 convictions out of 187 cases brought.

Meanwhile, the factory system was spreading to other sections of the textile industry, and in 1830 Richard Oastler became aware of conditions in the worsted factories of Bradford. Oastler was an Evangelical Tory, like Peel. He had been brought up a Wesleyan, and in his youth had worked among the poor of his native Leeds with his friend, Michael Sadler. Like most Wesleyans, he was a keen opponent of slavery. Realising that children were being employed in Bradford factories in worse conditions than slaves in the West Indies, Oastler sprang into action with all the zeal of a convert. He engaged in a lengthy and increasingly acrimonious correspondence in the local press, and Sadler in Parliament introduced a Bill to extend the protection of factory children to those working in the wool textile industry. A Select Committee was appointed in 1832 which had gathered evidence only from the reformers before its existence was terminated at the dissolution of Parliament. Sadler lost his seat in the first general election of the reformed Parliament, and the cause of factory reform was taken up by another Evangelical Tory, Lord Ashley.

In this story are some of the main ingredients of a reform agitation: the awakening conscience, limited legislation, and the use of a Select Committee biased towards the viewpoint of the sponsoring Member of Parliament to expose the need for further reform. The aim of the reformers was to limit children's work to 10 hours a day, but behind this moderate and acceptable aim was the intention to force a similar limitation on adult hours, for adult labour depended upon the assistance of children. The employers were naturally aware of this stratagem, and they had the opportunity to put their case when the new Whig government forestalled Ashley, appointing a Royal Commission led by three men influenced by Bentham – Edwin Chadwick, Thomas Southwood Smith (a doctor) and Thomas Tooke (an economist). The Commission's recommendations, bearing all the signs of Chadwick's handiwork, were embodied in the first really effective Factory Act (1833).

The Act was a very clever piece of legislation which supported the main case of the factory masters whilst conceding the moral basis of the reformers' position. Chadwick's intention was to prohibit the employment of children under the age of 9, and to limit the hours of those between 9 and 13 to eight a day. This met the demands of the humanitarians whilst leaving open the probability of children being worked in relays to support a lengthened 16-hour day for adults. A late alteration to the Bill modified the impact of this clause, though, by limiting the hours of young people between the ages of 13 and 18 to 12 per day, which in effect established the 12-hour day for adults as well. These provisions were to be applied to all textile factories except lace factories, although the clause prohibiting the labour of children under 9 did not apply to the silk industry. The most important clauses for the future concerned not hours but the Benthamite principles of Inspection and Education. Children were to be educated for two hours a day, and the Act was to be enforced by a salaried inspectorate.

Historians frequently comment on the ineffectiveness of these two points of the legislation, but this is to miss the point of their significance. The Inspectors were working in a totally new area of legislation; their aim was not to make factory masters into criminals, but to protect the workers; and they had to be confident of a successful prosecution before bringing a case. Penalties were certainly too light; the education clause was easily avoided; and there was no check on the ages of children before Civil Registration was begun in 1836. But the Inspectors did their work conscientiously and made some impact. In the first five full years of the Act in the major textile districts of England, an average of nearly 600 charges were laid each year, with success in three out of every four cases. Moreover, the Inspectors' experience in working the Act led them to demand further legislation. Their reports to the Home Office – especially those of Leonard Horner, who was responsible for Scotland until 1836 and then Lancashire – became propaganda for further reform, and the Inspectors gave their full backing to Ashley's efforts in the 1840s.

In 1840, Ashley secured a Committee of Inquiry into the working of the 1833 Act, and into child employment in industries not covered by the Act. The first report, published in May 1842, concerned conditions in coal mines. The Commissioners were Thomas Tooke, Southwood Smith and two of the most active factory inspectors, Leonard Horner and R. J. Saunders, who was responsible for the Yorkshire area. Their report so shocked the House of Commons that a Bill to prevent all children and women working underground in the mines and to establish a mines inspectorate passed through its first and second readings without a division early in June and, despite fierce opposition from coal-owners in the Lords, became law at the end of July. Seldom can the technique of inquiry, reaction and legislation have been exploited so effectively to secure a major reform. For the first time in the nineteenth century, Parliament had interfered with the conditions of labour of adults – though not yet of adult males.

The next achievement of the Child Employment Commission was a modest measure limiting child labour in print works. Meanwhile, the review of the 1833 Act produced a further measure in 1844 which tightened up procedures in accordance with the Inspectors' advice and forbade night work by women. In just over a decade public opinion had begun to move significantly, and in 1847, during a period of recession and slack working, John Fielden was able to secure a Ten Hours Act – that is, 10 hours for all but adult males; but the system of working other groups in relays, which the Inspectors believed had been prevented by the 1844 Act, was exploited to thwart the hopes of the reformers once the recession had ended. An important compromise was reached in 1850 which limited the hours of work of women and young persons to 10½ between the hours of 6.00 a.m. and 6.00 p.m., and created the Saturday half-holiday. With the inclusion of children within these provisions by an amending Act of 1853, an effective 10½–hour day was established for all adult employees in the textile factories of Britain. But the 10-hours provision was not restored until 1874, and adult males were still, in theory, excluded from the legislation.

The regulation of child and female labour in textile factories set the pace for other industries, but it must be remembered that most employees were not textile workers. When the Factory Acts' Extension Act in 1864 brought relief to about 50,000 workers not involved in textile production, fewer than 850,000 workers in all were covered by the legislation. Only in 1867 were the terms of the factory acts applied to all workplaces in which more than 50 people were employed; not until the Factories and Workshops Act of 1878 did the 10-hour day and half-day Saturday (56½ hour week) become standard; not until the 1886 Shops Act were the first steps taken to limit the hours worked by children and young persons in the retail trade; and not until the Coal Mines Act of 1908, which fixed underground working hours to a maximum of eight, did the state interfere with the hours of adult male labour. The principle of compulsion, which was so much a part of Edwin Chadwick's philosophy, was so alien to nineteenth-century ways of thought that it was conceded only slowly: to regulate the affairs of children, women, paupers, lunatics and, only in the last resort, adult males.

Public health

Public health issues caused great conflicts of principle for Victorians anxious to preserve freedom and health. For Edwin Chadwick the matter was straightforward: sickness was wasteful, cost money, caused pauperism and bred immorality. His task was to persuade others that legislation was necessary to improve the health of the people. In this he was aided by several distinguished doctors and recurrent outbreaks of Asiatic cholera. Concern about the state of British towns reached a peak in the early 1830s: Charles Turner Thackrah, a Leeds doctor, carried out a survey of occupational disease, morbidity and mortality in 1831–2, and James Phillips Kay of Manchester published his study of the cotton workers of Manchester in 1832. Further evidence was added by the London and Manchester Statistical Societies, whose reports on conditions in parts of London, the manufacturing districts and three parishes in Rutland were used by Chadwick in his *Report* of 1842.[40] Meanwhile, people's awareness of the health issue was heightened by the cholera epidemic of 1831–2, causing the Government to create a temporary Central Board of Health, with limited powers to supervise and receive reports from local boards set up in large towns to contain the disease. The major problem was a lack of understanding of cholera and other diseases and of how they spread. It was observed that the most insanitary and malodorous districts usually experienced the highest levels of disease, though sometimes better areas also mysteriously suffered. Although the dangers of contagion were known, many people (including Chadwick) believed that disease was carried in the bad smells of the heavily polluted atmosphere. They considered quarantine and isolation of cases a waste of time, and advocated cleaning up the environment instead. Accidentally this led them to concentrate on one of the main causes of disease, including cholera and typhoid – a polluted water supply.

Chadwick's interest in public health arose out of his experience with the Poor Law Commission. Following a letter from Chadwick to the Poor Law Commissioners on the subject in 1838, the government set up a Commission of Inquiry comprising Neil Arnot, James Kay and Thomas Southwood Smith. All three men, like Chadwick, had been influenced by Bentham, and all three were doctors with experience of urban conditions. Their reports on London pointed clearly to overcrowding, poor ventilation, inadequate refuse disposal and bad water as major causes of disease – not, as some politicians and moralists believed, individual moral weakness and culpability. Chadwick then persuaded the Bishop of London to suggest a further inquiry into conditions throughout the whole country, including Scotland. Meanwhile, in the House of Commons, R. A. Slaney secured a Select Committee on the Health of Towns. Chadwick's report was not ready until 1842, and aroused great opposition from vested interests opposed to his strong desire for centralisation and compulsion. The two volumes of evidence, together with a third volume by Chadwick, were published under his name alone as the *Report on the Sanitary Condition of the Labouring Population of Great Britain*. It was a masterpiece of propaganda which, together with the Slaney Committee Report, led the Conservative Home Secretary, Sir James Graham, to set up a Royal Commission on the Health of Towns which reported in 1844–5. To add further public pressure a Health of Towns Association was formed, with local associations in the provinces. After abortive attempts at legislation in 1845–7 Lord Morpeth, the new Whig Home Secretary, successfully introduced a Bill for Promoting the Public Health in 1848, the first major statute dealing with public health in Britain.

The Act provided for a General Board of Health in London, and required Local Boards of Health with medical officers to be set up in places where the death rate exceeded 23 per 1,000 (the national average was 21 per 1,000). It was carried amid great opposition, and its powers of compulsion were saved only at the last by the House of Lords. In scope it was limited, and applied neither to Scotland (which had to wait until 1875 for a similar measure) nor London. The latter was a legislative minefield of over 300 fragmented local authorities, and was given its own Metropolitan Commission of Sewers in a separate Act. The general tone of the Public Health Act was permissive, and it paid great respect to local initiative. Indeed, the main provisions of the Act had been anticipated in Liverpool, which had secured private legislation in 1846, creating W. H. Duncan the first Medical Officer of Health in the country.

A return of the cholera in 1848–9 immediately appeared to vindicate Chadwick's campaign, but as the panic waned so enthusiasm for the measure declined. The General Board of Health, with Southwood Smith as its first Medical Officer, had been given powers only until 1854, by which time nearly 300 towns had applied for local boards – mainly without compulsion – bringing about 2 million people under its provisions. But in 1854 the Home Secretary, Lord Palmerston (whose son-in-law, Ashley – now Lord Shaftesbury – was one of the three members of the Board) had to fight hard to secure a renewal of its powers. Chadwick had upset too many people with his doctrinaire and authoritarian manner. He was pensioned off, and yet subsequent Acts in 1866, 1871, 1872 and 1875, as well as a Royal Commission in 1868, vindicated his approach.

Chadwick's mantle as leader of the public health movement fell to John Simon, Medical Officer for the City of London (1848–55) and then Southwood Smith's successor at the General Board of Health. Following a further change in the law in 1858, he was appointed first Medical Officer of the Privy Council, a position he used to create an unofficial Ministry of Health. For 13 years he pushed forward the cause of public health in Britain, codifying and extending previous laws, at last securing the principle of compulsion in 1866 and its effective implementation by the Act of 1872, which set up a network of sanitary authorities with local medical officers in all parts of the country.

If the tone of this early legislation was hesitant and permissive, that cannot be said of two other areas of public health legislation in which the state did not hesitate to assume powers of compulsion such as the late twentieth century would regard as wholly improper infringements of individual liberty. The issues of compulsory vaccination for children, and control of venereal disease in prostitutes, show the other side of the Victorian state.

The Vaccination Acts of 1853 and 1869 were an important innovation in preventative medicine, but they were resented by parents as an intrusion on their liberty to control their own children. An Anti-Compulsory Vaccination League was set up, stories were spread of children who had died as a result of receiving the vaccine, and some parents were even prepared to go to gaol rather than submit. Strong feelings were aroused as two classic Victorian principles came into conflict – personal liberty and the public good. Liberty finally won, with the repeal of the Acts in 1898.

The Contagious Diseases Acts of 1864, 1866 and 1869 were intended to prevent the spread of venereal disease in the armed forces, and gave the police powers in 18 garrison towns and ports to arrest any woman suspected of being a prostitute, subject her to a medical examination, and confine her to a secure hospital for treatment if she were found to be infected. Any woman who refused to be inspected had to prove her virtue in court. Libertarians and women's leaders were outraged by the Acts, and when it seemed likely in 1869 that they would be extended to the civilian population in the North of England a campaign was mounted to have the Acts abolished, led by Josephine Butler of Liverpool and the Ladies National Association. Gradually opinion was won over, but the Acts were not repealed until 1886.

Changing attitudes, 1880–1914

By 1880 the Victorian State had assumed powers to control the worst abuses and ensure minimum standards of health for a majority of its citizens. Legislation had been introduced to control pollution of the environment (the Alkali Acts of 1863, 1868 and 1874), to prevent the adulteration of food (1860, 1872 and 1874), to compel landlords to improve insanitary dwellings (the Torrens Act, 1865) and to give local authorities powers for the compulsory purchase and demolition of slum housing (the Cross Act, 1975). The Education Acts of 1870 (England and Wales) and 1872 (Scotland) had created public responsibility for the provision of education, and the Factory Acts of 1867, 1874 and 1878 had limited the hours of working for women and young people in factories and workshops to no more than 10 per day, and had effectively established the Saturday half-holiday for industrial workers. The Public Health Act of 1875 had dealt not only with matters of drainage and sewerage, but had given local authorities unlimited rating powers to create municipally owned gas and water supplies and to purchase land for public parks. Inspectorates had been established to oversee working conditions in factories and mines, to prevent nuisances under the Alkali Acts and to watch over the operation of the poor law and education. Compulsion had been extended to the registration of births and deaths (1874) and school attendance (1872 in Scotland and 1880 in England and Wales). All this had happened piecemeal, without any overall policy of state action. Much of the legislation remained permissive, inadequately enforced or limited in scope. Local initiative was preferred to central state action: 'municipal socialism' was becoming acceptable, but state socialism was abhorrent. Yet beneath the surface a slow change was taking place, as men came to realise the scale and nature of the problems still to be tackled, the weaknesses of current legislation and the inadequacies of private and voluntary effort.

Socialist demonstrations and mounting unemployment made poverty once more an issue in the 1880s. The publication of Congregationalist Andrew Mearns's *The Bitter Cry of Outcast London* in 1883 roused a new wave of religious and philanthropic concern, while Salvationist William Booth's *In Darkest London and the Way Out* showed a remarkably secular approach to London's poor when published in 1890. Above all, the publication of a survey by the Social Democratic Federation in the *Pall Mall Gazette* in 1885 stirred Charles Booth to conduct his own investigations into conditions in the metropolis, resulting eventually in the 17 volumes of his *Life and Labour of the People of London*, published between 1889 and 1903. Booth's work in turn inspired Rowntree to examine York in 1899. To this literature was added a new awareness stimulated by the University Settlement movement, which brought undergraduates of the higher social classes to live and work among the poor of the inner cities, and to experience conditions of which they would otherwise have remained complacently ignorant.

The first Settlement House, Toynbee Hall, was opened in London in 1884 by Canon Samuel Barnett as a result of his work in the parish of St Jude's, Whitechapel. Barnett had been a founder of the Charity Organisation Society, but living among the poor had brought him to see the inadequacy of the Society's approach. His example was rapidly followed, and by 1913 there were 27 Settlement Houses in London, with a further 12 in the English provinces and five in Scotland. The impact which these places made on the sons of the political and social élite can scarcely be exaggerated. Out of compassion tinged with guilt a new social policy was formed. Among the people who spent time at Toynbee Hall were William Beveridge (sub-warden, 1903–5) who is rightly regarded as the main inspiration for the creation of the Welfare State; Robert Morant, W. J. Braithwaite and H. Llewellyn Smith, all of whom were leading civil servants responsible for much of the social-welfare legislation of the early twentieth century; and Clement Attlee, whose post-1945 Labour Cabinet created the welfare state.

Between 1880 and 1905 successive Governments of both political parties extended the volume and scope of welfare legislation and instituted inquiries into a range of social issues. Attitudes were softening towards the 'deserving' poor, though this had the effect of hardening the poor law towards the 'undeserving'. The process of removing the respectable poor from the poor law was hastened by democratic changes in the franchise, which made more burdensome the disqualification of paupers from voting. In health provision, the 1875 Public Health Act had empowered local authorities to set up hospitals out of the rates, and in 1886 Joseph Chamberlain, as President of the Local Government Board, instructed the Guardians to find work for the unemployed which would not stigmatise them as paupers. This approach culminated in the 1905 Unemployed

Workmen's Act, which gave local authorities powers to establish labour exchanges and labour colonies, and to create work for the unemployed at the ratepayers' expense. The main aim behind the flood of legislation carried by Liberal governments between 1906 and 1914 was to continue this process, by attacking those causes of poverty which Booth and Rowntree had helped isolate and publicise: family poverty, old age, sickness, death of the breadwinner, low wages and unemployment. There was no overall plan and no sharp break with previous practice, yet the cumulative effect of these individual measures was to mark an end to the old approach and a beginning of the new.

Legislation to help children included the provision of free school meals by those local authorities who wished to supplement parental payments and charitable efforts (1906), and the introduction of the schools medical service, with compulsory medical examinations (1907). An important development in family law was the Children Act (1908), which instituted juvenile courts and consolidated the work of the Prevention of Cruelty to Children Act (1889) which had first given the courts power to intervene against parents to protect children. Finally in this area, an effort was made to improve infant mortality rates, with the Midwives Act (1900), which aimed to raise the standard of care at birth through the training and registration of midwives.

Low wages were not easily legislated against, and there was little support for the idea of a national minimum wage, but something was done in response to the scandal of sweated labour through the Trade Boards Act (1909), which set up statutory machinery for regulating wages in several low-pay industries such as tailoring and shirtmaking, although only 100,000 workers were initially affected. In the same year the Labour Exchanges Act created a national network through which the unemployed could seek work. Help for those injured whilst at work was extended to all workers except higher-paid non-manual workers by the Workmen's Compensation Act (1906), which also for the first time made provision for disablement or death due to certain industrial diseases.

Old age had been shown to be a major cause of poverty. Canon Barnett had proposed an old-age pension in 1883, Charles Booth had been converted to the idea in 1892 and a Royal Commission on the Aged Poor had reported favourably in 1895; but it was not until 1908 that the first legislation was enacted to provide pensions, and then in only a very restricted measure, providing a maximum of 5 *s.* (25p) a week for poor but deserving cases over the age of 70: 490,000 people qualified for benefit, many of them women. This pension was entirely funded by the state, at a total cost of £8 million – £1.5 million more than expected. Warned by this experience of the cost of welfare, the government adhered to the principle of self-help through the device of a contributory national insurance scheme for its most important piece of welfare legislation, the National Insurance Act of 1911.

The Act was in two parts. The first provided compulsory insurance for most employed persons against the financial consequences of sickness, disablement and maternity, but not death of the breadwinner, which was to remain a matter for private insurance despite the wishes of Lloyd George. Each employee was to contribute 4*d.* (about 2p) per week, the employer would add a further 3*d.* (just over 1p) and the government 5*d.* (just over 2p). Sick pay was to be at the rate of 10*s.* (50p) a week, and the scheme was to be administered through approved societies registered under the Industrial and Provident Societies Act of 1893. The second part dealt with unemployment. Benefit of 7*s.* (35p) a week for 15 weeks would be paid to around 2.25 million workers in trades vulnerable to short periods of unemployment such as building, engineering and shipbuilding. The contribution was to be 2½*d.* (1p) each from employee and employer, with 25 per cent extra from the state, and again the scheme was to operate through approved societies.

The hybrid nature of this legislation, with its restricted and restrictive nature, typifies the Liberal reforms of the pre-First-World-War years. They covered new ground, and yet clung to old principles. They showed a more humane understanding of poverty, and sought to remove the respectable and deserving poor from the ambit of the poor law. Yet they still assumed that the function of the State was to supplement individual initiative, not to replace it, and they left the structure of the poor law to act as a safety net for those too poor or unworthy to benefit from the welfare legislation.

The poor law was clearly in need of overhaul by the beginning of the twentieth century. Quite apart from the changing attitude towards poverty which was reinforcing the view of those who wished to abolish the existing system, there was pressure from within for change, as the costs of institutional provision for the poor rose with the Local Government Board's policy of gradually improving standards of relief, and as the social composition of Boards of Guardians widened after the Local Government Act of 1894. With rising unemployment in 1904, the Conservative government decided to appoint a Royal Commission on the Poor Law and Relief of Distress to investigate the position. The Commission began its work in November 1905 and reported in February 1909. Of the 18 Commissioners, 14 reported in favour of replacing the Guardians with Public Assistance Committees, part elected and part nominated by voluntary organisations; they wanted to retain the workhouses but to continue the development of more specialised services; they advocated a more rigorous classification of applicants for relief, distinguishing between the short-term and long-term unemployed; and they favoured Labour Exchanges, a contributory national insurance scheme, old-age pensions and school clinics. The minority, whose report is associated with Beatrice Webb (who had been one of Charles Booth's assistants and whose husband, Fabian Socialist Sidney Webb, probably drafted the Minority Report) agreed with many of these points but took a more radical line, demanding the break-up of the poor law entirely, and a rationalisation of the administrative machinery which had grown up around it. Each case of poverty was to be analysed and then treated according to its cause by the appropriate local or (for the unemployed) national authority. The poor were victims, not criminals, and the state had an obligation to lay down a national minimum standard below which no poor person should fall.

The Webbs' propaganda on behalf of the Minority Report has meant that it has long been accepted by historians of the Welfare State as a great and progressive document, quite different in tone from the Majority Report, which reflected the views of the Charity Organisation Society. In fact, the two reports were agreed on many points, and the Minority was no less harsh than the Majority towards the unworthy poor. The Fabian Socialists possessed the same drive towards compulsion and re-education that had made Edwin Chadwick so unpopular. Nevertheless, it is true that the Webbs' vision contained important seeds for the future. At the time, however, it was politically unacceptable, and in pursuing it so vehemently they ignored their many points of agreement with the Majority, and left the Government (with the ineffectual John Burns as the responsible Minister) to do nothing beyond nibble away at the edges of the existing system in the time-honoured way.

When one has put the Liberal welfare legislation of 1906–14 into context, it hardly constitutes the origins of the Welfare State; but the spate of legislation in the decade before the First World War is unusual and needs some overall explanation. Some basic reasons for a change in attitude among key administrators have already been discussed, and credit should be given to the two ministers – Winston Churchill at the Board of Trade (1908–10), and Lloyd George at the Exchequer (1908–15) – who pushed the most important legislation through Parliament. Public opinion towards poverty was also changing, but only slowly, and many people, from Members of Parliament to members of the working class, were hostile to an extension of state control over the individual. On the other hand, Liberals were aware of growing political pressure from Socialists demanding more state action in defence of the poor. As Thomas Jones commented on Lloyd George's skilful if sly manoeuvres, he 'spiked the socialist guns with essentially conservative measures from the liberal arsenal'. More broadly, those with responsibility for shaping and making legislation were aware of the welfare legislation already in force in Germany, which was coming to be seen as Britain's great rival in international affairs; and there was widespread discussion of 'national degeneration' prompted by the eugenics movement and the low level of health among military volunteers at the time of the Second Boer War (1899–1902). National well-being and the security and glory of the British Empire were of major concern. The desire to rescue and elevate the poor came not only from philanthropists conscious of the injustice and waste of individual poverty, but from state-corporatists anxious to raise and strengthen the British 'race'.

The origins of the Welfare State

The First World War added weight to the arguments which had led to the welfare reforms of the pre-war period. In the peculiar circumstances of the wartime emergency, principles were breached, precedents set and expectations raised. The Government began to pay family allowances to members of the armed forces for the first time in October 1914, and pensions to the widows and orphans of those killed in the war from November 1915. Rent controls were introduced in 1915, and price controls in 1917. Unemployment insurance was extended to most of the workforce in 1916. On the other hand, the demands of war led to a deterioration in civilian health care and a rise in the incidence of tuberculosis, though infant care was improved with the provision of milk to infants at cost price from 1915 and the establishment of ante-natal and child-welfare clinics from 1918.

Politicians maintained morale during the war with promises of 'reconstruction' after it was over. Poor-law reform was again discussed. A Ministry of Labour (one of the recommendations of the Minority Report in 1909) was set up in 1917, taking over the labour functions of the Board of Trade, and a Ministry of Health was created in 1919 to replace the Local Government Board. A Ministry of Pensions was also set up in 1919 which immediately proposed a far-reaching reform of benefits. The record of the Coalition Government appears impressive: an Education Act (Fisher's Act, 1918) raised the school-leaving age to 14, extended the principle of free education to all local authority schools and provided grants for nursery schools; subsidies to encourage house-building were introduced by the House and Town Planning Act (Addison's Act, 1919); the Old Age Pensions Act (1919) raised the basic pension to 10*s*. (50p) a week and removed the pauper disqualification from old people in receipt of money from the Poor Law Guardians; unemployment benefit was increased to cover 47 weeks a year instead of 15 – the so-called 'extended benefit' – without an equivalent rise in contributions. Much was done, but far less than the advocates of change had hoped for. The forces of conservatism were marshalling even before the war had ended, and the Government became increasingly alarmed at the costs of a genuine reconstruction. By 1921 high taxation was leading to demands for economies, and Sir Eric Geddes was asked to make recommendations. With the first of his Reports in 1922 the 'Geddes Axe' fell. Education and housing suffered most.

Pensions escaped the initial cuts and, though the actual rate remained at 10*s*. (50p) a week throughout the inter-war period, the range and nature of the pensions scheme was gradually changed. In 1920, as a result of the war, blind persons over the age of 50 became entitled to a pension, and in 1924 the first Labour Government extended the old-age pension to all over-70s in need. The succeeding Conservative administration then brought in pensions for widows, orphans and wives on a contributory basis, with the intention of gradually phasing out the non-contributory means-tested pension altogether.

Two factors above all others shaped the development of social welfare policy between the 1922 and 1939: the need to limit public expenditure, and the rise in unemployment. The poor law broke down under the strain. Some Guardians paid out benefits to whole families during the major strikes of 1918–21 and 1926, although the law allowed payment only to destitute dependants of strikers. In 1921 Poplar Council refused to raise a high rate as a protest at having to contribute to general London County Council expenditure, thus raising the whole issue of equalisation of the rates, which had not been faced squarely even in 1834. Twenty councillors, led by George Lansbury (who had been one of the Minority in 1909), went to gaol. Guardians found themselves torn between local demands for increased expenditure, and central government's demands for cuts in expenditure. Some, as at Poplar, paid outdoor relief at higher than the recommended levels, and most refused to use their workhouses for the unemployed. The Government responded in 1929 by abolishing the Guardians and disbanding the poor law unions. Public Assistance Committees were set up to help the able-bodied; the workhouse test was ended in 1930, and the former workhouses passed either to the local authorities as hospitals or survived as Public Assistance Institutions used mainly to accommodate the 'feeble-minded' poor, incapable of supporting themselves. Through the Public Assistance Committees, which were financed partly out of the rates and partly by central government, the latter hoped to control outdoor relief more effectively than had the old Guardians. Ironically, the main framework of the poor law was thus abolished through the desire to save money and control the generosity of the Guardians.

The burden of unemployment also undermined the fabric of National Insurance. With the distinction made in 1911 between the insured and the non-insured, and the introduction of non-contributory 'extended benefit' in 1921, the scheme became unworkable. A means test was introduced in 1922 which conflicted with the insurance basis of the scheme, but the Labour Government abolished it again in 1924. The most significant change came in 1927 when the Conservative Government conceded 'extended benefits' as of right, thus undermining the contributory principle. Indeed, there seemed to be no consistent principle behind the policies of successive governments, with 18 Acts of Parliament passed between 1920 and 1930 in an effort to make and mend. The overall effect was a steady extension of welfare benefits and a retreat from the principles of both 1834 and 1911. By 1931 the National Insurance fund was £115 million in deficit and there were 2.6 million unemployed. The second Labour Government broke over pressure to make economies, and the new National Government cut benefits by 10 per cent. The system staggered on until 1934, when the Unemployment Act restored the cut but reduced benefit to 26 weeks, extended the scheme to include agricultural workers, and replaced the Public Assistance Committees with the Unemployment Assistance Board, a central body which finally removed from local authorities responsibility for the able-bodied. Slowly, both with pensions and with sickness and unemployment relief, the inter-war governments were groping their way towards a scheme of contributory, non-means-tested benefit for all, plus a supplementary means-tested hand-out ('the dole') to those most in need. Old ideas of 'less eligibility' persisted, and the need for economy kept benefits at a minimal level, but attitudes were changing in the 1930s as men like John Maynard Keynes, a Liberal, and Harold Macmillan, a Conservative, looked forward to economic growth within a planned economy, improved welfare services and greater social justice.

Further changes were inevitable once the Second World War had created new challenges and obligations. The blueprint for 'reconstruction' – the Beveridge Report, *Social Insurance and Allied Services* – was published in December 1942 and accepted by the House of Commons in February 1943. Freed from the blight of unemployment, the Labour Government of 1945 was able to make a new start. But the legislation of 1945–51 and the political propaganda which later surrounded it have been in danger of blinding the historian to the great achievements of the inter-war years and the part played by Conservative as well as Labour administrations in the process.

The Welfare State

The major difference between the pre-1939 and post-1945 benefit systems was that the former was still based on the negative and selective concept of means, while the latter concentrated on relief according to the positive principles of universality and need. Early in the war the new spirit could be seen in the development of family welfare, with free milk, free immunisation, free cod-liver oil and a subsidised school meals service for all children, irrespective of parental income. These provisions were also incorporated in the Education Act of 1944 (the Butler Act) which raised the school-leaving age to 15 and provided free secondary education for all following selection at the age of 11. But major legislation affecting the benefit system had to wait until the end of the war. In 1945 the Family Allowance Act gave mothers 5*s.* (25p) a week for every second and subsequent child – an important step towards reducing child poverty. Following the general election of 1945, which brought a majority Labour

Government to power for the first time, the main foundation stones of the Welfare State were laid in two important Acts carried in 1946: the National Insurance Act, which retained the language of insurance but in fact provided subsidies from general taxation to fund old-age pensions and sickness, unemployment and death benefits for all insured women, men and wives; and the National Health Service Act, which from 1948 created a free medical service for all, funded partly from National Insurance contributions, but mainly out of general taxation. In 1948 the poor law was formally abolished, though a last vestige of the old system survived when the Unemployment Assistance Board of 1934 was replaced by a new National Assistance Board which provided a means-tested safety net for those not adequately covered by the new legislation. A court decision as late as 1997 ruled that this National Assistance was still available for those, such as immigrants seeking political asylum, who did not qualify for other benefits.

These measures were at the time regarded as genuinely radical and, although the broad direction of policy had all-party support, Labour's insistence on universality went rather further than many Liberals and Conservatives would have wished. Indeed, the demands of the National Health Service were such that even Labour retreated a little in 1951, when means-tested charges were imposed for spectacles. The Conservatives followed this in 1952 with similar charges for prescriptions and dental treatment. Further inequalities were reintroduced by both parties in the 1960s, according to the theory that those who could afford to do so should pay higher contributions in exchange for higher benefits: the graduated pension scheme of 1961 (Conservative), followed by earnings-related supplements for sickness and unemployment benefits in 1966 (Labour). The Welfare State was still in danger of providing a two-tier system with low basic benefits supplemented by National Assistance and its successors, Supplementary Benefit (1966) and Income Support (1988) for the poor, and higher benefits for the rest, who could afford to pay more in the form of higher contributions and higher taxes. With the 'rediscovery' of the extent of poverty as defined by National Assistance levels in the 1960s, and the rising cost of benefits, governments resorted to the policy of seeking out specific need and applying to it a means test, with rate rebates for those with the lowest incomes (the 1966 Rating Act), new benefits for the disabled and very old (National Insurance Act, 1970), and Family Income Supplement (1971). At the same time the retreat from universality (condemned as a waste of scarce resources) was continued with the withdrawal of free milk for all children in state schools.

The Beveridge Plan, on which the concept of the Welfare State was based, assumed an expanding economy with minimal unemployment. With the experience of the 1930s in mind, Beveridge argued that this meant rigorous planning and central control over industry, investment and labour. In the event such controls were not necessary after 1945 and, despite the fears of Conservatives, they were not introduced by the postwar Labour government in anything other than a marginal way. But with full employment came the risk of inflation, and by 1960 Beveridge had seen that this could be the new enemy threatening the achievements of the Welfare State. He urged voluntary restraint by employers and trade unions:

> Should that effort fail, the issues facing us will be clear. If the organisations that now determine wages continue to demand and to give more money for less work, the people of Britain must choose between establishing some State control of prices and suffering endless inflation which will debase our currency, will make saving seemed absurd, and will reduce to want and to need for public charity a growing number and proportion of our men and women, in the sunset of their lives.[41]

Only the Liberal Party took this warning to heart and began to advocate statutory controls over incomes and prices. The Conservatives and Labour, for different reasons, contemplated such interventionism only as an unpalatable and temporary expedient. Inflation did continue. But what Beveridge did not see was that the resulting damage to British competitiveness in world markets and consequent rise in unemployment would not check the inflation rate. In the 1970s Britain found itself with accelerating rates of both inflation and unemployment. With more old people and more unemployed to support, and with rising expectations generated by the paradox of increasing living-standards among those in work, the Welfare State was put under increasing pressure. By the 1980s its future shape had become a matter of intense political debate and, despite a fall in inflation in the 1990s, persistent levels of high unemployment continued to be a drain on national resources, prompting the political parties in and out of government to consider whether assistance should not be directed towards those in greatest need, with a further erosion of universality, and even whether there should not be a return to private insurance for the better-off.

Law, order and restraint

Within any community there are pressures towards conformity and penalties imposed upon those who do not choose to conform. These penalties can be informal and customary, such as the 'rough music' performed by neighbours assembled outside the house of an offender, banging pans and trays to show disapproval; or formal, such as fines and periods of detention imposed through the courts according to the law of the land. What constitutes a criminal act depends upon whether or not disapproval leads to legislation prohibiting the anti-social behaviour. In this way, legislation in criminal matters reflects the values of society and the extent to which deviation is tolerated. A study of criminal activity has therefore to include not only those factors leading to the commission of an act, but also those leading to that act being described as an offence.

There are two major difficulties which stand in the way of an accurate understanding of trends in criminality: first, the lack of adequate national statistics before the mid-nineteenth century (1857 for England and Wales, 1869 for Scotland); and, second, the distinctions which have to be made between levels of committed crime (which remain unknown), reported crime, recorded crime, prosecutions and convictions. Crime rates depend in part upon the preparedness of victims to report offences and of the authorities to prosecute; and criminal statistics (where they exist) often tell the historian more about the effectiveness of policing than about the commission of offences.

Crime and criminals

The reason why people commit crimes has long been a matter of debate. Much of the evidence for crime is filtered through the assumptions and ideologies of contemporary observers, usually of a higher social class than the criminals they write about. One common argument links criminality with immorality. Evangelical Christians of the later eighteenth and nineteenth centuries firmly believed in the power of original sin, which only Christian redemption could cancel: hence their great interest in prison visiting. For them crime was a matter of individual moral failure. An alternative view which became popular in the Enlightenment was that man is intrinsically good and is corrupted only by his environment. For those who believed this, crime was a disease to be eradicated like any other. In practice these contradictory views tended to merge into one which held that, though children are evil by nature, they can be made good by nurture: the schoolmaster was society's most effective defence against crime. Nineteenth-century reformers, armed with the Christian Gospel, Education and Sanitary Reform, sought to purge their inner cities of the dark, seething mass of criminality which inhabited them. Individual hardened cases could be put into isolation to limit the dangers of infection, while the next generation could be rescued for Christianity and civilisation through education and moral reform.

Whether criminals were made by their environment or simply happened to congregate in dens of iniquity, they seemed to contemporary observers such as Henry Mayhew and Charles Booth to form a separate social class. Bad conditions, poverty, drunkenness, prostitution, begging and thieving went together. Children in such places appeared to be born criminals, and in the later nineteenth century, as Darwinism made its impact, anthropologists pondered the apparently hereditary nature of criminality.

Criminals might even belong to a lesser species, deficient in moral sense and rational intelligence. A paper read at the British Association in 1869 sought to show that the skulls of habitual criminals were smaller than average. The apparent correlation between mental weakness and criminality was carried over into the English Mental Deficiency Acts of 1913 and 1927, which included the legal category of 'moral defectives' for those who needed detention because they were thought to be potential criminals.

Modern theory seeks to reconcile individual and environmental explanations by recognising that there is no typical crime or criminal, still less a whole criminal class. Many factors producing criminal activity may co-exist without being causally related, and any one cause or group of causes can do no more than suggest a statistical vulnerability to criminality. With this in mind the historian can study patterns of the incidence of crimes in the past, and suggest which factors appear to have made the commission of such crimes more likely at some periods than at others.

Studies of criminal records suggest that there was a steady increase in the crime rate during the middle decades of the eighteenth century, especially in more densely populated parishes, followed by a sharp upswing from the 1770s until the 1850s; thereafter the trend was downwards until the early twentieth century, since when there has been an accelerating rise not unlike that of the early nineteenth century. England had the worst overall crime rates in Britain in the mid-nineteenth century. The Welsh figures were 20 per cent better and the Scottish figures 29 per cent better than the English, although a larger proportion of Scottish females was convicted. Within these broad trends, different crimes followed individual patterns. Society was probably becoming less violent during the course of the eighteenth and early nineteenth centuries, and the upsurge in crimes from the 1770s is accounted for largely by offences against property. While these declined from the mid-nineteenth century, prosecutions for moral delinquencies such as drunkenness, commercial crimes and offences against social-welfare legislation increased. In the twentieth century the 'moral' category has declined, while offences against property and, since the Second World War, crimes of violence have again increased. Clearly no single explanation will be adequate to account for all these trends.

Evidence for declining violence from the mid-eighteenth century is largely anecdotal, and must be viewed with caution, as it frequently comes from reformers anxious to demonstrate the progress of their age and the success of their own campaigns to change attitudes towards violence and gratuitous cruelty. Nevertheless, a local study of judicial records for Surrey and Sussex (including metropolitan parishes south of the Thames) supports the view that crimes of violence did decline in the second half of the eighteenth century.[42] However violent the early nineteenth century might still have been, conditions in London were far better then than during the era of cheap gin, before the Act of 1751 restricted outlets and raised prices. London also benefited from improvements in both street lighting and policing, beginning with Henry Fielding's reforms as Bow Street magistrate (1748–54) and culminating in Peel's Metropolitan Police Act of 1829.

Though a decline in violence did not necessarily means a decline in crimes of violence (and could mean a rise in prosecutions), the long-term effect of improved policing, changing public attitudes and environmental improvement was to make London a safer place in which to live. Whether this improvement occurred also in other parts of Britain, as newer centres of population growth struggled to cope with rapid social change, is less clear in the short term. Whilst some of the factors making for a reduction in violence apply generally, in the eighteenth century London suffered most from the criminal implications of urban growth, and had most scope for improvement.

The violence of the law was also in decline. Although the number of capital offences multiplied during the course of the eighteenth century to over 200, juries were often reluctant to convict when the sentence would be out of proportion to the crime. Even when a conviction was obtained, the maximum sentence was not always exacted. Capital punishment was intended as a deterrent. When this failed to deter, a reprieve might serve to reinforce respect for authority. In London two out of every three offenders sentenced to death during the period 1749–58 were actually executed, but by the end of the century the proportion had fallen to less than one in three.

The growing numbers of crimes against property can be explained in several ways: new laws turning old customs into new crimes as people became more sensitive about the rights of private property; increasing poverty and hardship; social protest; more energetic policing; and the values of an increasingly acquisitive capitalist society. The last is the most debatable and difficult to prove, for the rise in property crimes in the later eighteenth century predates a triumph of capitalist values – which included hard work, sobriety and thrift as well as the desire for material accumulation – but the theory may be of use to explain the growth in certain kinds of crime, such as fraud, in the later nineteenth century.

The link between employment, poverty and crime is more clearly established by their chronology. During periods of warfare, crime appears to have fallen away with the boost given to employment, not least in the armed forces. The return of peace brought depression and unemployment, and discharged soldiers and sailors with little means of support. In the sudden upsurge in crime that followed the ending of the French Wars in 1815 the number of committals for indictable offences in England and Wales almost doubled, from 7,818 in 1816 to 14,254 in 1819. The same correlation between unemployment and crime is found again in the depressions of 'the Hungry Forties': by 1837 the total number of committals had risen to 23,612, but it then soared to peaks of over 30,000 in 1842 and 1848, before falling back to 19,437 in 1856. But the rising overall rate to mid-century, and the fall thereafter, suggests that temporary surges in times of acute depression no more than overlaid deeper reasons for variations in the crime rate. Most poor people were not criminals, though some undoubtedly did turn to such crimes as poaching and petty theft, as well as prostitution (often associated with other criminal activities), to supplement deficient earnings.

Crimes of poverty are hard to distinguish from crimes of social protest and customary acts against new property laws. One could argue that in the eighteenth and early nineteenth centuries there were only two classes of men: those who made and enforced the laws, and those who broke them and were punished. Though upper-class law-breaking did exist, it was of marginal importance. Crime was, almost by definition, something which the poor did to the rich. While landowners, magistrates, clergymen and poor-law officials committed institutionalised violence against the poor, the latter responded with threatening letters, maiming of animals, machine-breaking and arson which reached a crescendo between 1815 and the 1830s, and which did not die away until the second half of the nineteenth century. Enclosure was greeted with the destruction of fences; crop thefts followed restrictions on customary rights of gleaning; rioting and looting frequently accompanied high bread prices as two value systems met in confrontation – the crowd's ideas of the just price and the miller's or baker's idea of his legitimate profit. Attacks on distilleries in Edinburgh in June 1784 were attributed to a common belief that 'the high price of provisions is solely attributed to the quantity of grain there manufactured into spiritous liquors'.[43] In Scotland in 1830, 93 per cent of offences brought before the High Court in Edinburgh were against property, many of them committed in the winter months. The poor law of 1834 hit young unmarried men particularly hard, as they could not plead sickness in the family to escape the workhouse which threatened in the hard winter months of unemployment. Partly for this reason, it was the young who turned to crimes of social protest. In rural Wales, men dressed in women's clothes enacted a ritual of destruction against toll-gates, enclosures and tithes – the 'Rebecca Riots'. In the industrial districts workmen threatened and attacked blacklegs during strikes, and smashed machinery which threatened their livelihoods. Men with blackened faces – the 'Scotch cattle' – who intimidated strike-breakers on the South Wales coalfield even disciplined the workers for rebellion in November 1839. Some historians are inclined to reject the ideologically charged definition of crime in such cases and regard them as legitimate expressions of righteous anger.

The connection between the growth in the crime rate and urbanisation is not so clear as has often been assumed. Many of the crimes discussed above belonged to the countryside, where the majority of the people still lived in the first half of the nineteenth century. There was practically no difference between the increase in the crime rate between 1805 and 1841 in the 20 most and the 20 least agricultural counties in England; but with a population increase in the latter nearly double that in the former, the amount of crime there seemed much greater. Urbanisation did, however, make a difference to the types of crime committed: most urban crimes were forms of petty theft, not involving violence. Lancashire, the most urbanised county after Middlesex, had a crime rate above the national average; but 89 per cent of committals in 1830 involved larceny or connected crimes. What disturbed contemporaries most was the extent to which crime in towns appeared to be organised, and involved children. Young pickpockets and prostitutes were the stereotypes of urban crime, as Dickens well knew when writing *Oliver Twist* (1837). In the 1840s between a fifth and a quarter of all persons committed for trial in England and Wales were aged between 15 and 19, compared with about a tenth in the population as a whole, and a further quarter were in their early twenties. Thus nearly half the crime was committed by that fifth of the population which was aged between 15 and 24, four out of every five offenders being male.

The growth in recorded crime may also be attributed to the increasing vigilance of the police. The pickpocket who would formerly have been dragged to the village pump and half drowned by the mob was now arrested and became a criminal statistic. As procedures were formalised and as public awareness of crime brought calls for action, police attention was directed towards those most marginal in society – vagrants, immigrants and prostitutes. Though there were grounds for the belief that an inclination towards crime might be high among such groups, the police undoubtedly went there to look for it. Policing was directed not towards those parts of towns where property needed defending, but towards the poorer areas in which the criminal class was believed to live.

Most offenders, however, were not drawn from a 'criminal class', still less did they belong to a separate 'race'. In fact, most petty crimes were committed by amateurs. Although criminal gangs were known in London and the larger provincial towns in the eighteenth and early nineteenth centuries, increased policing, slum clearance and legislation for the better control of juveniles had begun to break up those urban nests of crime described so vividly by Dickens, Mayhew and others by the second half of the nineteenth century. The majority of criminals were drawn from the ordinary working class; their crimes arose out of casual employment and low wages. The 'moral' improvement detected by contemporaries in the second half of the nineteenth century is a measure of improving conditions among the poor.

By the 1850s and 1860s the authorities were becoming confident that crime was being contained. The statistics show them to have been right, although historians might give rather less credit to the police and more to broader social changes, such as improved economic conditions and the decline in the proportion of juveniles in the population. As standards and expectations rose, so moral reformers came to concentrate on specific issues which they thought were undermining the fabric of Victorian society. There is no evidence that drunkenness and prostitution were more common in the mid-Victorian years than earlier; but public consciousness of them certainly was, and this led to a more deliberate attempt to reform society through the courts. Between 1857 and 1876 the number of offences of drunkenness and drunken and disorderly behaviour determined summarily in England and Wales increased threefold, from 75,859 to 205,567, while the total number of other offences less than doubled. This untypical rise appears to coincide with increased agitation over the licensing laws. The Vagrancy Act (1824), the Town Police Act (1847), the Criminal Law Amendment Act (1885) and various local Improvement Acts all contributed to greater police powers and surges in prosecution rates whenever the local police decided the time was right to attack some particular social evil. In Manchester, for example, offences under the Vagrancy Act increased in the late 1830s and early 1840s, then fell for 20 years before reaching new peaks in the later 1860s and early 1880s, as the poor-law Guardians urged measures against begging in the streets. A rise in offences was also produced by increased state regulation through Factory, Public Health and Education Acts. In 1892 there were 86,149 cases of infringements of the Education Acts alone. Most remarkably in the twentieth century, technology and the law created an explosion in the number of traffic offences: in 1900 2,548 persons were found guilty of highway and motoring offences; the figure topped one million between 1968 and 1986, by which time it represented around 60 per cent of all offenders found guilty in the courts of England and Wales. In Scotland the equivalent figure was much lower – around a third.

During the course of the twentieth century the lesser, poverty-related crimes have decreased and the more serious and organised crimes, with the exception of murder, have increased. The outcome of these two contrary trends is that, although the total number of convictions for offences in England and Wales (excluding traffic offences) actually fell from just over 18 per 1,000 of the population in 1900 to just under 16 in 1980, the proportion of offences which were in the serious (indictable) category rose from 6.5 per cent in 1900 to 46.5 per cent in 1980. Only about a half of all offences committed were reported to – and only half of these were recorded by – the police; and many more offences were recorded by the police than came to court or resulted in a conviction. In 1980, when a new system of recording began, there were in England and Wales 2.7 million notifiable offences (previously known as indictable offences) recorded by the police. These numbers rose steadily to a peak of 5.6 million in 1992 (105 offences for every 1,000 people in the population), before falling to 5.1 million in 1995. Even allowing for variations in the reporting and recording of crimes committed, this represented a steep upwards trend in the 1980s and early 1990s. The trend in equivalent crimes in Scotland was similarly upwards, but much less steeply, with 364,600 crimes in 1980, rising to a peak of 589,600 in 1991 and tailing off to 502,800 in 1995. At the same time the total number of summary (minor) offences remained roughly stable between 1980 and 1992, falling thereafter, while in Scotland the trend was consistently downwards.

Within these figures, each offence had its own history. Between the beginning of the century and 1963, larceny from a dwelling house increased 40-fold and forgery 20-fold; while the more old-fashioned offence of larceny from the person rose by no more than the general rise in population (46 per cent). During the period of rapidly increasing numbers of notifiable offences in England and Wales after 1980, robbery, criminal damage, theft from vehicles and violence against the person have all more than doubled. With the exception of the relatively small category of male sex offenders, 45 per cent of whom were over 35 years of age in 1995, over 80 per cent of all crimes committed by men were by those under 35; indeed, a third or more of all thefts, robberies and acts of criminal damage were committed by boys under 18. There were about five male criminals for each female; but the age distribution for females is even more striking. Whereas a quarter of all indictable offences committed by males was the work of boys under 18, the equivalent proportion for girls was over a third. Over half the burglaries and robberies committed by females were the work of girls under 18. A closer analysis of the figures shows that, since 1972, the peak offending year for girls has been around 14, whereas the peak offending age for boys has gradually increased, from 14 in 1971 to 18 in 1995, when 9 per cent of the age group offended. Though contemporaries have found these figures shocking, they merely show how little has changed, in this respect at least, since the nineteenth century. Dickens's Artful Dodger was alive and well on the streets of Britain in the 1990s.

The reasons for crime in the twentieth century have been much debated. Taking a long view, one could argue that an increasingly affluent society, with its ostentatious display of portable wealth, and the existence of relative poverty amidst a superfluity of enticingly advertised consumer goods, invites larceny (taking away goods for one's own use), robbery and burglary, while shoplifting is but the modern equivalent of pocket-picking as a major form of petty theft. At the same time, the increasing complexity of commercial society has given new opportunities for fraud, embezzlement and forgery – the so-called 'white-collar crimes', although these did not increase so rapidly after 1980 as the average rate for all crimes. In searching for an explanation for the marked upswing in the serious crime rate from the 1960s, and particularly from the 1980s, moral observers have not failed to notice parallel trends concerning the instability of 'traditional' family life and the rejection of traditional morality. A causal link between these various trends is very difficult to prove, though the Youth Lifestyles Survey conducted for the Home Office in 1992–3 found that young people not living with both their natural parents were more likely to *say* that they had committed an offence. Social observers, by contrast, have sought an explanation in the growth in unemployment, and the widening gap between the richest and the poorest in society. Other observers, including the police, have noted that many offences appear to be drugs-related, either being committed while under the influence of drugs or, in the case of robberies and theft, being undertaken to finance the purchase of controlled drugs, notably cannabis, heroin, ecstasy, crack-cocaine and LSD, seizures of which all increased more than five-fold between 1981 and 1994.

Fears of a youth crime wave were, however, exaggerated. It is true that the crimes favoured by young offenders grew rapidly from the 1980s, and at the same time the clear-up rates for these offences fell, increasing public disquiet. Yet the actual numbers of individual young offenders found guilty or cautioned halved in the 1980s. This could partly be explained by a failure to convict the offenders, not least because some of them were too young to come before the courts; and partly by the fact that, according to the Youth Lifestyles Survey, 25 per cent of offences were committed by only 3 per cent of offenders.

As a consequence of the change in the pattern of crime towards more serious offences committed by young adult males, the prison population rose. In the first half of the twentieth century longer sentences for those convicted were balanced by falling numbers of prisoners, but between 1950 and 1980 both the number of prisoners under sentence and the daily average prison population more than doubled. Throughout the 1980s and ealry 1990s, despite a fall in the numbers of offenders found guilty in all age groups and categories of offence, the prison population continued to rise as more offenders than ever were sent to prison each year to serve longer sentences.

The police

The enforcement of law and order has always been a major preoccupation of those in positions of authority, but in the relatively small communities of pre-industrial Britain much could be achieved by informal pressure and unofficial summary punishment. Where neighbours knew one another and strangers were instantly detected, criminals could survive only when the community was in basic sympathy with them, which undoubtedly was the case with smugglers, petty poachers and machine-breakers in the eighteenth and early nineteenth centuries. Under such circumstances the authorities had to place great reliance on spies and informers who, for a price or a principle, were willing to go against the sentiment of the majority. The traditional instruments of law enforcement – the part-time parish constable, the common informer, the magistrate and (originally) the Grand Jury – drew their strength from local knowledge. Excessive population mobility was always a threat to the effectiveness of local regulation, which is one reason why the Settlement Laws were originally passed and long remained important in the eyes of parochial officials, and why a new Vagrancy Act was carried in 1824. But it was urban growth which made most people aware of the limits of informal social control and turned the prevention and detection of crime into a more professional and institutionalised matter.

In some urban parishes, particularly in London, the constable was assisted by a beadle and one or more night watchmen; but they were scarcely adequate to deal with large-scale public disorder or the immense problems of a large city. The Justices had therefore to rely upon the Militia (less important after the eighteenth century), the Yeomanry (from 1794), or had even to ask for regular troops in cases of major disturbance, while private organisations were created for the prosecution of felons. At least 450 such associations were established, mainly in the more populous areas of England, between 1744 and 1856.

The beginning of a new form of policing in the metropolis is usually dated from Henry Fielding's appointment as the paid magistrate at Bow Street in 1748. He appointed half a dozen former constables to act for him as 'thief takers', and obtained a small allowance from Secret Service Funds to pay them. They later became known as the 'Bow Street Runners', the first full-time professional detective force in London. Policing developed slowly in this way in response to need, and Bow Street became a centre for criminal intelligence not only for the whole of the metropolitan area but for the whole country. By 1782 there was a regular night Foot Patrol of 68 men to provide a street watch system which would not be inhibited by parochial boundaries, to which a Horse Patrol was added in 1805. The Middlesex Justices Act of 1792 added seven more police offices for London with stipendiary magistrates and police officers on the Bow Street model, and the Thames Police Office was added to patrol the riverside in 1801. By 1822 Bow Street had four patrols, including a Day Patrol of 27 men. Though later reformers spoke scathingly of these forces they represented an important development in professional policing and laid the basis for Robert Peel's celebrated Metropolitan Police Force of 1829.

London thereafter set the precedent for developments elsewhere, but, like the Bow Street Office, the Metropolitan Police had a national as well as local significance. Except for the City of London, they were (after further legislation in 1839) responsible for policing a wide area in and around London; and, despite opposition from the parishes, they were under the control of two Commissioners responsible directly to the Home Office. The Home Secretary could use them to supplement local forces for the maintenance of order anywhere in the country, and 2,246 of them were sent out into the provinces between June 1830 and January 1838 as an alternative to the local Yeomanry, whose performance in Manchester in 1819 had discredited them as an efficient force for crowd control.

Following the example of the metropolis, locally controlled police forces were established after 1829, partly to cope with the threat allegedly posed by criminals fleeing the metropolis but mainly as a precaution against 'Swing' rioters and Chartist agitators. The 1835 Municipal Corporations Act required each borough to set up a watch committee and appoint constables; and the 1839 County Police Act empowered Justices to set up a rural police. By 1842 there were perhaps 10,000 policemen in England and Wales, and the Home Secretary grew reluctant to employ metropolitan policemen outside their own area. As with the reform of the poor law, the break with the old system was not so clear as the legislation implies. A number of the new constables were recruited from the ranks of the old parish officials; sometimes the old officials continued to exist alongside the new.

Initially the new police were greeted with suspicion. Like the factory inspectors whom the reformers of the 1830s had also created, police officers were mistrusted as enemies of liberty, akin to the army of Excise Officers who had long been regarded as instruments of oppressive government. Early policemen looked suspiciously like the hated government spies who had been employed through Bow Street during the unrest of the French Wars. Led by former army officers, and recruited from the same social order as many criminals, the police had a long struggle to achieve both internal discipline and acceptance in the working-class community. Although attitudes did begin to change in the 1840s many people continued to view the police with considerable hostility, especially when they were called upon to enforce unpopular legislation or protect blackleg labour during strikes. Police action in a lower-class inner-city area was always as likely to cause as to prevent a breach of the peace. The enforcement of morality was particularly difficult, with policemen required (sometimes against their will) to support a system of law at variance with popular notions of justice; and with most crime involving the theft of property, the police were inevitably seen in some quarters as protectors of private property and of the system which permitted great disparities of wealth. In fact, the rich could afford, if need be, to look after themselves. The greatest benefit from effective public policing was felt by small property-owners such as shopkeepers, especially in working-class areas.

A second form of hostility to the early police came from ratepayers. Far from seeing the police as the defenders of the propertied class, they thought of them as a burden on the rates. Some of the smaller municipal boroughs appointed as few constables as possible. In 1836, for example, Wigan (population 20,774) appointed a police force of six, which by 1856 had risen to 23; Oldham (population 52,820) had an establishment of 12 when its force was founded in 1849. The estimated strength required was 1:1,000, a level achieved in fewer than half the boroughs with police forces in 1848. Only in the larger centres, where voluntary associations were already active, were the citizens pleased to be able to transfer the expense of felon-catching to the rates. Liverpool, for example, began in 1836 with 290 police for its population of 205,954, and had 886 by 1856. London had a ratio of 1:443 in 1840. The County Act of 1839 was only permissive, and there were no elected authorities, as in the boroughs, to implement it. The initiative rested with the Quarter Sessions, and not all counties thought a police force worth the trouble and expense. Some of the most 'troubled' parts of the country – the West Riding, the Potteries, Lanarkshire – did not immediately adopt the Act, and some that did were still thinly policed. Montgomery, which the Home Secretary had refused to supply with an adequate force of metropolitan police before the Chartist disturbances of 1839, had appointed its own force by 1841 – 15 men, at a ratio of 1:4,045. In 1853 still half the counties were without police forces, and 13 boroughs were holding out against the 1835 Act. Even the County and Borough Police Act of 1856, which compelled all counties and boroughs to maintain police forces and introduced the principle of inspection, did not immediately remove all anomalies or ensure an adequate police system for the whole country. Edwin Chadwick had since 1829 been urging a centralised force, but the police system of Britain was to remain a part of local, not national government, developing gradually in response to local need, though increasingly under central supervision and inspection. By 1900 there were 179 police forces in England and Wales, and 64 in Scotland, with a combined manpower of 47,800, a ratio of 1:778 in England and Wales and 1:914 in Scotland. Since then the number of police forces has been reduced by amalgamations and reorganisation to 51, with 141,285 men and women as regular officers in 1995, a ratio of 1:409 in England and Wales and 1:355 in Scotland. Despite the rise in numbers, though, the number of police-hours worked per head of population has not greatly increased during the course of the twentieth century.

The reasons why Britain acquired a professional police force are not dissimilar from those which led to the establishment of a whole range of welfare services from the 1830s. First, there was the perception of a need, with increasing levels of crime, loss of social control in expanding urban areas, and disturbances in both town and country. Second, there was the influence of Edwin Chadwick with his passion for centralisation, compulsion and inspection, expressed in his evidence to Peel's Select Committee on the Police of the Metropolis in 1828 and to the Royal Commission on the Rural Constabulary in 1839. As with much of the social welfare legislation of the nineteenth century, no single explanation is sufficient, and no theoretical model of administrative change can be adequate which does not recognise that the actual process of change was unplanned, haphazard, permissive and local. A neat theory of class control is particularly vulnerable to the criticisms that contemporaries seemed more concerned to keep down costs, and that outside London and the major provincial centres policemen were actually very thinly spread on the ground until late in the nineteenth century.

This last point is relevant to a discussion of the effectiveness of the police. They have been given credit for their impact on public order, especially in London; but the lessening of social tensions in the second half of the nineteenth century is probably of more significance for the diminution of crowd violence. The 'social police' – schoolteachers, clergymen, missionaries and charity workers – made a greater impact on the character of British people than did the overt control exercised by policemen. Nevertheless, this process of social control occurred within a framework of public law maintained by an unarmed civilian force – an important legacy of the Victorians to twentieth-century Britain.

Institutions of restraint

Prisons, workhouses, asylums – and even schools (especially boarding schools) and factories – shared more than a common architectural style: their purpose was to shape the behaviour of the individual through control of the immediate environment. Though each institution has its own particular history, there is more than a coincidence in the growth and decline of the idea that people can be made fit for society by institutional means. Growth can be related to the popularity in the later eighteenth and early nineteenth centuries of sensationalist psychology and environmentalism, the search for less cruel ways of treating people, the need to reassert controls of all kinds in an age of population expansion, and the emergence of a society wealthy enough to contemplate the expense of constructing elaborate institutions for the correction of those unfitted for mature, adult society. Following the Second World War there has been a marked retreat from this position, with criticisms of lengthy and expensive prison sentences, the development of an alternative to the poor law, the discharge of sick, disabled and mentally ill patients into the community, and the 'deschooling' movement. Again, general common causes can be suggested: more sophisticated theories of human psychology, disillusionment with the effectiveness of institutions and a realisation of the dangers of institutionalisation, a rejection of controls on personal liberty and the desire to cut costs in response to rising expenditure on other welfare benefits. Though the rapid increase in violent crime has militated against a reduction in the daily average prison population, progress was made in reducing the number of long-stay patients in hospitals of various kinds.

Prisons

There were between 400 and 500 prisons in Britain in the later eighteenth century, most of them small, local and with limited purposes. Houses of Correction (or Bridewells), under the control of the Justices, were intended for petty criminals and 'sturdy beggars'. Common Gaols, the responsibility of the county Sheriff, were for prisoners awaiting trial, debtors, and serious felons awaiting transportation or death. Long-term imprisonment was envisaged only as a more humane alternative to these harsher punishments, but those reformers who began to advocate this had first to modernise and improve the prison system itself. Within the Common Gaols and Houses of Correction of eighteenth-century Britain conditions were squalid, discipline poor and organisation chaotic. Gaolers were paid a contribution towards the expense of running their gaol, but they were also allowed to collect fees from prisoners and make a profit on food, drink and privileges (licit or otherwise) sold to prisoners. Only as the supply of public funds became a little more generous during the course of the eighteenth century did the common gaoler begin the transition from private entrepreneur to member of the public judicial system.

The turning-point came in the 1770s, with the reform campaigns of John Howard for better conditions in prison, and Jonas Hanaway with his fervent belief in the moral efficacy of solitary confinement. This ideal was embodied in the Penitentiary Act of 1779 which envisaged the well-conducted prison as a more effective method of reforming criminals and deterring crime than transportation – the latter having been made difficult by the American War. Though a proposed model prison was not built at this time, the General Prisons Act of 1791 commended the wider application of the penitentiary system. New County Gaols were provided with more separate cells, conditions were generally improved, and in the more advanced gaols a system for the classification of prisoners was introduced. This move was further encouraged by Peel's Prison Act of 1823, which for the first time gave central government a direct interest in local prisons.

Much attention has been devoted by historians to the 'model' prisons which most closely embodied the latest penal theories of the age, beginning with the Millbank Penitentiary of 1816 and culminating in Pentonville in 1842. Millbank fell short of its ideals: solitary confinement was never complete, conditions were harsh, the prison health record was poor and discipline proved hard to maintain. Pentonville, on the other hand, brought the solitary, reforming system to theoretical perfection. Instead of instruments of punishment like the treadwheel, there was to be reform through solitary confinement and religious instruction. Pentonville was specifically designed as a government prison to reform prisoners over a short period before transportation to Australia, but its purpose was soon radically changed. In 1853 Sydney and Melbourne refused to take any more convicts, and the Government introduced the Penal Servitude Act to substitute longer prison sentences with prison labour as a substitute for transportation. The hulks, which had been used since 1779 for prisoners awaiting transportation, had in fact become a convict prison in their own right, but as such were clearly inadequate. New prisons were built: Portland (1849), Dartmoor (1850), Portsmouth (1852), Brixton (for women, 1853) and Chatham (1856). Long-stay sections were added to some County Gaols, and in 1877 the whole prison system was placed under the central control of the Home Office.

Theorists of total institutions might find in the development of the British prison system a clear exemplification of their argument. But there are two major limitations to be taken into account. Firstly, the evolution of penal policy followed the usual course of make and mend, not a neat line from theory to implementation. Conflicting aims of punishment and reform, confinement and hard labour, were pursued by reformers not sure whether they were supposed to be saving souls or insurance company premiums. Furthermore, to concentrate on the model prisons, especially Pentonville, is to ignore the survival of old habits in the largely unreformed County Gaols and local Houses of Correction. In York Castle, for example, the County Gaol for Yorkshire, the prison staff exercised very little supervision over the inmates, and exclusion from contact with the outside world could hardly be described as total. The major concern of the governor was not whether the silent system should be introduced, but whether enough prisoners could be found to keep the place reasonably full. Far from prisons being overcrowded at the high point of the nineteenth-century crime wave, they were in competition with one another for clients.

During the final third of the nineteenth century, the prison system of Britain reached its peak. The institution had triumphed in the war against crime, and early thoughts of reformation had given way to the call for punishment and deterrence. In the first half of the twentieth century the process was then put into reverse. The Probation of Offenders Act (1907) had the effect of keeping minor first offenders out of detention. Fines and non-custodial sentences began to replace imprisonment, and the proportion of custodial sentences given to those convicted of indictable offences ('crimes' in Scotland) fell sharply: 53.1 per cent in 1901, 45.5 per cent in 1931 and 16.8 per cent in 1951. As a result, the number of prisoners under custodial sentence in England and Wales fell from 149,397 in 1900 to 33,875 in 1950, and from 50,000 to 9,000 in Scotland. With the pressure thus reduced many Victorian prisons were left unmodernised. But with longer sentences for the increasing minority of serious criminals (almost all of whom were men) this policy failed to keep the number of prisoners down after 1950. The daily average prison population in England and Wales in 1950 was 19,367 men and 1,107 women, compared to 14,459 men and 2,976 women in 1900. By 1995 the total daily average had more than doubled, to 37,897 men (and 1,482 women) in England

and Wales and 5,451 men (and 175 women) in Scotland, despite the fact that only 30 per cent of all convictions of violence against the person, 78 per cent of all sex convictions and 4 per cent of all convictions for theft resulted in imprisonment. The prisons were overcrowded to bursting point. Cells designed by Victorians for solitary confinement were filled with two or three inmates. In 1986 protests by prison officers at conditions inside the prisons led to serious rioting by prisoners. Judges were officially urged to use to the full the range of non-custodial measures outlined in the Criminal Justice Act of 1972; but public opinion called for longer custodial sentencing to halt the crime wave. The policy of escaping the confines of Victorian social policy, so successfully pursued elsewhere, seemed here in danger of failure, and by 1997, with the total number in custody approaching 60,000, the Home Office even considered using former RAF bases, holiday camps and a prison ship to provide extra accommodation.

Reform schools

Recognition of the special needs of children came with the growing use of imprisonment as a method of punishment. In the eighteenth century the war against juvenile crime was conducted largely by philanthropists who provided refuges for delinquent and destitute children in the hope that, by removing them from their evil surroundings and subjecting them to religious influences, they might grow up free from the taint and temptations of criminality. Most famous was the Philanthropic Society, which ran industrial schools in Hackney and Southwark, as well as the Reform Institution at Bermondsey, which opened an experimental farm-school at Redhill in 1821. These children were the lucky ones. Delinquent children over the age of seven could be convicted and sent to prison, where they quickly learnt the ways of adult criminals. Serious offenders were sent to the hulks and then transported.

As attention was turned to the provision of a state penitentiary for adult offenders, a separate and parallel penal institution for boys was considered; and in 1838 the Parkhurst Reformatory was opened on the Isle of Wight for 102 boys under the age of 18 from the hulks and London gaols. The regime was meant to be hard but reformatory, with solitary confinement, physical punishment, religious instruction and regimentation. As a place for children it was scarcely better than Millbank, whence many of them had come.

A change in policy was brought about by the Juvenile Offenders Act of 1847, which raised the minimum age for adult criminality to 14 (16 from 1849). Parkhurst was now devoted to young men over the age of 18. An alternative for juveniles appeared with the spread of Industrial Schools. These grew, in many cases, out of the Ragged Schools movement, begun under the patronage of Lord Ashley in the 1840s to reach those children of the streets who were escaping the usual religious Sunday and day schools. Formal recognition was given to their work by the Industrial Schools Act of 1857. What this could mean at the local level can be illustrated from the experience at Manchester, where the Ragged School (1853) became the Manchester and Salford Reformatory after the 1857 Act. New premises were acquired at a farm site on elevated ground some 3½ miles from the town. Here, in wholesome surroundings, the example of Redhill was followed. Some of the boys came voluntarily, some were sent by their parents, some by committee members, some by the magistrates. Parents had to pay 5s. (25p) a week and the scheme was seen in part as a means of fining parents for the delinquencies of their offspring. The regime was hard, even cruel; the diet was Spartan, but no worse than poor boys would have received outside. As always, the best of intentions were rarely realised in practice, and the farm school here, as elsewhere, was self-supporting rather than educative. Boys were later sent into the army or as cheap agricultural labour to Canada. Other Reform Schools sent boys into the Royal Navy, the merchant navy and the fishing fleet; girls were sent into domestic service. This kept most of them out of trouble.

The 1908 Children Act finally abolished imprisonment for juveniles under 14, substituting 'places of detention' (called Remand Homes from 1948) and permitting early release on licence for children in Reform Schools. For minor offenders there were probation officers created under the Act of 1907; and for young recidivists Borstal training was introduced in the same year. Juvenile Courts were set up to complete the distinction between juvenile delinquency and adult crime. The Children and Young Person's Act of 1933 consolidated and extended this legislation, bringing the Victorian era of Reform Schools to a close and replacing them with Approved Schools, in which the emphasis was placed more firmly on reformative education.

New theories about the nature of juvenile delinquency led to further changes during the next half-century, the aim being the steady withdrawal of juveniles from the system of adult law-enforcement. The most notable Acts came in 1969, when Approved Schools were removed from the Home Office and replaced by 'community homes' run as part of the local authorities' welfare services; and 1982, when the whole framework of custodial sentences for offenders under 21 was reformed, with youth custody superseding imprisonment for offenders over 17 and a flexible alternative of compensation payments, reporting to attendance centres and community service. Younger offenders between 10 and 18 (8 to 16 in Scotland) were to be committed to detention only for the most serious offences; supervision orders and reporting to attendance centres were the preferred options. But, with mounting offences in the 1980s and 1990s, this approach too was seen to have its limitations, as the police appeared to have few effective powers to restrain the criminal activities of children, some of whom were below the age of criminal responsibility. The Criminal Justice Act of 1991 strengthened the sanctions on parents to maintain discipline over their children, but at the same time measures introduced after several scandals to limit the physical abuse of children in the home and in local authority care removed many of the traditional physical restraints upon the behaviour of such children. If, as many believed, the roots of anti-social and ultimately criminal behaviour lay in the home, no-one seemed able to suggest how such homes might be reformed. Lacking the aggressive self-confidence of Victorian reformers, happy to send the moral police into working-class homes and to apply institutional 'remedies' where necessary, their libertarian twentieth-century successors were left uncertain what to do for the best.

Asylums

In the eighteenth century, the mad in Britain were not generally confined unless dangerous. The majority of these were held in small private madhouses, which were little if any better than the Houses of Correction which served as the only public alternative. Some philanthropists sought to provide better care for the poor on the same basis as charity hospitals, but when the York Lunatic Hospital was opened in 1777 it was only the fifth in the country. Allegations were frequently made of even the best-intended institutions that their inmates were subjected to unnecessary physical restraint and cruelty, and after the death of a Quaker in the York Lunatic Hospital the local Friends decided to open their own Retreat (1796) in which the system of 'moral restraint' was pioneered. The publicity given to this work helped the idea spread that the proper place for mentally disturbed people (especially women) should be in the secure environment of an asylum.

Concern about the conditions under which lunatics were kept prompted the first provision for inspection in modern British social legislation. Under an Act of 1774 five commissioners were to be elected annually by the Royal College of Physicians to inspect private madhouses in London, while the Justices were to visit and license those in the provinces. Though this measure was largely ineffective in preventing abuses, it did provide the basis for a system of inspection which came to full maturity with the Lunatics Act of 1845. Provision for public asylums was first made under an Act of 1808, the first County Asylum being opened in Nottingham in 1810; but the building of County Asylums was not made compulsory until 1845. Under the poor law of 1834, lunatics were usually confined to the workhouse, though they could be sent to asylums if the Guardians so decided. Workhouses, though, unlike asylums, were not open to inspection by the Lunacy Commission. In 1844 there were 17,355 pauper lunatics and idiots in England and Wales, compared to 4,072 private patients. Of the paupers, 27 per cent were in workhouses, 24 per cent were in County Asylums, 17 per cent were in private madhouses and 29 per cent were 'with friends' – that is, in receipt of outdoor relief. After the provision of County Asylums in all places following the 1845 Act it was more common for paupers to be transferred to asylums, but in 1861 35 per cent of workhouse inmates who had been resident for five or more years were still lunatics, second only to the 42 per cent kept there by old age or physical infirmity. The Metropolitan Poor Act of 1867 removed responsibility for pauper lunatics from the Guardians in London and set up a new Board to provide separate hospitals for them, but elsewhere the workhouse continued to be one of society's solutions to the problem of mental illness.

With much official confusion between madness, crime and poverty, the poor lunatic could find himself (or, more usually, herself) in any one of a number of institutions. It was only in 1889 that the Home Office advised magistrates that mentally ill offenders could be sent straight to an asylum and not to prison, and the practice of sending mentally defective offenders to prison was not ended until 1913. Though conditions gradually improved in the later nineteenth century, with the more severe cases of mental illness being treated in asylums according to the best medical knowledge of the day, one is tempted to conclude that the main purpose of mental institutions was not to provide the sick with asylum from the outside world, but to prevent the outside world from noticing the plight of the mentally ill.

The biggest jolt to public complacency about the treatment of the mentally ill in institutions of confinement came with the First World War. In 1928 there were still 65,000 'shell-shock' victims in British mental hospitals. The Mental Treatment Act of 1930 then began to break down the idea of confinement, with its provision for the voluntary treatment of mental illness, but only with the National Health Service Act of 1946 was a serious look taken at community health care for the mentally ill. The dismantling of the Victorian apparatus of asylums for all but the seriously ill and dangerous then followed slowly, prompted by the Mental Health Act of 1959. Of the 130 large mental hospitals still open in 1961, all but 22 were to be closed by the end of the century, being replaced by smaller homes and 'care in the community'. The latter, though, did not adequately meet all cases, with inadequate protection for some former patients unable to look after themselves and inadequate protection for the general public from a minority who remained dangerous both to themselves and others. Further legislation was needed in 1994 in an attempt to keep track of discharged patients.

The institutions developed in nineteenth-century Britain to deal with the problems of criminals and lunatics suggest a general point about all institutions, namely, that they create their own demand. The institution exists so it is used to solve a problem which has been defined as having an institutional solution. The institution also defines the people whom it is meant to cater for, giving them a routine, distinctive clothing, a bureaucratically convenient number and a generic name – pauper, prisoner, patient. It subjects these people to the power of the expert and the bureaucrat. It makes them incapable of surviving without their institution to support them. Institutions are very difficult to escape – for both inmates and those who determine social policy. One of the most remarkable changes over the last 200 years has been the rise and fall of the institution as an instrument of social control and individual reformation. In the eighteenth century it was the great hope of reformers confident in the therapeutic value of a secure environment; in the nineteenth its necessity for restraint and deterrence became conventional wisdom; in the twentieth it has become the despair of reformers, acutely aware of the damage done to the individual by institutionalisation. Public policy is still striving, at the close of the twentieth century, to find the right balance between the treatment of the person, the protection of society and the freedom of the individual.

Notes

1. B. S. Rowntree, *Poverty: A Study of Town Life* (1901; 4th edn., 1902), pp. 136–8.
2. A. Somerville, *The Autobiography of a Working Man* (1848; new edn., 1951), p. 7.
3. E. Chadwick, *Report on the Sanitary Condition of the Labouring Population of Great Britain* (1842; new edn., Edinburgh, 1965), p. 329.
4. B. S. Rowntree and M. Kendall, *How the Labourer Lives: A Study of the Rural Labour Problem* (1913), pp. 31–2.
5. G. Bourne, *Change in the Village* (1912; new edn., Harmondsworth, 1984), p. 13.
6. Quoted in Anne Digby, 'The Rural Poor', p. 597 in G. E. Mingay (ed.), *The Victorian Countryside* (2 vols., 1981), ii, pp. 591–602.
7. Quoted by J. Burnett, 'Country Diet', p. 562 in G. E. Mingay (ed.), *The Victorian Countryside*, ii, pp. 554–65.
8. Rowntree and Kendall, *How the Labourer Lives*, pp. 81–3.
9. Rowntree and Kendall, *How the Labourer Lives*, ch. 3.
10. Chadwick, *Report*, p. 221.
11. Rowntree, *Poverty*, p. 121; C. Booth, *Life and Labour*, i, p. 147.
12. J. Foster, *Class Struggle and the Industrial Revolution* (1974), p. 96.
13. M. Anderson, *Family Structure in Nineteenth Century Lancashire* (1971), p. 31.
14. J. P. Kay, *The Moral and Physical Condition of the Working Classes Employed in the Cotton Manufacture in Manchester* (1832; new impression, Manchester, 1969), pp. 23–6.
15. M. Arnold, *Culture and Anarchy* (1868; ed. J. Dover Wilson, Cambridge, 1932; repr. 1966), p. 193.
16. G. Stedman Jones, *Outcast London* (1971; repr. 1976), pp. 52–66.
17. A. S. Jasper, *A Hoxton Childhood* (1969), pp. 13–14.

18. R. M. Hartwell, 'The Rising Standard of Living in England, 1800–50', p. 94 in A. J. Taylor (ed.), *The Standard of Living in Britain* (1975), pp. 93–123.
19. R. S. Neale, 'The Standard of Living, 1780–1844: A Regional and Class Study', in Taylor, *Standard of Living in Britain*, pp. 154–77.
20. J. Burnett, *Plenty and Want* (1966; republished Harmondsworth, 1968), pp. 24–6.
21. E. A. Wrigley and R. S. Schofield, *The Population History of England*, Table A9.2, pp. 643–4.
22. R. Floud, K. Wachter and A. Gregory, *Height, Health and History: Nutritional Status in the United Kingdom, 1750–1980* (Cambridge, 1990).
23. B. S. Rowntree, *Poverty and Progress: A Second Social Survey of York* (1941), pp. 108, 110.
24. Rowntree, *Poverty and Progress*, pp. 453, 457.
25. B. S. Rowntree and G. R. Lavers, *Poverty and the Welfare State: A Third Social Survey of York dealing only with Economic Questions* (1951), pp. 31, 35. The three Rowntree surveys are compared in S. Jenkins and A. Maynard, 'The Rowntree Surveys: Poverty in York since 1899', pp. 188–93, in C. H. Feinstein (ed.), *York, 1831–1981: 150 years of Scientific Endeavour and Social Change* (York, 1981), pp. 188–204.
26. Jenkins and Maynard, p. 199.
27. G. C. Fiegehen, P. S. Lansley and A. D. Smith, *Poverty and Progress in Britain, 1953–1973. A Statistical Study of Low Income Households: Their Numbers, Types and Expenditure Patterns* (Cambridge, 1977), pp. 31, 69.
28. S. P. Jenkins, *Winners and Losers: A Portrait of the UK Income Distribution During the 1980s*, University College of Swansea, Department of Economics Discussion Paper, 94–07 (1994).
29. J. K. Galbraith, *The Affluent Society*, p. 262.
30. K. Coates and R. Silburn, *Poverty: The Forgotten Englishmen* (Harmondsworth, 1970).
31. Quoted in R. Wells, *Dearth and Distress in Yorkshire, 1793–1802* (York, 1977), p. 12.
32. P. Colquhoun, *A Treatise on Indigence* (1806), cited in J. R. Poynter, *Society and Pauperism. English Ideas on Poor Relief, 1795–1834* (1969), p. 203.
33. Sampson Low, cited in E. Lascelles, 'Charity', pp. 320–1, 325, in G. M. Young (ed.), *Early Victorian England, 1830–1865* (2 vols., Oxford 1934), ii, pp. 317–47. For charity and the Hartley Colliery disaster, see N. McCord, *North East England: An Economic and Social History* (1979), p. 176.
34. Quoted in Louis Heren, *Growing up Poor in London* (1973), pp. 24–5.
35. Quoted in E. Royle, *The Victorian Church in York* (York, 1983), p. 39.
36. Rowntree, *Poverty*, p. 59.
37. Rowntree and Kendall, *How the Labourer Lives*, p. 83.
38. G. R. Porter, *Progress of the Nation* (1836; new edn., 1851), p. 616.
39. H. M. Hyndman and C. Bradlaugh, *Will Socialism Benefit the English People?* (1884), p. 16.
40. Chadwick, *Report*, p. 220.
41. W. Beveridge, *Full Employment in a Free Society* (1944; second edn., 1960), Prologue, p. 11.
42. J. M. Beattie, 'The Pattern of Crime in England, 1660–1800', *Past & Present*, 62 (February 1974), pp. 47–95.
43. Quoted in K. J. Logue, *Popular Disturbances in Scotland, 1780–1815* (Edinburgh, 1979), p. 51.

5

Life and leisure

Leisure – the freedom to do what one wants in otherwise unoccupied time – was a rare commodity in pre- and early-industrial Britain. Those who were leisured – i.e., had such freedom in abundance – were few indeed. The prerequisite of leisure is an income adequate for support without the necessity of long hours of hard labour. This is not to deny that the rich sometimes worked very hard; but their compulsion to do so was other than strictly financial. The poor could afford little time or money for other than work, if work were available, though what is necessary to subsistence is as relative as poverty itself. In the eighteenth century, as Arthur Young and other moralising writers grumbled, people who were paid above subsistence wages frequently preferred not to work a full week, but instead to supplement their meagre standard of living with a little leisure.[1] The modern choice is often to sacrifice leisure to increase earnings which are then used to purchase a higher standard of living. The rise of a consumer society is a part of the history of leisure. At the same time, leisure has itself become a consumer product.

Traditional manners, customs and amusements

Landed society

The country house lay at the heart of aristocratic life in the eighteenth and early nineteenth centuries. Through their patronage of architecture the political and social leaders of Britain proclaimed their wealth, power and influence to their equals and inferiors alike. Within the walls of their magnificent houses they entertained, conspired, arranged marriages and ran the country. The great country house is a lasting monument to the triumph of the aristocracy in eighteenth-century Britain. Gentlemen came back from the Grand Tour inspired by Palladio's work and commissioned new houses beyond the means of princes from some of the minor European states. Neighbours indulged in competitive ostentation, and gentlemen expected to be allowed to visit the great houses to look around. They were usually welcome, for the great houses were built for show. The Duke of Chandos was even able to subsidise his household expenses out of the money left by his visitors; while Thomas Coke built Holkham Hall in Norfolk more as a place in which to display his classical treasures than one in which to live. What the wealthy could scarcely afford, the less wealthy admired and copied on a lesser scale. In small parks, manor houses acquired classical fronts; detached villas on the edges of towns lacked an avenue of trees, but were given the illusion of space with a sweeping drive.

When business, politics or pleasure called the aristocrat to town, he had another house, smaller and usually with limited grounds, built with the same purpose and run in the same way as his country house(s). The London season occupied the first part of the year, when life in the country might feel cold and remote. By August at the latest, the smell of the town indicated a move back to the country until Christmas. The length and timing of the parliamentary year was conditioned by this migratory lifestyle of the political élite. In both town and country the aristocracy enjoyed considerable leisure, interspersed with work of a public or private nature. Their libraries were filled with elegantly bound books on estate management; plans were discussed with stewards, summary justice was dispensed, social power was exerted over lesser neighbours, and political allies were wooed and impressed. Leisure was possible because of the army of indoor and outdoor servants who did the real work, preparing the houses, moving the household like some great army, looking after the family, providing a hospitable welcome for endless streams of guests. British society until the twentieth century was divided into the servant-keeping and the serving classes.

The day in these circles was organised at an appropriately leisurely pace. Breakfast was usually taken at nine or ten o'clock, some three or four hours after the day-labourer had trudged to his work in the fields. The meal was informal, but could be an elaborate and prolonged affair, a time for discussing the affairs of the estate, reading and answering letters and preparing for the business of the day. Social breakfasts were for informally entertaining friends – a function assumed by afternoon tea in the nineteenth century. Dinner was served in the early afternoon, but the hour got progressively later during the eighteenth century until, by the early nineteenth century, only the old-fashioned were dining as early as four o'clock.

Healthy appetites among the menfolk were stimulated by energetic indulgence in blood-sports. The favourite sport with aristocracy and gentry alike was hunting. Deer had once been the prime quarry, but these were now prized more for their contribution to a 'Capability' Brown landscape. Hare-coursing was still popular, but the latest eighteenth-century fashion was for fox-hunting and one of the highest (and most expensive) positions available to any man in county society was to be Master of the Foxhounds. Another sport gaining in favour was shooting, which largely replaced the older art of hawking, despite the cumbersome nature of the weaponry before the introduction of the breech-loading rifle in 1853. With the growth in shooting came the deliberate breeding and preserving of birds for sport, which involved excluding all but the wealthy and privileged from taking game. Tenants were not allowed even to shoot over their own land, except by permission of their landlord (a concession granted in 1831).

Eating and drinking were major leisure-time activities, and were frequently indulged to excess. Both sexes in the mid-eighteenth century generally behaved in a manner which a later generation would have regarded as coarse and vulgar, but by the end of the century the ladies were accustomed to withdraw (to the drawing room) after dinner, while the men drank, smoked and gambled away the evening, rejoining the ladies later if they were still capable of standing. The ladies concerned themselves during the day with the overseeing of the household, took tea (blends were closely guarded secrets), played cards, gossiped and showed their skill on the harp, harpsichord or newfangled box piano. As the hour for dinner got to be as late as seven they adopted the practice of taking a light midday snack called luncheon, so as not to appear as greedy as the men home from hunting in the evening.

A change in manners came slowly during the later eighteenth and early nineteenth centuries, as French refinement and evangelical religion brought more delicacy and circumspection to public behaviour. Social orders evolved into classes; society grew more exclusive, and gave rise to the word 'Society' in 1823, meaning an exclusive body of the fashionable. This withdrawal of the social élite was to have important consequences for their attitude to the customs and amusements of the people, as sporting activities came to reflect the class and gender divisions of society. Ladies, like gentlemen, rode horses, but even in 1804 it was regarded as rather unwomanly of a Mrs Thornton to race on the Knavesmire at York. Lady Salisbury kept a pack of foxhounds in the eighteenth century, but few ladies were riding seriously by the mid-nineteenth century. They rarely shot, except with bows and arrows – archery enjoyed a fashionable revival in the late eighteenth century. Where gentlemen had supported such pastimes as cock-fighting and prize-fighting in the eighteenth century, they no longer felt able to do so with a good conscience in the early nineteenth century. The squire no longer thought it appropriate to get drunk at the village inn; he might even think it proper to stay sober in his own house. Aristocratic houses and entertainments became more private, and ladies of easy virtue such as Harriette Wilson were no longer in evidence at great social occasions. With the sons of George III, an era came to an end. Some of this change in public manners was, admittedly, superficial – the morals of the Regency 'bucks' were soon to be replicated in those of the next Prince of Wales's 'fast set' – but a sea-change occurred between the easy-going age of George IV, Melbourne and Palmerston, and the seriously conscientious age of Prince Albert, Peel and Ashley, which was to have important consequences for social conduct throughout the population.

Provincial life

The social pace was set by the aristocracy but, as the wealth of the gentry and merchants increased, aristocratic styles spread and the social functions of the great house were reproduced commercially for those of lesser wealth. Public assembly rooms, theatres and concerts, beginning in London, spread in the eighteenth century into the major provincial county towns, despite an Act of 1737 which reaffirmed the professional monopoly of Covent Garden, Drury Lane and a handful of licensed provincial theatres. At first such leisure-time activities were financed on a subscription basis, but in the second half of the century they were often commercial operations, with admission to the general public by ticket. The flourishing nature of eighteenth-century provincial society is well illustrated by the case of York, the leading provincial town of northern England, as recorded by Francis Drake, whose *Eboracum* was published in 1736.

The main inspiration for the development of eighteenth-century York was commercial. The city was in economic decline, and set out to attract the local gentry who might baulk at the long winter journey to London. The York season was not only cheaper than London, but also cheaper (Drake claimed) than their remaining in their own houses in the country. In addition to the Assizes, which customarily drew the gentry twice a year, the city promoted horse-racing from 1709, and soon made August the main month for social gathering in the city. The new racecourse on the Knavesmire was opened for Race Week 1732, with a grandstand designed by John Carr, builder of many grand town houses in the city as well as the future architect of Harewood House. At the same time a new Assembly Room was built to a design of Lord Burlington for dancing, conversation, cards 'and other innocent diversions' on Mondays at a cost of half-a-crown; musical performances were given in the same room on Fridays at a cost of a crown. York had also one of the earliest provincial theatres, opened with the encouragement of the corporation in 1734: a season at the plays cost 15*s*. (75p). As Drake pointed out, the total outlay for 'a quarter of a year's polite entertainment' was very modest. The city also appointed a huntsman in 1719 who rode twice a week at the mayor's request. Less formally, coffee houses sprang up to accommodate the market for news, gossip and gambling.[2]

Much the same could be written of the other major county towns of England, such as Norwich, Newcastle, Bristol and Exeter. Edinburgh, Scotland's premier city, was a little different with its university and large professional middle class of lawyers practising in the Edinburgh courts; but the social life of the New Town was very Anglicised and provincial, like that of York. The leading town outside London for enjoyment was Bath. Originally a health spa, it had already become by Defoe's day what he called 'the resort of the sound rather than the sick'. It grew to be one of the largest and grandest of provincial towns (population 34,000 at the end of the eighteenth century), with public buildings, terraces and crescents in the best classical style, informally laid out to match the social style of Richard 'Beau' Nash, the greatest arbiter of fashion in the town in the first half of the century. Social life was centred on the Pump Room and the Assembly Room, where the aristocracy gossiped and gambled, attended balls and sought marriage partners. Nash maintained the strictest of propriety, but Charles Wesley called Bath 'the headquarters of Satan'.[3]

Horse racing

Men gambled on anything, from cards to cricket, but an abiding favourite was horse racing, one of the great leisure pursuits of all classes: as Drake observed, this 'barbarous diversion . . . not only draws in the country people in vast crowds, but the gentry, nay even the clergy and prime nobility are mixed amongst them'.[4] It was the first great spectator sport, and gambling became such a passion with the lower classes that an Act in 1740 attempted to make the sport more exclusive. But popular enthusiasm only increased. New, shorter races developed for large prize money – the St Leger (1776), the Derby (1780), the 2,000 Guineas (1809) and the 1,000 Guineas (1814). The aristocracy kept the people at a distance by resorting to their favourite device of enclosure – within five years of the first St Leger, Doncaster racecourse had a stand for the greater comfort of the wealthy. Racing survived the change in manners and evangelical onslaught of the early nineteenth century. Temporary successes by the Evangelicals – as at Cheltenham, where the Rev. Francis Close stopped the races and prevented the rebuilding of the theatre – were short-lived. Aristocratic patronage and local commercial interests were too strong for the moralists who, throughout the nineteenth century, were to remain morally anxious as race week approached, with its crowds, drunkenness and gambling.

The leviathan of the early Victorian sporting world was Lord George Bentinck, second surviving son of the Duke of Portland, who rode hard and betted harder (it was rumoured he had lost £30,000 when the favourite did not win the St Leger in 1826). Despite his own practices, which were not always above board, he attempted to clean up some of the more obvious forms of corruption in the running of races, establishing rules of conduct which the Jockey Club was later able to enforce and build upon. In the 1840s he owned between 60 and 70 horses, and his establishment cost him £40,000 a year. This was the aristocratic lifestyle on the grandest of scales.[5]

'Traditional' customs and amusements

Though the common people of Britain in the eighteenth century had no leisure such as the rich enjoyed, their lives were more than unremitting toil. In the countryside with its chronic under-employment there were certain seasons of the year when there was plenty of time to spare for customary entertainments, providing they cost little or no money. This 'customary' world was never as static as the word 'traditional' implies. Far from being unchanging until swept away by the forces of evangelical religion, enclosure and urbanisation at the end of the eighteenth century, it should rather be seen as undergoing continuous change and adaptation, beginning before the Puritan Revolution of the seventeenth century, before even the Reformation of the sixteenth century, and reaching forward well into the nineteenth. Popular culture proved itself to be remarkably resilient. In 1844 William Howitt was lamenting the passing of ancient customs which oral historians have found still flourishing at the beginning of the twentieth century, along with adaptations and innovations from more recent times.[6] Even in the towns, before the mid-nineteenth century, life remained sufficiently undisciplined for many rural habits to survive in recognisable form.

The customs of rural life were regulated by the seasons and the Christian year: Christmas, with its mumming plays and Yuletide celebrations; Plough Monday (the first Monday after Twelfth Night), with ploughboys and morris dancers collecting money for feasting and drinking before the start of the agricultural year; Shrove Tuesday, with its pancakes and carnival, and football played in the village street before the sombre days of Lent; mid-Lent Sunday, a time for servant girls to visit their mothers; Easter, with its fairs and games in celebration of Spring; May Day, the great festival of youth, with garlands, May dolls and dancing, merging perhaps with 29 May – Oak Apple Day (in commemoration of Charles II's escape after the Battle of Worcester); Whitsun with its ales (revels), sports, dancing and fairs; harvest, with its procession as the last cartload of corn was brought to the barn, followed by feasting and revelling far into the night; Hallowe'en, when evil spirits were exorcised before the dark nights of winter. Finally there was 5 November, when anti-Catholic sermons rang out in the churches before the people celebrated the triumph of Protestantism with bonfires and fireworks. Practice varied from village to village and region to region. The Scots celebrated Hogmanay rather than Yuletide, but in much the same way, with mumming plays; and the Kirk's half-yearly Communion Day provided a further occasion for family reunions.

For many villages, the patronal festival of the parish church was the high point of the year and the excuse for a fair or carnival. The form these wakes or village festivals took varied from place to place. In parts of Lancashire the heart of the celebration was the annual rush-bearing, when fresh rushes were cut and brought to the parish church at the end of the summer. Long after the need arose, the ceremony continued with intricately decorated rush-carts representing each community or trade. It is tempting to sentimentalise these rural customs. Like the rambling rose on the wall of the rural slum, they mitigated but did not replace the harshness of daily life. They provided a useful safety valve of riot and licence for a people accustomed to the alternating disciplines of want and work.

No celebration was complete without its fair, with its pedlars' stalls, puppet shows, musicians, menageries, human and animal curiosities, dancing, fighting, drinking and wenching. Fairs were held at any time from Easter onwards, culminating in the autumn after harvest with the Michaelmas Statute or Hiring fair. They were the great social occasions of the year, when town and country came together in drunken revelry and delight, as in Nottingham with its October Goose Fair, or the celebrated Bartholomew Fair in London, not suppressed by the corporation until 1854.

The amusements of country and townsfolk alike naturally centred on animals: bull-baiting, bear-baiting and badger-baiting with dogs were regarded as great sport; bull-running through the streets provided some of the excitement of the bull fight, and cock-shies were set up, especially on Shrove Tuesday, for the sport of cock-throwing; cock-fighting with spurs and dog-fights were also very popular with all classes. In a bloodthirsty age, such innocent fun was not thought amiss; after all, humans were scarcely less brutal to one another. Wrestling, fisticuffs, stick-fighting and cudgelling all aimed to break bones, draw blood or loosen teeth. Football should also perhaps be added to this catalogue of blood sports, since in its most unorganised form it could amount to a mad scramble by opposing crowds to kick a pig's bladder the length of a street or even the distance between two rival villages. Other popular entertainments included more restrained activities, such as cricket, quoits, skittles and bell-ringing. Many of these rural sports survived the beginnings of rapid urban growth in the later eighteenth and early nineteenth centuries, because town and country were never so clearly differentiated as the contrasting words 'urban' and 'rural' might suggest. The streets of towns were filled with country smells and animals – not only horses, cats and dogs, but also bacon-pigs and milch cows, sheep and cattle on their way to market, and performing bears in the street. Even in London – the only really urban environment in Britain before the end of the eighteenth century – bull-running, bull-baiting and cock-fighting continued, though cock-shies were prohibited in 1758.

Artisan life

Just as agricultural work determined the pattern of rural leisure, so life in an urban workshop also had its customary style. The artisan enjoyed considerable independence, whether he worked with his family in the home, or in a workshop for a small master. Even when his raw materials, his tools or his products were owned or controlled by a merchant capitalist, he continued to enjoy considerable freedom in the management of his time. Skill, and control over entry to the trade through apprenticeship, gave the artisan status and a bargaining position in dealings with his master. The loss of this status and freedom, affecting different trades and sections of trades from the late-eighteenth to the late-nineteenth centuries, was to be one of the major grievances of that emerging working class of which the artisans were frequently leaders.

The artisan in his workshop, making shoes, clothes, furniture or small metalware, was – in the literal sense of the word – a manufacturer: he worked with his hands, and was not dependent upon noisy machines which drowned all conversation and whose ceaseless motion demanded constant attention and discipline. He had a reputation for working hard and playing hard, and was sometimes something of a scholar. The handloom weaver might prop a book on his loom to relieve the boredom of his somewhat mechanical task (his was one of the few skills which was incompatible with conversation). For the rest, one might break off from his work in turns to read to his fellow workers. In the 1790s the works of Paine were notoriously popular with the artisans, whose workshops often turned into debating chambers on the merits of various brands of politics and religion. This should not be idealised. The artisans were also great drinkers. Work, and talking, made men thirsty. Any excuse was seized for an adjournment to a local public house, or an apprentice might be sent out with a jug to fetch in some ale. Celebrations were frequent. 'Footings' – the practice whereby the entrant to a trade put up a few shillings to which others added a lesser amount to fund a drinking bout at a nearby public house – were almost universal. Work patterns were irregular. The practice of 'St Monday' – taking Monday off work – was common among skilled workmen and, though opposed by the larger employers seeking to discipline their workers, it survived in the engineering trades, where apprenticeship continued strong, into the second half of the nineteenth century. The artisans also had their own customary festivals: St Crispin (25 October) for the shoemakers; St Andrew (30 November) for the lacemakers; and 3 February, when the woolcombers held their great Bishop Blaise festival and procession.

The life of the artisan in Manchester in the early 1830s is vividly recalled by Lloyd Jones in *Progress of the Working Class*:

> In the highest-paid trades, work was not to be had on a Monday from the artisan; many men only began their week on the Thursday.

> The practice of 'footings' was universal, the amount of which was invariably spent in drink. Still, there were many good influences to be found in such workshops. There were grave men, who employed their leisure hours in reading or study – entomologists, florists, botanists, students in chemistry and astronomy . . . But these men were exceptional, and sometimes, notwithstanding their studies, they were as fond of a glass as their most graceless neighbours.[7]

Here was the making of Victorian respectability – but not quite. One old entomologist, as Jones recalled, even disappeared from his work for three or four days, not collecting insects but drinking to his own funeral with money he had taken out of the burial club. Time- and work-discipline had yet to make their impact.

The attack upon popular recreations

By the 1840s a full-scale campaign was under way to change the shape of popular behaviour. Pressure came from several related sources. First, as towns grew and became more completely urban in character – a development promoted by the railways – the scope for the more exuberant forms of popular recreation such as street football became progressively limited; second, industrialisation and the extension of large scale capitalism gradually produced a more disciplined working day and week, with little opportunity for the old informal customs; third, religious opposition to the cruelty and barbarity of many popular sports changed public opinion and the law to force their eventual suppression; fourth, political concern over rowdy crowds which appeared to threaten social stability led to a new emphasis on social control; and, fifth, awareness of the need to provide something more positive and uplifting for the poor led to the provision of alternative, 'rational' recreations. None of these pressures should be exaggerated: they operated imperfectly and gradually over a century or more. But by the 1840s they were making a considerable impact, as many of the customs of pre-industrial Britain were either modified or replaced by new and more closely regulated forms of commercialised popular entertainment. This was a process led by a variety of people, from working-class leaders to paternalistic employers, from clergymen to sanitary reformers, from schoolteachers to policemen. Popular, in the sense of the inclusive experience of the people, was being redefined as that which belonged to the 'inferior' classes and stood in need of reformation.

Enclosure and urban growth

Enclosure and urban growth provided the context within which other forces for change operated. Popular field sports required space, and it was difficult to play football when the common was enclosed. Only the squire's hunt was permitted to rush over private property and crash through hedges with impunity in pursuit of pleasure and a quarry; and street football in the town became an increasingly hazardous nuisance to traffic, as the volume of carts and cabs grew to meet the commercial needs of thriving urban centres. Though green fields lay close to the hearts of some of the largest provincial cities, enclosure frequently removed access to them. But the process should not be exaggerated before the 1830s and 1840s. Glasgow Green, Ardwick Green in Manchester and Bethnal Green were still what their names implied at the beginning of the nineteenth century. Bonner's Fields in east London were not enclosed until the 1850s (to make Victoria Park), and Plumstead Common remained to provoke an enclosure riot in 1876. Though Bolton in 1833 was said to have 'no public walks, or open spaces in the nature of walks, or public gardens',[8] many towns still held their horse races on great open spaces within walking distance of their centres – Kersal Moor, Manchester (until 1846); the Town Moor, Newcastle (until 1882). Radicals holding large protest meetings gathered in these or other convenient places such as Calton Hill, Edinburgh; Peep Green in the heart of the West Riding; Mottram Moor near Stockport; and Shipley Glen near Bradford. A day's ramble would take workers from the Potteries to Mow Cop; from Oldham, Rochdale and Halifax to Blackstone Edge; from Nottingham into Sherwood Forest. Londoners had access to Hampstead Heath, Kennington Common and, by custom, royal Hyde Park. Until the formation of municipal police forces after 1835, and the powers granted to them under the Town Police Act of 1847, the streets also served as open spaces for the people, though they were hardly adequate compensation for the loss of open fields. The provision of public parks from the 1840s did not so much follow a generation which had been denied access to open spaces, as completed the process of enclosure, bringing order to the disordered and neatly laid-out walks to where the people had once run free.

Factory discipline

The combined effects of long working hours, a population unused to discipline and the paucity of recreational facilities in many towns was disastrous for the factory population, of whom a majority were women and young people. Lloyd Jones recalled his experience of factory workers in Manchester in 1832:

> What were the amusements of the masses, thus over-worked, ill-fed, ill-housed, – left for the most part uneducated? Large numbers of working people attended fairs and wakes, at the latter of which jumping in sacks, climbing greased poles, grinning through horse

> collars for tobacco, hunting pigs with soaped tails, were the choicest diversions. An almost general unchastity . . . prevailed amongst the women employed in factories, and generally throughout the lowest ranks of the working population. But drink was the mainspring of enjoyment. When Saturday evening came, indulgences began which continued till Sunday evening. Fiddles were to be heard on all sides, and limp-looking men and pale-faced women thronged the public-houses, and reeled and jigged until they were turned, drunk and riotous into the streets, at most unseasonable hours. . . . In fact, sullen, silent work alternated with noisy, drunken riot; and Easter and Whitsun debauches, with an occasional outbreak during some favourite 'wakes', rounded the whole life of the factory worker.[9]

Jones was writing in 1867, and his words betray the voice of moral improvement; and yet there is sufficient supporting evidence in the accounts of other contemporaries to suggest that he was not exaggerating. What is interesting about his account is how much of rural custom had survived in the behaviour of the factory workers, despite the different social context of the town. The alternation of hard work and riotous leisure, the popular amusements, the centrality of drink, were all customary. What Jones is here describing is the rural worker in an urban setting, with the advantages of neither and the disadvantages of both.

This style of rough conduct survived longest where heavy manual work was common, and was associated with sub-contracting, where labourers completed a job and then relaxed until their earnings were spent and they were forced back to work. It was a lifestyle appropriate to the navvy, the quarryman, the miner, the common sailor and the casual worker on the docks or in the building trade. In the factory, life had to be regulated. Unlike the artisan's workshop, the steam-driven factory could not co-exist with undisciplined labour, and masters attempted to regulate the conduct of their employees both on and off the premises. It was dangerous to the operative as well as bad for productivity to mix drinking or horse-play with minding a machine. Moreover, to the capitalist, time was money, and his machinery could not be left idle while his workers stayed in bed or took a day off work. So the early factory masters developed an intricate system of timekeeping, foreign to an age in which public clocks were few and the rhythms of country life were governed by the sun. The factory community was regulated precisely by bells, hooters and the 'knocker-up'; discipline was maintained by fines deducted from wages.

At Strutt's Belper works forfeits were imposed not only for theft and failure to do proper work, but also for absenteeism – 'being off drinking', 'off to Derby races without leave'; failure to comply with mill discipline – 'calling thro' window to some Soldiers', 'dancing in room' (Strutt returned the forfeit money in this case); misconduct outside working hours

– 'putting Jos Haynes' dog into a bucket of hot water', 'rubbing their faces with blood and going about the town to frighten people'.[10] As Robert Owen realised, the factory was an wonderful instrument for the formation of character. He was unusual among early factory masters only in perceiving the moral harm as well as the moral 'good' which the factory system could produce.[11]

Moral reform

Religious and humanitarian improvers were clear that the lower classes had to be rescued from indulging in customary cruel and morally debasing sports, the evils of the public house and the demon drink, and from spending their Sundays in dissolution and sin. This attitude was not new. Societies for the Reformation of Manners had been set up in the early eighteenth century, and in Scotland the General Assembly had urged strong action against Sabbath breakers, but morals then grew lax and it was not until the evangelical revival that new impetus was given to the movement for reform, with the Society for the Suppression of Vice being founded in 1802 and the Lord's Day Observance Society in 1831. In 1803 the Vice Society (as it was popularly known) proposed the suppression 'of all Fairs whatever, unless they are really wanted for the purpose of useful traffic'. Between the evangelicals and popular culture was fixed a gulf of incomprehension. As William Howitt observed of the Nottingham Goose Fair:

> It is a time, in fact, of universal country jollity, pleasure-taking, love-making, present-making, treating and youthful entertainment, enjoyed to an extent that people of different tastes can form no conception of.[12]

Town and City Missionaries felt themselves descending to the nether world when they frequented such scenes to distribute tracts urging upon people the sinfulness of Vanity Fair. Yet the fair as a form of entertainment was never entirely suppressed, despite the elimination of particular examples in the mid-nineteenth century. Instead it was cleaned up, civilized and given a new lease of life. The best example of a 'modern' fair is the Hoppings on the Town Moor at Newcastle, started in 1882 by Temperance reformers for the former race-going crowds when horse racing was moved out to Gosforth Park.

Howitt was a lover of the old ways, yet even he was glad to see the suppression of cruel sports. Progress was slow. A Bill to prevent bull-baiting in 1800 was roundly defeated amid popular rejoicing, but in 1822 the principle of legislative interference to prevent cruelty to animals was established, and in 1835 this was extended to prohibit the keeping of places for 'running, baiting, or fighting any bull, bear, badger, dog, or other animal . . . or for cockfighting'. Prohibition was one thing; enforcement another, despite the efforts of the Society for the Prevention of Cruelty to Animals, founded in 1824 (RSPCA from 1840). An event as public as the Stamford Bull Run was ended, after repeated pressure from the RSPCA, in 1840, but cock-fighting and dog-fighting long persisted in public houses. Their virtual suppression came only with the extension of effective policing throughout the country, though the employment of policemen on such unpopular work did nothing to assist their acceptance by resentful local communities. Working people could not help noticing that the aristocratically patronised RSPCA seemed rather keener to suppress the sports of the poor than of the rich.

In the opinion of the higher classes, the drinking place lay at the heart of the social problem: poverty was caused by excessive expenditure on alcohol; riotous behaviour was attributable to the drunkenness of the poor; gambling and prostitution flourished in the dissolute environment of the public house; crimes and even political sedition were plotted within its walls. The old country alehouse had (of course) been quite different – or so argued William Howitt in 1844.[13] In fact, the alehouse had itself not been tamed until the century after 1660, and then chiefly only in closed rural parishes, where the vestry and overseers of the poor could exert pressure on its customers. Alehouses (kept by the poor and selling only malt beer), inns and taverns (larger places selling a wider range of drinks) were licensed by the magistrates, who could exercise some control by threatening to refuse renewal of the licence of a landlord whose premises were judged of ill repute. The City of London in the eighteenth century was ringed with such places just beyond the jurisdiction of the city magistrates, but many low alehouses and gin-shops escaped detection and remained unlicensed.

Concern about drinking-places mounted in the early nineteenth century. Many contemporaries were therefore astonished when, in 1830, the Government yielded to the free trade lobby and carried the Beer Act, which permitted any ratepayer to obtain a licence for £2 with the minimum of formality from the local excise officer, allowing him to brew and sell beer on his premises without reference to the magistrates – many of whom, in country areas, were clergymen. The worst fears of the moralists appeared to be fulfilled. Far from weaning people off spirits, or bringing the unlicensed houses under some kind of control, the Act was followed by a proliferation of outlets for the sale of alcohol to the poor, with all the attendant opportunities for Sabbath-breaking, immorality and crime. By 1833 there were 35,000 beer shops in England and Wales (the Act did not apply to Scotland), but there is no evidence in the medium term that the Act was responsible for any of the evils attributed to it. Beer consumption was already rising in the 1820s, and per capita consumption of malt actually fell between the late 1820s and early 1840s. The real sin of the Beer Act was to place the control of popular leisure in the hands of lowly beer-house keepers and beyond the jurisdiction of the magistrates and clergy. Magistrates were not given the power to restrict beer-house licences until 1869.

Beer was, for many reformers, a temperance drink; indeed, with milk infected and water polluted, it was the only safe drink for the poor man and his family. The real problem of drunkenness lay with spirits. In Scotland whisky drinking had been introduced from the Highlands in the early eighteenth century, and in England gin remained a problem even after the ending of the 'gin era' in 1751. The glittering gin-palace which flourished in the 1830s conformed much more to the reformer's image of a den of iniquitous pleasure than the humble beer-house ever did. But the extent of drunkenness was all too obvious in the streets of early Victorian towns, and in the 1830s a new movement was begun with the object of total abstinence from all forms of intoxicating drinks.

Unlike other aspects of the movement for moral reform, the total abstinence movement had working-class roots. Mere temperance in spirits meant attacking the poor man's whisky or gin but leaving the rich man's port or claret untouched. From the late eighteenth century there had been a move amongst a minority of working men away from the traditional culture of the public house and towards abstinence and self-improvement. This minority became increasingly vocal in the leadership of the emergent working-class as a political force. The coffee house, which had been an institution of the higher classes in the eighteenth century, became a working-class institution in the first half of the nineteenth century. Teetotalism developed as the ally of political and religious radicalism, although it was never an exclusively Nonconformist movement, and its principles were rejected by those working-class leaders like Feargus O'Connor and Joseph Rayner Stephens, who were most attuned to the feelings of the great majority of working men.

In mid-Victorian Britain the three issues of Total Abstinence, Sabbatarianism and Sunday Trading were seen as closely interconnected. Evangelicals had argued with increasing conviction since the late eighteenth century that, since Sunday (the Sabbath) was designed solely for the worship of God, all secular pursuits should be banned. Until the 1830s Sabbatarianism made little headway in Parliament, where most recent legislation was liberalising rather than restrictive. The powers needed to limit Sunday trading and public entertainments were already provided by the Sunday Observance Acts of 1677 (repealed 1969) and 1780. In Scotland, where the Sabbatarianism of the Westminster Confession was enshrined in an Act of 1661, the Kirk Sessions exercised considerable moral power to maintain the Sabbath according to the decrees of the General Assembly. In many rural parishes the pressure to conform was very strong, especially in the north and west, where the Free Church was dominant after 1843, but in Glasgow the Sabbath went virtually unregulated.

One of the few amusements open to the lower classes on a Sunday was the public house, and even this was closed during morning service after 1828. As one contemporary in Manchester in the 1840s observed, 'The operatives loiter on the threshold of their cottages, or lounge in groups, at the street corners, until the hour of service is terminated, and the public houses are opened.'[14] Lloyd Jones even recalled churchwardens earlier raiding public houses and enforcing attendance at church.[15] The next step for the Sabbatarians was to close public houses completely on Sundays. Beer-houses were already restricted under the 1830 Act to opening on Sundays only between the hours of 1.00 p.m. to 3.00 p.m. and 5.00 p.m. to 10.00 p.m., but public houses were not interfered with until 1854, when they were required to close on Saturdays at midnight, and not re-open until 4.00 a.m. on Mondays except for the hours of 12.30 p.m. to 2.30 p.m. and 6.00 p.m. to 10.00 p.m. on Sundays. This was the closest the Sabbatarians came in England to achieving their goal. In Scotland complete Sunday closing was enforced in 1853; Wales followed in 1881.

Sunday trading was an extension of the Sunday drinking problem. Employers paid out wages late on Saturday nights in public houses; churchgoers on Sunday mornings were given to complaining to the police at finding working folk rather the worse for drink, loitering on the pavements and doing their shopping from street traders, who blocked the thoroughfares with their barrows. The eventual answer to the problem was to prohibit the practice of paying out wages in this way; but, before that was generally enforced, the Saturday half-day holiday had done something to alleviate the situation. None the less, pressure was building up in the 1830s and 1840s for more immediate action. Restrictions on Sunday opening in 1854 were one response; a Bill in 1855 to strengthen the laws prohibiting Sunday trading was another. Both measures were clearly and consciously aimed at the lower orders, who in London reacted angrily. Throughout the summer of 1855 rioting occurred in Hyde Park against the rich, as they enjoyed their carriage-rides there, and windows were smashed. The 1854 Act was modified to permit Sunday drinking from 12.30 p.m. to 3.00 p.m. and 5.00 p.m. to 11.00 p.m., and the Sunday Trading Bill was dropped, but the older laws of 1677 and 1780 remained to be applied, often in petty cases, and pawnbroking was added to the prohibited list in 1872, as if to emphasise the basic lack of understanding among moral reformers of the needs and patterns of working-class life.

Having dealt with Sunday, the reformers next attacked the problem of round-the-clock opening during the working week, which was widely believed to be the reason for much drunkenness. Consequently, in 1864 public houses in London were required to close at night between the hours of 1.00 a.m. and 4.00 a.m. Then, in 1871, the Liberal government turned its attention to the drink question more generally. Amid violent protests and political controversy, the Licensing Act (1872) reorganised the system of licensing, and for the first time prohibited night-time drinking generally along the lines which already applied to beer-houses. After some moderating amendments in 1874, all drinking places were closed at night, between 12.30 a.m. and 5.00 a.m (London), 11.00 p.m. and 6.00 a.m. (provincial urban) and 10.00 p.m. and 6.00 a.m. (rural); Sunday morning and mid-afternoon closing remained, as did total Sunday closing in Scotland.

The Act, even in its modified form, appeared to be a victory for the Temperance movement, but in fact the slight fall in per capita beer consumption which occurred in the later nineteenth century was probably due less to legislation, or, indeed, the campaigning of the Temperance movement, than to the rise in alternative leisure facilities. Drunkenness nevertheless remained a serious problem in late-Victorian and Edwardian Britain, and was not significantly affected by legislation until the Defence of the Realm Act (1914) restricted opening hours further and weakened the strength of the beer. These restrictions on the opening of licensed premises, which set Britain apart from much Continental practice until a new Licensing Act in 1988, went back no further than the First World War.

Social control

The need to control crowds of poor people lay behind much of the legislation to restrict popular amusements of all kinds. Fear of disorder was a sign of insecurity among the propertied classes. For much of the eighteenth century they had a quiet confidence in their ability to maintain order and to contain the turbulent poor. Signs of unusual crowd activity – such as a Methodist outdoor preaching – were quickly and effectively dealt with by traditional means within the local community. Rioting was not unusual, but the incidents which occasioned the disturbances were usually local and temporary. They did not represent a threat to the social order – indeed, some popular customs involved the whole community – and the level of tolerance was consequently high.

Attitudes began to change towards the end of the eighteenth century, as the upper classes became socially more distant from the common people. The ability of the forces of law and order to cope with a major disturbance was severely questioned in 1780 during the Gordon Riots in London, in which 285 people died and £100,000's-worth of damage was done to property in a week of looting and burning. This was a psychological turning point for the propertied classes. Although they were occasionally in the future to dally with the 'mob' – notably at the Priestley Riots in Birmingham in 1791 – the worsening of the situation in France from 1792 confirmed the lesson that the lower orders were dangerous, and a threat not simply to the public peace but to the social and even political stability of the country. This social pessimism was in tune with the evangelical view of man as a sinful creature in need of restraint and redemption. Conservatives identified the French revolutionaries with the Anti-Christ; the war against France, against radicalism at home and against sin were all one war, a righteous crusade.

With the growth in population, the disruption of communities through enclosure, the breaking down of local and informal controls and the rapid growth of towns lacking effective institutions for maintaining authority, magistrates became increasingly nervous as they observed what appeared to be a mounting crime wave. In 1786 the Salford Hundred Quarter Sessions expressed its alarm at the numbers of 'idle, disorderly and dangerous persons of all descriptions' who were roaming the streets of Manchester, and called for the establishment of a Sunday School.[16] The fear was that the devil would always find mischief for idle hands, particularly factory hands on Sundays. All occasions which encouraged the gathering of large crowds came to be seen as potential threats to the social and political fabric. Traditional 5 November celebrations could easily turn nasty if the effigy being burnt bore a striking resemblance not to Guy Fawkes but to the local clerical magistrate or squire. What had once been coarse but good-humoured fun became very serious when crowds were driving aristocrats to the guillotine in France.

From the 1790s to the 1840s this political dimension to popular culture was never far from the minds of those responsible for making and enforcing the law, even when their primary motives were fear for property, moral revulsion against cruelty or the desire to save souls. In an age of 'Jacobin' radicals, Luddites, 'Swing' rioters and Chartists, the propertied classes felt they were losing control, and looked for new ways to reinforce their traditional authority. What the respectable feared was not the lower orders as such, but their infiltration and corruption by evil men with revolutionary designs. Crowds sodden with drink and deprived of any moral sense by repeated indulgence in cruel and mindless pastimes were open to the temptations of the devil who came in the form of that stereotypical figure, the 'agitator' or 'mysterious stranger', who would exploit the ignorance of the mob for his own nefarious purposes. When the Manchester Town Missionaries went to the Easter Monday fair at Knott Mill, near the edge of the then built-up area of Manchester, what horrified them most in 'that scene of folly and wickedness' was an exhibition put on by the local Owenite Socialists, showing devils, ghosts and hobgoblins and aimed at the overthrow of Christianity.[17] To the evangelical and official mind, this was tantamount to the overthrow of all morality, law and systems of government. The irony is that these very Owenite agitators (men like Lloyd Jones), along with their much-feared Chartist brethren, were among the first to denounce immorality, drunkenness, popular licence and disorderly behaviour. Far from seeing such characteristics as promoting revolution, they saw them as playing into the hands of the governing classes. For differing political reasons, the pleasures of the people were under attack from all sides.

Reformed customs and rational recreations

The response of reformers to the dangerous state of popular culture was not entirely repressive. There was also an attempt to purge some popular recreations of their less acceptable characteristics, and to provide other recreations, more in keeping with that 'progress of the intellect' on which the Victorian middle classes prided themselves. This was not simply a matter of class, although class played its part. It was also a conflict of cultures between old and new, rural and urban, pagan and Christian, oral and written, uneducated and educated. The reformers came from all classes (perhaps least from the very bottom and very top of society), and they were not all of one mind. There were total abstainers and publicans; Sabbatarians and free-Sunday men; cultural philistines and lovers of art and music; manufacturers and working-class leaders; commercial entrepreneurs with and without principles; but chiefly there were the people themselves, not passive recipients of what was provided, but creators and improvisors of new pastimes to suit changed circumstances.

The list of cultural pursuits and healthy recreations followed by all classes grew longer and more diverse towards the end of the nineteenth century. In the 1830s and 1840s attitudes against frivolous leisure were hardening, against a background of fear and suspicion of the idle poor; by the 1870s the process had been reversed. Greater material comfort for many (not all) of the lower classes, stabilisation of class relations and an increasing awareness on the part of the propertied classes that the poor could not be abandoned in a Christian country, all helped soften the impact of strict evangelical religion as the Victorian era drew to a close.

Reformed customs

In its war against pagan customs the Church had, since time immemorial, sought to substitute its own calendar of ritual for that of tradition, as at Yuletide and Easter. The transformation of Whitsun and harvest festivities in the nineteenth century are examples of this continuing struggle against the implicit (and sometimes explicit) paganism of popular culture.

Whitsun (it was never remembered as Pentecost) was one of the great popular festivals of the year. Traditionally a time for revels, maypoles and moral laxity, it was reborn during the nineteenth century as an occasion for Sunday School processions and Friendly Society parades. The first 'Whit Walk' is usually traced to Manchester in 1801, when the local Anglican Sunday Schools marched to celebrate their division from the non-denominational Sunday School the previous year. Soon the ritual of rival denominational walks was established, even in some of the smallest villages in the textile north, and in some places Whit Monday was the day for examining the children's progress in school, after which they were allowed to play field sports and were awarded prizes and fed buns and milk for their tea. The purpose of these new festivals was partly diversionary. By providing the children (and adults) with an alternative attraction, it was hoped to wean them away from old customs. This was also true of the Friendly Society parades, each preceded by a sermon and followed by a dinner. But it would be wrong to see these occasions solely as manipulation from above. Village Friendly Societies were not above choosing their own preacher (one could always play the church off against the chapel), and the Whit Walk became an ingrained part of working-class culture – so much so by 1839 that the great West Riding Chartist meeting on Peep Green in that year took the form of a mass Whit Walk. Though Friendly Society parades were themselves dying out by the later nineteenth century, Sunday School walks survived – mainly in their original heartland of the Lancashire and Yorkshire textile districts – and were still being celebrated in the later twentieth century in some places, with band, procession, sports and tea almost as they were when described by Charlotte Brontë in *Shirley* in 1849.[18] Outside the textile areas the pattern of Whitsun observance could be rather different. In Birmingham, in the first half of the nineteenth century, many people preferred to work the first three days of Whit week to save up for the fair which began on the Thursday. Only when Whit Monday became a Bank Holiday in 1871 did the focus of attention move to the beginning of the week.

Harvest festivities similarly survived in altered form, with some differences between town and country. In the countryside, where the harvest still had significance, the Harvest Home continued, though with an important change of emphasis as the old community celebration gave way to one patronised by the larger farmers of the village. From about the 1860s the religious and temperance element became more pronounced, special services of thanksgiving were held, and the art of corn-dolly making was revived to decorate the churches. The urban harvest festival seems to date from around the same time, possibly imported from the countryside by clergymen seeking to build on popular sentiment and to bring some colour – and congregation – into their rather drab town churches. One of the earliest of harvest hymns – *Come ye Thankful People, Come* dates only from 1844, and though *We Plough the Fields, and Scatter* is an eighteenth-century German peasant song, it did not appear in English until 1861.

In many communities the old calendar of rituals and festivities was most satisfyingly replaced by the Nonconformists, especially the ubiquitous Methodists, with their weekly, monthly, quarterly and yearly round of meetings and special services. New festivals unknown to the ecclesiastical calendar replaced the patronal festival and became high points of community life: the Missionary Tea, the Annual Bazaar, the Chapel Anniversary and (most important of all in some places) the Sunday School Anniversary – a time for new clothes (something also associated with Whitsuntide), family reunions, community display and much-rehearsed singing. Elsewhere it was the Friendly Society service, parade and dinner which took the place of the village festival, but in some parts of the country (notably the textile districts of Lancashire and Yorkshire) the Wakes and Feasts survived intact, to be tamed as the annual holiday, a time for 'going away' to the seaside. The traditional fair was reborn in the late nineteenth century as the Pleasure Beach at Blackpool, which 100 years later was still the most popular attraction in Britain, with 7.3 million visitors in 1995.

Rational pleasures

The urban middle classes took the lead in the provision of rational and useful pleasures in place of the more cruel and barbaric practices of the aristocracy and common people. The history of rational recreations therefore cannot be separated from the efforts of the middle classes to discover for themselves new forms of entertainment and amusement which were compatible with their religious and secular values and which, by extension, they thought everyone else should value too. The attraction of rational recreation was that it weaned the lower classes away from vicious habits and at the same time provided a common basis of understanding between the classes – not *too* common, of course: where necessary the same activity could be socially stratified in different clubs and societies, or by a graded system of subscriptions and entry fees.

The growth of this urban 'associationalist' culture has been seen by historians to be no less important than economic and political developments in the creation of a sense of 'middle-classness' in Victorian Britain; and it was not just the work of men. Women, the wives and daughters of the male urban élite, were also involved through their philanthropic organisations and social activities, and as participants in such public occasions as bazaars, lectures and concerts. Far from deserving Matthew Arnold's dismissal of this 'machinery of business, chapels, tea-meetings, and addresses' as 'philistine',[19] the urban middle classes developed in the nineteenth century a rich and distinctive culture, purged of the excesses of aristocratic licence, and fit to be propagated in a civilising mission throughout society.

Useful knowledge

Literary and Philosophical Societies founded in the late eighteenth century brought together leading scientists, men (and occasionally women) of letters, medical men, manufacturers and merchants in a number of provincial towns for debate and edification. They were the intellectual élite of their day, and the nearest England came to a philosophic Enlightenment such as flourished in contemporary Edinburgh, Glasgow and Europe. In the early nineteenth century they and their successors inspired, founded and subscribed to innumerable antiquarian, archaeological, botanical and zoological societies, libraries and museums. Their academies provided an intellectual leadership parallel to that of the Scottish universities, with which there were close connections. The Manchester Literary and Philosophical Society dated from 1781, that at Newcastle upon Tyne from 1793 and its Society of Antiquaries from 1813; the Leeds Philosophical and Literary Society was founded a little later in 1819. Other societies existed in Birmingham, Derby, Bristol, Bath, Sheffield, Hull and even Whitby, among other places. Unitarians played a leading part. In York, Charles Wellbeloved, the Unitarian minister and tutor at the Manchester Academy (which he brought to York in 1803), was a founding or leading member of the Subscription Library (1794), the Savings Bank (1816), the Philosophical Society (1823), the Institute of Popular Science and Literature (1827), the Cemetery Company (1836) and the School of Design (1842). From these sources sprang the intellectual life of provincial Britain, creating schools of medicine (such as that at Newcastle in 1822 and Leeds in 1831); mechanics' institutes (founded in Manchester in 1824, and in Birmingham in 1825) and other civic institutions, culminating, in the last third of the nineteenth century, in civic colleges to serve both the industries and the culture of their municipalities.

Most of the societies founded by the middle classes for themselves were beyond the means of ordinary working people. The Derby Town and County Library and Newspaper Room (1835) charged £1 5*s.* 0*d.* (£1.25) annual admission to shareholders, and £2 to other people on the nomination of two shareholders; members of the Yorkshire Philosophical Society (1822) paid £5 on election and £1 a year thereafter. Such places were not intended for the poorer classes, unlike the mechanics' institutes, which were founded following the example of George Birkbeck in Glasgow and London (1823). The lectures delivered in these institutes proved not to be as popular with working men as their founders had hoped. Instead they drew in clerks, warehousemen and others of the lower-middle classes, providing an important source of leisure for an expanding group of men for whom few (if any) other opportunities existed for improving use of their scanty leisure time. Most attempts to improve the minds of working men, whether sponsored by middle-class patrons or provided by earnest working men themselves, ended in this way. A minority of workers, often from the more skilled trades, together with the lower reaches of the middle classes, were the ones who aspired most to enjoy those intellectual pleasures previously reserved for the higher reaches of society.

The staple reading-matter of those of the lower classes who could read were chapbooks, traditionally hawked round the country by pedlars or colporteurs, and sold at fairs together with reports of the last dying confessions of murderers, broadsheets, ballads and works of pornography, sedition and blasphemy. To counter this outpouring of popular literature, which was held to imperil the soul as well as degrade the mind, publishers turned their attention to the market for improving literature. Religious tracts were poured out by the million by the Society for the Propagation of the Gospel, the Religious Tract Society, the Scottish Colportage Society and many others, mainly of evangelical inspiration. But there was also a Rational and Utilitarian tradition of improvement, owing more to the Scottish Enlightenment than to evangelical religion. The Chambers brothers in Edinburgh, with their *Chambers's Information for the People* (1833–5), *Miscellany of Useful and Entertaining Information* and other non-fiction series, sought to exploit this market for cheap, wholesome literature. Less acceptable to thinking working men was Charles Knight, who was similarly but more stridently occupied both on his own and as publisher for the Society for the Diffusion of Useful Knowledge, and whose *Penny Magazine* was commenced in 1832. It is difficult to know how many of these tracts actually reached their intended readers, and how many of the more overtly propagandist works which were bought by philanthropists for gratuitous distribution were used by the recipients for their intended purpose.

Improving non-fiction was acceptable to the religious, although some felt that only the Bible and religious tracts should be read on Sundays; but fiction was frowned upon. That did not stop the progress of the popular novel, serialised in penny parts – the so-called 'penny dreadfuls' – but the latter at least no longer monopolised the market. Typical of the Chambers's tradition was John Cassell, the great mid-Victorian entrepreneur of popular improving literature. He was said to be a reformed drunkard, a carpenter by trade, who became a temperance lecturer and coffee dealer. He started selling tea in shilling packets instead of large cases which the poor could not afford, printing his own labels and, in his evenings, running off the first of his many publications, the *Teetotal Times*. In 1852 he began *Cassell's Popular Educator*, a self-instruction course in penny numbers. Thomas Hardy was to teach himself German from it, and Thomas Burt, the Northumberland miners' leader, used it to acquire some knowledge of English, French and Latin. By 1862 Cassell was selling between 25 and 30 million copies of his penny publications each year, mainly to the working and lower-middle classes.

The attraction of this periodical literature was its cheapness. Books were still expensive in the mid-nineteenth century, and subscription libraries were beyond the means of the relatively poorer classes. To remedy this situation cheaper circulating libraries emerged, often as sidelines for barbers, tobacconists and newsagents; but their wares, hired out at a penny a time, were not always in the best improving taste. Of the contents of 10 such libraries in London in 1838, nearly half the volumes were 'Novels of the lowest character, being chiefly imitations of Fashionable Novels, containing no good, although probably nothing decidedly bad'.[20] To improve this situation clergymen formed parish libraries, and these became common after 1832 when the National Society arranged with the SPCK to receive its literature in its parish schools. By 1849 there were approaching 6,000 such libraries, each containing on average about a hundred volumes of religious tracts and other blameless literature. Parliament was finally persuaded to intervene with an Act in 1850 (1853 in Scotland) to permit large towns to levy a halfpenny rate (raised to a penny and extended to medium-sized towns in 1855) to provide a public library. Liverpool and Manchester responded immediately. The Manchester Library was housed in the former Owenite Hall of Science, bought for the city by the lord of the manor, Sir Oswald Moseley – and, to judge by its contents even today, it must have inherited the Owenites' library along with their building. But, like much Victorian social legislation, the Act was permissive. Despite the argument that public libraries were the cheapest insurance against social unrest, most ratepayers preferred to keep the rates down rather than subsidise reading matter for the poor. The great period for founding public libraries came between 1897 and 1914 and owed much to private benefactions, not least from Andrew Carnegie. Before this period most working people had to rely upon literature largely donated (that is, 'improving' or discarded works) to libraries in mechanics' institutes, churches and chapels, co-operative societies and people's institutes; the self-taught working man was left to scrape around in second-hand bookshops.

The argument that the middle class wished to control the working class through reading-matter therefore needs examining very carefully. Despite the intentions of religious and Utilitarian propagandists, most people in the middle classes were not really interested in paying for libraries to keep the poor in order, any more than they were keen to pay for policemen. The argument for sober enlightenment remained a minority one, led by radical intellectuals. Evangelicals gave only selective encouragement to working-class self-improvement and did not see it as an alternative to true religion. For example, they were not prepared to countenance any relaxation in the laws governing the use of Sundays which would allow Sunday lectures of an uplifting, though not specifically religious, kind. The Sunday Observance Act of 1780, which forbade charging for lectures on a Sunday, was used indiscriminately to suppress Owenites in the 1840s and T. H. Huxley in the 1860s. The only way round the law was for a lecturer to register as a Dissenting preacher under the Toleration Act. After Huxley's lectures were terminated prematurely at the St Martin's Hall, London, in 1866 the struggle for a free and rational Sunday was continued by the

Sunday Lecture Society (1869) and the Sunday Society (1875), but with little success. It is doubtful whether more than a tiny minority of working men ever actually wanted to attend this kind of lecture anyway. When the law was finally changed in 1932, it was done chiefly to satisfy the cinema-going public.

Access to the arts

Museums and art galleries, like libraries, were intended primarily for the middle and upper classes. The Derby Town and County Museum, for example, which opened in 1836, was run by nominated subscribers who paid an annual subscription of half a guinea; the Manchester Art Union (1840) had an annual subscription of a guinea. In 1845 the Museums Act allowed a halfpenny rate to be levied to provide local funding for public museums for which the admission charge was not to exceed a penny (the public had been charged sixpence for admittance to the Derby museum), but this permissive Act was no more effective than the subsequent Libraries Acts. Their importance was not what they achieved, but what they represented – the idea that the provision of cheap, improving leisure-time facilities should be a public, municipal affair.

Rational recreation was given great encouragement by the success of the Great Exhibition of 1851, which was attended by 6 million people of all classes. In 1854 the Crystal Palace was re-opened on a permanent site at Sydenham, where it became the centre of a new-style pleasure garden, eminently respectable, with concerts, exhibitions, tropical trees and full-scale bronze dinosaurs. The old eighteenth-century pleasure gardens had rather degenerated into fun fairs, frequented by drunks, pickpockets and prostitutes; the last of them, at Cremorne in Chelsea, was closed down in 1877. Crystal Palace set the fashion for Alexandra Palace in north London (1875) and the People's Palace in east London (1886), which was inspired by the same spirit as the University Settlement movement to bring civilising influences into the poorest areas of the metropolis. In the provinces, the most famous equivalent was Belle Vue Gardens in Manchester.

The Great Exhibition also inspired Manchester to put on its own Art Treasures Exhibition in a Crystal Palace-like building erected on the Old Trafford cricket ground in the summer of 1857. With the patronage of Prince Albert, 16,000 art treasures were gathered from aristocratic collections throughout the country and were seen by 1,336,715 people. As with the Great Exhibition of 1851, a profit was made. It resulted in no permanent public legacy to the visual arts in the city, but £4,515 was given by the committee to a young German pianist and conductor to enlarge his orchestra and give daily performances at Old Trafford. His name was Charles Hallé.

To provide facilities for leisure was one thing; to ensure that they were available on Sundays when the poor were free to enjoy them was another. In 1829 William Lovett drew up a petition for the opening of 'the British Museum, and other exhibitions of Art and Nature, on Sundays'. He made no progress at the time, but in the 1850s 'the moral and religious influence which had been produced among the minds of the many who flocked to witness the glories of the late Crystal Palace' – in the words of Sir Joshua Walmsley[21] – led to a campaign for the opening of both the Crystal Palace and the British Museum on Sunday afternoons. But the argument that civilisation was better than the public house on a Sunday cut little ice with members of the Lord's Day Observance Society, and others who thought that all the people ought to do on Sundays was go to church. Pitted against them was the National Sunday League, founded by Robert Morrell of the London goldsmiths and silversmiths in the wake of the Sunday Trading riots of 1855, with Walmsley as its President and parliamentary spokesman. Walmsley's motion, 'That in the opinion of this House, it would promote the moral and intellectual improvement of the working classes of the metropolis if . . . the British Museum and the National Gallery were open to public inspection after morning service on Sundays', which he put in 1856, was defeated by 376 votes to 48, with 629,000 signatures on petitions against his motion. Government policy was to leave open those few institutions which were already open, and to keep closed the many which were already closed. So the British Museum was to remain closed, but a legal subterfuge by the Crystal Palace Company did allow the working classes access to its premises by 1860. Museums and galleries were not generally opened on Sundays until 1932.

The theatre

Between 1800 and 1850 the nature of theatres and theatre audiences was transformed as thoroughly as any of the habits and amusements of the people. Until the Theatres Act of 1843, only Drury Lane, Covent Garden and the Haymarket in London, and a few provincial theatres licensed by the Lord Chamberlain, were permitted to perform 'straight' drama which consisted of Shakespeare (tidied up by David Garrick), Italian operas and harlequinades. The other 'minor' theatres put on 'burlettas', a mixture of drama and music with the emphasis on comedy and farce. The popular theatre was a rowdy and unruly affair, with the audience crowded into the pit, standing around the projecting stage and engaging the actors in banter and heckling. The atmosphere was akin to that of the circus, which was the most popular form of all theatrical entertainments. Shakespeare, when performed in the full text, belonged to the people. The crowds flocked to see Edmund Kean as Othello and the clown Grimaldi, fashioning pantomime out of harlequin, native mumming traditions and endless transformation scenes. Under Charles Kemble Covent Garden thrived, but when he tried to put the prices up from 3*s.* 6*d.* to 4*s.* (17½p to 20p) for the pit in 1809 the crowd stormed into the newly rebuilt theatre and tore out the stalls, demanding a restoration of the old prices and the old pit. One historian has likened the occasion to an enclosure riot.[22] The price issue was almost irrelevant, for even 3*s.* 6*d.* was too much for the poor to pay, and audiences were often let in free to the second half of a performance.

Until the mid-nineteenth century most theatres made concessions to popular taste. Burlettas, melodramas and performances with a social or political edge were the favourites. Ambitious actor-managers in the big London theatres put on ever more extravagant productions. Drury Lane went over to burlettas, with a song or two for Ophelia and Hamlet. Charles Southwell, Owenite lecturer and melodramatic actor, delighted his atheistic followers by playing Shylock as the hero of *The Merchant of Venice* at the Canterbury Theatre. The pit audiences knew and loved their Shakespeare as well as or better than the actors themselves: he spoke to the vulgar, jovial crowd of the nineteenth century as he had spoken to them in the sixteenth. Theatres were bawdy, disreputable places, frequented by drunks and prostitutes, where the people enjoyed themselves. By 1850 all this was changing. Thomas Bowdler had cleaned up Shakespeare, pantomime had become a fairy-tale with only one slapstick scene and a single, respectable transformation at the end; seats and carpets were turning the pit into the stalls, and the stage was retreating behind its proscenium arch. 'Legitimate' theatre was born with the Theatres Act in 1843, and the Queen gave royal patronage to the acting profession in 1848. The common people were banished to the galleries, out of sight of the boxes and almost out of sight of the stage. The rougher presentations and audiences were driven out to smaller, less reputable theatres, public houses and music halls.

In the provinces fashions were rather behind those in London. The middle classes were rather less willing to patronise the new, respectable family theatres – an antimacassar on every seat-back – but 'sons of toil . . . who liked good acting and plenty of it'[23] crowded the galleries, where prices were lower than in London, perhaps as little as 3*d.* (just over 1p). Pantomime did not come to Birmingham until 1841, and Bradford until 1846, but by the 1850s the Christmas season was running into March. Manchester had two theatres, the Royal, which received the great actors and actresses on tour from London, and Egan's, where melodramas appealed to a lower class of audience. Liverpool was rather more cultured, with four theatres, but 'society' there still preferred the older fashion of assembly balls. Provincial theatres were actually closing down in the 1840s and 1850s, to the accompanying jubilations of Evangelicals, Methodists and strict Presbyterians. The dramatic arts were the least regarded of cultural entertainments in Victorian Britain.

Music

Music was acceptable to every social class. In the eighteenth century aristocratic and court patronage had supported Italian operas and chamber music, but fashions were changing by the 1830s. In London, taste was progressive and continental performers could be attracted for large fees, but the provinces were decidedly more conservative. When Hallé brought the dying Chopin to Manchester his recital left the audience unmoved. Hallé 'seriously thought of packing up and leaving'.[24] Nevertheless, the musical world was expanding rapidly. Subscription concerts were the means by which gentlemen financed their leisure. In London, annual seasons of Ancient Concerts (so-called because no music could be performed which was less than 20 years old) were begun in 1776 and lasted until 1848. They were supported at the highest level of society. In the 1770s Manchester also began a series of Gentlemen's Concerts, which by 1839 were attracting 600 patrons paying five guineas each. Their taste in each case was for Handel, Haydn, Mozart with a little Beethoven, and Bach towards the middle of the nineteenth century. Public musical concerts grew rapidly in number and popularity from the 1830s, and by 1870 had assumed their modern form. Between the seasons 1826/7 and 1845/6 the number of concerts given in London increased from 125 to 381. The more popular end in musical taste preferred Rossini, Liszt and the singing of Jenny Lind. Mendelssohn was all the rage after his first visit to Britain in 1829, and his concerts did a great deal to heighten public awareness of good music. Indeed, the development of musical taste in Britain owed much to German influence: cotton merchants in Manchester, refugees like the incomparable Charles Hallé, and Prince Albert, whose example encouraged the fashion for concert-going. His most important contribution to British culture, the Crystal Palace, had its own orchestra from 1854, and became the home for many music festivals and concerts.

More important than all this, though, was the middle-class Nonconformist devotion to choral music, an art form completely compatible with the strictest of religious principles. Huge chapels, with an organ and gallery of serried choir pews, facing a horse-shoe gallery of benches with a sweep of comfortable pews below, were built by the prospering middle classes so that they could enjoy a good sermon; but the buildings had marvellous acoustics, and made excellent concert halls. Increasingly in the second half of the nineteenth century, they rang to the strains of Handel's *Messiah* (1742), Haydn's *Creation* (1798) and Mendelssohn's *Elijah*, first performed at the Birmingham Festival in 1844. Thriving Victorian municipalities built Town Halls, some of which looked like chapels, with huge auditoria for orchestral and choral concerts of the highest quality. Local amateur orchestras and choral societies were formed for the amusement of their members and the entertainment of their communities. In West Yorkshire alone over 240 choral societies were founded between 1800 and 1914. The annual performance of the *Messiah* became a ritual no less important than Christmas itself.

These choral societies in the chapel lands of industrial Britain were drawn in equal proportions from the upper-working class, the lower-middle class and the 'substantial' middle-class of manufacturers and their families. Their audiences (or should one say 'congregations'?) were similarly composed. In this they reflected the chapels from which they came. Contemporaries hoped that music would sweeten the divisions of class. To some extent it probably did, in individual cases. It certain produced some unusual combinations of outlook, as when the 'infidel' Stalybridge Secular Choir performed Mozart's *Gloria in Excelsis Deo* to changed words, and appealed for someone to write a new libretto for the *Messiah* so they could perform it with a good conscience!

Alongside the choral society and the oratorio, brass bands were an equally popular form of musical entertainment, both at village festivals and in great national competitions held at Crystal Palace or Belle Vue. Early bandsmen played drums and fifes, or mixed reed and brass instruments, but the latter became easier to play after 1824 when valves were invented, and the modern brass band was fully developed by the 1850s. Most bands grew out of their local communities, chapels or temperance organisations – with an important additional contribution from the Salvation Army in the later nineteenth century. A minority, including some of the most famous, were the products of paternalism in mines, factories and workshops, where large employers might take on workmen especially for their musical skills. Doubtless there was here an element of social control through the promotion of rational leisure, though John Foster of Black Dyke Mills was himself a French-horn player and probably found business and personal interest closely harmonised. Patrons certainly were welcome, for the instruments represented a considerable capital outlay.

Singing and instrumental work required a musical ability rarely taught in the schools of nineteenth-century Britain. Sometimes the talent and skill ran in families, passed down the generations like any artisan craft; choirmasters trained their choirs to sing by ear; bandsmen started as apprentices with the cornet, and learned by example from their seniors; children learnt oratorios by heart, simply by listening to them. Music-making was popular because it was part of a popular oral (and aural) tradition.

The biggest technical advances in music making came in the 1840s, when J. Alfred Novello began to publish cheap editions of oratorios and other choral works, making sheet music widely available for the first time, and when John Curwen popularised the Tonic Sol-Fa notation for sight-singing. Together with the perfecting of the upright piano in London in 1829, these innovations made possible a revolution in domestic music-making among all but the poorest classes. Not only were Arthur Sullivan's tunes and W. S. Gilbert's words on practically every lower-middle-class lip in the last third of the nineteenth century; Sullivan's *The Lost Chord* sold half a million copies of sheet music between its publication in 1877 and 1900. Domestic music-making was an essential aspect of middle-class culture, especially for the ladies, with the soirée a favourite kind of social gathering; but by the 1860s the piano was penetrating even the homes of the relatively poor. When the cotton famine struck Lancashire contemporaries noticed how many pianos were being sent to the pawn shops. For those who could not afford or find room for a piano, the concertina (invented 1829) might give hours of pleasure. Needless to say, the *Hallelujah Chorus* was a favourite competition piece with concertina bands.

Fresh air and fun

The appalling revelations of social investigators in the 1830s and 1840s brought home the importance of healthy bodies as well as enlightened minds, and the need for fresh air in an age which accepted the 'miasmatic' theory of disease led to a movement to provide public parks out of the last remnants of common land. Hitherto most parks and gardens within towns had been private property. Birkenhead was the first provincial town to provide a public park, followed closely by Manchester, which opened three in 1846 paid for by public subscription. One of them, Peel Park (Peel donated £3,000), had facilities for playing ninepins and bowls, gymnastic exercises and swings and see-saws for the children. Pessimistic contemporaries were amazed that the working classes could frequent such places without tearing up the flower beds; supporters of the move attributed their success to the 'march of intellect'.

From the mid-nineteenth century the evangelical grip on middle-class recreations weakened. Physical recreations became increasingly popular with the young once they had ceased to be identified with the profligate upper classes and the disreputable lower classes. Cricket, for example, flourished. It had originated as a village game, but was also taken up by the gentry in the eighteenth century, and acquired a governing code which became synonymous with gentlemanly conduct. Under aristocratic and gentry patronage it attracted heavy gambling, which was not brought under control until the early nineteenth century. Bookmakers were banned from Thomas Lord's ground at Marylebone only in 1825, 38 years after the Marylebone Cricket Club had been founded there. But by 1844, when William Howitt wrote *The Rural Life of England*, he could hold cricket up as an example of a healthy, reformed sport which brought out the best in competitors and crowds alike.[25] By this date it was being played at all levels, from village green to All England, and by both gentlemen and 'players' (that is, those primarily of a lower class who were paid for their services) – a distinction which remained until the 1960s.

Members of the Manchester Athenaeum cricket club in 1845 were also able to indulge themselves with archery, quoits, fencing, boxing and singlestick fighting. These last four were purified versions of rough popular sports which were then being denied to the lower classes. There was also a rowing club, and the first Manchester regatta was held in 1842. Other modern sports were virtually unknown. The popular sport of 'pedestrianism', or foot-racing, did not develop into amateur athletics until after 1850. Football, similarly, was still to be purified through the public schools of the mid-nineteenth century, and codified into its carrying and dribbling varieties before being made fit for 'gentlemen' as well as 'players'. One of the most popular of late-Victorian middle-class sports, lawn tennis, did not exist until its rules were patented by Major Wingfield in 1874 under the name 'Sphairistike'. The All England Croquet Club at Wimbledon (founded 1868) then modified the rules and added 'and Lawn Tennis' to its title in 1877. Its first championships for men were held the same year. Golf was a traditional game only in Scotland until late in the nineteenth century. The Royal and Ancient Club at St Andrews dated from 1754, but in 1860 there was only one English club – at Blackheath – and that was for Scotsmen. The first truly English club was the Royal North Devon at Westward Ho, opened in 1864. Not until the twentieth century did the suburban English gentleman take to wearing plus-fours and playing a good round in lieu of other exercise or to impress a business partner.

The range of sports and facilities available to the middle classes expanded rapidly from the 1860s. Ironically, in view of the old evangelical attitude, the churches were partly responsible for this. The Young Men's Christian Association had been begun in 1844 to rescue young men of the lower-middle classes from the evils of music halls and other dens of vice. Its motto was 'Amusements are not necessary to your happiness, religion is'.[26] By the 1860s, local YMCAs and Sunday Schools were adopting more positive strategies for weaning young people away from their preferred pleasures. The religious organisations of late-Victorian Britain could offer their members a wide range of social activities, from cricket and football, swimming and cycling, to billiards and bowling in competition with secular clubs which flourished for all manner of recreations and pastimes. The prosperous citizen of a medium-sized town such as Bolton had the choice of joining clubs for the enjoyment of cricket (1833), billiards (1840), bowling (1854), swimming (1871), tennis (1896) and golf (1896), in addition to ice-skating (1876) and bicycling, which became all the rage in the 1890s. At the same time, a new form of entertainment appeared for the really wealthy who had formerly kept horses and a carriage: by 1900 the motor car had arrived.

A feature of many of these genteel recreations was their appeal to women as well as men. Ladies had always played some cricket, but had to bowl round arm on account of their skirts. More to their taste was croquet, introduced from France in 1852. Golf and tennis also caught on rapidly with both sexes. Ladies were admitted to play full rounds of golf in 1885, and the first Wimbledon tennis final for ladies was held the following year, but in this – as in other sports demanding flexibility of movement – women were inhibited by their clothing. The crinoline did not pass out of fashion until the 1870s. On the tennis court ladies were permitted the laxity of wearing a blouse with long skirt, but this was only just becoming an acceptable fashion elsewhere at the very end of the nineteenth century. Mrs Bloomer's eponymous replacement for the skirt caught on with the new cycling public, but was otherwise thought more suitable for the socialist salon than the capitalist drawing room.

Cricket, bowls, billiards and athletics had some attraction for the urban working man, especially when facilities were attached to a public house or provided at a works club; tennis and golf were definitely middle-class, and have retained this image long after it has ceased to be true. The 'people's game' par excellence was football.

The traditional game of football – unorganised, violent and disturbing to the peace – epitomised all that was wrong with older forms of leisure. The game had all but been killed off by the reformers when it was revived and transformed in the public schools. Public-school boys meeting up at Oxford or Cambridge and wishing to continue to play football found it necessary to draw up common regulations for the conduct of their games. The crucial distinction between those who picked up the ball and those who did not was formalised in 1863, with the formation of the Football Association. The Rugby Union followed in 1871. Many of these public schoolboys became clergymen in the Church of England or schoolmasters. Their influence percolated downwards, and the new, regulated game was popularised. After 1870 school, works and church clubs spread, along with the Saturday half-holiday. In 1880 Birmingham had 344 football clubs, 83 of them with religious affiliations; Liverpool in 1885 had 112, 25 of them religious. These teams rapidly outgrew their origins and became the property of professional clubs. Unlike cricket, where amateurs and professional managed to coexist, association football at the highest level was rapidly dominated by professional teams. Rugby went the other way, amateurs dominating the game until, in 1895, those working-class players who needed financial compensation for lost working time broke away to form their own Rugby League. The Rugby Union did not permit paid professionals to play their game until 1995.

Whether the new game was any better than the old was open to doubt in some minds. T. H. S. Escott, writing in 1897, thought that only a strenuous referee could prevent professional football from resembling 'the revival of the prize ring in disguise'.[27] There were also numerous complaints about the behaviour of football crowds, both in the streets and on trains. What is remarkable is that there was little sign of that fear of mob violence and revolution which would have greeted such crowds before the 1840s.

Football was received back as a 'respectable' sport not simply because it now had rules, enclosed grounds and public-school approval; it was acceptable because society was again sufficiently stable to accommodate it.

A 'bleak age'?

The notion of a 'bleak age' in working-class culture is hard to sustain. Many of the old ways were destroyed, but some survived and much was added which rapidly became 'traditional'. These new forms of leisure were provided by the middle classes in the sense that, if they were not directly responsible for them, they had conditioned the social environment in which they grew. The theory of hegemony involves the willing participation of the dominated as well as the dominating partners in a social relationship. This is what the transformation of leisure achieved. Nevertheless, many of the middle classes were also victims of the puritanism of their age. Their problem in the mid-nineteenth century was that they neither approved of nor had access to the lax countrified pursuits of the gentry; they did not, as Matthew Arnold observed in *Culture and Anarchy* (1869), have the refinement to patronise Culture; and they did not care for the rowdiness of popular recreations.[28] 'We really do not know how to amuse ourselves,' admitted the *Saturday Review* in 1870. This was an exaggeration, but it is true that, before the 1870s, evangelical opinion dissuaded many of the middle classes from 'secular' leisure as unbecoming a true Christian. Great energies were devoted instead to philanthropy, especially by wives and daughters. Charitable works among the poor, teas and bazaars to raise funds for missionaries at home and overseas, and religious meetings of every description were the strict diet of many middle-class families.

While the middle classes were imprisoned in their own values, the irony of their situation is that their efforts to share those values with other classes were only partly successful. The diffusion of rational recreations was indeed impressive. Any comparison between the beginning and end of the nineteenth century will show how much had been achieved in curbing what were seen as vicious, degrading and demoralising customs and amusements. Civilisation had progressed. But those members of the working class who wholeheartedly responded to the new rational leisure were probably a minority. Many continuities with the past remained, and old ways died hard.

Leisure and the consumer revolution

Leisure in the twentieth century has been dominated by the greater spending-power of the majority of the people. This has led to higher standards of comfort in the home which, with shorter working hours, has itself become a focus of leisure. At the same time, labour-saving devices have released men and – especially – women from many domestic chores, and provided a ready audience for commercialised leisure products outside the home. Standards and expectations which were once the experience of only the very wealthy have gradually been democratised until they have reached all but the poorest sections of society. Nowhere is this more clearly exemplified than in the history of holidays. These developments have taken place against a background of technological change: cinema, radio and television; steam train, motor car and aeroplane; gas and electric light and power; vacuum cleaners, refrigerators and washing machines. Never in the history of British society have so many of the people had so much money, so wide a choice and so many opportunities for diverse experiences. Even the very poor, whose poverty is made harder by the riches which surround them, are wealthy in comparison with their predecessors in the eighteenth and nineteenth centuries and with many of their contemporaries in the economically under-developed countries of the Third World.

Paradoxically, this freedom has also brought new constraints. Leisure has become big business, even a mainstay of the British economy. Human wants and behaviour are conditioned by the demands of the leisure and consumer industries through the medium of advertising, both overt and implicit in the presentation of ready-packaged culture. The transition from the irregular leisure patterns of the eighteenth century to the neatly clocked and calendared leisure-time and holidays of the later twentieth century has involved persuading people to want certain things in a certain way, and to be prepared to work for them. Economic growth depends upon rising productivity and consumption. Giving the people what they want has become giving the people what it is profitable to supply them with. The moral 'evils' of former generations – drinking and gambling – have become consumer 'goods'. Within commercialised leisure is a controlling force more subtle than the crude evangelising of the Victorian moral reformers, but none the less potent.

The commercialisation of leisure refers not simply to the provision of recreational facilities to the public for private gain, but the ownership and control of such facilities by large commercial organisations. The divorce between ownership and management which was a noted feature of industrial development in the later nineteenth century applies to the leisure industry as well. It has affected all aspects of leisure: holidays, professional football, betting and gaming, the press, theatres and cinemas, and even the humble (and not-so-humble) public house.

Holidays

The earliest holidays, in the sense of time away from home, were the seasonal peregrinations of the wealthy in the eighteenth century and before. Not only did they travel up to London for the Season, and back down to the country in the heat of August, but they also found it increasingly fashionable to spend a month or so at a spa town, 'taking the waters' for their health. Tunbridge Wells was fashionable in Restoration England; Bath became the premier resort in the eighteenth century. Their success led other spas to exploit more fully the commercial possibilities of their waters – Malvern and Cheltenham (patronised by George III in 1788) in the west, Buxton, Harrogate and Scarborough in the north. The aristocracy also ventured overseas, to sample the classical culture of Italy or the more convenient delights of Paris, the heart of eighteenth-century European civilization. The French Revolution and Napoleonic Wars put a stop to this, but after 1815 the quest for culture, romance and adventure continued. Switzerland drew eccentric English aristocrats wishing to climb Mont Blanc – cost £12, including guides and food for four days. Cannes attracted them in old age, where Lord Brougham set the fashion for English geriatrics to mellow beside the balmy Mediterranean sea. Those who could not afford the luxury of Continental travel, or could not bear the thought of foreigners or the four-hour sailing from Dover to Calais, could take the coach to Shap Wells at the edge of the Lake District, where the Earl of Lonsdale built a hotel with 70 beds in the 1830s. Scotland, Snowdonia and the Lake District provided tourists with the delights of romantic wilderness and whetted their appetites for the Alps or Wordsworth's poetry.

Rivalling the mountains for fresh air and the spas for their waters was the seaside. The idea was not to get sunburnt on the beach – a reddened skin was a sign of commonness – but to dip in and even drink the salt water. Scarborough, with the advantage of both sea and spa water, developed early in the eighteenth century and, with gaming room, theatre, and horse racing, it tried to rival York as a centre for fashionable northern society. For London and the south a string of seaside resorts developed from Weymouth round to Ramsgate and Margate. Brighthelmstone was transformed from a fishing village of six streets in 1760, into Brighton, a pleasure resort with 15 streets and a population of 7,000 in 1780. The Prince of Wales came in 1783, and the following year started his celebrated, extravagant Pavilion. Within a short time Brighton rather than Bath was the resort for fashionable society at play. The King, though, preferred Weymouth, the Princess of Wales went to Worthing, and little Princess Charlotte was sent in 1801 on a visit to Southend. With this kind of patronage the seaside holiday was established as an essential part of the yearly routine of the leisured class.

For this pattern of behaviour to percolate further down society, three things were needed: transport, time and money. Steam locomotion provided the first. The first pleasure steamers were run on the Clyde, soon to be followed by the Thames and the Mersey. London to Gravesend steamers were started in 1815, and Margate followed in 1819. In 1820–1

Margate pier handled nearly 44,000 passengers, over twice as many as eight years earlier. The social tone fell, and it became a vulgar, middle-class sort of place – though not yet working-class, for the return fare alone cost between 5*s.* and 7*s.* (25p–35p). The working man and his family were likely to travel no further than Greenwich fair.

This began to change with the railways, which provided rapid transport for the middle classes, drove the rich to ever more exclusive resorts, and gave the better-off members of the working class the chance of a day's excursion to the seaside. Special excursion trains were run by railway companies in the 1840s. Sunday trains left Manchester at 6.00 a.m. for Blackpool and Fleetwood: 3*s.* (15p) return for men, 1*s.* 6*d.* (7½p) for females and children. Scarborough, the only large resort not on the south coast, wondered whether the railway would damage the spa's exclusive reputation, but nevertheless accepted its link with York in 1845 and welcomed the rich manufacturers of the West Riding. To make them feel at home the Grand Hotel was built in 1867 to designs by Cuthbert Broderick, the architect of Leeds Town Hall. Brighton was reached by the railway in 1841, but its reputation was already declining in royal and therefore aristocratic circles as its popularity increased with the wealthier middle classes. In 1835, before the railway was built, 117,000 passengers travelled to Brighton by coach; in the second half of 1844 360,000 travelled by train – the cheapest fares on the new 'parliamentary train' were 4*s.* 2*d.* (21p) single. The major resort on the west coast was Southport, popular with Liverpool merchants, with whom New Brighton (projected in 1832) never quite caught on. But it was Blackpool which became synonymous with cheap, popular holidays in the nineteenth century, with its fine sands (quite unlike the shingle at Brighton) and healthful 'ozone' in the atmosphere. The wealthy moved away a few miles to Lytham and St Anne's.

The commercial possibilities of popular holidays quickly became apparent to the moral improvers of early-Victorian Britain, especially after Parliament had refused to exclude cheap Sunday trains from the 1844 Railway Act. Thomas Cook was the symbol of his age. In 1841 he arranged with the Midland Railway Company for a special excursion train to run from Leicester to Loughborough, bringing people to a temperance meeting in Loughborough Park. Other similar trips followed, and then in 1845 he took to organising Midland Railway Company excursions for a percentage on the tickets he sold. He also issued hotel tokens, and was soon arranging complete holidays: Leicester to Glasgow, by rail to Fleetwood and steamer to Ardrossan – one guinea (£1.05); the Great Exhibition from Leeds and Bradford – 5*s.* (25p); Leicester to Calais for the 1855 Paris Exhibition – £1 11*s.* 0*d.* (£1.55). For the wealthy there was a grand tour in 1856 of the Rhineland and Paris; for the poorer classes, moonlight trips to Scarborough so they would get a full day at the sea. Day-excursions were provided by philanthropists for children:

2,000 children went from Newcastle to look at Edinburgh in 1856; there were Sunday-School trips, which had the additional advantage of taking children away from temptation when the fair came to town. By 1864 Cook was taking parties of tourists (the word dates from 1780) to Switzerland and beyond. The Italians believed a story that the British were convicts sent to Italy because they had been refused by Australia; the British thought the Italians insanitary, avoided them as much as possible, and avidly rushed to see what the guide books told them they ought to see. The modern tourist industry was born.

For the working classes to share in this new experience, time was needed. Much is often made of the fact that the number of 'official' holidays (when the Bank of England and Stock Exchange were closed for business) was dramatically reduced in the early nineteenth century, from 44 in 1808 to only four (Christmas, Good Friday, 1 May and 1 November) by 1834; but this is largely irrelevant to the history of leisure in the manufacturing districts, where customary breaks were taken without official leave. Factory masters in Lancashire and Yorkshire had little choice but to concede to their workers up to a week at Christmas and Whitsun and at the time of the local Wakes or Feast, usually in the early autumn. Indeed, one suspects that many employers did not object to seeing their works close, for holidays were without pay and the steam engine had to be halted some time each year for maintenance. The necessity of saving for the holiday weeks was good for discipline, though the dissolute manner in which the traditional Wakes were spent caused increasing disquiet among moral improvers. The day-trip to the seaside proved to be an excellent diversion, and as the day grew into a weekend or a week later in the century, whole communities went to the sea together. The shops could shut, for there was no trade, and even the policemen could take a break.

The official modern definition of a holiday is four or more nights away from home. This was rarely possible for significant numbers of the lower-middle and upper-working classes before the last quarter of the nineteenth century, and did not reach the working class generally before holidays with pay were introduced. Paternalist employers, churches and chapels, Sunday Schools and back-street missions, friendly and co-operative societies all ran day-trips for their workers, members or the poor of their communities. Landlords of public houses collected for and organised a day out for their customers – all drinks taken with them, of course – to Southend, Epping Forest, or whatever local beauty-spot or seaside beach was nearest. Few workers were as fortunate as the employees of the great railway companies. Not only did they enjoy cheap travel, but, for example, the great majority of North Western Railway Company employees in Crewe (outside the actual works) were receiving some holidays with pay by 1914. In 1901 20,000 quarter-fare tickets were sold for the annual holiday in Crewe. Most people went to Blackpool, but many went to the

Isle of Man, the North Wales coast or even as far as Scotland, Ireland and the Continent.

The creation of public holidays made little difference to the industrial worker with his traditional Wakes week, but was significant for the lower-middle class, whose hours of leisure, as Charles Dickens pathetically illustrated in *A Christmas Carol* (1843), were very restricted. Only Good Friday was a parliamentary holiday (by an Act of 1800), though Christmas Day was a customary holiday in England and Wales (except among Jews) when Dickens wrote. In 1871 Sir John Lubbock sponsored an Act to add four further public holidays (disguised as Bank holidays) on Boxing Day (New Year's Day in Scotland), Easter Monday (not in Scotland), Whit Monday (first Monday in May in Scotland) and the first Monday in August. This Act extended the holidays of commercial clerks and shopkeepers, but probably restricted those of workers accustomed to take every Monday off work – the so-called 'St Monday' holiday. Gradually the traditional calendar was rearranged round the new holidays, with Easter and Whit Mondays merging with the newly developed 'weekend' (see pages 270–1) in place of customary breaks, and the August holiday establishing itself in the first week in August except where a later Wakes week was already common.

The patterns of holidaymaking fixed in the later nineteenth century continued, except for interruption during two World Wars, until the 1950s. The changes were matters of numbers and duration, rather than type. The wealthy went abroad, or to the country, or to the more select resorts in the South-West like Torquay or Sidmouth; in Scotland they went to St Andrews for the golf. The comfortably off went for a week to a small hotel in Tynemouth rather than a boarding house in Whitley Bay, Llandudno rather than Rhyl, Bournemouth rather than Margate. The better-off members of the working class saved up for a few days in Blackpool or its equivalent: Cleethorpes for the East Midlands, Hunstanton for the Cambridgeshire Fens, Southend and Margate for London.

In 1937, about 3 million workers had some holidays with pay; the Holidays with Pay Act of 1938 added another 11 million. By 1948 three-quarters of the highest social group, and half the lowest social group, were taking an annual holiday. The potential market for cheap mass-produced holidays was detected by William ('Billy') Butlin, pioneer of the large holiday camp. Skegness was opened in 1937 and Clacton two years later; but Butlin's flair for publicity should not conceal the fact that there were over 200 smaller holiday camps in Britain in 1939, with room for 30,000 visitors per week. Further camps were opened by Butlin after the war at Filey and Pwllheli. Butlin's importance is that he caught the imagination of a public which wanted to be entertained, fed and told what to do in glorious irresponsibility for £1 a day, all in. Perhaps it was too regimented, for he failed to attract large numbers of the working class. 'Butlinism' was a lower-middle-class phenomenon.

In 1951 25 million British people went on holiday in Britain and 2 million went abroad; 20 years later the figures were 34 million and 7 million respectively. In the next quarter of a century the number of holidays taken rose by 43 per cent. Those choosing to spend their time in Britain reached a peak in the mid-1970s, but had fallen again to 33 million by 1995. In the latter year, however, a record 26 million people took holidays abroad, over a third of them in Spain, and about 58 per cent of these holidays were arranged by 'package tour' companies such as Thomas Cook. Whereas in 1971 only one-third of adults in Great Britain had been abroad on holiday at some time in their lives, by 1996 less than one-third had not done so. Most of these were in the lower social classes. As in all matters of consumption, what could be purchased reflected social class. Whereas only 18 per cent of the professional classes did not take a holiday in 1995, over half the unskilled did not; and whereas over half the professional classes took their holiday abroad, only 20 per cent of the unskilled did so.

These bald facts about holidays spell out the extent of the revolution that had taken place in leisure after the Second World War. As austerity gave way to affluence, the thought of a wet week in Blackpool drove increasing numbers of the moderately well-off to seek the sun abroad. As more went, so prices came down, and more still could afford to go. Intense competition between tour companies produced temptingly advertised offers during the bleak winter months. The style of holidays was also changing, as more people acquired motor cars and the freedom to tour both at home and abroad. The pleasure of the 'old-fashioned' boarding-house family holiday had been for the wife: someone else to wait on her hand and foot while she had a real break. But with motor cars and caravans, self-catering chalets and camping sites, holidays ceased to be restful experiences for physically exhausted people and became, rather, extensions of a lifestyle in which leisure played an important part during 52 weeks of the year.

Commercialised pleasures

One of the most characteristic features of British leisure is the weekend. Initially it comprised the Saturday half-day holiday, when manufacturing industry came to a halt, and Sunday, when everything stopped; it was created unintentionally out of factory legislation to protect women and young persons together with evangelical Sabbatarianism. Though the case for some relaxation of Sunday strictness was recognised by liberal Christians in the later nineteenth century, as strict Sabbatarianism weakened, opponents of Sunday employment then came to the aid of the evangelicals with 'social Sabbatarianism', that is, opposition to the commercialisation of Sunday and a defence of the customary right of the working man to freedom from toil on that day. The Victorian Sunday thus survived almost intact well into the twentieth century, even after Saturday had become a full holiday for many workers. As late as 1986 a combination of Christian and trade-union opposition proved surprisingly effective in foiling an attempt by free-market Conservatives and commercial interests to repeal the Sunday trading legislation; but in 1994 the law was finally changed to permit all categories of shops to open for up to six hours on a Sunday.

One reason for the strength of the long opposition to Sunday trading was that the Saturday half-day was not available to many shopworkers, employed mainly in small retail outlets. Their hours were not regulated at all until 1928, long after the bulk of the workforce had achieved a 54-hour week. This lack of protection for retail workers contrasted with the favoured position of industrial workers, whose hours had long been regulated: the 1850 Factory Act had prohibited women and children from working in the majority textile factories after 2.00 p.m. on Saturdays; and the 1867 Workshops Act had similarly restricted the labour of the young people on whom many workshops depended, thus forcing most adults to take a half-day on Saturday rather than 'St Monday'. Though the hours of adult males were not formally restricted, the Saturday half-holiday had arrived *de facto* by the 1880s for a large section of the working class, for whom new leisure opportunities soon developed.

Football

The development of professional football as a mass spectator-sport would not have been possible without the Saturday afternoon holiday. Fixtures were put on a more regular basis with the establishment of the Football League of 12 northern and midland clubs in 1888; the Scottish League followed in 1891, and a second English League in 1892. The first 'international' game took place between England and (in effect) Queen's Park in Glasgow in 1872, but most away fixtures did not involve long journeys, as only six clubs out of 40 had joined the English Leagues from outside the founding areas before the First World War. The English Football Association Cup Final was usually played in London, though: 45,000 spectators made their way to Crystal Palace when it first staged the Final in 1895; in 1913, the crowd was 120,000. Football had emerged as big business.

The amateurish Football Association was rather squeamish about money, but not so the northern and midland clubs. Aston Villa started out as the Villa Cross Wesleyan Chapel team, collecting *5s. 2d.* (26p) at a match in 1874, but their takings for a match 30 years later were £14,329. Professionalism in football was reluctantly accepted by the Football Association in 1885. Players, who were often only part-timers, could now be paid small wages; top players were tempted with wages as high as those of a skilled artisan, perhaps 30 to 40*s*. (£1.50 – £2.00) a week. It was but a short step to transfer fees, as high as £1,000 in 1905. The money for the big clubs came from local businessmen and politicians with a flair for self-publicity. In the 1890s clubs became limited liability companies, in which their directors were shareholders. Capitalism was in control, and the players correspondingly formed a union in 1898. Not until 1963, though, did Jimmy Hill lead the union to shake off the outward forms of the class relationship between employers and employees. Before that date a maximum wage was enforced (£20 a week in 1958); thereafter a free market operated, and players could be paid whatever they could command. Wages for the very best players rose rapidly, making them as wealthy or wealthier than their directors; transfer fees soared into hundreds of thousands of pounds; in 1996 the highest transfer fee had reached £15 million. The leading teams became public companies, and their players little more than a negotiable currency in a transfer market that extended across the European Union and beyond. The smaller clubs could not compete, and several faced bankruptcy.

Betting and gambling

Horse racing, like football, drew great crowds, but with local meetings confined to a few days in each year, usually mid-week, few members of the working class travelled outside their own immediate areas to attend them except at holiday times. The transformation of horse racing from its eighteenth-century origins was largely due to the railway, which enabled both horses and supporters to travel easily and quickly between the hundred and more courses which provided the country with an extended season of events. The number of horses in training doubled between 1837 and 1869. As racing became more popular, increasing control was exercised over both the conduct of meetings and the crowds who came to them. Courses were enclosed, and entrance money began to be taken from spectators. New enclosed park courses were opened at Sandown (1874) and Kempton (1878), but some of the older, popular, rowdy courses in London were closed by the Racecourses Act of 1879, and the total number of courses in the country fell from 130 in 1874 to 65 10 years later.

The most popular aspect of racing was the gambling. Betting by aristocratic owners like Lord George Bentinck reached its peak in the first half of the nineteenth century, but the problem of gambling by working people was exacerbated by the growing popularity of racing, better communications and the rise of the sporting press. An Act of 1853 forbade off-course cash betting (credit betting was still permitted, but that was only for the wealthy) in an attempt to control the widespread working-class betting which went on in tobacconists, public houses and specialised betting shops. Though the law was not repealed until 1960, it was unable to stamp out the practice. In the 1930s Rowntree estimated that about half the working men in York bet on the horses, some of them every day, but their stakes were usually no more than 6*d*. As one gambler told one of Rowntree's investigators in the 1930s, he would rather 'have six penn'orth of hope than six penn'orth of electricity'.[29]

All sports attracted this kind of illegal cash betting, not least football, and before the First World War large-scale betting was organised, with commercial companies sending circulars through the post. The Football Association tried to prevent this, and in 1920 secured an Act of Parliament. The organisers of the 'Pools' got round it by collecting their wagers after the results were known. The resultant gambling industry became bigger than football itself. By the 1930s more than 16 people were gambling on the results for every one who actually went to a game. Stakes were as high as 2*s*. 6*d*. (12½p); prizes as high as £22,000. Littlewoods and Vernons in Liverpool became huge companies, employing about 30,000 people (mainly women) on checking coupons alone. In York, 48,000 coupons were delivered each week; between 18,000 and 20,000 were returned. In the football season in October 1938, 12,513 additional postal orders were bought at a value of over £900; other money went straight to pools' agents in the city, or by cheque for collective stakes from factories, offices, works and clubs. And this was one relatively small city.[30] Across the nation, £800,000 a week was being collected. Gambling on the pools was and was to remain a national craze: the hope of a fortune for a small stake. It had become a major pastime – and more. As one working man explained to Rowntree, 'A man spends three days in considering next week's football, a day filling in his coupon, and three days in keen anticipation of the following Saturday's results.'[31] Most people did not, in fact, think of 'having a flutter' on the football pools as gambling. Perhaps that is because, deep down, they realised they were unlikely to win. As Rowntree pointed out, few would bet on a horse with odds of 100:1, yet the best odds of winning on the pools were 394:1.[32] For most people, the 2*s*. 6*d*. (12½p) stake for a week's excitement was justification in itself. Winning was a bonus to be dreamt about. In 1949 11,250,000 people were estimated to have gambled on the pools (over a quarter of the adult population); this seems to have been about the peak. By 1983 the proportion had fallen to around a fifth: 28 per cent of men and 12 per cent of women over the age of 16, compared with about 5 per cent of men and under 1 per cent of women who bet on the horses.[33]

Another form of gambling which became popular in the 1960s was 'bingo', previously known as 'housey-housey'. This was popular in working-men's clubs as a means of raising funds for an outing but, with the decline of cinema audiences in the 1960s, many former picture-houses were turned into 'bingo halls', which especially attracted married women and the elderly. Bingo reached its peak in the mid-1970s, with about 1,600 clubs, but, although this number had been halved by the early 1990s, takings were still around £800 million a year. Like the football pools, bingo was not thought of as gambling, and was regarded as an essential feature of many old people's 'Darby and Joan' and 'Good Companions' clubs. Social workers even defended it on the grounds that the bingo halls provided warmth and company for many elderly and lonely people for the cost of a few penny stakes – rather less than their heating at home would have cost had they stayed there. Indeed, even Seebohm Rowntree, who in his York surveys did not approve of gambling, was forced to conclude in his last survey in 1949 that minor gambling did not contribute much to secondary poverty, and that the football pools should be nationalised rather than suppressed, with the profits put to good use.[34]

This changing attitude led the National Savings movement to introduce its Premium Bonds in 1956, the first state-organised gambling since the early nineteenth century; but it was the introduction of a National Lottery in late 1994 that transformed the nature of popular gambling in Britain. Municipal lotteries had earlier been organised to fund hospitals and other local charities, with £43 million of stake money in 1993–4, but in the first year of the National Lottery, ending February 1996, around £5,200 million was spent, with nine in every 10 adults in the country having participated, and two-thirds of the population over 16 regularly buying tickets. Average household expenditure on the lottery in the first year amounted to £106, nearly double that spent in charitable giving, but nearly three-quarters of this sum appeared to have been diverted from other forms of gambling, such as the football pools.

Though moralists worried about the effect of this expenditure on the poor, and economists pondered its anti-inflationary effect on the national economy, the lottery for most participants was no more to be taken seriously than the football pools or betting on the horses. Real gambling continued to exist, as it always had, not as the vice of the poor but as the pleasure of the rich. In 1992–3 there were 118 casino clubs licensed in Britain, with takings of over £2,000 million; three-quarters of casino stakes were placed in just 20 London clubs.

Newspapers and magazines

The wide publicity given to such sporting activities as football and horse racing would not have been possible without the sporting press or the sports pages of the popular press. A major leisure activity over the past hundred years and more has been reading the newspaper.

The popular newspaper dates back to the early nineteenth century. In 1829 the Sunday press with its scandal, crime, sports news and radical politics had a circulation of 110,000 copies a week, four times as large as that of the seven London morning papers. The leading papers were *Bell's Weekly Dispatch* (founded in 1801), the *Illustrated London News* (1842), *Lloyd's Weekly Newspaper* (1842), the *News of the World* (1843) and *Reynolds's Weekly Newspaper* (1850). Of these, the *Illustrated London News* was the most respectable, *Lloyd's* the least so; indeed, Edward Lloyd can be regarded as the common man's response to Charles Knight, whose *Penny Magazine* he put out of business.

When the newspaper stamp was removed in 1855 it helped the middle-class daily press, but made little impact on the popular press. The first penny London daily, the *Daily Telegraph* (1856), became the highest-circulation middle-class daily paper, with a circulation of about a quarter of a million in the 1880s; *Lloyd's* in the same period was selling three-quarters of a million with that traditional recipe of sport, crime and sensationalism which has remained the hallmark of the Sunday newspaper.

The so-called 'revolution of the popular press' which occurred in the 1880s and 1890s needs to be put in the context of this long tradition of the Sunday press. In 1880 George Newnes began *Tit-Bits*. He was followed by Alfred Harmsworth's *Answers to Correspondents* and Cyril Pearson's *Pearson's Weekly*. These three offered a diet of scraps of information, competitions, jokes and other ephemera. By the later 1890s each had a weekly circulation of between 400,000 and 600,000. Harmsworth (created Lord Northcliffe in 1905) also went into the daily press in 1896 with the *Daily Mail*, a halfpenny paper run at a loss and dependent upon mass advertising. He followed this in 1903 with the *Daily Mirror*, intended for a female readership, but soon converted into the first morning daily picture paper. In 1911–12 it became the first daily paper to achieve a circulation of over a million. His efforts to break into the Sunday field were thwarted in 1899 by Sabbatarians, who rather inconsistently did not mind their Monday papers being produced on a Sunday, but wished to spare the souls of the newsboys who sold the Sunday press. Harmsworth's brother (created Lord Rothermere in 1919) started the *Sunday Pictorial* in 1915, which in later times became the *Sunday Mirror*. Pearson responded to his rival in 1900 with the *Daily Express*, but was unable to continue his journalistic career when his sight failed. William Maxwell Aitken (created Lord Beaverbrook in 1917) acquired control of the paper in 1919. In 1910 the Pearson Group, the Northcliffe Group and the *Morning Leader* Group led by George Cadbury controlled 66.9 per cent of the London morning press, while H. J. Dalziel of *Reynolds's*, G. Riddell of the *News of the World*, Lloyd and Northcliffe controlled over 80 per cent of the London Sunday press.

This was the real 'Northcliffe revolution': not so much the creation of a popular press, as its transformation from independent private enterprise to large scale capitalist combination. The thriving provincial press followed. In 1920 there were 20 Scottish newspapers, all Scottish-owned; in 1940 there were 19, 11 Scottish and eight English; by 1980 there were only 15, four Scottish, two English and nine owned by multinational companies. The 'press barons' bought and sold newspapers like football players would be sold in a later age. Two of the most successful entrepreneurs in the inter-war years were the Berry brothers, one of whom (Lord Kemsley) founded Kemsley Newspapers Ltd, an empire which included 13 provincial dailies. In 1937 nearly half the provincial press was owned by the large newspaper chains. Between the wars the daily press began to assume more of the characteristics of the Sunday and magazine press, especially after Julius Elias (later Lord Southwood) of Odhams Press bought the Trade Union Congress out of their *Daily Herald* and relaunched it, with sales gimmicks including anything from free tea services to sets of Dickens.

After the Second World War the initiative passed to Rothermere's nephew, Cecil King, who revitalised the *Daily Mirror* and built up round it the largest press empire, eventually called Reed International and controlling Kemsley's magazines and Odhams Press as well as the country's second largest newsprint and paper company. The second postwar figure to shape the British press was Roy Thomson (a Canadian, like Beaverbrook, created Lord Thomson in 1964) who began by purchasing the *Scotsman* in 1953, then the Kemsley chain of newspapers in 1959 including the *Sunday Times*, and finally *The Times* itself in 1966. The third major force was Rupert Murdoch (an Australian educated at Oxford), who took over the *News of the World* in 1969, and then bought the ailing *Sun*, which had been started in 1964 as a trade union paper. He turned it into a tabloid like the *Daily Mirror*, and proceeded on the basis of sex, sport and sensationalism to outstrip the circulation of the *Mirror*. The *Daily Mail* and the *Daily Express* followed suit, along with a new tabloid, the *Daily Star*. Intellectually capable of being read on a crowded bus, they were physically designed for the same purpose. Part picture-paper, part comic, part magazine, their news content was minimal, and even their sports pages dwelt more on scandals than games.

In 1984 the Mirror Group Newspapers, publishers of six newspapers including the *Daily Mirror*, was purchased by Robert Maxwell, a Czech refugee who had been a Labour MP between 1964 and 1970, as part of his international publishing empire. His principal rival in the 1980s was Rupert Murdoch, whose News International company bought both *The Times* and the *Sunday Times* in 1981. Murdoch's management of *The Times* was controversial, and following a strike at the paper a number of former employees started a rival paper, the *Independent*, in 1986. In 1991 Maxwell's businesses were in serious financial trouble, a fact which emerged following his drowning at sea. Meanwhile Murdoch's empire grew ever wider, as he moved into satellite broadcasting with Sky Television in 1989, which in 1990 merged with its rival, British Satellite Broadcasting, to form British Sky Broadcasting.

The circulation of the Sunday press increased rapidly from about 1910, and that of the daily press did so from after the First World War. In 1937

10 million daily papers and 15.3 million Sunday papers were being sold; this had risen to 15.6 million dailies and 28.3 million Sundays by 1947. Thereafter the Sunday market began to decline and the daily market to catch up, perhaps as the daily press assumed some of the characteristics of the Sundays: in 1975 there were 14.1 million dailies and 19.7 million Sundays. Overall about 70 per cent of the adult population took at least one newspaper each day. Thereafter sales of all newspapers began to fall as television news coverage became more pervasive. In 1996 the 10 leading national daily papers were selling just over 13 million copies, while the nine leading national Sunday papers were selling only two million more – a difference almost wholly accounted for by the tabloid papers. Only 62 per cent of men and 54 per cent of women now read any national daily paper, though two-thirds did see a Sunday paper, the *News of the World*, leading the field with about a quarter of all readers. Of the national daily papers, the *Sun*, with a circulation of over four million, was the leader among the tabloids, with a quarter of all men and a fifth of all women reading it. The *Daily Telegraph*, with over a million circulation, was the leading broadsheet.

In so far as the tabloid press considered politics, all but the *Daily Mirror* were on the right. Significantly, this did not damage their popularity, though it is unclear how far the popular press created and how far it was created by the political attitudes which it presented. The *Sun* was widely given credit for the electoral successes of the Conservatives between 1979 and 1992. In fact, the readership of the press closely reflected the social structure and voting behaviour of the population at large. While the *Sun* and *Mirror* were the best-selling papers among the skilled working classes and below, the *Mail* and the *Express* were behind only the *Daily Telegraph* in their appeal to the highest social categories. The *Daily Telegraph*, *The Times*, the *Guardian*, the *Financial Times* and the *Independent* were all heavily dependent upon the upper social classes. The *Sun* reader who voted Conservative (and about a third of them did) was but the latest embodiment of a feature of political conduct reaching back to the anti-radical mobs of the eighteenth century, when loyalism had proved a more attractive political creed than a programme of foreign-inspired revolutionary change. It was therefore an interesting development when in 1997 Rupert Murdoch decided that the *Sun* would support Labour, perhaps indicating the extent to which Labour had successfully won over the support of readers of the paper; or perhaps to correct the fact, that in 1992, only a fifth of Labour voters read the *Sun* compared with over half who read the rival *Daily Mirror*.[35]

In addition to the popular press there was also a large market for weekly magazines, which had become popular in the inter-war years. Apart from the most popular, which in 1995–6 was the monthly *Reader's Digest* among older readers (circulation 1.65 million) and *Take a Break* among the younger (1.4 million), over a quarter of all readers took one of the four million guides to television and radio sold each week. Women's magazines also remained popular, the top five having a combined circulation of nearly 20 million, with around a quarter of the readers being men. These papers reflected changing women's interests in the later twentieth century, but the longer-established ones continued to find favour with older readers, to whom they offered a familiar selection of cooking recipes, knitting patterns and – a respectable survival from the nineteenth-century periodical press – serialised romantic fiction. For many older working-class women, the expression 'a book' referred not to the usual meaning of the term, but to a weekly woman's magazine. Like newspapers, they were heavily dependent upon advertising for their revenue.

Women were also more likely than men to visit the public library and to list reading as a pastime, with those over 55 more likely to spend their time in this way than the younger age groups. In 1996, four of the top five popular authors were also women. Younger people, on the other hand, were more likely to seek their pleasures outside the home.

Music hall, theatre, cinema and radio

The music hall and palace of varieties, which were the major source of public entertainment between the mid-nineteenth century and the First World War, evolved out of many earlier forms – the fairground and circus, the pleasure garden and burletta theatre – but the public house and the singing saloon were their immediate forebears. With so many drinking-places available in each town and village, many publicans sought to extend their businesses by pioneering new forms of leisure. Between 1829 and 1849 applications for singing and dancing licences in Middlesex increased by 800 per cent. Manchester in 1850 had 475 public houses and 1,143 beer houses (one drinking-place for every 80 adults in the population, not counting illicit premises). Regular musical entertainments were held in 49 of the public houses and 41 of the beer-houses. In these singing saloons the performances embodied many features of popular culture. At the *Star* in Bolton, opened in 1832 to counter the threat from the beer-house, there was a museum of curiosities and a menagerie, like the ones at the fair. The main business was singing: a chairman/soloist would be engaged for the evening, but what people enjoyed most was joining in the choruses in a free and easy way. These singing saloons and 'free and easies' had developed by the 1850s into the Victorian Music Hall.

The process of turning public houses into places of variety entertainment was partly the work of entrepreneurs like Thomas Sharples of the Bolton *Star,* and partly of large brewers anxious to increase trade and rival the gin-palaces of the distillers. But it was the discriminatory use of the licensing system against the free and easy public house which led in many cases to the building of larger music halls for socially mixed audiences and with a generally more favourable (though not quite 'respectable') image. Large halls – some of which, like the Alhambra in Leicester Square, seated 3500 in 1860 – required huge amounts of capital. Some publicans could extend their operations with the profits on their music saloons, but for many the only recourse was to the brewers, and the formation of limited companies under the Companies Act of 1862. Gradually the large halls killed off the smaller saloons: they could afford to pay higher fees for their 'stars' and charge lower admission prices as well. By 1914 the capital investment in London's major music halls amounted to £5 million, with ownership concentrated in a few companies.

With the success of the halls in London, they spread to the provinces. A handful of proprietors established chains across the country: H. E. Moss, for example, with his Empires in Newcastle, Edinburgh and Birmingham, who then moved into the London suburbs with the Palace in Stoke Newington and the Broadway in New Cross. These modern music halls were really theatres. Too much capital was at stake to risk offending the licensing authorities, so fixed seats replaced the old benches; eating and drinking (and sometimes even smoking) were banished from the cheaper seats; the coarse language of the performers was toned down to innuendo; songs were milked of biting social or political comment and turned into cosy romanticised presentations of human experience laced with 'jingoism' – a word derived from a popular song at the time of the Turkish crisis in 1878. The Edwardian music hall was a tamed beast compared with the popular theatres and song saloons of the early-Victorian period.

As the music hall reached its peak a new form of public entertainment appeared which was able to bring 'star' performances every week, on film. The first public showing of films was in London in 1896. The new enthusiasm spread rapidly. Motion pictures or 'movies' were much more realistic than the old magic-lantern shows, and entrepreneurs rushed to meet the new demand. Initially most picture shows took place in music halls or other adapted premises, but soon purpose-built Picture Theatres, Palaces and Houses appeared and, with them, in 1910, the word 'cinema'. Birmingham alone had at least 57 cinemas by 1915, and there were around 3,000 in the country as a whole.

As yet these films were silent, accompanied only by a pianist. 'Talkies' arrived in 1929; colour films appeared in the 1930s. Cinema audiences (in the full meaning of that word for the first time) increased still further, and included Sundays after the Sunday Entertainments Act of 1932. The old buildings – and even some built in the 1920s – proved inadequate. Grander cinemas than ever went up, in a variety of outlandish styles aiming at the middle as well as the lower classes. With greater capital expenditure, cinema chains appeared: Gaumont and British International, followed by Oscar Deutsch's Odeons, with their characteristic 'Odeon style', the epitome of 1930s modernist architecture. By 1939 even a modestly sized city like York had 10 cinemas and estimated weekly audiences of 50,000. Half of those who attended were children and young people; of the rest, three-quarters were women. Cinema-going had become part of national culture, with its Hollywood productions, British and American stars and – just as important, according to many contemporary recollections – 'two-penn'orth of darkness' on the back row. By 1939 there were approaching 5,000 cinemas in Britain, with weekly audiences of around 30 million.

The 'live' theatre responded to this challenge in three ways: first, by the quality of new work and acting in an age dominated by such names as James Matthew Barrie, George Bernard Shaw and John Galsworthy; second, by turning to light comedy and musicals, with the works of Ivor Novello and Noel Coward; and, third, by provincial theatres abandoning expensive touring companies and substituting local repertory companies, following the example of Annie Horniman at the Manchester Gaiety Theatre in 1908. Rowntree believed that the change to repertory saved the Theatre Royal in York, which became a non-profit-making organisation run in the interests of the community. With gallery prices at 4*d.*, upper-circle at 7*d.* and pit at 9*d.* (about 2p to 4p), the theatre was able to compete both with cinemas and the music hall.[36]

The principal challenge to theatrical entertainments of all kinds in the inter-war years was the dance hall, which appealed to young people in particular as another public forum in which 'courting' could take place. The fashion for public dancing owed much to the presence of American troops in Britain in the closing stages of the First World War. Old-fashioned waltzes gave way to quick-steps, foxtrots, tangos, and 'crazes' like the Charleston, Black-Bottom and Stomp. Jazz arrived, passing through its various forms from Ragtime, Blues and Dixieland to Chicago-style and 'big-band' swing in the 1930s. For those who wished to enjoy themselves at home the gramophone brought international artists – from music-hall stars like George Formby and Harry Lauder, to singers like Gracie Fields and band-leaders like Benny Goodman – to every fireside at the drop of a needle.

The gramophone began a revolution in home entertainment. For the first time, one could buy professional entertainment for home consumption. The process was continued by the radio, or 'wireless', as it was invariably known. Radio broadcasting was begun by the British Broadcasting Company at the end of 1922. Four years later it was taken over by a public body with a statutory monopoly, the British Broadcasting Corporation. During these four years the number of receiving licences, which cost 10*s.* (50p) each, increased from 35,744 to over 2 million; by 1939 there were nearly 9 million. As curiosity changed to enjoyment, listeners could tune into a single National Programme with alternative Regional Services, or commercial stations beyond the reach of British control, such as Radio Luxembourg. The latter specialised in light music and short serialised stories (a format going back to the 'penny-dreadfuls' of the early nineteenth century). These were often sponsored by soap manufacturers, and became known as 'soap-operas'. Luxembourg also provided a Littlewood's Pools Programme. All this was in stark contrast to the BBC under its first Director-General, John Reith, who saw his main responsibility as supplying rational and moral improvement, not entertainment. Light entertainment was strictly limited, though light music was encouraged with the formation of the BBC Radio Dance Band in 1926. More seriously the radio punctuated the day, week, month and year with a new series of rituals: news bulletins, but only after 6.00 p.m. so as not to threaten the newspapers; daily and Sunday religious broadcasts, but nothing except the weather forecast before 12.30 p.m. on Sundays, so as not to threaten the churches; the Christmas service of lessons and carols from King's College, Cambridge, begun in 1928; the monarch's Christmas message, pre-recorded and delivered annually from 1932; and sports reports on such important events as the Oxford and Cambridge Boat Race, the Grand National and the FA Cup Final. Commercialism here, at least, was kept at bay as the Victorian spirit of responsible, middle-class leadership found its last resting place in the newest form of entertainment at the BBC.

One striking feature of the 'How some typical families spend their leisure' section of Rowntree's *Poverty and Progress* (1941, relating to 1938) is how small a part the public house played in the lives of his working-class families. Certainly, drinking had declined considerably since the First World War; but this was not the only explanation, for many of the men, alongside such pastimes as football, wireless, cinema and gardening, wrote down 'Spend evening at Working Men's Club. Two pints of beer 1*s*.' or some such similar statement.[37] This was an important social development.

Working men's clubs had originated in the mid-nineteenth century as the most realistic attempt to control the working man's preference for the public house. The models for the first clubs are often held to be the Manchester lyceums, set up in the 1840s to attract working men after the failure of the Mechanics' Institute to do so. The lyceums provided libraries, evening schools, music, dancing and gymnastics for 2*s*. (10p) a quarter. Several similar institutes and clubs appeared in the 1850s, patronised in many cases by clergymen and the temperance interest. In the north of England temperance hotels also became an important part of the more respectable end of the working-class scene. The man who brought some of these local initiatives together was a Unitarian minister, Henry Solly, founder of the Lancaster Working Men's Mutual Improvement and Recreation Society (1860), who in 1862 formed the Club and Institute Union. Most of the early clubs were in small towns, run by middle-class patrons for the working classes, and offered coffee, not beer, to drink. Gradually Solly realised that these latter features were not conducive to success, and in 1875 the clubs were allowed to sell beer. This immediately gave them financial independence, and over the next 10 years the movement evolved towards full democracy.

The working-man's club failed as a method of social control, but by making the fundamental concession to beer the founders of the movement did succeed in removing much social drinking from the commercial pressures of the public house – although (or perhaps because), unlike the public house, the club was an exclusively male affair. When Seebohm Rowntree surveyed working-class life in York in 1899 he found nine drinking clubs which were patronised by the working class. Two of these were in the poor Irish quarter, and there was much drunkenness; the other seven were in newer parts of the city, and were respectably conducted; they were the scenes of heavy drinking (drink was 33 per cent cheaper than in public houses, and clubs were not restricted by the 1874 Licensing Act), but there was little drunkenness or gambling.[38]

Not only did the club replace the public house for some workmen, it also became the central institution of many working-class communities, especially those in areas like the coalfields in which male employment and male culture were dominant. Ironically, this meant that the clubs developed rather like the public houses of the 1850s, until by the 1960s some of them had become highly commercialised places of large-scale entertainment, with heavy financial commitments to the breweries, and which spent hundreds of thousands of pounds on concert rooms and extravagant night-club cabaret shows, the last resort for artists in the musical-hall tradition.

By the 1970s the newest form of entertainment, television, seemed to be carrying all before it. Cinema attendance was in steep decline. The number of cinemas more than halved between 1971 and 1984; audiences fell from 176 million to 52.7 million. By the mid-1980s fewer than half the population over seven ever went to the cinema. Ten years later this figure was up again to over three-quarters, and total attendances had increased to about 124 million a year. Old single-screen cinemas, which had been abandoned to bingo or ten-pin bowling, were now replaced by modern multi-screen complexes in newly designed buildings which recaptured some of the glamour and excitement of cinema in the 1930s. As in the earlier years of cinema's success, the appeal was to the young – over two-thirds of the 16–24 age-group went regularly, compared with the theatre, which attracted only 17 per cent.

The consumer society

Production for the market, and its corollary, purchasing for consumption, are essential features of almost any society. Already in the eighteenth century, techniques had become so highly sophisticated that historians have written of 'the birth of a consumer society' – that is, one in which the production, sale and consumption of non-essentials had become a major part of economic and social life. Josiah Tucker observed in 1758 how manufacturers in Britain were producing not merely for the luxury market of princes and nobles, but for all sections of society.[39] Despite the fact that, a hundred years later, William Howitt could describe the cottager as having no more possessions than 'a few wooden, or rush-bottomed chairs; a deal or oak table . . . a few pots and pans', Tucker's point was valid.[40] Britain had a growing number of consumers, though in describing them in any age one must make reservations for the poorest, who had the least.

The market was actively exploited in the eighteenth century by entrepreneurs determined that the new wealth of consumers should be channelled into their own pockets. Josiah Wedgwood opened showrooms for his pottery in London and Bath, and cleverly exploited social snobbery to persuade the middling classes to buy his wares. Early provincial newspapers were little more than advertising sheets. Pedlars brought to fairs the latest trinkets for fashionable domestic servants to wear. Robert Owen recalled in his own experience in the 1780s the development of the modern shop, contrasting McGuffog's sedate draper's shop in Stamford, where the gentry's needs and the appropriate prices were discreetly discussed, and Flint and Palmer's shop on London Bridge, at which goods were set out ready-priced for customers to take or leave with no haggling: 'The favour appeared to be more to the purchaser than to the seller of the articles.'[41] Francis Place also recalled the new kind of shop which was appearing in London. When he fitted up his Charing Cross shop in 1801 he spent nearly £300 on 'the largest plate glass windows in London', illuminated with Argand oil-lamps as well as candles. The foundations of his commercial prosperity were laid on the ready-money sales he made from these windows, and he did not bother about tailoring himself: it was more important to ingratiate himself with his customers.[42] Place was typical, but not unique: there were 153 shops in Oxford Street in 1800. Where London led, the provinces were not far behind. News of the latest fashions spread quickly, and shopkeepers throughout the country eagerly met their customers' wishes for drapery and household goods, furnishings and furniture.

It was food and clothing, though, which people needed to buy most frequently, so these were the most common shops in towns and villages: cobblers and tailors, butchers and bakers, selling their own products; groceries and greengroceries, available from small shops, or from market stalls. In villages and working-class sectors of growing towns, general shopkeepers kept a variety of wares, but in town centres more specialised traders emerged.

Retailing methods began to change in the 1860s and 1870s. In the larger centres of population drapers extended their businesses and started stocking a wider range of household goods: Kendal, Milne and Faulkner in

Manchester and Bainbridge in Newcastle-upon-Tyne had grown into department stores by mid-century, followed by Lewis's in Liverpool, Peter Robinson in Oxford Street and their lesser equivalents in lesser centres of population. A little later, multiple retailing developed in the grocery trade against a background of rising real wages, out of the peculiar circumstances of dealing in imported goods – initially tea and sugar, but by the 1880s a whole range of meat and dairy products from as far away as New Zealand. Thomas Lipton, one of the greatest names in this context, set up shop on his own in Glasgow in 1871 with £100; by 1914 he had around 500 shops. His success rested on bulk buying, cheap selling, a large turnover, and mass advertising – the same techniques as Harmsworth used with his *Daily Mail*. Other trades soon followed where the grocers had led: Jesse Boot with his 'pure drug' shops; Marks and Spencer with their Penny Bazaars; Montague Burton with his ready-made clothing. A third influence on this 'retailing revolution' was the co-operative movement, expanding rapidly after 1860 in groceries and, later, non-foodstuffs as well. By 1914 they had three million members and a turnover of £88 million. In many prospering northern working-class communities, the 'co-op' was the main, if not the only store. Nevertheless, among the poor the small, often struggling shopkeeper was the norm. Robert Roberts recalled how in his corner of Salford there were:

> fifteen beerhouses, a hotel, and two off-licences, nine grocery and general stores, three greengrocers (forever struggling to survive against the street hawker), two tripe shops, three barbers, three cloggers, two cook shops, a fish and chip shop (*déclassé*), an old clothes store, a couple of pawnbrokers and two loan offices.[43]

This remained the pattern of shopping until the 1950s. Corner shops struggled, but many survived; the co-operative movement faltered, caught between its commitment to small community shops and the competition of the large chain-stores, but was still a force to be reckoned with. Town-centre high streets were dominated by national chains: Marks and Spencer, Boots, F. W. Woolworth (an American import), W. H. Smith and Montague Burton. Other chains were regionally strong, such as Sainsbury (mainly in the south of England). As in the newspaper trade, rivals amalgamated and capital concentrated in a few hands: Lipton, Broughs, Meadow, Maypole and Home and Colonial, for example, despite their different shop-fronts, were all the same company.

Change began in the 1950s with postwar rebuilding schemes creating new shopping centres and developers tearing the hearts out of Victorian cities, like Bradford, as effectively as German bombs had destroyed the centres of others, like Coventry. Commerce and property development marched on: the pedestrian precincts and covered shopping arcades which had been a feature of many Victorian townscapes were swept away and replaced by others, larger and more functional, but less elegant. Shops multiplied, selling all manner of goods on the 'buy now, pay later' principle of hire-purchase. Self-service grocery stores emerged, and old market leaders, such as the Home and Colonial Group and the Co-op, fell behind the rapidly expanding Sainsbury chain and a relative newcomer, John Cohen's Tesco.

The revolution in consumer spending began, on the demand side, with rising real incomes. In 1914 the average working-class family spent three-quarters of its income on food and housing; in 1938 this had fallen to under half. The surplus money went on little luxuries, like tobacco, of which consumption doubled and on which expenditure rose by 500 per cent to over £200 million by 1939. But the beginnings of a trend can also be seen among the better-off towards the purchase of consumer durables, many of which were dependent upon electricity: by 1939, two out of every three houses were wired for electricity and could plug into the modern age. A family's status was henceforth to be measured not by whether they kept a servant (and how many), but whether they had more domestic gadgets than their neighbours: radios, washing machines, electric cookers, vacuum cleaners, electric irons before the Second World War; and televisions, refrigerators, deep-freezers, colour televisions, dishwashers, video-recorders, home computers and electric toothbrushes and carving knives in more recent times. This spending revolution gained pace in the 1930s, resumed in the 1950s and 1960s, and raced ahead in the 1970s. In 1900 2.5 per cent of total consumer expenditure went on furniture, electrical goods, other consumer durables and motor cars (excluding running costs); in 1938 the figure was 5.9 per cent; in 1950, 4.7 per cent (the effect of the war). The figure then rose to 7.5 per cent in the 1950s and remained at around the same level in the 1960s, before rising again to 9.7 per cent by 1980. In 1983 97 per cent of families owned a television set and a refrigerator; 81 per cent owned a washing machine; and 62 per cent a motor car. By 1990, as ownership approached saturation point, there was little further growth in the percentage of households with televisions, telephones, washing machines, refrigerators and freezers. These had now become 'necessities', and the new growth areas were in video-recorders, microwave ovens, home computers, dishwashers and, above all, compact-disc players, which were owned by about a quarter of households in 1991–2 and half in 1995–6. Nevertheless, the depression which followed the economic recovery of the late 1980s shook consumer confidence, and, with rising unemployment, retail sales slowed or even stagnated in the early 1990s. The credit and consumer boom had, at least temporarily, come to a halt. Whilst there was very little difference between the percentage of income spent on household goods and services across the income groups, this naturally meant that the poorer households were spending far less. Whereas 41 per cent of professional households owned a dishwasher, this was true of only 4 per cent of unskilled households.

The lubricant to make the consumer society function smoothly was advertising, which was made all the easier with the advent of television. Although experiments had been conducted with televised broadcasting before the Second World War, the service was not developed until after the war. Licences were introduced in 1946, and in 1947 just 15,000 were issued; this had risen to 4.5 million by 1955, when the BBC's monopoly was broken with the opening of Independent Television, funded from advertising. Before this date, advertising on film had been confined to the commercial break at the cinema. Now products could be recommended within the privacy and security of 18.7 million homes, and the message repeated every quarter of an hour with all the sincerity an actor or actress could summon until the image of the product was firmly planted in the viewers' minds. People were persuaded to want bigger, better and allegedly different goods. Anything could be sold, from soap powders to politicians. Perceiving the shift in the age structure of the population in the 1960s towards the 10–19 age-group (of whom there were 22 per cent more in 1961 than in 1951), the advertisers created 'teenagers', and persuaded them to need clothes, 'pop' music records and teenage magazines in which their 'problems' were magnified and then discussed. The money from advertisements (and from shares held in television companies) kept the newspaper industry alive, and provided heavy subsidies for commercialised sport.

The way we lived, then and now

A generation grew up in the 1960s too young to know the hardships of the war, too young even to have been 'called up' for National Service, which was ended in 1960. Its only memory was affluence. Yet grandfathers were still alive to recall how, in their teens, they had experienced the horror of the trenches in the First World War. Grandmothers remembered years of disciplined drudgery 'in service' with some wealthy family. Parents still bore the scars of unemployment and the fear of unemployment from the early 1930s, and looked for gratitude for having held Hitler at bay a decade later. The 'generation gap' was real.

The working class whom Rowntree studied in 1938 still lived, despite a World War, in an intellectual and social climate which was recognisably 'Victorian'. A labourer aged 50 worked five days a week and Saturday mornings. His main leisure pursuit was looking after his hens and his allotment; he spent one night at the pub, one at the club, and Saturday afternoon watching football; he took his wife out on Saturday night, and visited relations with her on Sunday night. She washed, dried and ironed the clothes, cleaned the house and did the shopping. Their elder son, aged 18 and single, was a butcher's assistant and so worked six days a week including late on Saturdays; he went to the theatre with his girlfriend on Mondays, to her house on Tuesdays, for a walk with her on Wednesdays, and to the cinema with her on Fridays; she came to his house on Sundays; on his one night at home alone (Thursdays) he filled in his football coupon. The younger son, aged 16, was not yet courting and so kept company more with his own sex: Boys' Club twice a week, cinema twice a week, dancing once a week; he played football or cricket on a Saturday afternoon, and went out for walks with his chums on Saturday and Sunday evenings. Both boys spent Sunday mornings in bed. None of the males helped the mother much: the husband helped with the housework on Sundays, and the younger son ran a few errands on Saturday mornings.[44]

This one example illustrates a type which can be recognised in oral history back to the late nineteenth century. The details change – no cinema or football coupons – but the emphases remain the same. The woman's sphere is within the home, and housework and washing the clothes takes nearly all her time. Male leisure is nearly all conducted outside the home.

What might remain of this experience 60 years later? In an unskilled manual worker's family, the wife is likely to go out to work, perhaps having a part-time job as an office cleaner or working at a supermarket till. A washing machine and spin-drier (88 per cent of her class had washing machines in 1992) enable her to compress two days' work into a few hours, and the bulk of the clothes are of man-made fibres and do not need ironing. Shopping is done on a Thursday or Friday evening at the supermarket, and perishables put in the refrigerator (90 per cent of her class have refrigerators and 87 per cent have freezers). The husband is less likely to keep hens and an allotment and does not work such long hours, unless overtime is available. The sons are likely to visit the cinema, a fast-food restaurant and a night club, and almost certainly go to the public house, even though the younger son is under the legal age for drinking. The younger son has probably only just left school, though, and might be looking for a job, in which case his ability to spend on leisure depends on whether he pays his parents anything for board. The father is also likely to go to the public house, for this is the most popular activity in all social classes and all age groups except the elderly. If he goes out for a meal, though, he is likely to go to a non-fast-food restaurant.

One thing which has changed surprisingly little is the sexual division of labour within the home. Though there is a 42 per cent chance that a boy always cleans his own room and a 34 per cent chance that he always makes his own bed, there is a less than 14 per cent chance that he does anything else about the house. With his sister, though, there is a 64 per cent chance that she always cleans her own room, and a 56 per cent chance that she makes her bed. Moreover, there is a better than 25 per cent chance that she washes her clothes, makes her own meals, does the shopping and the washing-up and cleans the rest of the house. In this behaviour the children are following their parents' example. Women spend, on average, 62 hours a week on household tasks, compared with 23 hours spent by men; men devote under six hours a week to cooking, cleaning, washing and ironing; women spend nearly 36 hours a week on these chores, and still manage to spend twice as long with their children. These averages, though, probably conceal a widening variation between those households where the man is still the chief 'breadwinner' and those in which he is unemployed and a reversal of roles has, to some extent, been forced by circumstances.

The biggest change over the 60 years is the amount of time spent in the home. The family as a whole spends a large part of the leisure time saved by modern equipment and shorter working hours watching television. Different surveys of the actual time spent watching television have produced different results – perhaps an indication that people are not always willing to admit how much of their time is spent in front of a television set – but the average figure would appear to be something in excess of 20 hours a week, with the figure increasing to over 30 with the elderly or the lowest social class. The modern unskilled worker's family is also likely to be one of that 30 per cent in England and Wales (or 40 per cent in Scotland) who do not own a car; but if they do it is probably an old one, requiring regular do-it-yourself mechanical attention.

This unskilled-working-class example illustrates change at the level in society where it has always been at its most conservative. Higher classes with greater material means at their disposal are able to adapt to new opportunities more quickly. Though society is no longer divided between the leisured and the non-leisured, and though the circumstances of almost all families have much improved during the second half of the twentieth century, in a consumer society those with most money have remained clearly differentiated from those with least. Leisure and consumption patterns in this sense are clear indicators of relative social inequality.

Notes

1. A. Young, *A Six Month Tour through the North of England* (4 vols., 1770, 2nd edn., 1771), i, pp. 172–3.
2. F. Drake, *Eboracum, or the History and Antiquities of the City of York* (1736), pp. 240–4.
3. Quotations from R. Porter, *English Society in the Eighteenth Century* (Harmondsworth, 1982), pp. 245–6.
4. Drake, *Eboracum*, p. 241.
5. See N. Gash, 'Lord George Bentinck and his Sporting World', in *Pillars of Government and Other Essays on State and Society, c. 1770–c.1880* (1986), pp. 162–75.
6. W. Howitt, *The Rural Life of England* (1838; 3rd edn., 1844), ch. xvi: 'Lingering Customs', pp. 582–92.
7. J. M. Ludlow and L. Jones, *Progress of the Working Class* (1867), pp. 18–19.

8. Quotation from R. Poole, *Popular Leisure and the Music Hall in 19th-Century Bolton* (Lancaster, 1982), p. 6.
9. Ludlow and Jones, *Progress of the Working Class*, pp. 17–18.
10. Cited in R. S. Fitton and A. P. Wadsworth, *The Strutts and the Arkwrights* (1958), pp. 234–7.
11. R. Owen, *Observations on the Effect of The Manufacturing System* (1815).
12. Howitt, *The Rural Life of England*, p. 501.
13. Howitt, *The Rural Life of England*, pp. 491–2.
14. Translator's footnote in L. Faucher, *Manchester in 1844* (1844), pp. 53–4.
15. Ludlow and Jones, *Progress of the Working Class*, p. 17. Church attendance was compulsory under the Act of Uniformity (1551), though Dissenters were excepted by the Toleration Act of 1689. It was repealed in 1969.
16. The quotation is taken from A. P. Wadsworth, 'The First Manchester Sunday Schools', p. 100 in M. W. Flinn and T. C. Smout (eds.), *Essays in Social History* (1974), pp. 100–22.
17. *Visit of the Manchester and Salford Town Missionaries, to the Knott Mill Fair, held Easter Week, 1841* (Manchester 1841).
18. C. Brontë, *Shirley: A Tale* (1849), chs. 16–17.
19. M. Arnold, *Culture and Anarchy* (1868; ed. J. Dover Wilson, Cambridge, 1932; repr. 1966), pp. 101–2.
20. 'Moral Statistics of Parishes in Westminster', *Journal of the Statistical Society* (1838), quoted in R. D. Altick, *The English Common Reader* (Chicago and London, 1957; paperback edn. 1963), p. 218.
21. Quoted by J. Wigley, *The Rise and Fall of the Victorian Sunday* (Manchester, 1980), p. 105.
22. A. Rattenbury, 'Methodism and the Tatterdemalions', p. 52, in E. and S. Yeo (eds.), *Popular Culture and Class Conflict* (Brighton, 1981), pp. 28–61.
23. Quotation in J. H. and M. M. Clapham, 'Life in the New Towns', pp. 240–1 in G. M. Young (ed.), *Early Victorian England* (2 vols., 1934), i, pp. 227–44.
24. For Hallé, see G. S. Messinger, *Manchester in the Victorian Age: The Half-Known City* (Manchester, 1985), pp.128–30.
25. Howitt, *The Rural Life of England*, pp. 526–9.
26. Quotation in P. Bailey, *Leisure and Class in Victorian England: Rational Recreation and the Contest for Control, 1830–1885* (1978), p. 93.
27. Quoted in H. E. Meller, *Leisure and the Changing City, 1870–1914* (1976), p. 235.
28. M. Arnold, *Culture and Anarchy*, pp. 102–5.
29. Rowntree, *Poverty and Progress* (1941), p. 403.
30. Rowntree, *Poverty and Progress*, p. 403.
31. Rowntree, *Poverty and Progress*, p. 404.
32. B. S. Rowntree and G. R. Lavers, *English Life and Leisure: A Social Study* (1951), pp. 132–4.
33. Rowntree and Lavers, *English Life and Leisure*, p. 135 compared with *Social Trends* (1986), pp. 164–5.
34. Rowntree and Lavers, *English Life and Leisure*, pp. 136–9.
35. D. Butler and D. Kavanagh, *The British General Election of 1992* (1992), p. 190; I. Crewe, A. Fox and N. Day, *The British Electorate, 1963–1992: A Compendium of Data from British Election Studies* (Cambridge, 1995), p. 447.
36. Rowntree, *Poverty and Progress*, pp. 413–15.
37. Rowntree, *Poverty and Progress*, pp. 428–49. The quotation comes on p. 432.
38. Rowntree, *Poverty and Progress*, pp. 326–31.
39. See N. McKendrick, 'Home Demand and Economic Growth', pp. 191–2, in N. McKendrick (ed.), *Historical Perspectives. Studies in English Thought and Society* (1974), pp. 152–210.

40. Howitt, *The Rural Life of England*, p. 404.
41. R. Owen, *The Life of Robert Owen, Written by Himself* (1857), p. 19.
42. M. Thale (ed.), *The Autobiography of Francis Place* (1972), p. 215.
43. R. Roberts, *The Classic Slum* (Manchester, 1971; republished Harmondsworth, 1973), p. 16.
44. Rowntree, *Poverty and Progress*, pp. 432–4.

6

Religion

Religion in the age of reason

The image of the eighteenth-century Church is one of urbanity, classical restraint and tolerance. Gone were the bloodlettings of the sixteenth- and seventeenth-century conflicts. The natural political and social order had been re-established, and vulgar 'enthusiasm' was frowned upon. Faith now rested on reason, which harmonised the complementary revelations of God in nature and Scripture. Gentlemanly conduct, morality, style, tolerance and good works had replaced the old, uncomfortable message of the puritan saints, with their fanaticism and stress upon grace, the dangers of hell and the temptations of the devil. This, at least, is how the leaders of the eighteenth-century Church saw themselves; but the reality was far more complex. Beneath the surface a different spirit moved, still turbulent, undisciplined and superstitious. The institutional history of the Church is only half the story of the religion of the people.

The crisis of the established churches

The eighteenth century saw the political subordination of national churches throughout Europe. In England and Wales the Anglican Church had been restored in 1660, but was dealt a severe blow in 1689 when the political revolution against James II caused divided loyalties among the bishops and also opened the way for the permanent toleration of non-Anglicans. Since the Reformation in the 1530s Church and State had been closely connected, and the eighteenth-century taming of party spirit and consolidation of oligarchy in the secular sphere naturally had its counterpart in spiritual affairs. In Scotland the consequences of the defeat of James VII were even more far-reaching, for with the old Stuart monarchy went the hopes of both Catholics and Episcopalians, and the struggle for supremacy which had been going on since the Reformation of the 1560s was resolved by Parliament in favour of a Presbyterian Church of Scotland. In the eighteenth century it too settled down to a relatively tame existence under the union of 1707 and the solidly Protestant House of Hanover, while the Episcopal church almost withered away after the defeat of Jacobitism in 1745.

One major problem faced by all the Established Churches was their administrative inflexibility in the face of social change. In England there were 23 dioceses, in Wales four, and one for the Isle of Man. They were of unequal size and wealth, the four Welsh ones all being notoriously poor and of low status in the Church. Of the English dioceses, all but six served the southern half of the country, where about two-thirds of the country's 10,000 parishes were situated. In other words, with the exception of London the church was administratively weakest precisely in those areas in which social change was to be most rapid in the later eighteenth century. The Scottish Church, which comprised about 900 parishes, was similarly ill-placed to respond to the rapid growth of population on Clydeside. With their parochial structures, the Churches had been designed to serve small, clearly defined rural communities, not the sprawling industrialising districts of northern England, or the densely populated centres of major seaports and manufacturing towns like Glasgow, Liverpool, Birmingham or Manchester.

A connected problem was that of the poverty of many livings. Although the income from a rectory might be £500 a year and more (though usually less in Scotland), most parish clergymen received under £100, and many of them less than £50. Rectories, with their rights to the great (especially corn) tithe, were frequently held not by clergymen but by lay impropriators, whose vicars (deputies) received a stipend from the rector – 'the leavings, not the livings'. Sometimes parochial income had been diverted to endow charitable institutions such as colleges and schools, but more usually the lay impropriator was a squire who had inherited his rights from those gentry who had bought up monastic endowments after the Reformation. As a result of this poverty, clergymen looked for other sources of income, such as schoolteaching, farming their own glebe land, or holding more than one living in plurality. Some parochial clergymen even served as curates for their richer neighbours, who were happy to take their incomes and employ another to do their work. In 1743 about half the clergymen in the diocese of York held more than one living, the majority for reasons of poverty. Pluralism, though, often meant non-residence and neglect of pastoral work.

A third source of weakness in the Church was political. In England quarrels between High and Low Church factions in the Anglican Church meant that neither of its provincial Convocations was permitted to meet for serious business between 1717 and 1852, except for one brief session in 1741. This robbed the Church of any independent voice in its own affairs, and left control in lay hands. At the bottom of the ecclesiastical order, lay rectors appointed vicars to livings; at the top, politicians (through the monarch) chose bishops who would provide a reliable body of ministerial support in the House of Lords. Though the bishops were mostly conscientious men when not required to be in London during parliamentary sessions, they had neither the means nor the time to supervise their dioceses with the degree of care necessary for the well-being of the Church. An additional problem in Wales was the alien nature of the Anglican Church. Between 1714 and 1870, no Welsh-speaking bishop was appointed to a Welsh see, and many of the clergy also were unable to preach in the native language (sometimes the only language) of the people. In Scotland, an attempt was made to throw off lay control in 1690 but, despite the Act of Union in 1707 promising to uphold the Presbyterian Church, the British Parliament restored lay patronage in the Scottish Church in 1712. The tendency was for lay patrons in Scotland, Wales and England to chose men amenable to themselves. The richer livings fell into the hands of younger sons of the gentry.

These failings in the structure of the Churches were compounded by their spiritual weaknesses. The seventeenth century tradition of Anglican spirituality tended to be strongest among High Churchmen, such as Thomas Ken and William Law, whose continued support for James II and his heirs took them out of the mainstream of ecclesiastical life. The safe Latitudinarianism of a Church buffeted by political upheaval and uncertainty was spiritually tepid, and the great Church societies – notably the Society for the Promotion of Christian Knowledge and the Society for the Propagation of the Gospel – lost their initial fervour. The Moderates similarly set the tone in Scotland, with their Calvinism diluted through contact with the civilising influences of Enlightened thought. Those who did not like this development seceded and thus accelerated the process. In this more relaxed atmosphere, pastoral visiting and public rebuking declined in Scotland; and public worship in the Church of England became less and less frequent, perhaps no more than once on a Sunday and not at all during the week. Communions were most commonly held quarterly, a custom already well-established in the seventeenth century in the Church of Scotland.

The story of the Churches is not one of entire gloom, though. Much of the criticism which has been levelled at them in the eighteenth century has been made by people looking back through the evangelical revival and (in England) the Oxford Movement. The eighteenth-century Church has to be seen on its own terms. It was far more tolerant than in previous ages. Its better-off clergy were men of culture and learning, amateur scientists and men of letters. Spirituality was not entirely dormant, for the Wesleyan revival is best understood within the High Church tradition of William Law. High Church traditions did survive to an extent not appreciated by nineteenth-century critics, and some churches, especially in the larger towns, did maintain double service on Sundays and monthly communions. Even the closeness of Church and State, which a later generation was to repudiate, was an advantage which kept the Churches at the heart of the secular, political process, while the poverty of many parish ministers and clergymen at least helped them identify with their parishioners. The Churches were weakened rather than strengthened in the later eighteenth century when increasing numbers (never a majority) of parochial clergyman moved perceptibly into the arms of the local gentry or became gentlemen themselves.

This latter process was in part due to agricultural prosperity, which added to the value of tithes, and partly to enclosure, which consolidated glebe land, often on favourable terms, or involved an award of land in lieu of tithes. As a consequence some clergymen were joining the ranks of the propertied élite at a time when the social gulf between the propertied and the unpropertied was getting wider. The promotion of clergymen to the bench of magistrates neatly symbolised the union of Church and State which reached its climax between 1790 and 1830, as the Establishment in both closed ranks against the subversive threat posed by the Revolution in France. Though the actual number of clerical magistrates increased by only 18 per cent between 1760 and 1820, many of the new faces were those of clergymen and the proportion of clergy on the bench doubled to a national average of 22 per cent. In the counties of recent enclosure the figures were much higher: 47 per cent in Lincolnshire in 1831; 45 per cent in Cambridgeshire; and 41 per cent in Bedfordshire.

The weakness of Dissent

Catholicism should be seen as the oldest form of Dissent, for the Catholic Church was not so much a survival from pre-Reformation times (except through the influence of a few families) as a revival of the seventeenth and eighteenth centuries. In Scotland the major centres of Catholic strength were in the North-East, where the house of Huntley provided leadership, and the North-West, which was converted to Catholicism by Franciscan missionaries from Antrim in 1624. In the main, the Highland Jacobites were not Catholics but Episcopalian Protestants. It has been estimated that, throughout Scotland, the number of Catholics was rising from around 14,000 in the mid-seventeenth century (all but 2,000 of them in the Highlands) to 30,000 in 1779 and 50,000 in 1800, including by this last date religious refugees from Ulster bringing with them to Clydeside a new kind of Catholicism. In England and Wales the Catholic community may have numbered around 60,000 in the mid-seventeenth century, rising to around 80,000 by 1770. This community was gentry-based and, despite the Penal Laws, well-integrated into English society. The character of eighteenth-century Catholicism began to change only as refugee priests from France and immigrants from Ireland arrived with new and sometimes disturbing ways.

Protestant Dissent was in decline in the eighteenth century. In 1662 about a fifth of the parochial clergy in England and Wales had been ejected from their livings for refusing to conform to the Act of Uniformity, but toleration in 1689 brought weakness rather than strength. The total number of Independents, Baptists and Presbyterians fell from around 300,000 in 1700 to only 50,000 in 1740. With this decline in numbers came an even more decisive collapse in social support. Unlike Catholicism, the strength of which remained with the gentry, Protestant Dissent lost most of its aristocratic and gentry patronage, and became almost exclusively a religion of the middling and lower orders. Though the Penal Legislation of the 1660s was no heavy burden in the eighteenth century, the social stigma of second-class citizenship meant that, with increasing prosperity and social advancement, many Dissenters found the path to their rather lax and unexacting parish church an easy one to take.

The Dissenting congregations themselves lacked organisation and purpose. An attempt to formulate common doctrine failed in 1719 and independent congregations evolved in sectarian isolation. Their only national voice came from the Protestant Dissenting Deputies, a pressure group of Dissenting ministers from within 10 miles of London, formed in 1727 to press for the repeal of the Test and Corporation Acts. From mid-century, as the evangelical revival began to make its impact, the broad consensus of Dissent started to disintegrate. Some Presbyterians ministers, who, unlike Independents and Baptists, were not directly answerable to their congregations, took up a rationalist interpretation of the Bible which led them to adopt Arian and later Socinian theological positions which denied the complete equality of Christ with the Father in the Trinity. These views were shared by many General (that is, Arminian) Baptists, as well as by a minority of Independents (such as Joseph Priestley) and a few Anglicans, led by Theophilus Lindsey, who left the Established Church in the 1770s to lay the foundations of what was to become Unitarianism. Their hope was that one day the National Church would be reunited on rational, Scriptural principles (perhaps not unlike the Church of Scotland in the heyday of the Moderates during the Scottish Enlightenment), but this was thwarted as most Independents and Particular (that is, Calvinist) Baptists adopted evangelical principles and a New Connexion of Trinitarian General Baptists was formed in 1770. While the numbers of these orthodox groups showed signs of recovery towards the end of the eighteenth century, those of the rationalists continued to decline. Finally, the support the latter gave to the principles of the French Revolution weakened what remained of their influence and social standing, as 'Church and King' mobs attacked their chapels and destroyed the homes of their leaders.

In Scotland, the main group outside the Established Church was the Episcopalians, who were perhaps in a majority in 1689, especially north of the Tay, where half the population lived. Between 1688 and 1716 the ministers in 664 out of 926 parishes throughout Scotland were ejected. Yet, 50 years later, Episcopalianism no less than English Dissent was ceasing to be significant in the life of the nation. Despite the granting of toleration by the High Church government of Anne in 1712, the implication of the Episcopalians with Jacobitism led to further penal legislation, culminating in 1746 in almost complete proscription, which lasted until 1792. The Presbyterian Church under the Moderates seemed closer to the traditions of the National Church than an Episcopalianism increasingly out of touch with both Hanoverian politics and the Anglican Church south of the border.

Popular religion

What people believed was seldom what they were taught or expected to believe. Fear of evil spirits and the power of witchcraft were still common in the later eighteenth century. The law might have abolished the crime of witchcraft in 1736, but that did not stop people believing in the evil power of witches or prevent both offensive and defensive measures being taken against them. There was a thriving market in lucky charms and magic potions, and the Bible and Prayer Book were held to have talismanic properties. Popular versions of orthodox religion appeared in many cases to mean more than official teaching. The folk rite of christening was regarded as a form of inoculation against bad luck and illness; the churching of women after childbirth was an essential preparation for re-admission into the community, and women might be excluded from their neighbours' homes as bearers of bad luck until they were purified. Moss from the churchyard, rainwater from the roof, or even lead scraped from the church windows were all thought to have healing properties. This was the popular face of religion in the age of reason. It answered the needs of a people who had few defences against ill health and ill fortune.

Alongside an almost superstitious belief in the powers of the clergy to exorcise ghosts and ward off evil spirits ran a strong current of popular anti-clericalism. Sometimes this arose out of a failure to fulfil expectations: Parson Woodforde was once threatened by a parishioner for refusing the privilege of a private baptism for his second child because he had not brought his first child back to church after its baptism. The man said he would take his child to the Dissenters' Meeting House instead.[1] A common cause of friction between the clergy and their parishioners was tithes. Payment of the corn tithe soured relations between small landowners and tithe owners, but more significant was the attempt by clergy to exact their lesser tithes on cottage pigs, or increasingly common crops, like potatoes grown in cottage gardens. Added to this grievance was the prevalence of clerical magistrates. So the clergyman was portrayed in popular cartoons in a less-than-flattering manner – in his rural surroundings greedily choosing his tithe pig (by Isaac Cruikshank, 1797), and in his urban context calling out the cavalry at the 'Peterloo' massacre (by George Cruikshank, 1819). 'More pigs and less parsons' was a familiar toast among the common people; 'may the last king be strangled in the bowels of the last priest' is how political radicals envisaged the coming republic.

Popular beliefs also found an outlet in a variety of religious sects: 'Alchymists, Astrologers, Calculators, Mystics, Magnetizers, Prophets, and Projectors, of every class', is how one alarmed contemporary described them in 1800 after the French Revolution had re-opened that can of worms sealed with difficulty after the turbulence of the seventeenth century.[2] Followers of Jacob Boehme (1575–1624), Lodowicke Muggleton (1609–1698) and the Camisard Prophets of the early eighteenth century abounded. Women identified themselves with roles cast for them in the apocalyptic books of the Bible: Ann Lee of Manchester, influenced by the Camisard Prophets and the Quakers, who founded the Shakers in the early 1770s; Mary Evans of Anglesey, who left her husband in about 1780 to become the Bride of the Lamb (*Revelations* 19); Elspeth Simpson (Mrs Luckie Buchan) of Ayr, who started the Buchanites in 1784; and Joanna Southcott from Devon, who heard voices and began to prophesy in 1792.

Southcottianism and its derivatives were the most popular forms of millenarianism in Britain. In 1796 Joanna discovered that she was the Bride of the Lamb, began to publish her prophecies (in doggerel verse) in 1800 and moved to London in 1802, where she collected a following among the disciples of Richard Brothers, 'The Nephew of the Almighty', who had been sent to a lunatic asylum in 1795 for identifying Britain with Anti-Christ and prophesying the fall of George III. Joanna's belief was that she was to bear a child – the Shiloh of *Genesis* 49: 10, or the Man-child of *Revelations* 12: 5 – and in 1814 she had a false pregnancy on her deathbed at the age of 64. Her disciples maintained their faith despite their disappointment, some of them becoming disciples of the 'False Prophets', John 'Zion' Ward in London, and John Wroe of Bradford, who called the faithful to await the Second Coming of Christ in his New Jerusalem at Ashton-under-Lyne. Their successors were still waiting, in Bedford, in the early twentieth century.

Millenarianism (or chiliasm) was the belief that Christ was about to inaugurate his thousand-year rule on earth. Millenarian sects flourished in Britain between about 1780 and 1850, and it is tempting to associate them with the social and political tensions of those years – perhaps the chiliasm of despair for the cotton spinners of Ashton, but for Brothers and Ward their political message was more a chiliasm of hope. The French Revolution gave great impetus to millenarian thought: the French Revolution had overthrown the Catholic Church – the Anti-Christ – and so heralded the end of time; to attack the revolutionaries was therefore to support Anti-Christ. So potent did this message appear that conservative millenarians were encouraged to produce the alternative view that the Revolution was Anti-Christ, and that to fight it was thus a godly task. But orthodox Southcottianism was apolitical, and its appeal may have been social and, more particularly, feminist. Of 7,000 Southcottian names to survive, 63 per cent are those of women; moreover, two-thirds of the followers were unmarried, like Joanna herself. A number of the millenarian sects involved the renunciation of sexual relations, which were identified with original sin, and it may be that they in part embodied a protest against the sexual subordination and exploitation of women – or a sublimation of sexual failure and frustration. The part played by female prophets from the Camisards (one-third of whom were women) to the Shakers and Southcottians is very marked, and also suggests continuity with popular beliefs in wise-women or white witches such as Mother Shipton. Whatever their many and mixed motivations, the millenarian sects show, above all, the extent and nature of the dense spiritual undergrowth beyond the carefully cultivated gardens of rational, institutional religion. It was partly from this wilderness that the religion of the evangelical revival drew its strength and support.

The evangelical revival

The origins of the revival

The evangelical revival cannot be understood solely in national terms, for it affected religious life from Silesia to New England. Its origins are to be traced to the growth of Pietism within the Lutheran Church of the later seventeenth century, centred on the new university of Halle, founded in 1694. The Pietists were Arminian in theology; that is, they believed that God's grace was available to all and not just the elect. This was a missionary theology, and Halle became a powerhouse for new religious endeavours across Europe and beyond, from Greenland to India. One of the most determined missionary groups were the Moravians, Protestant refugees who settled on the estate of the Pietist Count Ludwig von Zinzendorf at Bertholdsdorf in 1722, where, in 1727, they reconstituted the ancient Hussite Moravian Church of the United Brethren under his leadership. In 1735 a group of these Moravian missionaries happened to be on the same boat, bound for the new colony of Georgia, as a young missionary from the Society for the Propagation of the Gospel named John Wesley. Three years later, when searching for spiritual renewal, Wesley met up again with a Moravian group in London. On 24 May 1738 at an Anglican religious society in Fetter Lane, Aldersgate Street, he felt his heart 'strangely warmed'. Wesley was a High Churchman, Arminian rather than Calvinist in theology, having much in common with the Lutheran Pietists. Though he was eventually to break with the Moravians over their

Quietism – their waiting on the Holy Spirit instead of learning God's will through action – they had fired his energies and made him the single most important figure in the revival of religion in eighteenth-century Britain. But he was not the only, or the first leader of the revival.

A new spirit was also beginning to run through many Independent congregations of Calvinists. In 1707 Isaac Watts published his *Hymns and Spiritual Songs*. Hitherto, Calvinists had frowned upon hymns as mere human contrivances, in contrast to the Psalms, which were the Word of God, even in their metrical form. New hymns and sacred poetry had belonged more to the High Church tradition of George Herbert and Bishop Thomas Ken. Watts opened up a new art form, which was to be exploited by Charles Wesley. A liberal Calvinist theology was also emerging at this time from the Northampton Academy under Philip Doddridge (1729–51) which was to have a profound influence on all sections of Protestantism. While these new ideas were stirring within Calvinism in Northampton, a revival led by Jonathan Edwards known as the Great Awakening was shaking Northampton, Massachusetts, in 1734–5, an account of which was published in London in 1737. Edwards's writings were to have far-reaching consequences in Britain, inspiring revivals in Cambuslang (1742) and missionary endeavours among the Particular Baptists of the English Midlands (1784). More immediately, the Great Awakening stimulated one of Wesley's Oxford friends, George Whitefield, who set out for New England just as Wesley was returning, disillusioned, from Georgia in 1738. From America he brought back experience of open-air evangelism and a conviction that liberal Calvinism rather than Arminianism offered the correct theology of salvation.

Meanwhile, in Wales, a young shepherd named Griffith Jones had a dream, became a curate in the Church of Wales in 1710, and broke parochial discipline by preaching outside his own parish, drawing large crowds to open-air meetings and inspiring others to become travelling teachers of the people in 'hedgerow schools'. One of his converts, Howell Harris, became a successful itinerant lay preacher who met and also influenced Whitefield.

Scotland, too, was caught up in the spirit of revival, as both moderate and strict Calvinism developed amid evangelical cross-currents. Periodic outbursts of dissatisfaction with the Church had, on occasions since the seventeenth century, led to the formation of Praying Societies among the devout; and one emigré in this tradition, Walter Ker, had taken an active part in the Great Awakening. Some members of these Praying Societies joined with congregations who had seceded from the Church in 1733 over the question of lay patronage, a touchstone of evangelical awareness. Between 1737 and 1740 the number of seceding congregations grew from 15 to 36 as evangelicals declared their independence of the increasingly secular-minded and lay-dominated Church of Scotland. Their leaders invited Whitefield to come to Scotland to preach for them in 1741, but he found them too exclusive and unwilling to admit that they did not hold a monopoly on revival. This became apparent when revival hit Cambuslang near Glasgow in 1742. The Praying Societies were already strong in the parish, and had compelled the patron to supply a pastor of evangelical opinions. Inspired by the Great Awakening, spiritual revival swept through the parish, and at a great communion held in August 30,000 people were present (including Whitefield), with 3,000 receiving the elements even though the usual communion had been held only the month before. The majority of evangelicals remained a troubled and troublesome group within the Church of Scotland, though they did not oust the Moderate leadership until 1834. The Seceders divided among themselves, and then divided again; others joined them, and some eventually rejoined the original Church. The net result was the growth of a new Presbyterian nonconformity in Scotland. When the United Secession Church was formed in 1820 it had 280 congregations, chiefly in the Glasgow area, where 40 per cent of the population were Dissenters.

Methodism

The movement known as 'Methodism' and associated chiefly with the Wesley brothers cannot be understood except as part of this great evangelical revival which swept through all the Churches and religious bodies of Britain (and beyond) in the second and third quarters of the eighteenth century. John and Charles Wesley are important because they not only contributed to the wider revival, especially within their own Anglican Church, but eventually created the largest and most enduring of the new religious bodies.

Methodism was a hybrid creation, born of the unlikely alliance of High Church pietism, Moravian evangelicalism and Calvinist revivalism. Wesleyan Methodism, the major branch of the movement, was in form a religious society within the Church of England, not unlike the SPCK or the SPG, for spreading 'scriptural holiness through the land'. Yet it gradually fell into the ways of Dissent, despite the intentions of John Wesley himself. The paradoxes of the movement are present in Wesley's own life and background. Both his grandfathers had been ejected in 1662, yet his father, rector of Epworth in Lincolnshire, was a High Church Tory like many country clergymen, and his mother – the dominant influence in his life – might even be described as a Jacobite. He was educated at Oxford where, as a fellow of Lincoln College, he was an unusually assiduous tutor and helped a number of undergraduates, including his younger brother Charles, to start a Holy Club for study, religious observance and practical good works. It was the methodical approach of this Club which gave Wesley's followers their name of Methodists.

After his evangelical conversion in 1738 Wesley began evangelising within the Established Church, and gradually the special features of

Methodism evolved. Influenced by Whitefield, he started open-air preaching in 1739; influenced by his mother, he used lay preachers from 1740; from 1744 he called an annual Conference of preachers to assist and advise him, though the body had no power until his death in 1791, when the 'Legal Hundred' of senior preachers inherited the role of directing Methodism, which had hitherto been the personal responsibility of 'Pope' John alone. Wesley was a great preacher, and used the legal freedom of an Oxford Fellowship to preach the length and breadth of the country; but his real genius was organisation. What he found in the 1740s was an apparently spontaneous outburst of revivalist preaching in parishes throughout Britain. Other Anglican clergymen were active before Wesley – men like William Grimshaw of Haworth in Yorkshire, whose conversion began in 1734. Laymen, too, were preparing the way: John Nelson, a Yorkshire stonemason, heard Whitefield and Wesley, was converted in 1739, and returned home to spread the movement in his native county. Benjamin Ingham, a Holy Club member, also missioned his native Yorkshire, first as a Moravian and later as leader of the Inghamites.

Wesley broke with the Moravians in 1739 and began his own special mission, gradually linking up with other preachers and local revivals to shape a new religious movement. He made little headway in Scotland, where the Praying Societies were able to exist within the Established Church and where Episcopalianism (Wesley was no Presbyterian) was in severe decline; and in Wales, where the revival spread chiefly through Calvinist Nonconformity, closer to Whitefield than to Wesley; but in England both clergy and laymen were responsive to his leadership. Little societies were formed to strengthen new converts. Their activities were supplementary to those of the Established Church, providing preachings outside the infrequent hours of the parish service, prayer meetings, Bible study and encouraging attendance at services of Holy Communion. The little Methodist societies were divided into classes of 12 for spiritual oversight and public confession. Discipline was strict, and members were expelled for backsliding in both moral and spiritual matters. Slowly, as these societies grew, buildings were acquired, and soon the religious society was halfway to being a denomination. Open-air preachings, the unauthorised use of laymen and unauthorised preaching by parochial clergymen outside their own parishes were against ecclesiastical discipline. The Methodists were probably also in breach of the Conventicle Acts (1664, 1669) which prevented more than five people meeting outside the household for non-Anglican worship. Was Methodist worship 'non-Anglican'? Should their buildings be licensed for Dissenting worship under the Toleration Act? Wesley was quite clear: he was no Dissenter; but not all his followers were of like mind. From 1760 increasing numbers of Methodists preachers took out Dissenters' licences under the Toleration Act and applied for licences for their meeting places.

Despite efforts to hold Calvinists and Arminians together, the revival eventually split along theological lines. The Calvinist Methodists themselves fell into four groups which worked in close co-operation: the followers of George Whitefield, Benjamin Ingham, Howell Harris and Selina, Dowager Countess of Huntingdon, who was Ingham's sister-in-law. Lady Huntingdon's strategy was to appoint evangelical preachers as her chaplains and build proprietary chapels for them in the hope of converting people of her own rank within the Church of England. In this she had some success. Her first chapel was at Brighton in 1760, followed by Bath (1765), Tunbridge Wells (1767), Worcester (1773), Basingstoke (1777) and Spa Fields (1779). Georgian Evangelicalism (the capital 'E' is used to denote the movement within the Established Church) became a fashionable affair, with an influence out of all proportion to its numbers. Her convert the Earl of Dartmouth, for example, placed Henry Venn at Huddersfield (1759–71), and John Newton (a converted slave-trader) secured the curacy at Olney in Buckinghamshire (1764–80) by similar means. At Olney, which already had an important Baptist congregation, Newton deepened the spiritual life of the parish church with prayer meetings for which he and William Cowper wrote the celebrated Olney hymns. Unlike other Methodist organisations, Lady Huntingdon's Connexion was to remain at its strongest in London and the adjacent counties. She also founded a preachers' college for Howell Harris at Trevecka (later moved to Cheshunt, and later still to Cambridge) to provide gospel clergymen for the Established Church; but most of them disappointed her by becoming pastors to Independent congregations instead.

The breach between the Established Church and Methodism came slowly, reluctantly and pragmatically. In 1779 Lady Huntingdon felt compelled by legal disputes to establish her own Connexion, registering it under the Toleration Act as a Dissenting body which, in 1783, formally broke with the Church over non-episcopal ordinations. She did this with little enthusiasm, and in Wales the Calvinistic Methodists under Howell Harris's leadership continued within the Church until 1811. In 1784 John Wesley followed the Countess of Huntingdon's Connexion in ordaining preachers for work in the newly independent United States but, despite this serious challenge to episcopal authority, he still refused to recognise where his actions were leading. George Whitefield, on the contrary, was always prepared to work for revival outside as well as inside the Church, and after his death in 1770 many of his preachers slipped into Independency, reinforcing its liberal Calvinist elements and helping transform them from inward-looking isolation and stagnation into a growing evangelical body with an international outlook for mission. Dissenting voices also grew stronger within Wesleyan Methodism after John Wesley's death in 1791, and in 1795 a compromise agreement in Conference resulted in Methodists being allowed, after strict safeguards, to receive

Holy Communion from their own ministers and to hold services at the same time as the parish church. A separate denomination gradually evolved over the next generation.

The impact of Methodism

Contemporaries of the Revival had no difficulty in explaining it as the work of the Holy Spirit, but historians are agnostic on such matters and deal only in secondary causes. One obvious reason for revival at this level is dissatisfaction with the existing Churches, a reaction against the rationalism of the Established Churches and the introspection of Dissent, just as these in turn had been reactions against the excesses of the seventeenth century. Reasonable religion and exclusive Dissent did not speak to the needs of popular religion. The revivalists certainly did, with their familiar talk about evil spirits and offer of talismanic salvation to all who accepted the blood of the Lamb. Wesley, who believed in ghosts and wrote a book on popular medicine which mixed sound common sense with the magical remedies of the wise women, was able to communicate with people for whom the dry homilies of the orthodox pulpit had little meaning. He often spoke of himself as 'A Brand Plucked from the Burning' – a reference to his escape as a child from a fire at the Epworth rectory, but also an echo of the title of a Camisard book written by Samuel Keimer in 1707. The hysterical prophesyings of the Camisards were not unlike those witnessed at revival meetings addressed by Wesley, Whitefield and their preachers. Keimer described one scene, extreme even by Camisard standards, in which Dorothy Harling, 'she that called herself the Permanent Spring . . . would lift up her clothes before a company of men and women believers, crying out, "Come in Christ, come in"'.[3] Whatever his different meaning, this language is not far from Charles Wesley's in a hymn written in 1739:

> Come, Holy Ghost, all-quick'ning fire,
> Come and in me delight to rest,
> Drawn by the lure of strong desire,
> O come and consecrate my breast! ...

Years of familiarity have destroyed the sensual power of Charles Wesley's imagery, as erotic as any modern popular love song, just as the printed versions of John Wesley's highly erudite and theologically complex sermons now fail to convey the power of preachers to communicate in common language to the common man (and woman) the startling evangelical truth of spiritual equality with the rich and morally upright.

Furthermore, the new organisations of Methodism had most success in communities where the need was greatest. Wesley concentrated his preaching tours along a triangle from London to Bristol and Newcastle, all great ports with shifting populations. He had least success in London, where churches and chapels of all denominations were competing in close proximity. In Bristol his appeal was directed outside the commercial centre to the colliers of Kingswood. His message was heard most frequently among those whose lives were rootless or precarious: miners, sailors, fishermen, those uprooted from their communities by enclosure or the attraction of life in growing towns. In settled communities, whether dominated by the Established Church or by Old Dissent, there was least room for Methodism. In great, sprawling, industrialising Pennine parishes like Halifax, and in rapidly growing towns like Leeds, where the Church was thin on the ground, the early Methodist preachers found receptive audiences. 'Go not to those who need you, but to those who need you most' was Wesley's advice to his preachers.

Methodism also took root in another kind of environment. Most historians stress how Methodism grew to fill the gaps left by the Established Church, its success being an indictment of the poverty of spiritual provision by the Church of England. Yet, if Methodism in the eighteenth century is regarded primarily as a movement from within that Church, a different perspective emerges. Methodism was strong in parishes where Anglican evangelicals were active: in Venn's Huddersfield, for example, or – more surprisingly – William Richardson's York. The premier cathedral city of the north of England was hardly a place of spiritual destitution, with its Cathedral and 23 parish churches, and yet it was a stronghold of Wesleyan Methodism to such an extent that in 1837 total Methodist Sunday congregations amounted to 5,240 compared with 5,863 for the Church of England. The reason for this appears to have been the success of Evangelical clergy within the Church in stimulating a demand for services which was beyond their own resources to satisfy: that is, the institutional failure of the Church was underlined by its spiritual vitality. Methodism succeeded in such places as an auxiliary movement, much as Wesley had intended.

Nevertheless, in explaining the appeal of Methodism the case should not be exaggerated, for Methodism was not outstandingly popular in the eighteenth century. Though crowds were drawn to hear the preachers, as crowds might be drawn to a fairground entertainment or theatrical performance, few stayed or were allowed to stay as members of Wesley's spiritual élite. Among the 64 members expelled from the Newcastle society in 1743 were 17 for drunkenness and 29 for 'lightness and carelessness'; and among the 76 who left it were 14 (chiefly Dissenters) 'because otherwise their ministers would not give them the sacrament', nine 'because their husbands or wives were not willing they should stay in it', 12 'because their parents were not willing', five 'because their master and mistress would not let them come', one 'because she was afraid of falling into fits' and one 'because people were so rude in the street'. This is not a picture of a 'popular' society.[5] Though evangelical preachers liked to stress how 'miserable sinners' were eager to hear the message of salvation, there were doubtless many happy sinners who resented the message and its implications. In smaller communities Methodists were often seen as intruders, and were greeted with rough music and such rituals as daubing in mud, ducking in the village pond and being paraded round the bounds of the village before being expelled.

The authorities also had cause to object to the Methodists. Magistrates saw in the crowds they caused to assemble a threat to the peace. Clergymen found Methodist preachers rude, crude and intrusive. Worse still, they were 'enthusiastic'. This word of condemnation is best explained in Bishop Butler's famous rebuke to John Wesley: 'Sir, the pretending to extraordinary revelations and gifts of the Holy Ghost is a horrid thing, a very horrid thing'.[6] Enthusiasm denied authority and was subversive. It led to the antinomian heresy – the belief that those who are in the Holy Spirit are exempt from the moral law. Wesley was all too well aware of the dangers, and he deplored those who fell about in fits during his services. His great achievement was to discipline a movement which was potentially explosive, to control enthusiasm, to fight against antinomianism and to marry popular superstition with institutional religion.

Evangelicals, politics and reform

In 1906 the French historian, Elie Halévy, advanced the theory that a major difference between revolutionary France and stable Britain was evangelical religion – put crudely, Methodism saved Britain from revolution.[7] The idea that culture – in this case, religious belief – can affect political behaviour is an attractive one in theory, but hard to substantiate in individual cases. Methodist teaching was opposed to political radicalism, and encouraged an attitude of mind which shunned worldly rebelliousness; but its spiritual message could equally encourage a democratic levelling, even a sense of moral superiority over the rich.

The idea that Methodism could have made any significant impact on political attitudes has been challenged largely on the grounds that there were not enough Methodists around to make much difference. Far from preventing revolution, social unrest was greatest in those parts of the country in which Methodism was strongest. This is not to claim that Methodism caused unrest, but merely to observe that both would appear to have been prompted by common factors in areas of rapid social change and where there was least supervision from squire and parson. The connection between Methodism and unrest was given a new twist in 1963 by the historian and ex-Methodist Edward Thompson, when he argued that Methodism grew up in the wake of radical defeat and suppression – 'the great Methodist recruitment between 1790 and 1830 may be seen as the Chiliasm of despair'.[8] Whilst it is true that Methodist numbers grew irregularly, the chronological and geographical match between religious activity and political suppression is imperfect. Not only was Methodism weak in London, where radicalism knew many defeats, but the start of some of the great periodic revivals appears to precede, rather than succeed, political setbacks. Moreover, official Methodism (unlike Anglican Evangelicalism) was never chiliastic, and its leaders did their best to control the millenarian fringe which inevitably attached itself to the Connexion. Thompson's argument is at best only a partial explanation of the extraordinary fervour which preachers were able to whip up on occasions in the 1790s and early 1800s.

Methodism has also been credited with the transformation of the moral character of the people. William Howitt considered this view in 1838, and rejected it. As he pointed out, the character of the people was changed in High Church villages where no Methodist influences were permitted, as well as in Methodist strongholds. What Howitt did concede, though, was that

> In the manufacturing districts, where the Methodists have gained most influence, it is true enough that they have helped to expel an immense quantity of dog-fighting, cock-fighting, bull-baiting, badger-baiting, boxing, and such blackguard amusements.[9]

'Methodist' became a byword for a puritanical kill-joy, though many who used the term as one of abuse were intending to include also Evangelicals within the Church of England.

These Anglican Evangelicals included a highly organised pressure-group of well-placed laymen, known as 'the Clapham Sect' through their association with the parish of Clapham in London where John Venn was rector from 1792 to 1814. Members of the 'sect' included William Wilberforce, Granville Sharp, Zachary Macaulay, James Stephen, Charles Grant, John Shore and John Thornton of Clapham, patron of both Henry and John Venn and founder of the group. These men became famous for their strenuous efforts to end slavery and the slave trade in the British Empire, to open India up to Christian (that is, Anglican) influences, and to purge the realm of vice and inhumanity. Social historians have treated them with ambivalence. Their humanitarian campaign against the slave trade is generally praised; their Indian policy which led to the opening up of India to Anglicisation and Anglicanisation in 1813 is less popular in a post-colonial era. Their moral puritanism at home is frequently condemned. Yet all their policies were as one in their own minds: a single-minded desire to bring the whole world to true religion and right conduct. Least popular with recent historians has been their political position. Led by Wilberforce in Parliament, they were loyal supporters of William Pitt in the 1790s, and fervent anti-Jacobins. If they prevented revolution in Britain, it was less through their influence over the masses than through their encouragement of the firm policies adopted against reformers by the Pitt government.

The political position of the Methodists was less clear. Wesley himself was a Hanoverian Tory and a lover of order in all things. Politically, if not theologically, he was a quietist, and he urged his followers to concentrate on winning souls. The oppressed were assured the comforts of salvation in the next world and, though adherence to Methodism often brought improvements in this world also, it was no part of Wesley's theology to encourage social mobility or political aspirations among the poor. Nevertheless, seen from the point of view of those in authority, Methodism was a threat to stability. During the Revolutionary Wars Methodist itinerant preachers were hard to distinguish from radical rabble-rousers, and the leaders of the Connexion went out of their way to protest their loyalty to the government and House of Hanover for fear of legislation restricting itinerancy under the Toleration Act. They faced the choice of putting their own house in order or having it done for them, and they chose the former. All signs of excess were suppressed within their ranks. This led to their removal of Alexander Kilham from the Connexion in 1796, branded as a Paineite for criticising the leaders of Wesleyanism and defending the traditional rights of the freeborn Englishman. His followers formed the small New Connexion in 1797. More serious was the threat posed by Lorenzo Dow, a crazy Irish-American revivalist whose arrival in Liverpool in 1805 led to an upsurge of popular religion which put the Wesleyan leadership in a panic. In this state the Wesleyans failed to distinguish between excess and a revived zeal worthy of early ('primitive') Methodism. Expulsions followed, and Primitive Methodism came into being as a separate denomination in 1810. The nature of Methodism cannot, therefore, be neatly described with reference only to the official pronouncements of the leaders of the Wesleyan Conference, led by Jabez Bunting who was rapidly emerging as a leading voice in Connexional counsels during the first decade of the nineteenth century. If Methodists did learn from their leaders that true religion involved obedience to the secular powers, they did not always practise what was preached.

Church and State

'The Church as it now stands,' lamented Thomas Arnold in 1832, 'no human power can save.'[10] Despite the extent of the evangelical revival of the eighteenth century, its impact on the established Churches of England, Wales and Scotland had been patchy, and institutional reform and renewal had scarcely begun. The Church of England Pluralities Act of 1803 was a limited measure: of 10,558 livings in 1813, only 4,183 had their clergyman resident within the meaning of the Act, though this does not mean that all the other livings were spiritually destitute. The only traditional source for supplementing the pay of the clergy was Queen Anne's Bounty, funded by income from the ancient ecclesiastical taxes on First Fruits and Tenths, but the money available was never adequate to supply all needs. In 1810 3,998 livings were worth less than £150 a year; 1,061 of them were worth less than £50. There were gross disparities between the dioceses: the Bishop of Durham received £19,066 a year; Llandaff was paid £924. The Church was unpopular on account of tithes, Church rates and clerical magistrates. Much ground was being lost to the administratively more flexible Methodists. Welsh-speaking Calvinistic Methodists and Baptists had virtually captured Wales for the Nonconformists. In Scotland tensions between evangelicals and Moderates were mounting over the old issue of lay patronage, and matters seemed to be coming to a head when the evangelical leader, Thomas Chalmers, became Moderator in 1832. In the same year Parliament was reformed amid much talk of representation of the people. The State was already felt by some Anglicans to have betrayed the Church with the repeal of the Test and Corporation Acts in 1828 and Catholic Emancipation the following year. Tories and friends of the Church feared what a majority Whig government might do for its Dissenting and Catholic allies.

Reform of the Church of England

The State Church was seen as having a special claim on the State for assistance in its plight. Accordingly, from 1809 an additional £100,000 was given to Queen Anne's Bounty for the augmentation of poor livings, and in 1818 £1 million (with a further £500,000 in 1824) was granted for the building of new churches. Also in 1818 the law relating to the creation of new parishes was simplified. The Church of England at last began to catch up on the chapel-building efforts of Methodists and Nonconformists. In the 1820s 308 new churches were consecrated; in the 1830s, 600; and in the 1840s, 929. Far from threatening the Church, Whigs as well as Tories collaborated in the 1830s to reform its structure. An Ecclesiastical Commission was appointed in 1832, renewed by Peel in 1835 and then made permanent by Melbourne with the brief 'to consider the state of the Established Church'. There followed in 1836 the Established Church Act, which equalised the stipends of all but the most senior bishops at £4,000 and proposed to amalgamate the sees of Bristol with Gloucester, Sodor and Man with Carlisle, and St Asaph with Bangor, new sees being created at Manchester for Lancashire and Ripon for the West Riding. Though only the first of the amalgamations took place, the two new sees were created in 1836 and 1847 respectively. A more effective Pluralities Act followed in 1838, and cathedrals were reformed by the Ecclesiastical Duties and Revenues Act of 1840 which attacked sinecures and took some cathedral revenues to augment poor livings and fund new parishes. Added to this important legislation were further measures to remove major grievances against the Church, notably the Marriage Act and the Commutation of Tithes Act, both of which were carried in 1836. Though further reforms remained necessary, including the abolition of Church Rates (not achieved until 1868) and the appointment of more bishops (not secured until the re-introduction of suffragans in 1870), the structure of the Church of England was in far better shape to counter the challenges of population growth, urbanisation and Dissent in 1850 than it had been in 1800.

Not everyone agreed with the method of legislative reform, for in the process much autonomy was sacrificed and, whereas the measures introduced in England and Wales were moderate, the State's attitude towards the Established Church in Ireland appeared to many honest Churchmen to amount to no less than the promotion of rape and plunder. In the late summer of 1833 a group of Oxford academics led by the Vicar of St Mary's, John Henry Newman, gathered to discuss the need to safeguard the apostolic succession of bishops and the integrity of the spiritual Church. Tracts were issued, and the Oxford Movement was born.

This meant that in the early-Victorian period there were three parties contending for influence within the Church of England: the Evangelicals, whose lay leader in the generation after Wilberforce was Lord Ashley; the Latitudinarians or Broad Church, whose cause was advocated by Thomas Arnold at Rugby, his pupils and disciples; and the High Church party of John Keble, Edward Pusey and (until his conversion to Roman Catholicism in 1845) John Henry Newman. They were distinguished by their attitudes towards the Church, their theology and their politics. The Evangelicals were inclined to be Tory in politics and mistrustful of any party which appeared to countenance Roman Catholicism; they did not put great emphasis on the physical Church, and were sometimes prepared to co-operate with fellow-evangelicals among Dissenters to spread the Word of God. In theology they were liberal Calvinists, and in biblical scholarship inclined towards what is now known very loosely as 'fundamentalism' with a touch of millenarianism at the fringes. The Broad Church tended towards liberalism in politics and theology, and, as its name implies, hoped for organic reconciliation with Nonconformists to re-establish a National Church for England and Wales, even if this meant sacrificing traditional Anglican shibboleths. The High Church placed their emphasis on the authority of the visible Church, the sacraments and tradition. They saw the Church of England as the true representation of the Catholic Church in England – those who ceased to believe this were, in time, driven to recognise Rome as the one true Church – and they looked not to the Reformation but to the medieval Church for inspiration. They resented State interference in spiritual matters.

These divisions loom large in traditional ecclesiastical histories, but mean little to the social historian. Down in the parish they did not make much immediate difference; neither did the reforms of the 1830s. Change worked its way only slowly through the Church, as is shown in the Rural Dean's survey of the state of the parish churches in and around York in 1845. On the rural parishes he noted: 'Several of these have no resident curate & in some instances he lives at least three miles or more from the Parish Church . . . Many of the churches too are in an unsatisfactory state as to their proper keeping . . . Some check should be put to the pasturing of Church Yards with cattle.' Services were said as infrequently as in the eighteenth century, and many of the livings were very poor. Within the city, things were not a great deal better. At Holy Trinity, Goodramgate, 'The houses on the South side are occupied by poor people who have windows opening into the Church yard from which slops and broken pots are thrown.' The interior of the churches was usually unprepossessing: 'All the Pews are high and square & of course lined with dirty baize originally of a green colour'; 'the rest of the Church is filled with Pews, square, high & appropriated & as usual lined with dirty green baize' were typical comments. Pulpits were usually centrally placed at the head of the nave, for churches were preaching-houses, not places for the administration of sacraments. In only one church could the Rural Dean observe, 'The pulpit is well placed & not as usual impeding the view of the altar.' When he turned to the central parish of Holy Trinity, King's Court (population 685) he found the incumbent, Robert Inman, was resident on his rectory near Rotherham. From the £87 value of the living he paid a curate under £40, for which the latter said afternoon service weekly and administered Communion four times a year.[11] Inman held the cure from 1808 until 1866, but was never resident. His churchwardens were to grumble in their Visitation Return in 1849: 'The Minister is only Curate. The Rector has not preached in the parish above 20 yrs. Know nothing of Catechising the Youth. Sacrament four times in the year. Visits the sick when sent for.' Of the parish clerk they wrote, 'Old age & infirmities prevent a faithful discharge.' As to Psalmody, 'Know nothing of it.'[12]

If this is the other face of the early-Victorian Church in the age of reform, improvements were at least around the corner. In other parishes keen Evangelical clergy had been active for over a generation, with morning and afternoon services, plus an evening lecture on Sundays as well as monthly on Fridays before Communion. Where they were pluralists they appointed diligent curates of their own persuasion. This is how true reform spread, as the character of the clergy was changed. Whether Evangelicals or High Church 'Puseyites', the transformation of the Church of England was ultimately determined by the quality and devotion of its parochial clergy. Slowly their impact can be observed. The Rural Dean in 1845 called for two services in each church on a Sunday and (what would make this possible) a clergyman for every church. The double service alone had a remarkable effect in York, pushing Sunday congregations up from 5,863 in 1837 to 10,712 in 1851, which produced an increase in the

Church's 'market share' of churchgoing from 37.9 per cent to 48.2 per cent.[13]

This Anglican recovery was not unusual. Leeds was a Methodist town in 1837 when W. F. Hook became vicar. By 1859 he had transformed the situation, and it was the Methodists who were struggling. A High Churchman with a strong social conscience and dedication to the Anglican parochial ideal, Hook's achievement was one which few Leeds Anglicans would have dared predict in the 1830s. The same was happening across the country. Congregations were growing; the number of communicants and the frequency of communions were increasing; new churches were being built and old ones rebuilt; pews were giving way to benches; additional free seats were being created in place of the old appropriated pews; pulpits were being pushed aside to reveal altar tables – though in some High Churches medieval choir screens were then reappearing to conceal the mysteries of the east; curates were brought in to assist, not replace, incumbents; clergymen began wearing distinctive dress, the hard 'Roman' collar replacing the gentleman's white choker, and the pastoral office was becoming more professionalised. By the third quarter of the nineteenth century the Victorian Church was better-organised and more confident than at any time since the early eighteenth century. The call for disestablishment, which rang out from the councils of the Society for the Liberation of Religion from State Patronage and Control (1853), had ceased to be a serious threat by the 1870s, despite the fate of the minority Irish Church in 1869 and the continued vulnerability of the Welsh Church, which was to be disestablished in 1914.

The education question in England and Wales

One of the most important aspects of the revival of the Church of England, and also one of the most controversial issues in Church-State relations, was education. The major Anglican educational enterprise at the beginning of the nineteenth century was the SPCK, but its effectiveness depended on local support for charity schools. Where parochial life was moribund, the educational work of the Church had withered away. An attempt to remedy this situation was made by members of the SPCK who founded 'The National Society for Promoting the Education of the Poor in the Principles of the Established Church throughout England and Wales' in 1811. Some Anglicans, though, gave support to the British and Foreign Schools Society, which was a non-denominational, though largely Quaker and Congregationalist, society. In 1833 the State made a grant to the two societies of £20,000 for school building. Nonconformist, Methodist and Catholic schools received nothing. With its national system of funding through its dioceses and parishes, the National Society was far more effective than the British Society at raising money for school buildings, and so was able to earn 70 per cent of the annual grant between 1833 and 1838.

Then, in 1839, the advantageous position enjoyed by the National Society was challenged by a proposal from the Committee of the Privy Council on Education (secretary Dr James P. Kay, later Kay-Shuttleworth) to provide funds for other denominational schools, to set up non-denominational training colleges for teachers and to provide for the State inspection of Church schools. Tories and Anglicans protested at this secularisation of the educational work of the Church; Wesleyans wanted to accept the proposal to give money to their schools, but felt obliged to denounce it because they did not want money to go to Catholic schools; Nonconformists, led by Edward Baines, asserted the Voluntaryist principle that the State should not use public money to fund any denominational form of education. This unholy Tory–Anglican–Wesleyan–Voluntaryist alliance triumphed over the Whig government and Kay's proposals for increased State involvement. Inspection was introduced, but subject to Church control in Church schools; and the voluntary societies were to run their own training colleges, which meant that the Church of England maintained its upper hand. During the next decade the National Society secured 80 per cent of a rapidly increasing government grant, while diocesan committees set up training colleges and raised funds locally for schools. The British Society was subsequently weakened by the withdrawal of the Congregationalists, who no longer wished to be implicated in the receipt of State funding.

Though the Anglican diocesan societies maintained the local momentum of the later 1830s and 1840s with difficulty, the National Society spearheaded the Anglican revival across the country. Especially in villages, education was made synonymous with 'the principles of the Established Church'. The ideal Anglican parish, with its rebuilt Gothic church, resident incumbent and comfortable parsonage also had its neat school filled with happy children learning their catechisms and growing up safeguarded against the wiles of Dissent and the Devil. The Voluntaryist argument remained strong, though, and the limits of direct State support for the State Church were drawn in 1843, when the Conservative Home Secretary proposed to make Anglicanism the basis of an extended system of compulsory factory-schooling. Methodists, Catholics and Dissenters all opposed the proposal, which was withdrawn. Despite their victories in 1839 and 1843, the Wesleyans nevertheless knew that their educational effort could succeed only with public funding, so in 1847 they accepted public money, and the Catholics followed them a year later. Dissenting Voluntaryists held out, but by the 1850s they too had realised that the religious bodies could not, on their own, raise sufficient funds to provide all the elementary education needed to create schools for all. One proposal offered by radicals of the National Public Schools Association was for a locally controlled, publicly financed, national system of secular education, which a majority of Christians (and not only Anglicans) found unacceptable.

The compromise embodied in the Liberal government's Education Act of 1870 was to set up two parallel systems: one of state-funded denominational schools (of which the majority were Anglican) supported through voluntary donations and national taxation; and one of non-denominational public schools, to be set up where the level of denominational provision was inadequate. This meant that in many rural areas and small towns Anglican supremacy was confirmed, but that in the larger urban areas there was genuine choice, with local taxation being used to fund non-sectarian education. This compromise lasted until 1902, when the Conservative government put all elementary education, including denominational schools, under the authority of education committees of local borough and county councils, funded in part through local taxation. The cry went up of 'religion on the rates', but subsequent Liberal governments were unable to secure a majority in the House of Lords to repeal the 1902 Act. State support of denominational schools survived as the last vestige of that initial commitment of the State to support the educational work of its State Church.

The Disruption in the Church of Scotland

Despite the large number of secessions from the Church of Scotland in the eighteenth century, there was no exodus comparable with that of the Methodists in England or Wales. The majority of evangelicals stayed within the main body of the Church, and were still hoping for reform from the General Assembly in the 1830s. Against a background of political reform agitation (more significant in its implications for Scotland than England) the demand was raised for a restoration of congregational rights over the presentation of ministers. There was also need for reform to adapt the institutional structure of the Church to the changing social and demographic needs of the country. In 1798 the Assembly had authorized the creation of chapels-of-ease where parishes were inadequately provided for, but the status of such chapels had to be approved by the local presbytery, on which the chapels had no representation. Among the first chapels to be built were ones for those Gaelic-speaking Highlanders who had settled in Glasgow, and for the populations of new mining and industrial areas, such as the parish of New Monkland which had grown into the industrial town of Airdrie. Such places were fertile soil for evangelical mission, and the evangelicals therefore felt that they were being denied full representation by the non-parochial status of their new chapels. By 1833 only 42 chapels had been recognised by presbyteries, which is one reason why secessionist congregations were strong in the Glasgow area. In addition, a further 40 unendowed district churches had been erected in the Highlands and Islands under an Act of 1824 which paralleled the English Act of the same year but without the same generosity of grant.

Had these mainly evangelical churches all had full parochial status the evangelicals would have been able to outvote the Moderates in the Assembly in 1832. When they did secure their majority in 1834 they proceeded, without reference to Parliament, to confer parochial rights on the chapels-of-ease.

This did not settle the matter, for the rapid industrialisation of Scotland in the 1820s and 1830s made the need for more and more churches increasingly urgent. In conflict with the secessionist/evangelical view that the central feature of mission was the congregation, the Church view was that the only basis for organisation was the endowed parish. In 1828 the Church made a concession when it formed a committee to raise private funds for church extension, but it continued to hope that the government would provide the majority of the funds for the State Church's work. This aid was not forthcoming, and when Thomas Chalmers joined the committee in 1833 he proceeded to demonstrate the ability of the Church to act alone: in seven years £306,000 was raised and 222 churches built. The power of congregations to reshape the Church outside the bounds of tradition had been conclusively demonstrated.

The issue which continued to attract most attention, though, remained the right of presentation, and in 1834 the Assembly carried a measure by 184 votes to 139 in favour of giving congregations a veto over the appointment of their ministers. In 1838 an excluded minister appealed against the Assembly to the secular Court of Session and won his case. The evangelical majority in the Assembly had now been denied by the State over both the funding of Church extension and the congregational veto. Passions were rising, as the Assembly confronted the Court of Session in case after case. On 24 May 1842 Chalmers moved in the Assembly the adoption of 'The Claim of Right', asserting the independence of the Church. The government dismissed the document, and the evangelicals met to plan the repudiation of the State by the Church. But before the Assembly could meet in May 1843 the evangelicals' majority had been whittled away by the defection of a 'middle party' and a legal decision which appeared to remove the rights of all ministers of former chapels-of-ease. Accordingly, when the Assembly met, the retiring Moderator accepted the inevitable and in 1843 led the evangelicals out of the Establishment. Of 1,203 ministers in the Church, 451 seceded to form the Free Church of Scotland. Within 10 years, with 850 congregations and 760 ministers, Scotland had a second National Church.

The consequences for Scotland were immense, for since the seventeenth century the General Assembly had been more the embodiment of Scotland than its Parliament. The union of Parliaments in 1707 had therefore never meant in Scotland what it meant in England. The Church of Scotland, allied through the Moderates to the gentry class and lawyers of Edinburgh, had remained the government of Scotland for all intents and purposes save foreign affairs. The universities, the law, education and poor-law provision were all matters for the Church. The division of the Church therefore meant a disruption of the whole fabric of the nation, forcing change in all aspects of social life, and weakening the ability of the Scots to withstand further encroachments on their culture by Anglicisers from the south. It represented not simply a theological split between evangelicals and Moderates, but also a social split between the old élite of gentry and lawyers and the newer commercial and industrial families who were upwardly socially mobile. The Disruption of the Church is therefore to be seen also as part of the wider reform movement which destroyed the national and local political power of the burgh corporations in 1832 and 1833.

There was also a geographical side to the Disruption. Despite their Covenanting style, the evangelicals were strongest not in the lowlands and borders, but in the Highlands and Islands, where they had led the missionary effort of the Church. Here the people were ready, if need be, to lead their ministers out of the Church. They were rejecting not simply gentry patronage of livings, but a whole social order, and the landlords in many parts tried to prevent the building of churches for the Free Church. In part the events of 1843 were a result of the social antagonism produced by the forcible removal of families in the Highland clearances, but they should also be seen as an indication of the success of evangelical missionary work among the people of the Highlands where the traditional Church of Scotland had been weakest.

The effect of the Disruption on the Established Church itself was less serious than the Free Church liked to think. The vacant livings were filled without great difficulty. The Established Church was still the National Church, and saw itself as such: its great problem was not the Free Church, but the indifference of large numbers of the people. Reforms demanded by the evangelicals were granted surprisingly quickly. In 1843 Parliament passed a Benefices Act similar to one which it had rejected in 1840, to permit a presbytery to refuse a patron's nominee under certain circumstances, and this was accepted by the Assembly in 1844. In the same year the Church was given the authority to create new parishes where an annual income of £120 could be provided, though no State funds were made available for endowment. With 200 chapels of ease it was calculated that £600,000 was needed for endowment. Where the Disruption weakened the Church was in its ability to raise money. Left with the national responsibility for the care of the poor, it had fewer resources for its work. Free Churches were erected in parishes in competition with parish churches, whilst elsewhere Church accommodation was lacking altogether. By 1854 only £130,000 had been raised and 30 new parishes endowed. The reforming legislation had come too late from a Parliament at Westminster that had not understood the urgency of the Scottish situation. Not until 1929 were the wounds of the Disruption sufficiently healed for the Church of Scotland to be again reunited. By this date the State had eliminated several sources of contention by taking over the schools of both Free and State Churches (1872), abolishing patronage rights (1878) and ending all parliamentary interference in the spiritual freedom of the Established Church (1921).

Dissent

Evangelical missions and the rise of denominationalism

One consequence of the revival in religion was a willingness on the part of evangelicals in all denominations to collaborate in the great work of spreading the Gospel. Interdenominational Sunday Schools were organised in many places, especially in the rapidly expanding industrial communities of late-eighteenth-century England, and adult schools were begun on the same basis in Wales by Thomas Charles of Bala in 1811. Organisations like the Sunday School Society (1785), the Sunday School Union (1812), the Religious Tract Society (1799), the British and Foreign Bible Society (1804) and the various Town and City Missions started in the 1830s, all expressed the willingness of like-minded Christians to work together irrespective of traditional divisions between Church and Dissent. Though social and political tensions led to the withdrawal of some Anglicans from community Sunday Schools in the 1790s and early 1800s, other forms of evangelical co-operation survived and multiplied, encouraged by a common interest in evangelism and, in the case of the Evangelical Alliance (1846), anti-Catholicism.

At the same time the needs of mission led to a growth in denominational particularism, with increasing organisation and cohesion among even the most independent of sects. The Baptists formed the first of their County Associations in Northamptonshire in 1764, and in 1797 a society was started in London 'for the Encouragement and Support of Itinerant and Village Preaching' (later, the Baptist Home Mission Society). The Independents created their first County Associations in the 1790s, followed by a Home Missionary Society in 1819 to assist where County Associations were weak or not yet formed. Even more important in bringing scattered congregations together was denominational support for missions overseas. In 1792 the Northampton Association set up the Particular Baptist Society for Propagating the Gospel among the Heathen and sent William Carey out to India. The experience of working in this society led to the formation of the General Union of Baptist Ministers and Churches in 1813, a loose grouping of Baptists of all kinds 'to furnish a stimulus for a zealous co-operation in our own denomination, and especially to encourage and support our missions'.[14] A letter home from William Carey in 1795 prompted a group of Independent ministers in

London to start a non-denominational missionary society, known from 1818 as the London Missionary Society. Though it remained nominally without denominational affiliation, the London Missionary Society was, in fact, an Independent (that is, Congregationalist) society. When the General Congregational Union was formed in 1831 to bring together the various County Associations, the third reason given for its formation was that 'the intercourse already so widely promoted by means of the London Missionary Society and other kindred institutions has produced a general acquaintance and mutual confidence between many of the churches and ministers in our Denomination'.[15] The Wesleyans had been engaged in missionary activity overseas since 1786, but they too set up a Missionary Society in 1813 on the grounds that each denomination should have its own fund. And within the Established Church, the Clapham Sect in 1799 started what was to become the Church Missionary Society. In this way, the missionary societies helped define their respective denominations and parties within the Church and gave them greater coherence.

Protestant Dissent in England and Wales

Despite their organisational differences, the various Protestant denominations in the nineteenth century had many similarities: all were affected by the evangelical revival, and all three of the major groupings (Baptist, Congregational and Methodist) experienced similar growth patterns. All experienced divisions and difficulties between traditionalists and modernisers as they evolved during the course of the nineteenth century from a sectarian 'chapel' outlook to a position in which they could regard themselves as Churches equal and outwardly similar to the Established Church. Among the common reasons for this development were the gradual removal of legal disabilities (not finally accomplished until 1880), and the growth in the size, wealth and social respectability of their congregations.

After their harrowing experience in the 1790s, the Unitarians recovered under a new generation of leaders and were free to develop as a denomination following the amendment of the Toleration Act in 1813. In that year the Scottish Unitarian Association was created, followed by the British and Foreign Unitarian Association in 1825. The new spirit of Unitarianism was expressed at a meeting of the Association at Cross Street Chapel, Manchester, in 1830, when the decision was taken to begin Domestic Missions in Britain. The first two Domestic Missionaries for the Manchester Domestic Mission, founded in 1833, belonged to a sect of Methodist Unitarians, the followers of Joseph Cooke who had been expelled by the Wesleyan Conference in 1806 for preaching against the excessively subjective and emotional nature of the Methodist conversion experience. Further dissident Methodism was injected in the early 1840s after Joseph Barker and his followers had left the New Connexion in 1841. They made strange company for old-fashioned Unitarians who adhered to Priestley's scriptural rationalism. The latter also found themselves challenged by a more romantic school of Unitarian thought associated with the names of W. E. Channing in America and James Martineau in England, and the Unitarians were among the first to take up Gothic 'church' architecture for their chapels in the 1840s.

The Religious Society of Friends (the 'Quakers') had much in common with the Unitarians, including an undogmatic theology and numerical weakness. They too had their evangelical side, resembling the Moravians with their emphasis on Quietism – waiting on the Spirit – and the Wesleyans with their strict society discipline, and they influenced the development of new religious bodies as different as the Shakers, Primitive Methodists and Plymouth Brethren. During the early nineteenth century evangelical Friends emerged as a strong force in many Meetings, urging the Bible rather than the 'Inner Light' as their source of authority, and diluting some of the stricter Quaker conventions. One of their leaders, the rich banker, Joseph John Gurney, who ministered to the Norwich Meeting from 1818 to 1847, had close connections with local Anglican Evangelicals. Where the new attitude did not prevail, Friends were often lost to other denominations. In Kendal the Meeting was wrecked when the evangelicals split away to form an early congregation of the Brethren in 1836.

Both the Unitarians and the Friends constituted a social élite among Dissenters. Though their Domestic Missions enabled the Unitarians to reach out to groups of working men and women, their main appeal was to a prospering middle class of merchants and manufacturers. Their influence was out of all proportion to their numbers as they provided civic leadership through Literary and Philosophical Societies and as members of reformed corporations after 1835 in towns such as Manchester, Birmingham and Liverpool. The Friends, similarly, with their close family networks and powerful social sanctions against bankruptcy, provided more than their share of entrepreneurs for the early industrial revolution, as well as country bankers whose firms are now household names; and as advocates of temperance, they included in their numbers several celebrated brewing families when beer was a temperance drink and, later, an unusual number of tea and cocoa dealers. Like the Unitarians, their influence was considerable, especially in the campaigns to reform prison conditions and against slavery.

At the time of the Religious Census on 30 March 1851, both Unitarians and Friends were in numerical decline, and in this respect were quite different from the rest of Dissent, which was expanding rapidly. Information about the Unitarians is scanty, but it is a measure of their weakness that no more than 40 per cent of their churches ever bothered to join the Unitarian Association, which was disbanded in 1867. On

Census Sunday there were 229 congregations which called themselves Unitarian, with 50,061 attendances. Geographically, they were strongest in the North (Lancashire, Cheshire and the West Riding had 38.4 per cent of all Unitarian attendances), in the South-West and along the south coast (Somerset, Devon, Dorset, Hampshire and Sussex – 17.5 per cent), and the West Midlands (Worcestershire and Warwickshire – 12 per cent). The Friends, with their much tighter organisation of Meetings at local, district and national levels, have left a far clearer picture of their position. At the beginning of the nineteenth century they numbered around 19,800; in 1864 they reached a low point of only 13,755. In 1851 there were 371 places of worship in England and Wales, with a total attendance of 22,478. The Friends were traditionally strong in the North (Westmorland, Lancashire and Yorkshire), East Anglia (especially Norwich), the South-West (especially Bristol) and London.

The immediate reason for this decline among the Friends, apart from dissension between traditional and evangelical parties, was their marriage rule, enshrined in the Marriage Act of 1836, which stated that both partners had to be Friends; to marry outside the sect meant disownment. This remained the rule until 1860, when it was amended to permit one or even both partners merely to be in sympathy with the Friends. This proved to be a turning-point in the history of the denomination. As John Stephenson Rowntree, an avid gatherer of demographic statistics in support of liberalisation, pointedly stated in *Quakerism Past and Present* (1859), ecclesiastical history did not record 'another instance of so deliberate an act of suicide on the part of a Church, as to persevere for a series of years in disowning from one-quarter to one-third of all its members who married'.[16] After the changing of the rule numbers began to increase gradually, and reached 19,942 in 1914. The Unitarians also experienced institutional growth in the later nineteenth century – to a peak of 378 ministers (not necessarily the same thing as congregations) in 1911 – but this was more by attracting other congregations dissatisfied with their own denominations than by direct proselytism.

Unlike the Unitarians and Quakers, the Independents and Baptists experienced the full impact of the evangelical revival in the late eighteenth and early nineteenth centuries. The number of Independents (or Congregationalists, as they were coming to be known) in England increased from 26,000 in 1790 to 35,000 in 1800, 128,000 in 1838, and stood at around 165,000 at the time of the religious census in 1851. Membership, though, was never a good measure of attendances at worship. On Census Sunday 1851, congregations at morning services alone amounted to over half a million, and total attendances for the day were 1,214,059 in 3,244 places of worship. The pattern of growth among both Particular and New Connexion General Baptists closely resembled that of the Congregationalists. In 1790 there were 17,000 Particular Baptists and 2,843 in the New Connexion. By 1851 these figures had risen to 122,000 and 18,277 respectively. According to the census in 1851 there were 2,789 Baptist congregations of various kinds in England and Wales, with total attendances of 930,190, rather fewer than the Congregationalists.

The Methodists were the largest religious grouping outside the Established Church and, despite divisions among themselves, they, like the Congregationalists and Baptists, grew rapidly in the half-century following Wesley's death in 1791. Membership of the original Wesleyan Connexion rose from 87,010 in 1801 to 135,863 in 1811, 188,668 in 1821, 232,883 in 1831 and 305,682 in 1841. The Methodist New Connexion (1797) was never so large, rising only from 4,815 in 1801 to 20,506 in 1841. The Primitive Methodists (1810), on the other hand, increased from 16,394 in 1821 to 75,967 in 1841. These two groups represented different forms of Methodist division. The first was a secession from the main Wesleyan body. It was followed by other groups, notably the Protestant Methodists of 1829 and the Arminian Methodists of 1833, who together made up the Wesleyan Methodist Association in 1836. The second was a revivalist body which recruited mainly from outside Wesleyan ranks, and was parallelled by William O'Bryan's Bible Christians (1819), whose main strength lay in the South-West. In 1841 there were 22,072 members of the Wesleyan Methodist Association and 11,353 Bible Christians.

The figures for Methodist membership at the time of the 1851 census are somewhat distorted by the fact that the Wesleyans were then in the middle of their largest secessionist controversy. The fundamental problem was one of the nature of authority and ministry within the Connexion. A growing storm against the High Wesleyanism of Jabez Bunting, who defended the tradition of centralism handed down by Wesley himself, broke in the later 1840s when the suspected authors of a series of anonymous Fly Sheets were expelled from the Connexion in 1849. Those local delegates who subsequently attended a Reform Conference in London were similarly drummed out of office in their local circuits. Between 1846 and 1856 Wesleyan numbers fell from 319,770 to 242,296, a loss of 77,474. During these years the New Connexion increased by fewer than 3,000, and the Primitives by under 19,000. Yet when the Reformers joined up with the Wesleyan Methodist Association in 1857 to form the United Methodist Free Churches, the membership of the latter was only about 34,000 larger than the Association alone had been in 1846. Taking these figures together, one can see that the effect of the controversy was a net loss to Methodism of some 20,000 members in the decade, whereas over three times that number had been gained in the 10 years before 1846; and all the time the population of the country was rising. Methodism had ground to a halt.

The 1851 figures show 11,007 Methodist places of worship, with total attendances of 2,416,353 in England and Wales. Of these, 60 per cent of

Table 6.1 Areas of Church of England weakness in 1851

	Index of Attendance less than 33%	and Percentage Share less than 50%
Durham	14.4	33.8
Northumberland	15.6	37.2
West Riding	18.1	34.2
Lancashire	18.8	42.6
Cornwall	19.2	27.2
East Riding	21.8	37.0
Stafford	22.5	46.1
Derby	23.7	40.8
Nottingham	24.0	41.4
Cheshire	24.3	46.5
North Riding	26.4	41.6
Lincoln	27.4	43.3

Source: B. I. Coleman, *The Church of England in the Mid-Nineteenth Century* (1980), p. 40.

the places of worship and 64 per cent of the attendances were in the Original Connexion, and 26 per cent of the places of worship and 21 per cent of the attendances were Primitive. In addition, there were 828 congregations of Calvinistic Methodists with 264,112 attendances (chiefly in Wales and the Welsh border counties) and 109 congregations in Lady Huntingdon's Connexion with 44,642 attenders (principally in the south-east of England, from Cambridgeshire to Sussex).

The areas of geographical strength for the principal denominations in 1851 show marked contrasts between the Established Church, New Dissent (Congregationalists and Baptists) and Methodists. The relative effectiveness of the churches is measured by the total attendances for each denomination, expressed as a percentage of the total population (the 'Index of Attendance' or IA) and the percentage share of total attendances taken by each denomination ('Percentage Share' or PS). In these terms the main areas of weakness for the Church of England were those shown in Table 6.1.

This table clearly shows that the Established Church was relatively weak in Cornwall and every county north of the Wash, except Cumberland and Westmorland, where the Church had a more than half share in a low overall attendance.

The Congregationalists and Baptists were also at their strongest in the southern part of England. Their areas of strength are given in Tables 6.2 and 6.3.

What is striking about these figures is the strongly regional nature of two older Dissenting denominations. Though the Congregationalists were represented in all parts of the country, their strength was concentrated in only two areas, East Anglia and the central south; the Baptists were even

Table 6.2 Areas of Congregationalist strength in 1851

	Index of Attendance more than 10% and Percentage Share more than 15%	
Essex	16.9	23.0
Suffolk	13.2	16.1
Dorset	11.7	15.1
Hampshire	10.4	15.4

Source: B. I. Coleman, *The Church of England in the Mid-Nineteenth Century* (1980), p. 40.

Table 6.3 Areas of Baptist strength in 1851

	Index of Attendance more than 10% and Percentage Share more than 15%	
Bedford	20.8	19.9
Huntingdon	20.6	21.9
Cambridge	17.3	20.5
Buckingham	16.1	18.4
Suffolk	12.4	15.1
Leicester	11.7	16.2
Gloucester	10.2	15.5

Source: B. I. Coleman, *The Church of England in the Mid-Nineteenth Century* (1980), p. 40.

more narrowly based, in the eastern counties and Gloucester, a reminder of the times in the seventeenth century when the West Country had been a Baptist stronghold.

By contrast, the distribution of Methodism was quite different, as Table 6.4 shows. With the exception of Cornwall (and the Isle of Wight, which does not show up in these county totals) Methodist strength lay across the North Midlands, from Cheshire to Nottinghamshire, in Yorkshire, and up the eastern side of England from Norfolk to Durham. This distribution shows Methodism to have been very much a religion of the gaps. Except for Norfolk, all the counties of greatest Methodist strength (Table 6.4) were counties of greatest Anglican weakness (Table 6.1); and except for Northumberland and Lancashire, all the counties of greatest Anglican weakness were counties of greatest Methodist strength. The main areas of influence for the Original Connexion were Cornwall, Lincoln and the West and North Ridings, and for the Primitives Norfolk and the East Riding. Just as Methodists had originally succeeded where the Church was relatively weak, so the Primitives had their greatest successes where other forms of Methodism were least strong. They were able to make an impact on Norfolk, despite the relative strength of the Church there, because it was not a strong Wesleyan or Dissenting county; but they failed to make

Table 6.4 Areas of Methodist strength in 1851

	Index of Attendance over 15%	and Percentage Share over 30%
Cornwall	43.8	64.5
Lincoln	29.5	46.5
North Riding	28.8	45.4
East Riding	27.8	47.3
Derby	23.9	40.9
West Riding	22.3	42.3
Norfolk	20.5	31.3
Durham	19.6	46.0
Nottingham	19.1	33.0
Stafford	18.1	37.0
Cheshire	17.5	33.4

Source: B. I. Coleman, *The Church of England in the Mid-Nineteenth Century* (1980), p. 40.

much impression on Suffolk and Essex, where Dissent was already strong, and they were unable to make any showing in Devon, which was Bible Christian territory. Yet the point should be emphasised that the Established Church, with 14,077 places of worship in 1851 and attendances of 5,292,551, was the only denomination to aspire to national coverage in any meaningful sense, even though it came second to the combined forces of Methodism in Derby, Durham, Lincoln and the three Ridings of Yorkshire, and second to the Wesleyans alone in Cornwall.

The situation was rather different in Wales, where the Established Church had lost a great deal of ground since the eighteenth century and was ceasing to have any realistic claim to be regarded as the National Church. By the middle of the nineteenth century there were 52,600 Calvinistic Methodists, 30,000 Particular Baptists (compared with 9,000 in 1798), 60,000 Independents (15,000 in 1800) and about 18,000 Wesleyans, many of whom belonged to Welsh-speaking congregations. The Religious Census recorded 246,000 Calvinist Methodist attendances,

Table 6.5 Index of Attendance and Percentage Share of the major denominations in Wales in 1851

	Anglican IA/PS	Methodist IA/PS	Independent IA/PS	Baptist IA/PS
Monmouth	16.4/22.4	21.5/29.3	11.2/15.3	20.4/27.9
S. Wales	15.6/18.3	23.9/28.7	23.7/28.5	17.7/21.3
N. Wales	15.1/17.4	48.9/56.4	13.8/15.9	7.4/8.5

Source: B. I. Coleman, *The Church of England in the Mid-Nineteenth Century* (1980), p. 40.

197,710 Congregationalist, 135,717 Baptist and 96,450 Methodist attendances, compared with only 155,066 for the Anglicans. Nowhere in England, not even in Cornwall, did the Established Church perform so badly as it did in Wales.

The number of Dissenters continued to grow in the second half of the nineteenth century, and at first sight the results are impressive. After the traumas of the early 1850s the various sections of Methodism resumed a pattern of intermittent but overall growth, numbers almost doubling between the low point of 1856 and the high point of 1906, when there were over 800,000 Methodists in England. The Congregationalist reached a peak of 291,102 in 1908; and the Baptists 267,737 in 1907. Increasing numbers, though, did not mean an increasing strength relative to the population as a whole.

Table 6.6 Nonconformist membership/total adult population, 1801–1914 (%)

	1801	**peak (year)**	**1914**
Methodists	1.60	4.50 (1841)	3.20
Congregationalists	0.65	1.56 (1863)	1.21
Baptists	0.45	1.31 (1880)	1.11

Source: A. D. Gilbert, *Religion and Society in Industrial England* (1976), pp. 32, 37.

The illusion of growth coincided with a period of prosperity and chapel-building, during which time many of the rugged characteristics of Dissent were exchanged for a more comfortable existence. This was apparent in three areas: church-building, theology and attitudes towards 'the world'.

Gothic chapels were erected, with spires, chancels, altars, side-pulpits and stained glass, instead of the old-fashioned square preaching-box chapels. The Unitarians had set the trend in the 1840s with chapels like Mill Hill in Leeds (1848), and the others followed suit in the next few years. Congregational Gothic was well-established by the 1870s, when it was used for the City Temple, opened in London in 1874 at a cost of £80,000. Albion Congregational Church in Ashton-under-Lyne cost £50,000 in 1896, with windows designed by William Morris and Edward Burne-Jones. These were comfortable buildings for comfortable people.

Doctrine also became more comfortable. For some Unitarian congregations James Martineau's abandonment of the old rationalist theology meant a slow slide into 'free Christianity' and theism – a doctrineless doctrine based on the principles of humanity. With rather less cause for alarm, orthodox Calvinists in their Baptist and Congregational churches feared this was where they also were being led. The great period of expansion in the first half of the nineteenth century had seen evangelical Calvinism dominate the pulpit. Towards the end of the nineteenth century such views were challenged. The extremities of Calvinist tolerance were tested by R. J. Campbell, who proclaimed from the City Temple pulpit the humanity of the Gospel. His book, *The New Theology*, published in 1907, caused such a storm that Campbell had to withdraw it in 1911. He resigned in 1915 for ministry in the calmer waters of the Church of England. Even the strict Calvinism of the Baptists was so moderated during the later nineteenth century that in 1891 it was possible for the New Connexion led by Dr John Clifford to join with the Particulars to form a new Baptist Union embracing both Calvinist and Arminian traditions.

The price of liberalism, as always, was a certain amount of dissention. The key issue for the Baptists was the long-running question of whether the true and baptised Calvinist elect should admit others to their communion table. Among those who wished for a strict exclusion of outsiders were the followers of William Gadsby, minister at Back Lane Chapel, Manchester from 1805 to 1844. As Particular Baptists lost their strictness, these Gadsbyites or Strict Baptists came together to defend their sectarian cause. They were always a small group, a few thousand strong, organised in county associations but with no national union. They were not able even to win the support of one of the most powerful of late-nineteenth-century Baptist preachers, Charles Spurgeon, who shared much of their conservatism and left the Baptist Union in 1888 over the new theological liberalism, but never wavered in his support for the principle of open communion. Few followed Spurgeon out of the Union. The future lay with Clifford, liberalism, the social gospel and the Free Church movement which he helped lead in the 1890s.

The 'social gospel' was, for many conservative evangelicals, a poor substitute for the message of individual salvation. Whereas they had always worked unstintingly for social reform, they had also believed that sin was personal and that the redemption of society would be achieved only by the redemption of all sinners. The new teaching was corporate, and matched the growing importance of the State in social affairs. Perhaps for this reason the State Church was more receptive to it than Nonconformists, with their suspicion of the State and all its works. The theology of Christian Socialism was largely the work of Frederick Denison Maurice (whose father had been a Unitarian). His ideas were taken up between 1848 and 1854 by Charles Kingsley and J. M. Ludlow; they passed into the co-operative movement through E. V. Neale, and into the Broad Church through Thomas Hughes and other pupils of Arnold at Rugby. More importantly, they were picked up again in the 1880s by the High Church, most vocally by Stewart Headlam and the Guild of St Matthew in Bethnal Green, and most influentially by Henry Scott Holland and the Christian Social Union.

The 'social gospel' was discovered in London in the 1880s in the debates about poverty which affected all the churches. In their different ways the

Settlements, the Salvation Army and the 'Forward Movement' in Methodism were all expressions of the new mood (see below, pages 336–7). So too was the changing attitude towards leisure and worldly enjoyment. It was but a small step from being 'in the world' to being 'of the world'.

Nonconformity became much more political in these years, led by men like John Clifford of the Baptists and Hugh Price Hughes of the Wesleyans. Before 1870 the mixture of religion with politics had meant the evil of an Established Church. By the later nineteenth century the Nonconformists had gained sufficiently in confidence and numbers to think of themselves as an alternative establishment, with the political power to shape national policies. The Liberal Party was their natural vehicle for self-expression, and they sought to influence it on such matters as drink, personal morality, peace and – above all – education. Not everyone welcomed this politicisation of Dissent – the 'Nonconformist Conscience', as it was called. Wesleyans in particular were reluctant to identify themselves wholly with it, especially after 1885, when, for both social and anti-Catholic reasons, many of them passed into the Liberal Unionist camp – though Hugh Price Hughes worked hard to associate the more radical wing of Wesleyanism with Liberalism and the Free Churches. The Liberal electoral victory of 1906, coming in the wake of the religious revival which swept through South Wales in 1905, appeared to many Nonconformists like a victory for their own cause. They were probably mistaken, but in any case it was to prove a hollow victory for both Liberals and Nonconformists. Lloyd George was still to play the Nonconformist card when it suited him, but all this was a far cry from the days when Dissent and Methodism had been claiming the allegiance of an increasing proportion of the population. Though they scarcely knew it, the great days of Nonconformity were over.

Scottish Dissent

The Presbyterian Church had lost small groups of Dissenters from time to time throughout the eighteenth century. With the exception of the Relief Church of 1761, most of these had been consolidated in the United Secession Church of 1820, which in 1839 had 431 congregations. The Relief Church joined in 1847 to form the United Presbyterian Church with 518 congregations. Though other, smaller secessionist churches continued in independence, Scottish Presbyterianism was in effect divided into three main parties: the Established Church, the Free Church and the United Presbyterians. The 1851 Religious Census showed what every Scotsman already knew: the National Church was no longer the Church of the Nation.

No other denomination had more than 25,000 attendances. Even allowing for some exaggeration in the Free Church returns, this was a remarkable achievement by a Church which was less than 10 years old.

Table 6.7 Major Scottish denominations in 1851

	Attendances	Churches
Established Church	566,409	1,183
Free Church	555,702	889
United Presbyterians	336,412	465
Roman Catholics	79,723	117
Congregationalists	68,531	192
Episcopalians	43,904	134

Source: Parliamentary Papers, 59 (1854), *Religious Census of Worship: Scotland.*

The Presbyterian Churches were affected in the later nineteenth century by the same problems of liberalisation which concerned Calvinists south of the border, but there was also the added problem of attitudes towards the Establishment. Discussions on a merger between the Free Church and United Presbyterians broke down on this point in 1873. The United Presbyterians were 'free churchmen' in the English sense of Voluntaryists; the Free Church was not. The latter was also more theologically conservative than the former, and this proved to be the next stumbling-block when negotiations were resumed in the 1890s. When union was agreed in 1900 the hard core of strict Calvinists who had been the principal supporters of the Disruption in the Highlands in 1843 maintained their independence and the title of Free Church. The United Free Church of 1900 then rejoined the Established Church in 1929 after the last formalities implying monarchical rather than divine headship of the Church had been reformed.

During the course of the nineteenth century, the Presbyterian form of worship became somewhat less austere. Chanting was replaced by singing with musical accompaniment; hymns were introduced in addition to metrical psalms. The first hymn book was produced in 1792 by the Relief Church, the most liberal of the Presbyterian churches, and this was taken over and completely revised by the United Presbyterians in 1851, with many English hymns from sources as varied as Isaac Watts, the Wesleys and John Keble. Not till 1870, though, did the Established Church agree on *The Scottish Hymnal*, and the Free Church with its strongly conservative party held out until 1872. The Relief Church was also the most responsive to the laity's demand for church organs, but not until 1872 were the United Presbyterians persuaded to authorise their use. By the end of the decade pipe organs were becoming common in all three Presbyterian Churches. Hymn-singing was given a great stimulus in 1874, when Moody and Sankey brought American-style revivalism to Scotland and shook the staid ways of the older generation of Presbyterian elders and ministers. Only in the Highlands was the Free Church able to keep the modern world at bay.

This picture of slowly mellowing Calvinism is in stark contrast to the experience of Episcopalianism. The Episcopal Church was divided into two parts at the end of the eighteenth century. North of the Tay it had been a Jacobite High Church, proscribed until 1792. Here were preserved many of the features of Stuart Episcopacy, including the Scottish Communion rite. In Central Scotland and the Borders was the 'qualified' (under the Toleration Act) Episcopal Church, which used the English Book of Common Prayer and corresponded in theological outlook to the 'High and Dry' Anglican tradition. The two sections were reunited in 1804. As the balance of population moved during the nineteenth century from North to Central Scotland, so the old Non-Juring Church declined in relative importance and the former qualified church grew, reinvigorated by the Oxford Movement from England. In 1863 it was decided that the Scottish Rite would continue only where it was already in use. All new congregations would follow the Book of Common Prayer. Scotland's Episcopal Church became the safest home of Tractarianism in the British Isles.

Socially, the Episcopal Church was traditionally the church of the gentry and the sort of people who bought houses in the Edinburgh New Town. As it expanded in the nineteenth century it attracted wealthy and influential support among those who found the Established Church too cold and the other Presbyterian Churches too bleak, but for the mass of the people it remained a somewhat alien body. Queen Victoria disliked it as much as she hated the narrowness of the Free Church, and in this she probably represented the feeling of many of her subjects outside the Highlands. But one consequence of the High-Church nature of the Episcopal Church was the weakness of the Roman Catholic Church in Scotland. Its strength lay principally in the Clyde valley, among immigrants from Ireland. Scots Catholic priests from the Highlands who initially ministered to them viewed them with some alarm. Presbyterians felt rather more strongly. But when the Catholic hierarchy was restored to Scotland in 1878 (27 years later than in England) there was relatively little commotion. Honest Calvinists, accustomed to the Episcopal Church, were, perhaps, used to Papist ways.

Roman Catholicism

The Church of the English Catholic gentry was rudely shaken in the early nineteenth century by the hordes of poor Irish who streamed into Liverpool and other western seaports and then spread out along the main lines of communication through Lancashire and Cheshire, across to the North-East and down through Birmingham to London wherever employment in agriculture, construction work and general labouring was available. In 1851, when they were the smallest of the major denominations,

Table 6.8 Areas of Roman Catholic strength in 1851

	Index of Attendance over 2%	and Percentage Share over 5%
Lancashire	7.2	16.3
Durham	3.0	7.0
Cheshire	3.0	5.7
Warwick	2.8	5.8
Northumberland	2.7	6.3
Stafford	2.6	5.3
Surrey	2.2	5.2
Middlesex	2.1	5.7
Cumberland	2.1	5.6

Source: B. I. Coleman, *The Church of England in the Mid-Nineteenth Century* (1980), p. 40.

the Census recorded 570 places of worship and attendances of 383,630. In Lancashire, Durham and Northumberland they outnumbered both the Congregationalists and the Baptists.

The concentration of Catholic numbers in western Lancashire and neighbouring parts of Cheshire, and in parts of Durham and Northumberland, resulted from a combination of traditional Catholic support in the countryside on the estates of Catholic gentry, and Irish immigration into the towns. The latter soon overwhelmed the former, and by the late nineteenth century Cardinal Manning could estimate that over 80 per cent of the Catholics in England were Irish.

A second important development in the Catholic Church during the nineteenth century was the conversion of a number of Anglicans to the Catholic faith. This attracted widespread attention at the time, and yet the numbers involved were insignificant; nor were they the result of insidious proselytising, as Protestants often feared. The converts came for a variety of reasons: Kenelm Digby and Ambrose Phillipps, who became Catholics in the 1820s, were romantic medievalists; others, notably Newman and Manning, came through the Oxford Movement in the 1840s and 1850s. But there was no one type. Newman was very much an English Catholic, not uncritical of the Papacy, whereas Manning was more Roman than the Romans. Old English Catholics viewed these Anglican converts with suspicion as likely to provoke anti-Catholic feeling in the country. Both worried about the Irish, who might bring fleas into church.

Slowly a new Church was forged from these three disparate groups, though the distinctions never entirely disappeared. In 1850, when the Catholic hierarchy was restored to England amid anti-Catholic demonstrations, there were 587 churches in England and Wales and 168 priests; 20 years later there were 1,151 churches and 1,528 priests; by 1900 there were 1,529 churches and 2,812 priests, and the Catholic community is estimated to have been around 1.5 million compared with an estimated 700,000 in 1851 – a rather faster rate of growth than was experienced by the main branches of Protestant Dissent.

Church and people

The midwife of class

'Reluctant to be born, the new class society needed a midwife to help it into existence. It found one in the unexpected form of sectarian religion.'[17] This observation sums up the central place of religion in the formation of modern society. It also points to the central place of class in defining sectarian religion. But one must be cautious: matters of belief are not reducible to social forms. Nevertheless, it is true that certain denominational groupings appealed to some social classes more than others, and each of the denominations acquired a class image. The Established Church was identified with the upper classes, Nonconformity with the middle classes, and the more exclusive forms of sectarianism and irreligion with the working classes. Many qualifications need to be made to these generalisations, not least if the theory is to be extended from England to Wales and Scotland, but they remain not entirely without foundation.

The Established Church was the Church of the governing classes. Except for a few Catholics in England and Episcopalians in Scotland, few members of the upper classes dissociated themselves from a Church which was part of the legal and educational fabric of their country. Acceptance of the Church was implicit in acceptance of the social order, and the social order itself was constructed upon religious sanctions administered through the Established Church. This was a source both of strength and weakness. Within an unquestioned hierarchy the Church's position gave it a natural authority; but when that hierarchy came to be challenged, whether in the seventeenth or nineteenth centuries, the Church was often the most visible symbol to be attacked. Dissent was therefore both religious and political, and appealed to those social groups who felt themselves to be excluded from landed and aristocratic society by birth or lack of landed wealth. Dissenting congregations were likely to attract those with a certain amount of independence and a modest but comfortable income. This view is supported by occupational references scattered in baptismal and other chapel records, and in the impressionistic comments of contemporaries. A. D. Gilbert has analysed non-parochial registers for the period 1800–37 and concluded that Nonconformists (including Methodists) as a whole were under-represented at the very top and bottom of the social scale and among farmers, but were slightly over-represented among tradesmen, and considerably over-represented among artisans.[18] There were, of course, differences between the denominations. The Friends in York at the beginning of the nineteenth century were drawn most heavily from the tradesman class, whereas the Independents were almost all artisans. In Gilbert's analysis about 63 per cent of Wesleyans, Congregationalists and Baptists were skilled workers or artisans, but the Congregationalists and Baptists had slightly more appeal among tradesmen and farmers, and slightly less among labourers and miners. The Primitives had the most distinctive profile, with only 48 per cent artisans, fewer shopkeepers than any of the other groups, but more labourers and miners.

These are rough figures and refer only to the early nineteenth century, but impressions suggest that they give a fair guide over much longer period. Among the comments on the social composition of Dissent to be gleaned from Anglican Visitation Returns of the clergy for York are to be found 'The Upper Classes . . . belong to the Church but the majority of the Poor . . . who attend any place of worship are dissenters' (1865), 'the Tradespeople are principally Dissenters' (1871), 'nearly all the tradespeople go to chapel and do not support their parish church' (1900).[19] Another piece of evidence which can be used to suggest the social composition of congregations is the relative popularity of morning and evening services. Generally speaking, the higher the class of congregation, the higher the morning attendance compared with the evening, and vice versa. There were good reasons for this. Shopkeepers and tradesmen, as well as members of the working class, were up late on Saturday nights either serving or buying food and other goods, and preferred to stay in bed on Sunday mornings. Servants, and those families without servants, were kept at home preparing the Sunday dinner. Leisure time on a Sunday morning was the privilege of the employer class. If this rough rule is applied to the various denominations on Census Sunday 1851, the results confirm the picture suggested by Gilbert. The Church of England, Quakers and Unitarians were morning churches; the Congregationalists and Baptists were evenly divided; the Methodists were evening churches, the Primitives more so than the Wesleyans. The Catholics are a special case, for mass was said only in the mornings. What is striking, at least in York in 1851, is that the 'English'-gentry Catholic Church was overwhelmingly a morning church, while the 'Irish' slum-church had a majority of evening attendances.

These can only be generalisations. The actual social composition of individual denominations and Churches varied from county to county, town to town, and district to district within a town. The Wesleyans in Cornwall were far more 'popular' than in the West Riding; the Free Church in the Highlands of Scotland was quite different in composition and temperament to the Free Church in Edinburgh. As a general rule, in the countryside the Church appealed to the landowners, the Wesleyans to the farmers and the Primitives to the labourers, but the Wesleyans in a small village chapel might well be of a lower social class than the Primitives of a principal chapel in a strong urban centre like Hull or Sunderland. The social history of religion at this level of detail has to be a local history.

More important than nice distinctions of social class between different branches of Dissent is the social role of Dissent as a whole in relation to the Church. It was primarily a means of asserting independence, something much easier in the town than in the countryside, where social and economic pressures could demand conformity. Dissent also offered greater freedom and scope for initiative among laymen. The Nonconformists' chapel was a lay institution. In Congregational and Baptist churches, the congregation hired and fired the pastor; that is, the Deacons were in charge. To be a Deacon was far more prestigious than being a churchwarden, and carried far more power. It was an entrepreneurial position for a man of substance and business. Similarly among the Methodists, the system of itineracy, whereby ministers moved on every three years, coupled with the fact that one minister had several chapels under his care, meant that the laity were in fact the leaders of the church at the local level, as society stewards, local preachers and trustees. The latter, with their legal responsibility for chapel property, were the businessmen of Methodism, and many of the tensions within nineteenth-century Methodism (especially Wesleyanism) can be understood locally as conflict between prosperous trustees and the lesser leaders of congregations and Sunday Schools.

The tensions between hierarchy and independence came to a head in the 1790s against a background of revolution and fears of revolution. Dissent was identified with Radicalism. Methodists were suspected of being Jacobins. As political class hardened around the issue of reform, Church and chapel symbolised the deep division in society. Methodists found themselves drawn towards the chapel position despite protestations to the contrary from their leaders. As the new society began to take shape, different social and political forces clustered around different religious institutions. In Wales, Dissent gave the Welsh a religion of their own in their own language. In Scotland, the Disruption of 1843 was a religious counterpart of the reforms of 1832. In England, Municipal Corporation reform in 1835 was the corollary of the repeal of the Test and Corporation Acts in 1828. Political campaigning took on a religious guise. The Anti-Corn-Law League, despite all denials, was anti-landlord, anti-tithe and anti-State-Church, for the Church as a landlord and tithe-owner benefited from the protection of high corn prices. The League was organised along chapel lines, and pitched its appeal towards Dissent. Its leaders had been campaigners against Church Rates in the 1830s, and were to demand secular education in the 1850s. Chapel, middle class and Liberalism were moving in one orbit as clearly as Church, gentry and Conservatism were moving in another.

The Churches and the working classes

'I feel there is a dangerous want of sympathy at present between the better informed working class of the manufacturing districts and the clergy,' was how Sir Charles Lyell summed up the problem of the Established Church in his evidence to the Public Schools Commission in 1864.[20] Charles Kingsley, in *Politics for the People* (1848), knew why: 'We have used the Bible as if it was a mere special constable's handbook – an opium-dose for keeping beasts of burden patient while they were being overloaded – a mere book to keep the poor in order.'[21] Both men were making party points, and yet the evidence in support of their arguments is overwhelming. The Church – and, indeed, the chapel – as an institution did not command the confidence of the majority of working men in the industrial towns, where there was widespread hostility to organised religion.

The 1851 Religious Census was intended primarily to determine levels of Church accommodation, but, from the moment that Horace Mann began to process the returns, two other issues emerged as more important: the relative strengths of the various Churches, and the low level of attendance at worship. Since the questionnaires were not designed to elicit this information, the actual conclusions drawn must be suspect. Mann suggested that the number of attendances recorded could be turned into the number of attenders by assuming that those who went to church in the morning would make up half the afternoon congregations, and all but a third of the evening congregations would already have been to church earlier in the day. Even if the returns for attendances were completely reliable, this assumption was without foundation. Mann also had the problem of making allowance for those people who would have attended church if they had not been sick, at work, or otherwise prevented from attending, and again he made an arbitrary adjustment to allow for this. Finally he had the problem of the untypicality of Census Sunday. Clergymen complained as they filled in their Census forms that the Nonconformists had urged maximum attendances on 30 March to make a good showing in the returns. They also blamed the weather, and pointed out that 30 March was mid-Lent Sunday (Mothering Sunday) when the custom was for grown-up children to be away from home visiting parents. We do not know whether 30 March 1851 was typical or, even if it were, whether similarly sized congregations in other weeks contained the same or different people.

Bearing all this in mind, certain general statements can be made. Only about half the adult population went to church, Wales being better than Scotland which was better than England. Within England, only about half of those who went to church attended the Established Church; rather fewer in Scotland (about a third) and fewest (under one-fifth) in Wales. Of the rest, in England the Methodists made up just under half. In general, attendance was higher in the countryside than in the towns, and higher in small and slowly growing towns than in large and rapidly growing towns.

Horace Mann also had an interesting social observation to make:

> The middle classes have augmented rather than diminished that devotional sentiment and strictness of attention to religious services

> by which, for several centuries, they have so eminently been distinguished. With the upper classes, too, the subject of religion has obtained of late a marked degree of notice, and a regular church-attendance is now ranked among the recognised proprieties of life. It is to satisfy the wants of these two classes that the number of religious structures has of late years so increased. But while the labouring myriads of our country have been multiplying with our multiplied material prosperity, it cannot, it is feared, be stated that a corresponding increase has occurred in the attendance of this class in our religious edifices. More specially in cities and large towns it is observable how absolutely insignificant a portion of the congregations is composed of artizans. They fill, perhaps, in youth, our National, British, and Sunday Schools, and there receive the elements of a religious education; but, no sooner do they mingle in the active world of labour than, subjected to the constant action of opposing influences, they soon become as utter strangers to religious ordinances as the people of a heathen country.[22]

The first point to note here is that, however disappointing, the Census results came after two generations of religious revival and renewal. From what we know from Church-growth figures, the Census represents the beginning of a high plateau in Victorian religion, when not only the bulk of the middle classes but also many of the higher classes took church attendance seriously. It is not simply that believers among the lower classes had lost their faith when community patterns were disrupted on the move to unchurched towns; the weakness of the nineteenth-century Churches must be understood against a background of inadequate provision in the countryside, which meant that many people had little religious allegiance to shed.

The second point is the important distinction between children and adults. The main thrust of evangelism since the late eighteenth century had been towards children, through education. Education was about denominational rivalry, the great war against ignorance (of religion) and infidelity. Though many of these children as adults did not attend church or chapel, in March 1851 or at any other time, the fundamentals of a folk religion were laid which created a climate of opinion broadly sympathetic towards a version of the teachings of Christianity which might be compatible with a cynicism of, or even hostility to, the institutional Church. When Victorians lamented the irreligion of the lower classes they meant their lack of response to institutions of religion, and frequently confused the two.

Finally, the implications of Mann's attendance figures should not be ignored. If, as has been suggested (above, page 89), 81 per cent of adult males in 1851 belonged to the working classes, and if about half of all adults attended public worship in 1851, then even if all the upper 19 per cent of society were in church on Census Sunday, at least as many more from the working classes must also have been present. The paradox is that, although a majority of the working class seems not to have attended church, it is possible that a majority of those who attended church were of the working classes. The question is, as with discussions of working-class politics, who were the members of this broadly defined working class who attended church and chapel? The answer is probably the same as for politics, and for the same reason: the better-off members of the working class. As Thomas Frost recalled,

> the paucity of worshippers was not due either to unbelief or dissent, both of which indicate more exercise of intellect than is compatible with such a low material condition as then prevailed among the masses . . . whose minds were engrossed almost constantly with the one thought – how to get the next meal, to replace some worn-out garment, or to pay the rent.[23]

Towards the end of the nineteenth century, as the working-class proportion of the population declined and this upper stratum expanded into a lower-middle class, it is also likely that the churches became much more lower-middle-class in composition. Nevertheless, such definitions of class are often subjective. When Rowntree's observers were asked to comment on the social composition of congregations in York in 1901, they reported that 66 per cent of attendances were 'working' class and 34 per cent 'upper' class.[24]

Both Rowntree and the *Daily News* census of London worship (1902–3) also provide information on the gender division of congregations at the beginning of the twentieth century. In both York and London, women made up two-thirds of Anglican congregations (65 per cent in York, 66 per cent in London), a rather smaller proportion among Catholics (59 per cent and 61 per cent respectively), and the smallest of all among Nonconformists (51 per cent and 58 per cent respectively). These figures confirm the impression that the Nonconformists were rather more successful than the other churches in attracting men, even though, overall, women were more likely to attend church than men. Moreover, in York at least, men outnumbered women at Nonconformist morning services, suggesting that some women who attended chapel in the evenings were either domestic servants or had domestic duties of their own to attend to on Sunday mornings.[25] Partly for lack of data, the gender composition of congregations has so far attracted rather less discussion among historians than their class composition.

Following discussion at the Church Congress in 1881, newspapers across the country began to conduct their own censuses of religious worship, 30 years on from Mann's official attempt. They largely confirmed the picture in 1851, showing the relative weakness of the Established Churches, especially in Wales and Scotland, the large numbers of non-attenders and the problem of the towns.[26] But what the figures also showed was that, although the growth of the Churches relative to the population as a whole had ceased, at a time of increasing population the Churches were holding their own. From the 1880s a note of pessimism creeps into contemporary reports, as Church growth fell behind population growth. At the same time, discussion was renewed about the nature of poverty in the inner cities. The Churches redoubled their efforts to make some impact on the urban poor. For Anglicans this meant an intensification of parochial efforts, to which a new spirit was brought by ritualistic High Churchmen, whose dramatic visual appeal to the poor was inspired not only by theology but by the success of the Catholics with their own poor. The Churches also approached the poor through the Settlement movement (see above, page 204), and through other less conventional means.

One of the most striking new developments was the Salvation Army, founded by William and Catherine Booth in 1870 as a breakaway Methodist Connexion after William Booth had been refused leave by the New Connexion (of which he was a minister) to become a travelling evangelist in 1861. Military metaphors multiplied over the next few years, and the name Salvation Army dates from 1878. Booth's first mission was in a tent in the (closed) Quaker burial ground in Whitechapel: by 1868 this had multiplied to 13 preaching stations in London, and by 1881 he had 29 stations and 'congregations' of over 12,000. Army corps were also started in the provinces, the first in Coventry in 1878. From the start women had complete equality with men. With their music, rousing hymns and uniforms, they became a distinctive feature of street corners in poorer city areas. When greeted with derision and cat-calls, they turned to the brass band as a means of making themselves heard. Policemen were worried about the public peace and invoked the Town Police Act of 1847, but the Army persisted until eventually accepted by the authorities. As well as evangelism, Booth was also led to develop a social side to his work, and from the mid-1880s Salvation Army hostels and soup kitchens were set up in needy areas of the inner city. Many dignified Christians felt initially that the Booths were demeaning the Gospel, but their impact was undeniable. In 1880, the Wesleyan Conference asked William Booth to address them, and the Established Church paid him the compliment of imitation with the Church Army in 1882.

The official Wesleyan response to the problem of the cities came with the so-called 'Forward Movement'. This was begun in 1884, when Conference appointed committees to consider 'Old Chapels in Large Towns' and 'Spiritual Destitution in London'. The outcome was a policy to convert large inner-city chapels, the congregations of which had departed for the suburbs, into Mission Halls with social and evangelistic work outside the normal constraints of the circuit and itinerant systems. By 1909 there were 41 central missions in London and most large cities across the country. Their success seemed spectacular: 'The Forward Movement has saved London Methodism. A new world has been called into existence to redress the balance of the old,' is how one contemporary journalist put it.[27] Yet London remained a Methodist 'desert', and even in the provinces the Missions had little more than a local and temporary impact. The effort sustained by all the Churches to reach the poorer classes failed; and by the end of the nineteenth century the upper classes also were beginning to slip out of the regular churchgoing habit. After a century and more of growth, the Churches were about to experience progressive decline.

Working-class religion

This sense of pessimism, though, was partly generated by the class perspective of the leading organisers of religious activities in the nineteenth century. The idea that the working classes were 'infidels' or 'heathen' in need of 'missions' was a very middle-class one. The lack of working-class support for the institutional Church, though exaggerated, was a real enough problem – for the middle classes. But, in defining the working classes as a 'problem', they were lamenting the failure of the working classes to share their religious priorities and perspectives. 'Honest doubt' in the Victorian age was an affliction of the intellectual classes. The sense of religious decline after about 1880 was a reflection of the weakening of middle-class churchgoing. Not only were these institutionalised Christians prone to under-estimate the extent of working-class religion; they were also insensitive to the way in which those who rarely identified with or responded to the institutional Churches also had their own concept of true religion.

The nature of working-class religion was aptly summed up by the Manchester (Unitarian) Domestic Missionary in 1848:

> The bulk of the people in humble circumstances, do not attend any place of worship, or observe any religious forms, with the exception of those connected with baptisms, marriages and funerals. They appear, for the most part, to have lost all interest in the public celebration of divine worship. Most of those who do still value Christian privileges belong, I think, to the churches of England and Rome, and these probably will be found on inquiry to be the denominations which take most pains, in this town at least, to attract and attach them. Let me not, however, be supposed to say that the great mass of the working class have no religion. Many of them have a religious feeling, of a rude and peculiar character, dormant and uninfluential and peculiar in character, indeed, in ordinary circumstances, and little addicted to public, or perhaps, to any acts of habitual devotion, but which, nevertheless, restrains them from much evil, and awakens their hopes and fears in times of affliction.[28]

This was the essence of popular religious belief: a folk religion of the rites of passage; a basic non-institutionalised belief; Catholicism among the Irish poor; and a basic Church of England Protestantism among the rest, which could periodically be stirred up by Evangelical fervour into anti-Catholicism.

After 1836 civil marriage was available for the first time in England and Wales. Before that date all marriages (except among Quakers) had to take place according to the rites of the Church of England. Those who wished to avoid this had to go to Scotland, where marriage was an extremely informal civil affair. In 1844 out of every 1,000 marriages in England and Wales, 907 took place in the Church of England, 49 in Dissenting chapels, 17 in Roman Catholic chapels, 1 was Jewish and 26 were civil. In 1904 the respective figures were: 642 Church of England, 131 Dissenting, 41 Roman Catholic, 7 Jewish and 179 civil.[29] Not all Dissenting chapels were registered for marriages, and some Nonconformist groups took the Scottish view that marriage ought to be a civil ceremony, but there is no ambiguity in the continuing popularity of the Church of England, even at the end of the nineteenth century, as the 'proper' place for a wedding. The church building and the clergyman had a magical or mystical power not apparent in the civil registrar and his rather dingy office.

When Horace Mann attempted to describe the masses in 1851 he spoke of them as '*unconscious Secularists* – engrossed by the demands, the trials, or the pleasures of the passing hour.'[30] Secularism was, at the time that Mann was writing his report (in 1852–3) highly topical, having just been organised and named by its leader, George Jacob Holyoake, as a kind of working-class anti-sect, devoted to the proposition that, since mankind knows for certain of no other existence except the present one, morality and happiness must be founded in the here and now. But when Holyoake read Mann's words he rejected them with the implication that he could more truly have called the masses 'unconscious Christians'.[31] He was right. Working-class religion emphasised fate and good works, not salvation and justification through faith as was taught by the Evangelicals, but it was conceived within a religious framework: if not exactly St Paul's Epistle to the Romans, then at least the Sermon on the Mount. Popular Christianity meant good works, for without good works faith was mere hypocrisy. Most churchgoers were hypocrites; the poor who did not go to church were the real Christians, because they lived decently and helped their neighbours.

So far as the institutional Church was concerned, the Roman Catholics were the only denomination capable of reaching out to people at this level. Methodism had tried in the eighteenth century, but had largely given up the attempt to compromise with popular beliefs as it grew more self-consciously respectable. Yet even the Catholic Church was not entirely successful at maintaining its links with the Irish poor, despite common ties of culture and language between the priests and the people. In 1851 the

Irish community in England and Wales numbered about 700,000, but only 252,783 Roman Catholics are estimated to have worshipped on that day. In Liverpool the figure was 38,123 Catholics out of 83,813 Irish-born. From the earliest days of the mass Irish immigration into Britain, the priests had the problem of 'leakage' to contend with. Nevertheless, Catholic chapels were crowded with many people of a class which was noticeably absent from most Protestant churches.

The counterpart to this Irish Catholic presence was a variety of popular Protestantism which belied the so-called 'apathy' of the masses, and brought to England and Scotland some of the popular sectarianism of Ulster. Its leaders were men like Hugh McNeile of Liverpool, who stamped his personal brand of Irish Protestantism on the city during his ministry between 1834 and 1868; and Hugh Stowell of Manchester, a Manxman who became a curate in Salford in 1828 and so filled his church to overflowing that a new one had to be built for him in 1832, where he remained until his death in 1865. Both men were staunchly Protestant orators in the Ulster tradition, immensely popular, and as capable of calling out a mob against the Owenites in 1840 as against the Catholics over the Maynooth grant in 1845. The Stockport Riots of 1852, the Garibaldi Riots in Hyde Park in 1862 and the Murphy Riots in 1867 all bore witness to an intensity of popular Protestantism in Britain in the nineteenth century which in the later twentieth century thrives only in Ulster.

It is therefore not easy to categorise working-class religion, except to say that it certainly was not secular. How far it was Christian might be a matter for debate, depending upon whether one takes the view from the church door looking out on to 'the world' or the view from the world peering into the unfamiliar surroundings of 'the church'.

Decline and de-Christianisation

Institutional patterns in the twentieth century

In their statistical study, *Churches and Church-goers* (1977), Currie, Gilbert and Horsley have suggested two complementary models of church growth.[32] The first considers why people join Churches, and the second asks where Churches recruit members. According to the first model, people join religious organisations for at least three reasons: they desire to gain access to the supernatural; they experience social, aesthetic or intellectual pleasure in the means by which the supernatural is approached; and they feel satisfaction through being involved in the organisation of religion. However important the second and third reasons may be, for specifically religious growth to take place the first is essential: if interest in the fundamental object of religion begins to fail then rituals and Church organisation become mere hobbies, in competition with other activities which yield intellectual, cultural, emotional or social satisfactions.

The second model of growth suggests that Churches recruit from people with these aspirations from within the circle of their adherents and offspring, but for sustained Church growth to take place over a long period they need also to bring in people from a wider constituency. External recruitment depends upon the existence of a large body of sympathetic people who need or can be persuaded to need what religion has to offer, or whose needs have stimulated the religious organisations to supply such satisfactions as will draw the people in.

These conditions were met – to some extent at least – in the later eighteenth and early nineteenth centuries. The evangelicals responded to a need which was not being met, and offered a system of religion which promised spiritual equality, hope for the future if not the present, and a new formulation of popular religion, with its emphasis on supernatural interventionism. They also, more controversially, offered freedom from a guilt which they had first to awaken in their audiences. The chosen means, especially the emotional release involved in the conversion experience and the singing of hymns to familiar tunes, were attractive and less forbidding than formal liturgies. In their societies and other religious organisations, they provided a means of social satisfaction and identity. Society was sufficiently religious and accustomed to a broadly Christian culture for this kind of external recruitment to be possible, and the number of Church members and attenders grew accordingly.

In the later nineteenth century the major Churches ceased to recruit in this way, and their principal source of growth became internal. That is, the number of people with an outlook favourable to the Christian message was shrinking to those already within the Churches' sphere of influence, largely the offspring, families and friends of members. The Society of Friends before 1860 is an extreme example of deliberately restricted recruitment, and the result was a sharp decline in numbers. The major Churches continued to have a sufficiently wide penumbra of support in the later Victorian years for absolute growth to continue even if, relatively speaking, membership was falling behind the total rise in population. The great 'staged' revivals associated with American evangelists such as James Caughey in the 1840s, Moody and Sankey in the 1870s, Torrey and Alexander in the early 1900s or Billy Graham in the 1960s succeeded in bringing converts in from the fringes of the Churches rather than from completely outside. As one York incumbent observed when asked about the results of the Archbishop of York's special mission in 1888, 'I think the spiritual life of our communicants deepened but I did not observe any startling results.'[33] This was to be the pattern of internal growth in the twentieth century.

The initial response of the institutional Churches to intensifying denominational rivalries, the decline in external recruitment and the 'problem' of the unchurched masses was to broaden the front of their appeal by diversifying their product in an expanding consumer market. In other words, they expanded that provision of leisure-time activities examined above (page 262), with more services, more weekday meetings, more clubs, societies and activities. But this proved to be a short-term solution. The expansion of the institution proved costly. New buildings reaching out into new suburbs, with church halls attached, cost money, and soon the activities for which they were designed became necessary to raise funds to pay for them. As non-religious providers moved into the commercial provision of rival and more attractive forms of leisure, the institutional Churches were left with costly buildings they could no longer afford, and which were no longer appropriate for their original purpose as places for the worship of God.

Patterns of growth and decline among the Churches in the twentieth century have varied from denomination to denomination, but generally speaking the major Protestant Churches began to experience absolute decline shortly before the First World War. A possible effect of the war was to reverse this decline in the 1920s and to bring the Churches to their highest-ever level of membership – almost six million in 1927, compared with just over five million in 1900. Then began an accelerating decline to under five million in 1947, followed by a recovery to the mid-1950s, and then a prolonged period of further decline in the 1960s, which began to level off only in the later 1970s at around one million members/communicants in Scotland and a little over three million in England and Wales. The Catholics, on the other hand, continued to grow throughout much of the twentieth century, partly because the mechanisms for internal growth proved more successful in raising children – including the children of Catholic/Protestant parents – in the Catholic faith, and partly through sustained immigration from Ireland. Whereas there were around two million Catholics in Britain in 1900, and three million in 1940, there were four million in 1957 and approaching five and a half million in 1971. Attendance at mass, though, was less than half this figure and declining.

Like any secular organisation under threat, the reaction of the institutional Churches to this loss of numbers and decrease in attractiveness has been the amalgamation and consolidation of increasingly scarce resources. The ecumenical movement, which gathered pace in Britain from 1912, was based on sound theological reasoning, but support for it also has a social explanation. As the threat of institutional decline became clear, denominations which had multiplied by division in the nineteenth century started coming together again. The Baptist Union of 1891 was followed by a long-discussed amalgamation of Methodists from the New Connexion, Bible Christians and Free Churches in 1907 to form the United Methodist Church; this body in turn joined with the Primitives and Wesleyans in 1932 to reunite the principal sections of the once-fragmented Methodist movement. Even the Unitarians drew together once more in 1928 in the

General Assembly of Unitarian and Free Christian Churches. After the Second World War attempts were made to heal two of the great historic divisions within English Protestantism, between Anglicans and Methodists, and between Presbyterians and Congregationalists. Discussions between the former broke down in the 1960s, but looked like coming together again in the 1990s as the implications of severe demographic decline were appreciated. The Presbyterians and Congregationalists did achieve unity in 1972, as the United Reformed Church. Between 1975 and 1979 the membership of the United Reformed Church fell more sharply than that of any other denomination. Far from restoring Church growth, the union of Churches appeared to shake the institutional loyalties of members for whom little else remained, leaving an aging rump of believers to maintain the contracting structures.

Even so, institutional membership figures do not tell the whole story of contraction and decline. Whereas in the nineteenth century congregations might number two or three times the membership, in the twentieth century the reverse has become true. The penumbra of the Churches have so contracted by the 1990s that even part of the Churches' own membership in reality belongs only to the fringe. On the other hand, the decline of the Victorian institutional Church should not be dated from too early in the twentieth century. Despite the sense of failure which many Victorian clergymen felt in 1900, significant trends away from traditional patterns of religion have been a feature only of the later twentieth century. Before that, the devotional practice of some Church members changed and possibly intensified, despite the general decline. The numbers attending Anglican Easter Communions followed the general pattern of rise and fall but the figure of 1,899,000 in 1966 was higher than at any time in the nineteenth century.

Distinctions also need to be drawn between different Churches and various age groups. Those Protestant Churches which emphasised adult commitment in membership showed rather less decline than Protestant Churches with infant baptism, and the numbers of conversions and attendances actually rose again in the late 1970s among the Baptists. Though this was not sustained into the 1980s, in general the more theologically conservative and evangelical Churches and congregations declined less sharply than the more liberal Churches and congregations, while some minor sects and charismatic Churches even expanded. The most liberal Churches have suffered most, and their heaviest losses have been among the young. Whereas 46,000 children were baptised into the Methodist Church in 1961 and 24,000 youngsters came into full Church membership, in 1983 29,000 were baptised but only 9,000 came into membership. Between 1970 and 1995 membership of the Church of England electoral roll fell from 2.6 million to 1.7 million, and the Methodists, the largest body of Nonconformists, went down from 657,000 to 408,000. Even the Roman Catholics began to contract in the closing decades of the century, with numbers attending mass down from 2.7 million in 1970 to 2 million by 1995. Whereas, in 1970, 9.1 million people were members of the main Trinitarian Churches, this figure had been reduced to 6.4 million by 1996. In a survey conducted in 1979, 21 per cent of all children under 15 in England attended Church, and 23 per cent of the 45–64 age-group, but only 8 per cent of those aged between 15 and 19, and 14 per cent of those aged between 20 and 29.[34] By the 1980s the liberal Protestant Churches could look back on the 1960s as the decade of a missing generation. This boded ill for the future, as the reserves of support built up in the 1920s passed into old age and died.

Institutional decline of historic churches, though, should not be taken to imply wholesale religious decline – that would be to make the mistake of the nineteenth-century commentators. Even in 1995, participation in religious services remained the single most popular voluntary activity, with over a million people attending Church of England services alone each Sunday. Moreover, other varieties of religious experience – not all of them Christian – were springing up. Between 1970 and 1995 the number of Mormons doubled to approaching 200,000, and of Jehovah's Witnesses from 60,000 to over 100,000. Even more striking was the growth in immigrant religions. Like Catholicism and Judaism before them, Islam, Sikhism and Hinduism expanded rapidly as believers entered Britain bringing with them their own cultures and faiths. Between 1970 and 1995 the number of Muslims increased from an estimated 250,000 to over 600,000, half as many again as the number of Methodists. There were also perhaps as many as 400,000 Sikhs and 140,000 Hindus. All together the number of non-Christian believers in Britain rose from 540,000 in 1970 to 1.3 million in 1995.[35]

Such figures suggest that easy generalisations about secularisation cannot be made. As in the eighteenth century, the story at the end of the twentieth century might be one of shifting allegiances and decline among established religious forms, rather than the complete decay of religion as such. The appropriate question might be not was Britain a secular country in the later twentieth century but was it a Christian country?

De-Christianisation and secularisation

The most frequently offered explanation for this overall failure by the institutional Churches is secularisation, but this is to avoid the question. Secularisation is the process, not the cause of the process. 'Secularisation' is the shift across a range of human institutions, activities and beliefs from views rooted in the transcendental and supernatural to ones rooted in the present and the natural world. It is a process that has been going on throughout the entire period covered in this book, though the decline in orthodox forms of Christian religion has been a marked feature of British life for rather less than 100 years. What is new about the twentieth century is the increasing availability of non-religious options and an increasing willingness of people to choose them. Why this should be so is not clear. Social theorists used to associate secularisation with concepts such as 'urbanisation', 'modernisation' and 'industrialisation'. Particularly for nineteenth-century rationalists, progress towards the secular was linear and unstoppable. In fact, the history of religion in Britain challenges this view. The eighteenth century, when the word secularisation was first used in the sense of taking Church property out of Church hands, was in some respects more secular than the nineteenth, but the religious revival which Britain experienced between the mid-eighteenth and later-nineteenth centuries coincided with a period of rapid urbanisation and industrialisation. The most 'modern' western society at the end of the twentieth century – that of the United States of America – is also the most religious in terms of support for institutional Churches and avowal of religious beliefs. In the Islamic world, similarly, revivalism began in one of the most advanced states – Iran.

Historians are therefore no longer so willing as they once were to view religious change as a story of inevitable decline into the modern age. Nevertheless, whatever the reason, secularisation has been taking place alongside religious growth. On 21 March 1832 the nation was called to fast against the cholera; a generation later the more natural reaction was to pass public health legislation. Science was becoming the new providence, in place of divine intervention. The magic was departing out of ordinary life. Historians, geologists and anthropologists were bringing forward new theories which challenged the divine status of the Bible. Biblical criticism may not have produced such a great wave of unbelief as contemporaries feared, except where minds were already predisposed to doubt; but it did help undermine the supernatural status of the Book at the heart of Protestantism.

The Churches shared in this general process of secularisation even as they expanded. The Clapham sect had sought reform 'in the world'; their sons became reformers 'of the world'. Many aspects of life, such as education, the organisation of leisure, the sanctions of morality and indeed politics, in which religion had played a central part, were becoming increasingly secular during the course of the nineteenth century. Religion was being pushed to the margins of human experience even when it remained a central feature of weekly routine for many people. The paradox of religious history is that, in the nineteenth century, even atheism was religious, in that it existed in a religious context and took its questions (though not its answers) from traditional theology. Great Secularist leaders like G. J. Holyoake and Charles Bradlaugh were profoundly religious men, who knew and took their Bibles seriously. Their followers founded local societies which had every appearance of back-street Bethels. They declined at precisely the same moment as the Churches whose mirror image they were. In the twentieth century the reverse has been true. The Churches now exist in an increasingly secular environment, taking their colour from it. Religion in the traditional sense of the quest for the supernatural or transcendental seems to have little part in the activities of many Churches, especially in the liberal Protestant tradition, which appears preoccupied with secular social welfare schemes or mere institutional survival.

In Britain at least, therefore, at the end of the twentieth century, religion has come to hold a central place in the lives of fewer people than it did a hundred years ago, and this has led to a dwindling of that wider constituency of potential support from which external recruitment to the Churches might draw. As increasing numbers of people have – for whatever reason – ceased to believe in the supernatural, so their fundamental need for religious institutions has gone. Rituals persist because some people like them, and the Churches continue to serve certain secular functions, with limited appeal, in direct competition with other leisure-time activities. People may not be any the more or less 'religious' than they were, but they have more opportunities to appear less religious.

More significant than the decline of the institutions of religion in the later twentieth century has been the secularisation of British culture. The religious dimension to life seems strangely unfamiliar. The very terminology of Christianity is foreign to a generation not brought up in Sunday Schools. The language of the Prayer Book and the Bible, on which the foundations of the English literary tradition rest, have lost meaning and relevance. Even within the Churches, the attempt to explain the meaning and symbolism of sacred texts, hymns and liturgies has been abandoned in favour of simpler and less textually rich versions. As T. S. Eliot wrote in 1934:

> But it seems that something has happened that has never happened
> before: though we know not just when, or why, or how, or where.
> Men have left GOD not for other gods, they say, but for no god; and
> this has never happened before.[36]

Yet the case must not be overstated. The word 'de-Christianisation' is used to make an important distinction between the phenomenon of secularisation – the progressive elimination of transcendental, supernatural and mystical religion – and the process whereby the specifically Christian version of such a religion is in decline. The argument remains that the basic paganism of popular religion still survives in modern Britain. Though social institutions are largely secular, personal beliefs are not. Here there is a parallel with the eighteenth century, in which a Latitudinarian Church of England and a Moderate Church of Scotland were too 'civilised' or 'urbane' for the less rational religion of the people. Twentieth-century theology has emphasised the immanence of God, the Incarnation and the Kingdom in this world. The transcendental God, the God in a heaven above the clouds who sits like a kindly old gentleman working miracles for those who believe in him, has been pronounced dead. When this view was popularised by the then Bishop of Woolwich in his book, *Honest to God*, in March 1963, the result was astonishing.[37] At a time when the institutional Church was in severe decline, theology became a bestseller and was discussed in the popular press. The Bishop of Durham had the same effect in 1985 when he publicly uttered some of the commonplaces of theologians about the doctrine of the Resurrection of Christ. What was remarkable about these outcries in defence of traditional, miraculous and magical religion was not simply their volume, but the fact that they came from outside as well as inside the traditional Church, perhaps less from the latter than the former. People apparently did not wish to go to church, but they did not wish to be deprived of the old religion.

A survey of social attitudes in 1995 found that three-quarters of the population professed some sort of belief in the supernatural; three-fifths of people surveyed claimed a religious allegiance; and a third said they belonged to the Church of England.[38] This confirmed the findings of an earlier survey, conducted at the University of Leeds in 1980–3. Despite the fact that across West Yorkshire as a whole only 10 per cent of the population went to church as frequently as once a month, a random survey of nearly 2,000 people in Leeds found that 72 per cent of the sample believed in God; 56 per cent believed in fate or destiny; and 40 per cent believed in life after death. These popular beliefs could not be called Christianity as the orthodox would understand it, but yet they showed a strong survival of or instinct for belief in something beyond the institutional Church. This 'something' finds expression in various ways. The popularity of the horoscope, for example, is a manifestation of a widespread half-belief in fate. Closer to the Churches is the continued attraction of religious broadcasting for a people whose religious experience seems to be private and individualistic rather than public and communal. Hymn-singing is still one of the most popular forms of religious activity, with the BBC's Sunday-evening religious broadcasts, contrary to all predictions, retaining a strong if aging following.

All this suggests that four varieties of religion must be distinguished in modern Britain: first, traditional, institutional Christianity, which is in decline, though it remains the most popular form of voluntary activity; second, the institutionalised expression of other faiths, which is growing rapidly; third, residual Christianity which, though weakening among young people, is still a powerful but declining influence over beliefs and attitudes; and fourth, a broader paganism which can no longer be described as Christian and yet which is not secular either. As the third of these varieties is increasingly diluted and blends into the fourth, some within the institutions of religion have reacted in the classic sectarian manner, emphasising not points of liberal contact with 'the world', but points of difference from it. The success of the Pentecostalists and the Charismatic movement in establishing growth against the trend suggests that those tensions between established and evangelical religion which underlay the eighteenth-century crisis and revival are still present, though there is no reason to believe that history is about to be repeated. Since the evangelical revival of the eighteenth century the entire historical context of human material existence has changed. As T. S. Eliot put it:

> We toil for six days, on the seventh we must motor
> To Hindhead, or Maidenhead.
> If the weather is foul we stay at home and read the papers. [39]

This was written in 1934, two years after cinemas were opened on Sundays. In 1996 he might have added 'or go to the supermarket or to a football match, or watch television'. In the consumer society the Church has become a marketable product, and religious activities have suffered from secular competition.

Notes

1. James Woodforde, *Diary of a Country Parson*, passages selected and edited by John Beresford (Oxford, 1935; paperback edn., Oxford, 1978), p. 137: entry for 1 October 1777.
2. W. H. Reid, *The Rise and Dissolution of the Infidel Societies in this Metropolis* (1800), p. 91.
3. S. Keimer, *A Brand Pluck'd from the Burning* (1718), quoted in J. F. C. Harrison, *The Second Coming. Popular Millenarianism, 1780–1850* (1979), p. 234, n. 42.
4. Charles Wesley, *Hymns and Sacred Poems* (1739).
5. J. Wesley, *Journal*, 12 March 1743, quoted in S. Andrews, *Methodism and Society* (1970), pp. 104–5.
6. Quoted in H. Rack, *Reasonable Enthusiast: John Wesley and the Rise of Methodism* (1989), p. 209.
7. E. Halévy, 'La Naissance du Méthodisme en Angleterre', *Revue de Paris* (August 1906), pp. 519–39, 841–67, transl. by Bernard Semmel as *The Birth of Methodism in England* (Chicago, 1971).
8. E. P. Thompson, *The Making of the English Working Class* (1963; republished Harmondsworth, 1968), pp. 411–40.
9. W. Howitt, *The Rural Life of England* (1844), p. 415.
10. Quoted in S. C. Carpenter, *Church and People, 1789–1889* (1933), p. 62.
11. Borthwick Institute of Historical Research, York, RD.AIN.1, manuscript notebook.
12. Borthwick Institute of Historical Research, V1849/AE, Articles of Enquiry exhibited to the Churchwardens, Holy Trinity, King's Court, York, quoted in E. Royle, *The Victorian Church in York* (York, 1983), p. 9.
13. See E. Royle, *Nonconformity in Nineteenth-Century York* (York, 1985), p. 2.
14. Part of the third founding resolution, as given in E. A. Payne, *The Baptist Union: A Short History* (1958), p. 24.
15. Quoted in A. Peel, *These Hundred Years. A History of the Congregational Union of England and Wales, 1831–1931* (1931), p. 58.
16. J. S. Rowntree, *Quakerism Past and Present: being an Inquiry into the Causes of its Decline in Great Britain and Ireland* (1859), p. 156.

17. H. J. Perkin, *The Origins of Modern English Society* (1969), p. 196.
18. A. D. Gilbert, *Religion and Society in Industrial England* (1976), pp. 63, 67.
19. Borthwick Institute of Historical Research, V1865/Ret (St Olave), V1868/Ret (St Michael le Belfrey), Bp.V1900/Ret (St Margaret).
20. Quoted from *Report of the Public School Commission* (1864) iv, p. 376 in B. Simon, *Studies in the History of Education, 1780–1870* (1960), p. 306.
21. Quoted from *Politics for the People* (1848), p. 58 in T. Christensen, *Origin and History of Christian Socialism, 1848–1854* (Aarhus, 1962), p. 77.
22. H. Mann, *Religious Worship in England and Wales: Abridged from the Official Report* (1854), p. 93.
23. T. Frost, *Forty Years' Recollections* (1880), p. 225.
24. B. S. Rowntree, *Poverty: A Study of Town Life* (1902), pp. 347–8.
25. R. Mudie-Smith (ed.), *The Religious Life of London* (1904), p. 267; Rowntree, p. 346.
26. Most of the results of these newspapers censuses were republished in A. Mearns, *The Statistics of Attendance at Public Worship, 1881–2* (1882).
27. Jane T. Stoddart, 'The *Daily News* Census of 1902–3 Compared with the *British Weekly* Census of 1886', p. 293, in Mudie-Smith, pp. 280–93.
28. John Layhe, *14th Report of the Ministry to the Poor* (Manchester, 1848), pp. 25–6.
29. Calculated from the figures in R. Currie, A. Gilbert and L. Horsley, *Churches and Church-goers. Patterns of Church Growth in the British Isles since 1700* (Oxford, 1977), pp. 223–4.
30. H. Mann, *Religious Worship Report*, p. 93.
31. *Reasoner*, 16 (5) (9 April 1854), p. 252 and 17 (18) (29 October 1854), pp. 273–4.
32. Currie, Gilbert and Horsley, *Churches and Church-goers*, pp. 5–9, 116–23.
33. Borthwick Institute of Historical Research, Bp.V/Ret.2 (St Sampson, York).
34. Bible Society, *Prospect for the Eighties: From a Census of the Churches in 1979. Undertaken by the Nationwide Initiative in Evangelism* (1980), p. 13.
35. The figures here, taken from *Social Trends* (1997), p. 224 are for 'Church membership'. The actual communities were probably twice as large – see *Britain: An Official Handbook* (1997), p. 472–3.
36. T. S. Eliot, *Choruses from 'The Rock'* (1934), vii.
37. J. A. T. Robinson, *Honest to God* (1963).
38. *British Social Attitudes Survey* (1995), as summarised in *Social Trends* (1997), p. 224.
39. T. S. Eliot, *Choruses from 'The Rock'*, i.

7

Education

Education can be defined as 'that process whereby one generation consciously transmits its skills and values to the next'. In other words, it is a form of overt socialisation, manipulative and usually conservative. But there is a second definition which describes education as 'that process by which an individual strives to realise to the full his or her physical and mental potential'. Such education can be liberating – even revolutionary – and exists in tension with socially defined education. Throughout history it has scarcely been considered appropriate for the mass of the people, yet without an understanding of this individual motivation much of educational history will be meaningless. Education cannot be understood simply as an economic function of society, meeting utilitarian needs in a mechanical kind of way, for in all educational history there are two sides to be considered: the providers – teachers, philanthropists, churches and governments; and the recipients – children, families, communities and social classes.

Literacy

The measurement of literacy

The definition of literacy has changed over time to match rising expectations. For the early eighteenth century, it may be enough to suggest that basic literacy involved no more than the ability to read a simple passage of Scripture, but by the end of the century there was also some expectation of elementary writing skill – perhaps enough to be able to sign one's name. In the mid-nineteenth century the basic standard was to be able to read and understand a paragraph in a newspaper, though elementary writing ability was probably also assumed. In the twentieth century the expectation is that the literate person will be able to use the written word as a means of communication through the sending and receiving of simple written documents such as official forms and letters.

There are enormous problems with all these definitions. In Britain reading and writing (as opposed to penmanship) have traditionally been taught together, but they are in fact separate skills, and proficiency in one need not imply anything about the other. Levels of performance are also impossible to measure: how difficult should the level of comprehension be; can writing be divorced from composition (creative writing as opposed to copying)? There are no completely satisfactory solutions to these problems, and so one can write a history of literacy only by making certain assumptions upon which to base a statistical study of trends.

There are two main assumptions behind most studies of literacy in Britain since the mid-eighteenth century. The first is that the ability to sign one's name suggests an elementary reading capability and is a satisfactory indication of basic literacy; the second is that the volume of popular literature in circulation will reflect the size of the reading public and hence the extent of popular literacy.

The reasoning behind the first was spelt out by the Registrar General for Births, Marriages and Deaths in England, writing in 1861:

> If a man can write his own name, it may be presumed that he can read it when written by another; still more that he will recognise that and other familiar words when he sees them in print; and it is even probable that he will spell his way through a paragraph in the newspaper.[1]

This assumption is highly convenient for the historian, since signature-signing on legal documents provides a rich source of evidence. This is particularly true of England and Wales after Lord Hardwicke's Marriage Act tightened up the legal side of weddings south of Gretna Green in 1753. Henceforth, all marriage partners were required to sign the parochial register, or to make a witnessed mark if they were unable to sign. From 1754, therefore, the parochial registers of England and Wales are available to show what percentage of the male and female population who married in any given year were able to write their own names. Whatever the defects of the method, it is likely that the comparative accuracy of the information so gained will be useful even if the absolute levels have still be to be treated with great caution. With the coming of civil marriage and the central collection of data by the Registrar General (after 1836 in England and Wales and after 1855 in Scotland), national data are available and the comparative task is relatively simple.

The other principal method of measuring literacy – book circulation – is also best used comparatively rather than absolutely. There is no knowing whether books were read at all, and if so by how many people. Increasing numbers of publications could mean that the same number of people was reading more, or – in an age of rising population – that the same percentage of the population was reading proportionately the same. But if one looks at commercial literature requiring a very elementary level of reading ability – chapbooks, broadsheets and so on – it is likely that the publishers knew their market, and that it was expanding faster than the population as a whole. Taking the two approaches together, with other scraps of local evidence, an overall picture emerges of steadily increasing literacy. The value of the signature method is that it enables one to detect local variations in this national trend, which are extremely important in a consideration of the reasons behind changes in levels of basic literacy.

Levels of literacy and illiteracy

Studies of England, Scotland and France have all shown great regional variations in levels of literacy, suggesting that the causes of literacy lie not in national policies but in local cultural and economic circumstances. When the Registrar General produced his first summary of literacy statistics in 1839 he found the regional distribution was as given in Table 7.1. The high levels of literacy in London and the four northernmost counties of England illustrate the problems of explanation. The northern levels are very little different from those over the border in Scotland, despite formal differences in educational provision. Except for mining and economic development along the coasts of Durham and south Northumberland, the

Table 7.1 Literacy in England and Wales, 1839

Male (per cent)		Female (per cent)	
London	88.4	London	76.1
North	79.4	South-East	60.0
South-West	67.6	North	57.7
South-East	67.4	South-West	53.0
N. Midlands	67.2		
Yorkshire	66.4		
Average	*66.3*	*Average*	*50.5*
West	60.3	N. Midlands	49.9
North-West	58.3	E. Counties	48.3
S. Midlands	57.3	S. Midlands	47.3
E. Counties	54.9	West	46.4
Wales	51.8	Yorkshire	43.1
		North-West	35.8
		Wales	30.4

Source: G. R. Porter, *Progress of the Nation* (1851), p. 700.

area was thinly populated and largely pastoral. London, by contrast, was a rapidly growing, densely concentrated population centre. Yet, traditionally, both were areas of relatively high literacy, with Newcastle being a major provincial centre for the book trade. What is also striking is the relatively low level of male literacy in those heartlands of seventeenth-century Bible-reading puritanism, the South Midlands and Eastern Counties – lower than in any of the major industrialising regions of the country. There are also interesting contrasts between the sexes. The difference in levels of literacy between men and women are least in the southern part of England, and greatest in the northern industrialised counties, especially the North-West (Lancashire and Cheshire) and Yorkshire. Wales is a special case. Work on the similar case of Brittany suggests that where the language of the oral culture is different from that of the written culture, literacy is likely to be unusually low.[2]

A similar analysis can be applied to Scotland after 1855, showing literacy in the lowland rural counties to have been over 90 per cent for men and 80 per cent for women, with some of the Border counties recording almost universal literacy for both sexes. Levels were a little lower in the eastern industrial and semi-industrial counties, especially in Stirling and West Lothian. Literacy scores in the Highlands and Far North varied a great deal, from 99 per cent men and 95 per cent women in Orkney to only 64 per cent men and 53 per cent women in Inverness, the lowest score throughout Scotland. With the exception of the Gaelic Highlands, though, the worst region comprised the four western industrialised counties of Dunbarton, Renfrew, Ayr and Lanark, where the levels for men ranged from 83 to 87 per cent and for women 69 to 75 per cent.[3]

Regional explanations for these differences, even if possible, are scarcely adequate, for within regions levels of literacy varied even from parish to parish. A comparative study of several parishes that have been studied in detail suggests that, while literacy levels between 1750 and 1840 were rising in most places, they were falling slightly in Northampton (South Midlands), and catastrophically in Halifax.[4] Was Halifax an exception, or a type of rapidly industrialising parish in which local literacy levels ran counter to the national trend? Further research has suggested the latter. A study of Lancashire parish registers shows literacy scores in the 1830s as different as 79 per cent in Kirby Ireleth (Furness District) and 19 per cent in Rochdale and Wigan. The lowest scores were mainly in the south-eastern corner of the county where textile production predominated. Here the range of scores was typically between 20 and 30 per cent, compared with 40 to 50 per cent in the more rural areas.[5]

This correspondence between the rapidly growing towns of the early industrial revolution and low levels of literacy, especially among women, is no coincidence. An explanation of the phenomenon takes one to the heart of the educational experience and the social consequences of the industrial revolution. There appear to be three stages in the creation of a literate community: in the first stage, the individual wants or needs to acquire literacy, however difficult this might be; in the second stage, the acquisition of literacy is made easier through the provision of schools; in the third stage, all children, irrespective of their own motives, are compelled to attend these schools. In the early industrial revolution numbers at the first stage were reduced by the removal of both opportunity and incentive, women being affected more severely than men. In the second stage, which came between about 1830 and 1880, literacy levels began to climb for both sexes, with women gradually closing the gap on men as opportunities for basic education expanded. But only with the third stage, towards the close of the nineteenth century, were literacy rates for both sexes pushed up to the level of around 95 per cent regarded as full literacy.

The rapid expansion and urban concentration of population in areas such as Lancashire and the West of Scotland during the second half of the eighteenth century meant that the pattern and level of educational provision were no longer appropriate to the needs of the area. Resources were in most demand where they were least available, and in industrial Lancashire literacy levels began to fall from the middle of the eighteenth century. In response, a moral and religious crusade was launched to provide new educational facilities for the poor. The decline was halted in 1815 at around 58 per cent illiteracy for men and 81 per cent for women, suggesting that some couples who grew up in the 1790s were benefiting from the impact of Sunday Schools which first appeared in the 1780s. Increasing numbers of day-schools followed in the early nineteenth century, and by the 1830s the position was showing clear improvement.[6]

However, the towns of industrial Lancashire and Clydeside were to remain behind the national average (especially for women) well into the nineteenth century, and it is not sufficient to account for low literacy scores solely in terms of the lack of opportunity caused by a deficiency in the number and quality of schools. At the elementary level of signature-signing there is a less-than-perfect correspondence between the availability of or attendance at schools and literacy. In the neighbouring Nottinghamshire parishes of Bingham and Radford, for example, the literacy scores for boys in the mid-nineteenth century were the same in both parishes, though a lower percentage of boys in Radford (an industrialised parish) attended school than in Bingham (an agricultural parish); there is, however, a correspondence between the low attendance of Radford girls and high illiteracy rates.[7] This corroborates the general conclusion to be derived from Table 7.1: that in the industrialised areas it was women rather than men whose literacy suffered most from the lack of educational opportunities. As late as 1864, of 963 young women aged between 16 and 23 who were attending the Manchester Domestic Mission sewing school, only 21 per cent could both read and write, and 46 per cent could neither read nor write. Though the provision of a school could remedy this situation, the higher literacy rates for men suggest that in the first stage of the literacy process one needs to look closer at individual opportunity and motivation.

The demand for literacy

In strictly economic terms, there was little incentive to acquire literacy in the early industrial revolution. The number of people needing to be able to read or write to act in a supervisory capacity was growing, but relatively small, and almost exclusively male. Ordinary workers did not need literacy for their jobs. On the contrary, opportunities for the employment of children discouraged parents from prolonging the period during which a child might be formally taught. The girls who went to work in the factories of Lancashire or Lanarkshire had no need of education. There appears to be a significant connection between low levels of literacy, and areas in which there were abundant opportunities for child and female employment. From the strictly utilitarian point of view, the question must be why so many people bothered to acquire literacy at all.

Among those who did become literate there were many motives, apart from some parental compulsion of children – the only form of compulsion widespread in popular education before the last quarter of the nineteenth century. One striking feature of descriptions of the poor by contemporary observers among the higher classes is the contrast between laments about the ignorance of the poor and criticism of the low trash which they read. Education was indeed equated with a preference for the improving publications of Charles Knight or John Cassell rather than the degrading rubbish of James Catnach or Edward Lloyd. Behind this value-laden paradox one glimpses a view of the working-class reader, eagerly spelling his or her way through the report of a scandalous murder with the help of a crude wood-cut illustration. The principal reason for wanting to be able to read was the enjoyment it afforded. A more elevated picture is provided in the reminiscences of Joseph Barker (born 1806) about his father, who was in the army and away from his native Yorkshire when he was converted among the Methodists of Kent. Eager to inform his wife of this miraculous event, he bought himself a *Reading Made Easy* – a basic alphabet book:

> By a little help he learned to put the letters into words and spell; and was soon able both to read and write. He now sent word to my mother about all that had taken place. She, poor woman, was quite overpowered, and resolved to be religious too.[8]

Barker did not say whether his mother could read or had to get a neighbour to read the letter out to her. Among the Barker children growing up in a West Riding weaver-clothier's family, education was not easily come by:

> Almost the only opportunity I had of learning anything, except what I might learn at home, was by attending the Sunday-school. When we had work, we had no time to go to school; and when we had not work, we had nothing with which to pay school wages, so that a Sunday-school was our only resource. What little learning, therefore, I did get, I got at home from my brothers and sisters, and at Sunday-school. I recollect my eldest sister and my elder brothers teaching me my letters from a large family Bible that we had, and I also recollect teaching my younger brothers their letters afterwards from the same great Book.[9]

This passage sums up the essence of much family-based working-class education in the early nineteenth century. Within a literate family the acquisition of literacy was taken for granted, however hard the fight to obtain it. Working men and women learned to read because reading opened up access to whole new worlds of experience, whether secular pleasure or religious knowledge. This is a story which can be told without reference to those denominational charity schools which loom so large in institutional histories.

Where literacy was not strong within families, or the incentives were not powerful enough to overcome the problems of lack of time, money and candle-light, the story could be very different. The first steps in socialisation and education took place within the home; to middle-class reformers such as Dr James Kay of Manchester (later, Kay-Shuttleworth), the social disaster of the early nineteenth century was the failure of the working-class home as a place of religion, social discipline and education. Accordingly he devoted his life to providing schools, not so much as agencies of enlightenment as of mission and social reconstruction.

Elementary schooling

Schools were provided for many and mixed reasons. Many were founded or funded by philanthropists anxious to support the cause of true religion and morality and to enable the poor to read the Bible; others were simply commercially motivated, run to satisfy demand and to produce an income for the schoolteacher. Some educators wished to ensure that the poor were brought up with the 'right' ideas about politics and society; others perceived an economic need for a literate work-force. In England and Wales the State played only an indirect part in the provision of education before 1870. In Scotland, by contrast, the State took a central part in the education of the people.

Private and informal schooling

The great mistake of the educational and moral reformers was to underestimate the resources of the working classes to educate themselves, and to over-estimate the importance of formal schooling provided by others. Most children before the second half of the nineteenth century were not educated in the formally provided schools of the various religious bodies, and they were not directly exposed to the various doctrines of religious, moral, political and economic control which have seemed so important to subsequent historians of the working class. As Michael Anderson has shown for Preston (see above, page 53), families in an expanding industrial town were not isolated or bereft of help. Kinship networks ensured that grandmother, if not mother, was often available to help rear the children. Additional support was available from within the working-class community. Elderly or disabled men and women frequently earned their keep by looking after their neighbours' children. These so-called 'dame schools' were maligned by the educational reformers, who delighted to quote examples of ignorant childminding as all that such 'schools' could offer. In fact, there were many different levels of dame schools. Some were as bad as their critics maintained, but others did offer a little basic education: reading for a penny or twopence a week; writing as well for threepence or fourpence. At this point they graded imperceptibly into common day-schools, which provided more advanced subjects. Although both dame schools and Sunday Schools were criticised by reformers for their educational ineffectiveness, it is likely that these institutions reached more of the poor than any others and did more to lay the foundations of basic literacy, if little else. In Manchester in the 1830s the Statistical Society found that 54 per cent of those children attending any kind of school whatever were attending only Sunday Schools; for the rest the two largest categories were common day-schools (16 per cent) and dame schools (11 per cent). The figures were similar for Salford and Bury.[10]

The missing dimension in the reformers' view of popular education was parental and individual choice. The dame and common day-schools cost parents money, and yet the subsidised endowed and charity schools of Manchester attracted only 8 per cent of all those attending schools, and there were empty places available. Parents were suspicious of the control implicit in provided education, and preferred the often inferior teaching of dames from within the working-class community.

The provision of schooling, from whatever source, could only increase the educational level of the people as far as they themselves were prepared to go. Lack of money, time and interest meant that the levels achieved were very basic indeed, and that a considerable minority of the population remained totally outside the scope of educational provision. Literacy levels appear to have followed the social order closely, and it is probable that those working-class families which strove to win an education were from a minority among the better-off or those with traditions which went with a once-higher status, like the handloom weavers. These were the sort of people who sought education, and then continued to deepen it as adults. Here women appear to have slipped behind men. Even if they were permitted as children to attend school for a few years on a more or less regular basis, they had little opportunity or incentive to maintain their skills as adults. Female labour, even in domestic service, was likely to require little other than reading. Most of a family's dealings with the outside world were conducted by men. Without practice and incentives, the hard-won and barely learnt lessons of childhood were quickly forgotten amid the pressures and anxieties of working-class domestic life. The men, on the other hand, were in constant contact with the literate world, at work, in their clubs, unions and political associations. They could learn to read or practise their reading in radical discussion groups and other self-help organisations. Some went to their local Mechanics' Institutes, not to learn science or be indoctrinated in the ways of sound Political Economy, but to receive basic instruction in the elements of reading, writing and arithmetic. At the Birmingham Mechanics' Institute in the late 1830s, 405 of the 485 members were from the working classes; none was a woman. In most Institutes the elementary classes were by far the most popular. Among those classes which had to fight for education, its acquisition should not be identified either with school or childhood.[11]

The provision of public elementary education before 1870

For those parents who wanted their children to receive an elementary education, an increasingly wide variety of institutions was offered to them by private and public bodies concerned about the condition of the poor. Scotland, in theory, was the best-supplied part of Britain, with its network of parochial schools provided by the Church and funded mainly by the heritors of the parish. These were supplemented in the Lowlands and Borders by private schools, and in the vast Highland parishes by Scottish SPCK and additional General Assembly schools organised by the Church. In the Borders the network of schools appears to have been effective in creating a highly literate society in the eighteenth century, but levels of literacy among the Highlanders flocking into Glasgow from the late eighteenth century were low, and produced the same kind of crisis as was experienced in Lancashire. In 1825 only 30 per cent of Scottish children were receiving formal education, and only one-third of these was doing so in parochial schools, though many of the remaining 20 per cent were being educated in additional schools maintained by the Kirk Sessions in parishes which needed more than the one statutory school. But the awkward fact remained that the majority of children were not being educated at all, and after 1843 much effort and finance were wasted in denominational rivalry. Despite myths about Scottish superiority in literacy and the provision of schooling, in fact the experiences of comparable regions in England and Scotland were not dissimilar. Despite all the efforts of the Churches and mounting government grants, the number of school places available was not brought up to that needed to provide an education for all children until the Education Act of 1872.

The effort to extend elementary education in the countryside in England and Wales rested largely with the Churches and private charity, which in practice meant the Established Church through its National Schools. The standard reached was not always high, or the curriculum relevant to the needs of the countryside. In the towns there was more variety, but denominational rivalries prevented the full resources of public finance being called upon to make the haphazard system more effective. In addition to Sunday Schools, dame schools and other private schools of varying quality supported solely by parents, there were also charity schools supported through the SPCK and by private benefactors or annual charity sermons. From the early nineteenth century most parochial charity schools were brought under the control of the National Society, whilst other denominational schools were provided by the British Society and other religious bodies. State finance for education was provided indirectly through these religious organisations after 1833 (see above, pages 311–13). In two special cases the state took a more direct interest in the education of the poor – the children of paupers in England and Wales after 1834, and children employed in large factories throughout Great Britain – though in neither case was the policy of compulsion matched with finance to carry it out.

The 1802 Factory Act required factory masters to provide schooling for their pauper apprentices. Though this measure was patchily implemented and affected only a small number of children, it opened the way for further State action. In 1833 the new Factory Act laid down two hours of compulsory schooling each day for children employed in factories covered by the Act, but it removed from factory masters the obligation to provide the education. Instead, children had to produce certificates of attendance at any school in order to secure employment the following week. This law was hard to enforce: there were no means of telling a child's age, and no system for approving schools or even preventing the forgery of certificates. Factory masters who wanted to keep the children on their premises could start a factory school, which might be no better than the poorest dame school, in order to comply with the law. As a result of their experience working this Act the Factory Inspectors pressed for change, and in 1844 the simpler and more effective half-time system was introduced. The effect of this legislation was to double the number of factory children receiving an education, with most of the increase going to the religious (especially the National) schools.

This increase would not have been possible had not greater State funding been made available to the religious societies in 1839 as a result of James Kay's work. Thereafter the religious schools were to become the main channel for public education in England and Wales, with the power of the purse being used to maintain standards. By 1858, according to the Newcastle Commission, 860,000 children were being educated in private schools and 1,675,000 in schools run by the religious societies – though only one-third of the latter were in receipt of a State grant. The total charge to the Exchequer in 1861 was £800,000 compared with £125,000 in 1848.

Despite these efforts, it was becoming clear by the middle of the nineteenth century that neither the Scottish nor the English systems would be able to bring a satisfactory level of elementary education to all the poorer classes. In 1866 the Argyll Commission found that, of 490,000 children requiring education in Scotland, 200,000 were receiving it in uninspected schools of doubtful merit, and 90,000 (18 per cent) were not being educated at all. In England and Wales in 1868 there were 2,531,000 children in the 6–12 age group, of whom 950,000 were in State-aided (and therefore inspected) schools and 697,000 were in unaided schools, leaving 839,000 (33 per cent) not being educated in any schools at all. Despite the considerable achievements of voluntary effort, school places were still in short supply in the major centres of population, and standards were appallingly low even in inspected schools.

This serious situation was hardly new, but the evidence in the reports of the Newcastle Commission (1858–61) for England and Wales and the Argyll Commission (1864–67) for Scotland could hardly be ignored. Pressure for change was organised by radicals in such cities as Birmingham and Manchester, where the need for further schools was regarded as desperate. Those who pointed to the low level of popular education could talk of the dangers presented to the country by the Reform Act of 1867, which enfranchised large numbers of the urban working class, and they could point to the international threat to British industrial supremacy posed by the success of the Paris Exhibition, also of 1867. Within weeks of the Education Bill being submitted to Parliament in 1870, Prussia's literate army was triumphing over France's relatively illiterate army. Reformed education seemed a matter of political rather than moral or religious urgency for perhaps the first time.

Elementary education under the School Boards

Forster's Education Act (1870) created for England and Wales locally elected School Boards in places in which the existing provision of schools was inadequate. It was a policy not of State education, but of filling the gaps. Boards were created almost immediately in most major cities, and soon large Board Schools were erected, like mission stations, in working-class urban areas, charged with bringing basic education and social discipline to the children of the poorer classes. The Boards had the power to waive school fees and also to compel attendance, but as yet, in most places, education was neither compulsory nor free. A further Act in 1876 created school attendance committees with similar powers in places where there was no Board, and then in 1880 attendance was made compulsory for all children between the ages of 5 and 13 – although part-timers could begin work from the age of 10 if they had reached a sufficient standard. The grant system was not changed to enable Boards to remit all fees until 1891.

The equivalent Act for Scotland was Young's Education Act of 1872, which was quite different in scope. It created a nationwide network of nearly a thousand School Boards – one for every burgh and parish – which took over the existing schools and ran them as a single national system. This was in the traditional of Scottish educational provision before the Disruption, and there was little denominational opposition, since the three main Presbyterian groups could agree on a common form of religious education in the Board Schools. Attendance was made compulsory from the start.

The attempt which had been made in the Revised Code of 1862 to confine the activities of State-funded schools to a narrow, elementary curriculum was hard to implement in practice and increasingly irksome to School Boards. Not only did it run contrary to Scottish tradition, but it proved unacceptable to many English educators. The Wesleyans, for example, caused problems of definition because they were accustomed in their schools to cater for a slightly higher class of pupil than in the National Schools, and yet they too received the grant. The attempt in the Revised Code to cut back on support for non-basic subjects succeeded for a time in reducing costs and narrowing the curriculum, but under the School Boards pressure from the schools resulted in a considerable bending of the rules. Some Boards set up Higher Grade schools for more advanced work: in 1882 there were some 1861 children in Board Schools doing work above Standard VI. The legality of this development was dubious, for School Board rates were intended only for elementary instruction.

Confusion was multiplied by administrative chaos. Schools teaching advanced subjects could also apply for grants from the Science and Art Department (created in 1853 after the Great Exhibition), while alternative government funding was available after 1890 for technical education. Sometimes this went to the Boards, but in some cases – notably the West Riding – the money was spent directly by the new County Councils which had been empowered the previous year to levy a penny rate in support of technical education. This West Riding initiative showed the way for all educational activities to be concentrated in the hands of the counties and county boroughs, and led in 1902 to the abolition of School Boards in

England and Wales and their replacement by local education committees, nominated by elected borough and county councils and responsible for both elementary and secondary education. The equivalent Act was carried for Scotland in 1901, but the Scottish Boards survived until 1918, when they were replaced by larger *ad hoc* education committees; local authorities were not made the responsible bodies, as in England and Wales, until 1929. What was significant about the 1901 Education Act in Scotland, though, was its abandonment of the term 'elementary' to describe the basic education of the poor. Though the same significant alteration of language did not come south of the border until 1944, it signalled a new development in educational history.

Schooling and social class

The term 'primary education' suggests a stage in the educational process through which all must progress. It hints at an educational ladder which the able will be able to climb, however humble their backgrounds. On the contrary, elementary education was – by definition – exclusively for the working class. The purpose of the charity schools, National Schools and Board Schools of England and Wales was to provide the poor with education in the elements of knowledge – that is, reading, writing, arithmetic and religious knowledge – and nothing more. Parents were meant to pay some part of the cost, but the expectation was that the bulk of the funding would come from private charity and, increasingly, the public purse. The schools were not supposed to lead anywhere. Education meant a series of separate starting-points and goals appropriate to each class. Nowhere can the class structure of nineteenth-century England and Wales be seen more clearly than in the educational system. The aim was to educate children for their station in life. Publicly funded schooling smacked of charity, and parents who could bear the full cost of educating their children expected to do so, if only to maintain status.

In Scotland the tradition was quite different. Here the State had a part to play in the education of all classes, and the parochial schools had always been intended for all the children of the parish. Public funding was primarily to provide an endowment for the schoolmaster, who was expected to be a graduate and capable of teaching children up to the level of university entrance. In practice, this ideal system had largely broken down under the strains of urbanisation and population growth, and in the towns the burgh schools (equivalent to parochial schools elsewhere) were often dominated by the middle class, the poor being left to attend charity mission schools created especially for them in working-class districts. But the classless ideal always remained behind the Scottish system. When the 'Revised Code' was introduced in 1862 to restrict the grant-qualifying subjects to reading, writing and arithmetic, the Scots felt even more than the English that this was an unwarranted attack on the broad curriculum appropriate to their schools.

The one possibility of social advancement was for those who had attended elementary schools to become teachers themselves within the system. Before the later 1830s many schools operated some version of the monitorial system, whereby a master or mistress taught the older pupils, who then passed on their knowledge to the young. It was a cheap, but hardly efficient, approach. The teachers themselves had probably received no more than a few months' training at the British Society's school in Borough Road, London, or the National Society's school in Westminster. Though Scottish parochial schoolmasters were ideally graduates, in the poorer city areas this was not so, and in 1838 the Glasgow Educational Society pioneered a large 'Normal School' at which to train students to teach. The National Society was moving in the same direction with a system of pupil-teachers, and these developments were encouraged and assisted by James Kay and the Education Committee of the Privy Council from 1839. Their scheme, as it finally emerged in 1846, provided for a five-year apprenticeship, during which time the pupil-teacher would be paid and would receive further education from the schoolmaster. He or she would then be eligible to try for a Queen's scholarship to a training college. A study of the first training college for women, Whitelands, has shown that, whereas initially 52.6 per cent of the pupils were lower-middle class and only 36.8 per cent working-class, by 1857 76.3 per cent of the students came from working-class backgrounds.[12] Preparation for a career in teaching thus opened the way to secondary education for bright working-class children, both boys and girls. It was a small but necessary concession, and did little to qualify the prevailing view that a secondary education proper was a liberal education, the prerogative of the leisured classes.

Secondary schools

The eighteenth-century grammar school

The most common form of school in England and Wales before the charity schools of the early eighteenth century was the grammar school, which was an endowed school for the gratuitous teaching of Latin and, less frequently, Greek grammar to boys, to which was frequently attached a petty school in which a more basic English education was offered to both boys and girls. By the mid-eighteenth century many of these schools were ancient and decayed, like the Established Church with which the majority were associated. They had been established or re-established in the century and a half between the Reformation and the beginning of the eighteenth century, and provided no more than a thinly scattered network of schools to educate boys in the classics and prepare them for university.

In this they differed from the parochial schools of Scotland, which were founded and endowed by public authority. According to an Act of 1696 every rural parish was to have a school, open to both boys and girls, with a schoolmaster maintained at public expense to teach both elementary and university entrance subjects such as Latin and mathematics. Every burgh also was to maintain a similar school. The problem was that only one school was required by law for each parish, which was as inadequate at the end of the eighteenth century in the thinly populated, though large, Highland parishes as it was in the thickly populated towns of the Clyde Valley.

The English grammar schools were caught in conflicting currents which determined whether they would become 'public schools', local grammar schools, mere charity schools or nothing at all. If a school's endowment were invested in land, as land values rose with agricultural improvement and urban development, the future was assured. If funds remained invested in government stocks at a time of inflation during the French Wars, then the school might no longer be able to exist as a 'free' grammar school. There were also tensions between the two original functions of the grammar school, to provide a classical education free and to educate poor boys. By the later eighteenth century few poor boys wanted a classical education; those who did were not poor. Which should the schools cater for? To emphasise the classics would drive away the poor, which in some remoter quarters would mean there would be no scholars left; but to educate the poor would be to go against the founders' intentions of providing a classical education, and cut the poor off from the education and scholarships which led to university. Some grammar schools responded by teaching elementary subjects free as well as classics; others charged. The curriculum was shaped largely by market forces. In the nineteenth century, as other schools were created to provide an elementary education for the poor, town grammar schools shook themselves free of the obligation to provide the poor with an education which few of them wanted, and concerned themselves with more advanced studies. There remained the problem of whether these studies should be modern as well as classical and, if so, whether they should be free. After a period of legal confusion, the latter was permitted by the Grammar School Act of 1840, which can be taken as the starting-point for the history of the modern grammar school.

The public schools

A minority of ancient classical foundations was distinguished from the ordinary run of grammar schools by their association with the aristocracy and by national recruitment. Most such schools were situated in and around London, but the two most ancient were the medieval foundations of Winchester (linked to New College, Oxford) and Eton (linked to King's College, Cambridge). The other 'great' schools of the later eighteenth century were Henry VIII's refounded school at Westminster, Charterhouse and Harrow, to which Shrewsbury was added at the end of the eighteenth century, and Rugby in the early nineteenth. By the time of Lord Clarendon's Commission into the public schools in 1861, two London day-schools had been added to the list of 'great' schools, St Paul's and Merchant Taylors'. Others, such as Manchester Grammar School, were knocking on the door, but were excluded from both the 'great seven' and the 'Clarendon nine'.

The seven great public schools of the early nineteenth century were socially exclusive, not least because of their fees and classical curriculum. Eton, for example, took 38 poor boys out of a total intake of over 3,000 between 1753 and 1790. Only one of the famous Reformation refoundations kept its charitable role intact: Christ's Hospital, intended for the children of poor clergymen and of Londoners without the means of educating their children.

The fortunes of the public schools fluctuated considerably in the eighteenth century. Winchester was small and struggling until the 1790s. Eton recovered from a Jacobite taint in the 1720s to become highly fashionable when George III made Windsor his favourite residence. Harrow thrived on Whig opposition to Tory Eton. Westminster sank as London grew dirtier and Eton or Harrow beckoned. Much depended on the enterprise of the headmaster. Shrewsbury was rescued from oblivion in 1798 by Samuel Butler. By the 1830s all the public schools had received a new lease of life and were inspiring imitators on all sides.

The reasons for this renaissance can be exemplified in the history of Rugby School, which acquired new school buildings at a cost of £46,000 between 1809 and 1813. The attendant publicity helped John Wooll, who became headmaster in 1808, build up his intake to over a hundred, the largest of any school in England at that time. Numbers then fell, but rose again when Thomas Arnold succeeded Wooll in 1828. He made several important improvements which, while not unique or entirely successful, helped create a favourable impression in parents' minds, and a model for other schools to follow. First, he was determined to raise the status of his assistant masters. Hitherto they had held curacies elsewhere and their pay from the school had been low. Now he put his masters in charge of the school's boarding-houses, and brought in boys who had previously lodged in the town. This had the effect not only of supplementing the masters' salaries, but of instituting a new form of discipline and moral supervision. The eighteenth-century public school had been a riotous sort of place, in which education and morals were neglected and violence was institutionalised in a republic of boys. Slowly parental expectations changed and schools adapted accordingly. Butler built Shrewsbury up by emphasising academic matters; Arnold tried to make Rugby moral. He adapted the hierarchies of power among the boys to produce the sixth-form and the prefect system, a self-regulating mechanism which maintained order and gave the older boys the responsibilities of leadership. Though his successes were never complete and his reputation was built partly on the mythology woven by his disciples, what mattered in the school's success was the image rather than the reality. Parents affected by the revival of religion could feel confident that their boys would be safe with the eminent Dr Arnold.

The expansion of the public-school system was aided by the revival in religion, the growing wealth of the gentry and professional families with aspirations to gentry status, and the coming of the railways, which made national boarding schools easily accessible to a wider clientele. The growing demand for a public-school education also completed the exclusion of poor local boys from Harrow, Rugby and other grammar schools aspiring to follow them, for the gentry did not send their children to be educated in the company of tradesmen's sons. Indeed, even sons of the more prosperous middle classes were rare creatures at the older public schools. Their parents instead turned to other schools which were able to provide them with a public-school education. Some were old endowed grammar schools like Repton, Sherborne and Uppingham, where Edward Thring established his reputation after 1853 by attempting to modernise the curriculum. Some were newly endowed, like Wellington (1859) in memory of the Duke and originally for the education of the sons of army officers. Many were joint-stock proprietary (that is, non-profit-making) schools, like Cheltenham (1841), Marlborough (1843), and Lancing (1848). The latter was part of an ambitious scheme of Nathaniel Woodard for re-Christianising England. Between 1837 and 1869, 31 classical boarding schools were founded, though not all immediately achieved public-school status.

All these schools were Anglican, like the two English universities which they fed. With the growth in Dissent, though, a parallel system of boarding schools was created for the children of those parents who could not accept – and, indeed, wished to protect their children against – the Anglican ethos of traditional public schools. Several Catholic schools were founded in the aftermath of the French Revolution which cut off the former route to a continental education: Stoneyhurst and Oscott (1794), Downside (1795) and Ampleforth (1802). The Methodists founded schools for the children of travelling preachers, notably Kingswood (1748), and to staunch the loss of the sons of well-to-do Methodists to the Church (the Leys, Cambridge, 1875). Rather different were the Friends' schools, such as Ackworth (1771) and Bootham, York (1828); Mill Hill, set up by the Congregationalists in London in 1808 with a curriculum unfettered by tradition; and the Hill brothers' experimental school at Hazelwood, Birmingham (1819).

In Scotland the situation was rather different from that south of the border. The English public schools really served the whole of Britain. Parents who wished their sons to succeed in public life could not afford to ignore those institutions in which British public life was shaped. As a result, there were very few public schools on the English model in Scotland itself. Rare exceptions included Glenalmond, founded by the Episcopalians near Perth in 1847, and Fettes College in Edinburgh, opened in 1870 after the bequest of Sir William Fettes (died 1836) had been diverted from its original purposes.

Middle-class education

As Matthew Arnold argued in *A French Eton* (1864), the English provided charity schools for the poor and endowed schools for the rich, but nothing for the middle classes.[13] Whilst this was an exaggeration, it was certainly true that the education available for those who could not afford the boarding fees of a public school, did not want a classical education and expected their sons to leave school at 16 for useful employment, was scarcely adequate. Some were provided for in local grammar schools, but a majority attended private schools which varied from high-quality proprietary schools to all manner of 'educational homes' which advertised their unguaranteed qualities in the national and local press. Provision for the education of girls was far worse than that for boys.

The whole question of educational provision in Britain was subjected to a series of Royal Commissions in the mid-nineteenth century. After the Newcastle Commission had reported on elementary education in 1861, and the Clarendon Commission on the nine great public schools in 1864, the Schools Inquiry or Taunton Commission was set to work, and reported in 1868 on the rest – some 791 endowed schools providing higher-than-working-class education. The main recommendations of the Commission for a sweeping reorganisation of endowments were not accepted, though considerable changes were introduced as a result of the Endowed Schools Act of 1869, which brought greater flexibility in the use of endowments and allowed the grammar schools to pursue the course on which they were already embarked, providing a modern as well as classical education for a fee-paying clientele to the exclusion of the lower-middle classes and poor.

The limited Endowed Institutions (Scotland) Act (1869) and more extensive Educational Endowments (Scotland) Act of 1882 did for Scotland what the Endowed Schools Act of 1869 did for England. The retreat from the ideal of open-access schools to the reality of a middle-class monopoly can be illustrated in the experience of Edinburgh, which had a third of all Scotland's educational endowments. Here the ancient burgh High School had been challenged in 1824, when the Edinburgh Academy was opened to provide a truly secondary education up to English standards. It was a proprietary day school, situated in the New Town and charging higher fees than the old High School. The town council responded by rebuilding the High School on a new site on Calton Hill and appealing to the same middle-class clientele. Unlike their counterparts in other towns (excepting Glasgow and Aberdeen), these were élite institutions for the middle classes, and admitted only boys. For the poor there were the various endowed hospitals, notable George Heriot's School, founded in the seventeenth century on the model of Christ's Hospital; the Merchant Maiden Hospital, founded for the daughters of the members of the Merchant Company in 1695; George Watson's (1741) and Daniel Stewart's (1855). All but Heriot's were turned from boarding schools for the poor into day-schools for the middle class in 1870; Heriot's followed, after much controversy, in 1885. There was some justification for this, as it permitted far more children to be educated than under the old 'hospital' boarding system, and the children of the poor could be catered for in schools administered by the School Board after 1872, including the reluctant High School; but it was a controversial development, which appeared to cut across the traditions of Scottish education.

One consequence of the rearrangement of endowments was a transfer of some funding to secondary education for girls. The Taunton Commission had accepted the need to consider girls' education only under pressure from Emily Davies, but the outcome justified the concession. In some places endowments were divided and a small part devoted to the creation of sister schools for girls – for example, Haberdashers' Aske's; the Perse, Cambridge; and King Edward's, Birmingham. Whereas in the 1860s there were only 12 endowed schools for girls in England, by the 1890s there were 80. Similarly in Scotland, where there was a much longer tradition of schooling for girls, George Watson's charity was used to create schools for both girls and boys in 1870.

Other new educational institutions were created for girls in line with those being provided for boys, though rather later and to a lesser extent. The first proprietary boarding school for girls was Cheltenham Ladies College, founded in 1823. Its example was followed by St Leonard's, opened at St Andrews in 1877, and Roedean, started in Brighton in 1885. The most influential day-school was the North London Collegiate, opened by Frances Mary Buss in 1850 as a private school with some boarding, and handed over to trustees as a wholly day school in 1871. Cheltenham Ladies' College, under its most famous early headmistress, Dorothea Beale, was an élite school for the daughters of the gentry; at the North London Collegiate, Miss Buss took not only the daughters of the professional classes of Camden Town, but also those of local tradespeople.

Miss Buss's school was the inspiration for Maria Grey and her sister Emily Shirreff, who set up a National Union for the Education of Girls of all Classes above the Elementary in 1871, which in turn created the

Girls' Public Day School Company in 1872 to form and assist in the creation of high schools for girls across the country. Their first school was opened in Chelsea in 1873; others followed in the London area and then further afield – even as far north as Gateshead. In 1901 there were 38 High Schools aided by the company, which was renamed the Girls' Public Day School Trust in 1906. The Company was copied by the less successful Church of England Schools Company in 1883, which also opened a number of schools for girls across the country.

Public examinations

As Matthew Arnold had observed in 1864, the major problem with middle-class education was the maintenance of standards.[14] This was even more important for girls than boys, for the former had to prove that they were as intellectually capable as the latter. The development of middle-class – and especially girls' – schooling cannot therefore be separated from the history of public examinations.

Public examinations were widely regarded in the mid-nineteenth century as a suitable method for eliminating favouritism and the irrational use of resources, and putting in their place a fair, impartial and open system of selection. They appealed to reformers in the universities of Oxford and Cambridge, and in the public schools. The hopes of the reformers were not entirely fulfilled. The attempt to open up the public schools, for example, by reducing the numbers of closed scholarships, simply meant that only those parents who could afford a good preparatory school could secure entry to the public schools. And the same was largely true of entry to the universities. The old system had been sufficiently irrational to let through the occasional poor scholarship boy; whereas the reformed system offered equality to all who could pay.

Nevertheless, the desire for public examinations had a beneficial effect upon educational standards. The idea was pioneered by T. D. Acland in Exeter in 1857, and then taken up by the universities of Oxford and Cambridge, which created the new qualification of Associate in Arts in 1858. The 'middle-class examinations', as they were called, were sat at two levels: juniors, up to 15 or 16; and seniors, at 18. They were sat at local centres throughout England, and hence came to be called the Local Examinations. At the junior level, non-university subjects such as English grammar, geography and history were included, and so the new examinations were looked down upon by the public schools. In the early examinations mathematics was less well done than classics, and very few candidates were entered in scientific subjects. The new examination system proved popular with middle-class schools, but the public schools remained aloof, and separate arrangements were made for them when the Oxford and Cambridge Schools Examination Board was created in 1873.

The introduction of the Locals was of the utmost importance in the development of education for girls both in schools and at the universities. In 1863 Cambridge agreed to Emily Davies's request to let girls try the Locals privately when the examination was sat at their London centre; this was made official two years later, when 126 girls took the examination at six centres. The Locals were enthusiastically supported by Miss Buss, but Miss Beale spoke for the public schools in not welcoming them. Next, in 1869, Cambridge agreed to provide a higher level of examination for girls of more mature years (men also were allowed to sit the examination from 1873, but few did so); Oxford followed in 1877. The aim here was to provide women with some kind of certification in higher education to help them in their careers as teachers or governesses, but the need to prepare adequately for the examination led to residential teaching, and so stimulated the demand for women's colleges at the universities and full admission to degree examinations instead. They were helped in this direction in 1877, when a senior certificate in the Locals was accepted in lieu of the first stage in the degree course (the Previous Examination at Cambridge; Responsions at Oxford). The extent to which the Locals were important for girls can be seen from the proportions of the sexes taking the examination. In 1878, 69 per cent of candidates taking the junior level were boys, but 61 per cent of the seniors were girls.

The ancient universities dominated public examinations in schools in the nineteenth century, although theirs were not the only ones available. The University of London's matriculation examination, started in 1858 (and opened up to women 20 years later) came to be regarded as a qualification in its own right, although it was never intended as an assessment of academic achievement in schools, and did not formally become a schools examination until 1902. In Scotland, where university entrance examinations were introduced in 1892 to raise standards in schools and thereby in the first year at university, the State also took the initiative, introducing the Leaving Certificate in university subjects in 1888 in an effort to influence developments in secondary schools outside the control of the School Boards. Concern with university entrance was to remain central to examinations for senior students in schools in the twentieth century, leading to repeated charges that the universities were dictating and distorting the curriculum in schools for their own convenience and to the detriment of the many pupils who were not interested in university entrance. This was the opposite of what had been intended in 1858.

Secondary education in the first half of the twentieth century

The provision of secondary education for the middle classes in England and Wales was still largely beyond direct State control when the Bryce

Commission looked at schools in the mid-1890s. There were 1448 grammar schools in England and 31 in Wales which came within the scope of the Endowed Schools Act. These varied in quality, from major classical schools like Manchester Grammar School and Dulwich College at the top, to struggling local schools like that at Hull (which was almost handed over to the School Board in the 1880s) at the bottom. Additionally, there were many private and proprietary schools offering modern subjects, and the School Boards' higher-grade schools. Further pressure in the 1890s led to the opening of several day-training centres to offer improved secondary education to pupil teachers. Though scholarships existed to enable children from elementary school to gain access to secondary education, few were able to benefit from them. The odds against a child from an elementary school gaining a scholarship to secondary school in 1894 were 270 to 1.

The aim of the 1902 Education Act was to build on the experience which local authorities had acquired under the Technical Instruction Act of 1889, and to provide a national public system of secondary education. Struggling grammar schools were able to receive grants both from the Board of Education (established 1899) in London and from their local authorities, in exchange for places being made available to able children from the elementary schools. In 1907 grants were increased on condition that 25 per cent of places were allocated free to children from public elementary schools who had passed a qualifying examination. Competition for the free places became so fierce that the examination became competitive instead of merely qualifying. New secondary schools were also created where necessary, for both boys and girls, modelled on the ancient grammar schools with entrance by qualifying (that is, competitive) examination, and all pupil teachers were required to receive full-time (preferably secondary) education up to the age of 16. By the outbreak of the First World War there were over a thousand grant-aided secondary schools in England and Wales, with nearly 188,000 pupils. Though this represented considerable progress, it was only a beginning. Most children continued to attend their elementary schools until the age of 13 (14 after 1918) with little prospect of educational or social advancement. Out of every 1,000 children aged 10 to 11, only 56 children from elementary schools found their way to secondary school free of charge.

In Scotland the Education Act of 1901 made a formal distinction between elementary and secondary education, with transfer at the age of 12 for all pupils capable of benefiting from the latter. The Scots appeared for a time to be moving towards a tripartite system of Supplementary Courses in elementary schools for those who would leave at 14; Higher Grade Schools for those who would leave at 16; and Higher Class schools, which would offer an education up to 18 and lead to university. The distinction between these last two types of school gradually faded after

1908, when all secondary schools were required to work towards an Intermediate Certificate after three years of secondary education both for those leaving school at 15 or 16, and as a preliminary to the Leaving Certificate taken by those staying on until 17 or 18. Thus by 1920, in Scotland as in England, a two-tier system was operating, with elementary education for the majority to the age of 14, and secondary education for a minority who remained in education beyond the age of compulsory education.

After 1918 secondary schools in England and Wales were required to choose between local authority support and a direct grant from the Board of Education. Competition and financial necessity brought many grammar and proprietary schools into the local authority system, but by 1944 there were 232 schools with 18 per cent of the total grammar-school population in receipt of direct grants. These schools differed little in theory from local authority grammar schools, but in practice they were closer in spirit to the public schools. Their defenders saw them as a bridge between the two systems, offering what was regarded as the best form of education to an able minority from the lower classes as well as to the middle classes. Their opponents saw them as socially divisive, and detrimental to the ordinary grammar schools to which the majority of able children went.

A further development of the inter-war period was the emergence of schools which provided a non-academic secondary education for children not qualified for entry to grammar school. This approach, which had long been advocated by the Fabian Society, was recommended by the Hadow Committee in 1926. Local authorities were urged by the Board of Education to implement the scheme for separate secondary education for non-academic children, and many did introduce what were known as central or modern schools, though the full implementation of the Hadow Report had to wait until 1944. In Scotland the Hadow Report was partly implemented in 1936, when it was recognised that all children were entitled at the age of 12 to transfer either to non-academic 'junior secondary' schools offering three-year courses or to academic 'senior' schools offering the five-year course up to university entrance. This structure was confirmed by the Scottish Education Act of 1945.

The development of separate secondary education went furthest in the towns. In the countryside, practice lagged far behind theory. It was still possible to walk into an English village school in the 1930s and find one room divided by a curtain, with the younger children in one half and the older ones in the other. The single schoolmistress taught one half at a time, while a senior pupil minded the other half for her. Most of the pupils went to work in the fields as soon as legally able to leave school. Only a few left at 11 for secondary school in the town, and they were the sons of farmers.[15]

Secondary education in the second half of the twentieth century

The Education Act of 1944 finally abandoned the idea of elementary education in England and Wales and established the principle of secondary education for all children over the age of 11, replacing the qualifying examination by the selective 'eleven-plus' which was taken by all. The theory was that children would be allocated to three types of school according to aptitude: grammar for the academic; technical for those with special abilities of a more practical nature; and modern for the non-academic. In fact, there were grammar school places for only about 20 per cent of children and technical places for no more than 5 per cent, so most children were classified as non-academic and allocated to the residual category of modern schools. Outside large cities it was unusual for local authorities to offer the technical option at all, and in some places there were even too few secondary modern places; and so all but those pupils destined for grammar school continued, as before 1944, to remain in their elementary schools until Standard VI at the age of 15.

In these circumstances, the criticisms which had been levelled against the direct-grant schools came to be levelled against grammar schools as a whole. The idea that children could be tested and divided at the age of 11 was also subjected to intellectual criticism. Although intended as an academically selective test to open education up to talent irrespective of birth, in practice the eleven-plus examination was seen as socially divisive, and a new move began in the 1950s to abandon selection in favour of comprehensive schools at the secondary level for all children between the ages of 11 and 15 (16 from 1973). In 1965 the Labour government required local authorities to draw up plans to phase out selective schools and the eleven-plus examination. By 1970, when a new Conservative government withdrew the instruction, about a third of children in the secondary age-group in England and Wales were being educated in comprehensive schools, and rather more in Scotland, where some rural schools had always functioned as both 'junior' and 'senior' secondary schools. National policy was reversed again with the swing of the political pendulum in 1976, when the Labour government's Education Act again required local authorities to reorganise secondary education along comprehensive lines.

More controversially, the 1976 Act withdrew support from direct-grant schools. Some of the latter were drawn into the local authority network, but many decided to become wholly private, thus strengthening the public-school sector of education and underlining the traditional divide in English educational provision between a State sector of free education for the poor, and a private sector of fee-paying education for the rich. This was not what the Labour government had intended, and with the return of a

Conservative administration in 1979 the aim of the direct-grant system was restored with an assisted places scheme (1980) to enable children to compete on ability for means-tested places in private schools.

The history of schooling in Britain in the 1980s and 1990s was influenced by two major issues: how to ensure both equality of opportunity in a society in which life-chances were not equal, and at the same time to maximise the talents of the most able in the service of the State; and how to direct the content and quality of education so as to ensure that the needs of the State (especially the national economy) were indeed being met. Though the approach taken by Conservative administrations between 1979 and 1997 was markedly different from that adopted by Labour in the 1960s and 1970s, by 1997, when Labour regained political power, it had accepted the logic of many of the policies adopted by the Conservatives, whilst retaining a preference for public over private control, and against selection on principle, if not always in practice.

The educational purposes and social consequences of selection were of primary concern. By 1984 selective secondary schooling had virtually disappeared in Scotland, and catered for only 1.6 per cent of children in Wales and 8 per cent in England. Even in some strongly Conservative areas the falling birthrate was suggesting sound financial reasons for amalgamating schools, ending selection and concentrating post-compulsory education in sixth-form colleges. Only a few local authorities were still holding out in defence of their grammar schools when the government reversed the policy back towards selection with a specialist-schools policy in 1993. This created 15 non-fee-paying independent city technology colleges, funded by government and private enterprise. At the same time, sixth-form colleges were removed from local authority control and given further education status. Policy was now moving to reverse the 1902 structure which had made local education authorities primarily responsible for the provision of public education locally. Individual schools were now allowed to 'opt out' of local authority control and attain 'grant-maintained' status, with central funding. In 1996 it was proposed to allow these schools to select up to half their pupils. Specialist language and technology colleges would be able to select up to 30 per cent, and new grammar schools would be encouraged. By 1996 18 per cent of secondary schools in England (and 5 per cent in Wales) were grant-maintained, and another 14 per cent were in the independent sector.

Concern that the education provided should give the State a return on its investment was prompted by invidious international comparisons, which suggested that the schools were failing to achieve adequate standards, especially in mathematics and technology. The response was to impose, alongside greater autonomy for schools in their administration, a degree of State intervention in the curriculum and standards achieved in schools unknown since Robert Lowe had introduced the Revised Code in 1862. In 1988 a National Curriculum was laid down for all publicly funded schools in England and Wales for all pupils aged 5 to 16, with core and foundation subjects (including Welsh in Wales), the aim being to ensure proficiency in English, mathematics and science, and to ensure that all pupils were taught modern languages, design and technology and information technology. In Scotland such a broad curriculum was 'recommended', although Scottish educational provision, especially after the age of 16, had traditionally been broader than that offered south of the border.

With a closer definition of the curriculum came the need for pieces of paper to show what standards had been achieved. In England and Wales the system of externally set school examinations after 1951 consisted of a General Certificate in Education qualification in individual subjects at Ordinary Level, intended for about 20 per cent of the age group at 16, and an Advanced Level in individual subjects for those aged 18, intended for that small minority who might choose to extend their schooling beyond the projected school-leaving age of 16. In Scotland the Scottish Certificate of Education (Ordinary or Standard Grade) was taken at the end of the fourth year of secondary education, the equivalent of the GCE, with a Higher Grade examination in the fifth or sixth year of study. In 1960–1 over half the children of parents in the semi-skilled and unskilled social classes attending grammar schools left without any qualification whatever, compared with only about a quarter from the professional classes; and of those attending other secondary schools (excluding secondary modern schools, which frequently did not offer any external examinations) nine out of 10 pupils from the lower social classes left without any qualification. Following the Newsom Report on this state of affairs in 1963, an additional examination, the Certificate in Secondary Education (CSE), was introduced in 1965 to meet the needs of 60 per cent of the age-group. This in effect became a school-leaving examination when the age of compulsory education was raised to 16 in 1973. In 1988 the two examinations were combined to form the General Certificate in Secondary Education (GCSE), which served as both a school-leaving examination and a qualification for entry into further education. Numbers of pupils achieving high grades in these examinations increased rapidly in the 1980s and 1990s. In 1974 just under a quarter of pupils achieved the equivalent of five or more GCSE subjects at grade C or above (what was commonly referred to as a 'pass'); in 1995, two-fifths of boys and nearly half the girls did so. And, whereas 21 per cent of boys and 19 per cent of girls left school with no qualifications in 1975, these figures had fallen to 9 per cent for boys and only 6 per cent for girls by 1991. Not only was this a striking improvement, especially marked after 1987, but it signified a considerable change in the comparative achievement of girls, who were now outperforming boys at every level and in most subjects. They did better than boys not only in humanities and social sciences, but also in many areas traditionally regarded as boys' subjects. Those girls who chose to study such subjects as physics and chemistry, as well as new subjects such as design and technology, business studies, craft design and technology, computer studies and information systems, had a higher success rate than boys. Though sexual stereotyping in subjects and careers was far from dead, this trend has signalled an important social change in attitudes which promises to unlock the hitherto under-used skills of half the population. In the longer term this revolution in education seems likely to confirm trends in adult employment not only away from unskilled to skilled labour, but also from traditional male jobs to new sectors of the economy increasingly employing women.

In marked contrast to these changes in the nature of school examinations at the stage of compulsory schooling, the GCE A-Level survived as both a leaving examination at the higher level and as an entry qualification to University, despite many debates and proposals about its replacement. The same trend was observable at A-Level as at 16, with more girls than boys taking A-Levels or their equivalent, and with the overall number and standard of passes rising rapidly. This in turn fuelled a greatly increased take-up by girls of places in higher education.

Universities

The decline and revival of Oxford and Cambridge

The ancient universities of England were clerical institutions, an integral part of the Established Church, and as such shared in the general weakness and lethargy of the Church of England in the eighteenth century. From an estimated peak of over 500 freshmen each year in the 1630s, Oxford was admitting under 200 in the mid-eighteenth century, and numbers did not again rise to over 500 until the 1870s. Cambridge reached a similar peak in the 1620s, and fell to a little over 100 in the 1760s, before recovering once more to over 500 in the 1860s.[16] Why was this?

The first point to note is that the decline of Oxford and Cambridge was not unique. Throughout most of Europe, universities were in similar decline in the eighteenth century – the Netherlands and Scotland were rare exceptions. This suggests a general crisis of confidence among the educated classes of Europe in the culture and pedagogy of universities. Within England, the weakness of the universities must also be linked to the decline of the grammar schools that fed them many of their students, though their weakness was as much caused by as a cause of the problems of the universities. Fundamental to the rejection of the universities was a revulsion against their narrow clericalism and pedantry. They were seen not as preparing students for the broad, humane and civilised world of the eighteenth century, but as narrowing horizons and encouraging outmoded sectarianism. Intellectually they were backwaters, despite the presence of individual classical and scientific scholars of repute. Even at Cambridge, where Isaac Newton made mathematics a central feature of the teaching, his very dominance prevented an appreciation of the critical importance of the work of Descartes for the future of the subject. The political turmoils and purges of the later Stuarts had undermined morale in the colleges, and Oxford was tainted with Jacobitism under the early Hanoverians. Furthermore, the universities were not safe places for the young. As Lawrence Stone has shown, there is a correspondence between the popularity of the universities and the extent of close moral supervision of students offered by the colleges.[17] As a few senior tutors collected to themselves large numbers of students (and fees), so their ability to offer an adequate moral and intellectual supervision of their charges declined. The tone of the Colleges was set not by the fellows but by their aristocratic students, who were less interested in scholarship than pleasure.

An analysis of the social composition of the student body suggests that the decline of the universities did not take place among all classes. The peerage were well-represented throughout the century, but the numbers of knights and gentlemen fell, and there was a steady decline in 'plebeians'. The universities were serving two functions: educating the clergy, and consolidating the social élite. Parents who wanted other things for their children had to look elsewhere.

The weakness of the universities is further indicated in their lack of patronage. As with the grammar schools, the number of endowments fell drastically. Only three new colleges were founded in the eighteenth century – Worcester College (1714) and Hertford College (1740) at Oxford, and Downing at Cambridge, which, because of a legal dispute, was not actually started until 1800. All three were intended to bring reforms, but all, for different reasons, were soon assimilated into the existing system. Some royal patronage was offered to the universities: George I established Regius Chairs in History, and gave Cambridge a library; but it may be significant that George II's great educational foundation was at Göttingen (1734) in his native Hanover.

Student numbers began to recover in the later eighteenth century, but not appreciably so until after 1800. The origins of this recovery are as obscure as the earlier causes of decline. The rise in land values may have stimulated more members of the gentry to educate their sons at university: 40 per cent of matriculants were 'esquires' in 1810, compared with 30 per cent of a lower total a generation earlier. There are also signs that academic life was being taken more seriously. A man's academic class was still determined, in the medieval fashion, by oral disputation (the Tripos) at Cambridge, but from 1780 his position in the class list was decided by the Senate House Examination, in which written answers were required to oral questions in mathematics, logic and moral philosophy over a four-day period. Written questions were introduced in 1827. At Oxford a written examination was introduced in 1800, and the Classics and

Mathematical Schools were separated in 1807 (Peel in 1808 was the first to gain the distinction of a 'double first'). Gradually new subjects were carved out of the old curriculum. The Classics Tripos was introduced in Cambridge in 1824, followed in 1848 by Triposes in Moral Sciences (including history) and Natural Sciences; by the mid-nineteenth century Oxford had Schools in Natural Science, Law, Modern History and Theology.

Despite these changes, the universities remained primarily clerical institutions and, as such, their recovery was inseparable from the revival in religion. This made its impact most obviously at Cambridge, where Charles Simeon influenced undergraduates from his rooms in King's College (1788–1830) and the pulpit of Holy Trinity Church. Though only a minority of undergraduates ever became 'Sims', the pervasive influence of evangelical religion was widely felt. Young men at the universities, no less than the working classes, felt that moral discipline which sought to erode their wilder pleasures and establish order during the turbulent years of the French Revolution. The Colleges reasserted themselves as instruments for the control of the young, but most fellows did not as yet see their role as involving serious teaching. Lectures were seldom and badly given, and sparsely attended; tutors confined themselves to moral matters; and that minority of students who wished to prepare for examinations had to turn to private coaches or crammers. Academic reform came mainly after 1850.

Pressure for change also came from Scotland, with its quite different and apparently more successful university system. Scottish criticism of English ways can be seen right across the social and political scene in the early nineteenth century, voiced especially through the pages of the *Edinburgh Review*. Edinburgh-educated Whigs sought rational and utilitarian change in every quarter, especially in the Church. The universities could not remain apart from this process. Though the main consequence of the reforming movement was to establish a university in London, by mid-century there was also considerable pressure for change within the ancient universities, and a memorial was presented to the Prime Minister, Russell, in 1849 asking for a Royal Commission into the state of Oxford and Cambridge. This reported in 1852, and resulted in legislation which cleared the way for internal reforms over the next 20 years.

The Oxford and Cambridge University Acts of 1854 and 1856 respectively made the governing bodies of the universities more representative and abolished religious tests up to the BA level (except for Divinity students). These reforms were completed in 1871 when Dissenters were admitted to higher degrees, fellowships and the government of the universities. Admission to the colleges were also reformed, with closed scholarships and fellowships being thrown open to competition. This did not affect the social composition of the student body, for few poor boys had ever climbed the flimsy educational ladder which closed scholarships had provided; but it did lead to a greater emphasis on intellectual merit, and stimulated the public schools to ensure that their pupils received good teaching. A further Act in 1877 ended the requirement of clerical celibacy among the college fellowships (hitherto, only heads of colleges had been allowed to marry) and resulted in a flowering of academic family networks, with sons and daughters to be educated in future generations.

A second important step in opening up the universities came when Oxford (1868) and Cambridge (1869) decided to admit students who were not also members of colleges. This had two consequences. First, an institution was created in each university through which non-collegiate members could be admitted, but which offered no teaching or corporate life. These gradually acquired a quasi-collegiate existence as St Catherine's at Oxford and Fitzwilliam at Cambridge and, after nearly a century of providing a cheaper method of entry to their universities, became full colleges in the 1960s. Second, as a consequence of the opening up of the universities to Dissent, a number of denominational hostels were created. Two of these – Keble at Oxford (1870) and Selwyn at Cambridge (1882) – were intended to provide a relatively cheap and safely Anglican environment for undergraduates at what were now seen to be secular universities. Others, such as Mansfield in Oxford, were for Nonconformists.

The third area of reform concerned teaching and the curriculum. The revival in College teaching gradually made its impact after 1850, although undergraduates still had to rely on crammers. With the development of inter-collegiate lectures in the 1870s, some college tutors began to take responsibility for the personal oversight of the pupils' academic work, and by the end of the century additional coaching was considered remedial rather than central. The tension between what the Colleges could provide and what should be more properly university-based was not always so fruitful. In the sciences, heavy financial investment was needed which could be provided only on an inter-collegiate or university basis. This led some colleges to guard their independence and income by holding back on the development of expensive science teaching. University laboratories were created at both Oxford and Cambridge in the 1850s and 1860s, but not until 1877 did Parliament compel the colleges to give greater support to the university teaching of science.

Even then, teaching in science and technology made slow progress at the ancient universities, especially at Oxford. Though classics were declining, it was history rather than science which grew, as can be seen by comparing examination results at the two universities in 1900 and 1914. In the Oxford Class Lists for 1900, Classics led the field with 34 per cent, closely followed by History with 33 per cent; Natural Sciences were a mere 8 per cent and Mathematics 6 per cent. At Cambridge, the largest single group passing Part I of the Tripos was in Natural Sciences (27 per cent) followed by Classics (25 per cent), Mathematics (16 per cent) and History (10 per cent). In 1914, the Natural Sciences had declined proportionately but were still the largest group at Cambridge (22 per cent), followed by History (19 per cent); but at Oxford, History claimed 31 per cent and Classics 22 per cent, leaving Natural Sciences with only 14 per cent. The strength of the sciences at Cambridge can partly be attributed to its mathematical tradition, but even this was highly philosophical, and there were few signs before 1914 that the ancient universities saw their role as being anything other than to provide a liberal education for gentlemen.

The Scottish universities in the age of the Enlightenment

The contrast between the ancient universities of England and Scotland is one of the most marked features of the later eighteenth century, though the qualities and differences which distinguished Scottish education should not be allowed to mask its defects and similarities. First, the Scottish universities were as much as part of the Established Church as those in England, and their primary function was to prepare boys for ministry in the Church. Second, the five Scottish universities did not share equal distinction. St Andrews was always small and struggling; Aberdeen's two universities – King's and Marischal, not united until 1858 – were highly localised, and more like secondary schools than places of higher education. The reputation of Scotland really rested on the universities of Glasgow and Edinburgh.

Their rise was partly accidental, the product not of idealism but poverty. In 1708 Edinburgh City Council – which controlled the University of Edinburgh – had reformed it along Dutch lines, abolishing the system of regent masters, whereby one tutor taught all subjects to his pupils, and appointing instead a number of specialist professors. But, lacking adequate endowments, the university required its professors to charge for their lectures to make up the bulk of their incomes. Since the fee was to be three guineas per student per course, a popular lecturer could be richly rewarded. The other universities developed similarly, Marischal being the last to adopt the professorial system in 1753. The result was a cluster of outstanding professors and other academics, living quite literally off their wits, and providing some of the finest intellectual influences in Europe. Whereas before about 1750 many Scotsmen had gone to other universities, especially in Holland, to complete their education, now they received men from England: not only Dissenters barred from the English universities, but also leading Whig politicians cut off from the Continental tour by the French Wars – Russell, Palmerston and Brougham. In 1824 Edinburgh had about 2,300 students, Glasgow 1,240 and Aberdeen 730, and only St Andrews was languishing with under 200.

The success of the professorial system enhanced another feature of the Scottish universities – their open access. At a time when Oxford and

Cambridge were growing ever more exclusive, with fees increasing from around £100 in the mid-eighteenth century to as much as £250 a year by the 1830s, a student could attend his local Scottish university for a few pounds. The lectures were open to anyone willing to pay the relatively small fee; and divinity was usually free, enabling poor boys to aspire to social advancement through the Church or schoolmastering. Most students lived at home, or travelled to university with their bags of meal and lived frugally in lodgings. At Glasgow at the end of the eighteenth century, about half the students came from commercial and industrial backgrounds, and about half of these can broadly be called 'working-class'.[18] Many were destined for the Church. The Aberdeen universities were particularly well-served from the 1830s by the Dick bequest, which supplemented schoolmasters' salaries in the North-East, maintaining a high level of university-qualified teachers who could prepare their pupils to win bursaries to King's or Marischal. For this reason, the tradition of the parochial school and popular entrance to university remained in the North-East even after it had begun to collapse elsewhere with the increasing social stratification of the schooling system.

Nevertheless, the Scottish universities were not without their critics. Overall academic standards among students were very low. This was a product partly of the very young age of entry – as low as 15 – and partly the emphasis in the four-year Arts course on a broad and highly generalised education, in contrast to the more specialised Classics teaching at Oxford and Mathematics at Cambridge. At the very time that Scotland was still enjoying the autumn of its Enlightenment reputation, and Scotsmen were telling Englishmen how to run their education system, a Royal Commission (1826–30) told Scotsmen to make their universities more like the English ones, a message not fully accepted before 1889. Whatever the arguments about the curriculum, reform of the administrative structures of the universities was badly needed. They had become professorial oligarchies no less corrupt and inefficient than College fellowships and, as in England, the issue of academic reform cannot be divorced from the wider movement to open up all oligarchies of power to more popular and responsible control. The leading figure in the movement for the reform of the Scottish universities was, in fact, Joseph Hume, MP for Aberdeen, who was also instrumental in the reform of municipal corporations and the establishment of London University.

Alternative institutions

For those dissatisfied with or excluded from the universities in the eighteenth century, Academies provided an alternative. The first of these were set up in the later seventeenth century by tutors ejected from Oxford and Cambridge, and many of them served the dual purpose of seminaries for Dissenting ministers and colleges offering advanced education with a modern syllabus. Many of them were short-lived, or migrated with their tutors, but they made an invaluable contribution to the literary, scientific and philosophic education of a wide social group among the middling classes of all denominational loyalties in the eighteenth century. The chemist John Roebuck attended the Northampton Academy, before going on to study at Edinburgh and Leyden; John Wilkinson, the iron-master and an Anglican, went to the Kendal Academy. Archbishop Thomas Secker went to Tewkesbury, as did Bishop Joseph Butler, who then found Oxford a disappointing anticlimax. At the celebrated Warrington Academy (1757–83) where Joseph Priestley (LL,D, Edinburgh) was tutor, at least a quarter of the graduates went into commerce. 'The chief and proper object of education is not to form a shining and popular character, but a useful one, this being also the only foundation of real happiness,' wrote Priestley in 1778.[19]

The same modern spirit inspired the Academy movement in Scotland, though here the initiative was taken by local burgh councils, not private individuals. The first was Perth, opened in 1760 to offer a two-year course in scientific and utilitarian subjects instead of the rather philosophic courses of the universities, as well as being nearer home and even cheaper. Though by the end of the century many of these academies had merged with their local high schools, one consequence of the demand for a more utilitarian approach to education which they represented was the modernisation of courses at the universities. Two institutions which survived in this scientific tradition were the Andersonian Institute at Glasgow, founded in 1796, and the Watt Institution in Edinburgh, begun as the Edinburgh School of Arts in 1821 and taken over at the redistribution of the Heriot endowment in 1885 to form Heriot-Watt College. Both eventually became universities (Strathclyde, 1964; and Heriot-Watt, 1965).

The single most important educational institution to be founded by the reformers in the early nineteenth century was the University of London, opened in Gower Street in 1828. The leadership came from Henry Brougham (great-nephew of William Robertson, Principal of Edinburgh University at the height of the Scottish Enlightenment), George Birkbeck (Professor of Natural Philosophy at the Andersonian), James Mill (University of Edinburgh), Jeremy Bentham (Westminster and Oxford), George Grote (Charterhouse and banking), Thomas Campbell (University of Glasgow) and Joseph Hume (University of Edinburgh). Their University was secular and utilitarian, professorial and non-residential, inspired by Scotland and the revived university system of Germany. In response, the Anglican King's College was opened in the Strand in 1831. In 1836 it was agreed that the Gower Street institution should be called University College, and a separate University of London was created with power to grant degrees to members of either college or to candidates from other institutions of approved status. By 1851 there were 29 general colleges and nearly 60 medical colleges affiliated to the University from as far away as Yorkshire and Carmarthen as well as from overseas – Ceylon, Bengal, Malta and McGill in Canada. One-third of the graduates were medical students. In 1858 the necessity of being registered with an approved institution was removed for all non-medical students. London thus both encouraged the development of provincial and metropolitan institutions offering courses in higher education, and after 1858 became a kind of 'open university' for any individual who had prepared himself (or herself after 1878) for the London examinations. Although King's was founded in reaction to University College, its curriculum was little different. Both provided a strongly practical, scientific education for the middle classes.

In this respect the third foundation of the early nineteenth century, at Durham, was quite different. It was established in 1837 out of the riches of the Bishopric of Durham by the Bishop and Chapter in the shadow of reform. It was intended to provide a cheaper form of Oxbridge education for the northern clergy and, unlike London, was a residential university. Although the curriculum was soon broadened to include such subjects as engineering, Durham did not at first succeed. The market for Oxbridge on the cheap was clearly not extensive. This was discovered also by the executors of the will of John Owens, who opened Owens' College in Manchester in 1851 to provide a liberal education area without religious tests for the young men of Manchester.

Liberal, scientific or useful education?

When J. H. Newman found himself in the tortuous position of having to defend the ideal of an Oxford liberal education before an audience of Irish parents seeking a professional training for their sons in the proposed Catholic University in Dublin in 1851, he produced an argument worthy of his subtle, theologically trained mind. His words have been repeated on many occasions since then to justify the direction in which British higher education developed, for better or worse, up to the 1980s:

> A University training is the great ordinary means to a great but ordinary end; it aims at raising the intellectual tone of society, at cultivating the public mind, . . . at giving enlargement and sobriety to the ideas of the age, at facilitating the exercise of political power, and refining the intercourse of private life. It is the education which gives a man a clear conscious view of his own opinions and judgements, a truth in developing them, and eloquence in expressing them, and a force in urging them. It teaches him to see things as they are, to go right to the point, to disentangle a skein of thought, to detect what is sophistical, and to discard what is irrelevant. It prepares him to fill any post with credit, and to master any subject with facility.[20]

A liberal education was for gentlemen of leisure, and was beneficial (and hence useful) because it was not undertaken to serve narrow utilitarian ends.

In the traditions of Oxford and Cambridge, any branch of knowledge could serve the purposes of a liberal education, though there was a prejudice against the natural and applied sciences on the grounds of intellectual narrowness. Mathematics at Cambridge or Classics at Oxford were, however, equally liberal studies. The Scots saw matters differently, and found the approach in the English universities too narrowing to be truly liberal; whereas the English found the Scottish degree courses too superficial to serve the purposes of a liberalising education. The Scots lost the argument, partly because the English had the political power and partly because, as many Scots knew, their courses were academically shallow. After 1889 the two systems were brought closer together, with only the four-year course and general introductory first year surviving from the old Scottish system in the later twentieth century. As knowledge grew ever more complex and specialised, the British academic ideal became 'true breadth in depth', though American educators might still disagree.

While the ancient universities were debating and redefining a liberal education, newer foundations were pursuing more practical lines, such as had distinguished London from its earliest years. Owen's College in Manchester began to recover from a rather feeble start when it was made to appear relevant to the local community through the efforts of Henry Roscoe, Professor of Chemistry from 1857, and roots in local industry were also important for new civic colleges created in the 1870s and 1880s: the Newcastle College of Physical Science (1871), the Yorkshire College of Science at Leeds (1874), Firth College, Sheffield (1874), University College, Bristol (1876), the Mason College of Science, Birmingham (1880), University College, Liverpool (1881) and University College, Nottingham (1881). Initially the majority of their students were local, studying at below degree level and on a part-time basis. Leeds, for example, opened in 1874 with 80 day-students, 101 afternoon students and 145 evening students. Each institution had its own history and development, but all had certain features in common. They arose out of a concern by industrialists for the future of British industry and commerce, prompted by an awareness of increasing foreign competition; but they also expressed the civic pride and cultural aspirations of an educated provincial élite. Dundee College, founded in 1883 with money from the Baxter linen family, was intended to elevate the culture of the trading community, and had an Arts faculty and Chair in English from the start. To escape the confines of the Scottish system, its students were prepared for London degrees.

The determination of civic leaders to provide liberal as well as applied studies ensured that, over a generation, the earliest civic colleges would move towards university status. Owen's College was the first, becoming the Victoria University in 1880; Liverpool joined in 1884 and Leeds in

1887. A gift of £50,000 from Andrew Carnegie helped Birmingham achieve University status in 1900, and this precipitated the break-up of the Victoria University. Manchester and Liverpool became independent universities in 1903, Leeds followed in 1904 and – not to be upstaged by its Yorkshire rival – Sheffield followed in 1905. H. O. Wills then put up the money for Bristol University in 1909.

Somewhat different in inspiration from the civic colleges and universities of industrial, provincial England was the federal University of Wales, created in 1893 out of local colleges in Aberystwyth, Bangor and Cardiff. Here science was not important; culture and national identity were, and the majority of students in the early years became either schoolteachers or ministers of religion. The first College, opened in the Castle Hotel, Aberystwyth in 1867, was as remote from industrial Wales as was possible, and within the Principality had to rely chiefly upon the small donations of relatively poor people. Indeed, over half the money raised between 1863 and 1881 was expatriate Welsh money from England, and the College was saved only by an annual government grant given on the recommendation of the Aberdare Committee from 1882. The Committee thought there should be only two colleges, one for North Wales and one for the South, but Aberystwyth was confirmed as a third college in 1889. The College at Bangor, opened in 1884, was similarly dependent upon small subscriptions; indeed, Bangor might rightly be regarded as the people's own Welsh college: the Penrhyn and Dinorwic quarry workers alone raised over £1,250, while Lord Penrhyn himself could manage only a paltry £1,000. The main support came from Liverpool and a bequest of £47,000 from Dr Thomas Evans of Manchester. Cardiff (1883) lacked both popular and local industrial support, although alone of the Welsh colleges it was industrially based. The largest donations came from the London Drapers' Company, the coal-owners preferring to set up their own mining college at Treforest.

Meanwhile, Colleges had been multiplying in London to prepare students for London degrees. Most important after University and King's were the various medical schools, the London School of Economics (1895) and the constituent parts of Imperial College (1907) – the Royal College of Science, the Royal School of Mines and the City and Guilds Colleges – which provided much of the technological education available at the higher level in the metropolis. The constitution of London University itself was changed in 1898 to prevent the colleges developing into separate universities; from 1900 it consisted of two elements: affiliated colleges and external candidates. Most of the London and provincial colleges became affiliated (a notable exception being Newcastle, which gave Durham degrees). Although university extension work from Cambridge and Oxford lay behind the creation of other colleges at Nottingham (1881) and Reading (1892) respectively, London was, in effect, the midwife of the British university system as it developed up to the expansion of the 1960s.

Higher education for women

The cause of higher education for women was inextricably linked with the need to improve the educational standards of middle-class women generally, especially those who had to support themselves by working as governesses, or who aspired to enter higher professions hitherto exclusively reserved for men.

In 1847 Frederick Denison Maurice of King's College, London, began a series of lectures for governesses, and the following year opened Queen's College in Harley Street, next door to the offices of the Governesses' Benevolent Institution which had been set up to help indigent governesses in 1843. Though the College was no more than a secondary school, it educated some of the leading pioneers of women's education – among them Frances Mary Buss, who came to the evening classes, Dorothea Beale, and Sophia Jex-Blake, who was to lead the fight to win entry for women to the medical profession. The next year Elizabeth Reid opened a house in Bedford Square for lectures which she had been arranging for women since 1847. On her death in 1866 she left an endowment to continue her work, and Bedford College achieved full status preparing women for the London degree when it was made available to them in 1878. Other women's colleges followed: Westfield (1882) to provide an Anglican equivalent to the non-denominational Bedford; and Royal Holloway (1886). Before this, a long struggle had taken place to secure the right of women to matriculate, and it was the refusal of London to allow Elizabeth Garrett to study medicine in 1862 which determined Emily Davies to pursue her life's work in opening up higher education to women.

Emily Davies wished to raise the standards of women's education in schools and to open up the universities to them at the same time. It was a tall order. Her efforts led to the establishment in Hitchin in 1869 of a College linked with Cambridge to prepare girls for the Previous Examination and the Ordinary Degree. The College was moved to Girton, a village two miles safely outside Cambridge, in 1874; but it was not until 1880 that women were allowed to sit the same Tripos examinations as men. Even then their results were given on a separate class list and women were not entitled to take their degrees.

Other reformers within the university had different ideas, and considered Emily Davies too headstrong and unrealistic. Conscious of the inadequate preparation received by girls aspiring to university studies, and wishing to set an example of reform, a group of Cambridge academics and their wives – including Professor and Mrs Henry Sidgwick, F. D. Maurice and James Stuart – met at the home of Professor and Mrs Henry Fawcett (the latter being Elizabeth Garrett's sister) in 1869 to plan courses of lectures for women. In part the inspiration for this came from the lecturing experiences of James Stuart, a young mathematics lecturer at Trinity. He had been invited (on the recommendation of Josephine Butler) by Anne Clough of the Liverpool Ladies' Educational Association to give a series of lectures to women in Liverpool, Sheffield, Manchester and Leeds in 1867. He chose to give his lectures on astronomy and applied science; they were a great success. There was nothing unusual in this, for the professors at Edinburgh and Glasgow were well-known for the popular extra-curricular lectures which they delivered to augment their incomes, and which drew large numbers of women to hear them. Indeed, Stuart's work cannot be understood without reference to his Scottish background, and his awareness of the great differences in cost and social recruitment at the two universities – St Andrews and Cambridge – of which he had first-hand experience. As a result of his lectures in Lancashire, Josephine Butler (wife of the Principal of Liverpool College) set up the North of England Council for Promoting the Higher Education of Women, with Anne Clough as secretary. Although she had been involved with Emily Davies's campaigns in London before returning to her native Liverpool, Clough's ideas for women's education were far less ambitious.

Stuart's lectures resulted in requests to repeat them the following year at the Crewe Mechanics' Institute and the Rochdale Pioneers Society, and so began the extra-mural work which was to lead to the University Extension movement (1873). Also in 1868 he started giving inter-collegiate lectures at Cambridge, the first non-professor to offer lectures outside his own college, and in 1869 he gave his open lectures both in Cambridge (where they were attended by women as well as men) and at Hitchin, where the girls were chaperoned by Emily Davies, knitting.[21] The lectures planned at the Fawcetts' house in 1869 were a continuation of this work, so it was natural, when Sidgwick opened accommodation for women wishing to attend the lectures from outside Cambridge, that he should invite Anne Clough to take charge of it. She came, and in 1875 permanent premises were opened at Newnham, primarily to prepare women for the Higher Local Examination which had been instituted in 1869. Unlike any other Cambridge College, Newnham College (as it became in 1880) was a purely secular institution, with no college chapel. Girton was a men's college for women; Newnham was closer in spirit to university extension, and part of the wider movement for radical change.

Oxford soon followed. Mark Pattison had envisaged in the 1860s a scheme of post-school classes for men and women in every large town, and had begun such classes in Oxford; but, unlike Stuart's work in Cambridge, these came to nothing. More resulted from the pressure of liberal academics, especially the Professor of Political Economy, J. E. Thorold Rogers, whose daughter Annie was accidentally offered a scholarship to Worcester College in 1870 on the strength of her results in the Local Examination. (Her sex was disguised by her use of her initials only.) In 1877 a separate women's examination was held for the first time at Oxford. Annie Rogers was the sole candidate to take honours. She realised how difficult the work was, and in 1879 helped set up the Association for the Education of Women to organise the tuition of women for the examination. In this respect, her efforts were parallel to those of Anne Clough. Two halls were opened at Oxford, Lady Margaret (Church of England) and Somerville (undenominational) in 1879, as well as a non-collegiate institution (later, St Anne's); these were followed by St Hugh's (1886) and St Hilda's (1893).

The struggle for equality of treatment for women took a long time. The anomalous position of women at Cambridge was illustrated in 1890, when Philippa Fawcett of Newnham (daughter of Henry and Millicent Fawcett) was placed 'above the Senior Wrangler'; that is, better than anyone else in the senior Mathematics Tripos, the most prestigious of all academic achievements for an undergraduate. The lie had been given to the charge that women were intrinsically inferior to men, but Cambridge still managed to delay granting titular degrees to women until 1921, and did not admit women to full degrees as equals until 1948. Women were gradually admitted to the Oxford Schools between 1884 and 1904, but were not permitted to take their degrees until 1920. By this date not only London and all its colleges but every other university in the country had admitted women to its degrees: Victoria (1880) and Wales (1893) from their foundation, the Scottish universities from 1892, and finally Durham from 1895.

This was a great triumph of principle, achieved over a comparatively short space of time. But the actual numbers of women in higher education were not high. Family and social expectations, lack of schooling and poor economic prospects were long to hamper the development of true equality of opportunity in higher education. As late as 1961, on the eve of the great expansion in university places, there were only 593 female undergraduates at Oxford and Cambridge (13 per cent). The real breakthrough there came only in the 1970s, when most Oxford and Cambridge colleges became co-educational.

Higher education in the twentieth century

Between 1914 and 1963, when the Robbins Committee reported on Higher Education, development followed the lines established between 1870 and 1914. Historically there were seven groups of universities to be considered by the Committee.[22] First, there were Oxford and Cambridge, which accounted for between 5,000 and 6,000 students (22 per cent of the total) before 1939 and about 9,000 (16 per cent) in 1963.

Second came the four ancient Scottish foundations (St Andrews, Glasgow, Aberdeen, and Edinburgh), which had grown from 10,000 students before the Second World War to 20,000 in 1963. Of the four, only St Andrews was largely residential, having been forced by poverty to recruit students from England in the later nineteenth century. The Dundee College had become a part of St Andrews in 1953. Third, there was the University of London, given greater coherence by an Act of 1926, but still an enormous conglomerate, over twice the size of any other two universities put together, with 13,000 students before the Second World War, increasing to 23,000 by 1963. Then, fourth, there was Durham and the older civic universities, which had achieved their full status before 1914 (Manchester, Birmingham, Liverpool, Leeds, Sheffield and Bristol). Of these, Manchester had 8,000 students in 1963, and Leeds between 5,000 and 6,000.

Fifth came the three Welsh Colleges which had made up the University of Wales in 1893, to which a fourth College at Swansea had been added in 1920. Together with the Welsh National School of Medicine, the Welsh Colleges had only 8,000 students between them in 1963. Sixth, there were the University Colleges, of which Reading, Nottingham, Southampton and Exeter had been founded before the First World War, and Leicester and Hull shortly afterwards. Reading became a full university in 1926, but the others were only recent creations, achieving university status between 1948 and 1957. Additionally, there was the only post-Second-World-War University College, Keele in North Staffordshire. This college was unusual in that it offered a four-year course with a general foundation year and taught for its own degrees under the sponsorship of three other universities. It became a full university in 1962. Of these institutions, only Nottingham had over 2000 students in 1963.

Finally, there were eight 'new' universities, founded between 1961 and 1965, at Brighton, Canterbury, Colchester, Coventry, Lancaster, Norwich, Stirling and York. Unlike the civic colleges of the nineteenth century, these were full universities from the start, deliberately planned as residential institutions on 'green-field' sites, with a broad range of cultural as well as scientific subjects. In inspiration they owed less to London than to Oxford and Cambridge, but they were also – like Keele – expected to use their novel positions to bring fresh thinking to bear on academic structures and courses.

The commitment of the government to the support of these institutions represented a considerable reversal of policy over the previous hundred years. Apart from the Scottish universities, which received state finance under the terms of the Act of Union, and the Welsh grant from 1882, there was no systematic support for higher education until treasury grants were begun in 1889. These were at a very low level – £15,000 only in the first year. Though Scotland was much better supported than England, the main source of finance for the Scottish Universities before the First World War was the Carnegie Trust, which after 1901 dispensed £100,000 annually to support fellowships and research projects, and to pay the class fees of about half of Scotland's undergraduates. The Carnegie administration of financial support became the model in 1919 for the University Grants Committee, set up by the government to administer public funding of the university system, which had by then grown to about a million pounds. By the early 1960s this had risen to over £80 million, excluding the support given to students to assist with their living expenses, which became mandatory on local authorities in 1962.

Nevertheless, only a small proportion of the country's youth was able to attend university. Numbers rose from about 20,000 in 1900 to 50,000 in 1938, and had reached 113,150 in 1961–2, of whom 43 per cent were reading Humanities and Social Studies. The number of students actually going to university represented only about 4 per cent of their age-group. Within this number the bias was strongly against women and the working classes: only about a quarter of university entrants belonged to the working class, and fewer than a third were women.

The Robbins Committee outlined plans to remedy this situation, and to extend higher education in Britain to all who were qualified to enjoy it. It recommended the expansion of existing universities and the creation of new technological universities out of existing technical institutions, as a result of which the number of universities in Britain grew to over 40.

A further recommendation was the creation of a new body – the Council for National Academic Awards – to give degrees for higher-education work done in institutions outside the university system. A number of colleges of technology then became Polytechnics in 1968, when the Labour government removed the monopoly of the universities for the first time and created the 'binary' system of higher education. In effect, the CNAA was fulfilling for the later twentieth century the role which London University had earlier played for the civic colleges. Despite the alleged equality of status between the two halves of the system, though, there were signs in the 1980s of the Polytechnics wishing to follow the former civic colleges towards full independence as universities, a move confirmed in 1992, when the Polytechnics and several other Colleges of Higher Education became universities in name as well as intent, bringing the total number of such institutions to over 90.

A third important development, also envisaged by Robbins, came in 1969 when the Open University was founded. It too had been foreshadowed by London University in the nineteenth century, but with two important differences. First, it was designed specifically for adults; and, second, it was able to exploit the new media of radio and television to provide direct teaching to individual students in their own homes. Between 1970 and 1995 the Open University awarded 143,828 first degrees, and in 1996 it accounted for over 100,000 undergraduates, well over half the students enrolled on part-time first-degree courses in British higher education.

As a result of these measures, considerably more of the country's population was being introduced to higher education than ever before. Between 1970 and 1990 the number of full-time undergraduate students in higher education rose from 400,000 (42.5 per cent women) to 664,000 (48 per cent women). Four years later the total was 1,024,000 (50 per cent women). Whereas in 1968 only about 6 per cent of the population of Britain between the ages of 18 and 21 were in full-time education, in 1994 the figure was 25.6 per cent. Moreover, this expansion took place across all the major subject groups, so that of every 10 students to receive a first degree in 1992 four were in science, technology and medicine, four were in the social sciences and humanities, and two were in law and business studies.

Education and society

Education is a part of society, not a separate lever by which society can be moved. Despite the long-cherished beliefs of educational theorists, it has very little power of itself to reshape the social order. As Utopian philosophers since Plato have recognised, only by using education to obliterate all other forms of socialisation in the very young can educators hope to rebuild society. Otherwise, education is essentially a conservative force which reproduces in each generation the experience and values of its predecessors; and even when the power of the modern centralised State is called upon to enforce schemes of social engineering and reconstruction, change comes at best only slowly. But because society is never wholly static, the conservative circle is seldom completely closed, and in periods of rapid social change education may exert some influence over the direction and pace of that change.

Popular education and social change, 1750–1870

In Britain since the mid-eighteenth century educators have sought to influence society in a number of ways to direct or inhibit the process of change. Many people among the English upper classes in the eighteenth – and well into the nineteenth – century believed that the sole purpose of popular education was to fit people for the station in life into which they were born. For the poor this meant a practical training for manual work, and sufficient religious teaching to know that the social order was the will of God. Though philanthropists might wish to improve the lot of the poor, they were anxious not to encourage social mobility except among a few of rare academic gifts, whose education might be carefully sponsored and controlled. Ignorance of book-learning was the safest policy towards the majority. The theory in Scotland was a little different, placing greater emphasis on the religious duty to provide a basic education for all and social advancement for the 'lad of parts', but actual attitudes towards the social order were very similar to those south of the border.

There were two major impediments to this policy of social control through education. First, until late in the nineteenth century there was no effective central authority to enforce it. The State as such barely existed. That authority which was supposed to maintain moral and educational control, the Church, had in practice lost its monopoly in England in the seventeenth century, and was effectively undermined in Scotland by the pace of social change and urbanisation long before the Disruption completed a similar process there. Second, because English had long since replaced Latin as the major language for written communication, there were few barriers to the transition from an oral to a written (that is, literate) culture, except in parts of Wales and Scotland where English was not the spoken language of the people. When Joseph Barker's father taught himself to read and write simply by mastering the alphabet, he demonstrated the futility of attempts to control the poor through ignorance. Indeed, the policy had already failed before the eighteenth century began, as the founders of charity schools and the SPCK had recognised.

In a Protestant country it was very difficult to deny to people access to the Word of God in the Bible. Calvinists in Scotland and Puritans in England were theologically committed to basic education in the seventeenth century. Evangelicals followed them in the eighteenth. Hannah More and others who distributed religious tracts at the end of the eighteenth century knew that the poor needed to be able to read for the good of their souls – no less, but certainly no more. The founders of Sunday Schools were quite explicit about their objectives. In the words of the York Sunday School Committee (1786) they were for 'rescuing the children of poor parents from the low habits of vice and idleness and initiating them in the principles of the Christian religion'. To this end the children were to be 'restricted to reading in the Old and New Testament, and to spelling as a preparation for it'.[23] Dissenters and Methodists shared these motives, but originally taught writing as well, for Sunday was the one day in the week when children were available for instruction. However, unlike reading, writing was seen as a secular pursuit from which children might gain worldly advantage; to teach it on the Sabbath was a profanation. As Sabbatarian feeling grew, so the teaching of secular subjects declined. Writing was condemned by the Wesleyan Conference in 1814 and again in 1823 and 1837, which suggests that the ban was not easily enforced. A further reason why the Sunday Schools were suspicious of writing was that it encouraged people to think and express themselves. Reading was thought to be a passive pursuit which could be contained. But in the years following the French revolution the confidence of supporters of the social order was shattered by the insidious circulation of radical tracts by Thomas Paine and others who were able to exploit the Bible skill of reading for quite other purposes. The poor were no longer ignorant, so educational policy had to become aggressively positive in defence of religion, morality and the social order. The early nineteenth century saw a major drive by the Churches, aided by an increasingly interventionist State, to provide schools for the poor.

Education became a major plank in social policy. For crusaders like James Kay-Shuttleworth it was the means by which the evils attendant upon the new urban and industrial society could be eliminated. For Utilitarians like Henry Brougham it was the basis of a progressive society in which the poor would be equipped to play their allotted part. For leaders of working-class radical opinion it was the foundation of a democratic society. For supporters of the Established Church it was the way to rescue the poor from that ignorance which left them prey to the propaganda of the radical demagogue and infidel socialist, the evils of drink, the delusions of Rome and the competition of Dissent. Educational theorists and would-be educators abounded, confident in the belief that society could be upheld/transformed/redeemed through education.

Control was exerted through the discipline of the institution and what was taught there. In both respects the voluntary nature of education weakened the efforts of those who sought to use it. Nevertheless, the Churches (and especially the National Society) made considerable progress in providing an education in relatively disciplined surroundings which could bring to bear more 'elevating' influences than those to which children were exposed in their own homes, without teaching them anything which would lead them to challenge the established order. In this respect, the provision of elementary education before 1870 was successful in reforming those controls by which a society remains coherent, and in promoting peaceful adaptation in an age of rapid social and economic change. But there was still the possibility that some troublesome individuals, not content with an elementary education, might seek to develop their education as adults and question existing social, religious and political structures. These often became the leaders of working-class opinion, and were regarded as dangerous by aristocracy and clergy, and by middle-class industrialists and Utilitarian reformers alike.

This independent and largely self-taught working-class opinion was inspired by radical editors and publishers like William Cobbett, William Hone, Richard Carlile, Henry Hetherington and William Lovett, who championed the cause of popular rights. They sought for the working classes not simply an education appropriate to their station, but – in the words of a report of the Birmingham Mechanics' Institute in 1835 – 'The SAME Education; and THE BEST – for ALL CLASSES'.[24] So working-class autodidacts rose at five o'clock in the morning to learn Latin, Greek and even Hebrew precisely because it was not useful. They wanted it because it was a liberal education in which they had a democratic right to share. For a minority of self-educated working men, education enabled them to become critically aware citizens. Fortunately for those who wished to maintain the hierarchy of education, reserving a liberal education exclusively for gentlemen, the working-class autodidacts were untypical of their class. Their influence, though, was sufficient to cause considerable anxieties among the upper and middle classes in the generation before

1850, as supporters of the Society for the Diffusion of Useful Knowledge and patrons of Mechanics' Institutes redoubled their efforts to incorporate the working classes within the capitalist system by teaching them the fundamental realities of classical Political Economy.

It is easy to gain a distorted picture of the place of education in class conflict during the early nineteenth century. The radical periodicals give an impression of the onward march of a righteous cause in which all 'the people' were involved. There is, indeed, much autobiographical evidence of the effect which the radical press had on working-class opinion, and a protest movement like Chartism cannot be understood unless the impact of radical literature is taken seriously. But even Chartism was ultimately dependent upon wider social influences. Educated radicalism gave shape, direction and coherence to the movement, but it did not cause those anxieties about social conditions, jobs and status which brought supporters forward in their thousands. Education may have heightened class awareness in the major urban and industrial areas of Britain in the years between the French revolution and the defeat of Chartism, but it did not cause it. Similarly, the efforts of middle-class educators anxious to soften class tensions were probably less successful than might at first glance seem the case. If one reads the speeches of those soliciting patronage for Mechanics' Institutes and similar places, one learns a great deal about the objective of gaining social control through education, but the connection between intent and outcome in education is, at best, rather tenuous. If education contributed towards the reduction in class tensions in the second half of the nineteenth century, it was more through helping working men to participate in trade unions, co-operative societies, working-men's clubs, building societies, chapels and political parties than through success for the cruder forms of indoctrination attempted by some educators of the earlier nineteenth century.

By the mid-nineteenth century, the cross-conflicts of ideological and educational struggle had begun to resolve themselves along new lines. The radical working-class challenge was incorporated within a changing view of society and the State. Radicals who had feared the State and sought to create their own education outside its indoctrinating reach received the vote in 1867 and came to see State power as the only effective means of obtaining educational change and social justice. This brought them close to the middle-class reformers' position expressed by Richard Cobden in the National Public Schools Association and Joseph Chamberlain in the National Education League. In 1870 compromise was institutionalised. Radicals and reformers accepted the State as educator, with coercive powers subject to a measure of local democratic control. With considerable reluctance, the Church of England acquiesced. What the experience of the previous hundred years had shown was that, despite fears of popular education, the problem was not too much education, but too little. The focus was shifting from questions of moral control and religious revival to ones of economic need and national welfare. What did not change – and was recognised in Scotland for the first time – was the class basis of educational provision, and the attitude that the education of the poor was not so much for their own benefit as for the good of society and the maintenance of the social order. The School Boards, with their powers of compulsion, continued the work, bringing discipline, order, and eventually welfare to children whom educators in the tradition of Kay-Shuttleworth were anxious to rescue from the viciousness of their home-lives and to elevate into tomorrow's citizens.

Education and the preservation of the élite

In the later eighteenth century Britain was governed by a narrow, self-confident, aristocratic élite bound together not only by family but by education and culture. A hundred years later, that élite had adapted itself to rule one of the foremost industrial powers in the world. It remained united by education and culture. This extraordinary ability of the British social and political élite to survive, and to continue surviving into the later twentieth century, is partly attributable to the educational institutions of England – its public schools and ancient universities.

The élite survived, by intelligent adaptation, without serious dilution. If one compares Britain with Germany in 1848, the contrast is clear. The German states, most of which had at least one university, were producing a well-educated middle class without access to political power. Among the many causes of the revolutions of 1848 was the presence of this discontented surplus of intellectuals. In Britain, on the contrary, the middle classes were allowed the semblance of political power in 1832, and just sufficient upward mobility to satisfy the social ambitions of the wealthiest among their numbers. High fees limited access to public schools which guarded the gates to social influence and real political power. The friends made at school and university constituted a charmed circle from which the great and the good were selected. Fathers aspiring to introduce their sons to the closed councils of the élite had first to send them to a public school. Until the second half of the nineteenth century only a few from among the commercial and industrial classes chose to do so – Peel and Gladstone being the most famous. When competitive examinations replaced patronage and connection in the mid-nineteenth century, the importance of the public schools was enhanced, for the schools were geared to coach their pupils to satisfy the examiners. Ambitious middle-class parents knew they would have to make the necessary sacrifices to buy a public-school education for their sons if they were to make their marks in the world. Purchase of office had been the eighteenth-century method; purchase of education replaced it in the nineteenth. At a time when theory was proclaiming the opening-up of British government to talent, the practice was for education to consolidate the position of the élite by limiting recruitment to the new wealthy.

Scottish experience might suggest that this was not the position north of the border. Although the current academic fashion is to challenge the myth of open access to education in Scotland, compared with the English system the Scottish schools and universities were relatively open to boys of low social and economic status. In 1866, for example, around a quarter of students entering Glasgow and Edinburgh universities were from working-class families, though practically all were the children of either artisans or skilled workers.[25] The products of the Scottish system, though, were not openly competing to join the British élite. Indeed, the nature of the unreformed Scottish degree handicapped Scottish students in competitive examinations for entry into the Civil Service, and the need to compete effectively was one reason for the decline in the distinctively Scottish nature of the degree course. Scottish students went into teaching, the Church or the professions. Their doctors, like those from London, found employment in the Empire. University for the British upper classes did not mean Glasgow or Edinburgh, or London or Manchester, but Oxford or Cambridge – indeed, at times it meant Balliol College, Oxford.

This attitude did not end with the nineteenth century. As the prestige and value of land declined, so the nature of the élite began to change and recruitment became rather wider. But what the educational system did was to preserve the values of the old élite even as it changed, so that social continuities were preserved. Long after the extension of the franchise to the bulk of the people, Britain remained in essence a political aristocracy. The narrow educational background of the leaders of British society even in the twentieth century is remarkable. A study of the Civil Service shows that in 1929 22.6 per cent of higher civil servants in Britain had attended one of the 'Clarendon Nine' public schools; in 1939 the proportion had fallen to 16.5 per cent, but it was still 10.8 per cent in 1950, and nearly a quarter of top civil servants had attended an independent boarding school of some kind.[26] Similarly in the political parties, especially in the Conservative Party, recruitment long depended upon a few select institutions (see above, pages 117–19, 157–9). An analysis of the people listed in *Who's Who?* in 1961 showed that a third of those named had been at a public school, with no fewer than one in six having attended Eton.[27]

What the public schools – and the ancient universities of England – achieved was an extraordinary sense of common purpose based on the ideals of a liberal education. This gave a coherence and confidence to the élite, and brought a stability to British institutions which sat strangely with the country's advanced economic state and emerging democratic system of government. The word which summed up these mystical qualities, imparted through the public schools and considered essential in a member of the élite, was 'gentleman'.

A gentleman was, by definition, male and wealthy. He had a natural moral superiority and self-assurance, was used to taking responsibility and being obeyed. His largeness of mind and generosity of spirit were based upon a classical education. He was a man of leisure, an amateur capable of detachment and philosophical reflection. He was instantly recognisable as someone at ease with the world, civilised, urbane, cultured, cosmopolitan and public-spirited. He liked to think of himself as a patrician in Cicero's Rome. Gentlemen lived by a code of behaviour enforced by peer-group pressure – the 'house spirit' at school; at university they were good 'College men'. They believed in teamwork and the team spirit, developed at school by playing such games as rugby and cricket. They became rulers, not through ambition, but through duty and a commitment to public service. If they worked hard, they liked not to show it.

In the last quarter of the nineteenth century, gentlemen (whether by birth or merely by education) constituted the British ruling class. They ruled not only a group of islands off north-west Europe, but an empire across the world. And they did it rather well. The qualities engendered in a gentleman's mind at school and university fitted him to rule India with conscientious impartiality. The British Civil Service and Judiciary established a reputation which was second to none. The same spirit later made the BBC respected throughout the world. But it was a limited education and did not, as Newman had claimed, prepare the gentleman 'to fill any post with credit'. The very qualities which made a good team member could easily stifle individual initiative, intelligence and eccentricity. The British Army discovered this in its contest with irregular soldiers in the Second Boer War; and the amateur spirit of the officer corps died in the trenches of the First World War. Less dramatically, the education of a gentleman hardly fitted him to became a thrusting man of business, ruthless in exploiting new opportunities in the greedy pursuit of personal wealth. Indeed, the purpose of education was to transform the sons of such people into gentlemen.

Education and the decline of Britain

As the de-industrialisation of Britain gathered pace in the 1970s and 1980s, a historical inquest began into where Britain had gone wrong, and an influential thesis was argued by an American professor, Martin Wiener, to the effect that British culture had never been reconciled to industrialism, and that the drive and initiative shown by the entrepreneurs of the First Industrial Revolution before 1850 had been progressively sapped by the anti-industrial ideals of élite culture.[28] The 1851 Exhibition was the high-water mark of industrial culture, but at that point it failed to take over and transform the older values of gentry society. Instead, the reverse occurred, leaving Britain ill-equipped to withstand the international competition which gathered pace in the second half of the nineteenth century. British decline was not, in Wiener's view, to be seen as a recent or cyclical problem, but as a long-term consequence of educational and cultural failure.

This thesis had a respectable pedigree. It was in effect an application in reverse of the thesis advanced by Max Weber in *The Protestant Ethic and the Spirit of Capitalism*, that economic development can have a cultural explanation.[29] There are at least three responses to Wiener's argument. The first is to accept it – with pride. If the model being opposed to the British way of life is that conventionally associated with America – brashly commercial and ruthlessly competitive – then the gentlemanly ideal has its attractions. Materialism and the profit motive seem shallow gods for the human spirit to worship. Matthew Arnold may well have been right when he wrote:

> Culture begets a dissatisfaction which is of the highest possible value in stemming the common tide of men's thoughts in a wealthy and industrial community, and which saves the future, as one may hope, from being vulgarised, even if it cannot save the present.[30]

Yet this very defence of the gentlemanly ideal may well be a symptom of the problem, for the values which inform the defence are the very ones which are under attack. Arnold is hardly an impartial witness.

The second response is to accept the thesis – with regret. Covering a broad sweep of history, it has a power to explain the economic failure of Britain which is as attractive as it is pessimistic. Much of the argument is valid, and hardly new. As Arthur Koestler argued in 1954, 'a subtle distortion of our intellectual values is caused by the emphasis in public schools on the humanities and the corresponding neglect of the sciences', and the case against the public school 'ethos' was also acknowledged in the conclusion to T. W. Bamford's *The Rise of the Public Schools* in 1967.[31] The failure of Oxford and Cambridge to provide a scientific and technological education in the nineteenth century has long been recognised. As G. C. Allen argued in 1976, 'the "establishment" was the victim of anachronistic institutions in the English class system and the educational arrangements associated with it'.[32] The ancient English universities provided only limited opportunities for social mobility, and none for social change. Their undergraduates were ill equipped to cope with the demands of industrial society. The spirit of amateurism which suffused the boardrooms of British industry contrasted sharply with the professionalism of the Germans, Americans and Japanese. Even in the City, no stranger to materialism, gentlemen traditionally preferred finance to industry, and preferred to make their money out of foreign trade, services and investments rather than domestic industrial development.

The third reaction is to recognise the validity of parts of the argument without being misled by the whole. The thesis shows several characteristics of a historical myth, providing an easy answer to a difficult problem for which contemporaries demand an answer, and containing just enough truth to be plausible. Economic historians are now far less confident than they were that the British economy in the later nineteenth century was experiencing a 'great depression'; and, when considering the depression of the inter-war years, they have concluded that Britain suffered rather less than her major competitors. Thus one cannot paint a picture of continuous decline since the mid-nineteenth century, interrupted only by a brief revival of traditional exports in the first decade of the twentieth century, financed by the export of capital. After allowance has been made for the fact that one small island could not hope forever to remain the workshop of the world, British economic achievements even as late as the 1950s were not disgracefully behind those of other major industrial nations. If the difficulties which beset the British economy from the 1960s onwards were attributable to long-term cultural failure, that cannot be the whole story. Either the cultured amateurs were not unsuccessful, or Britain was not quite such an amateur country as the dominance of the public schools and the humanities might suggest.

Historians of education are doubtful about taking too far the pessimistic comparisons between British and German education which figured so prominently in nineteenth-century inquests into the success of German competition. German universities were revived after 1806 with a modern rather than classical curriculum, but the spirit of education was still a humanist one not unlike that provided at Oxford and Cambridge. *Wissenschaft* (the pursuit of knowledge for its own sake) was their principal feature; narrow utilitarianism was frowned upon. Similarly, the *grandes écoles* of Paris were highly élitist, and professionally rather than industrially oriented. Oxford and Cambridge were not unique in fulfilling the role of providing servants for the state rather than private industry.

Where the Germans excelled was in extending their concept of *Wissenschaft* to pure science. Here the British universities certainly lagged behind Germany, but by 1914 they were catching up in most subjects except chemistry. The problem lay not in the capabilities of the British universities to develop pure science, but in the neglect of applied science by industrialists and government alike. In Germany after 1870 industrialists sought closer links with the universities in the development of applied science, but the universities did not always welcome them. Instead, increased funding went to other institutions, notably the *Technische Hochschulen* (technical high schools). The government encouraged these advanced technical colleges, and by the end of the century they had achieved parity with the universities.

A comparison between education in Britain and Germany points to three areas in which the British were inferior: first, in the lack of parity of esteem between technology and the humanities; second, in the low level of provision for education at all levels in technology and applied science; and third, in the scale of the entire educational enterprise. Only the first of these can be attributed directly to an anti-industrial culture. Advocates of a liberal education could appreciate the virtues of *Wissenschaft*, but not its application to scientific knowledge, especially when directed to practical ends. As late as 1890, 80 per cent of all science graduates in England were mathematicians from Oxford or Cambridge.

The failure to provide adequate schooling and higher education in technology and applied science is more complex. To some extent it was a consequence of the reluctance of the State to invest in public education. With the exception of the efforts arising out of the Great Exhibition and the development of South Kensington, there was no expansion in technical education in Britain in the third quarter of the nineteenth century to match that which occurred at the elementary level. Not until the Technical Instruction Act of 1889 were public funds made available for local technical colleges. The London university institutions and civic colleges and universities made some contribution, but it was a modest one by German standards. In 1901–2 there were just 3,370 science and technology students in British universities, technical schools and colleges; Germany had 10,740 students in her technical high schools alone.

The reasons for this lack of scientific and technological education are not straightforward. In part they reflect the third factor, the dearth of higher education in all subjects. It is not that students were studying humanities instead of science; they were simply not studying at all. On the eve of the First World War, Germany had as many students studying science and technology as there were undergraduates in all subjects put together in British universities. This lack of provision for higher education has remained a constant theme of British history for much of the twentieth century. But there was also the problem of attitudes within British industry. The civic colleges attempted to forge links with local industry and to serve their communities, but they found British industrialists remarkably unresponsive compared to their German rivals. And they were unresponsive not because they had suffered a classical education, but because they did not see the value of scientific research, especially in its early, theoretical stages. It was not the academics but the entrepreneurs who failed to emulate their German counterparts. There is a marked contrast here also with American practice, where universities proved more open than those in Germany to direct involvement in sponsored industrial research for private companies, and where industrialists showed themselves more prepared than in Britain to support such enterprises.

In the twentieth century the British education system has proved itself capable of producing first-class minds to meet the needs of the modern state. There were many reasons why Britain was able to win two world wars, but not least were the administrative skills and scientific expertise of its people. But the two fundamental weaknesses of the later nineteenth century remained: the lack of adequately funded technical education at all levels, and the lack of parity in esteem between 'pure' and 'applied' knowledge in general, and between the humanities and technology in particular.

The 1902 Education Act enshrined the principles of a liberal education for all. In retrospect, the decision to model the new local-authority secondary schools on the old public and grammar schools – which owed much to the influence of the leading civil servant involved, Robert Morant – was a mistake. It enshrined the belief that a liberal education was the best; applied science was for those who could not understand Latin. Parental and public opinion accepted this view so readily that the principle of selection after 1944 came to mean a choice between a grammar-school education and 'failure'. Technology was devalued in schools among teachers, pupils and parents. Upward social mobility meant movement into the professions and public service, away from the dirt and commercialism of industry.

Several efforts were made after 1945 to increase the provision of technical education at the intermediate and higher levels, culminating in 1956 in the establishment of a hierarchy of institutions, with ten Colleges of Advanced Technology at the top. Within 10 years these Colleges were becoming technological universities with humanities departments, illustrating the persistence of the belief that higher education is properly the function only of a liberal university. Twenty-five years later the Polytechnics moved down the same path, convinced that within the binary system they were second-class citizens. Technology was recognised neither as the equal of pure science and the humanities, nor as an integral part of a liberal education for all. It is at this point that one can accept the argument put forward by Professor Wiener. The British educational system in its entirety – and not just Oxbridge and the public schools – has remained infused with a value system which has percolated down from the public schools and continues to accept a traditional liberal education as the ideal. As the Hungarian-born Koestler recognised, in Britain 'professions related to the humanities, the arts and letters rank higher than those connected with engineering and the applied sciences'.[33] The attempt to expand technological education in the 1960s foundered not because policy was lacking, but because students could not be found in the same numbers and of the same quality as humanities students to fill the places provided for them. Education policy was demand-led, for this was the essence of liberalism in education.

Much was claimed for educational advance in the optimistic days of the 1960s. It was assumed that to rebuild the education system – from comprehensive schools at the bottom, to new universities at the top – would be to lay the foundations for national regeneration. Twenty years later, it was not surprising that a disappointed and frustrated generation came to blame its teachers for failing to deliver the promised goods, which led to a rather mechanistic effort to 'raise standards' by politicians eager to be seen to be doing something. But this is to misunderstand the nature of the relationship between education and society, in which society forms as well as is formed by its education system. The historian of British decline has to look at many other factors beyond educational systems. For example, the cost of the Second World War was considerable, in terms both of the drain on British manpower and resources, and on the advantages which the war brought to Britain's major competitors. The United States received thousands of refugees from Europe in the 1930s and 1940s, some of them among the best-educated minds in the country. In Germany and Japan, social systems were destroyed and could be rebuilt to face the new age after 1945. In Britain, the wars modified but did not destroy old practices and attitudes. These were not wrong in themselves, but they were increasingly irrelevant to the modern age. Britain's educational institutions continued to reflect the values and needs of a past age, but were powerless on their own to transform society either as fast or as thoroughly as total defeat in war would have done. Between 1964 and 1974 politicians spoke of the need for a technological revolution, but had accomplished little before inflation, an oil crisis and a slowing-down in the world economy dampened enthusiasm for change and introduced a note of excessive caution into industry. Only in the 1980s were there at last signs of a significant renewal, with a determined effort by government to lead a cultural shift in British thinking.

Even so, as the century draws to a close, it is still unclear how far this has been permanently successful. In 1992 15 per cent of British graduates were engineers; in Germany and Japan the figure was 22 per cent. Britain is still better at invention than innovation. The City of London still prefers commerce to industry, and short-term profits to long-term investment in industrial development, though significant amounts of overseas capital have been attracted to establish new industries with a high scientific and technological content. Government and much of industry, though, remain reluctant to fund basic research where there is no apparent or immediate gain.

The legacy of past neglect still weighs heavily with a country that has failed to inspire a scientific culture in its citizens. The problem is readily recognisable in British intellectual life at all levels. In a survey of 37-year-olds conducted in 1995, 47 per cent were found to have low numeracy skills, compared to only 18 per cent with low literacy skills. Among those who had remained in full-time education until they were over 21, 12 per cent had low numeracy skills in what was a wholly literate group. Parity of esteem between what the scientist and novelist C. P. Snow in 1959 called 'the two cultures', is still some way off, and British society remains the weaker for it.[34]

Notes

1. Quoted by L. Stone, 'Literacy and Education in England, 1640–1900', p. 98 in *Past & Present*, 42 (February 1969), pp. 69–139.

2. F. Furet and J. Ozouf, *Reading and Writing: Literacy in France from Calvin to Jules Ferry* (Cambridge, 1982), pp. 282–99.
3. See R. D. Anderson, 'Education and the State in Nineteenth-Century Scotland', p. 524 in *Economic History Review* 36 (1983), pp. 518–34.
4. Stone, 'Literacy and Education in England, 1640–1900', pp. 104–5.
5. M. Sanderson, 'Literacy and Social Mobility in the Industrial Revolution', *Past & Present*, 56 (August 1972), pp. 75–104.
6. See T. W. Laqueur, 'Debate. Literacy and Social Mobility in the Industrial Revolution', p. 98, and M. Sanderson. 'A Rejoinder', in *Past & Present*, 64 (August 1974), pp. 96–112.
7. R. J. Smith, 'Education, Society and Literacy in Nottinghamshire in the Mid-Nineteenth Century', *University of Birmingham Historical Journal* 12 (1969), pp. 42–56.
8. J. T. Barker (ed.) *The Life of Joseph Barker, Written by Himself* (1880), p. 14.
9. Barker, *Life*, pp. 34–5.
10. *Report of a Committee of the Manchester Statistical Society, on the State of Education in the City of York, in 1836–1837* (1837), p. 16.
11. E. Royle, 'Mechanics' Institutes and the Working Classes, 1840–1860', *Historical Journal* 14 (1971), pp. 305–21.
12. F. Widdowson, *Going up into the Next Class: Women and Elementary Teacher Training, 1840–1914* (1980), p. 27.
13. M. Arnold, *A French Eton* (1864), pp. 106–7, repr. in P. Smith and G. Summerfield (eds.), *Matthew Arnold and the Education of the New Order* (Cambridge, 1969), pp. 76–156.
14. Arnold, *French Eton*, pp. 110–12.
15. Interview with the school teacher (1929–1951) at Millington Church of England School, East Riding, in 1980.
16. Estimates in L. Stone, *The University in Society*, (2 vols., Princeton, 1974) i, pp. 91–2.
17. L. Stone, 'Social Control and Intellectual Excellence: Oxbridge and Edinburgh 1560–1983', in N. Phillipson (ed.), *Universities, Society, and the Future* (Edinburgh, 1983), pp. 3–28.
18. W. M. Mathew, 'The Origins and Occupations of Glasgow Students, 1740–1839', *Past & Present*, 33 (April 1966), pp. 74–94.
19. J. Priestley, *Observations relating to Education* (1778), pp. xiii-xiv, quoted by H. C. Barnard, *A History of English Education from 1760* (1947; 2nd edn., 1971), pp. 29–30.
20. J. H. Newman, *Discourses on University Education* (Dublin, 1852), quoted in M. Sanderson (ed.), *The Universities in the Nineteenth Century* (1975), pp. 124–5.
21. James Stuart, *Reminiscences* (1912), pp. 150–5, 158–79.
22. *Higher Education: Report of the Committee appointed by the Prime Minister under the Chairmanship of Lord Robbins 1961–63*. Cmnd 2154 (1963), pp. 22–4.
23. J. Howard, *Historical Sketch of the Origin and Work of the York Incorporated (Church of England) Sunday School Committee* (1887; 2nd edn., York, 1896), pp. 7, 11.
24. *Report of the Committee of the Birmingham Mechanics Institute*, 10 (May 1835), p. 11.
25. R. D. Anderson, *Education and Opportunity in Victorian Scotland: Schools and Universities* (1983), pp. 150–1.
26. R. K. Kelsall, *Higher Civil Servants in Britain from 1870 to the Present Day* (1955), p. 123.

27. *The Times Education Supplement*, 20 Oct. 1961.
28. M. J. Wiener, *English Culture and the Decline of the Industrial Spirit* (Cambridge, 1980).
29. M. Weber, *The Protestant Ethic and the Spirit of Capitalism* (1904–5; English edn. 1930).
30. M. Arnold, *Culture and Anarchy* (1869; ed. J. Dover Wilson, Cambridge, 1932; repr. 1960), p. 52.
31. A. Koestler, 'An Anatomy of Snobbery' (1954), p. 90, printed in *The Trail of the Dinosaur and Other Essays* (1955), pp. 69–94; T. W. Bamford, *The Rise of the Public Schools* (1967), pp. 307–30.
32. G. C. Allen, *The British Disease: A Short Essay on the Nature and Causes of the Nation's Lagging Wealth* (1976), p. 48.
33. Koestler, 'Snobbery', p. 91.
34. C. P. Snow, *The Two Cultures and the Scientific Revolution* (1959).

Conclusion

The pace of social change in Britain over the past 250 years has increased beyond all but the wildest dreams of men and women alive when those economic changes began which historians have since labelled the 'industrial revolution'. Change became significant when its extent was so great as to impress itself on the experience of a single generation. This began to happen in the later eighteenth century, but only very selectively. Economic and technological developments affected the industrialising (especially textile) regions of the country, but left other parts relatively undisturbed. Only gradually did the impact of the industrial revolution spread throughout society and the political system. This process was hastened by the long period of war between 1793 and 1815, but even after that much remained within British society that was recognisably of the eighteenth century. To the social historian, oblivious of traditional chronology, the nineteenth century did not begin until some time between 1830 and 1860. Only by the latter date can one point to extensive urbanisation, a revolutionary transport network, the stabilisation of a class-structured society, the emergence of an administrative state, a clear rise in living standards and an extension of schooling to a majority of children. The change in demographic trends came even later, in the 1870s. What is popularly thought of as Victorian society is, to a large extent, late Victorian society.

If the eighteenth century lasted, in social terms, another 50 years or so beyond its natural span, the same is true of the nineteenth. Far from the century ending at the conventional political date of 1914, it continued in many respects until after the Second World War. Despite the considerable impact of the Great War of 1914–18, social trends established in the second half of the nineteenth century can be traced throughout the inter-war period in demography, household and family structures, education, religion and welfare. Though the absence of a national census in 1941 makes it difficult to establish which trends were modified before

1939, and which changed only during or after the Second World War, it was not until 1951 that marked differences were registered which then became the distinguishing features of late-twentieth-century Britain. Only as the country recovered from war in the 1950s can 'modern' British society be said to have come of age – with its demographic and sexual revolutions, rapid commercialisation, State welfare, universal secondary education, de-Christianisation and the diffusion throughout society of technological innovations such as the motor car, electrical goods and television. Contemporaries became self-consciously aware of their new society in the 1960s, but the 1950s should more accurately be seen as the turning point.

The speed of social change since the 1950s has meant that people in every generation now have to learn several times over to live as part of a different society from that into which they were born. Since the 1970s discoveries in molecular biology have transformed people's understanding of life, while developments in micro-electronics have revolutionised their capacity to organise and transmit human knowledge. At the same time, accelerating social trends have emphasised the extent to which human relationships and expectations have been recast within half a lifetime. In such an age, when the only certainty is that nothing is certain to remain the same, there is all the more reason to study the past, for no society – however new and iconoclastic – can escape its roots. Much which determines the shape of British society in the late twentieth century can be understood only by going back to the unfamiliar territory of what preceded it in the nineteenth and eighteenth centuries – or even earlier.

'Our tendency,' wrote J. K. Galbraith in 1977 (*The Age of Uncertainty*, p. 324), 'is to reflect on failure.' The social historian of modern Britain finds this inescapable. Social problems appear to beset us as never before: an impending environmental crisis; inner-city decay; the decline in traditional moral values; rampant materialism; increasing crime; the persistence of gross inequalities in life-chances; and a Welfare State struggling to meet increasing demands with decreasing hopes of satisfying them. There is little comfort in noting how many of these characteristics of the contemporary mood are to be found in every generation – not least in those which appear to us now to have been the most confident and successful. The sense of failure comes not because there has been an absolute deterioration in the quality of life – far from it – but with the knowledge that so little progress has been made, despite the scientific knowledge and technological wonders increasingly at the disposal of mankind since the industrial revolution. Like eighteenth-century rationalists, we continue to believe in the existence of absolute solutions, and feel frustrated that they have so far eluded us.

In fact, a study of history over the past two centuries suggests that solutions have often been found to social problems, but that out of each solution a new problem has arisen or a new standard of expectation has been created. Achievements have been many, but of their very nature they have been temporary. Progress is a word which historians like to avoid, for it encourages a simple belief in cause and effect linking improvement to improvement down the generations, and militates against the attempt to understand each generation for itself without reference to what comes after. Whilst this is true, for no generation knew what the future would make of its inheritance – and would be surprised if it could know now – the historian can also be permitted a little hindsight. In a complex and unpredictable way, the present has emerged out of the past, and so a better understanding of the present can be attempted through a better understanding of the past.

The perfect society is *utopia* – literally, nowhere. History provides no answers to our problems, but can prompt some of the questions which have to be answered in the struggle to rebuild society anew for every generation. If historians, like philosophers, exist to interpret the world but not to change it, those who read what historians write may at least aspire to the latter. If so, then no better goal may be found than that which inspired those reformers striving to cope with the problems of early industrial Britain 200 years ago – that the greatest happiness of the greatest number is still a worthy end, towards which human society should devote its physical, intellectual and moral resources.

Further reading

The following list is divided roughly according to the major subject headings in the book. A few works are repeated in more than one section. Students wanting brief introductions, with bibliographies, to many of the themes raised in this book are advised to start with the Studies in Economic and Social History series, published for the Economic History Society by Macmillan before 1995, and thereafter by Cambridge University Press. These booklets are designated by the initials SESH. These and other works useful for introductory reading are indicated thus *. The place of publication is London, unless otherwise indicated.

Useful collections of sources

Annual Abstract of Statistics (annually).

Britain: An Official Handbook (annually).

Butler, D. and G., *British Political Facts, 1900–1994* (1963; seventh edn., 1996).

Cook, C. and Stevenson, J., *The Longman Handbook of Modern British History, 1714–1995* (1963; third edn., 1996).

Halsey, A. H. (ed.), *Trends in British Society since 1900: A Guide to the Changing Social Structure of Britain* (1972).

Mitchell, B. R. and Deane, P., *Abstract of British Historical Statistics* (Cambridge 1962).

Mitchell B. R., and Jones, H. G., *Second Abstract of British Historical Statistics* (Cambridge, 1971).

Social Trends (annually).

General works

Bédarida, F., *A Social History of England, 1851–1975* (Paris, 1976; transl., 1979; second edn., 1991).

Berg, M., *The Age of Manufactures: Industry, Innovation and Work in Britain 1700–1820* (1985).

Best, G., *Mid-Victorian Britain, 1851–1875* (1971; new ed. 1979).

Briggs, A., *A Social History of England* (1983; second edn., 1994).

Clarke, P., *Hope and Glory: Britain, 1900–1990* (1996).

Deane, P. and Cole, W. A., *British Economic Growth, 1688–1959* (1962; second edn., Cambridge, 1967).

Daunton, M. J., *Progress and Poverty: An Economic and Social History of Britain, 1700–1850* (Oxford, 1995).

*Evans, E. J., *The Forging of the Modern State: Early Industrial Britain, 1783–1870* (1983; second edn., 1996). Good bibliography and statistical appendix.

Flinn, M. W. and Smout, T. C. (eds.), *Essays in Social History* (Oxford, 1974), i. Reprints some of the most important essays in British social history.

Floud R. and McCloskey, D. (eds.), *The Economic History of Britain since 1700* (1981; second edn., 3 vols., Cambridge, 1994). Excellent for up-to-date essays.

*Halsey, A. H., *Change in British Society* (1978; fourth edn., Oxford, 1995).

Harris, J., *Private Lives, Public Spirit: Britain, 1870–1914* (1993).

*Harrison, J. F. C., *The Common People: A History from the Norman Conquest to the Present* (1984).

Harrison, J. F. C., *Early Victorian Britain, 1832–1851* (1979).

Harrison, J. F. C., *Late Victorian Britain, 1875–1901* (1990).

Hay, D. and Rogers, N., *Eighteenth-Century English Society 1688–1820* (Oxford, 1997).

Hopkins, E., *A Social History of the English Working Classes* (1979).

Hunt, E. H., *British Labour History 1815–1914* (1981).

Marwick, A., *British Society since 1945* (Harmondsworth, 1982; second edn., 1995).

Obelkevich, J. and Catterall, P. (eds.), *Understanding Post-War British Society* (1994). Essays, useful for recent trends.

Porter, R., *English Society in the Eighteenth Century* (Harmondsworth, 1982).

Price, R., *Labour in British Society: An Interpretative History* (1986).

*Robbins, K., *The Eclipse of a Great Power: Modern Britain, 1870–1992* (1983; second edn., 1994). Good bibliography and statistical appendix.

Rule, J., *Albion's People: English Society, 1714–1815* (1992).

Stevenson, J., *British Society, 1914–45* (Harmondsworth, 1984).

Thane, P. and Sutcliffe, A. (eds.), *Essays in Social History* (Oxford, 1986), ii. A second series of some of the most important recent essays in British social history.

Thompson, F. M. L., *The Rise of Respectable Society: A Social History of Victorian Britain, 1830–1900* (1988).

*Thompson, F. M. L. (ed.), *The Cambridge Social History of Britain, 1750–1950* (3 vols., Cambridge, 1990). Excellent introductory essays on several central themes.

Wilson, A. (ed.), *Rethinking Social History: English Society 1570–1920 and its Interpretation* (Manchester, 1993). For the way the subject is developing.

General works: Wales

Herbert, T. and Jones, G. E. (eds.), *People and Protest: Wales 1815–1880* and *Wales, 1880–1914* (Cardiff, 1988). Essays on social themes.

*Howell, D. and Baber, C., 'Wales', in Thompson, F. M. L. (ed.), *The Cambridge Social History of Britain, 1750–1950* (Cambridge, 1990), i, pp. 281–354.

Morgan, K. O., *Rebirth of a Nation: Wales, 1880–1980* (Oxford and Cardiff, 1981).

Williams, D., *A History of Modern Wales* (1950; second edn., 1977).

Williams, G. A., *When Was Wales? A History of the Welsh* (Harmondsworth, 1985).

General works: Scotland

Checkland, S. and O., *Industry and Ethos: Scotland, 1832–1914* (1984).

Devine, T. and Mitchison, R. (eds.), *People and Society in Scotland: 1760–1830* (Edinburgh, 1988).

Dickinson, T. and Treble, J. H. (eds.), *People and Society in Scotland: 1914 to the Present* (Edinburgh, 1991).

Fraser, W. H. and Morris, R. J. (eds.), *People and Society in Scotland: 1830–1914* (Edinburgh, 1990).

Harvie, C., *No Gods and Precious Few Heroes: Scotland, 1914–1980* (1981).

Lythe, S. G. E. and Butt, J., *An Economic History of Scotland, 1100–1939* (Glasgow, 1975).

Lenman, B., *An Economic History of Modern Scotland, 1660–1976* (1977).

Lenman, B., *Integration, Enlightenment, and Industrialization: Scotland, 1746–1832* (1982).

*Mitchison, R., 'Scotland, 1750–1850', in Thompson, F. M. L. (ed.), *The Cambridge Social History of Britain, 1750–1950* (Cambridge, 1990), vol. 1, pp. 155–207.

Smout, T. C., *A History of the Scottish People, 1560–1830* (1969).

Smout, T. C., *A Century of the Scottish People, 1830–1950* (1986).

*Smout, T. C., 'Scotland, 1850–1950', in Thompson, F. M. L. (ed.), *The*

Cambridge Social History of Britain, 1750–1950 (Cambridge, 1990), i, pp. 209–80.

Historical geography

Butlin, R. A., 'The Historical Geography of Britain', in *The Ordnance Survey Atlas of Great Britain* (1982), pp. 144–57.
*Darby, H. C. (ed.), *A New Historical Geography of England after 1600* (Cambridge, 1976).
Dodgshon, R. A. and Butlin, R. A. (eds.), *A Historical Geography of England and Wales* (1978).
Langton, J. and Morris, R. J. (eds.), *Atlas of Industrialising Britain 1780–1914* (1986).
Pope, R. (ed.), *Atlas of British Social and Economic History since c. 1700* (1989).
Trinder, B., *The Making of the Industrial Landscape* (1982).
Turnock, D., *A Historical Geography of Scotland since 1707* (Cambridge, 1982).
Wise, M. J., 'Modern Britain', in *The Ordnance Survey Atlas of Great Britain* (1982), pp. 158–77.

The changing countryside

Armstrong, W. A., *Farmworkers in England and Wales: A Social and Economic History* (1988).
*Armstrong, W. A., 'The Countryside', in Thompson, F. M. L. (ed.), *The Cambridge Social History of Britain, 1750–1950* (Cambridge, 1990), i, pp. 87–153.
Butlin, R. A., *The Transformation of Rural England, c. 1580–1800* (Oxford, 1982).
Chambers, J. D. and Mingay, G. E., *The Agricultural Revolution, 1750–1870* (1966).
Grigg, D., *The Dynamics of Agricultural Change: The Historical Experience* (1982).
Howell, D. W., *Land and People in Nineteenth-Century Wales* (1977).
Howkins, A., *Reshaping Rural England: A Social History, 1850–1925* (1991).
Jones, E. L., *Seasons and Prices. The Role of the Weather in English Agricultural History* (1964).
Mingay, G. E., *English Landed Society in the Eighteenth Century* (1963).
*Mingay, G. E., *Rural Life in Victorian England* (1979).
*Mingay, G. E. (ed.), *The Victorian Countryside* (2 vols., 1981). Forty-six short essays covering all aspects, well illustrated.

Mingay, G. E., *Land and Society in England, 1750–1880* (1994).
Nelson, J. M., *Commoners: Common Right, Enclosure and Social Change in England, 1700–1820* (Cambridge, 1993).
Newby, H., *Country Life: A Social History of Rural England* (1987).
Parry, M. L. and Slater, T. R. (eds.), *The Making of the Scottish Countryside* (1980).
*Perren, R., *Agriculture in Depression, 1870–1940* (SESH, Cambridge, 1995).
Richards, E., *A History of the Highland Clearances: Agrarian Transformation and the Evictions, 1746–1886* (1982).
Thompson, F. M. L., *English Landed Society in the Nineteenth Century* (1963).
*Turner, M., *Enclosures in Britain, 1750–1830* (SESH, 1984).

Towns and cities

Adams, I. H., *The Making of Urban Scotland* (1978).
Briggs, A., *Victorian Cities* (Harmondsworth, 1968).
*Burnett, J., *A Social History of Housing, 1815–1970* (1980).
Cannadine, D. N., *Lords and Landlords: The Aristocracy and the Towns, 1774–1967* (Leicester, 1980).
Clark, P. (ed.), *The Transformation of English Provincial Towns, 1600–1800* (1984).
*Corfield, P. J., *The Impact of English Towns* (Oxford, 1982).
Dennis R., *English Industrial Cities of the Nineteenth Century: A Social Geography* (Cambridge, 1984).
Daunton, M. J., *House and Home in the Victorian City: Working-Class Housing 1850–1914* (1983).
*Daunton, M. J., 'Housing', in Thompson, F. M. L. (ed.), *The Cambridge Social History of Britain, 1750–1950* (Cambridge, 1990), ii, pp. 195–250.
Dyos, H. J., *Exploring the Urban Past: Essays in Urban History*, ed. Cannadine, D. N., and Reeder, D. A. (Cambridge, 1982).
*Dyos, H. J. and Wolff, M. (eds.), *The Victorian City* (2 vols., 1973). Thirty-eight essays covering all aspects, well illustrated.
Fraser, D. (ed.), *A History of Modern Leeds* (Manchester, 1980).
George, M. D., *London Life in the XVIIIth Century* (1925; second edn., 1930).
Morris, R. J. and Rodger, R. (eds.), *The Victorian City: A Reader in British Urban History, 1820–1914* (1993) .
Olsen, D. J., *The Growth of Victorian London* (1976).
Pooley, C. G. and Irish, S., *The Development of Corporation Housing in Liverpool, 1869–1945* (Centre for North West Regional Studies, Lancaster, 1984).

*Rodger, R. *Housing in Urban Britain, 1780–1914* (SESH, 1989; republ. Cambridge, 1995).

Tarn, J. N., *Five Per Cent Philanthropy: An Account of Housing in Urban Areas Between 1840 and 1914* (Cambridge, 1973). Covers a variety of types, well illustrated.

*Thompson, F. M. L., 'Town and City', in Thompson, F. M. L. (ed.), *The Cambridge Social History of Britain, 1750–1950* (Cambridge, 1990), i, pp. 1–86.

*Waller, P. J., *Town, City and Nation: England 1850–1914* (Oxford, 1983).

*Walvin, J., *English Urban Life, 1776–1851* (1984).

Transportation

Bagwell, P. *The Transport Revolution from 1770* (1974; second edn., 1988) .

*Barker, T. C. and Gerhold, D., *The Rise and Rise of Road Transport* (SESH, 1993; republ. Cambridge, 1995) .

Barker, T. C. and Savage, C. I., *An Economic History of Transport in Britain*, third edn. (1974).

Dyos, H. J. and Aldcroft, D. H., *British Transport: An Economic Survey from the Seventeenth Century to the Twentieth*, second edn. (Leicester, 1974).

Jackman, W. T., *The Development of Transportation in Modern England* (Cambridge, 1916; third edn., 1966).

Kellett, J. R., *Railways and Victorian Cities* (1979).

*Perkin, H., *The Age of the Railway* (1970).

Simmons, J., *The Railway in England and Wales, 1830–1914*, i (Leicester, 1978).

Industrialisation

Ashton, T. S., *Iron and Steel in the Industrial Revolution* (Manchester 1924; second edn., 1951).

*Berg, M., *The Age of Manufactures: Industry, Innovation and Work in Britain 1700–1820* (1985).

Berg, M., Hudson, P. and Sonenscher, M. (eds.), *Manufacture in Town and Country Before the Factory* (Cambridge, 1983).

Bythell, D., *The Handloom Weavers: A Study in the English Cotton Industry during the Industrial Revolution* (Cambridge, 1969).

*Chapman, S. D., *The Cotton Industry in the Industrial Revolution* (SESH, 1972; second edn., 1987).

*Clarkson, L. A., *Proto-Industrialisation: The First Phase of Industrialisation?* (SESH, 1985).

Hudson, P., *Regions and Industries: A Perspective on the Industrial Revolution in Britain* (Cambridge, 1989).
Jenkins, D. T. and Ponting, K. G., *The British Wool Textile Industry* (1982).
Timmins, G., *The Last Shift: The Decline of Handloom Weaving in Nineteenth-Century Lancashire* (Manchester, 1993).
Valenze, D., *The First Industrial Woman* (Oxford, 1995).

Population

Abrams, M., *The Population of Great Britain* (1945).
*Anderson, M., 'The Social Implications of Demographic Change', in Thompson, F. M. L. (ed.), *The Cambridge Social History of Britain, 1750–1950* (Cambridge, 1990), ii, pp. 1–70.
Banks, J. A., *Prosperity and Parenthood: A Study of Family Planning among the Victorian Middle Classes* (1954).
Banks, J. A., *Victorian Values: Secularism and the Size of Families* (1981).
Banks, J. A. and O., *Feminism and Family Planning in Victorian England* (Liverpool, 1965).
Barker, T. and Drake, M., (eds.), *Population and Society in Britain, 1850–1980* (1982). Useful essays for this and following sections.
Drake, M., *Population in Industrialization* (1969).
Drake, M. (ed.), *Population Studies from Parish Registers* (Local Population Studies, Matlock, 1982).
*Flinn, M., *British Population Growth, 1700–1850* (SESH, 1970).
Flinn, M. (ed.), *Scottish Population History from the 17th century to the 1930s* (Cambridge, 1977). The best work for Scotland.
Glass, D. V., *Population Policies and Movements in Europe* (Oxford, 1940; reprinted 1967).
Habakkuk, H. J., *Population Growth and Economic Development since 1750* (Leicester, 1971).
Higgs, E., *Making Sense of the Census: The Manuscript Returns for England and Wales, 1801–1901* (1989).
Higgs, E., *A Clearer Sense of the Census. The Victorian censuses and historical research* (1996).
Himes, N., *Medical History of Contraception* (1936).
Lawton, R. (ed.), *The Census and Social Structure: An Interpretative Guide to the 19th Century Censuses for England and Wales* (1978). A good starting point for using the census.
*McLaren, A., *Birth Control in Nineteenth-Century England* (1978).
McLaren, A., *A History of Contraception from Antiquity to the Present Day* (Oxford, 1990).
*Mitchison, R., *British Population Change since 1860* (SESH, 1977).
Szreter, S., *Fertility, Class and Gender in Britain, 1860–1940* (Cambridge, 1996).

Teitelbaum, M. S., *The British Fertility Decline: Demographic Transition in the Crucible of the Industrial Revolution* (Princeton, 1984).

*Tranter, N. L., *Population and Society, 1750–1940: Contrasts in Population Growth* (Harlow, 1985).

Tranter, N. L., *British Population in the Twentieth Century* (1995).

*Woods, R., *The Population of Britain in the Nineteenth Century* (SESH, 1992; republ. Cambridge, 1995).

Wrigley, E. A. and Schofield, R. S., *The Population History of England, 1541–1871: A Reconstruction* (1981). The major influence on modern demographic history.

Households and families

Anderson, M., *Family Structure in Nineteenth Century Lancashire* (Cambridge, 1971).

*Anderson, M., *Approaches to the History of the Western Family, 1500–1914* (SESH, 1980; republ. Cambridge, 1995).

Armstrong, A., *Stability and Change in an English County Town: A Social Study of York, 1801–51* (Cambridge, 1974).

*Davidoff, L., 'The Family in Britain', in Thompson, F. M. L. (ed.), *The Cambridge Social History of Britain, 1750–1950* (Cambridge, 1990), ii, pp. 71–129.

Gittins, D., *Fair Sex: Family Size and Structure, 1900–39* (1982).

*Laslett, P. with R. Wall (eds.), *Household and Family in Past Time* (Cambridge, 1972).

Lewis, J., *Women in England 1870–1950: Sexual Divisions and Social Change* (Brighton, 1984).

Lewis, J. (ed.), *Labour and Love: Women's Experience of Home and Family, 1850–1940* (Oxford, 1986).

Perkin, J., *Women and Marriage in Nineteenth-Century England* (1989).

Phillips, R., *Untying the Knot: A Short History of Divorce* (Cambridge, 1991).

Stone, L., *The Family, Sex and Marriage in England, 1500–1800* (1977; abridged, revised edn., Harmondsworth, 1979).

Wrigley, E. A. (ed.), *Nineteenth-Century Society. Essays in the Use of Quantitative Methods for the Study of Social Data* (Cambridge, 1972).

Migration

Alderman, G., *Modern British Jewry* (Oxford, 1992).

*Baines, D., *Emigration from Europe, 1815–1930* (SESH, 1991; republ. Cambridge, 1995).

Finnegan, F., *Poverty and Prejudice: A Study of Irish Immigrants in York, 1840–1875* (Cork, 1982).

*Fryer, P., *Staying Power: The History of Black People in Britain* (1984).
Gartner, L. P., *The Jewish Immigrant in England, 1870–1914* (1960).
Gilley, S. and Swift, R. (eds.), *The Irish in Britain, 1815–1939* (1989) .
Hammerton, A. J., *Emigrant Gentlewomen: Genteel Poverty and Female Emigration, 1830–1914* (1979).
*Holmes, C. (ed.), *Immigrants and Minorities in British Society* (1978). Useful essays with wide coverage of different groups.
Holmes, C., *Immigrants and Refugees in Britain, 1871–1971* (1986).
Jackson, J. A., *The Irish in Britain* (1963).
Jackson, J. A. (ed.), *Migration* (Cambridge, 1969).
Lees, L. H., *Exiles of Erin* (Manchester, 1979). On London Irish.
Lunn, K. (ed.), *Hosts, Immigrants and Minorities: Historical Responses to Newcomers in British Society, 1870–1914* (Folkestone, 1980).
Macdonald, D. F., *Scotland's Shifting Population, 1770–1850* (Glasgow, 1937; republ. Philadelphia, 1978).
Parr, J., *Labouring Children: British Immigrant Apprentices to Canada, 1869–1924* (London, 1980).
Pooley, C. G. and Whyte, I. D. (eds.), *Migrants, Emigrants and Immigrants: A Social History of Migration* (1991).
Redford, A., *Labour Migration in England, 1800–50* (Manchester, 1926; third edn., 1976).
Saville, J., *Rural Depopulation in England and Wales, 1851–1951* (1957).

Social and occupational structures

*Briggs, A., 'The Language of "Class" in Early Nineteenth-century England', in Briggs, A. and Saville, J. (eds.), *Essays in Labour History* (1960), pp. 43–73.
Carr-Saunders, A. M. and Caradog-Jones, D., *A Survey of the Social Structure of England & Wales as Illustrated by Statistics* (1927); second edn., *A Survey of the Social Structure of England and Wales as Illustrated by Statistics* (1937); third edn., with Moser, C. A., *A Survey of Social Conditions in England and Wales as Illustrated by Statistics* (1958).
Cole, G. D. H., *Studies in Class Structure* (1955).
Halsey, A. H. (ed.), *Trends in British Society since 1900: A Guide to the Changing Social Structure of Britain* (1972).
Galbraith, J. K., *The Affluent Society* (1958; republ. Harmondsworth, 1962).
Keating, P., *Class and Inequality in Britain: Social Stratification since 1945* (Oxford, 1996).
Marsh, D. C., *The Changing Social Structure of England and Wales, 1871–1961* (1965).

McKibben, R., *The Ideologies of Class: Social Relations in Britain 1800–1950* (Oxford, 1991). Miscellaneous essays.

Perkin, H. J., *The Origins of Modern English Society, 1780–1870* (1969).

Perkin, H. J., *The Structured Crowd: Essays in English Social History* (1981).

Perkin, H. J., *The Rise of Professional Society* (1990).

*Reid, A. J., *Social Classes and Social Relations in Britain, 1850–1914* (SESH, 1991; republ. Cambridge, 1995).

The working class

Benson, J., *The Working Class in Britain, 1850–1939* (1989).

Bourke, J., *Working Class Cultures in Britain, 1890–1960: Gender, Class and Ethnicity* (1993).

Clark, A., *The Struggle for the Breeches: Gender and the Making of the British Working Class* (1995).

Crossick, G., *An Artisan Elite in Victorian Society: Kentish London, 1840–1880* (1978).

Foster, J., *Class Struggle and the Industrial Revolution: Early Industrial Capitalism in Three English Towns* (1974).

Goldthorpe, J. H. and Lockwood, D., 'Affluence and the British Class Structure', *Sociological Review*, 11 (2) (July 1963), pp. 133–63.

Goldthorpe, J. H., with Llewellyn, C. and Payne, C., *Social Mobility and the Class Structure in Modern Britain* (Oxford, 1980).

Goldthorpe, J. H., Lockwood, D., Bechhofer, F. and Platt, J., *The Affluent Worker: i, Industrial Attitudes and Behaviour; ii, Political Attitudes and Behaviour; iii, In the Class Structure* (Cambridge, 1968–9).

*Gray, R., *The Aristocracy of Labour in Nineteenth Century Britain, c. 1850–1914* (SESH, 1981).

Harrison, M., 'Time, Work and the Occurrence of Crowds, 1790–1835', *Past and Present* 110 (February 1986), pp. 134–68.

Joyce, P., *Visions of the People: Industrial England and the Question of Class, 1840–1914* (Cambridge, 1991).

Kirk, N. (ed.), *Social Class and Marxism: Defences and Challenges* (Aldershot, 1996).

Ludlow, J. M. and Jones, L., *The Progress of the Working Class, 1832–1867* (1867; repr. Clifton, NJ, 1973).

*McCord, N., 'Adding a Touch of Class', *History*, 70 (230) (October 1985), pp. 410–19. An important and critical review article.

More, C., *Skill and the English Working Class, 1870–1914* (1980).

*Morris, R. J., *Class and Class Consciousness in the Industrial Revolution, 1780–1850* (SESH, 1979).

Neale, R. S., *Class and Ideology in the Nineteenth Century* (1972).

Neale, R. S., *Class in English History, 1680–1850* (Oxford, 1981).

Savage, M. and Miles, A., *The Remaking of the British Working Class, 1840–1940* (1994) .
*Stedman Jones, G., *Languages of Class: Studies in English Working-Class History, 1832–1982* (Cambridge, 1983).
Thompson, E. P., *The Making of the English Working Class* (1963; second edn., Harmondsworth, 1968).
*Thompson, E. P., 'Eighteenth-Century English Society: Class Struggle without Class?' *Social History* 3 (1) (May 1978).
Thompson, E. P., 'The Moral Economy of the English Crowd in the Eighteenth Century', *Past and Present*, 50 (February 1971), pp. 76–136.
Thompson, E. P., 'Time, Work-Discipline and Industrial Capitalism', *Past and Present*, 38 (December 1967), pp. 56–97.

The middle class

Anderson, G., *Victorian Clerks* (Manchester, 1976).
*Briggs, A., 'Middle-Class Consciousness in English Politics, 1780–1846', *Past and Present*, 9 (April 1956), pp. 65–74.
Corfield, P. J., *Power and the Professions in Britain, 1700–1850* (1995).
Crossick, G. (ed.), *The Lower Middle Class in Britain, 1870–1914* (1977).
Crossick, G. and Haupt, H.-G. (eds.), *Shopkeepers and Master Artisans in Nineteenth-Century Europe* (1984).
Davidoff, L. and Hall, C., *Family Fortunes: Men and Women of the English Middle Class, 1780–1850* (1987).
Morris, R. J., *Class, Sect and Party: The Making of the British Middle Class. Leeds, 1820–1850* (Manchester, 1990).
Reader, W. J., *Professional Men: The Rise of the Professional Classes in Nineteenth-Century England* (1966).
Smail, J., *The Origins of Middle Class Culture: Halifax, Yorkshire, 1660–1780* (Ithaca, NY, 1996).

The aristocracy and the governing élite

Beard, M., *English Landed Society in the Twentieth Century* (1989).
Beckett, J. V., *The Aristocracy in England, 1660–1914* (Oxford, 1986).
Burch M. and Moran M., 'The Changing British Political Élite, 1945–1983: M.P.s and Cabinet Ministers', *Parliamentary Affairs*, 38 (1) (Winter 1985), pp. 1–15.
Bush, M. L., *The English Aristocracy: A Comparative Synthesis* (Manchester, 1984).
Cannadine, D. N., *The Decline and Fall of the British Aristocracy* (New Haven and London, 1990).
*Cannadine, D. N., *Aspects of Aristocracy: Grandeur and Decline in Modern Britain* (New Haven and London 1994). Stimulating essays.

Cannon, J., *Aristocratic Century: The Peerage of Eighteenth-Century England* (Cambridge, 1984).
Clark, G. Kitson, *The Making of Victorian England* (1962).
Clark, J. C. D., *English Society, 1688–1832* (Cambridge, 1985).
*Guttsman, W. L., *The British Political Élite* (1965). A central study.
Mingay, G. E., *English Landed Society in the Eighteenth Century* (1963).
Rubinstein, W. D., *Men of Property: The Very Wealthy in Britain since the Industrial Revolution* (1981). An important interpretation.
Rubinstein, W. D., 'New Men of Wealth and the Purchase of Land in Nineteenth-century England', *Past and Present*, 92 (August 1981), pp. 125–47.
Rubinstein, W. D., 'Education and the Social Origins of British Elites 1880–1970', *Past and Present*, 112 (August 1986), pp. 163–207.
Stone, L. and J. C. F., *An Open Élite? England 1540–1880* (Oxford, 1984).
*Thompson, F. M. L., *English Landed Society in the Nineteenth Century* (1963).

Reform politics

*Adelman, P., *Victorian Radicalism: The Middle-Class Experience, 1830–1914* (1984).
*Belchem, J., *Popular Radicalism in Nineteenth-Century Britain* (1996). Covers late eighteenth to early twentieth centuries.
*Belchem, J., *Class, Party and the Political System in Britain, 1867–1914* (1990).
*Biagini, E. F. and Reid, A. J. (eds.), *Currents of Radicalism: Popular Radicalism, Organised Labour and Party Politics in Britain, 1850–1914* (Cambridge, 1991). Innovative essays.
Brewer, J., *Party Ideology and Popular Politics at the Accession of George III* (Cambridge, 1976). On the Wilkite movement.
Briggs, A. (ed.), *Chartist Studies* (1959). Mainly local studies.
Brock, M., *The Great Reform Act* (1983).
Calhoun, C., *The Question of Class Struggle: Social Foundations of Popular Radicalism during the Industrial Revolution* (Oxford, 1982).
*Cannon, J., *Parliamentary Reform, 1640–1832* (Cambridge, 1973).
*Dickinson, H. T., *British Radicalism and the French Revolution* (Oxford, 1985).
*Dinwiddy, J. R., *From Luddism to the First Reform Bill* (Oxford, 1986).
Epstein, J. A. and Thompson, D., *The Chartist Experience* (1982). Includes local studies.
*Evans, E. J., *Britain before the Reform Act: Politics and Society, 1815–1832* (1989). With source extracts and bibliography.
*Evans, E. J., *Political Parties in Britain, 1783–1867* (1985).
*Evans, E. J., *The Great Reform Act of 1832* (1983; second edn., 1994).

Finn, M. C., *After Chartism: Class and Nation in English Radical Politics* (Cambridge, 1993).

Gillespie, F. E., *Labour and Politics in England, 1850–1867* (Durham, NC, 1927; repr. 1967).

Goodway, D., *London Chartism, 1838–1848* (Cambridge, 1982). Good also for the London trades.

Goodwin, A., *The Friends of Liberty: The English Democratic Movement in the Age of the French Revolution* (1979).

Jones, D., *Chartism and the Chartists* (1975).

McCord, N., *The Anti-Corn Law League, 1838–46* (1958; second edn., 1968).

Prothero, I., *Artisans and Politics in Early Nineteenth-century London: John Gast and his Times* (1979).

*Rendall, J. (ed.), *Equal or Different: Women's Politics, 1800–1914* (1987).

*Royle, E., *Chartism* (1980; third edn., 1996). With source extracts and bibliography.

Royle, E. and Walvin, J., *English Radicals and Reformers, 1760–1848* (Brighton, 1982).

Royle, E., *Radicals, Secularists and Republicans: Popular Freethought in Britain, 1866–1915* (Manchester, 1980).

Rubinstein, W. D., 'The End of "Old Corruption" in Britain, 1780–1860', *Past and Present*, 101 (November 1983), pp. 55–86.

Smith, F. B., *The Making of the Second Reform Bill* (Cambridge, 1966).

Stevenson, J., *Popular Disturbances in England, 1700–1832* (1979).

Thomas, W., *The Philosophic Radicals: Nine Studies in Theory and Practice, 1817–1841* (Oxford, 1979).

Tholfsen, T., *Working-Class Radicalism in Mid-Victorian England* (London, 1976).

Thomis, M. and Holt, P., *Threats of Revolution in Britain, 1789–1848* (1977).

Thomis, M. and Grimmett, J., *Women in Protest* (1982).

Thompson, D., *The Chartists* (1984).

*Walton, J. K., *The Second Reform Act* (1987).

Wahrman, D., *Imagining the Middle Class: The Political Representation of Class in Britain, c. 1780–1840* (Cambridge, 1995).

Ward, J. T., *Popular Movements, c. 1830–1850* (1970).

*Wright, D. G., *Popular Radicalism: The Working-Class Experience, 1780–1880* (1988).

Local government

Fraser, D., *Power and Authority in the Victorian City* (Oxford, 1979).

Fraser, D., *Urban Politics in Victorian England: The Structure of Politics in Victorian Cities* (Leicester, 1976).

Hennock, E. P., *Fit and Proper Persons: Ideal and Reality in Nineteenth-Century Urban Government* (1973).

P. Hollis, *Ladies Elect: Women in English Local Government, 1865–1914* (Oxford, 1987).

The world of labour

Alexander, S., *Women's Work in Nineteenth-Century London: A Study of the Years 1820–50* (Journeyman Press and London History Workshop Centre, 1983).

Bourke, J., 'Housewifery in Working-Class England 1860–1914', *Past and Present*, 143 (May 1994), pp. 167–97.

*Belchem, J., *Industrialisation and the Working Class: The English Experience, 1750–1900* (1990).

Burnett, J. (ed.), *Useful Toil: Autobiographies of Working People from the 1820s to the 1920s* (1974).

Bythell, D., *The Sweated Trades: Outwork in Nineteenth-century Britain* (1978).

*Horn, P., *Children's Work and Welfare, 1780–1890* (SESH, 1994; republ. Cambridge, 1995).

Horn, P., *The Rise and Fall of the Victorian Servant* (Dublin, 1975).

*John, A. V. (ed.), *Unequal Opportunities: Women's Employment in England, 1800–1918* (Oxford, 1986).

Joyce, P., *Work, Society and Politics: The Culture of the Factory in Later Victorian Britain* (Brighton, 1980).

Joyce, P. (ed.), *The Historical Meanings of Work* (Cambridge, 1987).

*Joyce, P., 'Work', in Thompson, F. M. L. (ed.), *The Cambridge Social History of Britain, 1750–1950* (Cambridge, 1990), ii, pp. 131–94.

Lown, J., *Women and Industrialization: Gender and Work in Nineteenth-Century England* (Oxford, 1990).

Pinchbeck, I., *Women Workers in the Industrial Revolution, 1750–1850* (1930; third edn., 1981).

Prothero, I., *Artisans and Politics in Early Nineteenth-Century London: John Gast and his times* (1979).

*Rendall, J., *Women in an Industrializing Society: England, 1750–1880* (Oxford, 1990).

*Roberts, E., *Women's Work, 1840–1940* (SESH, 1987; republ. Cambridge, 1995).

Rule, J., *The Experience of Labour in Eighteenth-Century Industry* (1981).

Rule, J., *The Labouring Classes in Early Industrial England, 1750–1850* (1986).

Tilly, L. A. and Scott, J. W., *Women, Work and Family* (New York, 1978). Deals with both France and England.

The labour movement

*Adelman, P., *The Rise of the Labour Party, 1880–1945* (1972; third edn., 1996). With source extracts and bibliography.

Brown, K. D. (with Clarkson, L. A.), *The English Labour Movement, 1700–1951* (Dublin, 1982).

Brown, K. D. (ed.), *The First Labour Party, 1906–1914* (1985). Useful essays.

Burgess, K., *The Challenge of Labour: Shaping British Society, 1850–1930* (1980).

Clegg, H. A., Fox, A. and Thompson, A. F., *A History of British Trade Unions since 1889, Volume 1, 1889–1910* (Oxford, 1964).

Clegg, H. A., *A History of British Trade Unions since 1889, Volume 2, 1911–1933* (Oxford, 1985); *Volume 3, 1934–1951* (Oxford, 1994).

Cole, G. D. H., *Attempts at General Union, 1818–1834* (1953).

Dutton, H. I. and King, J. E., *Ten Per Cent and No Surrender: The Preston Strike, 1853–1854* (Cambridge, 1981).

Fraser, W. H., *Trade Unions and Society: The Struggle for Acceptance, 1850–1880* (1974).

Goldman, H., *Emma Paterson: She Led Women into a Man's World* (1974).

Harrison, B., 'Class and Gender in Modern British Labour History', *Past and Present*, 124 (August 1989), pp. 121–58.

Hinton, J., *Labour and Socialism: A History of the British Labour Movement, 1867–1974* (Brighton, 1983).

*Hunt, E. H., *British Labour History 1815–1914* (1981).

Kirby, R. G. and Musson, A. E., *The Voice of the People: John Doherty, 1798–1854, Trade Unionist, Radical and Factory Reformer* (1975).

Kynaston, D., *King Labour: The British Working Class, 1850–1914* (1976).

Laybourn, K., *The General Strike of 1926* (Manchester, 1993).

Laybourn, K., *The Rise of Labour: The British Labour Party, 1890–1979* (1988).

Laybourn, K. and James, D. (eds.), *The Rising Sun of Socialism: The Independent Labour Party in the Textile District of the West Riding of Yorkshire between 1890 and 1914* (Bradford, 1991). Essays on the key local area.

*Lovell, J., *British Trade Unions, 1875–1933* (SESH, 1977).

Lovell, J., *Trade Unions in Twentieth-Century Britain* (1996).

McCord, N., *Strikes* (Oxford, 1980).

Macdonald, D. F., *The State and the Trade Unions* (1960).

MacDoughall, I. (ed.), *Essays in Scottish Labour History* (Edinburgh, 1978).
*Musson, A. E., *British Trade Unions, 1800–1875* (SESH, 1972).
*Morris, M., *The British General Strike*, Historical Association G.82 (1973). Booklet.
*Pelling, H., *A History of British Trade Unionism* (Harmondsworth, 1963).
*Pelling, H. and Reid, A. J., *A Short History of the Labour Party* (1961; eleventh edn., 1996).
Pelling, H., *The Origins of the Labour Party* (Oxford, 1965).
Pelling, H., *Popular Politics and Society in late Victorian Britain* (1968). Important collection of essays.
*Phillips, G., *The Rise of the Labour Party, 1893–1931* (1992).
Soldon, N. C., *Women in British Trade Unions, 1874–1976* (1978).
Ward, J. T. and Fraser, W. H. (eds.), *Workers and Employers: Documents on Trade Unions and Industrial Relations in Britain since the Eighteenth Century* (1980).
Webb, S. and B., *The History of Trade Unionism* (1894; new edn., 1920).

Poverty and the standard of living

Abel-Smith, B. and Townsend, P., *The Poor and the Poorest* (1965).
Booth, C. *Life and Labour of the People in London* (17 vols., 1889–1903). See also Fried and Elman, below.
Booth, W., *Into Darkest England and The Way Out* (1890).
*Burnett, J., *Plenty and Want: A Social History of Diet in England from 1815 to the Present Day* (1966; republ. 1989). Important survey.
Burnett, J. (ed.), *Idle Hands: The Experience of Unemployment, 1790–1990* (1994). Based on working-class autobiographies.
Chadwick, E., *Report on the Sanitary Condition of the Labouring Population of Great Britain* (1842; ed. M.W. Flinn, Edinburgh, 1965).
Chinn, C., *Poverty amidst Prosperity: The Urban Poor in England, 1834–1914* (Manchester, 1995).
Coates, K. and Silburn, R., *Poverty: The Forgotten Englishmen* (Harmondsworth, 1970).
*Constantine, S., *Social Conditions in Britain, 1918–1939* (1983).
Davin, A., *Growing Up Poor: Home, School and Street in London, 1870–1914* (1995).
F. Engels, *The Condition of the Working Class in England* (1845; ed. V. Kiernan, Harmondsworth, 1987).
Fiegehen, G. C., Lansley, P. S. and Smith, A. D., *Poverty and Progress in Britain, 1953–1973. A Statistical Study of Low Income Households: Their Numbers, Types and Expenditure Patterns* (Cambridge, 1977).
Floud, R., Wachter, K. and Gregory, A., *Height, Health and History:*

Nutritional Status in the United Kingdom, 1750–1980 (Cambridge, 1990).

Fried, A. and Elman R. (eds.), *Charles Booth's London. A Portrait of the Poor at the Turn of the Century drawn from his Life and Labour of the People in London* (Harmondsworth, 1971).

Himmelfarb, G., *The Idea of Poverty: England in the Early Industrial Age* (1984).

Jenkins, S. and Maynard, A., 'The Rowntree Surveys: Poverty in York since 1899', in Feinstein, C. H. (ed.), *York, 1831–1981. 150 Years of Scientific Endeavour and Social Change* (York, 1981), pp. 188–204.

Kay, J. P., *The Moral and Physical Condition of the Working Classes employed in the Cotton Manufacture in Manchester* (1832; new impression, Didsbury, 1969).

Keating, P. (ed.), *Into Unknown England, 1866–1913: Selections from the Social Explorers* (Glasgow, 1976).

Llewellyn Davies, M. (ed.), *Life As We Have Known It: By Co-operative Working Women* (1931; republ. 1977). Accounts of working-class life sent to the Women's Co-operative Guild.

Mayhew, H. *London Labour and the London Poor* (1861–2; republ. in 4 vols., New York, 1968).

Mearns, A., *The Bitter Cry of Outcast London* (1883; ed. A. S. Wohl, Leicester, 1970).

O'Day, R. and Englander, D., *Mr Charles Booth's Inquiry: Life and Labour of the People in London Reconsidered* (1993).

Oddy, D. J., 'Food, Drink and Nutrition', in Thompson, F. M. L. (ed.), *The Cambridge Social History of Britain, 1750–1950* (Cambridge, 1990), ii, pp. 251–78.

Pember Reeves, M., *Round About a Pound a Week* (1913; republ. 1979). A classic account of poverty before the First World War.

Rowntree, B. S., *The Human Needs of Labour* (rev. and rewritten, 1937).

Rowntree, B. S., *Poverty: A Study of Town Life* (1901; fourth edn., 1902).

Rowntree, B. S., *Poverty and Progress: A Second Social Survey of York* (1941).

Rowntree, B. S. and Lavers, G. R., *Poverty and the Welfare State: A Third Social Survey of York dealing only with Economic Questions* (1951).

Rowntree, B. S. and Kendall, M., *How the Labourer Lives: A Study of the Rural Labour Problem* (1913).

*Snell, K. D. M., *Annals of the Labouring Poor: Social Change and Agrarian England, 1660–1900* (Cambridge, 1985).

Somerville, A., *The Autobiography of a Working Man* (1848; republ. 1951).

Spring Rice, M., *Working-Class Wives: Their Health and Conditions* (1939; second edn., 1981).

*Stedman Jones, G., *Outcast London: A Study in the Relationship between Classes in Victorian Society* (Harmondsworth, 1976).

*Taylor, A. J. (ed.), *The Standard of Living in Britain in the Industrial Revolution* (1975). Selected controversial essays.

Thompson, E. P. and Yeo, E. (eds.), *The Unknown Mayhew: Selection from the Morning Chronicle, 1849–50* (Harmondsworth, 1973).

Thompson, P., *The Edwardians: The Remaking of British Society* (1975). Based on oral history.

*Townsend, P., *Poverty in the United Kingdom: A Survey of Household Resources and Standards of Living* (Harmondsworth, 1979).

*Treble, J. H., *Urban Poverty in Britain, 1830–1914* (1979).

Vincent, D., *Poor Citizens: The State and the Poor in Twentieth-Century Britain* (1991).

Responses to poverty

Brundage, A., *The Making of the New Poor Law 1832–39* (1978).

*Checkland, S. G. and E. O. A. (eds.), *The Poor Law Report of 1834* (Harmondsworth, 1974). With a very helpful introduction.

Checkland, O., *Philanthropy in Victorian Scotland: Social Welfare and the Voluntary Principle* (Edinburgh, 1980).

Crowther, M. A., *The Workhouse System, 1834–1929: The History of an English Social Institution* (1981).

Digby, A., *Pauper Palaces* (1978). On workhouses.

*Digby, A., *The Poor Law in Nineteenth-Century England and Wales*, Historical Association G.104 (1982). Booklet, excellent brief introduction.

*Fraser, D. (ed.), *The New Poor Law in the Nineteenth Century* (1976). Very useful essays on different aspects of the poor law, including Scotland.

Gosden, P. H. J. G., *Self-Help: Voluntary Associations in Nineteenth-century Britain* (1973).

Harrison, B., 'Philanthropy and the Victorians', in *Peaceable Kingdom. Stability and Change in Modern Britain* (Oxford, 1982), pp. 217–59.

Heasman, K., *Evangelicals in Action: An Appraisal of their Social Work in the Victorian Era* (1962).

Hendrick, H., *Child Welfare: England, 1872–1989* (1993).

Hopkins, E., *Working-Class Self-Help in Nineteenth-Century England: Responses to Industrialisation* (1995).

Lascelles, E., 'Charity', in G. M. Young (ed.), *Early Victorian England, 1830–1865* (Oxford, 1934), pp. 317–47.

Levitt, I., *Poverty and Social Welfare in Scotland, 1890–1948* (Edinburgh, 1988).

Lewis, J., *The Voluntary Sector, the State and Social Work in Britain: The Charity Organisation Society/Family Welfare Association since 1869* (Cheltenham, 1995).

Marshall, D., *The English Poor in the Eighteenth Century: A Study in Social and Administrative History* (1926; second edn., 1969).
*Marshall, J. D., *The Old Poor Law, 1795–1834* (SESH, 1968).
Owen, D., *English Philanthropy, 1660–1960* (Cambridge, Mass., 1965).
Oxley, G. W., *Poor Relief in England and Wales, 1601–1834* (Newton Abbot, 1974).
Poynter, J. R., *Society and Pauperism: English Ideas on Poor Relief, 1795–1834* (1969).
Prochaska, F. K., *Women and Philanthropy in Nineteenth-Century England,* (Oxford, 1980).
*Prochaska, F. K., 'Philanthropy', in Thompson, F. M. L. (ed.), *The Cambridge Social History of Britain, 1750–1950* (Cambridge, 1990), iii, pp. 357–93.
Rose, M. E. (ed.), *The English Poor Law, 1780–1930* (Newton Abbot, 1971).
*Rose, M. E., *The Relief of Poverty, 1834–1914* (SESH, 1972).
*Slack, P., *The English Poor Law, 1531–1782* (SESH, 1990; republ. Cambridge, 1995).
Tebbutt, M., *Making Ends Meet. Pawnbroking and Working-Class Credit* (1984).

Social policy and welfare

Birch, R. C., *The Shaping of the Welfare State* (1974). With source extracts and bibliography.
Best, G. F. A., *Shaftesbury* (1964).
Brown, J., *The British Welfare State* (Oxford, 1995).
Bruce, M., *The Coming of the Welfare State* (1961; second edn., 1965).
Checkland, S., *British Public Policy, 1776–1939: An Economic, Social and Political Perspective* (Cambridge, 1985).
Cromwell, V. (ed.), *Revolution or Evolution: British Government in the Nineteenth Century* (1977).
Crowther, M. A., *Social Policy in Britain 1914–1939* (SESH, 1988; second edn., Cambridge, 1996).
Evans, E. J. (ed.), *Social Policy, 1830–1914: Individualism, Collectivism and the Origins of the Welfare State* (1978).
Fido, J., 'The COS and Social Casework in London 1896–1900', in A. P. Donajgrodzki (ed.), *Social Control in Nineteenth-Century Britain* (1977), pp. 207–30.
Finer, S. E., *The Life and Times of Sir Edwin Chadwick* (1952) .
Finlayson, G., *Citizen, State and Social Welfare in Britain 1830–1900* (Oxford, 1994) .
Fraser, D., *The Evolution of the British Welfare State* (1973).
Gilbert, B. B., *The Evolution of National Insurance in Great Britain: The Origins of the Welfare State* (1966).

*Harris, J., 'Society and the State in Twentieth-Century Britain', in Thompson, F. M. L. (ed.), *The Cambridge Social History of Britain, 1750–1950* (Cambridge, 1990), iii, pp. 63–117.

*Hay, J. R., *The Origins of the Liberal Welfare Reforms, 1906–1914* (SESH, 1975).

Hendrick, H., *Child Welfare: England, 1872–1989* (1993).

*Henriques, U. R. Q., *Before the Welfare State: Social Administration in Early Industrial Britain* (1979).

Henriques, U. R. Q., *The Early Factory Acts and their Enforcement* (Historical Association, 1971). Booklet.

Jones, H., *Health and Society in Twentieth-Century Britain* (1994).

Jones, K., *The Making of Social Policy in Britain, 1830–1990* (1991).

Lambert, R., *Sir John Simon, 1816–1904 and English Social Administration* (1963).

*Laybourn, K., *The Evolution of British Social Policy and the Welfare State, c. 1800–1993* (Keele, 1995).

Lubenow, W. C., *The Politics of Government Growth: Early Victorian Attitudes towards State Intervention, 1833–1848* (Newton Abbot, 1971).

MacDonagh. O., *Early Victorian Government, 1830–1870* (1977).

Midwinter, E. C. *Victorian Social Reform* (1968). With source extracts and bibliography.

Mowat, C. L., *The Charity Organisation Society 1869–1913: Its Ideas and Work* (1961).

Peden, G. C., *British Economic and Social Policy: Lloyd George to Margaret Thatcher* (Oxford, 1985).

Roberts, D., *Victorian Origins of the British Welfare State* (New Haven, 1960; repr. Hamden, Conn., 1969).

Rooff, M., *A Hundred Years of Family Welfare* (1972).

*Taylor, A. J., *Laissez-faire and State Intervention in Nineteenth-Century Britain* (SESH, 1972).

*Thane, P., *The Foundations of the Welfare State* (1982; second edn., 1996).

*Thane, P., 'Government and Society in England and Wales, 1750–1914', in Thompson, F. M. L. (ed.), *The Cambridge Social History of Britain, 1750–1950* (Cambridge, 1990), iii, pp. 1–61.

Medicine, disease and health

*Berridge, V., 'Health and Medicine', in Thompson, F. M. L. (ed.), *The Cambridge Social History of Britain, 1750–1950* (Cambridge, 1990), iii, pp. 171–242.

*Cherry, S., *Medical Services and the Hospital in Britain, 1860–1939* (SESH, Cambridge, 1996).

Digby, A., *From York Lunatic Asylum to Bootham Park Hospital* (York, 1986).

Digby, A., *Madness, Morality and Medicine: A Study of the York Retreat, 1796–1914* (Cambridge 1985). Illuminating history of pioneering Quaker asylum.

Hume, C. H., 'The Public Health Movement', in J. T. Ward (ed.), *Popular Movements, 1830–1850* (1970), pp. 183–200.

Jones, K., *Lunacy Law and Conscience, 1744–1845* (1955).

Parry Jones, W. L., *The Trade in Lunacy: A Study of Private Madhouses in England in the Eighteenth and Nineteenth Centuries* (1972).

Pelling, M., *Cholera, Fever and English Medicine, 1825–1865* (Oxford, 1978).

Porter, R., *Mind Forg'd Manacles: A History of Madness in England from the Restoration to the Regency* (1987).

*Porter, R., *Disease, Medicine and Society in England, 1550–1860*, new edn. (SESH, 1987; second edn., 1993; republ. Cambridge, 1995).

Scull, T.C., *Museums of Madness: The Social Organisation of Insanity in Nineteenth-Century England* (Harmondsworth, 1992).

Smith, F. B., *The People's Health, 1830–1910* (1979).

Walkowitz, J. R., *Prostitution and Victorian Society: Women, Class and the State* (Cambridge, 1980).

Crime and punishment

Bailey, V. (ed.), *Policing and Punishment in Nineteenth Century Britain* (1981).

Beattie, J. M., 'The Pattern of Crime in England, 1660–1800', *Past and Present,* 62 (February 1974), pp. 47–95.

Brewer, J. and Styles, J., *An Ungovernable People: The English and their Law in the Seventeenth and Eighteenth Centuries* (1980).

*Briggs, J., Harrison, C., McInnes, A. and Vincent, D., *Crime and Punishment in England: An Introductory History* (1996).

Bristow, E. J., *Vice and Vigilance: Purity Movements in Britain since 1700* (Dublin, 1977).

Chesney, K., *The Victorian Underworld* (Harmondsworth, 1972).

Donajgrodzki, A. P. (ed.), *Social Control in Nineteenth-Century Britain* (1977). Useful essays on different aspects.

Dunbabin, J. P. D., *Rural Discontent in Nineteenth-Century Britain* (1974).

*C. Emsley, *Crime and Society in England, 1750–1900* (1987; second edn., 1996).

C. Emsley, *The English Police: A Political and Social History* (1991; second edn., 1996).

Finnegan, F., *Poverty and Prostitution: A Study of Victorian Prostitutes in York* (Cambridge, 1979).

Gatrell, V. A. C., Lenman, B. and Parker, G. (eds.), *Crime and the Law: The Social History of Crime in Western Europe since 1500* (1980).

*Gatrell, V. A. C., 'Crime, Authority and the Policeman-State', in Thompson, F. M. L. (ed.), *The Cambridge Social History of Britain, 1750–1950* (Cambridge, 1990), iii, pp. 243–310.

Hay, D., Linbaugh, P., Rule, J. G., Thompson, E.P. and Winslow, C., *Albion's Fatal Tree: Crime and Society in Eighteenth-Century England* (1975).

Henriques, U. R. Q., 'The Rise and Decline of the Separate System of Prison Discipline', *Past and Present*, 54 (February 1972), pp. 61–93.

Hobsbawm, E. J. and Rudé, G., *Captain Swing* (Harmondsworth, 1973).

Ignatieff, M., *A Just Measure of Pain: Penitentiaries in the Industrial Revolution* (1978).

Jones, D. J. V., *Before Rebecca: Popular Protests in Wales, 1793–1835* (1973).

Jones, D. J. V., *Crime, Protest Community and Police in Nineteenth-Century Britain* (1982).

Jones, D. J. V., 'The Welsh and Crime', in C. Emsley and J. Walvin (eds.), *Artisans, Peasants & Proletarians, 1760–1860* (1985), pp. 81–103.

Logue, K. J., *Popular Disturbances in Scotland, 1780–1815* (Edinburgh, 1979).

Manton, J., *Mary Carpenter and the Children of the Streets* (1976).

Mather, F. C., *Public Order in the Age of the Chartists* (Manchester, 1959).

Midwinter, E. C., *Law and Order in Early Victorian Lancashire* (York, 1968).

Phillips, D., *Crime and Authority in Victorian England* (1977).

Quinault, R. and Stevenson, J. (eds.), *Popular Protest and Public Order: Six Studies in British History, 1790–1920* (1974). Essays.

Rule, J. and Wells, R., *Crime, Protest and Popular Politics in Southern England* (1997). Essays.

Steedman, C., *Policing the Victorian Community: The Formation of English Provincial Police Forces, 1856–80* (1984).

Stevenson, J., *Popular Disturbances in England, 1700–1870* (1979), revised as *Popular Disturbances in England, 1700–1832* (1992) and *Popular Disturbances in England, 1832–1939* (1997).

Taylor, D., *The New Police: Crime, Conflict and Control in Nineteenth-Century England* (Manchester, 1997).

Tobias, J. J., *Crime and Industrial Society in the Nineteenth Century* (Harmondsworth, 1972).

Tobias, J. J., *Crime and Police in England, 1700–1900* (Dublin, 1979).

West, D. J., *The Young Offender* (Harmondsworth, 1967).

Zedner, L., *Women, Crime and Custody in Victorian England* (Oxford, 1991).

Leisure and popular culture

Bamford, S., *Early Days*, ed. H. Dunckley (1893).

*Cunningham, H., *Leisure in the Industrial Revolution* (1980). An important interpretation.

*Cunningham, H., 'Leisure and Culture', in Thompson, F. M. L. (ed.), *The Cambridge Social History of Britain, 1750–1950* (Cambridge, 1990), ii, pp. 279–339.

*Golby, J. M. and Purdue, A. W., *The Civilisation of the Crowd: Popular Culture in England, 1750–1900* (1984).

Jones, S. G., *Workers at Play: A Social and Economic History of Leisure, 1918–1939* (1986).

Hartley M. and Ingilby, J., *Life and Tradition in West Yorkshire* (1976).

Hoggart, R., *The Uses of Literacy: Aspects of Working-Class Life with Special Reference to Publications and Entertainments* (Harmondsworth, 1958). A classic.

Holt, R. (ed.), *Sport and the Working Class in Modern Britain* (Manchester, 1990). Essays.

Howitt, W., *The Rural Life of England* (1838; third edn., 1844, repr. Shannon, 1971).

Ludlow, J. M. and Jones, L., *Progress of the Working Class* (1867; repr. Clifton, NJ, 1973). Useful for contemporary insights.

McKibbin, R., 'Working-Class Gambling in Britain, 1880–1939', *Past and Present*, 82 (February 1979), pp. 147–78.

*Malcolmson, R. W., *Popular Recreations in English Society, 1700–1850* (Cambridge, 1973).

*Morris, R. J., 'Clubs, Societies and Associations', in Thompson, F. M. L. (ed.), *The Cambridge Social History of Britain, 1750–1950* (Cambridge, 1990), iii, pp. 395–443.

Obelkevich, J., *Religion and Rural Society. South Lindsey 1825–1875* (Oxford, 1976). For popular religious culture.

Pimlott, J. A. R., *The Englishman's Holiday. A Social History* (1947).

Place, F., *The Autobiography of Francis Place*, ed. M. Thale (Cambridge, 1972).

Poole, R., *Popular Leisure and the Music Hall in 19th-Century Bolton*, Centre for North-West Regional Studies, University of Lancaster Occasional Paper No. 12 (Lancaster, 1982).

Porter, E., *Cambridgeshire Customs and Folklore* (1969).

*Reid, D. A., 'The Decline of Saint Monday, 1766–1876', *Past and Present*, 71 (May 1976), pp. 76–101.

Roberts, E., *A Woman's Place: An Oral History of Working-Class Women, 1890–1940* (Oxford, 1984). Vividly recreated from oral history.

Roberts, E., *Women and Families. An Oral History, 1840–1970* (Oxford, 1995).

Roberts, R., *The Classic Slum: Salford Life in the First Quarter of the Century* (Manchester, 1971; republ. Harmondsworth, 1973). Largely autobiographical.

Roberts, R., *A Ragged Schooling: Growing up in the Classic Slum* (Manchester, 1976; republ. Glasgow, 1978). Continuation of the above.

Rowntree, B. S., *Poverty and Progress: A Second Social Survey of York* (1941).

Rowntree, B. S. and Lavers, G. R., *English Life and Leisure: A Social Study* (1951). The social side of the third poverty study.

Russell, D., *Popular Music in England, 1840–1914: A Social History* (Manchester, 1987).

Strutt, J., *The Sports and Pastimes of the People of England* (1838).

Thompson, E. P., 'The Moral Economy of the English Crowd in the Eighteenth Century', *Past and Present*, 50 (February 1971), pp. 76–136.

*Thompson, E. P., 'Time, Work-Discipline and Industrial Capitalism', *Past and Present*, 38 (December 1967), pp. 56–97.

Walton, J. K., *The English Seaside Resort: A Social History, 1750–1914* (Leicester, 1983).

Walvin, J., *Beside the Seaside: A Social History of the Popular Seaside Holiday* (1978).

*Walvin, J., *Leisure and Society, 1830–1950* (1978).

Walvin, J., *The People's Game: A Social History of British Football* (1975).

Walvin, J. and Walton, J. (eds.), *Leisure in Britain, 1780–1939* (Manchester, 1983). Essays.

Wright, T., *Some Habits and Customs of the Working Classes, by a Journeyman Engineer* (1867; repr. New York, 1967).

Yeo, E. and S. (eds.), *Popular Culture and Class Conflict, 1590–1914: Explorations in the History of Labour and Leisure* (Brighton, 1981). Essays.

Young, G. M. (ed.), *Early Victorian England, 1830–1865* (2 vols., 1934). Dated, but still a rich collection of essays.

High society

*Cannadine, D. N., *Aspects of Aristocracy* (New Haven and London, 1994). Essays.

Davidoff, L., *The Best of Circles: Society, Etiquette and The Season* (1973).

Gash, N., 'Lord George Bentinck and his Sporting World', in *Pillars of Government and Other Essays on State and Society, c. 1770–c. 1880* (1986), pp. 162–75.

Gerard, J., *Country House Life. Families and Servants, 1815–1914* (Oxford, 1994).

Girouard, M., *Life in the English Country House: A Social and Architectural History* (New Haven and London, 1978).

Horn, P., *High Society: The English social élite, 1880–1914* (Stroud, 1992).

Mingay, G. E., *English Landed Society in the Eighteenth Century* (1963).

Thompson, F. M. L., *English Landed Society in the Nineteenth Century* (1963).

Moral reform

*Bradley, I., *The Call to Seriousness: The Evangelical Impact on the Victorians* (1976). Good introduction to Victorian Evangelicalism.

Burnett, J., *Plenty and Want: A Social History of Diet in England from 1815 to the Present Day* (1966; republ. 1989).

Harrison, B., *Drink and the Victorians: The Temperance Question in England, 1815–1872* (1971).

Harrison, B., *Peaceable Kingdom: Stability and Change in Modern Britain* (Oxford, 1982). Essays.

Hollis, P. (ed.), *Pressure from Without in Early Victorian England* (1974). Essays.

Thomas, K., *Man and the Natural World: Changing Attitudes in England, 1500–1800* (Harmondsworth, 1984).

*Wigley, J., *The Rise and Fall of the Victorian Sunday* (1980). Good introductory survey.

The press

Altick, R. D., *The English Common Reader: A Social History of the Mass Reading Public, 1800–1900* (Chicago and London, 1957; paperback edn., 1963). Includes some circulation figures.

Boyce, G., Curran, J. and Wingate, P. (eds.), *Newspaper History from the 17th century to the Present Day* (1978).

*Cranfield, G. A., *The Press and Society from Caxton to Northcliffe* (1978).

*James, L., *Print and the People, 1819–1851* (Harmondsworth, 1978). Well illustrated.

James, L., *Fiction for the Working Man: A Study of the Literature Produced for the Working Classes in early Victorian urban England* (Harmondsworth, 1973).

Jones, A., *Power of the Press: Newspapers, Power and the Public in Nineteenth-Century England* (Aldershot, 1996).

Lee, A. J., *The Origins of the Popular Press, 1855–1914* (1976).

*Neuburg, V. E., *Popular Literature: A History and a Guide* (Harmondsworth, 1977).

Webb, R. K., *The British Working-Class Reader, 1790–1848* (1955).
Williams, R., *The Long Revolution* (Harmondsworth, 1961).

Retailing

Adburgham, A., *Shops and Shopping, 1800–1914: Where and in What Manner the Well-Dressed Englishwoman Bought her Clothes* (1964).
Alexander, D., *Retailing during the Industrial Revolution* (1970).
*Benson, J., *The Rise of Consumer Society in Britain, 1880–1980* (1994).
Briggs, A., *Friends of the People: The Centenary History of Lewis's* (1956).
Corina, M., *Pile it High, Sell it Cheap: The Authorised Biography of Sir John Cohen, founder of Tesco* (1971).
Chartres, J. A., 'Country Tradesmen', in Mingay, G. E., *The Victorian Countryside*, i, pp. 300–131.
Cole, G. D. H., *A Century of Co-operation* (Manchester, 1944).
Fraser, W. H., *The Coming of the Mass Market, 1850–1914* (1981).
Jeffreys, J. B., *Retail Trading in Britain, 1850–1940* (Cambridge, 1954).
Lancaster, W., *The Department Store. A Social History* (Leicester, 1993).
McKendrick, N., Brewer J. and Plumb, J. H., *The Birth of a Consumer Society: The Commercialisation of Eighteenth-Century England* (1982).
Mathias, P., *Retailing Revolution: A History of Multiple Retailing in the Foods Trades based upon the Allied Suppliers Group of Companies* (1967).
Packard, V., *The Hidden Persuaders* (1957; republ. Harmondsworth, 1960).
Rees, G., *St Michael: A History of Marks and Spencer* (1969).
Winstanley, M., *The Shopkeeper's World, 1830–1914* (Manchester, 1983).

Religion – general works

*Armstrong, A., *The Church of England, the Methodists and Society 1700–1850* (1973).
Budd, S., *Varieties of Unbelief: Atheists and Agnostics in English Society, 1850–1959* (1977).
Chadwick, W. O., *The Victorian Church* (2 vols., 1966, 1970).
Cragg, G. R., *The Church and the Age of Reason (1648–1789)* (Harmondsworth, 1960).
Davies, E. T., *Religion in the Industrial Revolution in South Wales* (Cardiff, 1965).
*Gibson, W., *Church, State and Society, 1760–1850* (1994).
*Gilley, S. and Sheils, W. J. (eds.), *A History of Religion in Britain: Practice and Belief from Pre-Roman Times to the Present* (Oxford, 1994). Survey essays on all aspects of religious history.

Hastings, A., *A History of English Christianity, 1920–1985* (1986).
Henriques, U., *Religious Toleration in England, 1787–1833* (1961).
Machin, G. I. T., *Politics and the Churches in Great Britain, 1832 to 1868* (Oxford, 1977).
*McLeod, H., *Religion and the People of Western Europe, 1789–1970* (Oxford, 1981).
*McLeod, H., *Religion and Society in England, 1850–1914* (1996).
Norman, E. R., *Church and Society in England, 1770–1970: A Historical Study* (Oxford, 1976).
Obelkevich, J., Roper, L. and Samuel, R. (eds.), *Disciplines of Faith: Studies in Religion, Politics and Patriarchy* (1987). Essays.
*Obelkevich, J., 'Religion', in Thompson, F. M. L. (ed.), *The Cambridge Social History of Britain, 1750–1950* (Cambridge, 1990), iii, pp. 311–56.
*Parsons G. (ed.), *Religion in Victorian Britain* (5 vols., Manchester, 1988–97). A collection of thematic essays and sources which make essential reading.
Robbins, K., *History, Religion and Identity in Modern Britain* (1993).
Vidler, A. R., *The Church in an Age of Revolution* (Harmondsworth, 1961).
Ward, W. R., *Religion and Society in England, 1790–1850* (1982).
Wolffe, J. R., *God and Greater Britain. Religion and National Life in Britain and Ireland,* 1843–1945 (1994). An excellent overview of religion and nationalism.
Wolffe, J. R., *The Protestant Crusade in Great Britain, 1829–1860* (1991). On popular Protestantism and anti-Catholicism.

The Church of England

Christensen, T., *Origin and History of Christian Socialism, 1848–1854* (Aarhus, 1962).
Clark, G. Kitson, *Churchmen and the Condition of England, 1832–1885. A Study in the Development of Social Ideas and Practice from the Old Regime to the Modern State* (1973).
Edwards, D. L., *Leaders of the Church of England, 1828–1944* (Oxford, 1971).
Hole, R., *Pulpits, Politics and Public Order in England, 1760–1832* (Cambridge, 1989).
Jones, P. d'A., *The Christian Socialist Revival, 1877–1914: Religion, Class and Social Conscience in Late-Victorian England* (Princeton, 1968).
Knight, F., *The Nineteenth-Century Church and English Society* (Cambridge, 1995). A good short survey of rural Anglicanism.
Nockles, P., *The Oxford Movement in Context: Anglican High Churchmanship, 1760–1857* (Cambridge, 1994).

Paz, D. G. (ed.), *Nineteenth-Century English Religious Traditions* (Westport, 1995). Essays surveying recent research and an excellent guide to further work.

Royle, E., *The Victorian Church in York* (York, 1983). Booklet.

Soloway, R. A., *Prelates and People: Ecclesiastical Social Thought in England, 1783–1852* (1969).

Vidler, A. R., *F. D. Maurice and Company: Nineteenth-Century Studies* (1966).

Virgin, P., *The Church in an Age of Negligence: Ecclesiastical Structure and Problems of Church Reform, 1700–1840* (Cambridge, 1989).

Walsh, J., Haydon, C. and Taylor, S. (eds.), *The Church of England c. 1689–c. 1833* (Cambridge, 1993). Several important essays.

*Yates, N., *The Oxford Movement and Anglican Ritualism,* Historical Association, G.105 (1983). Booklet.

Scotland

*Brown, C. G., *The Social History of Religion in Scotland since 1730* (1987).

Drummond, A. L. and Bulloch, J., *The Church in Victorian Scotland, 1843–1874* (Edinburgh, 1975).

Drummond, A. L. and Bulloch, J., *The Scottish Church, 1688–1843* (Edinburgh, 1973).

Drummond, A. L. and Bulloch, J., *The Church in Late Victorian Scotland, 1874–1900* (Edinburgh, 1975).

MacLaren, A. A., *Religion and Social Class: The Disruption Years in Aberdeen* (1974).

Protestant Dissent and Nonconformity

Bebbington, D. W., *The Nonconformist Conscience: Chapel and Politics, 1870–1914* (1982).

*Bebbington, D., *Victorian Nonconformity* (Bangor, 1992). Booklet.

Binfield, C., *So Down to Prayers: Studies in English Nonconformity, 1780–1920* (1977).

Bolam, C. G., Goring, J., Short, H. L. and Thomas, R., *The English Presbyterians from Elizabethan Puritanism to Modern Unitarianism* (1968).

Briggs, J. H. Y., *The English Baptists of the Nineteenth Century* (Didcot, 1994).

Briggs, J. and Sellers, I. (eds.), *Victorian Nonconformity* (1973). Primary sources.

Everitt, A., *The Pattern of Rural Dissent: The Nineteenth Century* (Leicester, 1972).

Jones, R. T., *Congregationalism in England, 1662–1962* (1962).

Koss, S., *Nonconformity in Modern British Politics* (1975).

Payne, E. A., *The Baptist Union: A Short History* (1958).

Royle, E., *Nonconformity in Nineteenth-century York* (York, 1985). Booklet.

*Sellers, I., *Nineteenth-Century Nonconformity* (1977).

Thompson, D. M., *Denominationalism and Dissent, 1795–1835: A Question of Identity*. Thirty-ninth lecture, Dr Williams's Library (1985).

Thompson, D. M. (ed.), *Nonconformity in the Nineteenth Century* (1972). Primary sources.

Underwood, A. C., *A History of the English Baptists* (1947).

Ward, W. R., 'Swedenborgianism: Heresy, Schism or Religious Protest', *Studies in Church History*, 9 (1972), pp. 303–9.

Watts, M. R., *The Dissenters from the Reformation to the French Revolution* (Oxford, 1978).

Watts, M. R., *The Dissenters, Volume 2: The Expansion of Evangelical Nonconformity, 1791–1859* (Oxford, 1995).

Methodism

Andrews, S., *Methodism and Society* (1970). With source extracts and bibliography.

Currie, R. B., *Methodism Divided: A Study in the Sociology of Ecumenicalism* (1968).

Davies, R., *Methodism* (Harmondsworth, 1963).

Davies, R. and Rupp, G. (eds.), *A History of the Methodist Church*, i (1965). A collection of good, though now a little dated, essays.

*Davies, R., George, A. R. and Rupp, G. (eds.), *A History of the Methodist Church*, ii–iv (1978, 1983, 1988). Good collection of essays; vol. iv contains source documents and bibliography.

*Hempton, D., *Methodism and Politics in British Society, 1750–1850* (1984).

Hempton, D., *The Religion of the People: Methodism and Popular Religion, c. 1750–1900* (1996). Important collected essays.

Kent, J., *The Age of Disunity* (1966).

Moore, R., *Pit-Men, Preachers and Politics: The Effects of Methodism in a Durham Mining Community* (Cambridge, 1974).

Rack, H., *Reasonable Enthusiast: John Wesley and the Rise of Methodism* (1989). The best biography.

Rattenbury, A., 'Methodism and the Tatterdemalions', in Yeo, E. and S. (eds.), *Popular Culture and Class Conflict, 1590–1914: Explorations in the History of Labour and Leisure* (Brighton, 1981), pp. 28–61.

Semmel, B., *The Methodist Revolution* (1974).

Werner, J. S., *The Primitive Methodist Connexion: Its Background and Early History* (Madison, Wis., 1984).

The Catholic Church

Beck, G. A. (ed.), *The English Catholics, 1850–1950* (1950). Thematic essays.

Bossy, J., *The English Catholic Community, 1570–1850* (1975).

Heimann, M., *Catholic Devotion in Victorian England* (Oxford, 1995).

Norman, E. R., *The English Catholic Church in the Nineteenth Century* (Oxford, 1984).

Evangelicalism and revivalism

*Bebbington, D. W., *Evangelicalism in Modern Britain: A History from the 1730s to the 1980s* (1989).

Best, G. F. A., *Shaftesbury* (1964).

*Bradley, I., *The Call to Seriousness: The Evangelical Impact on the Victorians* (1976). Good introduction to Victorian Evangelicalism.

Carwardine, R., *Trans-Atlantic Revivalism: Popular Evangelicalism in Britain and America, 1790–1865* (Westport, Conn., 1978).

Hilton, B., *The Age of Atonement: The Influence of Evangelicalism on Social and Economic Thought, 1785–1865* (Oxford, 1988).

Hollis, P. (ed.), *Pressure from Without in Early Victorian England* (1974). Essays.

Howse, E. M., *Saints in Politics: The 'Clapham Sect' and the Growth of Freedom* (1953).

Kent, J., *Holding the Fort: Studies in Victorian Revivalism* (1978).

Wolffe, J. R. (ed.), *Evangelical Faith and Public Zeal: Evangelicals and Society in Britain, 1780–1980* (1995). Useful essays.

Church and people, attendance and attitudes

Best, G. F. A., 'Popular Protestantism', in R. Robson (ed.), *Ideas and Institutions of Victorian Britain* (1967).

*Coleman, B. I., *The Church of England in the Mid-Nineteenth Century*, Historical Association G.98 (1980). Booklet.

Cox, J., *The English Churches in a Secular Society: Lambeth, 1870–1930* (Oxford, 1982).

Currie, R. B., Gilbert, A. and Horsley, L., *Churches and Church-goers: Patterns of Church Growth in the British Isles since 1700* (Oxford, 1977). A collection of statistics with controversial introduction on church growth.

Evans, E. J., 'The Church in Danger? Anti-Clericalism in Nineteenth-Century England', *European Studies Review*, 13 (1983), pp. 201–23.

Evans, E. J., *The Contentious Tithe: The Tithe Problem and English Agriculture, 1750–1850* (1976).

Evans, E. J., 'Some Reasons for the Growth of English Rural Anti-Clericalism', *Past and Present*, 66 (February 1975), pp. 84–109.

Evans, H., 'Religious Statistics of England and Wales', *Contemporary Review*, 71 (1897), pp. 276–9.

Gay, J. D., *The Geography of Religion in England* (1971). Survey with maps using 1851 census data.

*Gilbert, A. D., *Religion and Society in Industrial England: Church, Chapel and Social Change, 1740–1914* (1976). Influential interpretation, now challenged, but still a good introduction.

Harrison, J. F. C., *The Second Coming: Popular Millenarianism, 1780–1850* (1979). Important and penetrating study.

Inglis, K. S., *Churches and the Working Classes in Victorian England* (1963). For long the standard work and still very useful.

Laqueur, T. W., *Religion and Respectability: Sunday Schools and Working-Class Culture, 1780–1850* (New Haven and London, 1976).

McLeod, H., *Class and Religion in the Late Victorian City* (1974). On London.

*McLeod, H., *Religion and the Working Class in Nineteenth-Century Britain* (SESH, 1984).

Morris, J., *Religion and Urban Change. Croydon, 1840–1914* (Woodbridge, 1992).

Mudie-Smith, R. (ed.), *The Religious Life of London* (1904). The *Daily News* census.

Norman, E. R., *Anti-Catholicism in Victorian England* (1968). Includes primary sources.

Obelkevich, J., *Religion and Rural Society. South Lindsey, 1825–1875* (Oxford, 1976). Important rural study of formal and folk religion.

Oliver, W. H., *Prophets and Millennialists: The uses of Biblical prophecy in England from the 1790s to the 1840s* (Auckland, 1978).

Paz, D., *Popular Anti-Catholicism in England, 1850–1851* (1979).

Prospect for the Eighties. From a Census of the Churches in 1979, undertaken by the Nationwide Initiative in Evangelism (1980). A modern survey.

Royle, E., *Radical Politics, 1790–1900: Religion and Unbelief* (1971). With source extracts and bibliography.

*Smith, A., *The Established Church and Popular Religion, 1750–1850* (1971). With source extracts and bibliography.

Snell, K. D. M., *Church and Chapel in the North Midlands: Religious Observance in the Nineteenth Century* (Leicester, 1991). Booklet with statistical analysis of the 1851 census.

Wickham, E. R., *Church and People in an Industrial City* (1957). Pioneering study of Sheffield.

Williams, S., 'Urban Popular Religion and the Rites of Passage', in McLeod, H. (ed.), *European Religion in the Age of Great Cities, 1830–1930* (1995).

Women and religion

*Malmgreen, G. (ed.), *Religion in the Lives of English Women, 1760–1930* (1986). Essays.

Valenze, D. M., *Prophetic Sons and Daughters: Female Preaching and Popular Religion in Industrial England* (Princeton, 1985).

Secularisation and religious change

*Bruce, S. (ed.), *Religion and Modernization: Sociologists and Historians Debate the Secularization Thesis* (Oxford, 1992). Essays from differing viewpoints.

Davie, G., *Religion in Britain since 1945: Believing without Belonging* (Oxford, 1994). A good survey.

*Gilbert, A. D., *The Making of Post-Christian Britain: A History of the Secularization of Modern Society* (1980). Argues the de-Christianization thesis.

Gill, R., *The Myth of the Empty Church* (1993).

Green, S. J. D., *Religion in the Age of Decline: Organisation and Experience in Industrial Yorkshire, 1870–1920* (Cambridge, 1996).

Hill, M., *A Sociology of Religion* (1973).

Hölscher, L., 'Secularization and Urbanization in the Nineteenth Century', in McLeod, H. (ed.), *European Religion in the Age of Great Cities, 1830–1930* (1995).

Martin, D., *A Sociology of English Religion* (1967).

Thomas, T. (ed.), *The British: Their Religious Beliefs and Practices, 1800–1986* (1988).

Wilson, B. R. (ed.), *Patterns of Sectarianism: Organisation and Ideology in Social and Religious Movements* (1967).

Wolffe, J. R. (ed.), *The Growth of Religious Diversity. Britain from 1945: A Reader* (Milton Keynes, 1993). Sources for the development of non-Christian religions.

Yeo, S., *Religion and Voluntary Organisations in Crisis* (1976).

Education – general works

Barnard, H. C., *A History of English Education from 1760* (1947; second edn., 1971).

Curtis, S. J. and Boultwood, M. E. A., *An Introductory History of English Education since 1800* (1960; fourth edn., 1966).

Jones, D. K., *The Making of the Education System, 1851–81* (1977).

*Lawson, J. and Silver, H., *A Social History of Education in England* (1973). Comprehensive introduction.

Lowndes, G. A. N., *The Silent Social Revolution: An Account of the Expansion of Public Education in England and Wales, 1895–1965* (1969).

Morrish, I., *Education since 1800* (1970).

*O'Day, R., *Education and Society, 1500–1800: The Social Foundations of Education in Early Modern Britain* (1982).

Paz, D. G., *The Politics of Working-Class Education in Britain, 1830–1850* (Manchester, 1980).

Simon, B., *Studies in the History of Education*, i, *The Two Nations and the Educational Structure, 1780–1870;* ii, *Education and the Labour Movement, 1870–1920;* iii, *The Politics of Educational Reform, 1920–1940;* iv, *Education and the Social Order, 1940–1990* (1960–91).

Stone, L. (ed.), *Schooling and Society: Studies in the History of Education* (Baltimore and London, 1976). Essays.

Sturt, M., *The Education of the People* (1967).

*Sutherland, G., 'Education', in Thompson, F. M. L. (ed.), *The Cambridge Social History of Britain, 1750–1950* (Cambridge, 1990), iii, pp. 119–69.

*Wardle, D., *English Popular Education, 1780–1970* (Cambridge, 1970).

Wardle, D., *Education and Society in Nineteenth-Century Nottingham* (Cambridge, 1971).

Wardle, D., *The Rise of the Schooled Society: The History of Formal Schooling in England* (1974).

West, E. G., *Education and the Industrial Revolution* (1975).

Literacy

*Graff, H. J. (ed.), *Literacy and Social Development in the West* (Cambridge, 1981). Very useful comparative essays.

Reay, B., 'The Context and Meaning of Popular Literacy: Some Evidence from Nineteenth-Century Rural England', *Past and Present*, 131 (May 1991), pp. 89–129.

Sanderson, M., 'Literacy and Social Mobility in the Industrial Revolution', *Past and Present*, 56 (August 1972), pp. 75–104.

Sanderson, M. and Laqueur, T. W., 'Debate. Literacy and Social Mobility in the Industrial Revolution', *Past and Present*, 64 (August 1974), pp. 96–112.

Smith, R. J., 'Education, Society and Literacy in Nottinghamshire in the mid-Nineteenth Century', *University of Birmingham Historical Journal*, 12 (1969), pp. 42–56.

Stephens, W. B., *Education, Literacy and Society, 1830–70: The Geography of Diversity in Provincial England* (Manchester, 1987).

*Stone, L., 'Literacy and Education in England, 1640–1900', *Past and Present*, 42 (February 1969), pp. 69–139. A key article.

Elementary schooling

Brown, C. K. F., *The Church's Part in Education, 1833–1941: With Special Reference to the Work of the National Society* (1942).

Burnett, J. (ed.), *Destiny Obscure: Autobiographies of Childhood, Education and Family from the 1820s to the 1920s* (1982).

Cook, T. G. (ed.), *History of Education Society: Local Studies and the History of Education* (1972). Several useful essays.

Dick, M., 'The Myth of the Working Class Sunday School', *History of Education*, 9 (1980), pp. 27–41. Challenges Laqueur (see below).

*Digby, A. and Searby, P. (eds.), *Children, School and Society in Nineteenth-Century England* (1981). Introduction and sources.

Gosden, P. H. J. H. and Sharp, P. R., *The Development of an Education Service: The West Riding, 1889–1974* (Oxford, 1978).

History of Education Society. Studies in the Government and Control of Education since 1860 (1970). Includes essays on Wales and Scotland.

Hurt, J. S., *Elementary Schooling and the Working Classes, 1860–1918* (1979).

Laqueur, T. W., *Religion and Respectability: Sunday Schools and Working-Class Culture, 1780–1850* (New Haven and London, 1976). Argues for independent working-class nature of Sunday schools.

McCann, W. P., 'Elementary Education in England and Wales on the Eve of the 1870 Education Act', *Journal of Educational Administration and History*, 2 (1) (December 1969), pp. 20–9.

Maclure, S., *One Hundred Years of London Education* (1970).

Maltby, S. E., *Manchester and the Movement for National Elementary Education, 1800–1870* (Manchester, 1981).

*Murphy, J., *Church, State and Schools in Britain 1800–1970* (1971).

Murphy, J., *The Education Act, 1870: Text and Commentary* (Newton Abbot, 1972).

Neuburg, V. E., *Popular Education in Eighteenth-Century England* (1981).

Sanderson, M., 'Education and the Factory in Industrial Lancashire, 1780–1840', *Economic History Review*, 20 (1967), pp. 266–79.

*Sutherland, G., *Elementary Education in the Nineteenth Century*, Historical Association G.76 (1971). Booklet, good introductory survey.

Wadsworth, A. P., 'The First Manchester Sunday Schools', in Flinn, M. W. and Smout, T. C. (eds.), *Essays in Social History* (1974), pp. 100–22.

Ward, G., 'The Education of Factory Child Workers, 1833–1850', *Economic History*, 3 (10) (February 1935), pp. 110–24.

Grammar and public schooling

*Bamford, T. W., *Rise of the Public Schools: A Study of Boys' Public Boarding Schools in England and Wales from 1837 to the Present Day* (1967).

Bishop, J. H. and Wilkinson, R., *Winchester and the Public School Élite* (1967).

Mack, E. C., *Public Schools and British Opinion, 1780–1860: An Examination of the Relationship between Contemporary Ideas and the Evolution of an English Institution* (1938).

Mack, E. C., *Public Schools and British Opinion since 1860: The Relationship between Contemporary Ideas and the Evolution of an English Institution* (New York, 1941).

Newsome, D., *Godliness and Good Learning: Four Studies on a Victorian Ideal* (1961).

Roach, J., *Public Examinations in England, 1850–1900* (Cambridge, 1971).

Sanderson, M. 'The Grammar School and the Education of the Poor, 1786–1840', *British Journal of Educational Studies*, 11 (1962), pp. 28–43.

*Tompson, R. S., *Classics or Charity? The Dilemma of the 18th-Century Grammar School* (Manchester, 1971).

Further, technical and adult education

Argles, M., *South Kensington to Robbins: An Account of English Technical and Scientific Education since 1851* (1964).

Cardwell, D. S. L., *Artisan to Graduate: Essays to Commemorate the Foundation in 1824 of the Manchester Mechanics' Institution, now in 1974 the University of Manchester Institute of Science and Technology* (Manchester, 1974).

*Harrison, J. F. C., *Learning and Living, 1790–1960* (1961).

Hudson, J. W., *The History of Adult Education* (1851; new edn. 1969).

Laurent J., 'Science, Society and Politics in Late Nineteenth-Century England: A Further Look at Mechanics' Institutes', *Social Studies of Science*, 14 (1984), pp. 585–619.

Roderick, G. W. and Stephens, M. D., *Education and Industry in the Nineteenth Century* (1978).

Royle, E., 'Mechanics' Institutes and the Working Classes, 1840–1860', *Historical Journal*, 14 (1971, pp. 303–21.

Summerfield, P. and Evans, E. J. (eds.), *Technical Education and the State since 1850* (Manchester, 1990). Useful essays on various aspects.

Wood, E. M., *A History of the Polytechnic* (1965).

Higher education

Anderson, C. A. and Schnaper, M., *School and Society in England: Social Backgrounds of Oxford and Cambridge Students* (Washington, 1952).

*Armytage, W. H. G., *The Civic Universities* (1955).
Ashby, E., *Technology and the Academics* (1959).
*Briggs, A., 'Development in Higher Education in the United Kingdom: 19th and 20th Centuries', in Niblett, W. R. (ed.), *Higher Education: Demand and Response* (1974), pp. 95–116.
Brooke, C. N. L., *A History of the University of Cambridge, Vol. IV, 1870–1990* (Cambridge, 1993).
Chaloner, W. H., *The Movement for the Extension of Owens College, Manchester, 1863–73* (Manchester, 1973).
Clark, G. Kitson, 'The Leeds Élite', *University of Leeds Review*, 17 (1974), pp. 232–58. The background to the foundation of the University of Leeds.
Dahrendorf, R., *LSE: A History of the London School of Economics and Political Science, 1895–1995* (Oxford, 1995).
Garland, M. M., *Cambridge Before Darwin: The Ideal of a Liberal Education, 1800–1860* (Cambridge, 1980).
Hans, N., *New Trends in Education in the Eighteenth Century* (1951).
Harrison, B. (ed.), *The History of the University of Oxford, Vol. VIII, The Twentieth Century* (Oxford, 1994).
Jenkins, H. and Jones, D. C., 'The Social Class of Cambridge University Alumni of the 18th and 19th centuries', *British Journal of Sociology*, 1 (1950), pp. 93–116.
McClelland, C. E., *State, Society and University in Germany, 1700–1914* (Cambridge, 1980). Useful for comparison.
Phillipson, N. (ed.), *Universities, Society and the Future* (Edinburgh, 1983).
Rothblatt, S., *The Revolution of the Dons: Cambridge and Society in Victorian England* (1968).
*Rothblatt, S., *Tradition and Change in English Liberal Education: An Essay in History and Culture* (1976). Actually a series of essays.
Sanderson, M., *The Universities and British Industry, 1850–1970* (1972).
Sanderson, M. (ed.), *The Universities in the Nineteenth Century* (1975). Good collection of illustrative source extracts.
*Stone, L. (ed.), *The University in Society* (2 vols., Princeton, 1974). Some important comparative essays.
Thompson, F. M. L. (ed.), *The University of London and the World of Learning, 1836–1986* (1990). Essays on different subjects.
Ward, W. R., *Victorian Oxford* (1965).
Winstanley, D. A., *Early Victorian Cambridge* (Cambridge, 1955).
Winstanley, D. A., *Later Victorian Cambridge* (Cambridge, 1947).
Wright, C. J., 'Academics and their Aims: English and Scottish Approaches to University Education in the 19th Century', *History of Education*, 8 (1979), pp. 91–7.

Women's education

Burstyn, J. N., *Victorian Education and the Ideal of Womanhood* (1980).

Dyhouse, C., *Girls Growing Up in Late-Victorian and Edwardian England* (1981).

*Kamm. J., *Hope Deferred: Girls' Education in English History* (1965).

McWilliams-Tullberg, R., *Women at Cambridge: A Men's University – Though of a Mixed Type* (1975).

Purvis, J., *Hard Lessons: The Lives and Education of Working-Class Women in Nineteenth-Century England* (Oxford, 1989).

Widdowson, F., *Going up into the Next Class: Women and Elementary Teacher Training, 1840–1914* (1980).

Scottish education

Anderson, R. D., *Education and Opportunity in Victorian Scotland: Schools and Universities* (Oxford, 1983).

Anderson, R. D., 'Education and the State in Nineteenth-Century Scotland', *Economic History Review*, 36 (1983), pp. 518–34.

Anderson, R. D., 'Secondary Schools and Scottish Society in the Nineteenth Century', *Past and Present*, 109 (November 1985), pp. 176–203.

*Anderson, R. D., *Education and the Scottish People, 1750–1918* (Oxford, 1995). Takes his earlier work further.

Davie, G. E., *The Democratic Intellect: Scotland and her Universities in the 19th Century* (Edinburgh, 1961).

Houston, R. A., *Scottish Literacy and the Scottish Identity: Illiteracy and Society in Scotland and Northern England, 1600–1800* (Cambridge, 1985).

Mathew, W. M., 'The Origins and Occupations of Glasgow Students, 1740–1839', *Past and Present*, 33 (April 1966), pp. 74–94.

Phillipson, N. and Mitchison, R. (eds.), *Scotland in the Age of Improvement* (Edinburgh, 1980).

Scotland, J., *A History of Scottish Education* (2 vols., 1969).

Smout, T. C., 'Born Again at Cambuslang: New Evidence on Popular Religion and Literacy in Eighteenth-Century Scotland', *Past and Present*, 97 (November 1982), pp. 114–27.

Education and society

*Anderson, R. D., *Universities and Elites in Britain since 1800* (SESH, 1992; republ. Cambridge, 1995).

Cannon, J., *Aristocratic Century. The Peerage of Eighteenth-Century England* (Cambridge, 1984).

Dintenfass, M., *The Decline of Industrial Britain, 1870–1980* (1992).

Dobbs, A. E., *Education and Social Movements, 1700–1850* (1919; repr. New York, 1969).

*Edgerton, D., *Science, Technology and the British Industrial 'Decline', 1879–1970* (SESH, Cambridge, 1996).

Johnson, R., 'Educational Policy and Social Control in Early Victorian England', *Past and Present*, 49 (November 1970), pp. 96–119.

Johnson, R., 'Really Useful Knowledge: Radical Education and Working-Class Culture, 1790–1848', in Clarke, J. *et al.* (eds.), *Working-Class Culture: Studies in History and Theory* (1979), pp. 75–102.

McCann, W. P. (ed.), *Popular Education and Socialization in the Nineteenth Century* (1977).

*Musgrave, P. W. (ed.), *Sociology, History and Education* (1970). Several important essays.

Musgrave, P. W., 'The Relationship between the Family and Education in England: A Sociological Account', *British Journal of Educational Studies*, 19 (1971), pp. 17–31.

Neuburg, V. E. (ed.), *Literacy and Society* (1971). Reprints two primary sources for the period 1790–1850.

O'Boyle, L., 'The Problem of an Excess of Educated Men in Western Europe, 1800–1850', *Journal of Modern History*, 42 (1970), pp. 471–95.

Rubinstein, D., *Capitalism, Culture and Decline in Britain, 1750–1990* (1994).

*Sanderson, M., *Education, Economic Change and Society in England, 1780–1870*, (SESH, 1983; second edn., 1991; republ. Cambridge, 1995).

Sanderson, M., 'Social Change and Elementary Education in Industrial Lancashire', *Northern History*, 3 (1968), pp. 131–54.

Silver, H., *The Concept of Popular Education; A Study of Ideas and Social Movements in the Early Nineteenth Century* (1965). Mainly on Owenite ideas.

*Silver, H., *English Education and the Radicals* (1975).

Wiener, M. J., *English Culture and the Decline of the Industrial Spirit* (Cambridge, 1981). An important and influential half-truth.

Index